INSTITUTIONS OF AMERICAN DEMOCRACY

THE EXECUTIVE BRANCH

THE
EXECUTIVE
BRANCH

Joel D. Aberbach
Mark A. Peterson

EDITORS

THE ANNENBERG FOUNDATION TRUST AT SUNNYLANDS

OXFORD
UNIVERSITY PRESS

OXFORD
UNIVERSITY PRESS

Oxford University Press, Inc., publishes works that further
Oxford University's objective of excellence
in research, scholarship, and education.

Oxford   New York
Auckland   Cape Town   Dar es Salaam   Hong Kong   Karachi
Kuala Lumpur   Madrid   Melbourne   Mexico City   Nairobi
New Delhi   Shanghai   Taipei   Toronto

With offices in
Argentina   Austria   Brazil   Chile   Czech Republic   France   Greece
Guatemala   Hungary   Italy   Japan   Poland   Portugal   Singapore
South Korea   Switzerland   Thailand   Turkey   Ukraine   Vietnam

Copyright © 2005 by Oxford University Press, Inc.

Published by Oxford University Press, Inc.
198 Madison Avenue, New York, New York, 10016
http://www.oup.com/us

Library of Congress Cataloging-in-Publication Data

The executive branch / Joel D. Aberbach, Mark A. Peterson, editors
v. <4> cm.—(Institutions of American democracy)
Includes bibliographical references and index.
ISBN-13: 978-0-19-517393-2 (alk. paper, cloth)
ISBN-10: 0-19-517393-7 (alk. paper, cloth)
ISBN-13: 978-0-19-530915-7 (alk. paper, pbk.)
ISBN-10: 0-19-530915-4 (alk. paper, pbk.)
1. Executive departments—United States.   I. Aberbach, Joel D.   II. Peterson, Mark A.
III. Institutions of American democracy series.
JK501.E94   2005
352.2´0973—dc22   2005017621

Book design by Joan Greenfield
Copyedited by Dorothy Bauhoff

Printed in the United States of America on acid-free paper

CONTENTS

DIRECTORY OF CONTRIBUTORS

Joel D. Aberbach (Editor)

Distinguished Professor of Political Science and Public Policy;
Director, Center for American Politics and Public Policy, University of California, Los Angeles

Professor Aberbach's research focuses on American and comparative politics, with emphasis on legislative-executive relations and broader issues of executive politics and policy making. His books include *In the Web of Politics: Three Decades of the U.S. Federal Executive*, which he coauthored with Bert A. Rockman, and *Keeping a Watchful Eye: The Politics of Congressional Oversight*. He is currently co-chair of the Research Committee on Structure and Organization of Government of the International Political Science Association. He has been a Fellow at both the Center for Advanced Study in the Behavioral Sciences and the Swedish Collegium for Advanced Study in the Social Sciences, a Visiting Fellow of the University of Bologna's Institute of Advanced Studies, and a Senior Fellow at the Brookings Institution in Washington, D.C.

Mark A. Peterson (Editor)

Professor, Public Policy and Political Science, University of California, Los Angeles

Professor Peterson is a scholar of American national institutions, focusing on the presidency, Congress, and interest groups, as well as national health care policy making, with publications that include *Legislating Together: The White House and Capitol Hill from Eisenhower to Reagan*. He previously held faculty appointments at Harvard University and the University of Pittsburgh, and has been a guest scholar at the Brookings Institution and a legislative assistant in the U.S. Senate. Former editor of the *Journal of Health Politics, Policy and Law* (1993–2002), he is currently chair of the National Advisory Committee for the Robert Wood Johnson Foundation's Scholars in Health Policy Research Program.

Colin Campbell

Canada Research Chair in U.S. Government and Politics, University of British Columbia, Vancouver;
Professor of Political Science, University of British Columbia, Vancouver

Professor Campbell founded and directed the Georgetown Public Policy Institute. Four of his nine books have drawn special recognition. This includes the 1987 American Political Science Association Neustadt Prize for *Managing the Presidency* and the 2004 National Academy of Public Administration Brownlow Award for *Preparing for the Future: Strategic Planning in the U.S. Air Force*. Campbell has also edited eight collections, including four books in a series of midterm assessments of presidents, and published numerous articles and book chapters.

Daniel Carpenter

Professor of Government, Harvard University

Professor Carpenter's research focuses on the development of political institutions, the political economy of regulation, bureaucratic politics, and health policy. His books include *The Forging of Bureaucratic Autonomy: Networks, Reputations and Policy Innovation in Executive Departments, 1862–1928* (winner of Levine Memorial Book Prize and the Gladys M. Kammerer Award), which advances a theory of bureaucratic autonomy and shows how federal bureaucracies came to occupy new policymaking roles in the early twentieth century, and the forthcoming *The Gatekeeper: Organizational Regulation and Pharmaceutical Regulation at the FDA*.

Matthew J. Dickinson

Professor of Political Science, Middlebury College

Professor Dickinson is the author of *Bitter Harvest: FDR, Presidential Power, and the Growth of the Presidential Branch* and has published numerous articles on the presidency, presidential decision making, and presidential advisers. His current research examines the growth of presidential staff in the post-World War II era.

James W. Fossett

Associate Professor of Public Administration and Public Health at the University at Albany of the State University of New York; Senior Fellow at the Rockefeller Institute of Government

A political scientist by training, Professor Fossett directs the Rockefeller Institute's health and Medicaid studies and has published extensively on political, financial, administrative, and intergovernmental issues around Medicaid and other domestic social programs.

Thomas L. Gais

Codirector, Federalism Research Group, the Rockefeller Institute of Government

Dr. Gais is Codirector of the Rockefeller Institute of Government, the public policy research arm of the State University of New York. In recent years, he has conducted research and written on federalism, American social policy, program implementation, and state spending on social programs. He is currently conducting research on the role and effects of faith-based institutions in delivering social services. His earlier work covered campaign finance laws and processes, state constitutional reforms, and interest groups.

Fred I. Greenstein

Professor of Politics Emeritus, Princeton University;
Director, Program in Leadership Studies, Woodrow Wilson School of Public and International Affairs, Princeton University

Professor Greenstein's books include *Children and Politics* (1965), *Personality and Politics* (1969), *The Hidden-Hand Presidency: Eisenhower as Leader* (1982), *How Presidents Test Reality* (1989, with John P. Burke), and *The Presidential Difference: Leadership Style from FDR to George W. Bush* (2004). He is a fellow of the American Academy of Arts and Sciences, former president of both the American Political Science Association's Presidency Research Group (and selected for its Career Service Award) and past president of the International Society for Political Psychology, as well as a recipient of its Nevitt Sanford Award and Harold D. Lasswell Award.

Patricia W. Ingraham

Distinguished Professor of Public Administration and Political Science, Maxwell School of Citizenship and Public Affairs, Syracuse University

Professor Ingraham was the Founding Director of the Alan K Campbell Public Affairs Institute and is a Fellow of the National Academy of Public Administration. She is the recipient of the Dwight Waldo Award, Donald Stone, and Paul Van Riper Awards for Distinguished Research Career and Distinguished Service from the American Society of Public Administration, and the John Gaus Award for Distinguished Career Contributions from the American Political Science Association. Her major research interests are the performance of public organizations and leading and managing the people within those organizations.

Lawrence R. Jacobs

Walter F and Joan Mondale Chair for Political Studies, Hubert H. Humphrey Institute and Department of Political Science, University of Minnesota

Professor Jacobs is Director of the Center for the Study of Politics and Governance. His recent books include *Inequality and American Democracy: What We Know and What We Need to Learn* (edited with Theda Skocpol, 2005), *Healthy, Wealthy, & Fair: Health Care and the Good Society* (edited with James Morone, 2005), and *Politicians Don't Pander: Political Manipulation and the Loss of Democratic Responsiveness* (with Robert Y. Shapiro, 2000), which won the American Political Science Association's Richard E. Neustadt Book Award, the American Sociological Association's Distinguished Book Award in political sociology, and the John F Kennedy School of Government's Goldsmith Book Prize.

Scott C. James

Associate Professor of Political Science, University of California, Los Angeles

Professor James joined the UCLA faculty in 1995 after winning the Schattschneider Award for his dissertation. His book, *Presidents, Parties, and the State: A Party System Perspective on Democratic Regulatory Choice, 1884–1936*, was awarded the American Political Science Association's 2001 Gladys Kammerer Award for the best political science publication in the field of U.S. national policy, and its 2002 Leon Epstein Award for the best book on political organizations and parties. His articles have appeared in the

American Political Science Review, the *British Journal of Political Science, International Organization*, and *Studies in American Political Development.*

Donald F. Kettl

Stanley I. Sheerr Endowed Term Professor in the Social Sciences and Director of the Fels Institute of Government, University of Pennsylvania;
Nonresident Senior Fellow, the Brookings Institution

Professor Kettl is the author of such books as *The Politics of the Administrative Process*, 3rd ed. (with James W. Fesler), *The Global Public Management Revolution*, 2nd ed., *Homeland Security: Politics and Policy, The Transformation of Governance* (winner of the National Academy of Public Administration's 2003 Louis Brownlow Book Award for the best book in public administration) and *Deficit Politics*. He is a fellow of the National Academy of Public Administration.

R. Shep Melnick

Thomas P. O'Neill, Jr. Professor of American Politics, Boston College;
Codirector, Harvard Program on Constitutional Government

Professor Melnick is the author of two books, *Regulation and the Courts: The Case of the Clean Air Act* and *Between the Lines: Interpreting Welfare Rights*. Before joining the faculty at Boston College he taught at Brandeis and Harvard and was a staff member at the Brookings Institution. Dr. Melnick has served as president of the New England Political Science Association and as an elected member of the New Hampshire House of Representatives.

Sidney M. Milkis

White Burkett Miller Professor and Chair, Department of Politics, University of Virginia;
Codirector, American Political Development Program, Miller Center of Public Affairs, University of Virginia

Professor Milkis' books include *The President and the Parties: The Transformation of the American Party System Since the New Deal* and *Political Parties and Constitutional Government: Remaking American Democracy*. He is coeditor of three volumes on 20th century political reform: *Progressivism and the New Democracy* (1999); *The New Deal and the Triumph of Liberalism* (2002); and *The Great Society and The High Tide of Liberalism* (forthcoming). His articles have appeared in *Political Science Quarterly, Studies in American Political Development*, and the *Journal of Policy History*.

Richard Rose

Director, Centre for the Study of Public Policy, University of Strathclyde, Glasgow

A native St. Louisan long resident in Britain, Professor Rose launched the comparative study of executive leadership by editing *Presidents and Prime Ministers*. It was followed up by *The Post-Modern President* and *The Prime Minister in a Shrinking World*. He has written more than 40 books on comparative politics and public policy. He has been a visiting fellow at the American Enterprise Institute, The Brookings Institution, the Woodrow Wilson Center, and the International Monetary Fund in Washington D.C. He is a fellow of the British Academy and an honorary fellow of the American Academy of Arts and Sciences.

Andrew Rudalevige

Associate Professor, Political Science, Dickinson College;
Visiting Research Scholar, Woodrow Wilson School, Princeton University

Professor Rudalevige's *Managing the President's Program: Presidential Leadership and Legislative Policy Formulation* won the American Political Science Association's Richard E. Neustadt Award as the best book on the presidency published in 2002. His second book, *The New Imperial Presidency: Renewing Presidential Power after Watergate* (2005), explores presidential-congressional relations over the past three decades. A graduate of the University of Chicago and Harvard University, he served as a staffer in the Massachusetts State Senate and then as an elected city councilor in his hometown of Watertown, Massachusetts.

Stephen J. Wayne

Professor of Government, Georgetown University

Professor Wayne's books include *The Road to the White House, Is This Any Way to Run a Democratic Election?, The Legislative Presidency,* and *Presidential Leadership* (with George Edwards). A Professor of Government at Georgetown University, he is also a founding member and former president of the Presidency Research Group, as well as former president of the National Capital Area Political Science Association. He lectures widely on aspects of the American presidency and the presidential electoral process in the United States and abroad.

Barry R. Weingast

Senior Fellow, the Hoover Institution;
Ward C. Krebs Family Professor, Department of Political Science, Stanford University

Professor Weingast is an elected fellow of the American Academy of Arts and Sciences and former Fellow at the Center for Advanced Studies in the Behavioral Sciences. His research focuses on the separation of powers system, and more generally, on the political foundation of markets, economic reform, and regulation. His publications have appeared in the *American Political Science Review, Journal of Law, Economics and Organization,* and *Journal of Economic History* and won numerous awards, including the Duncan Black Prize (public choice), Mary Parker Follett Prize (politics and history), and the Franklin L. Burdette Pi Sigma Alpha Award from the American Political Science Association.

GENERAL INTRODUCTION:
THE EXECUTIVE BRANCH
AS AN INSTITUTION OF AMERICAN
CONSTITUTIONAL DEMOCRACY

Jaroslav Pelikan

IN ONE OF HIS MOST WINSOME POLITICAL-THEOLOGICAL essays Reinhold Niebuhr made the dialectical case that what makes democracy necessary is the human capacity for pride, aggrandizement, and sin. Thereby he set himself against the usual Enlightenment justification for democracy, which was shared by some though not all of the framers of the Declaration of Independence and the Constitution, which grounded its case in an optimistic understanding of human rationality and of the human capacity for virtue.[1] A few years earlier, in the first series of his Gifford Lectures, delivered in the spring of 1939, he had identified himself with Immanuel Kant's critique of such Enlightenment doctrines; for while "in the basic trends of his thought Kant exhibits the moral complacency of the rational man which modern idealism shares with all forms of rationalism," Kant's doctrine of "the radical evil which corrupts the very basis of all maxims," as articulated in his Religion Within the Limits of Reason Alone, "penetrates into spiritual intricacies and mysteries to which he seems to remain completely blind in his Critique of Practical Reason," because it acknowledges "man's inclination to corrupt the imperatives of morality so that they become a screen for the expression of self-love."[2] It was that corrupting inclination that made democracy philosophically and politically necessary.

The framers had recognized this tendency above all in the British monarchy and in the actions of the ministers of King George III, as these are described in detail by the *gravamina* of the Declaration of Independence, and they sought to design the executive branch of the new republic in such a way as to obviate it. Therefore James Madison in *Federalist* 48 drew the contrast between "a representative republic" and both hereditary monarchy and untramelled democracy at this very point of the executive office:

> In a government, where numerous and extensive prerogatives are placed in the hands of a hereditary monarch, the executive department is very justly regarded as the source of danger, and watched with all the jealousy which a zeal for liberty ought to inspire. In a democracy, where a multitude of people exercise in person the legislative functions, and are continually exposed by their incapacity for regular deliberation and concerned measures, to the ambitious intrigues of their executive magistrates, tyranny may well be apprehended on some favorable emergency, to start up in the same quarter. But in a representative republic, where the executive magistracy is carefully limited both in the extent and the duration of its power; and where the legislative power is exercised by an assembly. . . , it is against the enterprising ambition of this [legislative] department, that the people ought to indulge all their jealousy and exhaust all their precautions.[3]

Yet a careful reading of the historical and political materials in this volume suggests that, contrary in some respects to such expectations, it has nevertheless been in the executive branch that Americans, too, have continued to see a chief source of governmental corruption and of the threat to the integrity of American constitutional democracy; in the familiar generalization of Edward S. Corwin, quoted by Scott James in his chapter, "the history of the presidency is the history of aggrandizement." Therefore it is instructive, and occasionally even amusing, to catalog the quite remarkable number of different epithets that are attached to the nouns "presidency" and "president" in one or another of the chapters of this volume and in the supporting secondary literature.

Pervading the volume is an awareness that the American presidency has evolved since its beginnings in Article II of the Constitution, and that this evolution has been in many respects more thoroughgoing than has the historical change at work in either the legislative or the judicial branch; therefore the epithet "the *modern* presidency," which Sidney Milkis still feels obliged to enclose in quotation marks. He makes clear what this specifically implies earlier in his chapter when he identifies this definition of "the modern executive office" as "arguably the most significant constitutional legacy of FDR's New Deal." Indeed, so dominating is the presidency of Franklin D. Roosevelt that Colin Campbell in his chapter on "the complex organization of the executive branch" can propose a periodization of the entire history of the executive branch from the beginning in which there are five distinct eras, the first of which extends all the way from 1789 to 1932, that is, from the Constitution to the New Deal—and then the remaining four periods are defined by the New Deal! An intriguing parallel to this lopsided periodization, from quite another historical discipline, was a history of the Christian doctrine of reconciliation and atonement published in 1838 by Ferdinand Christian Baur, in which that history of eighteen entire centuries was divided into three periods: from the beginnings of Christianity to the Reformation (about fifteen centuries); from the Reformation to Immanuel Kant (almost three centuries); and since Kant (thirty-four years).[4] One can argue that Franklin D. Roosevelt has defined not only "the modern presidency" but the very history of the executive branch, which has developed, to use the book title quoted from William E. Leuchtenburg by Scott James, "in the shadow of FDR,"[5] so that we can even read here of "the post-FDR presidency."

When the editors of this volume, Joel D. Aberbach and Mark A. Peterson, conclude it with questions about the future of the presidency, those have, as their baseline this redefinition of the office. Throughout the chapters leading up to that conclusion, they and their colleagues have been at pains both to take account of the fundamental changes that the presidencies of Andrew Jackson, Abraham Lincoln, Theodore Roosevelt, and Franklin D. Roosevelt have so visibly made in the original understanding of the office and at the same time to avoid the kind of hyperbole about the presidency that leads to what Hugh Heclo and Lester M. Salamon, as cited by Scott James, have labeled "the illusion of presidential government."[6] It seems that most of the characteristics of this "new presidency" envisioned by their concluding chapter will stand in some sort of recognizable continuity with "the modern presidency," so conceived and so dedicated, but that is will also display additional features.

One of those features will undoubtedly be a continuation and intensification of the qualities summarized by Matthew Dickinson under the rubric "the *politicized* presidency." After introducing the concept, Dickinson goes on explain why "further politicization of the EOP [Executive Office of the President] agencies' upper levels ought to be firmly resisted," but also why much of this resistance has, if anything, become "politically impracticable." Even a reader quite familiar with the provisions of the original Article II of the Constitution must be struck each time by the evident naiveté of its provision that "the person having the greatest number of votes [in the electoral college] shall be the President" and that "after the choice of the President, the person having the greatest number of votes of the electors shall be the Vice-president," on the assumption that "faction" or party simply would not play a role in so central a political institution as the executive office. Ironically, as Sidney Milkis argues, "the architects of the Constitution established a nonpartisan president who . . . was intended to play the leading institutional role in checking and controlling 'the violence of faction' that the framers feared would rend the fabric of representative government"; but the outcome has been the opposite, "the politicized presidency." As both a scholar and then a practitioner of this politicized presidency, Woodrow Wilson, as quoted here by Scott James, recognized that

> . . . [the president] cannot escape being the leader of his party . . . because he is at once the choice of the party and of the nation . . . [T]he president represents not so much the party's governing efficiency as its controlling ideals and principles. He is not so much part of its organization as its vital link of connection with the thinking nation. He can dominate his party by being spokesman for the real sentiment and purpose of the country, by giving direction to opinion, by giving the country at once the infomation and the statements of policy which will enable it to form its judgments alike of parties and of men.

The tragedy of his presidency and his personal tragedy was, in the battle over the League of Nations, his inability to be politically effective in doing precisely that.

An outgrowth of this trend towards the politicized presidency is "the *administrative* presidency,"[7] which can even become at one point in this volume "the *conservative administrative* presidency." Functionally, this involves the evolution of what Daniel Carpenter in his chapter describes as "the *bureaucratization* of the presidency." According to public choice theory, the administrative presidency produces "very strong emphasis on the part of presidents and their appointees at channeling the bureaucracy in directions that advance an administration's support and legacy." This requires them to "deploy strategies focused upon placing the state apparatus more at their disposal." The appeal of the Brownlow Committee, "The president needs help," which is quoted here more than once, underlies the evolution of the Executive Office of the President, whose permutations are charted in Matthew Dickinson's chapter. The federal bureaucracy thus becomes a principal obstacle to the freedom and efficiency of the administrative presidency—at least partly because its incumbents enjoy a term of office that outlasts the maximum eight years of a president's service (another unintended part of the legacy of FDR)—and at the same time the primary instrumentality by which, especially in his dealings with the Congress, the President is able to work his will. In his section on "the administrative presidency" Scott James pays special attention to what it has done to the departments of the Cabinet. At times in their history these have sometimes seemed to be quasiautonomous fiefdoms through which a powerful Cabinet officer has been able to exercise great latitude of action and, if anything, to shape presidential policy and action rather than being shaped by it. But "a distinctive feature in the evolution of the post-FDR presidency has been the diminution of Cabinet independence in personnel and policy matters, as presidents have increasingly centralized administrative appointments in the White House and inserted presidential loyalists into the cockpit of bureaucratic decision-making processes." By one set of criteria, it is possible (employing this set of presidential epithets) to measure a president's success or failure by the ability to manage the bureaucratic presidency in the interests of the administrative presidency.

What all of this amounts to can be encapsulated in the subtitle of Barry Weingast's chapter headed "*Institutionalized* Presidency," which has come into being as "all modern presidents have attempted to enhance their power, in part through institutionalizing their office and expanding those parts of the federal structure most closely allied with them, including the White House, the Executive Office of the President, and the Office of Management and Budget." Not surprisingly, several of these chapters connect this increasing institutionalization of the office of president with the presidency of Franklin D. Roosevelt, even calling it "arguably the most significant constitutional legacy of FDR's New Deal." The seemingly providential coincidence of the two crises, the Depression and the Second World War, brought together into his hands a unique combination of powers, many of which continue to adhere to the office even when it is occupied by an incumbent who is more reluctant to exercise them (or less skillful in manipulating them) than he was. If a modern Tocqueville were to study the institutional structure of the American democracy, he might well conclude that, materially though not formally, there are four branches of government, with the presidency a distinct though related branch unto itself.

Conversely, it is also possible to interpret the modern development of the separation of powers in another direction, which Andrew Rudalevige in his chapter labels, in an epithet borrowed from Stephen J. Wayne, "the *legislative* presidency."[8] The advantages and disadvantages of the American system, in its contrasts with the more common system of parliament and prime minister, have been fascinating students of comparative government for a long time, including Woodrow Wilson—*Professor* Woodrow Wilson, that is, not *President* Woodrow Wilson[9]—but the historical evolution of the office, especially during the twentieth century, made some of the conventional distinctions between the two systems considerably more fuzzy. That fuzziness has made itself evident at both ends of the legislative process by which a bill becomes a law. Many bills actually originate in the executive branch and then are submitted to the legislative branch for debate and decision. At the other end of the process, there has likewise been a dramatic increase in the resort to the presidential veto of a bill that comes out of the Congress. This is indeed envisaged in the Constitution, but as statistics cited here several times indicate, it remained quite rare. Patricia Ingraham is not exaggerating when she speaks in her chapter about a "sea change" having taken place in important respects in the Jackson presidency. As Scott James points out, for example, before the presidency of Andrew Jackson "the overriding constitutional function of the veto was to aid Congress in the performance of its deliberative functions, not to substitute the president's judgment for the Congress's on national policy matters"; he adds in a revealing historical footnote that "in the first forty years of the Republic, presidents exercised the veto power only ten times," but that "there would be twelve vetoes in the course of Jackson's two terms in office" alone. And, as Rudalevige points out, Franklin D. Roosevelt's vetoes were overridden nine times, which was almost as many times as the veto itself had been exercised by the presidents for the first forty years.

A "legislative presidency" is almost compelled to become as well a "*rhetorical* presidency."[10] But like the proverbial lady in Atlanta who was twenty years old before she realized that "damn Yankees" is two words, many Americans, including far too many professional political scientists, usually speak of "mere rhetoric" or otherwise disparage it as somehow dishonest and unworthy of serious scholarly attention. Because my professional responsibilities as the scholarly director of this project have included the teaching of a college course on rhetoric, usually on the basis of Aristotle's treatise, I have come to regret that this bias seems to have prevented scholars of the American presidency from analyzing the performance of "the rhetorical presidency" comparatively and historically. For the function of "rhetoric" is, as Aristotle defines it at the beginning of his treatise on the subject, "to find out in each case the existing means of persuasion";[11] and, in Andrew Rudalevige's neat phrase, building on Richard Neustadt, "since presidents cannot command, they must persuade." That has always been their job, which has become a vastly more important assignment, as well as a more complicated one, with the development of modern means of communication. Among the six factors that shape presidential performance, Fred Greenstein lists "effectiveness as a public communicator" as the first, adding his judgment that the only three modern presidents to have consistently lived up to the full potential of this criterion were Franklin D. Roosevelt, John F. Kennedy, and Ronald Reagan. Among earlier incumbents, who of course did not have at their disposal the modern technologies of being able to communicate instantaneously with the entire nation, Abraham Lincoln is in a special class, Thomas Gais and James Fossett argue, because "Lincoln's rhetoric . . . linked the federal government to a nearly religious conception of the nation." Even while affirming the power that comes from the veto, President George W. Bush, as quoted by Andrew Rudalevige, identified "persuasion" as "the best tool I have," and after the September 11, 2001 terrorist attack he rose to the rhetorical occasion with a power that even his detractors were obliged to recognize, and found his voice.

In some ways all of these many epithets of the presidency in the scholarly literature are overshadowed, at least in dramatic effect, by "the *imperial* presidency," or even, as it becomes in some formulations here, "the *imperial plebiscitory* presidency." Historiographically, this title is not without a certain irony. For it was created as a critique of the Nixon presidency by Arthur M. Schlesinger, Jr.,[12] who, as the chronicler of the presidency of Franklin Roosevelt, had charted the administrations of the president at whom, perhaps more than at any other, such derogatory epithets had long been directed. That

irony calls attention to a fundamental paradox in all of these presidential epithets and in the studies that have produced them. Students of the American
presidency as an institution of American constitutional democracy must begin
with the sparse and almost Delphic provisions of Article II, but then watch
the foliation of the presidency into the eye-filling office it has become; almost
on its first pages this volume identifies the "basic polarity between the wide
berth for discretionary action implicit in Article II and the modest grant of
formal powers attached to the presidential office." One may try to come to
terms with the fundamental oxymoron by coining an epithet like "the *semi-
sovereign* presidency";[13] yet there seems to be no way to avoid speaking, as Fred
Greenstein does here, of "presidential greatness," or, as Andrew Rudalevige
does, of "presidential leadership." I trust that I may not be the only reader of
these chapters to have occasionally closed my eyes and seen Mount Rushmore
(with or without Cary Grant and Eva Marie Saint draped over it). What would
the framers have said if they could have imagined these four massive stone
icons, especially with their own faces on two of them? Is it possible to con-
ceive of a similar creation for the judicial branch, with perhaps John Marshall
or Oliver Wendell Holmes, Jr. or Louis Brandeis or Benjamin Cardozo? Or is
the very idea of such a Pharaonic depiction inimical to the great traditions
of the Supreme Court? And if it is, what does that say in turn about the balance of powers?

Notes

1. Reinhold Niebuhr, *Children of Light and Children of Darkness: A Vindication of
   Democracy and a Critique of Its Traditional Defense* (New York: Charles Scribner's Sons,
   1944).
2. Reinhold Niebuhr, *The Nature and Destiny of Man* (2 vols.; New York: Charles
   Scribner's Sons, 1941–1944), 1:120, n. 12.
3. *The Federalist* 48, ed. Jacob E. Cooke (Middletown, Conn.: Wesleyan University
   Press, 1961), 333–334
4. Jaroslav Pelikan, *Credo: Historical and Theological Guide to Creeds and Confessions of
   Faith in the Christian Tradition* (New Haven, Conn.: Yale University Press), 366–367.
5. William E. Leuchtenburg, *In the Shadow of FDR: From Harry Truman to George W.
   Bush* (Ithaca, N.Y.: Cornell University Press, 2001).
6. Hugh Heclo and Lester M. Salamon, *The Illusion of Presidential Government* (Boulder,
   Colo.: Westview Press, 1981).
7. This epithet comes from two books by Richard P. Nathan: *The Plot That Failed:
   Nixon and the Administrative Presidency* (New York: Macmillan, 1975); and *The
   Administrative Presidency* (New York: Macmillan, 1982).
8. Stephen J. Wayne, *The Legislative Presidency* (New York: Harper and Row, 1978).
9. Woodrow Wilson, *Constitutional Government in the United States* (1908). New edition.
   Introduction by Sidney A. Pearson (Somerset, N.J.: Transaction Publishers, 2002).

10. Jeffrey Tulis, *The Rhetorical Presidency* (Princeton, N.J.: Princeton University Press, 1987).
11. Aristotle, *Rhetoric,* I.i.14 (1355b), Loeb Classical Library, 193:13.
12. Arthur M. Schlesinger, Jr., *The Imperial Presidency* (Boston: Houghton Mifflin, 1973).
13. Charles Tiefer, *The Semi-Sovereign Presidency: The Bush Administration's Strategy for Governing Without Congress* (Boulder, Colo.: Westview Press, 1994).

PRESIDENTS AND BUREAUCRATS: THE EXECUTIVE BRANCH AND AMERICAN DEMOCRACY

Joel D. Aberbach and Mark A. Peterson

TENSION AND PARADOX ARE EMBEDDED IN THE DNA OF the American republic. Essential features of the revolutionary impulse leading to independence, they soon became encoded in the U.S. Constitution and are today inescapable, and even more significant. The modern presidency and executive branch—as institutions, as sites of politics and policy making, as settings in which individuals seek and apply power—echo these tensions as many contemporary policy makers struggle to overcome them in a contemporary world filled with pronounced domestic and international challenges.

When the American experiment in republican government was launched by the thirteen new states nestled along the continent's eastern expanse, the emergent nation enjoyed both natural promise for future success and confronted self-made threats to its endurance. The United States, notes Joseph Ellis, benefited from the extraordinary advantages of "geographic isolation . . . and bountiful natural resources," but the revolutionary generation risked creating institutional traps that would snare the country's progress:

> the key insight, shared by most of the vanguard members of the revolutionary generation, is that the very arguments used to justify succession from the British Empire also undermined the legitimacy of any national government capable of overseeing such a far-flung population, or establishing uniform laws that knotted together the thirteen sovereign states and three or four distinct geographic and economic regions. For the core argument used to discredit the authority of Parliament and the British monarch, the primal source of what were called "Whig princi-

ples," was an obsessive suspicion of any centralized political power that operated in faraway places beyond the immediate supervision and surveillance of the citizens it claimed to govern. The national government established during the war under the Articles of Confederation accurately embodied the cardinal conviction of revolutionary-era republicanism: namely, that no central authority empowered to coerce or discipline the citizenry was permissible, since it duplicated the monarchical and aristocratic principles that the American Revolution had been fought to escape.[1]

In a realm of rich opportunity for nation building and development, even within the limited scope of eighteenth-century expectations, the governing apparatus appeared insufficient to the task.

With the ratification of the U.S. Constitution in 1789, what Gordon Wood describes as the "Whig science of politics" and its "localist . . . mistrust of governmental authority" yielded to the Federalists' determination to establish a more nationally oriented and more capable central government. Wood quotes the future Supreme Court chief justice Oliver Ellsworth's remark that the Constitution fulfilled its objective to be "a creation of power."[2] The constitutional arrangements, however, while invigorating national government by imbuing it with popular sovereignty, establishing a more functional legislature, and unifying the executive responsibilities in a single president, hardly centralized authority and control. Governing power was famously split among three independent legislative, executive, and judicial branches (which were also enmeshed in complicated ways with intersecting and overlapping responsibilities). It was further divided in a Congress with two legislative chambers of equal influence but profoundly disparate constituencies and orientations, and in a federal system that retained autonomous state governments with their own formal ties to the people's sovereignty. Finally, the availability of power to govern was obscured by the features of authority, responsibility, and influence the Constitution failed to elucidate fully and left open to competing, often entirely contradictory, interpretations.

Nonetheless, the Constitution under which George Washington assumed the office of president more than two centuries ago equipped the new government with the means to manage its most important affairs. It could handle the debt caused by the costly war of independence; secure and protect the nation's borders and trade routes; and establish a national currency, trade regime, and other infrastructure required to promote economic development and social stability. The pronounced, often vitriolic, early battles between the Federalists and Anti-federalists, and later between the Federalist party and Thomas Jefferson's Democratic-Republicans in the presidential election of 1800 (yielding the nation's first partisan transition in the presidency), leaves little doubt that the Constitution did not resolve all matters in the tension between Whig principles and a functional state. But the nation prospered in ways that were decidedly doubtful under the previous Articles of Confederation.

The president and executive branch of the twenty-first century operate largely within the same written constitutional framework as Washington and his early successors. Indeed, remarkably little has changed. The Seventeenth Amendment, ratified in 1913, offered the most significant institutional change by shifting the selection of senators from the legislatures of the states to the electorate, but without altering the allocation of two senators per state, their six-year terms, or the staggered selection of one third of the Senate in each congressional election year. The Twelfth Amendment, which redesigned the method of voting in the Electoral College in response to the rise of political parties, and thus arguably helped set the foundation for a president with a national constituency and more direct ties to the popular electorate, came early enough to involve the authors of the Constitution itself. Beyond the Senate modifications, the only features of the current written Constitution, as amended, that the founders themselves would not know from their own experiences are the amendments that have so dramatically expanded civil rights, civil liberties, and the population eligible to vote. What they would not even begin to recognize is the complex society now governed under the institutional provisions of the Constitution and the challenges it poses for executive leadership and administration.

The United States of George Washington's first inaugural had just under four million people (18 percent of whom were held in slavery), just a drop in the bucket compared with the current population of nearly 295 million. Then, as now, the largest city in the country was New York, but this most urban of locales in the young republic encompassed just 33,131 residents—smaller than the student body of UCLA and filling less than a third of the seats in the University of Michigan's football stadium. Today over 8 million people inhabit New York City alone. Among the "free" people of the original thirteen states, ethnic diversity had little meaning, certainly by the criteria used today. Eighty-five percent had white European backgrounds, the vast majority of whom had roots in the English-speaking British Isles. About 8 percent were free blacks. In the 2000 census, of those who reported just one race or ethnic background, 69 percent were non-Hispanic white, nearly 13 percent Hispanic or Latino, 12 percent African American, and 4 percent Asian American or Pacific Islander. About 14 percent of the non-Hispanic or Latino population identified with at least two races. The demographics are even more striking in California, not part of the republic at its founding but now the nation's largest state. In the most recent estimates, only 45.2 percent of the state's residents are non-Hispanic white, 34.3 percent are Hispanic or Latino,

11.7 percent Asian or Pacific Islander, and 6.9 percent African American. These broad categories only tap the surface of the mix of nationalities and enthnicities. Over 80 languages, for example, are spoken by students in the Los Angeles Unified School District, the second-largest district in the nation. One can also hardly compare the economies of the United States during the Washington and George W. Bush administrations. Over 90 percent of early Americans lived and worked in agriculture; the figure for today is less than 1 percent, with total workers in agriculture and related industries accounting for less than 2 percent of overall employment. Following the industrial revolution, giving rise to large-scale manufacturing, and the "post-industrial" growth of services and technology, employment in the modern American economy involves educational, health, leisure, and other services (33.9%); professional, business, financial, and information services (19.8%); construction and manufacturing (19.6%); wholesale and retail trade (15.0%); and government (4.5%). Where Washington and the first Congress had little to ponder with respect to social policy, today the federal government oversees direct expenditures, subsidies, regulations, and contracts and grants that empower a substantial public-private social welfare state. And rather than worrying about the fundamental vulnerability of being a small, albeit isolated, country in a world of vast empires and competing military powers, the current political leaders govern the lone remaining super power on the globe, with a massive nuclear arsenal and a defense budget nearly equal to the rest of the world combined, and a legacy of dozens of military or covert interventions in scores of countries.[3]

For the most part, the same constitutional configuration of government first derived when statesmen wore powdered wigs and breeches must make possible effective leadership and policy making under very different circumstances. Social conditions, once ignored, are now routinely viewed as public problems warranting some kind of government response. Indeed, the vast set of demands on government risks fomenting policy chaos unless there is some means to bring focus to the policy agenda. As the society and economy have grown in size and complexity, so have the reach and activities of the state and its administrative apparatus, posing extraordinary challenges to coordination and accountability. All of these transformations since 1789 have brought front and center four layers of core paradoxes affecting American government and politics that define the context for understanding and evaluating the performance of the modern executive branch. These paradoxes taken together establish the incentives that shape the ambitions of political leaders to achieve effective action as well as the simultaneous constraints on them that bind action, often frustrating energetic policy makers. The paradoxes play a major role in creating the tension between perceived responsibilities and actual capacities to perform, which, when most pronounced, has on occasion motivated chief executives to pursue constitutionally or legally questionable strategies to gain more effective influence.

Paradox 1: An Ethos of Individualism Mixed with a Call to Community

The first paradox is the current embodiment of the original clash between Whig principles, with their concentration on individual liberties, and the need for an effective government, which required harnessing concerted action to address problems that threatened the viability of the nation. The Constitution and the Federalists shifted the balance a notch towards greater centralization of power, but the core contradiction remains: a pervasive American political ethos that at once accentuates individual rights and autonomy while also recognizing the counter call to community and some version of collective action. The American polity has at root a commitment to the unfettered individual, protected from the interference of others, especially those wielding governmental authority. This tenet of rugged individualism has long been recognized as a feature of American politics, whether the product originally of the nation's extensive frontier, or its lack of feudal relations in the ages of agriculture or industrialization, or in the character of its immigrants, or simply its colonial experience vis à vis the British Crown and parliament.[4] The individual left alone remains winning political rhetoric. But so, too, is attention to "communal democracy" with its sensibility of "a united people . . . with the capacity, as John Adams put it, to 'think, feel, reason and act'" in search of solutions to inherently social problems.[5] There could not be, in Abraham Lincoln's words in his Gettysburg address, "a government of the people, by the people, for the people" without the expectation that the people can act in concert, with the state as their means and the president and executive branch playing instrumental roles. "Americans," writes James Morone, "have always managed to weigh the celebration of the individual with responsibility for community, market striving with civic caring, the private sphere and the public good."[6]

Paradox 2: A Distrust of Activist Government Mixed with Support for Government Benefits

The other three paradoxes have always been implied in the constitutional arrangements of the United States. The process of nation building early in the republic and certainly later on the effects of war, industrialization, and subsequent social change have brought them to the fore. Modern industrial democracies no longer remain on the sidelines of the economy or in the provision and protection of social welfare. In the second paradox, the American public—as one would expect from the first paradox—while distrusting activist government and worrying about threats to liberty of its interventions, as well as questioning its competence, today both desires and expects to receive the benefits of government domestic programs that have grown in response to market failures, economic downturns, insufficient provision of public goods, and resulting social disparities. For all of the disparagement of "big government" (even when it has not been so big compared to other nations), the two largest programs run by the federal government—Social Security and Medicare—have become so popular that they are considered the "third rail: touch them and you die."[7] At times the public even seems to favor greater expansions. In a September 20, 2000, Gallup Poll, for example, 64 percent of the public agreed with the position that "it is the responsibility of the federal government to make sure all Americans have health care coverage." One could find similar results for environmental protection, education, transportation, and other policy issues. As Lawrence Jacobs and Robert Shapiro put it most succinctly, "while Americans are philosophical conservatives who are committed to minimal government and maximum liberty for individuals to pursue their interests, they are also operational liberals who are devoted to specific and concrete government programs."[8] However, experience has also shown that when these two orientations, philosophical conservatism and operational liberalism, are posed in direct competition with one another on a specific policy issue, the political interests opposed to government involvement usually have a much easier time promoting the electorate's fear of government than policy advocates have in nurturing its desire for programmatic benefits.[9]

Paradox 3: Expectations of Presidential Leadership Mixed with a Fear of Presidential Power

The second paradox feeds the third. How can the nation tackle public problems effectively and coherently, given the complexity of the issues in both the domestic and international arenas, the size and diversity of the society, and the decentralization endemic in the American system of government (much of it, of course, required by the Constitution itself)? The answer is at first to be found in the broad public and elite expectations that the president should be the source of energetic leadership, that he or she is uniquely positioned to provide it, and will know how to execute it. The aura of greatness is associated with those chief executives who have fit this mold of personal leadership, at least in the American mythology: George Washington, proving the new republic could succeed; Thomas Jefferson, guiding the nation through its first transition from one governing party to the next and building upon the its great geographical expanse; Abraham Lincoln, preserving the union in the Civil War and ending slavery; Franklin Roosevelt, pulling the country out of the Great Depression and to a victory in World War II; and, most recently for some, Ronald Reagan, vanquishing the former Soviet Union to end the cold war. Other presidents floundered in this role. Jimmy Carter, for example, was unable to uplift the country in an era of perceived malaise, stagflation (the combination of high unemployment and high inflation), energy shortages, and the taking of U.S. hostages in Iran. George H.W.

Bush, devoid of a sense of vision, was unable to translate the regard for his leadership in the Persian Gulf War into effective management of the economy or domestic affairs as a whole. But hand-in-hand with the imagery of effective leadership is the other side of the paradox: the public's worries about actually granting the president unchecked authority to act, to lead independent of other public officials or armed with much more than persuasion and horse-trading. The Constitution offers little specific help to presidents, and the checks on executive leadership it embodies are necessary, from this perspective, to guard against the "imperial presidency" of the sort experienced during the Nixon administration and the Watergate scandals.[10] As Scott James poses it in his chapter for this volume, and as reflected in the ambiguity of Article II of the Constitution, the nation is caught "between a belief in executive leadership and a fear of executive power."

Paradox 4: Demand for a Responsive Bureaucracy Mixed with Expectations That a Competent Public Service Will Protect the Long-Term General Welfare

What programs or new directions are fashioned by the president and Congress, the executive agencies must implement and administer, which brings us to the fourth paradox. It begins with the general belief that the rest of the executive branch—the bureaucracy, in common language—should be reflective of and responsive to the public and its character, as expressed in the electorate's choice of elected leaders (both executive and legislative) and endorsement of their policy agendas. As part of what Morone describes as America's "democratic wish," rather than being ill-informed or incompetent subjects of public administration, Americans believe that "[t]he people are wiser than their governors." In each period throughout the nation's history, legitimacy for the bureaucracy has required "a different escape from the same threat—public officials who make independent judgments, [administrative] ministers who think."[11] From this perspective, the public fears that a bureaucracy left to its own devices—dislodged from the people—would be arrogant, wasteful, and prone to inertia, tying up action and responsiveness to public needs with red tape and organizational indolence. At the same time, along lines recognizable in Max Weber's idealized depiction of bureaucratic organization predicated on training, expertise, and specialization, attentive observers of government understand that the executive agencies should be the repository of policy-relevant knowledge, programmatic experience, analytical and administrative competence, and institutional memory, and have direct responsibility for fulfilling the programmatic dictates prescribed in laws that do not necessarily change with each new presidential administration or partisan regime.[12] In this same vein, agency officials, protected from the proximate torrents of politics, are believed to have a vital role in identifying what needs to be done rather than what may be most popular. Recalling Robert Dahl's criteria for democracy, executive branch institutions and officials are perhaps uniquely positioned among governmental actors to make possible the development and communication of an "enlightened understanding" of what best serves citizen interests and the society as a whole.[13] Too often it is not possible for the government and its administrative apparatus to be concurrently "of the people" or "by the people" while also being "for the people" in the largest sense.

The institutional arrangements of American government from the founding onward, including how they have been altered by law and interpretation, have necessarily reflected the governing ambiguities engendered by these paradoxes, as have the various efforts of disparate policy makers to either surmount or survive them. Both the Constitution and subsequent extra-constitutional developments—captured in Richard Neustadt's depiction of the president in a web of "separated institutions sharing powers" and picked up in the title of Charles O. Jones's book, *The Presidency in a Separated System*—pose the president and the executive branch in a highly decentralized system of governance with multiple competing institutional interests, each of which has a claim to public authority, and each now resident in a political-social milieu that is a wellspring of expectations, demands, and conflicts.[14]

When the national government was little more than the president, members of Congress, a limited set of judges and justices serving in the courts, and a few departments (with a small number of employees in Washington and a much greater quantity of postmasters throughout the country), the paradoxes were not much in play and the constitutional dispersion of power was significant but not of enormous consequence for executive officials. By mid-twentieth century, with the United States the world's leading economic engine and its dominant, internationalist military power, and with core norms of the social welfare state having begun to take root on America's shores, the contradictions embodied in the four paradoxes emerged full-blown. The resulting continuous contestation between individual interests, advantaged by the constitutional order, and new community interests, stimulated by economic and social change, has produced a potential for stalemate that satisfies no one, at least consistently, and has sometimes led to abuses of power. Individual-level incentives often overwhelm the capacity for successful collective action. Nonetheless, demands and opportunities for collective action (including opportunities to promote the interests of supportive constituencies in the name of collective interests) prompt presidents and their administrations, exploiting advances in information gathering and communications technologies, to identify and apply new strategies that they hope will permit them to advance their agendas in the complicated arena of American government.

Under the Madisonian design of American government, so named because among the founders James Madison was particularly instrumental in crafting the constitutional separation of the branches of government, a premium has always been placed on caution and incrementalism, rather than rapid acceptance of large-scale policy change. In this vein, Madisonian government typically favors one distinct side of the paradoxes: for example, individualism over community, philosophical conservatism over pragmatic liberalism, and fear of executive power over expectations of executive leadership. Madisonian government also favors thoughtful inertia in the administration of government and "republican virtue" (a commitment to an objective, public interest) over responsiveness to whatever popular passions may be sweeping the land at a given moment. Current sensitivities, though, may increase pressures on executive policy makers—whether liberal or conservative, Democratic or Republican—to strive to fulfill the opposite facets of the four paradoxes: emphasizing what they define as community needs at some risk to individual or specific group interests, pursuing programmatic action rather than showing restraint, empowering presidential leadership despite the fears of potential excesses, and pushing short-term administrative responsiveness over attention to competency and long-term societal interests. The paradoxes themselves, however, do not go away. The question thus remains: have presidents and the executive branch as a whole, especially in the modern era, been successful in negotiating the cross-cutting currents generated by the paradoxes embedded in American governance? Have they been able to govern effectively while also satisfying the dictates of the Constitution?

The Commission on the Executive Branch

To examine and evaluate the performance of the American presidency and executive branch as they have evolved since the founding of the republic, the Institutions of American Democracy project established a Commission on the Executive Branch, which we co-chaired. Our objective was to assemble for the commission an accomplished set of scholars, from distinguished emeriti to rising young stars, who represented diverse analytical orientations and political perspectives, and who could bring their specific and well-recognized expertise to bear on major topics that we identified as being of particular relevance to assessing the presidency, the executive agencies, and their engagement with the larger governing and political system. Some commissioners were engaged to author original chapters for this volume, the formal product of the commission. Others were invited to provide especially knowledgeable commentary on the draft chapters in progress and, along with the authors, to participate in whole-commission discussions of the issues both raised by us in formulating the plan for the book and emergent from the chapters themselves.

The commission held two multi-day meetings. The first was to critique and discuss as a group the initial chapter sketches submitted by the authors, and to develop a more thorough group understanding about the project's objectives, scope, and analytical approaches. The identification of the four paradoxes of American government grew naturally out of the authors' presentations and the commission's discussion of them. At the second meeting, completed first drafts of the chapters were subjected to detailed commentaries from both non-author commissioners and other authors writing chapters on related topics, joined by any other member of the commission who wished to offer additional insights and perspective. After each meeting we communicated directly with each author, providing our general guidance and specific suggestions for revisions, a process we repeated after the authors submitted revised drafts of their chapters. Consequently, this volume is the cumulative result of an ongoing, substantive dialogue among leading scholars in the country in which no chapter was produced or stands in isolation.

The deliberation at both commission meetings was open and wide-ranging, revealing both analytical points of consensus among these assembled specialists on the executive branch and areas of scholarly disagreement. We did not intend either the commission itself or the resulting edited book to hew to a particular "party line," whether political or intellectual. Our objective was to engage the issues with the best mix of research talent and analytical perspectives we could achieve. We believe that, as a result, this volume presents a fair representation of current scholarly assessment of the presidency and executive branch.

The authors in this volume, within their specific domains, first and foremost seek to explain the roles and behaviors of the president and those in the executive agencies given the nature of contemporary American government and the incentives created by the paradoxes in which it is embedded. At times, their analyses yield normative questions about how the president and executive branch should perform. From their individual perspectives, they give some consideration to what could be done to improve performance, sensitive to what is amenable to sensible "reform" and what is not, and with due attention to the long experience of adverse unintended consequences springing from the even the best intentioned changes. Because there is no official commission doctrine directing the authors in this volume, on some issues they may well disagree about either descriptive features of the system or normative ideas about improvements, or both. All, however, have wrestled with the challenges of modern American governance in the executive branch of the world's longest-running democracy, and provide sufficient evidence to permit readers themselves to formulate their own interpretations and normative conclusions.

Overview of the Book

Most edited volumes on the executive branch, indeed most scholarly books and articles on that subject, examine either the presidency or the administrative and regulatory agencies of government, not both simultaneously. Such is the curse of specialization in the academy. The design of the Commission on the Executive Branch permitted us to conduct an inclusive analysis that, under one cover, both focuses separately on the presidency and the executive agencies and considers them together as they influence—or are influenced by—other major institutions of American government and politics.

The first section of the book provides the historical and comparative context that is essential for understanding how the American executive branch has developed since the ratification of the Constitution and how much it differs from much of what has transpired in other advanced democracies, each with important implications for the contours and constraints of leadership. In Chapter 1, Scott James describes the most significant strategies undertaken by presidents throughout American history to manage the "yawning gulf between the duties of their office and the inadequate formal powers at their command." He sets the stage for the modern presidency and the subsequent efforts to achieve an "administrative presidency" with the chief executive in full control of the executive branch. Daniel Carpenter, author of Chapter 2, turns to the executive agencies, offering a "portable narrative, . . . a map that highlights the most important transitions and continuities in the history of American national bureaucracy." His essay highlights the inherited features from prior British administration, the dynamics of agency birth and death, the transformation of administrative personnel, and the role of war in building the bureaucracy. He also emphasizes the role of agencies as innovators and policy makers, the political context of agencies, and the nature of the most recent "contracting state." We next look at the executive in comparative perspective. Chapter 3 by Richard Rose shows how the institutional differences between the United States and other democracies create dramatically different contexts for leadership. He notes that "among the world's established democracies, the American presidential system is a deviant case. . . . The paradoxes of government . . . are resolved differently in Europe and in Washington. The dominant European political traditions . . . are collectivist rather than individualist. . . . Moreover, parliamentary leaders today benefit from being at the top of systems of government in which traditions of hierarchical authority are strongly entrenched and in which many citizens are prepared to accept the sometimes ponderous rule-bound ways in which public officials act in exchange for the social benefits that they deliver." These three chapters together underscore the core leadership and administrative challenges confronting the American executive branch.

Section II draws our analytical curtain around the White House establishment, addressing presidential behaviour and the institutions of the presidency. A good place to start is examining how presidents are selected for the august office they hold, the topic of Chapter 4 by Stephen J. Wayne. He provides a detailed description of the complicated process by which candidates emerge from the nominating process and ultimately "win" in the Electoral College. The attributes of presidential elections, he argues, "magnify a president's leadership dilemma by encouraging candidates to promise more than they can deliver, to exaggerate their accomplishments, and to present themselves as stronger, more confident, courageous, and visionary than they can possibly be in office." Matthew Dickinson investigates the Executive Office of the President (EOP), the most proximate organizational resources that presidents use to pursue their policy agendas and other objectives once in office. His concern, explored in Chapter 5, is the modern "paradox of politicization." Responding to heightened popular expectations of leadership, chief executives create a staff structure responsive to their immediate, individual political demands. Their "need for political loyalty has tended to trump [their] desire for nonpartisan expertise. The result is a pattern of institutional development in which administrative power within the EOP has gravitated toward the White House Office…The end result is a more thoroughly politicized, White House–dominated EOP, but one that is short on institutional memory, administrative expertise, and organizational continuity."

Presidents over the last few decades, according to Lawrence Jacobs in Chapter 6, have also sought to advance their objectives by making sweeping rhetorical claims that they represent the nation, the constituency as a whole, while simultaneously employing advanced public opinion polling to target strategically tailored communications to far more narrowly defined slices of the population. He concludes that "as presidents have promoted themselves ever more aggressively and visibly as defenders of the national interests, they and their advisors have devoted more attention to tracking and influencing narrow, discrete segments of the country to support the administration." These conclusions about campaigns, White House staffing and organization, and communications show modern presidents attempting to find ways to influence a governing system that would otherwise limit their impact. In this setting, do the characteristics of individual presidents make a difference? Fred Greenstein certainly believes so. In Chapter 7 he identifies six personal attributes of chief executives that can affect their chances for success in the American political system. Surveying the achievements and failures of exemplar presidents, he contends that "the personal qualities of the individual who happens to be president at a particular point in American history can have as great an impact as the impersonal forces and structures that command the bulk of attention in the scholarly literature on American government." However constrained, it matters whom the public selects to serve in the Oval Office.

In Section III, attention shifts from the president and White House to the bureaucracy. Colin Campbell opens the section with a study that illuminates the multifaceted array of executive agencies and the three models or approaches to public administration that have guided efforts to bring greater coherence to the "crazy quilt" American administrative state. Other nations, he notes, have "complex systems of departments, agencies, independent regulatory agencies and commissions, state and local government, nonprofit organizations, and private commercial contractors," but the United States "differs in the degree to which [various] factors . . . make coherent meshing of the contributions of these various elements exponentially more difficult than in most other advanced democracies." These agencies are run by the political appointees and career officials of the public service, the subject of Chapter 9 by Patricia Ingraham. Examining the characteristics of these officials and the challenging environment in which they work, she suggests that "[p]ublic servants are not 'bloodless bureaucrats,' they are people–the heart of government" who perform "tasks and jobs . . . [that] are more difficult and less predictable than at any point in our nation's history." As with the presidency, "the debate surrounding the public service has yet to address the problem of reconciling traditional constitutional tensions with more contemporary demands and expectations."

One source of tension or complexity is where the agencies and their personnel are located in the scheme of American national government. Although part of the executive branch, as Barry Weingast describes in Chapter 10, "[t]he federal bureaucracy is embedded in the American separation of powers system, implying a complex set of political relationships that I call the political-bureaucratic system. This system shapes bureaucratic behavior and policy making. In a real sense, the bureaucracy is 'caught in the middle' between Congress and the president," because the legislature plays a significant role in establishing, funding, and overseeing the agencies. A defining characteristic of the American administrative state, and the "logic of the political-bureaucratic system," are the efforts of both Congress and the president to exert control. Chapter 11, by Donald Kettl, explores one approach presidents in particular have often used to enhance control—the many guises of executive branch reform, part of what Kettl described as the American "system's remarkable ability to stretch, change, and adapt— without breaking—as new problems present themselves." In recent years, many democratic governments around the world have pursued "the new public management," a set of innovations whose overt aim is to improve the efficiency of administration. According to Kettl, the U.S. approach, including "reinventing government" during the Clinton administration, has proven to be "more ad hoc, more narrowly focused, and more pragmatic. . . . [Given the institutional decentralization of power,] Americans have tended more to use administrative reforms as political symbols, and to leverage those symbols for political gain." Still, the various waves of reform have had an impact, if only in increments. One way of summing across these assessments of the U.S. administrative state is that it appears to be firmly lodged in the middle—neither entirely responsive to presidential or congressional dictates, nor the paragon of competent and efficient management. However, it is also not addled by wanton red tape nor devoid of expertise, experience, and capacity. In fact, given the complex environment of the U.S. constitutional system, its growth and development are major achievements.

The presidency and agencies of the executive branch are deeply interwoven with other core institutions of American government and politics. These relationships are explored in Section IV. In Chapter 12, Sidney Milkis lends a textured historical analysis to political parties, an institution many of the founders faulted, did not think would be appropriate to the executive in the new republic, and ignored in the Constitution. But parties nonetheless flourished—"rooted in the states and localities; they penetrated deeply into American society between the 1830s and 1890s." As the president and the executive branch later led an expansion of the national administrative state, "[l]ocalized parties represented a formidable obstacle" until Franklin Roosevelt's institutionalized modern presidency "ruptured the limited but critical bond that linked presidents and parties." Since the Reagan administration, however, "a more national and issue-based party system [has been permitted] to develop, forging new links between presidents and parties," and offering another instrument of potential presidential influence over, even dominance of, the policy-making process. Partisan ties play a particularly critical role for presidents seeking to enact a legislative program, an issue discussed by Andrew Rudalevige in Chapter 13 on the executive branch and Congress. In the American system, the executive and the legislature are constitutionally separated from one another but need each other to accomplish their objectives. While executive agencies "remain important players in patterning policy for legislative perusal and maintain tight linkages to appropriations and authorizing committees," especially since FDR, "[t]he notion of a comprehensive presidential legislative program . . . has become an institution, a fundamental expectation of executive leadership." Presenting a legislative program is one thing, enacting it is quite another. Notes Rudalevige, "most of the time . . . presidents are facilitators, rather than directors, of change." Unlike prime ministers and their cabinets in parliamentary systems, presidents often see their initiatives ignored and are relative legislative giants when Congress accepts more than half of their proposals.

R. Shep Melnick, in Chapter 14, considers the other branch of government—the judiciary—with which presidents and agencies have also contended, sometimes sharply. Indeed, says Melnick, "American history is littered with dramatic confrontations between the president and the federal courts." Upon closer examination, however, "[g]iven the contrasting perspective of judges and chief executives, it is remarkable how rarely the federal courts have ruled that the president has exceeded his constitutional powers." As with the legislature, the "[s]truggles between the president and the courts have almost always centered not on the inherent constitutional powers of the executive, but on the important substantive political issues of the day." Because of the paradoxes embedded in the Constitution, this institutional relationship is also no stranger to the dual efforts of each branch trying to shape the other, from the courts presenting "shifting doctrines on the authority of administrative agencies" to the president trying to "to influence the judiciary through appointments and control over the federal government's litigational strategies. . . . Presidents with vision resolutely and unapologetically try to pack the courts with judges who share their vision. All great presidents have tried to do this." Finally, like the courts, federalism has historically constrained national policy making but also often been the instrument, however imperfect, of its implementation. As Thomas Gais and James Fossett argue in Chapter 15, the interactions and relationships of presidents and the national executive branch with state and local governments have also changed. Today "their policy agendas have become inextricably intertwined and overlapped." This result has "transformed the federal executive's role in the American federal system," shifting from indirect influence through the conventional legislative process to the use of "a growing range of administrative tools to negotiate directly with states over specific policies or to alter the context of state policy making without specific congressional approval." The new "executive federalism," however, comes with a cost. It may "undermine checks and balances *within* the national government; avoids national debates even while major policies spread through the federal system; and creates an even more complex and varied range of policies among the states." Each of these institutions—political parties, Congress, the courts, and federalism—have complicated the lives of presidents and executive agencies, not uncommonly blocking their desired policy agendas. In each case, presidents have eventually fought back, seeking to gain some degree of control over the policy levers that the Constitution denies them.

In our closing chapter in Section V, we offer our read of the status of presidential power and the administrative state based on the accumulation of evidence from the previous chapters. The paradoxes of American government and politics, fully actuated by the dynamics of a large, diverse, modern society, produce a constant struggle for control of policy making by multiple participants in the system, including the president and the political and career officials in the agencies. The central thrust of the modern presidency, particularly since the Nixon era and in full flower during the presidency of George W. Bush, is a grasping for a "unilateral presidency" as free as possible of the constraints enforced by competing institutions under the terms of the Constitution. Several presidents have sought to win decisively the battle for control of the executive agencies, applying the instruments of the "administrative presidency" to make the administrative state their own. The contending forces of American government, and the strategies of the modern presidency to centralize control in the White House, raise questions about the compatibility of such an empowered chief executive with the basic precepts of American constitutional design. The also put into sharp relief ambiguities about accountability: who is accountable, and to whom; who should be accountable, and to whom; and how—given the mix of constitutional arrangements and actual practice—the leaders of the policy-making process can and should be held answerable to the people.

Acknowledgments

An original and thorough examination of the major institutions of American government by a large group of the nation's academic specialists is not a trivial undertaking. Our collective study, resulting in this volume on the executive branch, is the product of the entrepreneurial spirit and collaboration of three institutions: the Annenberg Foundation Trust at Sunnylands, which underwrote the entire Institutions of American Democracy project; the Annenberg Public Policy Center of the University of Pennsylvania, which under the energetic leadership of its director, Kathleen Hall Jamieson, inspired the commissions and furnished our particular commission with excellent organizational support; and Oxford University Press, the publisher of all five Institutions of American Democracy volumes. We are grateful to have been chosen to co-chair the Commission on the Executive Branch, a task made both intellectually exciting and especially manageable because of this extraordinary institutional engagement and support.

We have also benefited from and are most thankful for the participation of Jaroslav Pelikan, the Scholarly Director of the Institutions of American Democracy project and leader of its National Advisory Board. He read all of the chapter manuscripts and was an engaged participant at the two meetings of the commission, both imbuing our sessions with good cheer and, with the keen sensibilities of a distinguished historian and man of letters, setting the elevated tone of our deliberations about core matters of democracy.

The Commission on the Executive Branch, of course, would have amounted to little absent the exceptional contributions of its members, who brought not only unparalleled expertise to the topics of our investigation but also a full sense of community and collaboration. The Commission may have involved hard work, but it was hard work of the best kind, facilitated by comradeship and mutual respect. We thank all of the chapter authors for their dedication to the enterprise, insightful essays, engagement with one another, and collegial partnership with us as editors. The chapter-writing members of the Commission have their labors memorialized in the pages of this volume. Here is our only formal opportunity to both name and extol the vital behind-the-scenes contributions of the distinguished non-author members of the Commission: Martha A. Derthick, George C. Edwards III, Hugh Heclo, Stephen Hess, Matthew Holden, Jr., Charles O. Jones, the Honorable Robert Katzmann, Richard P. Nathan, James P. Pfiffner, and Bert A. Rockman. Each one is a leading figure in the study of American national institutions and politics. They all provided the authors and us with thoughtful guidance, invaluable insights, and important concrete suggestions, for which we are all most appreciative.

Coordinating the simultaneous production and publication of five edited volumes, each with two coeditors and myriad chapter authors, cannot be an easy undertaking. We are indebted to our editors at Oxford University Press—Timothy DeWerff, Tim Bartlett, and Joe Clements—for their guidance, patience and good humor, accommodations, and effective management of a complex process.

Each meeting of the Commission at the Annenberg Public Policy Center ran smoothly, as if by magic, and with delightful fare, thanks to the sure organizational hands of Laura Kordiak and Annette Price. We would also like to thank Andrew Lee, Marc Pilotin, and Eric Torrence, Joel Aberbach's staff at the Center for American Politics and Public Policy at UCLA, for research and logistical assistance, as well as Holly Campbell, Mark Peterson's Graduate Research Assistant in the UCLA Department of Public Policy,

Notes

1. Joseph J. Ellis, *Founding Brothers: The Revolutionary Generation* (New York: Vintage, 2000), 7–8.
2. Gordon S. Wood, *The Creation of the American Republic, 1776–1787* (New York: W. W. Norton, 1969), chapters 1 and 13, quotes from pp. 519–520.
3. U.S. Census Bureau, Table 1, "United States—Race and Hispanic Origin: 1790 to 1990," Internet Release Date, September 13, 2002, http://www.census.gov /population/documentation/twps0056/tab01.xls; "Table 1: Annual Estimates of the Population of the United States and States, and for Puerto Rico: April 1, 2000, to July 1, 2004 (NST-EST2004-01), Source: Population Division, U.S. Census Bureau, Release Date: December 22, 2004, www.census.gov/popest/states /tables/NST-EST2004-01.pdf; Campbell Gibson, "Population of the 100 Largest Cities and Other Urban Places in the United States: 1790 to 1990," Population Division Working Paper No. 27, U.S. Bureau of the Census, Table 2, Internet Release Date, June 15, 1998, www.census.gov/population/documentation /twps0027/tab02.txt ; Darren M. Staloff, "The Learned Class of the 18th Century (Review Essay)," *William and Mary Quarterly* LVIII, no. 2 (April 2001), 464; Table on "Ethnic Division of the Colonial Population, 1775," Digital History Web site, www.digitalhistory.uh.edu/historyonline/us6.cfm; U.S. Census Bureau, *Statistical Abstract of the United States: 2004–2005* (Washington, D.C.), Table No. 21; Table No. 600; U.S. Census Bureau, *County and City Data Book: 2000* (Washington, D.C.), Table C-1; Program Evaluation and Assessment Branch, Los Angeles Unified School District; Jacob S. Hacker, *The Divided Welfare State: The Battle over Public and Private Social Benefits in the United States* (New York: Cambridge University Press, 2002); Niall Ferguson, "Think Again: Power," *Foreign Policy* (January–February 2003), 18–24; Ellen C. Collier, "Instances of Use of United States Forces Abroad, 1798–1993," Washington, D.C.: Congressional Research Service, Library of Congress, October 7, 1993, www.history.navy.mil/wars/foabroad.htm.
4. Frederick Jackson Turner, *The Frontier in American History* (New York: H. Holt, 1931); Louis Hartz, *The Liberal Tradition in America* (New York: Harcourt Brace Jovanovich, 1955); Alexis de Tocqueville, *Democracy in America* (Reprint, New York: Alfred A. Knopf, 1951).

5. James A. Morone, *The Democratic Wish: Popular Participation and the Limits of American Government* (New York: Basic Books, 1990), 5.
6. Morone, *The Democratic Wish*, 334.
7. Mark A. Peterson, "The Fate of 'Big Government' in the United States: Not Over, But Undermined?" *Governance* 13, no. 2 (April 2000), 251–264; Hacker, *The Divided Welfare State*.
8. "Do you think it is the responsibility of the federal government to make sure all Americans have health care coverage or is that not the responsibility of the federal government?," Gallup Poll, Release of Source Document: September 20, 2000; Lawrence R. Jacobs and Robert Y. Shapiro, "The American Public's Pragmatic Liberalism Meets Its Philosophical Conservatism," *Journal of Health Politics, Policy and Law* 24, no. 5 (October 1999), 1021.
9. Theda Skocpol, *Boomerang: Health Care Reform and the Turn against Government* (New York: W. W. Norton, 1996).
10. Arthur M. Schlesinger, Jr., *The Imperial Presidency* (Boston: Houghton Mifflin, 1973).
11. Morone, *The Democratic Wish*, 5, 323.
12. Max Weber, *The Theory of Social and Economic Organization* (Oxford University Press, 1947). Bureaucrats are also supposed to be neutral enough to completely and effectively administer new laws as well.
13. Robert A. Dahl, *Democracy and Its Critics* (New Haven: Yale University Press, 1989), 111–112.
14. Richard E. Neustadt, *Presidential Power* (New York: John Wiley & Sons, 1960), 42; Charles O. Jones, *The Presidency in a Separated System* (Washington, D.C.: The Brookings Institution, 1994).

THE EXECUTIVE BRANCH

THE HISTORICAL
AND COMPARATIVE CONTEXT

1

THE EVOLUTION OF THE PRESIDENCY: BETWEEN THE PROMISE AND THE FEAR

Scott C. James

PRESIDENTS CONFRONT A YAWNING GULF BETWEEN THE duties of their office and the inadequate formal powers at their command. This fundamental asymmetry is at the heart of the presidency's historical development. It has yielded an improvisational and opportunistic presidency, one whose incumbents are constantly on the make for short-term advantage in America's system of shared powers. That presidents remain at a competitive disadvantage in this struggle for influence can be gleaned from contemporary scholarship. Leading students of the office conclude that presidential influence over Congress occurs "at the margins" of the policy process; moments of presidential domination are episodic and contingent at best. Indeed, these studies indicate that the successful exercise of presidential leadership is shaped more by the configuration of situational variables outside the president's immediate control and less by the personal attributes of a particular incumbent or the institutional organization of his office.[1]

These impediments to effective leadership simply make presidents work harder, prompting them to explore the available mechanisms of political control and to challenge the political and cultural conventions that define appropriate presidential behavior. The results of these leadership efforts have been consequential. Historically, the presidential struggle for political influence has wrought several fundamental changes and, in the process, helped lay the foundations for the modern presidency: a profound conceptual reworking of the office, one that

3

stresses the popular underpinnings of presidential authority; the rise of a powerful and centralized presidential establishment; and basic alterations in the patterned relationships between presidents and Congress, presidents and the permanent bureaucracy, and presidents and citizens at large. On different occasions, presidential improvisation has also set presidents against public law, the standard operating procedures of government, or the Constitution itself, often in the name of short-term political success.

The purpose of this chapter is to trace the historical emergence of the modern presidency, to isolate its essential features, and to pinpoint the factors driving change over time. The modern presidency is often depicted as emerging virtually full-blown from the actions of Franklin Delano Roosevelt. In fact, its constituent elements emerged piecemeal over the long course of American history, the product of constitutional ambiguities, political and electoral necessity, developments in technology and social organization, and unvarnished presidential ambition. However, the fundamental dynamic driving the development of the presidency is constitutional in nature. It is rooted in a basic polarity between the wide berth for discretionary action implicit in Article II and the modest grant of formal powers attached to the presidential office—or, to put it more succinctly, between a belief in executive leadership and a fear of executive power. The former impels presidents to act; the latter sends presidents scrambling for fresh sources of political influence to sustain their leadership projects. The result has been a process of constitutional change and extraconstitutional innovation central to the presidency's historical development. As Emmet John Hughes has remarked, the Framers did not so much define the contours of executive power as defer the question to the future. The presidential office was left purposefully "to be shaped by the live touch of history."[2]

Independence, discretion, and wide-ranging responsibility are three constituent features of the modern presidency that help lay the predicate for the contemporary exercise of executive leadership. They have also helped to feed exaggerated characterizations of American government as "presidential government" and America itself as a "presidential nation."[3] While certainly not without empirical referents, such notions overstate the relative power of the office. The modern presidency is not a terribly strong presidency, let alone an imperial one. As an institution, it is inadequately endowed to meet the high contemporary expectations for national leadership; it is not fashioned for success. Of itself, independence does not create its own power resources; discretion does not necessarily yield political influence; and responsibility does not automatically foster its own requisite capacity. In the end, the modern presidency is a curiously paradoxical institution, one in which intrinsic institutional weakness stokes a latent cultural antipathy to executive power, as presidents in urgent search of ever greater political control erode public trust and fuel perceptions of an arrogant and aggrandizing office.

4

The discussion that follows will trace the evolution of the presidency from the era of the founders to the present day, examining in some detail the administrations of several chief executives deemed critical to the development of the presidential office. This evolution will be presented as a steady accrual of ancient traditions, conceptual innovations, and pragmatic experiments, elements that would be drawn together and synthesized by Franklin Roosevelt and posthumously labeled the "modern presidency." Some of the central scholarly writings on the post-Roosevelt presidency will also be examined, employing that literature as a device both for assessing contemporaneous attitudes toward the new "president-centered government" and for tracking that institution's continued transformation and growth. The conclusion of the chapter will return to a discussion of the paradoxes of the modern presidency and the challenges that confront the exercise of contemporary presidential leadership.

Founding-Era Contributions

Critical ideas regarding discretionary executive power are directly traceable to the Framers and, more broadly, to the political culture of the Founding Era. These understandings were rooted both in the ambiguities of the Constitution and in America's British political inheritance. They would provide a welcome cache of legitimacy for presidents seeking to justify ever-widening responsibilities and their authority to exercise independent leadership.

The Article II Vesting Clause

Some of the seeds of the modern presidency are sown into the fabric of the Constitution itself, especially the vaguely worded vesting clause that introduces Article II itself. Almost immediately, the founding generation would be forced to grapple with the ill-defined scope of the executive power. By comparison, the vesting clause that opens Article I was a model of exactitude. That article established a Congress of the United States and made clear reference to enumerated "powers herein granted"—language that precisely delineated and delimited the national legislative power. Article II was more open-ended—and by conventional rules of construction, intentionally so. It stated simply that "[t]he executive power shall be vested in a President of the United States." This description of "executive power" was left radically underspecified, though to enthusiasts of a strong presidency it implied a clear residuum of powers beyond those formally "herein granted." By this reading, the subsequent enumeration of particular powers served merely to exemplify the general grant of power contained in the vesting clause, and to delineate a set of specific limitations on that grant, as such in the requirement that presidents seek the advice and consent of the Senate in the making of treaties and executive appointments. Otherwise, the precise scope of the executive power was intentionally left to be interpreted in light of

5

concrete political exigencies, general constitutional principles, and accepted tenets of free government.

Future presidents would utilize the Vesting Clause, as well as the Take Care Clause and the Presidential Oath of Office (which together suggest the president's broader obligations to uphold the Constitution), to justify a wide berth for presidential actions not explicitly sanctioned by Article II's formal list of presidential powers.

Extra-Constitutional Traditions

EXECUTIVE PREROGATIVE. Many of the founding generation placed high value on an expansive understanding of the executive power. To them, Article II's underspecification of the executive power promised substantial returns to the commonweal. A well-structured relationship between the executive and the legislature required ample scope for presidential discretion. On this point, two of the founding era's most respected authorities, John Locke and William Blackstone, agreed. Writing in 1689, Locke had adjudged the good of society to require "that several things should be left to the discretion of him that has the executive power."

> For the Legislators not being able to foresee, and provide, by Laws, for all, that may be useful to the Community, the Executor of the Laws, having the power in his hands, has by the common Law of Nature, a right to make use of it, for the good of the society.[4]

In the preceding passage, Locke is elucidating the prerogative power, and independent executive action was at the heart of that power. In his most concise formulation, Locke defined executive prerogative as "the power to act according to discretion, for the publick good, without the prescription of the Law, and sometimes even against it."[5] It was a spontaneous and uncontrolled power, one therefore responsive to contingent circumstances affecting the community welfare. Writing in 1765, a period more contemporaneous with the founding of the United States, William Blackstone concurred in the general utility of the executive prerogative, even if its exact contours were hard to pin down. It was something "singular and eccentrical [sic],"[6] Blackstone wrote, though not necessarily arbitrary, for to be legitimate the prerogative was to be exercised to advance the public good. Because of its potential contributions to the public welfare, Blackstone further denied the authority of the legislature in many circumstances to limit the freedom of executive action: "For it would be of most mischievous consequence to the public," Blackstone wrote, "if the strength of the executive power were liable to be curtailed without its own express consent. . . ."[7]

In light of its historical association with British royal authority, political elites generally shied away from specific use of the term "prerogative." Moreover, the Constitution had denied to the American president many of the specific prerogatives traditionally enjoyed by the British king, such as the right to declare war. Nonetheless, the authority of Locke and Blackstone in the early republic lent credence to the notion that in any well-ordered political system, an independent and discretionary power must be lodged with some leader of high public trust in order to protect and advance the welfare of the community.

SALUS POPULI AND THE LIMITS OF THE LAW. As leaders of high public trust in their own right, it is worth reflecting upon the political dealings undertaken by the Framers themselves in pursuit of a new American Constitution. Their actions shed still more light onto the contemporaneous norms of leadership from which future presidents might draw. "Publius" (the pseudonym under which James Madison, Alexander Hamilton, and John Jay wrote their essays defending the proposed Constitution) was only conceding the obvious when he admitted that delegates to the Constitutional Convention had exceeded their legal authority both in the drafting of a new Constitution and in submitting their handiwork directly to the people for ratification (instead of to the state legislatures).[8] Such patently unlawful actions led Publius to consider the circumstances under which public-minded officers might legitimately abrogate rules expressly drawn to direct and delimit their own political autonomy. In Publius's formulation, the question was "how far considerations of duty ... [could supply] any defect of regular authority."[9] Publius's answer was bold and certain: When necessity clashes with the laws, when substance collides with forms, a concern for the public good requires that the latter yield to the former.

Publius grounded his defense of public-spirited lawlessness in the doctrine *salus populi suprema lex esto* ("the welfare of the people is the highest law"). In invoking the *salus populi*, he endeavored to tap a reservoir of political values that he and his readers shared in common. Here he argued that "the transcendent law of nature and of nature's God, which declares that the safety and happiness of society are the objects at which all political institutions aim . . ." stipulates that where adherence to law jeopardizes the public weal, the former must give way to the greater good. Indeed, Publius insisted that a defense of the law and of "ordinary forms" was often a haven for "those who wished to indulge, under these masks, their secret enmity to the substance contended for." Under such circumstances, it might be critical that leadership be seized "by some patriotic and respectable citizen or number of citizens" on behalf of some desirable but "informal and unauthorized propositions."[10]

Though unlawful, Publius considered such actions neither arbitrary nor illegitimate. What legitimated the actions of the Convention attendees—and what legitimates the unprescribed actions of any elected official of high public trust— is that they must ultimately submit those actions before the bar of public opinion. Nor could the public's verdict be taken for granted. Voters might register their disapprobation by rejecting both action and actor; conversely, they might sustain both. A public officer could never know for certain which side of the line he was on, but it was the leader's obligation to assume such risk as a part of his charge, to exercise, in Publius's words, "a manly confidence in their country, by whose confidence they had been so peculiarly distinguished."[11]

We can see the influence of the *salus populi* at work in the early history of the presidency, specifically in the writings of Thomas Jefferson. In the course of his eight-year presidency, Jefferson had been criticized for undertaking several unilateral actions for which no explicit constitutional authority could be cited. These included the Louisiana Purchase, the Chesapeake affair, and the so-called Burr conspiracy. The criticisms had cut, and the wound had not fully healed by the time Jefferson left office. Now in retirement, the ex-president found occasion to address more fully the question of "whether circumstances do not sometimes occur, which make it a duty in officers of high trust, to assume authorities beyond the law. . . ." Jefferson's response to this question is revealing for its explicit reliance upon the *salus populi*. Echoing Publius, the former president wrote:

> A strict observance of the written laws is doubtless *one* of the highest duties of a good citizen, but it is not the *highest*. The laws of necessity, of self-preservation, of saving our country when in danger, are of higher obligation. To lose our country by a scrupulous adherence to written law, would be to lose the law itself, with life, liberty, property and all those who are enjoying them with us; thus absurdly sacrificing the end to the means.[12]

This emphasis on communal danger and self-preservation might seem to delimit the situations under which recourse to the *salus populi* might legitimately be sought. However, the hypothetical scenario Jefferson subsequently developed to clarify his response is significant for the way it broadened the justification for unlawful presidential action beyond situations of dire necessity to reach more subjective calculations of "public advantage." Jefferson's hypothetical begins with a president who has been presented with an opportunity to purchase the Florida Territories (then in the possession of Spain) "for a reasonable sum." Congress is in recess, and, moreover, once back in session the president anticipates that congressional opponents might stymie timely action, closing the window of opportunity for the purchase. "Ought the Executive, in that case, and with that foreknowledge, to have secured the good of his country, and to have trusted to their justice for the transgression of the law? I think he ought, and that the act would have been approved." In closing, Jefferson reflected on the peculiar obligations of the presidential office and the mandate for independent and discretionary action implicit in them. Like Publius, Jefferson admits that in undertaking actions beyond the law, the president "does indeed risk himself on the justice of the controlling powers of the Constitution . . ." and of public opinion. Nevertheless, the obligations of his high station require that the risk be taken.

> It is incumbent on those only who accept great charges, to risk themselves on great occasions, when the safety of the nation, or some of its very high interests are at stake. An officer is bound to obey orders; yet he would be a bad one who should do it in cases for which they were not intended, and which involved the most important consequences. The line of discrimination between cases may be difficult; but the good officer is bound to draw it at his own peril, and throw himself on the justice of his country and the rectitude of his motives.[13]

The English tradition of executive prerogative, the doctrine of *salus populi*, and the discretion afforded officers of high trust each shaped the latent meaning of Article II's vesting clause. Though its interpretation would continue to be hotly contested, these traditions would be available to presidents seeking to legitimize the exercise of unilateral action. They prescribed independent executive action when, in the president's own judgment, the public welfare demanded it. They suggested a natural right of presidents to be bound by neither congressional law nor constitutional rule when the commonweal required political leadership. It indicated further that presidential actions undertaken without sanction of law could be legitimated retrospectively by popular acclamation. That is to say, it suggested that the principal constraint on independent presidential action might be plebiscitary in nature, not a reliance on formal constitutional mechanisms.

While the Cat's Away . . .

One final aspect of government in the early republic briefly requires our attention. As Figure 1 makes clear, during the first forty years of the Constitution's existence (1789–1829), Congress spent an average of almost two-thirds of a four-year presidential term of office in recess. Indeed, from 1789 to 1907 (the 1st through 59th Congresses) Congress was in session on average only 45.6 percent of a presidential term. By comparison, since 1969 the average Congress has spent close to 90 percent of this same time frame in session.

Governance through the regular promulgation of new law was not considered to be a full time job in the early Republic. Perhaps Locke's dictum still held sway, that "[i]t is not necessary, no nor so much as convenient, that the legislative should be always in being. . . ."[14] However, while legislation was an irregular activity, the administration of the law required the executive's almost continuous presence. The impact of this basic feature of early American government on the development of the presidency was significant and it should not be lost on us. It created a political environment in which presidential independence and discretion could more readily be asserted and their parameters more easily tested—

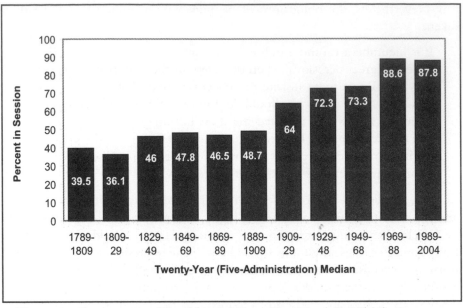

Figure 1   Percentage of Presidential Four–Year Term in Which Congress was in Session, 1789–2004

sometimes intentionally so. Indeed, many of the significant acts of discretionary leadership that punctuate American political history and that would provide precedents for subsequent presidents were undertaken while Congress was adjourned: Washington's Neutrality Proclamation; Jefferson's initiative in securing the Louisiana Purchase by treaty with France; Jackson's unilateral removal of government deposits from the second Bank of the United States; Lincoln's blockade of southern ports, his expansion of the army and navy, and his suspension of habeas corpus; Theodore Roosevelt's intervention to arbitrate the Great Anthracite Coal Strike of 1902. While there is insufficient space to pursue this theme in these pages, it is nonetheless worth posing the relevant counterfactual: Along what alternate developmental paths might the presidency have been pushed had Congress been in almost continual session, as it is today, from the very first days of the Republic?

The Jacksonian Revolution

The administration of Andrew Jackson (1829–1837) marks the first seminal juncture on the road to the modern presidency. When Jackson vetoed the bill to recharter the Second Bank of the United States in 1832, he set in train a series of events that would alter the constitutional foundations of the presidential office. Not the least of those transformations was to the veto itself. But in addition to that specific act of reinvention, Jackson's "little bank war" produced several novel constitutional doctrines, most of which we take for granted today: that the presidency is an equal and autonomous branch of government; that only the president speaks with a national voice and, as such, more effectively embodies the popular will in politics; and that the president is the responsible head of the administration (and is therefore justified in ensuring that the executive branch is responsive to presidential direction).[15] Each of these constitutional innovations will be examined here. The story of Jackson's war on the Bank of the United States (BUS) is as dramatic as its constitutional ramifications were transformative. When Congress took up the issue of the Bank's recharter in 1832, its original twenty-year charter was not due to expire for another four years. Anxious for an election-year issue that could cleave Jackson's Democratic coalition and prevent his reelection, the Kentucky senator Henry Clay, Jackson's presidential rival in that election year, arranged to have the recharter brought up for early consideration. Jackson's opposition to the BUS was widely known, his views having been made clear in two successive annual messages to Congress. Knowing Jackson never to shrink from a fight, Clay maneuvered the anti-Jackson Congress into passing the recharter bill to force a presidential veto. Jackson obliged. Still, more fundamental issues were implicated in the president's veto; with this action, Jackson had taken direct aim at the Jeffersonian doctrine of legislative supremacy. From this point on, Jackson now insisted, both the president's policy preferences and his constitutional convictions must be accounted for in the formulation of congressional legislation.

Policy Leadership

Jackson announced his veto of the Bank recharter on July 10, 1832, provoking an immediate and vehement congressional outcry. Prior to Jackson's administration, presidents had employed the veto power sparingly.[16] Settled practice authorized vetoes where Congress's authority to legislate in a given area was constitutionally murky, or where hasty consideration produced legislation with remediable technical deficiencies.[17] The overriding constitutional function of the veto was to aid Congress in the performance of its deliberative functions, not to substitute the president's judgment for the Congress's on national policy matters.[18]

Jackson directly challenged this practice. In his veto message, Jackson indicted the BUS as "inexpedient" and contrary to "sound policy."[19] In so doing, the president was directly expressing his personal programmatic judgment. The Bank was, in his view, an institution not conducive to the national welfare, and legislation inconsistent with his assessment would meet the full force of the president's power.

In taking these actions, Jackson was in fact asserting a leadership role for the president in the legislative process, signaling his intention to use the veto as a bargaining chip to force Congress's hand in the struggle over public policy.[20] The doctrine of congressional supremacy had been breached, with the president no longer willing to accept a constitutional station subordinate to the legislative power. Instead, Jackson had vindicated his institutional prerogatives as a coequal and coordinate branch of government, entitled to exercise the full measure of his personal discretion in the formation of national policy. The president, Jackson insisted, was the legislature's constitutional equal in matters of national policy and it was Congress's obligation to consult the president's views prior to legislative deliberations or face the consequences.[21]

Popular Mandate

Jackson concluded his veto message with one last departure from settled practice: a direct appeal to voters. Having denied the authority of Congress to limit the president's political independence, Jackson fastened onto the upcoming elections as yet another way to legitimate his attack on the BUS. However, Jackson did not invoke the special authority of *presidential* elections; that still lay in the future. Rather, he asked voters to vindicate his veto by repudiating the sitting Congress and sending new representatives to Washington to sustain the President's actions. Jackson wrote:

> A general discussion will now take place, eliciting new light and settling important questions; and a new Congress, elected in the midst of such discussion, . . . will bear to the Capitol the verdict of public opinion, and I doubt not, bring this important question to a satisfactory result.[22]

Another important precedent had thus been set. An incumbent president was turning to the electorate to sustain the authority of his policy actions. Unfortunately for Jackson, the new Congress only partly fulfilled his expectations. While the House would now be under Democratic control, the Senate remained under the sway of anti-Jacksonian forces. Undeterred, Jackson continued his assault on the Bank. Not content to wait four years for its original charter finally to expire, the President moved immediately to withdraw all federal deposits held by the BUS, thus bleeding the institution of its financial life's blood. But on what authority did Jackson propose to act? The deposits were under the direct control of the Treasury Department, and the First Congress had conferred upon the secretary of the Treasury statutory discretion and direct obligations to the legislature that seemed to defy presidential control.

Once again Jackson turned to voters to justify his course of action. However, now the President shifted his ground. Confronted with the ambiguous results of the most recent congressional elections, Jackson seized upon the special authority of presidential elections, an authority grounded in the uniquely communal act of choosing a chief executive. "We are one people in the choice of President and Vice-President," Jackson declared. "The people . . . are represented in the executive branch."[23] On September 18, 1833, Jackson notified his Cabinet of his intention to begin removing government deposits from the BUS. He also clarified the specific authority on which he would proceed. The president explained that Bank supporters had timed the recharter effort precisely to make it "a leading question in the election of a President of the United States. . . ." Indeed, "all steps deemed necessary had been taken" by his opponents "to procure from the people a reversal of the President's decision." Pro-Bank forces had put the matter before the people, the issue had been fully vetted on both sides, and the people had sustained the president. They had given Jackson a personal mandate to destroy the bank.

> It was to compel the President to take his stand that the question was brought forward at that particular time. He met the challenge, willingly took the position into which his adversaries sought to force him, and frankly declared his unalterable opposition to the bank as being both unconstitutional and inexpedient. On that ground the case was argued to the people; and now that the people have sustained the President, notwithstanding the array of influence and power which was brought to bear upon him, it is too late, he confidently thinks, to say that the question has not been decided. *Whatever may be the opinions of others, the President considers his reelection as a decision of the people against the bank.*[24]

Executive Unity and Responsibility

Jackson's war against the Bank also had lasting implications for the organization of the executive branch. In pressing forward his fight to remove the federal deposits from Bank control, Jackson was led to assert yet one further constitutional prerogative. The president insisted that his obligation to "take care that the laws be faithfully executed" required that all cabinet officers be placed in a subordinate relationship to him. Presidential responsibility for executive branch actions required Cabinet unity under presidential direction, and the only way that unity could be achieved was if administrative discretion resided solely with the president.

This doctrine of executive unity and responsibility was not fully elaborated when Jackson took office. As noted earlier, this was particularly true of the Treasury Department, which had enjoyed a close statutory relationship to Congress. The First Congress had granted treasury secretaries a considerable discretion in the execution of their duties; they were personally responsible to the legislature for all departmental actions; and they were required to submit to Congress in writing the reasons behind any such actions taken. This structural breach in the separation of powers set Jackson on a collision course with the Treasury once the president had determined his course of action. To him, the decision regarding where to store the federal deposits was purely an executive matter. Moreover, as chief executive, inferior executive officers were duty bound to follow his orders or be replaced by someone who would. In ordering his recalcitrant Treasury secretary to proceed, Jackson insisted: "A secretary, sir, is merely an executive agent, a subordinate. . . ."[25]

Jackson had finessed the problem early on by promoting his first secretary of the Treasury to secretary of State, installing a more pliant officer in his stead. However, the new secretary quickly asserted his independence. Jackson protested that any discretion vested in the Treasury secretary's office was *his* to exercise by authority of the Constitution, which had vested the whole of the executive power in the president of the United States. The secretary, however, reasserted his primary obligation to Congress and, moreover, refused to resign. The following questions were now ripe for resolution: Did the Treasury secretary "function under the direction and authority of the president" and did he serve at his pleasure? Could the president remove a duly confirmed Treasury secretary without the prior approval of Congress? Jackson answered each question in the affirmative, summarily firing the new secretary and replacing him with Roger Taney, a loyal Jacksonian. Of this action, the historian of public administration Leonard White would conclude: "No single change in the practical operation of the executive branch gave Presidents greater power than this, for the capacity to remove could be used to induce almost universal compliance among officeholders, either by its exercise or by mere threat or expectation of use."[26]

Lincoln's Legacy

Abraham Lincoln's precise impact upon the development of the presidency has been the subject of considerable dispute. Scholars on all sides of the debate acknowledge the unprecedented expansion of presidential power during the Civil War. Nevertheless, as many have rightly remarked, the transitory nature of this "Lincoln revolution" is equally striking, as is the tenacity with which old forms and practices were reasserted after the war's end.[27] This reversion to antebellum institutional habits appears so comprehensive that one skeptic of Lincoln's contributions to presidential development, Theodore Lowi, could justifiably remark, "By 1875 . . . you would not know there had been a war or a Lincoln."[28]

It is certainly the case that Lincoln was, in many respects, "a Whig in the White House."[29] A staunch member of the Whig Party, Lincoln grew to political maturity amid years of vigorous party opposition to a string of strong Jacksonian presidents and the inroads they had cut into traditional congressional prerogatives. Perhaps the clearest exposition of Whig principles had been set forth by President William Henry Harrison in his 1841 inaugural address. In that speech, Harrison expressly repudiated the Jacksonian model of the presidency. He denied the president's more intimate proximity to the people and lauded

Congress's superior popular foundations. He further disavowed the use of the veto on policy grounds and more broadly condemned presidential interference in the legislative process. Likewise, Harrison rejected the Jacksonian doctrine of Cabinet subordination to the chief executive and promised to seek congressional assent before removing his Treasury secretary from office.[30]

Harrison's views were largely Lincoln's, and as president, Lincoln put many of these orthodox Whig ideas into practice. In a clear repudiation of Andrew Jackson and subsequent Democratic presidents, Lincoln remained purposefully aloof from the legislative process and exercised his veto power sparingly.[31] He was also deferential to congressional Republicans in the matter of executive appointments and accorded his Cabinet members considerable autonomy in the day-to-day operations of their respective departments. Viewed from this angle, the Lincoln presidency would seem to have done more to retard than to advance movement toward modern presidential practices.

Emergency Powers

Still, to leave the discussion at this is to miss Lincoln's central contribution to the modern presidency. It is certainly the case that Theodore Roosevelt found more to draw from Lincoln's presidency than a strict Whig reading allows. What drew Roosevelt to Lincoln was the latter's elucidation of presidential emergency powers. Indeed, Roosevelt predicated some of his more controversial actions as president on his understanding of what he called "the Jackson-Lincoln theory of the presidency." As Roosevelt explained it, the theory held "that occasionally great national crises arise which call for immediate and vigorous executive action."[32] Roosevelt used this Jackson-Lincoln model of executive leadership as the basis for his "stewardship theory" of the presidency.

> The course I followed, of regarding the executive as subject only to the people, and, under the Constitution, bound to serve the people affirmatively in cases where the Constitution does not explicitly forbid him to render the service, was substantially the course followed by both Andrew Jackson and Abraham Lincoln.[33]

This is the Abraham Lincoln we want to recover here. To Roosevelt the lesson was clear: "great national crises" unlocked the latent authority of the president, and it was Lincoln's presidency that provided the model for the exercise of power under such conditions. After taking office, Lincoln had turned to the doctrine of emergency powers to justify a host of executive actions not otherwise justifiable by a strict reading of the Constitution: actions to blockade Southern ports; calling up the militia, expanding the size of the army and navy, and paying mobilized troops out of the Treasury without congressional appropriation; and suspending the writ of habeas corpus. Lincoln defended each of these actions on the basis of the civil emergency at hand and on a set of constitutional obligations mandating affirmative action. These included his authority as commander-in-chief, as well as obligations to "take care that the laws be faithfully executed" and to "preserve, protect and defend the Constitution of the United States." In Lincoln's judgment, such affirmative obligations "implied an inherent executive power—a power not specifically itemized in Article II—to take any action necessary to fulfill them."[34]

Lincoln was certainly not the first to recognize the fact that necessity—traditionally understood as military necessity—might require unilateral executive actions outside the boundaries of law. In the waning months of his presidency, Thomas Jefferson, reflecting on the threat posed by Aaron Burr's alleged secessionist movement in the Southwest Territories, would invoke the ancient Roman dictum *inter arma silent leges* ("in time of war the laws are silent"). In other words, Jefferson held, "self-preservation is paramount to all law." In Jefferson's judgment there were "extreme cases" in which "the laws become inadequate even to their own preservation, and where the universal resource is a dictator, or martial law."[35] But it was Lincoln who first and most fully explored such "extreme cases" and their implications for presidential power. In a memorandum to the newly inaugurated president, written at Lincoln's behest, Attorney General Edward Bates laid the groundwork for Lincoln's assertion of emergency powers. As Bates wrote,

> It is the plain duty of the President (and his peculiar duty above all other departments of Government) to preserve the Constitution and execute the laws all over the nation; and it is plainly impossible for him to perform this duty without putting down rebellion, insurrection, and all unlawful combinations to resist the General Government.[36]

Subsequent presidents would elaborate upon Lincoln's precedent and expand the concept of emergency powers beyond the contexts of formal war and domestic insurrection.[37] In so doing, they would significantly expand the president's field of independent action. To cite just three examples: In 1894, with the country suffering the effects of both economic depression and a massive railway strike, President Grover Cleveland would cite disruptions to interstate commerce and interstate mail service as emergencies justifying the dispatch of federal troops to suppress the strike and restore commercial life and postal service to the nation. Cleveland's deployment of federal troops was all the more significant because he possessed neither formal statutory authority for his actions nor the informal authorization of state and local authorities.[38] Likewise, in 1902, with a Pennsylvania-based, anthracite-coal strike threatening the nation's supply of winter home-heating fuel, Theodore Roosevelt took unilateral steps to resolve the dispute between operators and mine workers. To Roosevelt, "the crisis was only less serious than that of the Civil War."[39] Acknowledging the absence of a clear legal or constitutional basis on which to act, Roosevelt nonetheless took direct personal action to arbitrate the dispute, admitting that had his efforts proved unsuccessful, he was prepared to send the army into Pennsylvania to seize the mines and operate them in receivership until a settlement could be reached.[40] What Theodore Roosevelt was prepared to do in 1902, Harry Truman would do fifty years later, as labor disputes in the steel industry threatened to paralyze the national economy and jeopardize national defense. Receiving private assurances from Chief Justice Fred Vinson that the actions contemplated were indeed constitutional (assurances that would not be vindicated by the full Supreme Court), Truman signed executive order 10340 on April 8, 1952, directing the secretary of Commerce to take control of some eighty-eight steel mills the following day, explaining to his cautious treasury secretary, John Snyder, that "[t]he President has the power to keep the country from going to hell."[41]

Progressive Prototypes

The administrations of Theodore Roosevelt (1901–1909) and Woodrow Wilson (1913–1921) present us with many of the signature traits of the modern presidency. These two Progressive Era presidents riveted public attention on the White House and transformed it into the vital seat of national leadership. By the end of the Wilson years, most of the signposts of modern presidential leadership seemed to be in place, including the regular articulation of presidential agendas, proactive executive intervention in the policy process, and elaborate White House strategies of mass opinion formation. Indeed, Roosevelt and Wilson pioneered the strategy of "going public"—direct presidential communication with the mass public—in an effort to exert greater control over the details of the congressional policy process. Their legacy was a model for a new "rhetorical presidency," one that shattered the Founders' conception of a presidency aloof from partisan politics.[42] It would also widen considerably the legitimate scope of independent presidential action, thrust the president into the role of legislative party leader, and harness the power of public opinion to serve presidential policy ambitions.

Theodore Roosevelt and Opinion Leadership

As governor of New York, Theodore Roosevelt learned firsthand the power of public opinion and its ability to galvanize legislators into action behind executive leadership. In Albany, the reform-minded Roosevelt had confronted the almost continuous opposition of his own legislative party, under the control of Thomas C. Platt, "boss" of the state Republican machine. Roosevelt recognized that he could never match Platt and his allies in the deployment of party organizational machinery. In any such contest, Roosevelt was severely disadvantaged. Instead, Roosevelt circumvented party organization and took his case directly to voters; in his words, he "consistently adopted the plan of going over the heads of the men holding public office and the men in control of the organization, and appealing directly to the people behind them."[43]

> In theory the Executive has nothing to do with legislation. In practice as things are now, the Executive is or ought to be peculiarly representative of the people as a whole. As often as not the action of the Executive offers the only means by which the people can get the legislation they demand and ought to have. Therefore a good executive under the present conditions of American political life must take a very active interest in getting the right kind of legislation, in addition to performing his executive duties with an eye single to the public welfare. . . . I accomplished this only by arousing the people, and riveting their attention on what was done.[44]

As Roosevelt well understood, whatever control party bosses might have had over legislators, the latter were still, first and foremost, elected officials, and "in the last resort the people [i.e., voters] behind these legislators had a still greater control over them." It was a lesson Roosevelt never forgot. "I made up my mind that the only way I could beat the bosses whenever the need to do so arose . . . was . . . by making my appeal as directly and as emphatically as I knew how to the mass of voters themselves, to the people, to the men who if waked up [sic] would be able to impose their will on their representatives."[45]

Roosevelt's campaign as president on behalf of the Hepburn Act provides a useful case study in the lessons he had learned as governor of New York. The Hepburn Act was reform legislation, the purpose of which was to strengthen the regulatory powers of the Interstate Commerce Commission over railroad rate-making practices. For our purposes, what is significant here are the distinctly modern tactics Roosevelt employed to secure railroad reform.[46] The President used the occasion of his annual message to Congress to frame the basic policy problem and identify its salient dimensions, placing railroad reform firmly on the national agenda. In addition, to stoke the demand for reform, the attorney general, acting at Roosevelt's behest, coordinated a series of well-publicized lawsuits to fan public indignation with existing railroad practices. In the area of communications, Roosevelt was a pioneer in cultivating newspaper headlines to advance a presidential agenda and strengthen his leadership position. Roosevelt's "literary allies" in popular magazines like *McClure's, The Outlook*, and *The World's Work* wrote critical exposés of railroad practices and lambasted the Senate for holding up railroad reform. Roosevelt himself practiced the fine art of leaks, trial balloons, and off-the-record statements. In all, a coordinated and continuous stream of information poured forth from the White House and other federal agencies, fanning the fires for railroad reform. As one contemporary journalist observed: "The cannonade of head-lines took on a cumulative frequency—occasionally, indeed, two or more jostled each other on the same front page."[47] In yet another manifestation of the new presidential leadership, Roosevelt took control of the text of Hepburn Bill, the language of which was drafted in the executive branch, by the Justice Department, prior to its submission to Congress. Impromptu "press conferences" were also held, in which the president made himself available to reporters at prearranged times and places. There the president would discuss the details of the pending railroad bill legislation and outline the terms of acceptable amendment. Finally, much like a modern president, Roosevelt also took to the road, speaking directly to the public and beating the drum in support of railroad reform. In the course of eighteen months, Roosevelt campaigned for the Hepburn Bill in stops across the Southwest, the Midwest, and the Southeast. Finally, again in the style of modern presidents, Roosevelt bargained directly with legislative leaders on behalf of his bill, agreeing with Speaker Joseph Cannon to shelve tariff reform in return for passage of the Hepburn Bill in the House, and agreeing to a critical weakening amendment, sponsored by Republican majority leader Nelson Aldrich, to clear the way for passage in the Senate.

Woodrow Wilson and Legislative Party Leadership

Woodrow Wilson consolidated and extended the techniques practiced by Roosevelt. Prior to his entry into politics, Wilson had been a professor of political science at Princeton University. For decades, he had grappled with the problem of leadership in American politics. In his earliest writings, Wilson had proposed grafting a British-styled cabinet government onto the American constitutional system, as a means of bringing energy, leadership, and responsibility to national politics.[48] Ultimately convinced of the idea's impracticability, Wilson became a convert to presidential leadership and its potential synergies. The president, Wilson recognized, stood at the intersection of party organization and national popular opinion and, if he was willing to assume the charge, could harness each to great national effect. In combination, they were an irresistible force. More important, each element also offered the president a measure of freedom from the other. On the one hand, "[the president] may stand a little outside party and insist . . . upon the general opinion." On the other hand, the president could position himself to "stand within the party counsels and use the advantage of his power and personal force to control the actual programs." In one of Wilson's more arresting formulations, he maintained that,

> [The president] cannot escape being the leader of his party. . . , because he is at once the choice of the party and of the nation. . . . [T]he president represents not so much the party's governing efficiency as its controlling ideals and principles. He is not so much part of its organization as its vital link of connection with the thinking nation. He can dominate his party by being spokesman for the real sentiment and purpose of the country, by giving direction to opinion, by giving the country at once

the information and the statements of policy which will enable it to form its judgments alike of parties and of men.[49]

As president, Wilson took immediate steps to quicken the intercourse between the White House and Capitol Hill. For too long the tradition of submitting presidential messages in writing had dominated executive-legislative communications. The practice had been instituted by Jefferson as a way to buttress the formal separation of powers with an added measure of physical separation (as the two branches were situated at opposite ends of Pennsylvania Avenue). Wilson was convinced that if he could breach the physical separation, appearing directly before Congress to speak on matters of critical import, he could galvanize Congress and electrify the nation. If, as a consequence, the president appeared to dominate the legislature and compromise its autonomy, it was only that—appearance: "[I]f Congress be overborne by him . . . [it is] only because the President has the nation behind him, and the Congress has not. He has no means of compelling Congress except through public opinion."[50]

Like Roosevelt's before him, Wilson's presidency was in many ways a prototype of the modern presidency. It was in this period that a subset of congressional legislation first came to be identified as "administration bills"; that is, legislation "either drafted in executive department or known to constitute a part of the president's program."[51] As a matter of regular course, these presidential bills would also be introduced into Congress by friendly committee chairs or other administrative supporters, with administration officials testifying at committee hearings on behalf of those measures and legislative supporters speaking from the floor on behalf of the administration's position. Nor was it unusual for Wilson's chief dispenser of the patronage, Postmaster General Albert Burleson, to be observed at the Capitol counting heads and rounding up support for presidential initiatives. In the case of one World War I measure, the Overman Bill, which granted President Wilson authority to reorganize the War Industries Board, it was Burleson who carried the administrative measure physically to Capitol Hill on the day it was to be introduced, and who met with the measure's supporters in the president's room near the Senate chamber.[52] Writing in the last years of Wilson's presidency, H. C. Black described the nature of the new activist methods of presidential party leadership in the following way:

> [T]he modern president is in constant and free communication with the chairmen of important committees in both houses, with the parliamentary leaders of the party, with his individual friends and supporters, and even with those who are most conspicuous in their opposition to his polices. It has become a common practice, no longer exciting surprise or even comment, for the President to summon influential members of either house to conference at the White House, nor is it a secret that the purpose is to settle the details of an administration bill or to concert

ways and means for securing its passage, or perhaps to block the pathway of independent insurgents. Nor have the occasions been infrequent in which the President has himself gone to the room set apart for him at the Capitol and there summoned to his presence Senators or Representatives whose strong opposition threatened disaster to some favored measure. The object of such interviews is of course the taking of common counsel for the welfare of the country. But is it not the case that when the legislators return to their seats, their votes reflect the wishes of the executive?[53]

The Rooseveltian Synthesis

Franklin Delano Roosevelt was elected to office at the height of the greatest national emergency since the Civil War, circumstances which, as Lincoln well knew firsthand, afforded a great latitude to executive leadership. It was Roosevelt's genius to draw upon and synthesize many of the historical elements under review in this chapter, bequeathing to his successors both a system and style of governance that would make both independent action and program activism routine features of the post-Roosevelt presidency. Rightly or wrongly, FDR's presidency would be abstracted from its peculiar historical circumstances and held up as an exemplar for students of national political leadership, a benchmark for gauging the success of future presidents. As the historian William E. Leuchtenburg has vividly expressed it, subsequent presidents would operate "in the shadow of FDR."[54]

The Synthesis Deployed

The elements of the Rooseveltian synthesis are best observed in motion. The passage into law of the 1935 Public Utility Holding Company Act (PUHCA) provides a particularly compelling case study of modern presidential leadership in action.[55] The PUHCA was a profoundly controversial measure, fueled by a deep-seated Western animus against the public utilities industry. It was, in the words of Clair Wilcox, a student of American business regulation, "the most stringent corrective measure ever applied to American business."[56] Its politics also shattered Democratic Party unity, splitting it along conservative and liberal lines. The PUHCA forced the corporate restructuring of the public utilities industry and the divestiture of significant amounts of property. It also made the Securities and Exchange Commission (SEC) an effective regulator of electric and gas holding companies. Additionally, beginning on January 1, 1938, the SEC was required to undertake the reorganization of remaining holding companies into single integrated utility systems. Finally, and most controversially, the PUHCA mandated the dissolution of all utility holding companies beyond the second "degree." This was the so-called mandatory "death sentence" provision, and its retention in any final legislation was insisted upon by Roosevelt.

From the outset, Roosevelt embraced the role of national policy leader, taking full control over the substance and politics of the PUHCA. Where Woodrow Wilson had typically assumed a role of "first among equals" in substantive dealings with his congressional party, Franklin Roosevelt preferred a more complete direction of the policy process. The provisions of the PUHCA were thus authored exclusively in the executive branch along lines laid down by the president. While Sam Rayburn and Burton Wheeler, the respective chairmen of the House and Senate Interstate Commerce committees, were both present in White House during the planning and drafting phases, their presence was largely cosmetic, to help foster the fiction that the PUHC bill was a congressional measure, written by the relevant committees of jurisdiction. The White House was assisted in its drafting efforts by a growing and skilled cadre of government officials. In the period prior to 1939, before the creation of the Executive Office of the President, Roosevelt drew liberally on the executive branch's considerable talent and resources to buttress his policy leadership stance. In drafting the PUHC bill, for instance, Roosevelt made extensive use of experts available to him in several executive institutions, including the Treasury Department, the Federal Trade Commission, the Federal Power Commission, and the president's own National Power Policy Committee.

Roosevelt was also a skilled player in the field of opinion leadership. The opening rounds in the battle for reform were joined in a manner familiar at least since the days of Theodore Roosevelt. FDR seized the occasion of his State of the Union address to place the subject of utility holding companies firmly on the national agenda and heighten public awareness of the issues involved. In the aftermath of his address to Congress, the government released voluminous reports detailing the unsavory practices of the power industry and building the case for reform. At the same time, administration officials, congressional allies, and organized supporters took to the road and, in a coordinated series of speeches, newspaper interviews, and radio addresses, made the case for Roosevelt's reform initiative. The president also took his case directly to the people, using the instrument of the "fireside chat" to defend his stringent course of action.

With characteristic exuberance, Roosevelt also took the reins as legislative party leader. In Congress, Roosevelt relied heavily upon administration spokespersons like Edward C. Eicher, a second-term representative from Iowa and staunch New Dealer, to carry his battle for the PUHCA onto the floor of the House. When the House Interstate Commerce Committee stripped Roosevelt's prized death-sentence provision from its legislation, the administration made its case for reinstatement through the devise of a dissenting report— officially authored by Eicher—that accompanied the official majority and minority reports out of committee. Likewise, Eicher argued the administration's case for reinstatement before the full chamber and assumed the role of administration whip, mobilizing Democratic supporters of the death sentence to maximize turnout on votes deemed crucial by the White House. It was also Eicher who introduced (unsuccessfully) an amendment to reinstate the death sentence provision on the floor after its deletion in committee.

In the Senate, Roosevelt relied upon his vice president, John Nance Garner, who in his constitutional guise as president of the Senate turned aside both seniority and the preferences of committee leaders to ensure a conference committee delegation sympathetic to the President's death-sentence provision. FDR also sent expert advisors Benjamin Cohen, who had helped draft the original PUHC bill, and Dozier Devane of the Federal Power Commission, to accompany Senate conferees and aid them in swaying recalcitrant House conferees (and to ensure that Interstate Commerce Committee chairman Sam Rayburn did not pursue his own independent compromise). When all else had failed, Roosevelt enlisted the aid of Alabama senator (and future Supreme Court Justice) Hugo L. Black to launch an investigation into allegations of improper influence by the power industry. Black's charge was to scandalize the utilities industry, fostering public outrage and helping force House conferees to yield to the Senate on the death sentence. In the end, Roosevelt was forced to accept a watered-down death-sentence provision, one that could still be touted as a victory for Western progressives, but one more fully attuned to the realities of shared authority and countervailing power in American politics.

Roosevelt's tireless action on behalf of the PUHCA illustrates the operation of the modern presidency, its potential for excess, and its limits as an instrument of national leadership. In the end, it is as much a story of personal tenacity as institutional power. Roosevelt was required to pull out all the stops at every conceivable point to avoid outright defeat and salvage a partial, albeit politically important, victory. Clearly, it would be impossible to invest the president's limited political resources at similar levels on every important administrative measure. Indeed, Roosevelt's interventions on behalf of public utilities reform ultimately provoked a strong backlash among congressional representatives angry with Roosevelt's strong-arm tactics and his bold trespass upon their traditional prerogatives. In the end, the House would undertake its own investigation of undue influence—this one against the executive branch!—in an effort to embarrass the president and undermine his popular and legislative leadership. The episode underscores the paradox at the heart of the modern presidency, as constitutional inadequacies fed both the appearance and the reality of an encroaching and aggrandizing president grasping for personal power and influence. The battle for the PUHCA would ultimately take a toll on Roosevelt's presidency, presaging the diminishing returns his leadership would yield in his second term, when a conservative coalition of Republicans and Southern Democrats would slam the brakes on further New Deal reform initiatives.

23

The Synthesis Institutionalized

In 1939 Congress passed the Executive Reorganization Act. That landmark legislation had been sponsored by the White House, and though in the end it was considerably less than what Roosevelt had asked for, what he was given would supply permanent organizational support for the president's new leadership role.[57] It has been persuasively argued by Sidney M. Milkis that in institutionalizing national political leadership in the White House, Roosevelt was consciously seeking a way to reduce the president's reliance on traditional party mechanisms.[58] The heterogeneous composition of the Democratic Party and its conflicting ideological impulses cut against the formation of a national and programmatic party under Roosevelt's leadership, inhibiting unified action on liberal reform. Following the president's unsuccessful twelve-state effort to unseat conservative Democrats in the party's 1938 primary contests (he was successful in only two contests, one in Oregon, the other in New York), Roosevelt turned to building up the institutional powers of the executive branch as a way to vindicate liberal leadership. In Milkis's suggestive formulation, Roosevelt sought to institute a series of administrative reforms that would "help the president to govern in the absence of party government."[59]

The Administrative Reorganization Act of 1939 created the modern Executive Office of the President (EOP). It also established a formal White House Office as a principal subunit within the EOP, staffed with presidential assistants whose sole responsibility was to tend to the president's political and policy interests. This legislation also moved the Bureau of the Budget (the precursor of today's Office of Management and Budget) from Treasury to the EOP, strengthening presidential control over the budgetary and programmatic requests of the executive branch. Finally, Roosevelt also successfully extended civil service protection to federal personnel originally brought in to administer New Deal programs from outside the merit system, helping to institutionalize liberal expansionist tendencies within programs now permanently administered by the federal bureaucracy. Though modest in its initial endowment, the dramatic growth in both the size and complexity of the institutional presidency since the 1930s (see Matthew Dickinson in this volume) has provided presidents with an organizational capacity to project their leadership efforts into multiple political arenas simultaneously, progressively undercutting and marginalizing the role historically played by national party organizations.

Scholarly Assessments and Contemporary Trends

Roosevelt's synthesis and its subsequent institutionalization forever transformed both the character of the presidency and the structure of American politics. For better or worse, the president was now the acknowledged centerpiece in national politics—its prime mover—and the exaggerated expectations placed upon executive leadership sent presidents on an extended search for new tools of influence to justify their newfound preeminence. The rise of the modern presidency also stimulated new waves of scholarly interest in the office. Almost immediately, professional students of American politics undertook to assess the pathologies and potentialities of the new president-centered government. Political science scholarship on the post-Roosevelt presidency provides a unique window onto reactions by informed observers of political life to the rise of the modern presidency. These writings are also themselves a marker of the constantly evolving challenges that have confronted the exercise of modern presidential leadership since the New Deal.

Pathologies and Potentialities

Writing in the wake of "the Roosevelt revolution," the public law scholar Edward Corwin judged the transformation of legally prescribed roles and relationships wrought by FDR so comprehensive as to suggest that executive power had finally broken loose from its constitutional moorings.[60] To Corwin and others of his generation, the study of the Constitution and the laws was the study of a set of formal roles, rules, and standards regulating the actions of public officials, a set of external benchmarks or standards that defined the parameters of legitimate authority and established a bulwark against the aggrandizement of power by government. The problem was that presidential action resisted such formalization and regulation. Writing in 1953, some 166 years after the drafting of Article II, Corwin insisted that the "executive power [unlike the legislative or judicial powers] is still indefinite as to *function* and retains ... much of its original plasticity as regards *method*"[61] [emphasis added]. The intrinsic ambiguity of its provisions meant that its constitutional development fairly "bristles with alternatives."[62] That inherent flexibility made the presidential office spontaneously responsive to emergency conditions and fueled its growth. As Corwin famously stated, "Taken by and large, the history of the presidency is the history of aggrandizement."[63] The prevalence of both domestic and international emergencies since 1929, Corwin feared, had finally freed presidents from traditional legal and institutional restraints. Left unchecked, it would culminate in a highly personalized presidency, one in which effective leadership was too dependent on the accident of personality; one in which presidents would be required to consult no other authority save their own conscience as a guide to appropriate action; one which might, in its guise as popular tribune, trample upon the fundamental rights and liberties of non-majorities.

Other scholars eagerly embraced the emerging paradigm of presidential government.[64] For them, effective presidential leadership was now mandatory in American politics. It was also politically safe. In his *American Presidency* (1956), Clinton Rossiter took direct aim at the Corwinian perspective, arguing that it was not formal-legal constraints, but rather America's dense pluralistic network of overlapping restraints, that acted as the primary bulwark against the type of "presidential dictatorship" that so concerned Corwin. Congress, federalism, the party system, the pressure group system, public opinion, the sprawling federal bureaucracy, and the system of private enterprise all operated as checks on a gross and persistent misuse of presidential power. In Rossiter's words, "The power of the Presidency moves as a mighty host only *with* the grain of liberty and morality."[65]

To other advocates of presidential leadership, the implications of Rossiter's system of pluralist checks were less benign. While they might indeed function as effective political safeguards, they also constituted a host of institutional impediments that undercut purposeful presidential leadership. These scholars turned the time-worn problem of constraining presidential power on its head. The imperative now became that of liberating presidents from this system of pluralistic constraints, investigating in particular the personal attributes and organizational requirements needed to effectuate the potential of the modern office. In his seminal work *Presidential Power* (1960), Richard Neustadt tackled this problem head on. In a fragmented system of shared authority, no political actor possessed the authority to command obedience to his dictates; rather the art of leadership lay with techniques of persuasion. In one of his oft-cited passages, Neustadt wrote:

> When one man shares authority with another, but does not gain or lose his job upon the other's whim, his willingness to act upon the urging of the other turns on whether he conceives the action right for him. The essence of a president's persuasive task is to convince such men that what the White House wants of them is what they ought to do for their sake and on their authority.[66]

While the president's formal powers alone could not provide him with the power to command others, they were still relevant to the politics of persuasion. Neustadt recommended that presidents inventory their formal and informal bargaining advantages and deploy them purposefully—with skill and will—to harness legislative self-interest to presidential goals. In Neustadt's scheme, the president's "professional reputation" as a bargainer was the key to presidential policy influence, and this required that legislators routinely anticipate presidential success in the inter-branch bargaining game.[67]

In *Going Public* (1986), Samuel Kernell updates Neustadt's thesis, helping to clarify important reorientations in the leadership strategies of contemporary presidents.[68] Writing in an era of legislative decentralization, protracted divided government, and intense interest group surveillance of Congress, Kernell identified public opinion leadership, not traditional bargaining techniques, as the principal determinant of presidential policy influence. Employing a classic Neustadtian calculus, Kernell argued that to make bargaining techniques viable, mid-twentieth-century presidents had relied upon informal, backdoor party ties to powerful committee barons, as well as legislative norms of deference and reciprocity. These institutional conditions facilitated interbranch comity and legislative enforcement of bargains struck, making it cost effective for presidents to engage in direct bargaining tactics. By comparison, late-twentieth-century presidents faced a subcommittee system that fragmented power and made every legislator an independent actor and policy entrepreneur. Thus the traditional bargaining approach had become more costly, more time consuming, and less stable. Even with the resurgence of centralized legislative parties, the prevalence of divided government meant that presidents with the wrong party affiliation faced intense congressional resistance when presented with controversial presidential initiatives. Under such conditions, Kernell shows, presidents had rationally traded "bargaining" for "going public" as a principal technique of leadership. Contemporary presidents now had to possess the skill and the will to use their personal popularity as leverage in Congress. Presidents also required sophisticated systems of communications and outreach, allowing them to speak directly with targeted publics, tailor interest-group coalitions to immediate legislative needs, and send administration allies into the districts of critical swing legislators—all on behalf of presidential policy initiatives (see Lawrence Jacobs in this volume).[69]

The Continuing Evolution of the Presidency: Emerging Techniques of Unilateral Policy Leadership

As Kernell's analysis reminds us, divided government has been the norm for much of the post–World War II era. Indeed, if we include under the rubric of divided government interbranch ideological divisions as well as strictly partisan ones—to take into account the years in which the Conservative Coalition was ascendant in Congress—then the years of unified government have actually been quite few in number. Accordingly, presidents of all stripes have found it difficult to advance their policy agenda through legislative channels by relying solely on persuasion or opinion leadership. Instead, presidents have sought out additional tools with which to shape policy unilaterally—that is, without seeking Congress's statutory assent.

THE ADMINISTRATIVE PRESIDENCY. One way presidents have exerted unilateral policy leadership is through techniques of enhanced administrative control. Statements like "operations is policy" and "personnel is policy" express White House recognition of the thin line between policy implementation and policy formulation. In this regard, a distinctive feature in the evolution of the post-FDR presidency has been the diminution of Cabinet independence in personnel and policy matters, as presidents have increasingly centralized administrative appointments in the White House and inserted presidential loyalists into the cockpit of the bureaucratic decision-making processes.

Political scientist Terry M. Moe regards these developments as the product of fundamental changes in the institutional incentives facing all presidents since Franklin Roosevelt.[70] In the aftermath of FDR's presidency, Moe explains, the president alone is held electorally accountable for the performance of national government, a circumstance that arises because "the president is the only politician with a national constituency." Yet because public expectations for effective governance so far exceed the president's capacity to fulfill them, presidents have responded by "[seeking] control over the structure and processes of government."[71] In Moe's analysis, presidents are not driven to seek administrative control to achieve "efficiency or effectiveness or coordination per se"—that is, presidents are not motivated by values of neutral competence. Rather, presidents demand *responsive* competence from bureaucratic actors otherwise wedded to their own policy agendas, long-standing routines, and external standards of behavior. In search of greater political control, this modern "politicized presidency" has regularly bypassed Cabinet lines of authority, undercut traditions of neutral competence among career bureaucrats, and elevated ideology and personal loyalty (over expertise, objectivity, and experience) in the selection of political appointees.

As Moe notes, all modern presidents confront incentives to seek greater political control over national administrative processes. That said, it is hard to gainsay the fact that the boundaries of this "administrative presidency" have been explored most aggressively by presidents confronted with the peculiar challenges of divided government. The political scientist Richard P. Nathan was the first to give systematic attention to the techniques of administrative policy leadership, as they emerged in the presidency of Richard Nixon.[72] Nixon only slowly embraced these techniques. Taking office in 1969, the Nixon administration announced an ambitious domestic reform agenda, one spanning such diverse policy areas as revenue sharing, the environment, education, welfare, and urban policy. Nixon initially sought to accomplish these goals through customary channels, by seeking new statutory authorization in Congress. At the same time, Nixon adhered to the practice of appointing Cabinet members with independent national standing; his administrative selections subordinated matters of presidential control to the need to harmonize distinct constituency interests, ensure geographical diversity, and locate competence in party management and administrative oversight.

On both fronts, exasperation with political convention quickly set in. With the exception of revenue sharing, much of Nixon's domestic reform agenda was rebuffed by a Democratically controlled legislature. Simultaneously, presidential-Cabinet relations eroded, as White House officials complained of department heads "going native"—acting as representatives for the interests of career civil servants, departmental clientele interests, and congressional oversight committees, rather than serving as the president's loyal political and policy agents within the bureaucracy. By the start of Nixon's second term in 1973, efforts were well underway to redirect presidential energies away from traditional statutory and administrative practices in favor of enhanced techniques of administrative policy leadership. By systematically placing presidential loyalists in both Cabinet and sub-Cabinet positions—individuals without national reputations and con-stituency followings, and hence dependent on continued presidential favor for their position—and by seizing control of routine bureaucratic processes (rule making, grant writing, and budgeting), the administration hoped to effect a sig-nificant redirection of national policy, without seeking new statutory approval from Congress.

Nixon's administrative presidency was ultimately cut short by Watergate and its aftermath. However, these techniques were quickly redeployed by Ronald Reagan when he took office in 1981. There were differences of emphasis. Where Nixon had sought to infiltrate the major spending departments—Health, Education, and Welfare; Housing and Urban Development; Labor; Transportation; and Interior—the principal targets of Reagan's administrative presidency were the major regulatory agencies, especially the Environmental Protection Agency (EPA) and the Occupational Safety and Health Administration (OSHA). Regular line departments—such as the Department of Interior—were not ignored. Nevertheless, the administration's major focus was on reducing the regulatory burdens on American business, with an articulated aim of reducing operating costs, stimulating new investment, and reinvigorating American competitiveness in global markets. Perhaps most significantly, Executive Order 12291 initiated major institutional changes to advance these goals. It gave the Office of Management and Budget (OMB) the authority to review existing regulatory rules, and prohibited federal regulatory agencies from promulgating any new such rules until OMB had conducted its own cost-bene-fit analysis. By granting OMB final authority over both existing and proposed rules, E.O. 12291 effectively centralized presidential oversight over areas of regu-latory policy in which the Reagan administration sought change, especially environmental regulation, workplace safety and health regulation, and consumer protection regulation.

Techniques of unilateral administrative action continue to be employed. In the presidency of George W. Bush, this can be observed in the implementation of his Faith-Based Initiative.[73] Faced with congressional recalcitrance, the Bush administration has used all of the administrative tools at its disposal—the creation of new executive institutions, strategic political appointments, and the promulga-tion of new regulations and funding protocols—to provide faith-based service providers with expanded access to federal contracts and grants. The White House Office of Faith-Based and Community Initiatives was established with links to units in multiple federal agencies, "each with a carefully selected director and staff, empowered to articulate, advance, and oversee coordinated efforts to win more financial support for faith-based social services."[74] Additionally, relaxed administrative rules have permitted federally funded, faith-based groups accepting federal monies to take religion into consideration when hiring staff, construct dual-purpose facilities that provide both social services and facilities for religious worship, and use federal job-training vouchers to provide spiritual training for individuals seeking employment in religious institutions, or other faith-based organizations. Finally, federal agencies have simplified grant-application procedures to facilitate participation by smaller faith-based service providers, while many provide grant-application training to these same organizations.

EXECUTIVE ORDERS AND SIGNING STATEMENTS. In search of expanded opportunities for unilateral policy influence, post–World War II presidents have also made innovative use of such traditional instrumentalities as executive orders and presidential "signing statements."[75] Executive orders are directives to government officials and agencies instructing them on some facet of their job conduct. They can be quite straightforward, as when President John Quincy Adams issued an executive order directing members of the military to don black armbands to mark the death of Thomas Jefferson. Nevertheless, since Franklin Roosevelt, executive orders have grown into their own as instruments of unilateral policy leadership, as we saw in the case of Ronald Reagan's Executive Order 12291. In the area of social policy, presidents such as Ronald Reagan, George H. W. Bush, Bill Clinton, and George W. Bush have each used executive orders either to promote or discourage stem-cell research among investigators accepting federal funds. These same presidents have also used executive orders to lift or impose the "gag rule" on family clinics offering abortion-related counseling and referrals.

Of course, presidents have long turned to executive orders to assert leadership in civil rights policy. A few examples can suffice: In 1948, Harry Truman signed E.O. 9981, integrating the American armed forces; in 1957, Dwight Eisenhower signed an executive order sending federal troops into Little Rock, Arkansas, to enforce Supreme Court decisions banning racial segregation in public schools; in 1963, John F. Kennedy issued E.O. 11063 barring racial discrimination in federally subsidized housing (after Congress had blocked the statutory route); in 1965, Lyndon Johnson issued E.O. 11246 directing federal contractors to create minority hiring programs (after Congress had refused to do so in the Civil Rights Act of 1964); and in 1969, Richard Nixon established the so-called "Philadelphia Plan" by executive order, which established racial hiring quotas on federal projects. Bill Clinton's "don't ask, don't tell" policy toward gays and lesbians in the military is only the most recent manifestation of this long tradition of affecting civil rights policy unilaterally through the use of executive orders.

Presidential signing statements are perhaps the most exotic, because most recent, of unilateral leadership tools.[76] These signing statements—presidential messages written for the occasion of signing a bill into law—have been used by recent presidents to assert what has been termed a "quasi-judicial power" over the interpretation of laws passed by Congress. That is to say, recent presidents have sought to exploit statutory ambiguities in legislative statutes to construe legislative purpose in ways intended to ensure that policy implementation comports more closely with presidential policy goals.

Presidents have also used signing statements to stipulate the constitutional understandings they will employ in administering congressional statutes. In the most dramatic instance, Ronald Reagan asserted the right not to be bound by provisions of law he deemed unconstitutional. The 1984 Competition in Contracting Act (CICA) had empowered Congress's comptroller general to suspend contracts awarded by federal agencies to ensure a competitive bidding process. Reagan's signing statement asserted this provision to be unconstitutional, having granted executive responsibilities to an arm of the legislature. Echoing Andrew Jackson, Reagan maintained further that the president pos sessed the same authority as the judicial branch to void unconstitutional legislation—that is, to suspend its immediate operation—insisting that his administration would not honor the disputed provisions of the CICA until such time as it was upheld by the Supreme Court. In hearings before the House of Representatives, the Justice Department paraphrased Chief Justice John Marshall in *Marbury v. Madison*, arguing that "[I]n case of a conflict between the Constitution and a statute, the President's duty to faithfully execute the law requires him not to observe a statute that is in conflict with the Constitution, the fundamental law of the land,"[77] insisting further that the president had a duty to put his own interpretation of the Constitution ahead of any statute and obey it rather than the statute itself. To implement the president's understanding, OMB issued a government-wide executive order directing all agencies not to obey the act, but rather to "proceed with the procurement process as though no such provisions were contained in the act."[78] While this case was never heard by the Supreme Court, the lower courts did hold against Reagan, arguing that such a practice amounted to an absolute veto on the part of the executive and violated Article III by assuming a role reserved for the judicial branch. Here, with evident satisfaction, the court quoted *Marbury v. Madison* back to the Administration, citing John Marshall that "it is emphatically the province and the duty of the judicial department to say what the law is."[79]

Conclusion: Between the Promise and the Fear

At the heart of the American presidency are a series of contradictions not soon to be resolved. They can be listed virtually seriatim: A dread of executive power is as old as the Constitution itself, yet most citizens today demand a powerful and activist presidency. Presidential power has grown in absolute terms, but its relative influence in American politics bespeaks a much spottier record; cries of an "imperial presidency" stand virtually side-by-side with ruminations on the "illusion of presidential government."[80] The conventional model of presidential government presumes unified party control, yet divided government and inter-branch warfare have proved to be much more the norm.[81] The architects of modern presidential leadership conceived of that instrument as a unifying force in American politics, yet ironically its exercise has sparked a proliferation of hostile and competing centers of power.[82] Perhaps most profoundly, and in stark contrast to its origins as an office above party politics, the presidency today manifests a demagogic, aggrandizing, and politicizing impulse, one that feeds public perceptions of presidents as unbounded by law, standard operating procedure, and norms of official propriety.[83]

The paradox of the modern presidency is everywhere manifest. Yet it is something with which Americans have not fully come to terms. The reason for this seems clear: the paradox of the American presidency is at root the paradox of the American people. The presidential office is the institutional focal point for American political culture; it both receives and transmits basic data on core American values. The ways in which presidents speak to the nation reveals something essential about our national identity, our political traditions, our future promise, and, within this broad context, the appropriate solutions to our current-day problems. In a similar fashion, the ways in which presidents behave (or misbehave) before the nation both instruct us and remind us of our cultural models of exemplary moral and political behavior.

Presidential elections ritually reenact the original promise of the American experiment and its potentialities for political renewal. However, presidents in office quickly confront the cultural ambivalence of their office, a tradition of deep discomfort with the fear of concentrated and unaccountable personal power. To paraphrase political scientist James Morone, the promise of presidential power elicits a dread of that very same power.[84] It is evident everywhere in American history, from Edmund Randolph's identification of the presidency as the "foetus of monarchy" and Whig Party caricatures of "King Andrew" Jackson, to Edward Corwin's fears of an institutionally unbounded and personalized executive office and Theodore Lowi's indictment of an "imperial-plebiscitary presidency."[85] As has often been noted, the discrepancy between the promise of the presidency and the powers attached to it creates an almost unbridgeable "expectations/performance gap," one that presses presidents to the water's edge of constitutional propriety. But the complexities of presidential leadership run deeper still. The popular apprehension of executive power leaves contemporary presidents with a series of challenges: how to exercise power without the appearance of being powerful; how to give direction and momentum to governmental processes without appearing to subvert cherished constitutional principles and conventions; how to represent what is exemplary and rare in the American cultural tradition without losing a sense of being one with the people.[86]

Americans actively embrace this tension between the promise and the fear. Indeed, it might be said that *not choosing* between these two contradictory values constitutes one of our most cherished political traditions. Such a practice expresses the desire for a dynamic and evolving equilibrium between political safety and liberty, on the one hand, and the achievement of collective purposes, on the other. This straddling of cultural contradictions fosters a creative tension in the popular culture, a healthy skepticism of governmental power that stimulates critical engagement and sustains an ongoing national dialogue about its legitimate exercise.

There is, therefore, manifest value in the tradition of not choosing, but it comes at a cost, and these costs should be borne neither lightly nor in ignorance. This tradition is productive of costly political externalities, deleterious by-products of a system that fosters relentless calculating and opportunism by presidents and other political elites, and public cynicism and political disengagement among average citizens. Leadership requires trust, and trust is built upon the effective and responsible exercise of discretionary power. Yet, as noted, American constitutionalism is predicated on the distrust of effective power and its capabilities. Our institutional features purposely discourage timely and efficient governmental action, undercut clear lines of political responsibility, and in the process undermine trust, feeding an abiding public doubt that government can be an effective instrument for the resolution of difficult national problems.

This core cultural contradiction is most clearly manifest in the undersupply of formal resources required to sustain purposive leadership—leadership that for better or worse has, since the era of Franklin Roosevelt, been squarely placed upon the shoulders of the president. As has been suggested in these pages, armed with few formal resources, presidents have been left to fend for themselves in the struggle for influence in the American political system. What must remain the subject for future national debate is whether effective political leadership must ultimately be lodged *somewhere*. The contemporary structure of Congress and our great political parties makes them institutionally incapable of filling that national leadership role. In its 1937 *Report of the President's Committee on Executive Management*, the Brownlow Committee wrote, "Those who waiver at the sight of needed power are false friends of modern democracy. . . . Strong executive leadership is essential to democratic government today."[87] One can reasonably disagree with the Brownlow Committee's specific conclusions and prescriptions. Yet it seems equally reasonable to conclude that as long as the public continues to demand effective presidential leadership, presidents will rationally respond by doing what they must to succeed within the system they have been given.

Notes

* The author wishes to thank members of the Executive Branch Commission for many excellent comments and helpful suggestions. Special thanks are owed to R. Shep Melnick, Charles O. Jones, Hugh Heclo, and Mark Peterson.

1. Edwards, *At the Margins*; Peterson, *Legislating Together*; Skowronek, *The Politics Presidents Make*; Jones, *The Presidency in a Separated System*.

2 Hughes, *The Living Presidency*, quoted in Ralph Ketcham, *Presidents above Party*.

3. Burns, *Presidential Government*; Califano, *Presidential Nation*.

4. Locke, *Two Treatises*, 392.

5. Locke, *Two Treatises*, 393.

6. Blackstone, *Commentaries on the Laws of England*, vol. 1, 232.

7. Blackstone, *Commentaries*, 253–254.

8. "Publius" is the pseudonym under which James Madison, Alexander Hamilton, and John Jay wrote their essays in defense of the proposed Constitution, essays that would be published under the title *The Federalist Papers*. The immediate purpose of these essays was to secure ratification of the Constitution in New York state.

9. Madison et al., *Federalist Papers*, 263.

10. Madison et al., *Federalist Papers*, 264, 285. On the illegality of the Philadelphia Convention and its implications for constitutional development, see Ackerman, *We the People*, especially ch. 7.

11. Madison et al., *Federalist Papers*, 264–265.

12. "Thomas Jefferson to J. B. Colvin" (September 20, 1810), in Bergh, ed., *Writings of Thomas Jefferson*, vol. 11, 418 (emphasis in original).

13. Bergh, ed., *Writings of Thomas Jefferson*, vol. 11, 421.

14. Locke, *Two Treatises*, 415.

15. On Jackson's war with the Second Bank of the United States, see Remini, *Andrew Jackson and the Bank War*; Remini, *Andrew Jackson*, vols. 2 and 3.

16. In the first forty years of the Republic, presidents exercised the veto power only ten times; there would be twelve vetoes in the course of Jackson's two terms in office.

17. A statement of conventional presidential practice regarding the veto can be found in "Inaugural Address of William Henry Harrison," in Richardson, ed., *Compilation*, vol. 3, 1865. That statement reads, "But if bills were never returned to Congress by [any of the pre-Jacksonian] Presidents . . . upon the ground of their being inexpedient or not as well adapted as they might be to the wants of the people, the veto *was* applied upon that of want of conformity to the Constitution or because errors had been committed from a too hasty enactment." (Emphasis added.)

18. Tulis, *Rhetorical Presidency*.

19. "Jackson's Bank Veto," in MacDonald, ed., *Selected Documents*.

20. Remini, *Andrew Jackson*, vol. 2, 370.

21. Robert V. Remini, "The Constitution and the Presidencies: The Jackson Era," in Martin Fausold and Alan Shank, eds., *The Constitution and the American Presidency* (New York: State University of New York Press), 32–33.

22. "Jackson's Bank Veto," in MacDonald, ed., *Selected Documents*, 266.

23. Remini, *Andrew Jackson*, vol. 3, 20.

24. "Removal of the Public Deposits," in Richardson, ed., *Compilation*, vol. 2, 1225–1226.

25. Remini, *Andrew Jackson and the Bank War*, 123.

26. White, *The Jacksonians*, 34.

27. Fehrenbacher, "Lincoln and the Constitution" in *Lincoln in Text and Context*, 116.

28. Theodore Lowi is quoted in Fausold and Shank, eds., *Constitution*, 45.

29. Donald, "Abraham Lincoln: A Whig in the White House," in *Lincoln Reconsidered*, 187–208.

30. William Henry Harrison, "Inaugural Address," in Richardson, ed., *Compilation*, vol. 3, 1860–1876.

31. Lincoln only vetoed one major piece of legislation, the Wade-Davis bill, and this was likely a manifestation of Lincoln's strong conviction that reconstruction policy in the South was a wholly executive matter.

32. Roosevelt, *Autobiography*, 479.

33. Roosevelt, *Autobiography*, 378.

34. Benedict, "The Constitution of the Lincoln Presidency and the Republican Era," in Fausold and Shank, eds., *Constitution*, 48.

35. Jefferson, "Thomas Jefferson to Doctor James Brown," in Bergh, ed., *Writings*, vol. 12, 183.

36. *Official Opinions of the Attorneys General*, vol. 10, 85.

37. For an extensive historical review of presidential national emergency actions, see the dissenting opinion of Chief Justice Fred Vinson in *Youngstown Company v. Sawyer*, 343 U.S. 597, 681–700 (1952).

38. Welch, *Presidencies of Grover Cleveland*, 143–149; Nevins, *Grover Cleveland*, 611–628.

39. Roosevelt, *Autobiography*, 489.

40. Gould, *Presidency of Theodore Roosevelt*, 66–71; Roosevelt, *Autobiography*, 479–493.

41. McCullough, *Truman*, 897.

42. Tulis, *Rhetorical Presidency*; Ketcham, *Presidents above Party*.

43. Roosevelt, *Autobiography*, 290.

44. Roosevelt, *Autobiography*, 292.

45. Roosevelt, *Autobiography*, 290.

46. This discussion draws on the following sources: Cornwell, *Presidential Leadership*, ch. 2; Tulis, *Rhetorical Presidency*, ch. 4; Gould, *Presidency of Theodore Roosevelt*, 156–165.

47. Sullivan, *Our Times*, 235.

48. Wilson, *Congressional Government*.

49. Wilson, *Constitutional Government*, 67–68.

50. Wilson, *Constitutional Government*, 70–71.

51. Black, *Relation of the Executive Power*, 35.

52. Black, *Relation of the Executive Power*, 60–61.

53. Black, *Relation of the Executive Power*, 59–60.

54. Leuchtenburg, *In the Shadow of FDR*.

55. This discussion of the PUHCA and its politics are taken from James, *Presidents, Parties and the State*, ch. 4.

56. Wilcox, *Public Policies Toward Business*, 590.

57. The best overview of the institutional presidency and its evolution is still Greenstein, "Change and Continuity in the Modern Presidency" in King, ed., *New American Political System*, 45–85.

58. Milkis, *President and the Parties*.

59. Milkis, "The President and the Parties," in Nelson, ed., *Presidency and the Political System*, 360.
60. Corwin, *President*.
61. Corwin and Koenig, *Presidency Today*, 1.
62. Corwin, *President*, i.
63. Corwin, *President*, 310.
64. For an exemplary statement, see Burns, *Presidential Government*.
65. Rossiter, *American Presidency*, 52.
66. Neustadt, *Presidential Power*, 34.
67. On the importance of contemporary veto bargaining to presidential leadership, see Cameron, *Veto Bargaining*.
68. Kernell, *Going Public*.
69. On presidents and group mobilization see Peterson, "Interest Mobilization and the Presidency," in Petracca, ed., *Politics of Interests*, ch. 10; and Peterson, "Clinton and Organized Interests," in Campbell and Rockman, eds., *Clinton Legacy*, ch. 7. On the evolution of presidential communications organization, see Maltese, *Spin Control*.
70. Moe, "The Politicized Presidency." See also, Nathan, *Administrative Presidency*, and Weko, *Politicizing Presidency*.
71. Moe, "The Politicized Presidency," 239.
72. Nathan, *The Plot That Failed;* ibid., *Administrative Presidency*.
73. The following discussion relies upon findings contained in Anne Farris, Richard P. Nathan, and David J. Wright, "The Expanding Administrative Presidency: George W. Bush and the Faith-Based Initiative" (The Roundtable on Religion and Social Welfare Policy, Rockefeller Institute of Government, August 2004).
74. Farris et al., "The Expanding Administrative Presidency," executive summary, 1.
75. Tiefer, *Semi-Sovereign Presidency;* Mayer, *Executive Orders and Presidential Power;* Cooper, *By Order of the President*.
76. See Tiefer, *Semi-Sovereign Presidency;* Cooper, *By Order of the President*.
77. *Ameron, Inc. v. U.S. Army Corps of Engineers*, 610 F. Supp. 750, 755.
78. Tiefer, *Semi-Sovereign Presidency*, 32.
79. *Ameron, Inc. v. U.S. Army Corps of Engineers*, 787 F.2d 875, 889.
80. Schlesinger, *Imperial Presidency;* Lowi, *Personal President;* Heclo and Salamon, eds., *Illusion of Presidential Government;* Peterson, *Legislating Together*.
81. Ginsberg and Shefter, *Politics by Other Means*.
82. Skowronek, *Politics Presidents Make;* Milkis, *President and the Parties*.
83. Ketcham, *Presidents above Parties;* Moe, "The Politicized Presidency"; and Tulis, *Rhetorical Presidency*.
84. Morone, *The Democratic Wish*. For a full and insightful discussion of these presidential contradictions and more, see Cronin and Genovese, *Paradoxes of the American Presidency*.
85. Farrand, *Records*, vol. 1, 66; Corwin, *President;* Lowi, *Personal Presidency*.
86. For a full and insightful discussion of these presidential contradictions and more, see Cronin and Genovese, *Paradoxes of the American Presidency*.
87. The report of the Brownslow Committee is quoted in Polenberg, *Reorganizing Roosevelt's Government*, 21.

Bibliography

Ackerman, Bruce. *We the People: Foundations.* New Haven: Yale University Press, 1991.

Arnold, Richard S. "How James Madison Interpreted the Constitution." *New York University Law Review* 72 (May 1997), 267–293.

Benedict, Michael Les. "The Constitution of the Lincoln Presidency and the Republican Era." In *The Constitution and the American Presidency*, edited by Martin Fausold and Alan Shank, 45-61. New York: State University of New York Press, 1991.

Bergh, Albert Ellery, ed. *The Writings of Thomas Jefferson*, vol. 11. Washington, D.C.: The Thomas Jefferson Memorial Association, 1905.

Black, H. C. *The Relation of the Executive Power to Legislation.* Princeton, N.J.: Princeton University Press, 1919.

Blackstone, William. *Commentaries on the Laws of England*, vol. 1. Chicago: University of Chicago Press, 1979.

Bryce, James. *The American Commonwealth*, 2 vols. New York: Macmillan, 1888.

Burns, James MacGregor. *Presidential Government: The Crucible of Leadership.* New York: Avon Books, 1965.

Califano, Joseph. *Presidential Nation.* New York: W.W. Norton, 1975.

Cameron, Charles. *Veto Bargaining: The Politics of Negative Power.* New York: Cambridge University Press, 2000.

Carpenter, Daniel *The Forging of Bureaucratic Autonomy: Reputations, Networks, and Policy Innovation in Executive Agencies, 1862–1928.* Princeton, N.J.: Princeton University Press, 2001.

Cooper, Philip. *By Order of the President: The Use and Abuse of Executive Direct Action.* Lawrence: University Press of Kansas, 2002.

Cornwell, Elmer R., Jr. *Presidential Leadership of Public Opinion.* Bloomington: Indiana University Press, 1965.

Corwin, Edward S. *The President: Office and Powers.* New York: New York University Press, 1941.

Corwin, Edward S., and Louis Koenig, *The Presidency Today.* New York: New York University Press, 1953.

Crenson, Matthew A. *The Federal Machine: Beginnings of Bureaucracy in Jacksonian America.* Baltimore: Johns Hopkins University Press, 1975

Cronin, Thomas E., and Michael Genovese. *The Paradoxes of the American Presidency*, 2d ed. New York: Oxford University Press, 2004.

Dewey, Donald O. "James Madison Helps Clio Interpret the Constitution." *The American Journal of Legal History* 15 (1971), 38–55.

Donald, David Herbert. "Abraham Lincoln: A Whig in the White House." In *Lincoln Reconsidered: Essays on the Civil War Era*, 2d ed. New York: Vintage Books, 1961.

Edwards, George C., III. *At the Margins: Presidential Leadership of Congress.* New Haven, Conn.: Yale University Press, 1990.

Farrand, Max, ed. *The Records of the Federal Convention of 1787.* 4 vols. Rev. ed. New Haven, Conn.: Yale University Press, 1966.

Fehrenbacher, Don E. "Lincoln and the Constitution." *Lincoln in Text and Context: Collected Essays.* Stanford, Calif.: Stanford University Press, 1987.

Ginsberg, Benjamin, and Martin Shefter. *Politics by Other Means: Politicians, Prosecutors, and the Press from Watergate to Whitewater.* New York: W. W. Norton, 1999.

Gould, Lewis L. *The Presidency of Theodore Roosevelt.* Lawrence: University Press of Kansas, 1991.

Greenstein, Fred I. "Change and Continuity in the Modern Presidency." In *The New American Political System,* edited by Anthony King, pp. 45–85. Washington, D.C.: American Enterprise Institute, 1978.

Hamilton, Alexander. "Pacificus," no. 1. June 29, 1793. In *The Founders' Constitution,* edited by Philip B. Kurland and Ralph Lerner, vol. 4, pp. 64–65. Indianapolis: Liberty Fund, 2000.

Heclo, Hugh, and Lester M. Salamon, eds. *The Illusion of Presidential Government.* Boulder, Colo.: Westview Press, 1981.

Hughes, Emmet John. *The Living Presidency: The Resources and Dilemmas of the American Presidential Office.* New York: Coward, McCann & Geoghegan, 1973.

James, Scott C. *Presidents, Parties and the State: A Party System Perspective on Democratic Regulatory Choice, 1884–1936.* New York: Cambridge University Press, 2000.

Jones, Charles O. *The Presidency in a Separated System.* Washington, D.C.: The Brookings Institution, 1994.

Kernell, Samuel. *Going Public: New Strategies of Presidential Leadership.* Washington, D.C.: Congressional Quarterly Press, 1986.

Ketcham, Ralph. *Presidents above Party: The First American Presidency, 1789–1829.* Chapel Hill: The University of North Carolina Press, 1984.

Lessig, Lawrence, and Cass Sunstein. "The President and the Administration." *Columbia Law Review* 91 (January 1994), 1–123.

Leuchtenburg, William E. *In the Shadow of FDR: From Harry Truman to George W. Bush.* Ithaca, N.Y.: Cornell University Press, 2001.

Locke, John. *Two Treatises of Government.* [1689.] New York: Mentor Books, 1963.

Lowi, Theodore J. *The Personal President: Power Invested, Promise Unfulfilled.* Ithaca, N.Y.: Cornell University Press, 1985.

MacDonald, William, ed. *Selected Documents Illustrative of the History of the United States, 1776–1861.* New York: Macmillan, 1907.

Madison, James, et al. *The Federalist Papers.* [1788.] New York: Penguin Books, 1987.

Magliocca, Gerald N. "Veto! The Jacksonian Revolution in Constitutional Law." *Nebraska Law Review* (1999), 205–262.

Maltese, John Anthony. *Spin Control: The White House Office of Communications and the Management of Presidential News.* Chapel Hill: The University of North Carolina Press, 1992.

Mayer, Kenneth R. *Executive Orders and Presidential Power.* Princeton, N.J.: Princeton University Press, 2001.

McCullough, David. *Truman.* New York: Simon and Schuster, 1992.

Milkis, Sidney M. "The President and the Parties." In *The Presidency and the Political System,* 7th ed., edited by Michael Nelson. Washington, D.C.: Congressional Quarterly Press, 2003.

Milkis, Sidney M. *The President and the Parties: The Transformation of the American Party System since the New Deal.* New York: Oxford University Press, 1993.

Moe, Terry M. "The Politicized Presidency." In *The New Direction in American Politics,* edited by John E. Chubb and Paul E. Peterson. Washington, D.C.: The Brookings Institution, 1985.

Morone, James. *The Democratic Wish: Popular Participation and the Limits of American Government.* New York: Basic Books, 1990.

Nathan, Richard P. *The Plot That Failed: Nixon and the Administrative Presidency.* New York: John Wiley and Sons, 1975.

Nathan, Richard P. *The Administrative Presidency.* New York: John Wiley and Sons, 1983.

Nelson, Michael. "A Short, Ironic History of American National Bureaucracy." *Journal of Politics* 44 (August 1982), 747–778.

Neustadt, Richard. *Presidential Power: The Politics of Leadership.* New York: John Wiley and Sons, 1960.

Nevins, Allan. *Grover Cleveland: A Study in Courage.* New York: Dodd, Mead and Company, 1962.

Official Opinions of the Attorneys General, vol. 10. Washington, D.C.: W. H. & O. H. Morrison, 1868.

Peterson, Mark A. "Clinton and Organized Interests: Splitting Friends, Unifying Enemies." In *The Clinton Legacy,* edited by Colin Campbell and Bert A. Rockman. New York: Chatham House, 2000.

Peterson, Mark A. "Interest Mobilization and the Presidency." In *The Politics of Interests: Interest Groups Transformed,* edited by Mark Petracca. Boulder, Colo.: Westview Press, 1992.

Peterson, Mark A. *Legislating Together: The White House and Capitol Hill from Eisenhower to Reagan.* Cambridge, Mass.: Harvard University Press, 1990.

Polenberg, Richard. *Reorganizing Roosevelt's Government, 1936-1939.* Cambridge, Mass.: Harvard University Press, 1966.

Remini, Robert V. "The Constitution and the Presidencies: The Jackson Era." In *The Constitution and the American Presidency,* edited by Martin Fausold and Alan Shank, pp. 29–43. New York: State University of New York Press, 1991.

Remini, Robert V. *Andrew Jackson and the Bank War.* New York: W. W. Norton, 1967.

Remini, Robert V. *Andrew Jackson.* Vol. 2: *The Course of American Freedom, 1822–1832.* New York: Harper and Row, 1981.

Remini, Robert V. *Andrew Jackson.* Vol. 3: *The Course of American Democracy, 1833–1845.* New York: Harper and Row, 1984.

Richardson, James D., ed. *A Compilation of the Messages and Papers of the Presidents.* Washington D.C.: Bureau of National Literature, 1911.

Roosevelt, Theodore. *An Autobiography.* [1913.] New York: Da Capo Press, 1985.

Rossiter, Clinton. *The American Presidency.* New York: Harcourt, Brace and Company, 1956.

Schlesinger, Arthur M., Jr. *The Imperial Presidency.* Boston: Houghton Mifflin, 1973.

Skowronek, Steven. *The Politics Presidents Make: Leadership from John Adams to George Bush.* Cambridge Mass.: The Belknap Press of Harvard University Press, 1993.

Sullivan, Mark. *Our Times.* Vol. 3: *Pre-War America.* New York: Charles Scribner's Sons, 1930.

Tiefer, Charles. *The Semi-Sovereign Presidency: The Bush Administration's Strategy for Governing Without Congress*. Boulder, Colo.: Westview Press, 1994.

Tulis, Jeffrey. *The Rhetorical Presidency*. Princeton, N.J.: Princeton University Press, 1987.

Weko, Thomas. *The Politicizing Presidency: The White House Personnel Office, 1948–1994*. Lawrence: The University Press of Kansas, 1995.

Welch, Richard E., Jr. *The Presidencies of Grover Cleveland*. Lawrence: University Press of Kansas, 1988.

White, Leonard D. *The Jacksonians: A Study in Administrative History, 1829–1861*. New York: Macmillan, 1954.

Wilcox, Clair. *Public Policies Toward Business*. Boston: Houghton Mifflin Company, 1955.

Wilson, Woodrow. *Congressional Government: A Study in American Politics*. [1885.] New York: Peter Smith, 1973.

Wilson, Woodrow. *Constitutional Government in the United States*. New York: Columbia University Press, 1911.

2

THE EVOLUTION OF NATIONAL
BUREAUCRACY IN THE UNITED STATES

Daniel Carpenter

THE SIMPLE DETAILS OF AMERICAN DAILY LIFE REVEAL
the pervasive presence of the bureaucratic state—the dollars in our wallets, printed by the Treasury Department; the peanut butter we eat, subsidized and regulated by the U.S. Department of Agriculture (USDA); the pain medications we take, approved and governed by the Food and Drug Administration (FDA); the cars we drive, produced in factories regulated by the Occupational Safety and Health Administration (OSHA) and themselves regulated by the Environmental Protection Agency (EPA) and the National Highway Traffic Safety Administration; the national parks and forests, in which we ski, fish, hike, hunt, climb, and camp, governed by the Forest Service and the Department of Interior; and the $425.3 billion in checks that our elderly and disabled receive annually from the Social Security Administration.

These everyday facts have an enduring history. Despite revisionist accounts and casual impressions, national bureaucracies have figured prominently in American history. Take the case of war. From the early 1800s, through the world wars to the present, American military affairs have been guided through large bureaucracies: the Navy and the Department of War (1789–1947) and the Department of Defense (1947–present).[1] U.S. military and intelligence agencies have spread millions of persons and trillions of dollars in expenditure across the continent and around the globe. These bureaucracies have created new weapons, and even launched the Internet, which was once a network of electronic communications conceived and funded by the Pentagon's Defense Advance Research Projects Agency (DARPA). The presence of bureaucratic government in American history is vast, even when we step outside the military. In the early

1800s, the U.S. national government contained what was perhaps the world's largest and most complex administrative organization of any kind in the U.S. Post Office Department, which employed more than 8,000 people in the early nineteenth century, at a time when the largest private companies employed per-haps 10,000 workers.[2] Later, in the 1940s and 1950s, the Post Office Department swelled to half a million workers.

In the modern United States, virtually complete control over finance and the aggregate money supply rests in the hands of two federal government agen-cies: the U.S. Treasury and the Federal Reserve Bank. Some of the largest federal agencies spread tens of thousands of employees, thousands of structures and offices, billions of dollars in discretionary money, and formidable political sway across the entire continent: the Departments of Agriculture; Housing and Urban Development; Interior; and now, Homeland Security. The Department of Agriculture's annual budget in 2004 was $78 billion, which is three times the endowment of America's wealthiest university, Harvard. In some cases, the seem-ingly smallest of agencies exercises an immense regulatory impact upon our economy and society. The Department of Treasury issues all U.S. bonds and hence establishes and regulates the largest bond markets in the world, it prints all money in the United States, and it collects (through the Internal Revenue Service) almost all of the over $1.5 trillion in federal revenues collected each year by our national government. The Department of Interior directly manages one-fifth of the nation's land, over 500 million acres. The Food and Drug Administration explicitly regulates one-quarter of total U.S. gross domestic product (GDP), with the power to recall and inspect commodities amounting to over $1 trillion in economic activity. One of the two largest social welfare pro-grams in the contemporary United States—Medicare—is administered with considerable discretion by the Center for Medicare and Medicaid Services (CMS). Regulations with costs and benefits in the hundreds of billions of dollars are administered and enforced by the Environmental Protection Agency and the U.S. Fish and Wildlife Service.

Two and a quarter centuries after the creation of the American Republic, the history of national bureaucracy in the United States still warrants study and reflection. Why is it that the government of the United States—a nation born in revolt from regal power, a nation dedicated in theory to the rule of law, a nation so antibureaucratic in its talk and tenor—is now shot through with bureaucratic organization? Was our nation's executive branch always this way? How have new bureaucratic agencies been created, and when have they been terminated? What accounts for the powerful policy-making roles played by national bureaucratic officials—from the Departments of Education and Homeland Security to the Food and Drug Administration and the Federal Reserve? Has the present era of government downsizing and of privatization truly changed the federal bureau-cracy, and if so, how?

No brief essay can do justice to any of these questions. Still, it may be possible to offer something far short of a full narrative that is nevertheless valuable and informative. What follows, then, is aimed at providing a more or less portable narrative map of concepts and characterizations; a map that highlights the most important transitions and continuities in the history of American national bureaucracy. To preview, these are:

- Copying the Crown. Much as the American Revolution was energized by a revolt against executive power (King George III and his colonial governors), Americans quickly came to reembrace executive and bureaucratic institutions in the early Republic. In doing so, they both knowingly and unknowingly embraced and inherited organizational forms that they had attacked just decades earlier. An important feature of early American government, then, was a striking continuity of executive institutions inherited and copied from the reign of George III (1760–1820).
- Compromise and Continuity through Birth and Death. New agencies are often born of presidential and congressional compromise, but they are also built from existing agencies and institutions. The institutions of the future seem endlessly created from the organizations of the past, implicitly preserving the continuity of personnel and programs. This is as true of bureaucratic death as of bureaucratic birth. As concerns death, many more —anywhere from one-third to one-half of all agencies created in the last century—have been terminated than one might guess from popular and media accounts.
- Personnel Transformation. Important changes have occurred in the way that we staff our national bureaucracies. From the elite networks of the early Republic, we transited wrenchingly to the Jacksonian patronage system, then to the "merit system" of the Progressive Era, and slowly in the past century to a mixed system that contains broad but not universal civil service protections.
- War Begets Bureaucracies and Bureaucratic Power. Whether in civil war, in international conflict, or in the struggle against terrorism, war has often mothered bureaucratic expansion in two ways. First, wars often issue in new bureaucratic organizations that live on after peace has been achieved. Second, war and security issues give all sorts of agencies (including "domestic" agencies) rationales to expand their missions, their resources, and their policy influence.
- Executive Agencies as Policy-making Agents. In a way that Alexander Hamilton might barely have presaged or hoped, executive agencies have become powerful innovating forces in national policy making. The fact of bureaucratic innovation is as true in defense, security, and diplomacy arenas as it is in "domestic" policy. In some cases by rule making and regula-

tion, in other cases by sponsoring legislative proposals that are enacted into statute, in other ways by launching experimental programs, federal bureaucrats do not merely administer policy but play an immense role in making it.

- The Politics of Executive Agencies. National government in the United States has been dominated by executive agencies that lie officially under the purview of the President but are just as strongly influenced by Congress. (These include the Departments of State, Army, Navy, Defense, Agriculture, Interior, Commerce, Education, and others).

- The Rise and Plateau of the Contracting State. While privatization of public services has gathered momentum in the past twenty years, an equally important feature of government is the creation of a "contracting state" in which governmental services are provided less by career bureaucrats and more by companies who seek and operate through competitive grants and contracts. Along with this practice has come the increasingly visible metaphor of "government as business" with citizens as "customers" or "stakeholders," which is actually a rehearsal of Progressive Era discussions. But this is less accurate than meets the eye. Those aspects of bureaucracy that have been contracted out remain every bit as monopolistic and bureaucratic as the federal agencies they have replaced. And if recent international events (particularly the creation of the Homeland Security Department) tell us anything, seeing the clients of the state as "customers" is problematic. While subcontracting and privatization will remain, the idea of "government as business" has been around before, and was never very informative.

Copying the Crown:
The Continuity of Regal Organizations and Institutions

Much more than Americans (then and now) would care to admit, early U.S. administrative institutions copied the agencies of the very empire against which the colonists rebelled. Many features of the executive departments of the early American Republic were modeled explicitly upon bureaucracies under the regime of King George III, and the structure of new national agencies created in the 1780s and 1790s bore an appreciable resemblance to those of the English Crown. This is especially true of the most active departments during the early period (Post Office, State, Treasury, and War).

Before 1763, the colonial bureaucracies governing British North America were known for their administrative inefficiency. Revenues went uncollected, colonial governors and their officers depended heavily upon colonial legislatures for the slightest of provisions, and bribery and corruption continued largely unchecked. There was little for the American colonists to copy here, and the

44

colonists largely enjoyed this system of government because, despite its ineffi-
ciencies, it left them alone. With the arrival of Sir George Grenville to the chancellorship of the Exchequer in 1763, the forceful extension of colonial rule
following the Seven Years' War caught colonists unaware and left them alienated
from the mother continent. Under Grenville's plan, the relatively efficient
bureaucratic system governing England itself would begin to replace, in pieces,
the inefficient system of colonial government.

This process, particularly the more efficient extraction of revenues and the
new acts specifying excises and taxes, brought Parliament and George III into
direct and acrimonious conflict with the colonists. The rest of the story is well
known. By 1776 the colonists had declared independence from the Crown, and
by 1783 they had formed their own government under a peace with the British.

So direct and unflinching was the American hatred for monarchy that, at
first, the revolutionaries wanted to create their own, indigenous bureaus modeled in the spirit of small legislatures. Bureaucracies during the Continental
Congress were composed of "boards" or "committees." In military affairs there
was a Board of War and Ordnance chaired by John Adams. In financial affairs
there was not a "Treasury" but a Committee of Claims composed of five members of Congress. Naval affairs were, after 1779, led by a Marine Committee.
Diplomatic affairs were governed by Samuel Adams's Committee of
Correspondence. There were two distinctive features of these executive boards.
First, they were strict departures from English and French administrative practice
wherein administrative positions vested authority in a single individual. Second,
they were populated not by administrative experts but by appointed members of
Congress. In both form and personage, then, revolutionary American bureaucra-
cies were legislative bodies.[3]

The year 1781 would prove to be decisive in the history of American
government. Led by the young Alexander Hamilton, Americans rejected the
administration-by-committee model in favor of appointive departments governed by a single head or Secretary. Hamilton and George Washington argued
vociferously for the principle that individual men were to be appointed to
lead administrative organizations, whether military or civil. Hamilton and the
new Americans were borrowing from the French as well as the English, but
in some cases the resemblances with the British Crown were uncanny. Copying
a title directly from George III's realm, Congress appointed a "secretary at
War" to head a Department of War. The Treasury boards were abolished in
favor of a Treasury headed by a superintendent of Finance. This title, as far as
we can tell, was borrowed from French arrangements, not British. The Marine
Committee was replaced by a secretary of Marine in the War Department.
Adams's Committee of Correspondence was eventually replaced by a
Department of Foreign Affairs. In form and in philosophical vision, Americans
had gently reembraced bureaucracy.[4]

Hamilton's Vision: The Constitution and the Making of U.S. Bureaucracy

By the time the Constitution of 1787 was adopted and the first executive agencies of the new national government were built in 1789, the executive branch of the United States began to look even more like the administration of George III. The offices of the Crown that colonists most hated—the Exchequer and Treasury Board, and the Secretaries of State—reappeared as "Departments" in the U.S. executive, with functions substantially similar to those to which George III put his civil servants (customs, revenue collection, trade promotion, diplomacy). The Americans created an "attorney-general" much like the one that served the English crown. The form of the Post Office Department was borrowed almost entirely from the colonial post that had operated under Benjamin Franklin's purview, when it functioned as an appendage of the British royal post. Military affairs under George III were conducted under a secretary at War; in the new United States, they would be the realm of the secretary of War, who oversaw a Department of War. In Britain naval administration was centralized under the Board of Admiralty under His Majesty's Navy, superintended by the Lord High Admiral. The Americans soon constructed an arrangement like this one, with a secretary of Navy and (after 1798) a Department of Navy.[5]

Other forms of British administration were copied less in title and more in form. The early United States governed the expenditures of administrative agencies through appropriations acts of the Congress. This was copied almost exactly from British administration, where appropriations of the House of Commons governed the public expenditure of the Crown. And just as the Crown had appointed governors to rule weakly over colonial lands, so too the Americans began to appoint territorial governors and secretaries whose rule over territorial lands was weak and required constant protection from the U.S. Army. In the face of alternative arrangements—copying from state governments, from the government of the Articles of Confederation, or even from French or Habsburg arrangements—early Americans most often borrowed administrative arrangements from the Crown against which they had just rebelled.[6]

There were several reasons for this borrowing. For one, British administration of homeland affairs was well regarded, even if its colonial agencies were seen as inefficient. Second, and more important, the drafting of the U.S. Constitution was to some degree a rejection of the pro-legislative ideals of the Revolution and an embrace of strong executive power. Throughout the 1780s, a broad "repudiation of 1776" at the federal and state levels was underway, in which the absolute supremacy of purely legislative government was rejected in favor of mixed regimes with strong executive actors and executive bureaucracies.[7] The Federal Constitution and the early Federalist period were products of a "revolution in favor of government," as early Americans themselves saw it. While the moderate James Madison was perhaps "father of the Constitution," the devotee of executive and administrative power Alexander Hamilton was perhaps just as influential, and it was Hamilton who sponsored and penned most of *The Federalist Papers*. It was Hamilton, too, who expressed early American hopes for what their executive government would become. As Hamilton wrote in *Federalist* 72, the scope of affairs left to administrators in American government would be broad, and their influence would be far-reaching, touching upon "all the operations of the body politic."

> The administration of government, in its largest sense, comprehends all the operations of the body politic, whether legislative, executive, or judiciary; but in its most usual and perhaps in its most precise signification, it is limited to executive details, and *falls peculiarly within the province of the executive department* [emphasis added]. The actual conduct of foreign negotiations, the preparatory plans of finance, the application and disbursement of the public moneys in conformity to the general appropriations of the legislature, the arrangement of the army and navy, the direction of the operations of war—these, and other matters of a like nature, constitute what seems to be most properly understood by the administration of government.[8]

Of course, Hamilton expressed his vision at a time when the federal government did much less than it does now, and this statement may have seemed less sweeping at the time than it is now.

It is also true that not every American founder agreed with Hamilton's prescriptions. Elbridge Gerry and (especially) Thomas Jefferson saw a much more limited role for bureaucratic government. Yet as the early American Republic began to form its administrative institutions, Hamilton's vision generally won out over that of Jeffersonian democracy. Even as the Jeffersonians took over after the election of 1800, they implicitly accepted a Hamiltonian vision of government by keeping the bureaucratic apparatus of the Federalist period (1789–1801) in place. The central government would involve itself heavily in national finance and in the promotion of trade and commerce. Appointees would hail from the higher social classes and from backgrounds of pedigree. Positions, titles, tasks, and procedures would be copied wholesale from British administration. The construction of bureaucratic institutions in the early United States was completed not in a vacuum, but evinced immense historical borrowing (some of it intentional, some of it not) from the English Crown.

This borrowing from the Crown is not merely of historical interest, but had identifiable impacts upon the development of U.S. government. For one, administrative development in the early Republic took place within the confines of agencies created at its birth in 1789. Not until 1849 was a new executive department (Interior) created in the United States; until that time, politicians had seen fit to place new program authorities within the static structure inherited from the British. Second, patterns of recruitment for civil office were alike in Georgian England and in the early American Republic. In both nations, bureaucratic recruitment was conducted through social networks of elites, networks that were anchored by the leader of state (the king and prime minister in Britain, the president in the United States). As it turns out, these networks would also become the basis of the early parties in the American Republic: the Federalists (led by Washington and John Adams) and the Jeffersonian Republicans.

The commonality of English and early American bureaucracy goes deeper still. Administrators in the early American Republic knowingly and unknowingly participated in the creation of a vast body of administrative law by issuing regulations and ordinances. The postmaster general and secretary of the Treasury, for instance, both issued book-length summaries and compilations of the regulations governing national bond markets and the postal system, respectively. Most of these regulations were conceived by Treasury and Post Office administrators and were issued by top-level officials. Many of them "bubbled up" from administrative patterns that had been established at various levels of these departments, and were codifications of prevailing practice. All of them had the force of law. As far as we can tell, this practice was inherited from English administration, wherein regal officials frequently issued general rulings and edicts that accumulated in common-law fashion into a more or less coherent body of administrative precedent and practice. As Sir Norman Chester has described the English administrative system in 1780, this pattern of regulation meant a system of "diffused authority" in which much less power was exercised by politicians than was thought to be the case. Such a pattern of "regulation by administrators" was common in both French and British North America. In the early United States, grants of power to the secretary of the Treasury or the postmaster general "tended to flow down . . . to the second or third levels of administration," that is, well below the Cabinet. Included in these powers was the power to superintend basic administrative functions (collection of the revenue, delivery of the mails), and included within these supervisory powers was the authority to issue circulars, rulings, and instructions for the governance of the department. From the very earliest days of the Republic, then, "rulemaking" activity by executive agencies—the issuance of rules, instructions, circulars, and regulations that gave life to everyday government—was an acknowledged and accepted mode of administration.[9]

Bargains, History, and Bureaucratic Structure

The growth of American bureaucratic government has been slow and punctuated by fits and spurts. A list of selected U.S. bureaucratic agencies appears in Table 1, which also supplies the agency's date of creation and its approximate spending authority for 2003 or 2004. Not until sixty years after the birth of the American Republic in 1789 was a major new agency (the Department of

TABLE 1

Selected U.S. Government Agencies and Their Dates of Creation
[where available, approximate budget figures for FY 2004 are given in {brackets}]

Executive Agencies	Independent Commissions, Boards, Corporations
Federalist Period to Reconstruction (1789–1876)	
Department of State (1789) {$11B} Department of War (1789) Department of Treasury (1789) {$11B} Office of Attorney General (1789) Post Office Department (1792) • Built from colonial postal system Department of Navy (1798) Department of Interior (1849) {$10B} • Collection of existing agencies Department of Agriculture (1862) {$78B} • Some components from Interior Department Department of Justice (1872) {$22B} • from Office of Attorney General	Smithsonian Institution (1846) {$596M}
Gilded Age to Second World War (1877–1947)	
Department of Commerce and Labor (1911) Food and Drug Administration (1927) • in USDA, from USDA Bureau of Chemistry Agricultural Adjustment Administration (1933) • in USDA, built in part from Bureau of Plant Industry and Bureau of Agricultural Economics Social Security Administration (1935, 1946) {$510B} Department of Defense (1947) {$358B} • created from Departments of Navy, Army and Army Air Force	Interstate Commerce Commission (1887) Federal Trade Commission (1913) {$191M} Federal Reserve Administration (1914) Securities and Exchange Commission (1934) {$842M} Federal Communications Commission (1933) {$281M} • from Federal Radio Commission (1927), and originally, from bureau of maritime radio regulation in Navy Department National Labor Relations Board (1938) {$243M}
Cold War to Present (1948–present)	
Department of Health, Education, and Welfare (1953) [HEW] Department of Housing and Urban Development (1969) {$38B}	Consumer Product Safety Commission (1973) [CPSC] {$60M} United States Post Office (1970) [termination of existence as

TABLE 1 (continued)

Cold War to Present (1948–present) (continued)	
Environmental Protection Agency (1970) {$8B}	executive department; established as government corporation]
Occupational Safety and Health Administration (1971) [OSHA]	
• within Department of Labor	
Department of Education (1979) {$60B}	
• from HEW; Department of Health and Human Services [HHS] created in 1980 {$502B}	
Department of Veterans Affairs (1989) {$57B}	
Department of Homeland Security (2002) {$28B}	

Interior) created. As the table suggests, the largest agencies of government are executive departments, and the history of some of these (State, Treasury, Interior, Agriculture) has been one of relative constancy. For others—the Departments of Commerce and Labor, the Department of Health and Human Services, and the recently created Department of Homeland Security—endless mergers and separations have defined and redefined turf.

How were these agencies created? And what role did politics play? In the governmental history of the United States, new agencies have often been hammered out as bargains in cross-partisan debates or congressional-presidential compromises. So, for instance, the creation of the Interior Department in 1849 was deeply intertwined with battles between the two major parties of nineteenth-century American politics—the Whigs and the Democrats—and the Compromise of 1850. The creation of the Agriculture Department and other new agencies during the Civil War was facilitated by the rise of the radical Republicans of the 1860s, and the retrenchment of agencies during Reconstruction in part reflected interbranch tensions within the Republican Party of the 1870s. Later, the statutes creating the nation's first two independent commissions—the Interstate Commerce Commission (ICC) in 1887 and the Federal Trade Commission (FTC) in 1914—both relied upon partisan compromises for their passage. In both of these cases, Progressive Democrats from New York supplied crucial and pivotal votes for the bills that established new forms of regulation for railroads and corporate commerce. The administrative launching of New Deal welfare programs required President Franklin Delano Roosevelt to compromise with Southern Democrats, who saw to it that federal welfare programs would be administered in such a way as to exclude African Americans.[10]

Political interbranch compromises, then, have decisively shaped the structure of the executive branch. One reasonable conjecture is that new departments and agencies are frequently created as a necessary condition of congressional-presidential bargains. It may often be the case that, in order to strike an effective compromise, the president and Congress must agree to a new agency or set of agencies that stands effectively between or apart from the legislature and president.

There are also important presidential advantages in the creation of administrative agencies. As it turns out, a high number of federal agencies in the past century have been created by presidential executive order. The executive order is a form of "unilateral action," in the sense that the president need not seek the advice or consent of Congress before issuing one.[11] What this means concretely is that presidents have structured these agencies largely according to their wishes, so as to maximize presidential control and to minimize congressional influence, to the extent possible. As will become clear, however, Congress's power in shaping the form and behavior of executive bureaucracies is formidable.

Creation through Recombination

If the pattern of agency creation in the United States admits of one generalization, it is this: agencies are almost never created *ex nihilo*, but are instead cobbled together from bits and parts of existing agencies, programs, and personnel. The early Post Office was founded on the structure of the colonial postal system. In creating the Department of the Interior in 1849, Congress collected together a number of agencies previously scattered around the executive branch—the Patent Office, the Pension Office, the General Land Office, and others—so much so that political scientist Leonard White has called Interior "The Great Miscellany."[12] While technically created in 1933, the Federal Communications Commission took much of its personnel from the earlier Federal Radio Commission, which itself grew out of a bureau of marine radio regulation in the Navy Department. The modern Food and Drug Administration was enabled in 1938, but it grew out of the Bureau of Chemistry in the U.S. Department of Agriculture. The recent Department of Homeland Security was essentially created by cobbling together parts of other departments. Other well-known agencies of American government—the Environmental Protection Agency (EPA), the Central Intelligence Agency (CIA)—were also created by carving and collecting pieces from existing agencies.

What is true of agency creation is also true of program creation. When Congress and the president create a new government program, they only rarely create an absolutely new agency to carry it out. Much more commonly, in fact about 80 percent of the time, politicians give new program authority to an agency that already exists. Historical examples abound. In the New Deal, numerous new agricultural programs, such as commodity price support programs, were delegated to the Department of Agriculture. New programs for labor and worker safety regulation in the 1960s and 1970s were given to the existing Department of Labor. The welfare program Supplemental Security Income (SSI), begun and expanded in the 1970s, was placed within the Social Security Administration created in the late 1930s, in a way that political scientist Martha Derthick found was generally inefficient in that it strained SSA resources. Massive welfare reforms under the administration of Presidents Lyndon Johnson and Richard Nixon were placed in the Department of Health, Education and Welfare (HEW), which had been created during the Eisenhower administration in the 1950s (perhaps not ironically, Nixon had served as vice president during that time). The education policies of President George W. Bush (in particular, the "No Child Left Behind" Act and the Education Accountability Act) were given to the Department of Education (just ten years earlier, congressional Republicans had called for its abolition).[13]

In order to explain the genesis of new bureaucratic structures at any given time, then, the first place to start is not with the political coalitions acting during the period—though we would certainly wish to pay attention to these—but with existing administrative institutions. Existing agencies are most often the place where new government programs are placed. Very often the ideas (general or specific) for such programs originate within the very federal agencies that eventually administer the programs. Moreover, existing agencies do not stand idly by as politicians decide where in the government to place new program authority. While some agencies are content with the discretion and authority they have, others actively seek new programs and powers. Numerous agencies— ranging from the early Treasury Department, to the Progressive Era Agriculture Department and Post Office, to the Departments of Education and Energy today—actively lobby for a policy-making and discretionary role in the administration of government programs.

Myths of Termination

What, finally, of agency death? Are agencies ever terminated under our system of government, and if so, with what frequency? Agencies are in fact terminated. The Civil Aeronautics Board (which regulated commercial aviation) was abolished in 1984; the Interstate Commerce Commission (which governed interstate trucking and railroads) and the Resolution Trust Corporation (which responded to the insolvencies of about 750 savings and loan institutions) were abolished in 1995. Recent research by Professor David Lewis of Princeton University shows that, of all federal bureaucratic agencies created from 1947 to 1998, 57 percent were terminated.[14] There are some other counterintuitive features to agency termination. In most cases, government programs continue even after agencies die. In all three cases just mentioned, the functions and personnel of these agencies were generally transferred to other departments (the Department of Transportation for the CAB and the ICC, the Savings Loan Insurance Fund for the RTC). Another interesting feature of agency death is its timeline. In the postwar period, federal agencies appear most at risk of termination when they are five to twelve years old. And large government deficits appear to make agencies safer, not more at risk of death. The reason is simple: termination is costly to politicians because it requires that employees' careers be bought out, that viable programs be transferred to other agencies, and that considerable legislative activity be undertaken.

Personnel Politics: From Patronage to Protection

Another area of immense change in the American executive branch is the way in which federal officials come to their positions. In the early Republic, again, this process was elite-driven, expertise-seeking, and was managed informally through social networks. With the inauguration of President Andrew Jackson in 1829, matters changed irreversibly. Jackson's theory of "rotation in office" held that any man could perform the duties of administrative office as well as any other. Why not allow the president's party to claim the "spoils" of the election and appoint the officials of government? Why not return government to "the common man" by allowing the rank-and-file party faithful to claim government jobs?

Jackson's vision of a rotation-based government was perfected into a "patronage system" by his successor, Martin Van Buren. Under this "spoils" system, the party of the president appointed most federal officials, and American national bureaucracy literally flushed itself of employees every time that a new president came to power. The spoils system grew to encompass virtually the entire national government, and helped to sustain the large and cohesive mass parties of the 1800s. Federal workers contributed a portion of their salaries to the party coffers (they were fired if they did not), and the payment of such dues was a source of much political and administrative corruption in the late nineteenth century.

The emergence of a reform-based movement concerned with "corruption" in the patronage system, combined with the assassination of President James Garfield by a disappointed office seeker in 1881, paved the way for fundamental change. "Merit reform," which gave permanence to civil officials in the United States, was adopted in the United States in the Pendleton Act of 1883. The Pendleton Act and related legislation outlawed party dues-paying as a condition of officeholding in the federal bureaucracy, instituted competitive examinations and evaluations as a necessary step for federal hiring, and prohibited the firing of federal civil servants except for cause. The passage of the Pendleton Act also placed U.S. national bureaucracies in a position comparable to that of other nations. Other nations—Great Britain, Prussia, France, Japan, and Russia among them—also passed merit-based civil service reforms in the late 1800s. Still, it took several decades for the Pendleton Act to become widely implemented in the U.S. government, with the critical moves not occurring until the presidential administrations of Theodore Roosevelt (1901–1909) and Woodrow Wilson (1913–1921). Even so, the patronage system died a slow, incremental death. As late as the New Deal presidency of Franklin Delano Roosevelt, some 40 percent of federal positions were subject to patronage appointment, and the system persists in many local governments even today.

In theory, merit reform was supposed to insulate federal bureaucracies from partisan politics, and to some extent this was its effect. The patronage-based parties waned from national politics, and it is generally conceded that many national agencies became more efficient and less corrupt as a result. In two ways, however, merit reform replaced one form of politics with another. First, merit reform created an insulated class of federal employees who claimed new administrative power and who (in some cases) quickly organized to defend their interests. As interest groups and labor unions go, federal employee unions such as the American Federation of Government Employees are among the weakest organizations in American politics. Yet the emergence of protected federal officials shifted conflict from a pure Republicans-versus-Democrats axis to a more multidimensional conflict in which partisan conflict was accompanied by conflict along a bureaucrats-versus-politicians axis. Second, within specific departments, merit reform placed control over hiring in the hands of careerist bureau chiefs. In a number of agencies—the Post Office Department, the U.S. Department of Agriculture, the Social Security Administration, the Food and Drug Administration of the 1950s, and the Environmental Protection Agency of the 1970s—entrepreneurial bureau chiefs created administrative "communities" of experts and officials who slowly refashioned policy to their liking. The programs shaped by these officials—Social Security, national forest regulation, environmental regulation of industry, the anti-lottery laws of the 1890s, food and drug regulation, and the Agricultural Adjustment Act—are among the most significant and transformative policies of the twentieth century.[15]

The merit principle in today's federal agencies is now governed by Title 5 of the U.S. Code. Civil servants protected by Title 5 include laborers covered under the Federal Wage System as well as administrative, technical, and professional jobs covered by the General Schedule (GS). Since the administration of Dwight D. Eisenhower, the federal civil service system has retreated to a degree. The process has been piecemeal, as individual departments—the Post Office, the Defense Department, the Federal Aviation Administration, and the new Department of Homeland Security, for instance—have received authority to create their own personnel systems outside standard civil service laws. In short, more than half of all federal jobs are exempt from the provisions of Title 5, including individuals in the Senior Executive Service (SES) and agency-specific positions denoted variously as Schedule A, B, and C positions. The ranks of these positions have been expanded to increase the number of federal officials whose jobs are dependent upon presidential administrations.[16]

The Rise and Persistence of the Executive Policy-making State

What sort of impact do bureaucratic agencies exercise upon policy, and upon social and economic outcomes? No one doubts that the influence of federal agencies is immense today, yet an important historical point is that bureaucratic influence upon policy has changed immensely in the past 150 years. Executive branch agencies today engage in two activities—planning and policy making—in which independent commissions and other sorts of agencies now play a lesser role, and which executive agencies themselves used to do a lot less of. In some respects, this represents a departure from traditional models of policy making that students learn in civics classes. For much of the past century, executive agencies have been the fount of numerous bills, influential policy ideas, and executive plans. Not all of these have been politically successful, and in some cases, poor public policies have resulted. Yet the fact of extensive bureaucratic involvement in policy innovation is today undeniable. Think tanks and interest groups have certainly diminished the dominant role of the agencies in some areas, but it remains true that in policy domains such as food and pharmaceutical safety, transportation, energy, security, and intelligence, the federal bureaucracy continues to play a crucial planning role.

The Historical Form of Bureaucratic Policy Innovation

Executive agencies are sometimes as powerful in creating new programs as in administering them, as powerful in innovation as in execution. In the late 1800s and early 1900s, the Agriculture Department and the Post Office Department were home to considerable policy innovation of this sort. Long-tenured career federal officials (protected by the Pendleton Act, and reinforced through the bureau-based system of hiring and retention) launched new programs and offices, ranging from the anti-pornography and anti-lottery laws of postal inspector Anthony Comstock to the pure food and drug regulation championed by the Department of Agriculture's Harvey Wiley. Postal bureaucrats took the lead in launching the rural free delivery service, postal savings banks, and parcel post. Agriculture Department officials inaugurated the farm extension system, programs in agricultural economics and planning, and numerous applied scientific programs (soil surveys, insect and pest studies, forestry regulation, and others).

In one of the best-known examples of bureaucratic policy innovation, Social Security administrators such as Arthur Altmeyer, Robert Ball, and others helped to transform the Old-Age and Survivors Disability Insurance (OASDI) program into the dominant income protection program of the federal government of the

United States. Some of these moves were made during the formative years of the Social Security program in the 1930s, when Altmeyer and his lieutenants at the Social Security Board (SSB) carefully chose the personnel who would guide the program's development in the ensuing decades and orchestrated an agency-wide plan for program stability followed by growth. Other administrative moves occurred after the World War II—in 1946, the SSB was transformed into the Social Security Administration (SSA) that exists today—including the SSA's active role in promoting union- and corporate-based income protection programs that were jointly negotiated by labor and management (beginning with the United Mine Workers in 1947) and the deployment of the Social Security Administration's expertise in statistics and actuarial science in managing field offices and state income-protection programs.[17]

Such bureaucratic innovation is not confined to the domestic agencies. In the middle of World War II, Navy Department administrators fundamentally changed the way that American militaries procured their supplies. Under the leadership of Undersecretary of the Navy James V. Forrestal (later appointed the first secretary of Defense in 1947), Navy bureaus such as the Bureau of Ships and the Bureau of Aeronautics sidestepped the earlier regime of competitive bidding and began to take active and discretionary control over naval procurement. Naval attorneys developed the first incentive-based contracts for construction and supply. Naval offices used direct and indirect price controls to capture "excess profits" from naval contractors. The bureaus induced their contractors to further subcontract their work as a way of reducing costs. And, as World War II ended, the Navy Department launched its own "deprocurement program" that terminated tens of thousands of contracts with suppliers. After the 1947 National Security Act, which unified the armed forces in a new Department of Defense, the Navy retained many of its procurement capacities even as the Army surrendered its capacities to the new department. The result, as Bartholomew Sparrow describes it, is that naval procurement was a strong exception to the general characterization of a "military-industrial complex" during and after World War II.[18]

Some federal agencies have continued this pattern of policy innovation and entrepreneurship in contemporary American politics. Under the leadership of James Witt (1993–2001), the Federal Emergency Management Agency (FEMA) has redefined its core mission around an "all hazards" approach—protecting the United States from numerous forms of natural disasters, as opposed to military or terrorist threats—and has resisted congressional attempts to mold its functions and operations in line with those of the Department of Homeland Security.[19] Witt and his lieutenants at FEMA reorganized the agency so as to conform with the "all hazards" approach and reinterpreted existing statutes so as to permit a FEMA response to be set in motion before a natural disaster even occurred. Witt's "Flood Safe" program encouraged private landowners to purchase flood insurance before floods materialized, thereby reducing the "moral hazard" problem inherent to federal disaster insurance. Witt also focused his agency's operations on the most predictable of natural disasters, namely floods, hurricanes, and tornadoes, all of which have a seasonal or cyclical component. Finally, to secure these innovations, Witt developed a network of affiliations to members of Congress from both parties and made the services of his agency of electoral use to reelection-minded members of Congress. When the time came for national administrative reorganizations in the wake of the September 11, 2001, terrorist attacks, numerous politicians proposed eliminating FEMA and submerging its functions within the Department of Homeland Security, but Witt and FEMA successfully resisted this move, as they were able to convince Congress and the George W. Bush Administration that its inherent and unique expertise lay in management of and response to natural disasters. Today FEMA lies under the umbrella of Homeland Security but retains considerable autonomy.[20]

To observers of recent presidencies, and especially of the George W. Bush and Reagan administrations, this characterization of agencies as policy innovators may seem problematic. It is apparent, for instance, that there has been considerable centralization of policy making in the White House under the administration of President George W. Bush. Observers of the federal government routinely note that Bush has distanced the making of administration policy and new rules from career civil servants, instead concentrating authority in the top (political) echelons of the federal bureaucracy. The Bush Administration has also encouraged and strengthened the hand of the Office of Management and Budget in reviewing new proposed rules proffered by lower-level bureaus and agencies.

Yet in two respects, the administration of George W. Bush is a continuation of earlier trends.[21] For one, it was a considered reaction to the prominence of executive departments in policy making that led the Bush Administration to move policy-making authority ever higher in the federal administrative hierarchy. Bush's centralization, then, followed upon the Reagan Administration's reaction to a received status quo in which executive agencies played a prominent role. Second, even as the Bush Administration has centralized policy making in the higher echelons of the federal bureaucracy, it has also begun to rely more heavily upon executive agencies for planning and executing federal government activity. Examples here include: the role of the new Center for Medicare and Medicaid Services (CMS) in administering the complex prescription-drug benefit from the Medicare reforms of 2002; the enhanced role of the Department of Transportation; the role of its Federal Aviation Administration (FAA) in coordinating airline schedules (particularly at the nation's most crowded and delayed airports, such as Chicago's O'Hare Field); and the role of the Environmental Protection Agency in proposing and administering new emissions-trading and other deregulatory programs, such as the Administration's Clear Skies Initiative.

The Constitutional Status of Bureaucratic Policy Innovation

At this point, readers might be interested in knowing something about the constitutional status of bureaucratic policy innovation. Is such activity unconstitutional? What bearing do the Constitution and the received body of administrative law in the United States have on this activity?

There is nothing constitutionally problematic with bureaucratic policy innovation in the American system of government. The idea of bureaucracies coming up with new ideas has a long tradition in American politics, most prominently in Article II of the Constitution, where executive officers may offer their opinion and judgment on legislation to the president. If we take the additional step of taking Alexander Hamilton's *Federalist* 72 literally, the notion that the federal bureaucracy would have an active planning role in national policy making goes back to the earliest days and ideas of the American Republic. In addition, there is no necessary or inherent constitutional threat embedded within the practice of bureaucratic policy innovation. The American system of separated powers with numerous veto points essentially protects citizens against arbitrary policy making by bureaucrats. For one, no amount of information, advocacy, persuasion, and documentation ever truly compels Congress or the president to follow the wishes of a federal agency. Bureaucratic plans and programs, when proposed, will have to exhibit a sufficient degree of popularity or political organization in order to become law. In other words, bureaucratic policy-making influence, when exercised, is earned. Moreover, the American system of government is replete with ex post facto checks upon bureaucracies, ranging from judicial review (the ability of federal courts to reverse or remand administrative decisions) to legislative veto (the ability of Congress to pass a law reversing administrative action) to Congress's control over agency funding (often called the "power of the purse").[22]

The Role and Distribution of Expertise

An increasingly prominent feature of national bureaucracies in the United States, as Patricia Ingraham points out in her chapter in this volume, is the professional and scientific composition of their workforce. Government positions are ever more characterized by personnel with highly specialized educations and extensive training and specific experience. This transformation is not unlike many sectors of the U.S. and global economies, but unlike the U.S. economy, the federal bureaucracy has seen little expansion of the "service sector" in the government labor system. This profession- and science-based transformation of American national bureaucracy has had several identifiable implications. First, it has led to increasing average pay scales. The average salary of federal government workers (though not the salaries of high-level federal executives) exceeds that of private sector workers by a fair margin. Observers of American bureaucracy often note facts such as these and decry the pay disparity between the public and private sectors, but unless education and training are accounted for, the wrong conclusion will be reached: the typical federal employee is more educated and more specifically trained than is the typical private sector employee. Indeed, when "human capital" is accounted for, federal government pay is less (and has been increasing more slowly) than pay for comparable positions in the private sector.[23] Second, this specificity and expert nature of federal employment creates a massive personnel problem in the federal government. The training that federal employees receive is very highly valued in private sector positions, whether the skills be those of nuclear engineering (personnel in the Navy and the Department of Energy), pharmacology and chemistry (chemists and physicians employed at the U.S. Food and Drug Administration), law (antitrust specialists in the Department of Justice, or pension lawyers in the Department of Labor's Pension Benefit Guaranty Corporation) or finance (employees of the Federal Reserve Bank or the Treasury Department). Specialized positions in the U.S. federal government are often characterized by high levels of turnover that disrupt the continuity of administrative operations and exacerbate the liabilities of organizational memory. The problem is not easy to solve: the positions created in public agencies target skills that are well remunerated in private and nonprofit positions.

There is a political element to these linkages as well, noticeable especially in hiring within the social sciences. Within the federal government bureaucracy a slow but steady shift in hiring practices has replaced sociologists and demographers with economists. Indeed, the demand for skills in economics is much greater in the public sector of government (and in the nonprofit world of academia and think tanks) than it is in the for-profit private sector. Along with the rise in economic analysis (particularly the cost-benefit analysis of new federal rules and existing policies) has come a sharp rise in the demand for statistical training. With the 1960s and 1970s, American government was newly infused with professional statisticians, who now command a presence in health sciences (biostatisticians) as well as in welfare and budget agencies. Where sociologists played important policy-making roles in the federal bureaucracy in the 1950s through the 1970s, their power has waned considerably since the early 1980s. The influence and number of lawyers and political scientists (international relations and security specialists, for example) in the federal government has plateaued. Beyond these "social-scientific" professionals, there have also been broad expansions of the scientific workforce in U.S. government, marked by an increasing flow of natural and physical scientists to government positions ranging from agricultural chemists (USDA) to geologists and engineers (Interior, Mines, Reclamation) to nuclear and high-energy physicists (Atomic Energy Commission and NASA) to chemists and toxicologists (EPA, USDA) to pharmacologists and molecular chemists (FDA).

Today the bureaucratic policy-making state is more constrained than it used to be, for three reasons. First, the fiscal constraints operating at all levels of government have combined to reduce discretionary spending and programs. The primary constraint upon discretionary bureaucracies comes not from deficits but from entitlement programs that take up an increasing share of federal spending. Put differently, the growth of entitlement government has limited the growth of administrative government. Second, bureaucracies are under increasing "competition" from think tanks and interest groups for the roles of specialization and information provision that they have enjoyed in the past century. Even expert bureaucracies rarely enjoy information monopolies in the contemporary political system. Finally, the waning of the traditional merit system in civil service has made federal bureaucracies much more top-heavy and answerable to the White House.

WHAT DO BUREAUCRATS VALUE? The emergence of greater administrative discretion, and of policy-making roles, among federal officials suggests something striking about what bureaucrats really value. Since a greater and greater fraction of federal employees work in professional positions, intangibles such as autonomy, reputation, esteem, and policy influence loom much larger in the bureaucratic calculus than do budgets and power. Most federal bureaucrats do not maximize budgets, and they do not uniformly attempt to expand their turf. Federal officials are instead "maximizers" of their reputation, their esteem, and their autonomy.[24] This reputation-maintenance dynamic prevails among military and intelligence officials, among Department of Justice attorneys, among National Institutes of Health (NIH) and FDA scientists, and among social workers.

War, Bureaucracy Building, and the Security-Domestic Spillover

Numerous agencies—military, diplomatic, and domestic—have been created and remade in the face of civil and international wars. War often makes new demands upon national governments, commonly met through the creation of new administrative organizations or the refinement of existing agencies. The War of 1812 compelled lasting alterations to the U.S. Navy, and Andrew Jackson's Indian Wars of the 1830s forced numerous and far-reaching changes upon the U.S. Army. The creation of Indian policy also led to the creation of numerous "Indian affairs" bureaucracies in the 1800s—ranging from the Office of Indian Education to the Bureau of Indian Affairs. The Civil War and the Reconstruction period (1861–1877) resulted in substantial changes to the Department of Justice and empowered federal officials in the Treasury Department and the Post Office. World War I roiled domestic markets for agricultural labor and threw farm commodity prices into a period of extreme variation, events that eventually enabled the U.S. Department of Agriculture to expand its regulatory powers over farm labor and enhance its forecasting and planning powers in preparation for the New Deal. World War II pressed new social and economic demands upon the federal government that transformed the Social Security Administration, the National Labor Relations Board, and the Navy. Most recently, the exigencies of the global fight against terrorism have resulted in the wholesale merger of previous intelligence agencies into the Department of Homeland Security and the creation of new discretionary agencies devoted to transportation security.[25]

If the past of American bureaucracy is any guide to its future, one relevant point may be that national security politics "spill over" into domestic politics. Repeatedly in the political history of the United States, seemingly "domestic" agencies have responded opportunistically to war and security threats to expand or refine their activities and their influence. Examples of such abound, particularly in the twentieth century.

- the USDA and agricultural production coordination in World War I and II;
- the development and regulation of nuclear weapons by the Department of Energy in the Cold War;
- the coordination of civilian defense and transportation security by the Federal Security Administration and later the Department of Transportation during the Cold War and in response to the terrorist attacks of September 11, 2001;
- the role of the Food and Drug Administration, USDA, and Environmental Protection Agency in planning and preparing for acts of bioterrorism.

In summary, wars and national security crises often provide an opening for bureaucratic agencies to expand and redefine their missions in creative ways. They also provide opportunities for politicians and interest groups to refashion agencies and give them new mandates. Exactly who controls these processes depends upon the agency in question, and upon history. The key point is that agencies have interests in intentionally blurring the line between domestic and foreign policy, and astute bureaucratic entrepreneurs are sometimes responsible for this blurring.

The point here is not that all major wars in American history have been uniformly associated with bureaucracy creation. Wars sometimes issue in new agencies (as in the Civil War or World War II) but at other times issue in few or none (World War I and the Korean War). Just as often, however, war creates opportunities for bureaucrats to refine, expand, and hone their missions and capacities.

The Life and Politics of Executive Agencies

Observers of U.S. bureaucracy often refer to two types of agencies—"executive agencies," whose top appointees can be dismissed without cause by the president, and independent commissions, whose appointees cannot be dismissed except "for cause" (dereliction of duty, criminal or civil negligence, and the like).[26] The history of American national government is, in the main, a story of executive agencies. While technically defined by the ability of the president to dismiss their top officials, these organizations depend upon the presidency for much more than appointee tenure. Executive agencies are often proposed and created by, almost always staffed by, and generally governed by executive and bureaucratic officials. Yet the title belies a deeper reality. For executive agencies are just as answerable to Congress and its committees as they are to the White House (see Barry Weingast in this volume).[27]

Historical and International Comparisons

One implication of the predominance of executive agencies in the United States is that our government resembles that of other nations more than we might think. In other nations (Japan since the Meiji period, Britain since 1780, France since the Third Republic), bureaucratic affairs are divided into large government "ministries" (Great Britain, Japan), or "departments" (France). Small, independent commissions are exceedingly rare in these nations, and when created they rarely live for long. In this respect, the organization of U.S. national government is on a par with other states.

In another respect, U.S. bureaucracies are quite different from those of other similar nations. In the United States, the dominance of executive agencies implies that the president rests at the official center of the national administrative system.[28] Top-level administrative officials are appointed by the president and, at least in theory, answer directly to him. In parliamentary systems such as Britain, India, Ireland, Israel, and Japan, the national departments and ministries are headed by "ministers" who are members of the prime minister's majority party. If such a system prevailed in the United States, the Speaker of the House of Representatives would occupy the role of president and would serve as the appointer of top-level Cabinet officials.

The Importance of Congress

Because of the separation of powers between the two elective branches of government, executive agencies are often as responsive to Congress as to the president. Congress controls the funding of agencies by means of appropriations, controls the formal authority of agencies by means of statutory enabling, and the Senate passes upon many high-level agency appointees. Officials in every agency of the federal government are deeply concerned about the potential congressional response to their decisions (or indecisions). In numerous annals of agency life, nothing provokes more anxiety among federal agency officials than the prospect of being grilled in oversight hearings by congressional committees (often in both chambers). And, of course, there is the power of statute. At least officially, agencies cannot take actions unless their authorities are stated or implied in the statutory enactments of the national legislature.

Extended presidential involvement in executive agencies is itself a recent historical fact. The twentieth century witnessed an increasing bureaucratization of the presidency, with the creation of the Bureau of the Budget in 1920, the Executive Office of the President (EOP) in 1939, the synthesis of the Office of Management and Budget (OMB) in 1970, and the creation of regulatory oversight capacity within OMB in 1981 and 1982.[29] Moreover, the staff attached to the president's top appointees (Cabinet officials and undersecretaries) has also grown. Much of the presidential bureaucracy, and many of the top layers of the executive departments themselves, have been created for the purpose of controlling other bureaucracies and bureaucrats. Some commentators (Professor Paul Light of the Brookings Institution and New York University) have argued that such multiplication of bureaucratic controls is actually counterproductive, since by creating more layers of bureaucracy Congress and the president remove the daily actions of federal bureaucrats ever further the people and from political accountability. In other criticisms, observers argue that by multiplying positions to control bureaucrats, politicians waste fiscal resources.

The Emergence of the Contracting State, and the Plateau of "Government as Business" Models

In the last decades of the twentieth century, a turn against government, and against "big, bureaucratic government" in particular, suffused the American political landscape. Among the products of this political turn were the elimination and privatization of numerous government services and capacities (regulation of commercial airline entry and pricing, government provision of legal services for the poor, government provision of public housing for low-income families). Along with this reduction in government capacity has come a general reduction in government offices and personnel. Many agencies have been downsized, including the Agriculture Department, the Department of Housing and Urban Development, and much of the nation's military. The nation's civilian federal workforce is now about 2 million persons, or less than 2 percent of the total working age population in the United States. But Professor Paul Light has shown that nine times as many people work for the federal government through the "shadow government" of contractors implementing federal programs.[30]

Perhaps the biggest structural change in American national government is the increasing reliance upon contractors for the provision of government service. Accompanying and reinforcing this "contracting out" revolution is the growing reliance of the national government upon state and local government to perform functions that were once centralized at the federal level. Contractor firms now conduct most government construction, much billing and auditing, and even provide security in domestic and overseas government activities. The administration of President George W. Bush has accelerated this trend, although recent figures suggest that it may be reaching a plateau of sorts.

Along with changes in government procedure have come changes in the metaphors we use to understand government bureaucracy. The past two decades have witnessed a resurgence of "government as business" metaphors that were in parlance in the Progressive Era and again in the 1950s. Beginning in 1993, Vice President Albert Gore Jr. launched a "Reinventing Government" campaign that emphasized government offices as entrepreneurial businesses and cast American citizens as "customers" of government bureaucracies. The Price Waterhouse Coopers firm (now owned by IBM) launched a "Foundation for the Business of Government," awarding grants to researchers and agencies for the furtherance of business-like reforms in government agencies, and bestowing awards and publicity upon particularly entrepreneurial government administrators.[31]

It seems likely that these "business" and "reinvention" models of administration have run their course and will be ever less helpful to the U.S. government. (I am not persuaded that they were of much help over the last twenty years, for that matter.) It seems incredibly problematic to apply these metaphors to crucial policy arenas such as homeland security, counterterrorism, environmental protection, or food and drug regulation. While there has been significant privatization and outsourcing of government work, these activities still do not appropriately define the U.S. citizen as a "customer" of government services. The "Contracting State" is real and will endure. "Government as business" will endure in rhetoric only.

Conclusion: Recombination and Reputation

It is impossible to divorce the evolution of American national bureaucracy from the evolution of politics and government authority more generally. Partisan politics, sectional politics, and racial politics have all figured centrally in the evolution of U.S. administration, often in predictable ways.[32]

There are at least three general historical lessons to be derived from a survey of American national bureaucracy. First, agencies are rarely created anew but are usually "recombined" from parts or wholes of existing administrative institutions. We see this in the launching of new bureaucracies under the American Republic and under the presidencies of George Washington and John Adams. We observe this in the continual creation of new agencies (large and small) through recombination. We see it even in the creation of the Department of Homeland Security in 2002.

The meaning of this continuity is that much of our current executive bureaucracy has been around for quite some time. Agencies draw upon laws, norms, and traditions that reach back into the nineteenth and twentieth centuries and, in some cases, to the very beginnings of the Republic. We also see that the "creation" of new agencies does not always add to the overall size of government.

Second, the historical study of government bureaucracy consistently reveals the importance of such intangibles as reputation, prestige, professional esteem, and historical legacy as motivating factors driving bureaucratic behavior. Attention to the history of administrative agencies—ranging from military agencies to large departments to small government bureaus—alerts us to dynamics of administrative behavior that differ materially from the standard views. Scholars studying bureaucracy have posited variously that bureaucrats try to enhance their budgets, their power, and their turf. Yet the history of American bureaucracy provides case after case in which these generalizations fail utterly. Agencies often resist new powers that seductively come with bigger budgets (the Federal Emergency Management Agency and the Social Security Administration are examples). Agencies often seek a *reduction* of responsibilities to their core missions in which they have demonstrated and observed competence. Agencies and their leaders are just as likely to take steps to build, protect, and enhance their reputations as they are to seek new authority, try to expand their pay and their budgets, and move up the ladder of hierarchy and power.

If nothing else, a historical perspective on American bureaucracy is useful for combating the hubris that observers of American government often have in thinking that a simple set of generalizations can explain behavior and operations across diverse agencies or over centuries of time. Too often, pundits and scholars will try to generalize about bureaucratic organizations, as if the USDA of today were equivalent to the Agriculture Department of the Progressive Era, as if the same principles and norms governing the behavior of the Federal Trade Commission also explain behavior at the Department of Housing and Urban Development, the Department of Defense, or the Environmental Protection Agency.

If we pay attention to the specific reputations and cultures of different bureaucratic organizations, we can engage in more accurate analysis of bureaucratic behavior while combining the general and specific. The pursuit and crafting of reputation—the reputation of individual officers, of their bureaus, or of their entire agency—is something that federal administrators engage in all the time. Yet because the reputation and culture of each agency are different, the way that one agency (a military intelligence bureau, say) shapes its identity is invariably different from the way that others do so (a social welfare agency, for example).

Finally, U.S. national bureaucracy is firmly rooted in the executive branch. This does not belie the forceful harnessing power of Congress, which controls executive agencies every bit as much as (sometimes more than) the presidency does. But various attempts to create more "legislative" forms of bureaucracy—in councils and committees, in independent commissions, and in government corporations—have been dwarfed by the continued growth of hierarchical and

TABLE 2
Executive Agencies Active in Policy Making and Innovation since the Civil War

Agency	Policy Innovations
Post Office Department	Railway mail transport (1862); parcel post; rural free delivery (1892); postal savings banks (1914)
Department of Agriculture	Food and drug regulation; national forest regulation; farm extension (county agent) system; price stabilization and production control (1920s–1930s); conservation easements (1960s–present)
Military (Departments of War, Navy, Army, and Defense)	Transformation of Navy procurement, including incentive-based contracts, "deprocurement policy" (1941–1945); discretionary scientific programs for communications and munitions development (DARPA)
U.S. Food and Drug Administration	Clinical trial regulations of 1963; advertising regulations of 1960s and 1970s; regulation of tobacco (attempted but unsuccessful); bar-coding of prescription drugs
Federal Emergency Management Agency (FEMA)	"All hazards" policy; "Flood Fighting" insurance program
Atomic Energy Commission, later Nuclear Regulatory Commission	Regulation of commercial nuclear energy production, plant construction and operation

largely centralized executive departments. The executive nature of the U.S. administrative state remains its most enduring and telling feature.

Notes

* I thank Steve Balla, Matthew Holden, Scott James, Richard Rose, Michael Ting, and Barry Weingast for insightful comments. Joel Aberbach, David Lewis, Sid Milkis, Mark Peterson, and James Pfiffner, and especially Martha Derthick, offered particularly detailed comments on earlier versions of this essay. I have also benefited from numerous conversations with Colin Moore. This essay was first drafted at the Center for the Advanced Study in the Behavioral Sciences. I thank CASBS, the Hewlett Foundation, the Annenberg Foundation, and the Faculty of Arts and Sciences at Harvard University for support. All interpretations and remaining errors are mine alone.

1. This does not mean that all such campaigns have been centralized. The Civil War, for instance, was fought through organized state militia that retained a good deal of independence until the early twentieth century.

2. Until the consolidation of the Pennsylvania railroad in the 1870s, as Richard John points out in *Spreading the News* (p. 6), the U.S. Post Office Department was the largest administrative organization of any kind (economic, religious, social, political) in the United States and among the largest unified state bureaucracies in modern history to date.

3. I am indebted to Professor Stephen Wayne of Georgetown University for pointing up the significance and history of executive boards and committees during the Continental Congress, and for referring me to especially relevant and accessible sources.

4. See Jay C. Guggenheimer, "The Development of the Executive Departments, 1775–1789," in J. Franklin Jameson, ed., *Essays in the Constitutional History of the United States in the Formative Periods 1775–1789* (Boston and New York: Houghton Mifflin, 1889); Jennings B. Sanders, *Evolution of the Executive Departments of the Continental Congress, 1774–1789* (Gloucester, Mass.: Peter Smith, 1971).

5. On England, see Sir Norman Chester, *The English Administrative System, 1780–1870* (Oxford: Clarendon Press, 1981), particularly Part I, which describes the administrative system as it existed in 1780.

6. I thank Colin Moore for suggesting several of these ideas to me. Too little is known, I think, on the early development of executive institutions in America, and some of the judgments expressed in this section must be couched in due humility. The set of dependencies upon English, continental European, colonial, and even native American arrangements in the construction of early U.S. institutions is an incredibly fertile and under-tilled field for future research.

7. For more on the struggles of this period, consult Gordon Wood, *The Creation of the American Republic, 1776–1787* (Chapel Hill: University of North Carolina Press, 1998).

8. See Hamilton, Madison and Jay, *The Federalist Papers*, ed. Clinton Rossiter (New York: Mentor Press, New American Library, Penguin Putnam, 1999), pp 403–404

9. This paragraph sketches briefly (and terribly inadequately) a pattern of activity that probably deserves several book-length studies of its own: the origins and evolution of administrative rules as a form and extension of the English common law. I thank Colin Moore for several extended discussions of this pattern.

10. For the Interior Department and the Whig-Democrat battles over its creation, see Michael Holt, *The Rise and Fall of the American Whig Party* (New York: Oxford University Press, 1999). For independent commissions, see Scott C. James's striking and nicely conveyed argument in *Presidents, Parties and the State: A Party System Perspective on Democratic Regulatory Choice, 1884–1936* (Cambridge and New York: Cambridge University Press, 2000). For an illuminating study of partisan and racial influences upon the administrative development of New Deal welfare programs, see Robert Lieberman, *Shifting the Color Line.*

11. See William Howell, *Power without Persuasion: A Theory of Unilateral Presidential Action* (Princeton, N.J.: Princeton University Press, 2003).

12. See White, *The Jacksonians.*
13. Delegation rarely goes to a new "agent," but often becomes a redelegation of authority to an "agent" whose properties and past behavior are more or less well known (see David Epstein and Sharyn O'Halloran, *Delegating Powers: A Transactions-Cost Approach to Policymaking under Separate Powers* (Cambridge and New York: Cambridge University Press, 1999); Carpenter, *The Forging of Bureaucratic Autonomy.*
14. See Lewis, "The Politics of Agency Termination" (2002).
15. See Martha Derthick, *Policymaking for Social Security* (Washington, D.C.: The Brookings Institution, 1979); and Daniel Carpenter, *The Forging of Bureaucratic Autonomy.*
16. I am indebted to Professor David Lewis of Princeton University for urging upon me the importance of these 1950s developments. His paper (book chapter) "Understanding the Federal Personnel System" was particularly valuable in helping me to grasp these developments. I am responsible for any and all errors and interpretations regarding this evidence and argument. See also U.S. General Accounting Office (GAO), *The Excepted Service: A Research Profile* (1997), quoted in Lewis, *Politicized Administration*, unpublished book chapter manuscript, Princeton University.
17. See Martha Derthick, *Policymaking for Social Security* (Washington, D.C.: The Brookings Institution, 1979); Jerry R. Cates, *Insuring Inequality: Administrative Leadership in Social Security, 1935–1954* (Ann Arbor: University of Michigan Press, 1984); and Sparrow, "Social Security's Missing Years," Chap. 2 of his *From the Outside In.*
18. See Bartholomew Sparrow's excellent chapter "The Transformation of Navy Procurement," pages 161–257 in his book *From the Outside In.*
19. See Alasdair Roberts, "Reputation and Federal Emergency Preparedness Agencies, 1948–2003," unpublished manuscript (May 2004), forthcoming, *Studies in American Political Development.*
20. See Roberts, "Reputation and Federal Emergency Preparedness Agencies, 1948–2003," passim. The Federal Aviation Administration also successfully resisted Bush Administration attempts in 2001–2002 to house its operations under the Department of Homeland Security and make it take on a greater anti-terrorism role. I acknowledge David Lewis for this point.
21. See Richard Nathan, *The Plot That Failed: Nixon and the Administrative Presidency* (New York: John Wiley & Sons, 1975); and Joel Aberbach and Bert Rockman, *In the Web of Politics: Three Decades of the U.S. Federal Executive* (Washington, D.C.: The Brookings Institution, 2000).
22. Even these tools of political control have their slippage and imperfections. The force and reach of the legislative veto has been curtailed in an important Supreme Court decision, *INS v. Chadha* [462 U.S. 919 (1983)]. Research also suggests that budget shifts take some time to achieve their desired outcomes; see Daniel P. Carpenter, "Adaptive Signal Processing, Hierarchy, and Budgetary Control in Federal Regulation," *American Political Science Review* 90, no. 2 (June 1996), 283–302.
23. See the memorandum of the Congressional Budget Office, "Comparing Federal Salaries with Those in the Private Sector," CBO Memorandum, June 1999

(Washington, D.C.: Congressional Budget Office. Available at http://www.cbo.gov /ftpdocs/5xx/doc599/fedsal.pdf (accessed March 13, 2005).

24. See Carpenter, *Forging of Bureaucratic Autonomy*; and Wilson, *Bureaucracy*.

25. See Robert V. Remini, *Andrew Jackson and His Indian Wars* (New York: Viking Penguin, 2001); Richard Franklin Bensel, *Yankee Leviathan: The Origins of Central State Authority, 1857–1877* (New York: Cambridge University Press, 1990).

26. This seemingly minute distinction in fact underlies modern administrative law.

27. The practice of senatorial courtesy, by which appointments of some federal officials with administrative jurisdiction in a given state are referred to the junior or senior Senator from that state, marks a very small exception to this rule.

28. See White, *The Federalists*, p. 18 and chap. 3.

29. On the EOP, see the chapter in this volume by Matthew Dickinson. Soon after the beginning of the first administration of President Ronald Reagan in 1981, Reagan issued a now famous Executive Order 12291, which required OMB review of all proposed rules drafted by agencies in the executive branch. The Reagan Administration also established an Office of Information and Regulatory Affairs (OIRA) within OMB, which exists at the writing of this essay.

30. Paul C. Light, *The True Size of Government* (Washington, D.C.: Brookings Institution Press, 1999).

31. See the chapter by Donald Kettl in this volume. On the prevalence of government as business metaphors in Progressive Era administrative discourse, see Carpenter, *The Forging of Bureaucratic Autonomy*.

32. For racial influences on U.S. bureaucracy, see the references to works by Desmond King, Daniel Kryder, and Robert Lieberman in the bibliography.

Bibliography

Aronson, Sidney H. *Status and Kinship in the Higher Civil Service: Standards of Selection in the Administrations of John Adams, Thomas Jefferson, and Andrew Jackson.* Cambridge, Mass.: Harvard University Press, 1964. A sociological analysis of appointment patterns in the early federal bureaucracy.

Balogh, Brian. *Chain Reaction: Expert Debate and Public Participation in American Commercial Nuclear Power, 1945–1975.* New York: Cambridge University Press, 1991. In-depth examination of the role of professions in the bureaucratic state.

Barrow, Thomas C. *Trade and Empire: The British Customs Service in Colonial America, 1660–1775.* Cambridge, Mass.: Harvard University Press, 1967. Insightful historical analysis of what was perhaps the most active and controversial colonial bureaucracy in British North America.

Baugh, Daniel. *British Naval Administration in the Age of Walpole.* Princeton, N.J.: Princeton University Press, 1965. Arguably the best overall study of administration in Great Britain. For a useful trove of background material, see Baugh, *Naval Administration, 1715–1750* (London: Spottiswoode Ballantine, 1977). For more general treatments of bureaucracy in early modern Europe, see Hans Rosenberg, *Bureaucracy, Aristocracy and Autocracy: The Prussian Experience, 1660–1815* (3rd ed., Boston, 1968); Geoffrey Holmes, *Augustan England: Professions, State and Society, 1680–1730* (London: George

Allen and Unwin, 1982); John Brewer and Eckhart Hellmuth, eds., *Rethinking Leviathan: The Eighteenth-Century State in Britain and Germany* (London: Oxford University Press, 1999); and Philip Harling, *The Modern British State: An Historical Introduction* (London: Polity, 2001).

Carpenter, Daniel P. *The Forging of Bureaucratic Autonomy: Reputations, Networks and Policy Innovation in Executive Agencies, 1862–1928.* Princeton, N.J.: Princeton University Press, 2001. An argument about how executive agencies construct and enhance their reputations and gain policy-making autonomy in the process. Also an intensive empirical study of three federal departments from the Civil War to the Great Depression that combines in-depth archival research with statistical analyses of bureaucratic behavior and personnel patterns.

Derthick, Martha. *The Social Security Administration in American Government.* Washington, D.C.: Brookings Institution Press, 1990. An excellent study of bureaucratic adaptation to new statutory requirements, showing the constraints of existing organizational culture and procedure.

Edling, Max M. *A Revolution in Favor of Government: Origins of the U.S. Constitution and the Making of the American State.* New York: Oxford University Press, 2003. Useful study for understanding how the Constitution empowered executive government as much as limited it.

John, Richard R. *Spreading the News: The American Postal System from Franklin to Morse.* Cambridge, Mass.: Harvard University Press, 1995. A fine and instructive study of bureaucratic government in early America.

Kettl, Donald F. *Leadership at the Fed.* New Haven: Yale University Press, 1988. Illustrative study of internal hierarchy at one of the nation's most powerful independent agencies.

King, Desmond. *Separate and Unequal: Black Americans and the U.S. Federal Government.* Oxford and New York: Clarendon Press, 1995. Along with Kryder, the best study to date on the central role of racial segregation in the growth of U.S. federal bureaucracy.

Kryder, Daniel. *Divided Arsenal: Race and the American State during World War II.* New York: Oxford University Press, 1999. Detailed historical analysis of racial politics in the U.S. bureaucracy (especially its military) during the Second World War.

Labaree, Leonard. *Royal Government in America: A Study of the British Colonial System before 1783.* New Haven: Yale University Press, 1930. Still the best overall treatment of colonial government in British North America.

Lewis, David E. *Presidents and the Politics of Agency Design: Political Insulation in the United States Government Bureaucracy, 1947–1997.* Stanford, Calif.: Stanford University Press, 2002. A fine study of federal agencies created since World War II that offers historical insights and fine statistical generalizations. For two other studies that debunk some of the myths about the frequency and manner in which administrative agencies are terminated in the United States, see Lewis, "The Politics of Agency Termination: Confronting the Myth of Agency Immortality," *Journal of Politics* 64, no. 1 (2002), 89–107; and Daniel P. Carpenter and David E. Lewis, "Political Learning from Rare Events: Poisson Inference, Fiscal Constraints and the Lifetime of Bureaus," *Political Analysis* 15, no. 3 (Summer 2004), 201–232.

Lieberman, Robert. *Shifting the Color Line: Race and the Origins of American Welfare Policy.* Cambridge, Mass.: Harvard University Press, 1997.

Light, Paul. *Thickening Government: Federal Hierarchy and the Diffusion of Accountability*. Washington, D.C.: Brookings Institution Press, 1995. An incisive and accessible study of recent trends toward the thickening of political appointments in the federal bureaucracy of the United States.

Light, Paul. *The True Size of Government*. Washington, D.C.: Brookings Institution Press, 1999. The best overall discussion of the rise and operation of the "contracting state" in American government.

Moe, Terry M. "Interests, Institutions and Positive Theory: The Politics of the NLRB." *Studies in American Political Development* 2 (1989), 236–299. Clear and accessible analysis of the role of politics and institutions in the shaping of U.S. labor-management relations.

Silberman, Bernard. *Cages of Reason: State Rationalization in the U.S., Great Britain, France and Japan*. Chicago: University of Chicago Press, 1992.

Skowronek, Stephen. *Building a New American State: The Expansion of National Administrative Capacities, 1877–1920*. New York: Cambridge University Press, 1982. The consummate study of the transformation and modernization of national bureaucracy in the United States.

Sparrow, Bartholomew. *From the Outside In: World War II and the American State*. Princeton, N.J.: Princeton University Press, 1996. A revealing analysis of how a resource-dependent national government responded to the exigencies of world war. The chapter on naval administration is particularly instructive.

White, Leonard. *The Federalists: A Study in Administrative History, 1789–1801; The Jeffersonians: A Study in Administrative History, 1801–1829; The Jacksonians: A Study in Administrative History, 1829–1861; The Republican Era: A Study in Administrative History, 1869–1901*. New York: Macmillan, 1948–1958. The classic four-volume series on the administrative history of the U.S. federal government from its founding until the dawn of the twentieth century. Better at describing high-level secretarial developments than in portraying day-to-day administrative operations, but invaluable as a general source.

Wilson, James Q. *Bureaucracy: What Government Agencies Do and Why They Do It*. New York: Basic Books, 1990. An accessible general review of political science research on government agencies; impressively synthetic.

3

GIVING DIRECTION TO GOVERNMENT
IN COMPARATIVE PERSPECTIVE

Richard Rose

IVING DIRECTION TO GOVERNMENT IS A COMMON problem in all political systems. Because the outputs of government result from the interaction between elected leaders and bureaucrats, "power is in the administration of everyday things."[1] If they are to give direction to government in fact as well as theory, leaders must influence the executive agencies for which they are nominally responsible. Failure to do so means that a leader reigns but does not rule.

Democratic heads of government differ in how they seek to give direction to government. Differences between presidents may be explained by contrasting historical epochs (the federal government that George W. Bush leads is not the same as that of Benjamin Harrison); events (the world was more peaceful in the presidency of Calvin Coolidge than that of Franklin D. Roosevelt); personalities (Dwight D. Eisenhower and John. F. Kennedy differed in generations and style); and differences between parties (the intentions of a Republican president may differ from those of a Democrat).

Greater differences are found in comparisons of democratic leaders across national boundaries; among the world's established democracies, the American presidential system is a deviant case. The great majority of democracies are parliamentary systems in which the direction of the executive branch is collective; it is vested in a Cabinet accountable to Parliament rather than in a popularly elected president. Even the most pro-American East European countries writing democratic constitutions after the fall of the Berlin Wall in 1989 did not adopt the American system; instead, they adopted parliamentary government.

This chapter compares the government of the United States with parliamentary systems in which both executive and legislative branches are directed by the prime minister and departmental ministers that collectively constitute the Cabinet. Since there are dozens of parliamentary democracies in the world, a lengthy book would be required to scrutinize all of them. For clarity in exposition, this chapter concentrates on comparing the American president's role in the executive branch with that of leaders in established parliamentary systems of Europe within the European Union.[2]

National constitutions create fundamental differences between the office of president and that of prime minister, the highest political post in a parliamentary system. The U.S. Constitution separates the legislative and executive branches. Even when the White House and Congress are in the hands of the same party, they are separately elected by different constituencies and can have different agendas. By contrast, legislative and executive authority are integrated in a parliamentary system, because ministers in charge of government departments hold office only as long as they maintain the confidence of Parliament. As long as this is the case, ministers can be confident of winning legislative endorsement for major initiatives. However, the president cannot count on congressional approval. If British Prime Minister Margaret Thatcher had been president of the United States, she would not have been able to turn her political principles into legislation with the thoroughness that was possible in Britain. Likewise, if Bill Clinton had been a British prime minister, he could have secured much more legislation from the British Parliament than he did from Congress.

Political achievements depend on resources as well as on institutions. In the nineteenth century, presidents and ministers had little need to give direction to government, for governments had few programs, few employees, and not much money. The twentieth-century growth in government created dozens of agencies within the executive branch that collectively administer many more programs than any president or minister could ever keep an eye on. Today, ministers of the social welfare states of Europe can claim a much bigger impact on their society domestically than the American president, since they are responsible for a much larger part of their country's gross domestic product than are federal agencies in Washington.

Internationally, influence depends on a country's resources. The global importance of the American presidency today is not due to its eighteenth-century Constitution but to its twenty-first-century wealth, military strength, and population size. Whereas a parliamentary government can be very influential domestically, if a country has a population one-tenth that of the United States, as is the case of most European countries, its international influence will be limited. Furthermore, in the conduct of international affairs, the president is much less dependent on Congress and on bureaucratic procedures; he can negotiate with foreigners through White House national security advisors and can order military action in his role as commander-in-chief.

The paradoxes of government are resolved differently in Europe and in Washington. The dominant European political traditions—Christian democracy and social democracy—are collectivist rather than individualist. Whereas an American president can denounce government as part of the country's problem, most Europeans believe in a "social state" that collectively provides a high level of benefits financed by a high level of taxes and delivered by a large number of employees of bureaucratic agencies. Moreover, parliamentary leaders today benefit from being at the top of systems of government in which traditions of hierarchical authority are strongly entrenched and in which many citizens are prepared to accept the sometimes ponderous rule-bound ways in which public officials act in exchange for the social benefits that they deliver.

Identifying differences between presidents and parliamentary leaders does not mean that one is superior to the other. Depending on the criteria for evaluation, each form of democratic government has both strengths and weaknesses. Understanding that other countries are not just like us has practical importance as well. For a president as intent as George W. Bush to promote "a single sustainable model for national success: freedom, democracy and free enterprise,"[3] an awareness of differences in democratic institutions is essential for the successful exercise of international leadership.

Integration versus Separation of Powers

All heads of government must be good at politics. However, the rules of politics in a parliamentary system are as different from American politics as soccer is from American football. While the American president has a unique political position within the executive branch, the separation of powers means that Congress can pressure officials in executive branch agencies too. By contrast, in a parliamentary system, the executive's control of a majority in Parliament means that bureaucrats are much freer from pressure by the legislature.

Constitutional differences in institutions reflect contrasting historical experiences. Since the days of absolute monarchs, centralized authority has been the ideal of Europe's rulers. The initial challenge to monarchical rule came from an aristocratic Parliament that did not wish to curb the executive's authority but to take control of it. The modern European state was created by giving royal powers to the king's ministers and by creating a bureaucracy that would implement the instructions of these ministers. The twentieth century saw the popular election of Parliament, Cabinet ministers require the confidence of Parliament. This confers democratic legitimacy on ministers who continue to wield extensive powers inherited from an earlier era. The chief check on the Cabinet's authority comes from party politics. A government can be forced from office if it loses the confidence of members of Parliament (MPs) in the party or coalition of parties that support a government. In federal systems, checks on the executive are not institutionalized in a second chamber of Parliament with powers comparable to those of the U. S. Senate.[4]

The authors of the U.S. Constitution institutionalized their distrust of centralized authority by creating a system of checks and balances in which actions of the executive branch are checked by a separately elected Congress and are subject to review by a Supreme Court, and in which the president can veto legislation approved by Congress. Twentieth-century presidents have sought to expand their legislative and rule-making powers, and the executive branch has grown greatly. However, the State of the Union address that the president delivers each year to Congress is a catalog of measures that the president would like Congress to enact. It is not a list of bills that the president can confidently expect to be enacted, as is the case with the program that a Cabinet presents to Parliament.

Parliamentary Systems Integrate Collective Power

Although formally separate, the Cabinet and Parliament are politically interdependent. The prime minister is normally the leader of the largest party in Parliament, and the ministers are the leading figures in the governing party. When a coalition of parties is required to secure a parliamentary majority, some prime ministers will also lead coalition partners (partners other than those in the prime minister's party). A parliamentary system creates collective government, because the Cabinet ministers who head executive branch departments stand or fall together in a parliamentary vote of confidence. The integration of executive and legislative authority means that once a decision is made at the top of government, colleagues must back it or risk losing their office.

Collective government is not consensus government. Divisions within the executive branch result in turf fights for jurisdiction over important programs. For example, ministers in charge of spending departments (departments carrying out programs such as health and defense) often disagree with the finance minister's attempts to limit spending. Personal ambitions create tensions within Cabinet, too, as ministers compete with each other for prominence and a chance to become the next prime minister. In a coalition government, there is competition for electoral support between ministers representing different parties. Up to a point, the division of government into conflicting and competing subgovernment networks (consisting of departmental officials, pressure group representatives, experts and others who have an interest in policies in specific areas) is paralleled in Washington. The difference is that in a parliamentary system there is also a collective authority strong enough to resolve differences between departments and subgovernments.

Party politics is the chief determinant of the prime minister's position. If a single party has a majority of seats in Parliament, the prime minister is strengthened by being the top person in both the executive branch and in the legislature. Britain is the best known example of single-party parliamentary government, since its first-past-the-post electoral system regularly produces a majority of seats for one party, even if the governing party wins less than half the popular vote, because three or more parties normally compete for each seat in Parliament. Thus, both Margaret Thatcher and Tony Blair achieved landslide majorities in Parliament with less than 44 percent of the popular vote. A prime minister who leads a majority party can call on the partisan interests and loyalty of MPs. This is not always easy to achieve, for a party big enough to win a parliamentary majority is often a coalition of competing interests, or even factions.

The great majority of parliaments are elected by proportional representation, which allocates seats according to each party's share of the popular vote, and none wins a majority of seats in parliament. A party with a substantial plurality can form a minority single-party government and remain in office as long as opposition parties are so divided that they cannot unite against it. For example, in Sweden the Social Democrats can maintain a minority government as long as the far-left party does not unite with right-wing parties to vote "no confidence." In Denmark it is easy to form a minority government, since a positive vote of confidence is not required to install a government, while a majority vote is required to dismiss it. A minority government can rely on a "jumping majority," logrolling support from different parties on different bills. In the extreme, the Danish Liberal Party once held office for two years with only 12 percent of the seats in Parliament.

Most prime ministers head a coalition government. The leader of the largest coalition partner usually takes the prime ministership, but the price of coalition is that other parties determine the allocation of other major offices in the executive branch. Once a coalition is formed, the priority of a prime minister is to hold it together. A coalition can break up during the life of a Parliament due to a conflict between coalition partners, and a new government can be formed under a new prime minister without a general election being held. While the President also tries to form coalitions to support specific policies, the breakup of such a coalition does not force the President to resign. Alternatively, the breakup of a coalition can trigger a general election. Once a new Parliament is elected, the process of coalition formation starts again. Some parties from the previous Cabinet can remain in office, while others will be left out. American parties are also coalitions, offering a tent that tries to be big enough to provide an electoral majority for their presidential candidate. Moreover, executive agencies and the White House often need to build coalitions to win votes in Congress. Loss of support in Congress or in public opinion polls does not, however, force an incumbent president to resign, as a prime minister must if his or her coalition collapses and results in a parliamentary vote of no confidence.

Coalition government can take several forms. If one party has close to a majority of seats, it can form a coalition in alliance with a minor party. This is the norm in Germany, whether the party with a big plurality is the Social Democratic Party or the Christian Democratic Union and the minor party is the Free Democrats or the Green Party. When no party has a large share of seats, coalitions are likely to have three or even four parties. This is usually the case in countries such as Italy, Belgium, and the Netherlands.

France is unique in Europe because it has a hybrid system, with a prime minister and Cabinet accountable to Parliament and an elected president. (In other European countries, the president is a head of state with little power, and some retain a king or queen as head of state.) The 1958 French Constitution, written at the direction of General Charles de Gaulle, gives the president responsibility for foreign policy and for acting in national emergencies, while Cabinet ministers are responsible for the administration of those everyday areas that account for the great bulk of French public expenditure. If the president's party controls Parliament, the president can name or dismiss the prime minister. However, when Opposition parties win control of Parliament, the president and prime minister live together in a system of government that the French call *cohabitation*; it is analogous to divided government in the United States, when the White House and one or both houses of Congress are in the hands of different parties.

The collective nature of authority in a parliamentary system makes it misleading to talk about prime ministerial government, because it ignores the collective reality on which his or her claim to authority rests. To describe the system as Cabinet government is accurate insofar as direction to government comes from the departmental ministers who collectively belong to the Cabinet. But it is misleading insofar as it underestimates the extent to which coalition government encourages parties and ministers to regard their department as their personal fiefdom. It is also misleading insofar as it implies that all members of a Cabinet are equal. The prime minister is first among equals, and in some instances, as Margaret Thatcher and Tony Blair have demonstrated, first without equal.

Separate Institutions Divide Power in Washington

The president is the only officeholder elected by the country as a whole (see Scott James and Lawrence Jacobs in this volume), whereas a prime minister has been chosen to represent a parliamentary party. Because the president enjoys a fixed four-year term of office, he is not vulnerable to losing office after a negative vote in Congress or a poor rating in the public opinion polls, as happens to prime ministers. President Clinton benefited from this, for the U.S. Constitution requires a two-thirds vote of the Senate to remove a president from office. Thus, the Senate vote to convict an impeached President Clinton was insufficient to remove him from office, whereas in a parliamentary system it would have been sufficient as an expression of no confidence to remove the entire administration from office.

The separation of powers creates multiple veto points that are obstacles to action even when the president and executive agencies are in agreement. Legislative proposals can be rejected by the House of Representatives or by the Senate. To secure enactment of a proposal, the White House must consult with members of Congress in the president's party, who can oppose the president if they deem it in their constituents' interests, an option not available to MPs. If short of support in his own party, the president must seek votes from members of Congress in the other party. Bargaining is far more particularized and personalized than the bargaining between disciplined coalition partners in a parliamentary system. Because congressional committees and subcommittees have much more power over legislation than do parliamentary committees in Europe, this adds to the total number of veto points.

In many ways, the president is a chief but not a chief executive. Whereas a corporate chief executive officer sits at the top of a hierarchical organization and can give orders that subordinates follow without challenge (they may be dismissed if they do not), a president's capacity to compel action is limited by the Constitution, by acts of Congress, and by the action or inaction of bureaucrats who are subject to pressures from Congress and interest groups as well as from the White House. Whereas a parliamentary system challenges the government's opponents to find ways to check its authority, the American separation of powers challenges the president to find ways to exercise authority. In the words of President Harry Truman, "I sit here all day trying to persuade people to do the things they ought to have sense enough to do without my persuading them. . . . That's all the powers of the President amount to."[5]

Core Executive versus Lonely Eminence

While the president and prime ministers face common problems, they approach them with different institutional resources and rise to the top through different sets of experience. The collective nature of parliamentary government means that the prime minister is a team captain; the team consists of politicians and civil servants experienced in the entire process of legislating, budgeting, and administering public policies. The team constitutes an informal and effective core executive that arrives at decisions that the entire Cabinet, and thus Parliament, endorse. When an issue is important to the maintenance of the government's support, the prime minister will be the central figure in the core executive. For some key issues, such as the resolution of disputes about the budget, the minister of finance is usually the central player, while on other issues the ball may be passed to a departmental minister of a coalition partner, for example, the minister of agriculture as representative of an agrarian party.

By contrast, the president has a lonely eminence; winning the office is a personal challenge, more akin to winning a golf championship than to managing a baseball team. A president usually enters the White House as a stranger to the federal executive, having previously been a state governor or member of Congress. A large majority of close advisors are chosen for personal loyalty and skills in campaigning; few have had the experience of working in executive branch agencies. While the president's eminence in the executive branch is undoubted, in the absence of an experienced team he is short on the resources needed to monitor or even understand the day-to-day workings of executive branch agencies.

Professionals in Government or Campaigning?

Campaigning for public office is about stating ambitious goals; governing is about realizing these intentions. To do this, a leader must do more than deliver "sound bite" statements that catch the attention of the media; he or she must also master the organizational politics, budgets, and legislation that constitute the stuff of government.

The leaders in a parliamentary system are no strangers to government. The first step in the career of an ambitious politician is to be elected to Parliament. In a proportional representation system, this requires gaining the endorsement of a party caucus for a place on the ballot that assures a seat in Parliament. To gain endorsement, an ambitious young politician must involve himself or herself in party activities. To retain a seat in Parliament, it is more important to keep the endorsement of the party caucus and the respect of fellow MPs than to court media attention.

Once in Parliament, an ambitious politician undergoes an apprenticeship in government, starting with observation of senior ministers explaining and defending policies. When his or her party is in office, an MP will first be appointed to a junior post in a ministry and then will strive for promotion to become a Cabinet minister. Having hands-on experience in heading a major executive-branch agency is far better preparation for being at the top of government than is the limbo of the vice presidency or heading a committee of Congress that can influence but not manage an executive agency. The average British prime minister has served a quarter century as a member of Parliament and up to a decade as a minister before assuming office. In Germany the route to the top is often broader, including a third of a century or more of activity within the party, membership in the federal parliament and Cabinet, and years of being the administrative head of a German *land*, which includes more involvement in national government than in the United States because of the greater integration between levels of government in German federalism. When a new prime minister enters office, he or she is no stranger to national government.

By contrast, a presidential hopeful spends more time campaigning than learning to govern, for the American system of nominating and electing politicians favors candidates who spend many months campaigning nationwide. Since 1976 four presidents—Jimmy Carter, Ronald Reagan, Bill Clinton, and George W. Bush—have used a governorship to launch a national political career. Being president was the first job of each in Washington. While the state executive office can be a good place to learn political skills, it is no place to learn about foreign policy, national defense, or how to deal effectively with a Congress that is far more capable of enunciating policies independently than is a state legislature. Even moving from the Capitol to the White House can be like moving into another world. After more than a decade of experience as a member of Congress, John F. Kennedy found that being president held surprises because "the problems are much more difficult than I had imagined them to be."[6]

On winning election, it is natural for the president to turn to the people he knows and trusts to advise him in the White House. Many are also strangers to Washington. Their qualification is not that they know the federal executive but that they know the president. Insofar as a president runs a perpetual campaign for public approval and reelection, having skilled campaigners at hand makes sense. But the presidency is also about governing, and the inexperience and zealousness of White House office staff can get the president in trouble. The downfall of Richard Nixon did not come about because he ordered a break-in at the Watergate offices, but because he approved a cover-up for campaign staff who had done so on their own initiative.

Distributing Appointments in the Executive Branch

The appointment of people to top jobs in government is a unique responsibility of a government leader, whether president or prime minister. Appointments are about both patronage and policy. A leader uses patronage to assure personal support for himself or herself, for example, giving a post to an individual who represents a particular electoral constituency, such as women, blacks, or trade unionists. In a coalition government, a prime minister will have some ministerial appointments dictated by coalition partners. Appointments also send signals about policy, such as naming a person with strong and well-known views to head an agency in a contentious field such as environmental policy or the regulation of business.

Giving direction to the mass of executive branch agencies requires a combination of political and administrative skills. If appointees lack political skills, they will soon land the government in trouble by offending core supporters and making well-publicized gaffes. If appointees lack administrative skills, their policy pronouncements will be ignored by senior civil servants whose actions are required to carry out their intentions. Ideally, one individual can combine both political and administrative skills, but achieving this balance requires the investment of substantial effort in both party politics and in directing large government organizations.

From a comparative perspective, the American presidency is striking because of the critical presence of staff who are personally close, such as the "California mafia" of Ronald Reagan or the FOBs (Friends of Bill) under President Clinton. The loyalty and skills they bring to the White House tend to reinforce the profile the president developed in campaigning for office; they do not compensate for his lack of experience in dealing with executive branch agencies. Although the president has ten to fifty times the number of nominal staff of a prime minister, numbers can be misleading. Only a handful of people interact directly with the president on a major policy issue.

As a prime minister has a much smaller staff, he or she has much more direct contact with those giving advice and is much less vulnerable to the potential problem of junior staff "going into business for themselves" and causing political controversy or scandal. Moreover, the majority of people who work for a prime minister are able civil servants, appointed on merit to posts in the Treasury or the Foreign Office. They can offer advice based on decades of experience in the intricacies of government administration and politics. A limited number of appointments will go to non–civil servants, for example, press relations. Britain's Tony Blair has been exceptional in emulating the American practice of bringing in outsiders as personal appointees in his Downing Street office. The result has mirrored what happens in Washington: inexperienced political appointees have embarrassed the government through press releases that "stretch" facts and leaks that undermine ministerial colleagues in ways that have bred distrust.

In a parliamentary system, Cabinet ministers are important because they head the departments that collectively constitute the executive branch of government. Ministers have substantial discretion, since the prime minister must practice "management by exception," ignoring routine detail and even more important issues in order to concentrate on what is important for his or her own political interests and to deal with tasks that the head of a national government cannot delegate, such as meetings with heads of foreign governments.

The pool from which ministers are chosen is full of people with substantial political and administrative experience. In the British system, for example, ministerial office is restricted to members of Parliament. Before appointment, a minister is already familiar with the cut and thrust of debate in the House of Commons and with handling the media. Since every department has three tiers of ministers, with only the top tier qualifying for Cabinet rank, MPs normally undergo a lengthy apprenticeship in junior posts, thus giving them practical experience in administration within one or more departments before heading a department. This apprenticeship system also weeds out MPs who lack the political or administrative skills to be a top minister. British civil servants advising ministers are not reshuffled when government changes hands, on the grounds that their appointment was nonpolitical. However, this description is misleading, for the great majority are adept at offering advice to ministers of either party. Given the involvement of high-ranking British civil servants in promoting policies, they are better described as bipartisan than nonpolitical.

In some continental European countries, the pool of talent is expanded because senior civil servants can be appointed as ministers. France is an outstanding example of this practice: elite civil servants from the ministry of finance and the foreign ministry have found themselves promoted to posts as minister in charge of that department. The majority of prime ministers and presidents in the Fifth French Republic have started their careers in elite posts in the civil service. For example, President Jacques Chirac started his professional life as a civil servant monitoring public expenditure, and then became a civil servant in the office of Prime Minister Georges Pompidou and a leading civil servant in the departments of employment and of finance, before being appointed a Cabinet minister. Chirac then became prime minister and was subsequently elected mayor of Paris and, in 1995, president of France.

A party large enough to win a majority of seats in Parliament is usually a coalition of disparate interests and of politicians with competing ambitions. For that reason, a prime minister will offer posts to his or her chief rivals as well as to personal supporters, in order to avoid a leadership coup within the governing party. In Britain, for example, Tony Blair gave Gordon Brown, his rival for party leadership, the post of Chancellor of the Exchequer, in which Brown controls decisions about public expenditure affecting every aspect of domestic government. An enemy outside the Cabinet is a threat to the security of the prime minister. In 1990 Margaret Thatcher lost her job—despite her apparent political strength—after she was challenged by a vote of confidence among Conservative MPs.

In a multiparty coalition government, the assignment of ministerial posts is about sharing the benefits of office among coalition partners. The leader of the second biggest party in the coalition will want the second most important job in government, for example, the post of foreign minister in Germany. A small party whose support is critical will bargain hard for a ministry relevant to its electoral constituency, such as labor if it is linked to trade unions, or education if it is a Catholic party concerned with public policy toward Catholic schools. Once in office, the minister in charge can act like a feudal baron, resisting direction from the prime minister by threatening to resign and break up the coalition on which the prime minister depends for office.

The president too looks for political support when he makes appointments and, because party ties are weaker than in Europe, personal loyalty is more important. The pool of people from whom the president can draw appointees is potentially very large, because jobs are not restricted to those who are members of the legislature, as is often the case in a parliamentary system. The doctrine of the separation of powers requires a member of Congress to resign if given an executive branch post. An executive branch job thus appeals more to an ex-Congressman defeated in a bid for reelection or a member approaching retirement than to a secure incumbent with an important committee post. Members of the Senior Executive Service, the people who have the most experience in running executive agencies, are classified as nonpartisan appointees and must resign from the civil service if they accept promotion as a presidential appointee. Moreover, their service under both Democratic and Republican administrations makes senior civil servants suspect, especially when control of the White House passes from one party to the other (see Patricia Ingraham in this volume).

Superficially, the fact that the president can appoint far more people than a prime minister appears to give him more influence in the executive branch. However, the need to fill thousands of appointments also creates major difficulties. First, it takes months for White House staff to search for suitable candidates and to secure their acceptance of an offer that can involve significant financial loss and merciless grilling from members of Congress as part of the confirmation process. Newcomers to federal government also receive extensive background checks that can reveal embarrassing details that disqualify them from office, such as the revelation that they have employed and failed to pay social security taxes for illegal immigrants. Therefore, hundreds of executive branch appointments are unfilled for months after a new president is inaugurated. Additionally, many presidential appointees are unknown to the president and may be strangers to the national capital as well. This predicament is very rare in a parliamentary system. A British prime minister can enter office on Friday and by Monday morning have distributed a full set of ministerial appointments to people whom he or she has known and observed in action for years as members of a "Shadow Cabinet" consisting of Opposition MPs whose assignment is to criticize a departmental minister and to be prepared to offer alternative policies should the Shadow Cabinet become the government.

The interdependence of politicians and senior civil servants causes friction when political appointees inexperienced in government administration voice demands that experienced civil servants deem either impossible to achieve or so ridden with administrative difficulties that they are not worth the initial applause they might gather. The long period in office of Democratic presidents led their Republican successors, starting with Richard Nixon, to suspect that objections made to their proposals were motivated by a liberal bias among civil servants. In response, the Nixon White House sought to add layers of political appointees at the top of federal agencies, for example, appointing program associate directors, when the Office of Management and Budget was established within the Executive Office of the President. This was done in the belief that it would increase the input of White House influence. However, increasing the number of layers of inexperienced appointees at the top of departments created barriers to the flow of information from career officials most familiar with the programs for which presidential appointees are nominally responsible.

There are fewer barriers to cooperation between ministers and civil servants in European countries. When the number of personal and partisan appointees are very few, ministers are forced to turn to experienced civil servants for information and advice. Since many countries allow civil servants recruited on merit to belong to a political party, a newly elected government can identify officials who share their party loyalty and can secure their appointment to leading posts in their ministry. This system operates in Sweden and Germany and is accepted by civil servants and elected politicians. In Italy and Austria, it involves a greater element of sharing out the spoils of office between coalition partners. In addition, a minister can also draw on support from a personal cabinet (in the French practice) consisting of outside experts, civil servants, and personally and party-loyal staff, whose tasks include exploring fresh ideas, monitoring departmental activities for potential political benefits and booby traps, and advancing the minister's political position within the party and the media.

Managing the Politics of the Executive Branch

On both sides of the Atlantic, the formal unity of the executive branch is misleading. The programs and interests of government departments have little in common; the head of an agency concerned with social security will have responsibilities very different from a politician dealing with education or with the environment. Where departments do have overlapping interests, they may conflict; for example, commerce and labor are oriented toward different interest groups, and while departments of defense and foreign affairs are both concerned with national security, they bring different perspectives and resources to their task. Furthermore, all departments compete with each other to capture whatever money is available to boost their budgets and for places in the government's annual legislative agenda.

Reaching agreement requires continued informal as well as formal discussion among responsible ministers. A half century ago, Cabinet ministers met together as often as twice a week to make decisions collectively. In Sweden, any ministers who are in Stockholm at midday traditionally meet for lunch every day to exchange news and views. The volume and complexity of government business has led to formal and informal specialization. No minister has the time, the knowledge, the interest, or the departmental responsibility to be involved in every issue facing government. Ministers normally want to be involved in those core executive meetings that deal with issues concerning their department, and pass on participation in those that do not.

Much government business is now decided in Cabinet committees that deal with discrete topics such as trade or health. Members include all ministers whose departments are affected by an issue; those unaffected will be glad to spend their time elsewhere dealing with issues that affect them and that they can influence. Equally consequential is the amount of time spent in informal negotiations, preparing the ground for committee discussions through specialized analysis of complex issues, agreeing to compromises to avoid the risks of an undesirable decision, and building alliances in anticipation of substantial disagreement in committee.

Because a prime minister only has time to become personally involved in a limited number of issues, the first decision he or she faces is whether or not to participate actively in deliberations about a specific issue. Issues that do not affect confidence in the prime minister are usually left alone. If a senior minister important in maintaining a coalition government is involved, then the prime minister must defer to that minister's position or risk disrupting the coalition. When the media headlines a crisis, contemporary prime ministers often like to be the center of attention, but doing so has an opportunity cost: there is less time to spend on the administration of everyday concerns.

A prime minister's unique role is to balance competing political pressures between ministers in order to maintain the unity of the governing party or coalition and to maintain electoral support at the next election. For example, if there is a dispute between a spending minister (who runs an operating department) and the minister controlling the budget, the prime minister's job is to adjudicate not in terms of economic efficiency but rather in terms of political effectiveness. Likewise, when confronted with demands from the European Commission in Brussels, the prime minister's job is to balance pressures from abroad with domestic political pressures. When resolving conflicting claims of ministers, the prime minister can exercise substantial influence on what emerges as the collective decision of government for, once he or she delineates government policy, a minister who wants to challenge that judgment risks being dismissed from office.

In both presidential and parliamentary systems, government policy is often the outcome of bargaining. However, the systems differ in the ways in which bargains are struck. In a parliamentary system, bargaining occurs within a collective executive that can deliver legislative endorsement once a compromise is achieved. By contrast, in Washington a president cannot stand by and wait for department heads to bring their differences to the Oval Office for resolution, because executive agencies are also under pressure from committees of Congress, which control their appropriations and authorizations. Members of Congress can begin applying pressure on a presidential nominee when he or she first seeks confirmation in office from Congress. The president has the option of appointing a task force, with guidelines that set out presidential preferences and a membership favorable to his point of view, or he can ask personal staff to "knock heads" so that presidential appointees will reach agreement on terms the White House favors or risk being fired. When the president does take a public initiative, this is often the start of a behind-the-scenes bargaining process that involves a three-way tug of war between the White House, executive branch agencies, and Congress.

Presidents frustrated by the delays and compromises involved in bargaining with Congress have invoked a repertoire of tools to achieve their goals unilaterally. The means of doing so include national security directives, executive agreements with foreign governments, proclamations, and executive orders. The first two instruments have been invoked for more than a century by presidents confronted with war or the threat of war. Executive orders are used to influence the executive branch, for example, authorizing reorganization measures reflecting a president's priorities. Proclamations have been issued by presidents to respond to unexpected economic events such as the devaluation of the dollar and rises in the price of oil. Controversial unilateral actions can be challenged in Congress and in the courts. In a parliamentary system, such challenges are less likely because laws often delegate substantial discretion to Cabinet ministers, and in an emergency a government may secure parliamentary approval in a single day's vote or even by retrospective legislation.

Resources and Reach of Domestic Policy

While institutions reflect how government is organized, they do not determine what government does. To understand what a president or Cabinet ministers may influence, we must look at the reach of government, that is, the range and size of its policies that are the result of an accumulation of taxing and spending measures adopted over generations by many predecessors.

Contrasting Taxing and Spending Commitments

Established democracies today have unprecedented levels of national wealth, whether judged by their historic past or by comparison with the average developing government struggling to modernize its economy. Whatever the pressure of budget deficits, presidents and European prime ministers cannot claim that their countries are poor.

What citizens expect of their government differs greatly on opposite sides of the Atlantic. While Europeans do not expect their prime minister to decide the fate of the free world, they do expect their national government to provide generous social programs for health, education, social security, and employment. Americans have different expectations: there is a greater readiness to turn to the market or to not-for-profit organizations for health, education, and pensions and a preference for local and state governments to deliver or finance public services. Differences in expectations lead to big differences in the domestic financial resources of the executive branch president compared to a Cabinet in Europe.

While the trillions of dollars that governments at all levels in the United States collect in taxes each year is big money by any standards, it is only a limited proportion of a national economy with an annual gross domestic product of some 12 trillion dollars a year. In fact, Americans pay relatively low taxes: total tax effort is half that of Sweden and almost one-third less than in the average European Union (EU) country (see Table 1). Because of the federal system of government, the proportion of tax revenue that goes to Washington is even more limited. For every three dollars that Americans pay in taxes, only two dollars go to the federal government; the remainder is divided between state and local governments. By contrast, for every 20 pounds that a Briton pays in taxes, 19 go into the pocket of central government, and for every eight euros that the average EU citizen pays in taxes, seven go to central government. Since the total tax take in the United States is much lower than in Europe, the average parliamentary government collects almost twice the share of its national product in taxes than does the American federal government.

European governments collect high taxes in order to fund directly major domestic social programs. In nearly every advanced industrial society, social security claims the largest portion of government expenditures; American public-sector spending on social security as a proportion of the national product is a third less than spending by Germany, France, or Sweden. The financing of health care further illustrates cross-continental differences. While American spending on health care in total is higher than that of any European country per capita and as a percent of the national product, the federal government provides less than one-third that total in explicit outlays, to which state and local governments add an additional budgeted component. Most health care expenditures in the United States are nominally financed through private insurance, largely acquired through employer-sponsored plans, but a significant share is subsidized by tax provisions

TABLE 1

Tax Effort of Governments Compared

	Total revenue % GDP	% collected by:	
		central gov't.	state, local
Sweden	51	68	32
France	45	90	10
European Union (average)	41	88	12
Germany	37	71	29
Britain	37	96	4
United States	29	66	34

SOURCES: *Revenue Statistics of OECD Member Countries, 1965–2003* (Paris: OECD, 2004), 24; *OECD in Figures 2004* (Paris: OECD, 2004), 38f.

that permit employers to deduct their health care costs as a business expense and that do not count the value of coverage as taxable income for employees. Direct federal spending on health care is thus one-third less than direct central government spending on health in the average European Union country, and the "private welfare state" of health and pension benefits promoted by reductions in tax payments is less redistributive and less accountable to government than in other countries.[7] The limits on presidential power are also demonstrated by the failure of presidents from Harry Truman to Bill Clinton to get Congress to adopt their proposals to provide health care coverage for all American citizens.

Education is the one social program that Americans fund at a higher level than the average of EU countries. However, 90 percent of spending on education comes from state and local government funds and from private sources. The federal government's spending on all levels of education, including research and programs such as "No Child Left Behind," is less than one percent of the national product, one-tenth the proportion spent on education by the French central government. Moreover, the role of the federal courts in promoting school desegregation has given the courts a more pervasive influence on education than the White House.

To describe taxing and spending programs as reflecting the decisions of the president or Cabinet ministers of the day is a mistake; they are a legacy of decisions taken by governments in the distant past. For example, social programs administered under President Bush and Prime Minister Blair were initiated before they were born. In both Europe and the United States, the bulk of central government expenditure is officially described as uncontrollable, because benefits must be financed for all citizens legally entitled to claim them; for example, people who have paid social security taxes can automatically claim a pension for the rest of their lives when they reach retirement age. When there are more older people in society, spending automatically goes up on social security; an aging population pushes up health care costs as well. Uncontrollable expenditure, including defense spending and interest on the national debt, accounts for at least four-fifths of federal expenditure.

The European governments that are most effective in raising taxes and spending money are the parliamentary regimes in Sweden, Denmark, and Norway. The governments of these unitary states collect more than half the national product in taxation and spend most of that money on social programs. They are not headed by personally dominant individuals, but by prime ministers whose first aim is maintaining the parliamentary support that keeps their party in office in a minority or coalition government.

Institutions for Influencing the Economy

Politicians everywhere share the desire to take credit for economic success and to avoid blame when the economy is in recession. However, the American president has fewer institutional as well as financial resources at hand to give direction to the economy than does a Cabinet government in Europe. Institutional weakness compounds the limited financial clout, with Washington taking a much smaller share of the national product than do governments in Europe.

While all governors face the problem of balancing taxing and spending commitments, the budget-making authority of the president is far weaker than of a Cabinet government. Within the Cabinet, the most important office after that of prime minister is usually the ministry of finance, responsible for taxing, spending, and the management of the economy. Disputes between that ministry and spending ministers are settled by a collective Cabinet decision that both winners and losers must accept or resign from government. The budget is usually endorsed by Parliament with little or no amendment. In the extreme case of France, the budget may even be imposed by executive decree. The Federal Republic of Germany is exceptional in that its financial programs are also subject to votes in the upper chamber of Parliament, where German provinces can be an obstacle when their economic interests are threatened by the fiscal proposals of the central government.

By contrast, the spending agreements that the Office of Management and Budget (OMB) negotiates with executive branch agencies on behalf of the president are not binding. They constitute recommendations that the president sends to Congress as his annual budget proposals. Members of Congress who disagree with the president's budget can describe it as "dead on arrival" at the Capitol and work away in committees to rewrite it with a freedom that members of Parliament lack.

A Cabinet has the collective authority to manage the economy because it can coordinate the spending, taxing, and regulatory activities of different agencies in a parliamentary system. Although the federal government can collectively influence the American economy, the president lacks the centralized authority to manage the economy. Within the Executive Office of the President, the chair and members of the Council of Economic Advisers are expected to drum up support for economic proposals emanating from the Oval Office, even those that most economists predict, on grounds of academic theory, will have harmful consequences to the nation's economic condition. The council is staffed by up to two dozen academic economists who serve only a short time. It provides briefs that can be used to promote policies within the executive branch and more widely. The Treasury Department is the lead executive branch agency on tax matters and international economic policy, which is also the concern of the Office of the U.S. Trade Representative, the State Department, and the Department of Commerce. Interest rates and monetary policy are independently set by the Federal Reserve Board, whose members are appointed by the president and confirmed by the Senate for fourteen-year terms. Board members are subject to pressures from Wall Street and Congress as well as from the White House. So numerous and diverse are the federal agencies concerned with the economy that there is now a National Economic Council with a small staff charged with the political task of trying to promote and coordinate support for economic measures of concern to the president.

Spending Less and Buying Better?

A legacy of social spending commitments and political resistance to tax increases has pushed governments on both sides of the Atlantic to try to reform public policies to work better and cost less. The promotion of businesslike ideas of management efficiency began in the 1970s under Presidents Nixon and Carter in Washington, and received a major impetus in Europe under Conservative prime ministers Edward Heath and Margaret Thatcher. It is still going on, and George W. Bush, as the first president with a master's degree in business administration, is giving it his backing.

A variety of measures promising to save money and make government work better are now promoted under the slogan of "New Public Management" (see Donald Kettl in this volume). The New Public Management emphasis on market values treats citizens as consumers; it also implies that users of public services should be able to vote with their pocketbooks by having a choice between competing suppliers and by paying directly for what they want, rather than financing services through taxation. This ethos is opposed to social democratic and Christian democratic values that see the state's role as providing major services to all its citizens in the name of equality and solidarity.

In Europe the most widely accepted New Public Management reform has been the reduction of the reach of government by the privatization of state-owned enterprises such as telephone monopolies, airlines, steel companies, shipbuilders, energy producers, railways, and airports. Selling public enterprises has been doubly attractive to finance ministers because it delivers short-term capital gains that are used to reduce budget deficits, and it reduces the long-term burden of state subsidies to poorly managed loss-making enterprises. To make a profit, private sector owners have cut employment more than politicians were willing to do and have increased revenue by being more entrepreneurial and cost-conscious than public sector managers. In Britain, where privatization has gone furthest, the government has also adopted American-style regulatory agencies to protect the public interest in such matters as the health and safety of products and the avoidance of exploitation through monopoly price increases.

On both sides of the Atlantic, governments have adopted in part the New Public Management recommendation that ministries should devote more money to buying services through a process of competitive bidding rather than delivering services through their own public employees. When the services are routine, such as the supply of meals in government offices or the provision of a pool of cars for official use, contracting with the private sector through competitive bidding procedures is politically noncontroversial. Contracting out public services is attractive to politicians insofar as it immediately reduces the "body count" of public employees, for the employees of suppliers are not civil servants with lifetime jobs and civil service pensions. For the same reason, it is unattractive to many career civil servants.

Since most public agencies do not operate by selling services to citizens, efforts to apply abstract business school principles to government have run into similar technical obstacles in Europe and the United States. It is often difficult to arrive at an agreement about the specific services that a contractor is meant to deliver. For example, the term "well-educated children" can be interpreted and measured in many different ways. To reduce this goal to a target number of children passing examinations on a few subjects can be counterproductive insofar as it encourages cramming for examination results or "grade creep" in the evaluation of pupil achievement. It is also technically difficult to determine the extent to which the poor performance of pupils is the fault of poor teachers, lazy or misbehaved pupils, lack of parental encouragement, or social and economic deprivation in the neighborhood of a school.

The greater reach and scale of European governments makes ministers more vulnerable to blame when things go wrong with services that have been privatized or contracted out, for ministers remain politically accountable for the consequences of adopting new management methods. If prisoners escape from the custody of a private contractor, the minister responsible is asked to explain why this has happened. Admitting that a contracted agency has defaulted on a contract is politically embarrassing. If a school fails to meet its target for examination successes, its supervisors in a ministry of education cannot stop providing free education to its pupils. It is faced with the option of trying to run the school itself or transferring its pupils elsewhere. When a private sector railroad agency is held responsible for a series of fatal rail accidents, as has happened in Britain, the government has decided that returning the enterprise to public control is better than continuing to receive political blame for public interest services that it does not control.

Changing the Arena Changes Executive Leadership

All national leaders work at the intersection of three worlds. Immediately, they are caught up in the world of insider politics, where everyone focuses on whose political star is rising and whose is falling. Beyond the Beltway and the Old World settings of Parliaments in Europe is the everyday world in which citizens live and receive public services. Finally, there is the world beyond the nation's borders, in which more than 180 different national governments each has a national leader seeking to advance his or her national interests in an era of increasing international interdependence.

While every national government claims sovereignty, their leaders do not have the same amount of international influence. In international affairs, size matters. The institutions of American government are not what makes the occupant of the White House so important in foreign affairs; it is the material power at his disposal (see Figure 1). Even before the war in Iraq, the United States spent 3.3 percent of its national product on defense, more than double the effort of Germany and two-thirds more than the average country in the European Union. That difference has risen since. Even more important, the absolute size of the American economy makes American defense spending nine times greater than that of any single country in Europe (Figure 1). The American military response to the attacks of September 11, 2001, has boosted defense spending. The president's 2006 budget requested $419 billion for defense expenditure plus money to finance military operations in Iraq and Afghanistan. Thus, earlier comparisons in this chapter between aggregate public expenditure under central government control in a European state and spending by the executive branch actually understate the difference. Defense expenditure is a much more significant part of the federal government's expenditure, whereas social expenditure is much more important in European parliamentary systems.

Since the end of World War II, many American presidents have ordered troops into action on other continents. President Truman sent troops to the defense of the Republic of Korea in 1950; John F. Kennedy twice engaged in high-stakes military activities in Cuba and started the commitment of American

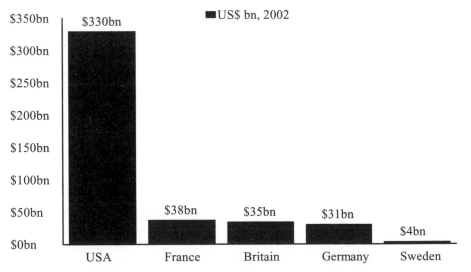

SOURCE: International Institute for Strategic Studies, *The Military Balance 2003–2004*. Oxford: Oxford University Press, 2003, 335f.

Figure 1   Public Expenditure on Defense Compared

forces in Vietnam. Lyndon Johnson and Richard Nixon maintained a Vietnam commitment that was costly in human lives. Jimmy Carter sought peace between Israel and Egypt, while his last year in office was blighted by frustrated attempts to gain the release of American hostages in Iran. Ronald Reagan launched a "Star Wars" initiative to put pressure on the Soviet Union, and committed troops in places as far apart as Lebanon and Grenada. George H. W. Bush led a coalition of forces that in 1991 liberated Kuwait after it was invaded by Iraq. Bill Clinton took military action in Somalia and Kosovo and launched missiles against Sudan. George W. Bush has committed troops to action in Afghanistan and Iraq.

Within the executive branch there is a de facto separation between the agencies chiefly responsible for international affairs—the Department of Defense, the State Department, and the Central Intelligence Agency—and domestic agencies. As commander in chief of the armed forces, the president can pull rank on generals in order to impose a decision. The Central Intelligence Agency briefs the president about America's enemies abroad, and the FBI provides files about enemies at home. The National Security Council staff gives the president enough personnel to deal with his diplomatic priorities and, as Henry Kissinger demonstrated, the chief national security advisor can act without consulting executive branch agencies. When "group think" emerges in Washington about issues of war and peace, the president's authority is central in deciding *what* the group thinks.

In foreign policy the constraints on the president are far fewer than in domestic affairs. The president can invoke war powers or implied powers to act unilaterally, leaving Congress to give last-minute or after-the-fact endorsement to what the president commands. While the legal definition of the president's war powers have been a subject of controversy since the time of Abraham Lincoln, presidents have wielded these powers with few effective restrictions from Congress or the courts. John F. Kennedy justified the assumption of exceptional powers in international affairs in words that George W. Bush would endorse: "There's a big difference between a bill being defeated and the country being wiped out."[8]

In recognition of differences between the president's authority at home and abroad, historian Aaron Wildavsky propounded a theory of the "two presidencies." In 1966 he stressed that the president's freedom of action abroad was enhanced both by the war powers of the office and by a political consensus about the national interest in international affairs. Following the Vietnam War, Wildavsky revised his theory to take into account congressional opposition to presidential initiatives abroad. The result has been a situation in which there are "two foreign policies competing for one presidency."[9] Yet disagreement at home is not sufficient to stop the president from acting unilaterally abroad.

As the chief executive, the president must deal with leaders of other governments about matters of war and peace, but the leaders of NATO (North Atlantic Treaty Organization) allies are in a fundamentally different position. A "two premierships" theory fits European countries today, because a prime minister can exercise much more influence at home than abroad. In domestic affairs, Cabinet ministers control a substantial share of the material resources of their country, whatever the size of its population, and the prime minister can balance disagreements between ministers.

In the international arena, however, the national resources of parliamentary democracies are limited. Germany, the largest democratic government in Europe, has less than one-third the population of the United States; thus, even if Germany spent the same share of its national product on defense as does the United States, the total amount would be scarcely one-tenth of what America spends. The population of the median European country is about 8 million people; if Sweden spent the same proportion on defense as the United States, it would be barely 2 percent of American defense expenditure (see Figure 1).

For the government of an average European country, the term "national" security is a misnomer. National governments rely for their security on international alliances and international institutions. This is true whether security is advanced by committing troops to a joint NATO action or by attendance at meetings of the United Nations. In either context, a prime minister's participation is more often that of a spectator than a decision maker.

As the head of government, every prime minister receives a steady flow of diplomatic, military, and intelligence briefings, but the information is rarely the basis for action. The Iraq War illustrates the limitations on European prime ministers on a global stage. Chancellor Gerhard Schröder of Germany and President Jacques Chirac of France opposed the war—but to no avail. By contrast, Prime Minister Tony Blair allied Britain with President George W. Bush in the belief that Britain would gain substantial influence in Washington. But while Blair's voice has been welcome when he endorses the dominant position in Washington, Britain has been unable to influence policies there or events on the ground in Iraq.

It is unusual for the prime minister of an average European country to have an impact in the world of international affairs. The chief military engagements fought on European soil since 1945 have demonstrated the weakness of parliamentary governments, for example, the thirty-year effort of the British government to end conflict with armed political groups in Northern Ireland. The development of transnational terrorist groups has increased national security concerns. However, countries such as France, Germany, and Spain have defined security problems as requiring domestic responses in the absence of the force that the United States has used to project its power in the Middle East.

The dollar's international importance as a reserve currency for the central banks of other countries gives the White House unique opportunities to exert economic influence abroad. When federal deficits have needed funding, Washington has literally passed the buck to the central banks in other countries, especially in Tokyo and Beijing. They have loaned money to the United States Treasury in order to prevent their national currencies from rising so much in value that Chinese and Japanese exports to the United States would be reduced. The White House also puts pressure on the International Monetary Fund and the World Bank to provide favored foreign governments with funds that the president cannot get Congress to appropriate, for example, making large and wasteful cash payments to help prop up the Russian government of Boris Yeltsin.

The European Union gives national prime ministers an opportunity to represent their country in discussions of economic and social policies of continental concern. However, the institutions of the European Union add a supranational layer to create a multilevel system of governance throughout the continent. In the councils of the EU, a prime minister cannot claim, as at home, to be first among equals. Instead, he or she is one among a crowd of national leaders, each promoting their own national priorities. The domestic advantage that a prime minister may gain by representing the national interest in the councils of the European Union is offset by the difficulties of advancing one's own national interest in competition with the interests of twenty-four other countries. Since no national government can dominate EU policy making, prime ministers must rely on bargains and compromises to get what they want.

Even though a parliamentary government is responsible for managing the economy to their national electorate, the country's economic conditions are no longer determined nationally. The Single Europe Market Treaty makes the European Union a free trade area. The treaty is used to expand the power of the European Union to regulate many aspects of national economies, as presidents have used the commerce clause of the Constitution to justify regulating activities said to affect the stream of commerce between the fifty states. In addition, twelve countries of the EU have abandoned their national currency in favor of the euro; their interest rates and monetary policy are no longer set in their national capital but in the headquarters of the European Central Bank in Frankfurt am Main.

Conclusion: Path Dependence and the Road Ahead

Constitutional differences between presidents and prime ministers are textbook examples of path dependence, the tendency of political institutions and policies, once adopted, to persist indefinitely. This is obviously the case for the American presidency, established more than two centuries ago, and even more so for the British Parliament, established in early medieval times. Because the constitutional framework limits changes in a system of government, it would take an extraordinary political upheaval to introduce a parliamentary system of government in the United States or to install a popularly elected president in place of Britain's prime minister. Yet the world moves on, and every national system of government must adapt to alterations in the international political environment or face the consequences of failing to adapt.

The transformation of the international system since the end of the cold war has greatly altered transatlantic relationships between the American president and the prime ministers of Europe. As long as the Soviet Union was seen as the chief threat to peace, European prime ministers compensated for limited military power by supporting NATO, and the military primacy of the United States in NATO justified describing the president as "leader of the free world." The disappearance of the Soviet Union has greatly reduced the importance that European prime ministers now give to military security and reliance on America's military strength. At the same time, the growing importance to the United States of countries such as Japan, China, and oil-rich Middle Eastern countries has reduced Europe from being the center of international affairs to being one among many centers.

The traditional division between domestic and international policies is concurrently being blurred by the growth of "intermestic" policies involving the interaction of domestic and international concerns, a trend recognized by European governments. In Europe, to cope with the growing influence of international activities on national economies, governments have given substantial economic powers to the European Union. In areas ranging from agricultural subsidies to regulations affecting trade, health, and safety at work, Cabinet ministers go to EU meetings to advance their national interests within a multinational framework of institutions.

The national security strategy promulgated by President George W. Bush explicitly recognizes the importance of intermestic policy: "Today, the distinction between domestic and foreign affairs is diminishing. In a globalized world, events beyond America's borders have a greater impact inside them."[10] The daily flow of information into the White House about international economic and security matters is of very high presidential concern.

The American economy is visibly becoming more intermestic, as American purchase of foreign goods is increasing foreign purchases of American goods, producing an annual trade deficit of up to half a trillion dollars. While the Office of U.S. Trade Representative gives the president more freedom to negotiate trade and tariff agreements with foreign countries, it also confronts him with a fact that European prime ministers have long recognized: one country cannot dictate trade measures to the rest of the world. Moreover, American membership in the World Trade Organization places constraints on the president's room for maneuver. The Bush administration's ability to win tax cuts from Congress without putting the brakes on federal spending has led to the biggest federal deficit in more than a decade. The ability of the Federal Reserve Board to finance the deficit without causing inflation depends on the readiness of foreign central banks to loan it money.

The al Qaeda terrorist attacks on New York City and Washington on September 11, 2001, have created a new form of intermestic politics, in which international security and America's homeland security are joined. President George W. Bush has replaced the cold war doctrine of deterrence with a strategy of preemptive military action, using America's great military power unconstrained by international organizations or alliances. In the words of an advisor to President Bush, "We're an empire now, and when we act, we create our own reality."[11]

The president can only be an international leader if other nations follow. This was the case in the United Nations–endorsed military action that liberated Kuwait from Iraqi invaders and in the military strike against Afghanistan because it offered a safe haven to al Qaeda leaders. However, President Bush's decision to declare war on the Iraqi regime of Saddam Hussein was not so supported. While American military power swiftly led to the collapse of Saddam's regime, subsequent events have shown that the success of American foreign policy depends not only on White House actions but also on what foreigners do. At the start of the twenty-first century, the American presidency confronts a challenge familiar to European prime ministers: governing in a world of intermestic policies and international interdependence.

Notes

*In addition to drawing on a number of my previous publications, this article benefited from very useful comments by Joel Aberbach and Jeffrey A. Weinberg.

1. Max Weber, *Wirtschaft und Gesellschaft*, 5th ed. (Tübingen, Germany: J. C. B. Mohr, 1972), 29.
2. For useful studies of Japan, see the book by Hayao cited in the bibliography; for Canada, see the book by Savoie; and for comparisons of Canada, Australia, and Britain, see the article by Weller.
3. *National Security Strategy Document* (September 17, 2002), accessed at www.whitehouse.gov/nsc/nssintro.html, December 27, 2004.
4. The Federal Republic of Germany is in part an exception. In reaction against the unconstrained power of Adolf Hitler's regime, its 1949 constitution institutionalized a check on the executive, which is accountable to the popularly elected chamber, the Bundestag, by conferring substantial powers on the Bundesrat, a second chamber controlled by delegates from Germany's sixteen federal states.
5. Quoted in Richard E. Neustadt, *Presidential Power* (New York: John Wiley and Sons, 1960), 9.
6. Quoted in Robert S. Hirshfield, ed., *The Power of the Presidency*, 2nd ed. (Chicago: Aldine Press, 1973), 134.

7. Jacob Hacker, *The Divided Welfare State: The Battle over Public and Private Social Benefits in the United States* (New York: Cambridge University Press, 2002).
8. Quoted in Rose, *The Postmodern President*, 17.
9. Wildavsky, *Beleaguered Presidency*.
10. *The National Security Strategy of the United States* (Washington, D.C.: The White House, September 2002), 31.
11. As quoted anonymously by Ron Suskind, "Without a Doubt," *New York Times Magazine* (October 17, 2004), 51.

Bibliography

Bache, Ian, and Matthew Flinders, eds. *Multi-level Governance*. New York: Oxford University Press, 2004. Shows how, in a variety of major areas of public policy, the European Union impacts national political institutions.

Elgie, Robert. *Political Leadership in Liberal Democracies*. London: Macmillan, 1995. A textbook look at Britain, France, Germany, the United States, Japan, and Italy.

Hayao, Kenji. *The Japanese Prime Minister and Public Policy*. Pittsburgh: University of Pittsburgh Press, 1993. A study of executive branch leadership.

Helms, Ludger. *Presidents, Prime Ministers and Chancellors: Executive Leadership in Western Democracies*. New York: St. Martin's Press, 2005. A systematic comparison of the American presidency, the British prime ministership, and the German chancellorship.

Howell, William G. *Power without Persuasion: The Politics of Direct Presidential Action*. Princeton: Princeton University Press, 2003. Catalogues important unilateral rule-making powers of the president that have few parallels in democratic European parliamentary systems.

Keohane, Robert O., and Joseph S. Nye, Jr. *Power and Interdependence*. 3rd ed. New York: Longman, 2001. A classic study of the politics of interdependence in a partially globalized world.

King, Anthony, ed. *Leaders' Personalities and the Outcomes of Democratic Elections*. New York: Oxford University Press, 2002. A calm social science analysis of the effect of a leader on election outcomes.

Lijphart, Arend, ed. *Parliamentary versus Presidential Government*. New York: Oxford University Press, 1992. A balanced collection of arguments for and against different forms of executive leadership.

Müller, Wolfgang C., and Kaare Strom, eds. *Coalition Governments in Western Europe*. New York: Oxford University Press, 2000. A good, up-to-date overview of political management when authority within the executive branch is divided among several parties in a coalition government.

Page, Edward C., and Vincent Wright, eds. *Bureaucratic Elites in Western European States*. New York: Oxford University Press, 1999. Detailed expert analyses of the roles of high-ranking civil servants in ten countries.

Riggs, Fred W. "The Survival of Presidentialism in America: Para-constitutional Practices." *International Political Science Review* 9, no. 4 (1988), 247–278. An outstanding study of how presidencies easily become dictatorships, based on comparisons between Latin American countries and the United States.

Rose, Richard. *The Postmodern President*. 2nd ed. Washington, D.C.: Congressional Quarterly Press, 1991. Examines the changes in the presidency arising from America's global interdependence.

Rose, Richard. *The Prime Minister in a Shrinking World*. Boston: Polity Press, 2001. Analyzes the British prime minister's rise in domestic importance and decline in international prominence in the past half century.

Rose, Richard, and Ezra Suleiman, eds. *Presidents and Prime Ministers*. Washington, D.C.: American Enterprise Institute, 1980. Systematic comparison of Britain, France, Germany, Norway, Italy, and Franco Spain, as well as the United States.

Savoie, Donald J. *Breaking the Bargain: Public Servants, Ministers and Parliament*. Toronto: University of Toronto Press, 2003. A major study of the changing relationship between elected leaders and the permanent bureaucracy, set in a Canadian context.

Sundquist, James. *Constitutional Reform and Effective Government*. Washington, D.C.: The Brookings Institution, 1986. A Washington insider makes the case for introducing parliamentary features to the presidential system.

Weller, Patrick. "Cabinet Government: An Elusive Ideal." *Public Administration* 81, no. 4 (2003), 701–722. A clear exposition of the different meanings given Cabinet government in British-style democracies.

Wildavsky, Aaron. *The Beleaguered Presidency*. New Brunswick, N.J.: Transaction Publishers, 1991. Contains Wildavsky's original article on the two presidencies and his subsequent revision of that thesis.

PRESIDENTIAL BEHAVIOR AND THE INSTITUTIONS OF THE PRESIDENCY

4

PRESIDENTIAL ELECTIONS AND AMERICAN DEMOCRACY

Stephen J. Wayne

EVERY FOUR YEARS, AMERICANS GO THROUGH THE process of electing their president. It is an exciting period, an illustration of American democracy in action. Thousands participate in the campaign; they contribute money, attend rallies, place bumper stickers on their cars, and discuss the candidates and issues. Millions more see the candidates on television, hear them on the radio, read about them in newspapers and on the Internet, and then vote.

Most of the time the results are clear. The losers concede, the winners organize their transition to government, and Americans get on with their business. The election cycle is temporarily over, and the governing cycle begins.

Occasionally, controversy ensues. The election outcome is in doubt and has to be resolved by the proper authorities, be they a state legislature, Congress, or the judiciary, but not by the people in the streets. The rule of law prevails. And even though many will not like the results and may even feel that they were cheated out of victory, they abide by the official outcome, knowing that in four years they will have another chance.[1]

But do presidential elections really achieve their goal of allowing the citizenry to make an informed judgment on election day? Do they provide every eligible voter with an equal chance to participate? Do they provide sufficient knowledge about the candidates and issues for an enlightened decision? Do they result in the selection of the people's choice, the most popular candidate, and also the most qualified? Do they indicate a policy direction for government and build a coalition for governing?

The answers to these questions are both yes and no. Presidential elections have become more democratic, but they also may have become less reflective of the views of the people as a whole. They are a consent mechanism in a system in which government rests on public consent, but usually only about one-fourth of the population give their consent by voting for the winner. Elections extend over a longer period of time, cost more money, and involve more people than in the past, but turnout remains disappointingly low and uneven among various population groups, network news coverage has declined, and the voters' knowledge of the issues remains rudimentary at best. Information about the candidates and the issues is readily available, but the news media, in choosing the information that is conveyed to the electorate, often base their coverage on its value as entertainment rather than enlightenment. The election of the president and vice president is the only national election in the United States, yet most of it is conducted in only a portion of the country, about one-third of the states. In theory, any person who meets the constitutional requirements (a native-born citizen, at least 35 years of age, and a resident for 14 years) can run, but in practice only a few have a realistic chance of winning. Elections provide an agenda for governing but not necessarily a body of elected officials who support that agenda.

These paradoxes raise serious question for the American presidency, the electorate, and the political system. For the presidency, the basic question is, do presidential elections facilitate or impede presidential leadership? For the electorate, the question is, do they allow people to make an informed judgment on the president's leadership skills, policy orientation, and personality characteristics, all of which affect that president's decisions, actions, and personal behavior in office? For the political system, the questions boil down to these: how democratic are presidential elections and how democratic should they be?

This chapter will answer these questions. It will do so by first describing the evolution of presidential elections in order to provide a foundation upon which those elections can be assessed: the expansion of suffrage, the changing modes of campaigning, the reforms in the nomination process, the increasing importance of money, the changing composition of the major parties, and communications technologies and their individual and collective impact on how candidates go about running for the presidency. The meaning of the election and its implications for governing will also be examined, as will the ways in which presidential elections have affected the operation of the presidency, the orientation of presidents, and their exercise of power.

One of the theses of this chapter is that presidential elections magnify a president's leadership dilemma by encouraging candidates to promise more than they can deliver, to exaggerate their accomplishments, and to present themselves as stronger and more confident, courageous, and visionary than they can possibly be in office.

The second part of the chapter will address the questions that relate to the democratic character of the political system. Are the Electoral College, the level of citizen participation, and the solicitation and use of campaign resources consistent or inconsistent with the basic goals, structures, and processes of a democratic election? Do state laws for the conduct of elections encourage the eligible electorate to participate? Do candidate communications and new coverage of the elections permit the citizenry to cast an intelligent vote and to exercise a meaningful choice when doing so? Does the electoral process extend or limit popular control and public accountability? Do federal elections facilitate or impede national governance?

Another thesis of the chapter contends that, even though presidential elections have become more democratic, serious inequities remain. Suffrage has been extended, but turnout has not increased in proportion to the expansion of eligible voters. There are more opportunities for people to participate, but participation remains skewed in the direction of the better organized and more affluent. The gap between the electorate and the populace remains large; many would say too large. This gap continues to have serious implications for the policy government makes.

Moreover, the winners of the election do not easily come together to form an effective government. Members of Congress usually get reelected regardless of who wins the presidency; others win on the basis of their own campaign and local issues, and perhaps with financial help from their party. The result is a government of individualists, with their own distinctive constituencies, competing with each other for visibility, stature, and influence. Consensus on the issues is often difficult to achieve, although the ideological orientations of the parties have worked to enhance a more cohesive partisan majority than existed two or three decades ago. With that cohesion has come diminished influence for the minority, particularly in the House of Representatives.

There is more information available, but the exaggeration of some of it and the negativism of much of it contribute to the disenchantment with the electoral process in general and with politicians in particular. High levels of cynicism and low levels of efficacy undermine the health and vitality of the American political system.

Finally, the electoral process often produces mixed messages and incompatible elected officials who in recent years have become far more ideological and more closely tied to their electoral constituencies. Fashioning national policy, building a consensus, reaching compromises, and engaging in deliberative discussions have all become harder. The difficulty of governing satisfactorily has led elected officials to engage in a permanent campaign for their policies and for themselves, one in which style trumps substance, imagery shapes reality, and the difference between leading and following becomes obliterated by nonstop public relations campaigns and constant polling and focus group activity.

Is this any way to run a democratic electoral process and a democratic government? The chapter ends with a balance sheet contrasting the costs and benefits of the presidential elections for American democracy.

A Short History of Presidential Elections

From start to finish, American presidential elections are public and participatory. They were not always that way. Indeed suffrage was initially limited by most states to white male Christians who owned property. There were no political parties. The candidates did not personally campaign. The election was decided by a small group of electors chosen by the states.

The system was designed by the framers of the Constitution to be consistent with a republican form of government, the separation of powers, and the internal checks and balances. It was thought to be reasonably efficient, given the state of communication and transportation at the time, politically acceptable to the large and small states and to the proponents of a federal system and those who favored a stronger national government, and above all, more likely to result in the selection of the most qualified candidate for president and vice president than any other system the framers could envision.[2]

According to the Electoral College provision, presidential electors were to be chosen by the states in a manner designated by their legislatures. To ensure their independence, the electors could not simultaneously hold a government position. The number of electors would equal the number of senators and representatives from the state. At a designated time, they would meet and vote for two people; however, they could not designate which of them they wanted to be president and which vice president. Nor could they cast both of their votes for inhabitants of their own states.

Under the original plan, the person with a majority of the votes would be elected president, and the one with the second highest number would be vice president. If no one had a majority, the House of Representatives would chose the president from among the top five candidates, with each state's congressional delegation casting one vote, and a majority required for election. If two or more individuals were tied for second, then the Senate would decide among them.

The system worked according to plan in the first two elections. George Washington was the unanimous choice of the electors, with John Adams coming in second. However, the development of political parties at the end of the eighteenth century quickly changed the dynamics of the system. The electors became agents of their party and were expected to vote for its candidates, not make an independent judgment on their own.

The tie vote in the election of 1800 between Thomas Jefferson and Aaron Burr, the two candidates of the Democratic-Republican Party, testifies to partisan voting by the electors. All Democratic-Republican electors cast their votes for Jefferson and Burr. To prevent such ties from reoccurring, the Twelfth Amendment, enacted by Congress in 1803 and ratified by the states one year later, provided for separate ballots for president and vice president and reduced the number of candidates from which the House could choose from five to three if no one received a majority in the Electoral College.

Nonetheless, the parties had captured the presidential electoral process. By doing so, they converted it into a contest between their respective nominees and platforms. The parties provided a structure, broadened participation, and introduced the public campaign.

Partisanship added a new dimension to the presidency. It made presidents more dependent on their parties, but it also provided them with a coalition for overcoming the constitutional separation of powers. The paradox is that presidents became more constrained by their party connection but at the same time more empowered by it.

The Expansion of Suffrage

The presidential election system has continued to evolve. The political parties have driven that evolution. They nominated candidates, first by congressional caucus and later by national conventions; they conducted the campaigns for their nominees and compiled the platforms on which they ran; and they influenced the selection of the electors who acted as their partisan agents.

As the parties expanded their popular base, the states began to remove property and religious restrictions on voting and moved to the direct election of the electors. Following the Civil War, the Fifteenth Amendment prohibited states from denying people the right to vote on the basis of race, color, or previous condition of servitude. Theoretically, the amendment extended suffrage to African American males. In practice, however, southern states effectively prevented most African Americans from voting for another one hundred years through the imposition of poll taxes, literacy tests, whites-only primaries, and social pressures. It was not until the 1960s, however, that Congress acted to eliminate these discriminatory practices by its enactment of the Civil Rights Act of 1964 and the Voting Rights Act of 1965.[3]

The movement to enfranchise women, begun in the 1870s, was initially directed toward the states. However, few of them changed their constitutions to permit women the right to vote. Women suffragists then turned to the federal government for relief. In 1920 a constitutional amendment, the Nineteenth, was ratified, providing for women's suffrage. Citizens living in the District of Columbia received the right to vote in presidential elections in 1961 (the Twenty-third Amendment), and a uniform voting age of eighteen was established by the Twenty-sixth Amendment in 1971.

Over a period of 183 years, suffrage had been extended to the entire adult citizen population. However, as the percentage of eligible voters has grown, overall turnout has generally declined and variations across subpopulations have become more pronounced.

Changes in Campaigning

Until the end of the nineteenth century, most presidential candidates themselves did not campaign. Their parties campaigned for them, sponsoring rallies, parades, and social events. The parties also distributed literature, printed ballots, and brought their supporters to the polls.

The invention of the telegraph and the building of an intercontinental railroad system made national campaigns feasible. The development of radio and later television extended the campaign into the homes of millions of Americans. The new electronic technology, however, carried a high price tag. Campaign expenses skyrocketed; performance skills, as projected through radio and television, became much more important; grassroots operations initially suffered and the party organizations weakened as the candidates devoted more and more of their time and resources to the new electronic media.

Television began to separate candidates from their parties by offering an alternative means of communication that individual candidates could control. That separation was evident in the conduct of campaigns, the imagery that was presented to voters, and the criteria by which the electorate rendered its judgment. Presidential candidates were more on their own, but so were the winners once they entered office—an unfortunate consequence in a system of divided powers.

Reforming the Nomination Process

Changes in the nomination process contributed to the personalization of presidential politics. In an effort to broaden and sustain their own partisan base, the parties instituted major internal reforms after the 1968 Democratic nominating process, a process in which the winning candidate, Vice President Hubert Humphrey, had avoided primaries that the other Democratic candidates had used to protest the Vietnam War.[4] The need to unify the party during a divisive convention prompted Humphrey's delegates to support his opponents' demand for a party commission to review the rules for delegate selection.

The commission recommended a series of reforms designed to encourage greater participation in the Democrats' nomination process and to ensure that convention delegates were more representative of the party's rank-and-file. To achieve these objectives, the party approved changes that increased the number of primaries and multi-tiered caucuses, and more fairly reflected the popular vote in these nomination contests in the actual selection of convention delegates.[5] Most state legislatures, particularly those controlled by the Democrats, changed their election laws to conform to the new party rules. The Republican Parties in those states were forced to follow suit. By the mid-1970s, both parties were selecting the bulk of their delegates through state primaries.

Naturally, the movement to primaries and multi-tiered caucuses affected the way in which candidates ran for the nomination. Campaigns began earlier. Fund-raising became more important. News media coverage became more intense. Campaign professionals—pollsters, media consultants, grassroots organizers, and policy and public relations experts—began to replace party officials in the organization and operation of the presidential campaigns.

The gulf between party officials and campaign professionals has extended into government, with each group providing the president with different targets of opportunities and skills of their trade. Party leaders wanted to satisfy their constituencies and expand their advantage in the next election. The campaign professionals wanted to use their newly honed skills to help presidents achieve their programmatic and personal goals. The net effect was to cloud the distinction between campaigning and governing. Over time, a "permanent campaign" has emerged as the White House uses its campaign-style public relations experts to advance the president's policy, political, and even personal agendas.

The Increasing Importance of Money

The expansion of the campaigns, combined with increased use of new communications technologies (electronic media, public opinion polls and focus groups, computer-based targeting of groups, media buying, and the Internet), inflated the financial costs of running and the political costs of governing. Public opinion polling and focus groups became standard fare, paid for by the parties to enhance the policy successes and reelection potential of their incumbents. One consequence of these developments is that candidates and even incumbent presidents now have to spend more time and energy fund-raising.

The negative fallout from these activities has forced Congress to keep revising the campaign finance laws. This process began in the early 1970s when the Federal Election Campaign Act was enacted to limit contributions, control expenditures, subsidize presidential nominations, fund the general election, and bring campaign finances into the open by requiring the filing of quarterly reports of contributions and expenditures. The Federal Election Commission was established to monitor these activities, oversee compliance, and make the information available to the general public.

The legislation, combined with the new communications technology, revolutionized presidential campaigns. The law required the candidates to establish their own organizations distinct from their party's. These candidate organizations rivaled and in some cases weakened the major parties. Nonparty groups, which were not subject to the contribution limits, proliferated and became much more active in the election process.

For a time, the parties successfully circumvented the limits that the law imposed on individual donors by using a 1979 amendment to the legislation that permitted them to raise unlimited amounts for party-building and get-out-the-vote activities. These additional revenues, referred to as "soft money" to distinguish them from the "hard money" that was regulated by law, enabled the parties to supplement their war chests by appealing to a small number of wealthy people. The appeals, which raised millions for the major parties in 1996 and 2000, led Congress to close the loophole in 2002 with its enactment of the Bipartisan Campaign Finance Reform Act (also known as the McCain Feingold Act), but that act did not stop nonparty groups from taking advantage of the loophole. Advocacy groups, known as "527s" (the number of the Internal Revenue Service code that permits tax-exempt organizations to raise unlimited amounts for political activities as long as they do not coordinate their activities with the parties or their candidates), solicited large contributions from wealthy donors and used them to supplement their parties' presidential campaigns.

As a consequence of these activities, three simultaneous campaigns now operate in presidential elections: one by the candidates, one by their parties, and one by their party-oriented advocacy groups as well as political action committees and other nonparty groups. One irony is that the campaign by the presidential candidates, which has been funded by the government since 1976, is the least well endowed of these three campaigns. A second consequence is that presidents have become more indebted to party and nonparty groups for their election. They make restitution in office by granting more access and influence to groups that helped them win. This behavior has led to a widespread perception of government of, by, and for special interests, and to policies that tend to advantage the advantaged.

The Shifting Political Environment

The political climate was also changing. The Democratic Party, which became the majority during the presidency of Franklin D. Roosevelt, began to suffer defections from its electoral base in the late 1960s and early 1970s. White southerners opposed the party's strong stand on civil rights and became increasingly Republican. Organized labor, a mainstay of the New Deal Democrats, shrunk as a percentage of the total electorate and also suffered slippage over the civil rights movement and affirmative action policies that followed it. Catholics, whose church opposed the Democrats' pro-choice position on abortion, became less loyal in their partisan affiliations and voting behavior. And Protestant fundamentalists, who had supported the Democrats through 1976 largely on the basis of that party's economic policies, became more concerned with social issues and more sympathetic to the Republicans' stands on them. The prosperity of the United States following World War II also worked to the Republicans' advantage by producing a larger middle and upper middle class. These losses to the Democrats' electoral coalition were only partially offset by larger and more cohesive Democratic voting by racial and ethnic minority groups. By the end of the 1980s, the parties were at rough parity with one another and have remained so since then.

The changes in the electoral bases of the Democratic and Republican parties resulted from shifts in American political attitudes. From the late 1960s to the beginnings of the 1990s, partisan allegiances declined in intensity and ticket splitting increased. Republicans won the presidency in seven of the ten elections from 1968 to 2004. In 1980 they won control of the Senate (for six years), the first time in twenty-six years. In 1994 they won majorities in both the Senate and the House of Representatives, the first time in forty years.[6] After their win in the 2002 midterm elections, the Republicans controlled Congress and the presidency for the first time in forty-eight years. A partisan shift within the electorate had occurred, but a new partisan plurality had not yet emerged.

The shifts in attitudes were reinforced by ideology. Conservatives became more Republican, and liberals stayed Democratic. Since a larger portion of the population identified themselves as conservatives, the Republicans benefited from the sharper ideological distinctions. The more ideological orientation of the parties increased partisan unity in government but made bipartisan cooperation more difficult. Partisanship also became a more important influence on the evaluation of the government's performance as well as on voting behavior itself.[7]

The more ideological the parties, the greater the polarization that has occurred in government. Republicans and Democrats have evidenced increasing difficulty in working together and finding common ground. In divided government, this polarization can lead to political stalemate; in unified government, it can reduce the minority's influence. The president's ability to influence legislative outcomes is correspondingly affected. The number of moderate legislators and the middle ground on which they stand are shrinking.

The New Communication Techniques

As changes were occurring within the body politic, so too were they occurring in the way campaigns were being communicated to the electorate. The candidates, the parties, and the groups that supported them turned increasingly to the tools of social science. Instead of relying on the old pros' "finger-in-the-air" approach to discern public opinion, the campaigns turned to survey research and focus groups to refine their appeals, put them in the most emotive language, and measure their impact on voters. As noted previously, these communication tools have also affected governing.

Some of the communications took the form of press releases, purposeful leaks to the news media, and candidates' speeches and events. The big increase, however, has been in political commercials, first employed in the 1952 presidential election. Today, about two-thirds of the campaign budget of the major party candidates is spent on the design and airing of political commercials.

Since the very beginning, candidates have depended on advertising special-ists to create and target their ads, buy airtime for them, and measure the effect they have had on voters. The techniques of Madison Avenue advertising firms are regularly used to sell candidates. Repetition, inference, and exaggeration are employed to make and remake points or paint an image. Taking advantage of the multiple channels on radio and television and the explosion of Web sites, the campaigns target specific messages to specific groups.

In constructing their appeals, candidates often use partisan stereotyping: Democrats describe Republicans as mean-spirited representatives of the rich, the conservative right, and business-oriented special interests; Republicans paint Democrats as tax-and-spend liberals, proponents of big government and big government programs. The candidates typically respond to this type of attack by emphasizing their moderation, in contrast to their more ideological appeals to party activists during the competitive state of the nomination process. The prob-lem here is that when elected, they tend to respond to the activists in their elec-toral coalition, thereby disillusioning those who wanted to believe in their more moderate rhetoric. George W. Bush is a good example. He emphasized his "com-passionate conservatism" in his two campaigns but has pursued neoconservative domestic and foreign policies as president that deviate from the tenets of tradi-tional conservatism.

Presidential candidates must also try to project an image of leadership when appealing to voters. Attributes of strength, decisiveness, courage, and vision are usually stressed. Any perceived character weakness of the incum-bent will be highlighted by the challenger, who will try to demonstrate those traits that the current president presumably lacks. Thus, in 2000, Bush said he would return honesty and integrity to the Oval Office, an obviously deroga-tory reference to the Clinton years; in 2004, Kerry said that he would never send American troops into battle on false pretenses, as he and others alleged Bush had done in Iraq.

Negative campaigning is a fact of political life. Name-calling, invective, and accusations of wrongdoing and unethical behavior have been part and parcel of presidential elections since 1796.[8] What seems to be different today is the increasing emphasis placed on confrontational ads by the candidates, the extent to which they have affected the tenor of modern campaigns, and the impact that they seem to have on voters. More than half the advertising of the major presi-dential candidates since 1988 has been negative.[9]

From the perspective of media consultants, negative ads work; they hit home because they come home, both on television and on the Internet. From the per-spective of the public, they are a subject of complaint, a reason given for the high level of cynicism and low level of voter turnout. Candidates regularly complain about the negative ads of their opponents, but use the same techniques them-selves in their own commercials.

One of the most recent communication innovations has been the use of the Internet to solicit funds, mobilize volunteers, and keep supporters informed and involved. Howard Dean raised millions on his Web site, which was also used as an ongoing political forum by his supporters. Officials of the Dean campaign spent hours communicating with people who asked questions or made comments on the campaign's Web log (or *blog*).[10]

The trend toward the increasing use of the Web to reach potential voters, particularly young ones, can be expected to continue in subsequent presidential elections. The White House has also used its Web site to trumpet the achievements of the administration, the decisions and actions of the president, and the activities of the First Family.

Contemporary Presidential Campaigns

The changes that we have noted in the financial, political, and media environment in which presidential elections occur could not help but affect the general election campaigns themselves: their timing, targeting, and strategizing. The general election campaign also begins earlier, well before candidates officially receive their party's nomination. During the period following the end of the competitive phase of the nomination contest and before the national nominating convention, biographical ads for the challenger, accomplishment ads for the incumbents, and negative ads for both are aired. The candidates try to maintain their visibility in the news with speeches, endorsements, and campaign events.

The conventions continue to be held, but primarily as public relations extravaganzas. Conventions educate the public, activate partisans, and generate enthusiasm. They are a time of learning and commitment during which much of the partisan electorate and some independents make their voting decisions. And they launch the presidential campaign, with the hope of providing their nominees with a bounce that carries them into the election campaign.

The general election campaign follows. Here the candidates make their appeals, try to project an image of leadership, and attack their opponent, as do their party and the nonparty groups that support them. The campaign is conducted with the state allocation of votes in the Electoral College in mind. The objective is to win the most electoral votes, not the most popular votes. The presidential campaign is not fought across the entire country. It is concentrated in the key battleground states in which polls indicate that the outcome is in doubt. Resources are thus expended where they will do the most good. The 2004 campaign began with each candidate targeting seventeen or eighteen states and ended with a focus on only a few.

In an age of partisan parity, campaigns matter. The economic, social, and political environment, unless overwhelmingly positive or negative, does not preordain the results, although it obviously has an impact on them. The importance of the campaign lies in its educational and mobilization functions. Both efforts are designed to convince partisans and independents to vote and for whom.

Who turns out matters almost as much as how people vote. "Get-out-the-vote" campaigns have therefore become increasingly important for the parties. Most of the campaign's policy message is directed toward turning out the base. It was no coincidence that eleven ballot initiatives opposing gay marriage were on the ballots of many of the key battleground states in 2004. These initiatives were a calculated part of Republican strategy to maximize the Christian Coalition vote, as was the president's highly publicized remarks favoring a constitutional amendment on heterosexual marriage, opposing the use of fetuses for stem-cell research, and nominating strict constructionists to the Supreme Court. More generic appeals and personal imagery are targeted to independents and weak partisans of the other party.

Understanding the Election Results

Partisanship also provides a framework for explaining the vote. Exit polls and public opinion surveys seek to determine why people voted as they did. They assess the importance of various issues and the candidates' stands on them, public perceptions of the candidates, and a host of demographic and attitudinal characteristics. The result is usually a complex picture, subject to multiple interpretations by political scientists, media pundits, the winning and losing candidates, their staffs, and party officials. Frequently, there is not a consensus.

But, of course, there are actual outcomes, winners and losers, and they present a portrait of the electorate as well. If one party wins control of the White House and both houses of Congress, especially by large margins, the meaning of the election is clear and the coalition for governing has been formed. When partisan control shifts as well, the charge is to change policy along the lines proposed by the winning candidate and party. When partisan control does not shift, and one party maintains control of government, the message is to continue the policies of the previous administration while pursuing the priorities that the victorious candidate articulated in the campaign.

Most elections fall well short of a mandate, even though the winning candidate may claim one, as Harry Truman did in 1948 and Bill Clinton in 1992. Both acted as if they had received public support for their policy initiatives but were only modestly successful in actually achieving them.[11] George W. Bush indicated that he intended to pursue his campaign pledges at the beginning of both of his terms. Moreover, he claimed that he had earned political capital following his and his party's victory in the 2004 elections, even though his margin of victory was small and the Republican gains in Congress were modest.

With the political parties at or near parity, with increasingly autonomous congressional and presidential elections, and with incumbents in Congress so advantaged, the election messages are mixed, the winners may be incompatible with one another, and the victorious presidential candidate starts out with high hopes but often with a weak coalitional base. The bottom line, however, is that the politics of the elections carries over into the politics of governing with many of the same political cleavages evident. The permanent campaign continues, with its headquarters at 1600 Pennsylvania Avenue in Washington, D.C.

Summary

Presidential elections have become part of the American political tradition. They have also become more democratic in the sense that more people can participate at more stages in the process. Candidates have more means available to them to reach the electorate. The public needs only to turn on television, radio, go on-line, or read a newspaper or a news magazine to learn about the campaign, acquire knowledge about the candidates and issues, and make an informed judgment on Election Day.

The winners take office, attempt to redeem their campaign promises, convert them into a governing agenda, and then pursue that agenda with the help of other partisans and like-minded legislators. The system is open, the campaign visible, public participation is encouraged, government officials are chosen, and they tend to remain responsive to the people who elected them. So what's the problem?

Are Presidential Elections Democratic?

To answer this question, we turn to the principles of a democratic election process and examine the extent to which contemporary presidential elections accord with those principles.

Basic Tenets of Democratic Elections

Elections are defining moments for a democracy. They represent the only official collective judgment of the people in deciding who will govern, how, and to what ends. The purpose of elections is to link citizens to their government; elections serve as a mechanism for exercising public choice. They also facilitate governing by providing an agenda and a coalition that a president can use to build and maintain support in Congress. Finally, periodic elections are a means by which the public can hold those in office accountable for their actions and at the same time give legitimacy to their policy decisions.

For elections to be democratic, they must be predicated on the principles of individual liberty, political equality, and enlightened judgment.[12] To satisfy these principles, elections must meet three criteria:

1. Universal suffrage. All adult citizens who are capable of making an informed judgment should be able to vote. They must be able to vote freely and without duress.

2. One person, one vote. All votes should be counted equally in determining the outcome of the election.
3. Enlightened understanding. People should have sufficient knowledge about the candidates and the issues to make an informed judgment.[13] To obtain such information, a free and competitive media is essential.

To what extent do presidential elections meet these democratic criteria? To address this important issue, we must first turn to a crucial feature of the system, the Electoral College, and then to the participants and the resources they use to affect election outcomes. Do people get sufficient relevant information to make an intelligent judgment? This question requires an examination of the communications process and how it may be distorted by partisan advertising and news media coverage. The final part of this section focuses on the impact of elections on government, the direction they provide and the coalitions they create. It addresses two very important questions: do presidential elections contribute to a president's ability to lead and do they contribute to effective governance?

The Electoral College System

The framers of the United States Constitution were not democrats; they were republicans. They desired a government that rested on popular consent, but not one that would be subject to the public mood of the moment, to the so-called "tyranny of the majority."[14] Although the delegates to the Constitutional Convention considered direct election of the president, they rejected this mode of selection as neither wise nor feasible. They believed it unwise because they lacked faith in the judgment of the masses; they considered it unfeasible because of the large geographic expanse of the country, its relatively slow means of transportation and communication, and the rivalries among the states and regions that made a fair and honest election problematic. They debated having the legislature select the president but could not agree on procedures that would ensure the independence of the office. The Electoral College, proposed as a compromise toward the end of the convention, was viewed as safe and workable, consistent with the politics of the time, the constitutional design, and a republican form of government.[15]

States had the option of choosing the electors in any manner they saw fit. Initially, most legislatures did so themselves. However, as the parties developed and reached out for supporters, state legislatures began to maneuver the process to benefit the party in power. This maneuvering resulted in the partisan selection of electors. Those states in which the electors were elected by popular vote also changed to a "winner-take-all" system to maximize their partisan influence. By 1832, all states but one, South Carolina, chose their electors on the basis of a popular, statewide vote.

The direct selection of electors made the Electoral College more democratic than it had been or was intended to be. However, the movement to a general ticket, winner-take-all system skewed the outcome. Not only did it deny the losing party any representation in the state's electoral delegation, it also created the possibility that the candidate who received the most popular votes in the country might not receive the most electoral votes, a possibility that became a reality three times in American history: 1876, 1888, and 2000.[16]

The winner-take-all system, practiced today in all states but Maine and Nebraska, also creates another democratic problem. It discourages turnout in states dominated by one party. Why vote if one of the candidates is practically assured of victory by virtue of the partisan composition and voting patterns of the state?

In addition, the winner-take-all system encourages candidates to concentrate their campaigns in the most competitive states. Using sophisticated polling to sample public opinion over the course of the campaign, candidates are able to direct their energy and resources where they will be the most beneficial. In 2000 and 2004, these battleground states constituted a little more than one-third of the country's population yet received the overwhelming amount of candidate appearances, political advertising, and grassroots activities.

A third undemocratic consequence of the Electoral College system is the overrepresentation of the very smallest and largest states. The small states are overrepresented by virtue of getting a minimum of three electoral votes, regardless of their size of their populations. In 2000 and 2004, George W. Bush carried more than twice as many small states than did his Democratic opponents. Bush thus disproportionately benefited from this small-state bias in the Electoral College.[17]

The largest states also exercise more influence than they would in a direct popular vote by casting their electoral votes as a unit. The Democrats in 2000 and 2004 carried five of the seven largest states, thereby gaining advantage of the big-state block-voting. Within the large states, sizable and cohesive voting groups also can exercise considerable clout, so candidates make specific appeals to these groups: Hispanics in the Southwest, Jews in New York, Arab-Americans in Michigan, and Asian Americans in California.

Any system that could upset a popular judgment, discourages turnout, and gives states of a certain size an advantage is undemocratic. So why not change the system to make it fairer to all concerned? The reason is simple—the beneficiaries of the current arrangement would probably not support the constitutional amendment required to change it.[18]

Despite the controversy arising from the elections of 2000, despite public opinion polls that indicate that a majority of the population favor direct election, and despite the undemocratic character of the Electoral College, there has not been significant public pressure to abandon the current system. Political traditions die hard, particularly for those who attribute the country's successful presidential leadership to such a system, those who perceive that they are advantaged by the system, and those who dislike the alternatives. Why fix it if it is not broken, or if it breaks down so rarely, proponents argue.

The most comprehensive "fix" would be to abolish the Electoral College entirely for a direct election. Such a change would simplify the election and prevent a discrepancy between the popular vote and the Electoral College vote, provided only a plurality was needed to win. If a majority were still required, however, another election, perhaps between the top two candidates or a congressional resolution of the matter, would probably be necessary to determine a winner.

A direct election would be fairer. It conforms to democratic criteria, maximizes turnout, and forces candidates to engage in a more national campaign than they currently do. Moreover, it might invigorate the major parties and could conceivably give third parties and independent candidates more clout than they have under the present arrangement.

What are the problems with a direct election? Critics contend that it would undercut the federal character of the U.S. political system,[19] elevate the importance of the large metropolitan areas and decrease the influence of rural areas, and in close elections, would magnify the problems of fraudulent voting, registration glitches, discriminatory practices by electoral officials, and machine tabulation problems. Instead of voting controversies being limited to one or a few states, as they were in 2000, they could potentially involve all of the states.

Allocating the electoral vote in proportion to the popular vote within states (the proportional plan) or allocating one vote to the winner of each congressional district within the state and two to the overall winner of the state vote (the district plan; the states of Maine and Nebraska use such a system) are two other alternatives. Both would result in a more equitable and closer vote than the current system provides; both might give third parties and independent candidates more influence. Neither one would have changed the outcome of the 2000 or 2004 election, however.[20]

But the Electoral College is only part of the problem. Even if its undemocratic features were modified, there are still other problems with it. They related to unsatisfactory turnout and unequal resources, to the electorate's capacity to make an informed decision, and to the conversion of the election results into a governing agenda and a coalition to support and sustain it.

Citizen Participation

Who participates how, and what difference does participation make for the perceived and actual outcome of the election? In theory, the United States has universal suffrage. All adult citizens have the right to vote. In practice, some states have restricted that right for those who are or have been incarcerated, in mental institutions, or have been dishonorably discharged from the military. In other cases, citizens have been turned away from the polls because their names did not appear on the precinct's registration list. The problem of restricting voting rights, while serious, particularly for African American males, has had much less impact in recent years than the problem of citizens simply not voting when they have the right to do so.[21]

Voter turnout has declined for much of the last fifty years. In 1960 an estimated 64.9 percent of the voting age population cast ballots in the presidential election; over the next twenty years that percentage declined to 54.7. Since then, turnout has reached a low of 51.5 percent in 1996 and a high of almost 60 percent in 2004.[22] Why do so many people not vote, and what difference does it make for a democracy? The reasons for not voting are varied. People give all sorts of excuses, from being too busy, to lacking interest, to contending that it doesn't matter to them, or to the country, who wins. Political scientists point to the weakening of partisan identification in the late 1960s and 1970s, the growing disillusionment with government in general and national politicians in particular, feelings of declining efficacy (the belief that one can make a difference), increasingly negative campaigns reinforced by a critical news media, and even the absence of defining events, since Vietnam and Watergate, in which government has played a major role in people's lives.[23] The list goes on, but the bottom line is that many people feel that voting just is not worth the effort. According to scholars Paul R. Abramson, John H. Aldrich, and David W. Rohde, about two-thirds of the decline in turnout since 1960 can be attributed to the combined effects of weaker partisan affiliation and feelings of less political effectiveness, with the latter being twice as important.[24]

Does it matter to a democratic society that so many people do not vote? Some say it does not, as long as people have the right to do so and can exercise that right freely. In fact, a few democratic elitists have argued that nonvoting actually reduces political discord, enhances social stability, and allows those with the most interest and information to make the electoral decisions.[25] Moreover, if apathy suggests some degree of contentment with existing conditions, then why consider nonvoting a problem?

Most democratic theorists, however, do not share this view; they do not see apathy as a positive social trait but as a sign of discontent, disappointment, and disempowerment.[26] Nonvoting weakens the link between citizens and their elected representatives; it widens the gap between the electorate and the population. If the electorate were representative of the entire population, such a gap would not be as much of a problem as democratic activists believe. But alas, people who vote more regularly distinguish themselves from those who do not by being older, more educated, with higher incomes and greater professional opportunities—the so-called "haves" of society. To the extent that elected officials respond more to the electorate than the general public, their policy decisions will reflect the interests of the "haves" more than the "have nots."[27]

There is a partisan dimension to turnout as well. The Democrats, who receive more support from those in the lower socioeconomic groups, are usually more often disadvantaged in a low-turnout election than are the Republicans. In an age of partisan parity, turnout matters; it can spell the difference between victory and defeat. The importance of energizing and turning out their base has led both major parties to design and implement massive get-out-the-vote efforts in recent elections, particularly in 2004, an election in which Republican turnout in the key battleground states exceeded that of the Democrats.

Voting matters for the country's foreign policy as well, especially for a country that sees democratization and human rights as principles upon which its policy toward other nation-states should be based. The incongruence between promoting democratic elections abroad with less than optimal turnout at home has not been lost on members of Congress. Over the years Congress has acted to ease the burden of registering to vote as well as the act of voting itself.

In addition to the Civil Rights Act of 1964 and the Voting Rights Act of 1965 (previously mentioned), Congress enacted legislation in 1993 known as the "Motor-Voter" bill which made registration forms available at motor vehicle, welfare, and military recruiting offices. Following the Florida vote controversy of 2000, an electoral reform law was passed. Entitled "The Help America Vote Act of 2002," the legislation was designed to aid states in automating their voter registration records, providing money to improve the technology of voting machines and computerize voting lists.[28] And the Civil Rights Commission has also looked into accusations of discrimination against African Americans and other minority groups by state election officials.

Some states have also moved on their own initiative to tackle voting problems. Florida enacted legislation to correct the problems it encountered in 2000. The state provided more training for election officials, more accurate registration procedures and up-to-date lists of eligible voters, and more money to replace the antiquated punch-card voting machines that caused so much of the tabulation difficulties. Oregon instituted a vote-by-mail system, while others have experimented with touch-screen voting, although machine malfunctions and the absence of paper ballots to check the accuracy of the vote count on some of the computers have raised questions about this technology. There have even been a few attempts to use the Internet as a vehicle for voting; however, security concerns persist and have discouraged election officials from turning to this method.

Despite educational campaigns and partisan efforts to get out the vote, and new laws that have eased registration and voting procedures, turnout did not significantly increase until 2004 when almost 60 percent of eligible voters cast ballots. What else can government do? One possibility that might make it easier for some people to vote would be to make Election Day a holiday, to hold elections on Sunday, or to combine Election Day with another holiday such as Veterans Day. Another alternative would be to extend the time for voting from 12 to 24 hours or even longer. A third possibility would be for every state to issue "no fault" absentee ballots on request. States have experimented with extending the period for voting and making absentee ballots easier to obtain, with modest success.

Those who bemoan the low participation rate and are leery of the efficacy of any adjustments that the state and federal government have made might consider a more radical change: require voting as an obligation of citizenship and penalize those who fail to do so. A number of countries, such as Australia, Belgium, and Chile, have such a requirement. Needless to add, they also have high turnouts. A principal merit of requiring voting is that it would effectively convert the citizen population into the electorate and thereby force elected officials to be responsive to more people. Policy decisions would reflect the needs and interests of all citizens, not just those who vote. Under these circumstances, the gap between the "haves" and "have nots" might decline.

One problem with requiring voting, however, is that it denies people the right not to vote, to protest the choices they have in the election by staying home. Another pertains to how informed the judgment of disinterested citizens would be if they were forced to vote. Although government may require its citizens to vote, it would be much harder to require them to acquire the knowledge to make an informed decision. Increasing the number of uninformed voters would not result in the selection of more qualified candidates. Public ignorance is certainly not the key to enlightened self-rule in a democracy.

The failure of a sizable portion of the citizenry to vote, the overrepresentation within this group of the young, the poor, the infirm, and the incarcerated, and the penchant of elected officials to respond to those who elected them rather than the population as a whole create a fission within the democratic political system that hurts some and benefits others. Since most of the nonvoting is by choice, one can argue that citizens get what they deserve. Such is not the case with the unequal distribution of resources.

The Campaign Finance Issue: Inequitable Resources

Private money directly impinges on the equity issue in presidential elections. Presidential elections are expensive, and someone has to pay for them. In the distribution of the resources, who gains and who loses?

Presidential elections became costly when candidates began to campaign personally across the country at the end of the nineteenth century. William McKinley raised and spent between $6 and 7 million in 1896, compared to William Jennings Bryan's $650,000. With the advent of the electronic media, expenditures increased sharply. John F. Kennedy and Richard Nixon spent about $10 million each in 1960; twelve years later, George McGovern and Richard Nixon combined to spend over $90 million. And that was just the beginning.

During the 2004 election cycle, expenditures on the presidential contest were estimated to be about $1.2 billion in current dollars.[29]

The sharp increase in expenditures is the consequence of the two campaigns that are required every four years—one for the nomination and the other for the general election. Of the two, nomination costs have risen faster than those of the general election. With prolonged campaigns starting the year prior to the election, an increasingly front-loaded primary schedule, and the need for simultaneous multistate campaigns, candidates for their party's nomination must raise millions just to be viable.

Although the Democratic 2004 nomination was effectively determined by March 2 of that year, and there was no Republican contest, both leading candidates for their party's nomination continued to raise and spend money—lots of it. By the time of their political conventions, Kerry had raised almost $250 million and George W. Bush over $290 million.[30] In addition, their national parties and the nonparty groups that supported their candidacies also continued to raise and spend millions.

What are the principal concerns for a democratic electoral process with large contributions and expenditures? One relates to the donors and spenders and what they get for their money; the other pertains to how the amount of money raised and spent and how that affects who runs, who wins, and how they govern.

There are three major sources of campaign revenue. One can be the candidates themselves, independently wealthy individuals who use their own resources: Ross Perot in 1992, Steve Forbes in the 1996 and 2000 Republican nomination contests, and, to some extent, John Kerry in the 2004 Democratic nomination.[31] Is it fair that wealthy individuals have an advantage, when those with more modest resources do not? Congress apparently did not think so when it enacted campaign finance legislation that capped the amount individuals could give to their own campaigns at $50,000, if they accepted federal funds. But why take federal funds and the spending restrictions that go with them if other options are available?[32]

The second problem stems from those individuals and groups that make large contributions or spend large amounts of money on behalf of the candidates. Federal law now limits the amount individuals can contribute to $2,000 per candidate per election; nonparty groups are limited to a maximum of $5,000. Large contributors, those who gave $1,000 or more, have comprised more than half the donors in the last two presidential nomination processes.[33]

The public perceives that money contributes to electoral success.[34] People also believe that large contributors receive preferential treatment from elected officials, especially from those who benefited from their contributions.[35] Such perceptions, whether true or false, reduce confidence and trust in government and contribute to public cynicism and feelings of alienation.

Those who raise the most—Bush called them "explorers" ($200,000) and "pioneers" ($100,000) and Kerry, the "100 Club" ($100,000)—gain special recognition and benefits, sometimes including offers of government positions, invitations to special events, and most importantly, access to key public officials. Contributors to the presidential candidates also give indirectly through their contributions to the national parties and nonparty groups.[36] They can also spend independently in support of or opposition to one of the presidential candidates.

The issue is one of equity. If the individuals and groups that contributed and spent the most were representative of the population as a whole, equity might not be a problem, but they are not representative. Business, labor, trade, and professional groups give and spend far more than do consumer groups and nonprofessionals, including unorganized labor. When was the last time that you heard of a group representing the unemployed, single parents, or prisoners spending a lot of money to influence the outcome of a presidential election?

Congress has tried to deal with the problem of campaign finance with a series of laws that have made more public information about campaign contributions and expenditures available, provide government funds to subsidize nomination campaigns and fund the major party candidates in the general election, and limit the amount that individuals and groups can give to federal candidates and the amounts that presidential candidates can spend if they accept government funds. But the legislation has had only mixed success because of the ingenuity of the candidates and their financial advisers in devising legal ways to circumvent the law, and because of the Supreme Court's decision in *Buckley v. Valeo* that campaign spending is protected by the First Amendment's guarantee of freedom of speech.

Proposals advocating free television time, more candidate debates, shorter campaigns, and more public funding with larger expenditure ceilings have been made and might help alleviate the problem. But they will not eliminate it entirely, as long as individual and nonparty expenditures are protected by the First Amendment, and the composition of the Federal Election Commission remains evenly divided under existing law between Republicans and Democrats.

In short, money can and does affect the democratic character of presidential elections. If a basic tenet of an electoral democracy is every citizen's right to an equal opportunity to influence an election outcome, then the unequal distribution of resources within society, combined with the protections that the Constitution affords the use of these resources, undermines that right.

Campaign Communications

To gain an enlightened understanding and make an informed judgment, the electorate needs ample information from diverse sources. The candidates supply a lot of it themselves; party and nonparty groups do so as well. The problem with this information is that it is provided by people and organizations that have an interest in a particular outcome. Not only is it not balanced, it may be misleading, exaggerated, even false. Obviously an enlightened understanding cannot be gained from this information alone, although it may still be valuable in understanding the positions of the candidates, their personal qualities and beliefs, and what they may do if elected.

POLITICAL COMMERCIALS. Today most of the information presented by presidential campaigns and those of other groups supporting their efforts comes in the form of political advertising. Studies have shown that people gain and retain more information about the campaign from advertisements than they do from the news.[37] Ads are repetitive; most news stories are not. Ads have been pretested and scripted to achieve maximum effect; news stories are not. Ads are targeted to specific groups; news coverage is directed toward a more general audience.

All political advertising is not beneficial to a democratic electoral process. Ads that make their point by exaggeration, inference, and misinformation do not contribute to an enlightened electorate but to a misguided one. Ads also tend to be more negative than positive, particularly as the campaign progresses.[38] Many are directed at a candidate's personal attributes; they tend to stereotype and often take statements, positions, legislative votes, and executive vetoes out of context. With the exception of a few major news organizations' ad watches, which evaluate the claims made in the advertisements, the only check on misinformation is the opposition candidate's statements and advertisements, which are also one-sided. One of the primary allegations about negative ads is that they make people more cynical and less likely to vote.[39] However, much of the empirical evidence collected by political scientists and the experience of media consultants who design such ads suggest otherwise. Negative ads are informative; they help mobilize the electorate, especially partisans.[40]

Doing something about misleading even untrue accusations and claims made in political commercials is very difficult because the First Amendment protects the right of candidates, their parties, nonparty groups, and individuals to express their views. Suing for libel is also problematic for public figures in light of the Supreme Court's decision in *Sullivan v. New York Times* that falsehood alone is not sufficient to win a judgment. Malice must be proven as well, and that is very difficult to do. Ad watches, such as those initiated by major newspapers, and stories on campaign advertising may help, but neither has the same impact as the ads themselves.[41] Nor can we expect a media organization that profits from the advertising to police itself and refuse ads that contain misleading information or factual errors.

NEWS MEDIA COVERAGE. Candidates, parties, and interest groups are expected to present their side; the electorate knows this and presumably considers the source when evaluating the content. But the news media are expected to present a "fair and balanced" view.[42] Moreover, with the electronic media serving as the principal communications link between the candidates and voters, what election news is reported, how it is reported, and what spin, if any, it has will affect what the public knows.

The news media are biased. Some of the partisan public perceives that bias to be ideological. Republicans view the news media as liberal and Democratic; Democrats see less ideological bias than Republicans, but those who do perceive bias see the media as conservative, a tool of corporate America.[43] Most political scientists see the bias as more institutional than ideological. They see it captured in the definition of what is newsworthy: that which is new, surprising, exciting, dramatic, and conflict oriented. The first utterance is more newsworthy than the second time it is stated; the unexpected development is more newsworthy than the expected one; and the contest, if it is perceived to be close, is more newsworthy than the substance of the issues, at least to most Americans.

A profit-oriented media want to maintain as large an audience as possible for as long as possible. News stories that achieve this objective are more likely to be reported than those that do not. To capture and sustain public attention, the press report elections as if they were sporting events. More attention is given to the horse race than to substantive policy;[44] polls indicate who is ahead; media pundits speculate endlessly on the candidates' strategies and tactics; other reporters provide color commentary; the wives, the children, even the pets become part of the overall portrait. Is this the information that the electorate needs to have an enlightened understanding and to make an informed judgment?

The news media's format is also a problem. Most news stories are short. The candidate's words and actions that appear on the screen are even shorter. In the 2000 and 2004 elections, the average "sound bite" of a presidential candidate on the broadcast networks' evening news shows was less than eight seconds.[45] The reporters and commentators shape the story; they put events into a context that the audience will understand; it is a continuing story, at least through the election. For most of the events that are reported, the correspondent solicits a few short comments meant to be reflective of the public or partisan reaction to what the candidate has said or done. The comments tend to be more critical than complementary. Overall the spin is negative, reinforcing the negativity of the campaign advertisements.[46]

A number of unfortunate consequences for a democratic electoral process follow from this type of election coverage. The electorate gets a jaundiced view of the campaign. It is an overly personalized perspective, seen more as a contest between candidates driven by their partisan and personal ambition, rather than as a debate over policy and its implications for the country. And to make matters worse, it is presented in the news media primarily by reporters and correspondents rather than by the candidates themselves.

Criticizing contemporary press coverage of presidential campaigns is much easier than making constructive suggestions to change that coverage. The electorate may be getting what it wants, but is it getting what it needs? On the other hand, what good would it do to present a detailed discussion of the issues, their costs and consequences, if most of the people had little interest, could not or would not follow it, or worse yet, were "turned off" by it? Besides, there is plenty of such information currently available, if people want to seek it out.

Debates by the candidates help inform the electorate, but these too are not without their problems. The format, which is contentiously negotiated by the candidates, tends to prevent long explanations. The candidates often seem rehearsed and overly cautious. They skirt some of the questions. But they also provide an opportunity for the electorate to compare the major party candidates in the same setting, at the same time, and on the basis of the same criteria.

Debates, however, emphasize style and performance skills. While both are important components of presidential leadership, neither address the substantive questions that the election poses for a democratic populace. The analysts are preoccupied with winners and losers; campaign strategists try to influence post-debate coverage and, above all, the public's response.

Giving candidates free air time to express their views and make their appeals might also contribute to a more informed electorate, but it might also have a negligible impact, or one that was equivalent to a free advertisement. Who would watch? Would a profit-oriented news media be willing to provide free time when they could profit from selling that time?

Perhaps the issue is not as dire as it seems. Although the public ritually complains about media coverage, and many people perceive the news media as ideologically biased, voters still claim that they have sufficient information to make an informed voting decision, according to surveys conducted by the Pew Research Center for the People and the Press following the election.[47]

Elections and Governing: A Tenuous Connection

In theory, elections should provide guidance for government; they should help forge and reinforce the governing coalitions; they should be the mechanism that holds those in elected positions responsive to the people who voted for them and accountable for their decisions and actions during the next election cycle. Do presidential elections currently meet these criteria?

As previously discussed, most presidential elections do not provide a policy mandate for the winner, even though many newly elected presidents proceed as if they received one. For a policy mandate to exist, the presidential candidates must take clear and compatible positions on the issues, and people must vote for them primarily because of these positions.[48] Presidential candidates do take differing stands on some issues, but they also fudge their positions on others, and take similar positions on a few of them. The electorate, for its part, votes for candidates for a combination of reasons: their record, their leadership skills, their partisan affiliation, and their policy positions, among others. The results of the vote rarely indicate which of the reasons was dominant.

Presidents do try to redeem their campaign pledges, but often with mixed results.[49] Bill Clinton failed on two of his three major priorities: an economic stimulus and national health care reform during his first year in office.[50] President George W. Bush's only major legislative achievements prior to the terrorist attacks of September 11, 2001, were his fiscal year 2002 budget, the outlines of which Congress supported in its budget resolutions, and a large, but not permanent, tax cut. During most of this period of time, both presidents dealt with a Congress controlled by their party. What's the problem?

Part of the president's difficulties lies with unrealistic expectations that were created during the campaign; part of them lies with the incompatibility of the elected officials with one another and with the president; part has to do with the federal character of the political system.

Presidential candidates typically overpromise and underinform to get elected. They pledge to pursue different policies for different groups, and purposefully do not establish clear priorities in order to maximize their potential support from these groups. They also may not discuss the economic or social costs of achieving their policies nor indicate the trouble they may encounter in getting Congress to support them.

Presidential candidates run as if they will lead in a presidential system. Rarely do they temper their promises or modify their leadership by pointing out that they cannot achieve their policy goals alone. Yet they have only minimal influence on who else gets elected to the national government, even on the same party label. The absence of presidential coattails since 1980 adds to the president's woes. Running behind members of Congress in their districts decreases a president's leverage over those members. Divided government, the rule not the exception from 1968 to 2002, magnifies the president's leadership problem.

Newly elected members of Congress may not know one another. They may not agree on the issues. The one thing they have in common, however, is their promise to represent their constituency faithfully and to act in its interests. In other words, on most issues, especially those in the domestic arena, their focus is parochial and the president's is national, although his national constituency comprises many groups with different interests. The problem is systemic and political: the federal system, gerrymandered legislative districts, and autonomous electoral processes all contribute. Add to these problems limited turnover, resulting from safe legislative districts, incumbency advantages, and overlapping terms in the Senate, and the president has his persuasive work cut out for him.

In short, elections raise false hopes and create unrealistic expectations of presidential leadership. The presidential candidates contribute to these hopes and expectations by the way in which they run for office, which in turn is driven by their need to win in order to govern. The bottom line is that presidential elections make presidential leadership more difficult.

Presidential Elections and American Democracy: A Balance Sheet

Presidential elections were not designed to be democratic; they were designed to be consistent with a republican form of government, to maintain the independence of the executive institution, to comport with the country's political environment, and to result in the selection of the most qualified candidate. The good news, at least as far as the first three criteria are concerned, is that the Electoral College system has met these criteria and continues to do so. Whether it has achieved the fourth is debatable. But surely that criterion—selecting the *most* qualified person in the country as president—would always be problematic in actual practice.

The framers' system has changed with the times. It has become more democratic in the sense that more people exercise greater influence on the nomination and election of the president than ever before. Here are some of the ways in which democracy has been enhanced:

- voting rights have been extended;
- impediments to voting have been reduced;
- more people have greater opportunities to run;
- political parties have become more inclusive;
- nonparty groups now span the political spectrum, reflect much of the country's social and economic diversity, represent a wide range of interests, and actively participate within the electoral arena.

Moreover, there are numerous ways in which individuals can become involved in presidential campaigns, from making contributions to volunteering to help distribute literature, make telephone calls, or ring door bells, to attending political rallies and other events, and to voting. Further, much information is easily and readily available to make an informed judgment, although it is buried in various sorts of sources whose credibility may be difficult to judge. It comes in many forms, from advertisements to speeches, from live coverage of the conventions and debates to news reports about all aspects of the campaign, from talk show hosts to political analysts, from documentary films (*Travels with George*) to entertainment shows (*The Oprah Winfrey Show, Larry King Live, Saturday Night Live*) to movies (*Fahrenheit 9/11*). A push of the remote control button or a turn of the dial is all that is necessary to become exposed to a variety of opinions, analyses, and other campaign-related information.

The system has endured for over two hundred years and for the most part has achieved decisive results, accepted by the vast majority of people. It has conveyed legitimacy for those elected to office and for the policy decisions they make in government. It has also worked to hold first-term presidents accountable.[51] What more should Americans ask of their presidential election process?

Plenty, say those who believe that the democratic trends have not gone far enough. They contend that voting has actually become less rather than more equitable:

- the Electoral College is an anachronism that undercuts the very principle on which a democracy is based: one person, one vote;
- the system turns off voters rather than encourages them to participate;
- registration procedures, voting restrictions, complicated ballots, tabulation controversies, negative advertising, and critical press combine to make the public more cynical, detract from political efficacy, and contribute to feelings of alienation.

The equity issues are related: voting restrictions disproportionately affect minority voters; the lowest turnout exists among those with the lowest income, lowest education levels, and the least skilled, professional jobs; and elected officials are more responsive to the electorate than to the populace. Compounding this inequity are additional factors: the access and influence that big money brings to electoral politics; special interests who pursue their economic or ideological goals within the electoral arena; and the profit orientation of the media conglomerates that provide voters with much of the information they need to make informed judgments. The result: major undemocratic consequences are undercutting the democratic character of the presidential electoral process.

There are tradeoffs in any electoral system. Increasing equity decreases liberty. Do Americans want to reduce their ability to pursue and protect their own interests, to use their own resources as they see fit, or to not vote, if they so desire? Do they want to increase their own tax burden by having the government pay for more of the costs of campaigning, particularly for candidates and parties they do not like? Do they want the news media to give them an endless diet of policy analysis? Do they want to increase the size of the electorate if it means that more people with less information will be deciding who the next president will be?

And what about the criticism that the electoral system does not easily convert into a governing system, that it reduces, not enhances, the president's ability to exert strong leadership? Any electoral system that regularly produces mixed messages, divided government, and fragile governing coalitions cannot be an effective instrument of and for democratic government. Yet, do Americans want Congress to dutifully follow the president's lead all or most of the time? Do they want to upset the checks and balances? Do they want to reduce or abolish the federal system of representation in the electoral process in general or in the Electoral College in particular?

These are tough questions for most Americans. The strength of American democracy is that they will continue to be debated, that change is possible as society evolves. However, given the potential impact of electoral change on governing and on public policy, change should be deliberative and derivative of the entire system, not just elections and democracy or the Electoral College and the presidency.

Notes

1. The Supreme Court's resolution of the 2000 presidential election is a case in point. A divided Court ruled in favor of Bush in the case of *Bush v. Gore*. Despite the strong partisan emotions that the Florida vote controversy and Supreme Court's decision generated, Americans accepted the judgment. According to a Gallup poll conducted after the Court's verdict, almost half the population believed that Bush had won the election fair and square, 32 percent thought he had won it on a technicality, and 18 percent felt he had stolen it. See David Moore, "One Year after Election, Controversy over Winner Appears Less Serious," Gallup News Service Press Release, November 6, 2001. After Bush's first few weeks in office, 57 percent of the population approved of the job he was doing. See "Presidential Ratings: Job Approval," Gallup Poll, February 2001. In short, the public had accepted the Court's verdict and had moved on.

2. Jack N. Rakove, "Presidential Selection: Electoral Fallacies," *Political Science Quarterly* 119 (Spring 2004), 24–30.

3. The Voting Rights Act did away with literacy tests in federal elections for all citizens who had received a sixth-grade education in an American school. Where less than 50 percent of the people in an electoral district were registered to vote, the law authorized the government to send federal registrars to facilitate their registration. Subsequently, Congress also reduced the residence requirement for voting in federal elections to 30 days.

4. In 1968, only about one-third of the convention delegates were selected in primary elections; four years later that percentage had increased to 60 for the Democrats and 53 for the Republicans. Today between 85 and 90 percent of the delegates are chosen in state primaries. See Wayne, *The Road to the White House 2004,* 12.

5. In theory the percentage of the vote that candidates won was to be reflected in the percentage of the state's delegates they received. But candidates also had to reach a certain threshold, usually 15 percent of the vote, in order to be eligible for delegates.

6. Democrats won back control of the Senate in 1986 and maintained it through 2000. A 50-50 tie in the 2000 election gave Vice President Cheney the tie-breaking vote and the Republicans a majority until Senator James Jeffords defected from the Republican Party and threw his support to the Democrats. In 2002 the Republicans won a majority and expanded it in 2004.

7. Significant gender differences also began to emerge in the 1980s, with women more Democratic and men more Republican. Religious differences have also become evident, with Republicans receiving more support from sectarian communities and Democrats from those with more secular views.

8. Keith Melder, *Hail to the Candidate* (Washington, D.C.: Smithsonian Institution, 1992), 48–49.

9. Lynda Lee Kaid and Anne Johnson, "Negative versus Positive Television Advertising in U.S. Presidential Campaigns, 1960–1988," *Journal of Communications* 41 (Summer 1991), 54; L. Patrick Devlin, "Contrasts in Presidential Campaign Commercials of 1988," *American Behavioral Scientist* 32 (March/April 1989), 389; L. Patrick Devlin, "Contrasts in Presidential Campaign Commercials of 1992," *American Behavioral Scientist* (November 1993), 288; L. Patrick Devlin, "Contrasts in Presidential Campaign Commercials of 1996," *American Behavioral Scientist* (August 1997), 1064; West, *Air Wars*, 69.

10. By the end of 2003, over 500,000 names had been collected from those who accessed the Dean Web site and listed their e-mail addresses.

11. For a study of election mandates, see Conley, *Presidential Mandates.*

12. For an excellent discussion of democracy, see Dahl, *On Democracy.* Dahl has written extensively on the subject. Three of his other well known works on democracy and its application to the United States are: *A Preface to Democratic Theory* (Chicago: University of Chicago Press, 1956); *Democracy and Its Critics* (New Haven, Conn.: Yale University Press, 1989); and *How Democratic Is the American Constitution?* (New Haven, Conn.: Yale University Press, 2001).

13. Robert A. Dahl, *Democracy, Liberty, and Equality* (London: Norwegian University Press, 1986), 198–199.

14. James Madison argues in *Federalist Paper* 10 that one of the advantages of a large republican government was that it made it difficult for factions to coalesce and dominate the government.

15. The Electoral College compromised two contentious issues: the influence of the large and small states and the division of authority between the federal government and the states in the selection of the president.

16. In 1876, a dispute over 20 electoral votes and a resolution of it by a congressional commission, accepted by Congress, resulted in the election of Republican Rutherford B. Hayes, who had fewer popular votes than his opponent, Samuel J. Tilden. In 1888, Republican Benjamin Harrison received a majority of the electoral votes while his opponent, President Grover Cleveland, received a majority of the popular votes.

17. For an excellent critique of the faulty premises on which the perceived small state advantage is based, see Edwards, *Why the Electoral College Is Bad for America.*

18. To enact such an amendment requires a vote of two-thirds of the House and Senate and three-fourths of the states.

19. Judith Best, *The Case against Direct Election of the President: A Defense of the Electoral College* (Ithaca, N.Y.: Cornell University Press, 1975); Judith Best, "Presidential Selection: Complex Problems and Simple Solutions," *Political Science Quarterly* (Spring 2004), 39–59.

20. For a critical discussion of these proposals and their consequences see Wayne, *The Road to the White House 2004*, 321–325.

21. Thirteen states permanently disfranchise felons and those who have been dishonorably discharged from the military. The restrictions disproportionately affect one

demographic group: African American males. Of the 10.5 million African American males, 1.5 million have been temporarily or permanently disfranchised.

22. Curtis Gans, "President Bush, Mobilization Drives Propel Turnout to Post-1968 High," Center for the Study of the American Electorate, November 4, 2004.

23. The terrorist attacks of September 11, 2001, the U.S. response to them, and the continuing threat of domestic and international terrorism may become such a defining event for younger Americans who come of voting age during this period.

24. Paul R. Abramson, John H. Aldrich, and David W. Rohde, *Change and Continuity in the 2000 Elections,* 88.

25. This argument was expressed by Bernard Berelson, Paul F. Lazarfeld, and William McPhee in their book *Voting* (Chicago: University of Chicago Press, 1954).

26. There is considerable empirical data that lends support to this position. See *Why Don't Americans Trust Government?* (*Washington Post,* Kaiser Family Foundation, and Harvard University, 1996) and *Deconstructing Distrust* (Pew Research Center for the People and the Press, 1998).

27. Verba, Schlozman, and Brady have also found economic and education differences among people who try to influence policy decisions and those who do not try to do so. See Sidney Verba, Kay Lehman Schlozman, and Henry E. Brady, *Voice and Equality: Civic Volunteerism in American Politics* (Cambridge, Mass.: Harvard University Press), 512.

28. The law also requires provisional voting for those whose registration is challenged at the polls.

29. "'04 Elections Expected to Cost Nearly $4 Billion," Center for Responsive Politics, October 21, 2004, at http://www.opensecrets.org/pressrelease/2004/04spending .asp (accessed November 8, 2004.)

30. "2004 Presidential Race," Center for Responsive Politics, at http://www.opensecrets .org/presidential/summary.asp (accessed December 21, 2004).

31. After a lackluster start, Kerry ran out of funds and lent his campaign $6.4 million, which he obtained from a mortgage on one of his houses. Without those funds, he probably would not have been able to mount effective campaigns in Iowa and New Hampshire and might not have won the nomination. His campaign subsequently repaid his loan.

32. There are individual state spending limits based on the size of the state and overall expenditure limits for the nomination period. In 2004, the overall limits were about $49 million, which included money for fund-raising, campaign advertising, salaries, office expenses, and legal and accounting costs.

33. Campaign Finance Institute, "CFI Analysis of the Presidential Candidates' Financial Reports Filed June 20," July 23, 2004.

34. A survey conducted for the Center for Responsive Politics in 1997 found that more than half of those surveyed believe that money often affects whether candidates win or lose. "Money and Politics: A National Survey of the Public's Views on How Money Impacts our Political System," question 20B.

35. According to the "Money and Politics" survey, 50 percent believe that money often "gets someone appointed to office who would not otherwise be considered," and 55 percent believe that money often "gives one group more influence by keeping another from having its fair say." Ibid. See also Pew Research Center for the People

and the Press, *Deconstructing Distrust* (Washington, D.C., 1998). Another national survey, this one conducted by the Center on Policy Attitudes in January 1999, found a majority believing that the government is run by special interests, not for the benefit of all the people. See "Expecting More Say: The American Public on Its Role in Government Decisionmaking," Center on Policy Attitudes, question 12.

36. Party committees can receive up to $57,500 per election cycle from individuals, and nonparty groups can receive unlimited amounts. For example, in the 2004 election cycle, financier George Soros and insurance magnate Peter Lewis each gave Democratic-oriented groups millions of dollars.

37. Thomas E. Patterson and Robert D. McClure, *The Unseeing Eye* (New York: Putnam, 1975), 58; Craig Leonard Brians and Martin P. Wattenberg, "Comparing Issue Knowledge and Salience: Comparing Reception from TV Commercials, TV News, and Newspapers," *American Journal of Political Science* (February 1996), 172–193.

38. A study by the Annenberg Center for Public Policy of issue-advocacy ads in the 2000 election found that about two-thirds of the party ads contained some attack against the opposing candidates. This figure rose to 84 percent in the last two months of the election. See *Issue Advocacy in the 2000 Election Cycle,* February 1, 2001.

39. Ansolabehere and Iyengar, Going Negative, 147–150.

40. Richard R. Lau, Lee Sigelman, Caroline Heldman, and Paul Babbitt, "The Effects of Negative Political Advertisements: A Meta-Analytic Assessment," *American Political Science Review* 93 (December 1999), 860.

41. In his study of campaign advertising, West notes that people tend to remember the ad more than the criticism of it. West, *Air Wars,* 86.

42. In distinguishing itself from other news networks, Fox claims that its news is "fair and balanced" and implies the other networks are not; most liberals see it the other way around.

43. Pew Research Center for the People and the Press, "Media Seen as Fair But Tilting toward Gore," October 15, 2000, 12, and "Voters Liked Campaign 2004, But Too Much 'Mud-Slinging,'" November 11, 2004.

44. Stephen Hess, "Hess Report on Campaign Coverage in Nightly Network News," Brookings Institution, November 7, 2000. See also Farnsworth and Lichter, *The Nightly News Nightmare.*

45. "Take This Campaign—Please," *Media Monitor* (September/October 1996), 2–3; Center for Media and Public Affairs, "Journalists Monopolize TV News."

46. Hess, "Hess Report." See also Jeff Leeds, "Study Finds Negative Media Political Coverage—Especially for Gore," *Los Angeles Times* (November 1, 2000).

47. Pew Research Center for the People and the Press, "Campaign 2000 Highly Rated," November 16, 2000, and "Voters Liked Campaign 2004, But Too Much 'Mud-Slinging,'" November 11, 2004.

48. For a discussion of mandates see Robert A. Dahl, "A Myth of the Presidential Mandate," *Political Science Quarterly* 105 (Fall 1990), 355–372.

49. Jeff Fishel, *Presidents and Promises* (Washington, D.C.: Congressional Quarterly, 1994), 38, 42–43.

50. Clinton succeeded on the third, legislation to achieve deficit reduction, but was forced to modify his original proposal significantly before he could to gain sufficient congressional support to get it enacted into law.

51. Second term presidents are not eligible for reelection, thereby diminishing their accountability to the electorate. They may still be impeached, however.

Bibliography

Abramson, Paul R., John H. Aldrich, Phil Paolino, and David W. Rhode. "Third-Party and Independent Candidates in American Politics: Wallace, Anderson, and Perot." *Political Science Quarterly* 110 (1995), 349–367.

Abramson, Paul R., John H. Aldrich, and David W. Rhode. *Change and Continuity in the 2000 and 2002 Elections.* Washington, D.C.: Congressional Quarterly, 2003.

Ansolabehere, Stephen, and Shanto Iyengar. *Going Negative: How Political Advertisements Shrink and Polarize the Electorate.* New York: Free Press, 1995.

Bennett, Stephen Earl, and David Resnick. "The Implications of Nonvoting for Democracy in the United States." *American Journal of Political Science* 34 (1990), 771–802.

Conley, Patricia Heidotting. *Presidential Mandates: How Elections Shape the National Agenda.* Chicago: University of Chicago Press, 2001.

Dahl, Robert A. *On Democracy.* New Haven, Conn.: Yale University Press, 1998.

Dahl, Robert A. *How Democratic Is the American Constitution?* New Haven, Conn.: Yale University Press, 2001.

Edwards, George C., III. *Why the Electoral College Is Bad for America.* New Haven, Conn.: Yale University Press, 2004.

Erikson, Robert S. "The 2000 Presidential Election in Historical Perspective." *Political Science Quarterly* 116 (2001), 29–52.

Farnsworth, Stephen J., and S. Robert Lichter. *The Nightly News Nightmare: Network Television's Coverage of U.S. Presidential Elections, 1988–2000.* Lanham, Md.: Rowman & Littlefield, 2003.

Fishel, Jeff. *Presidents and Promises.* Washington, D.C.: Congressional Quarterly, 1985.

Fortier, John C., ed. *After the People Vote: A Guide to the Electoral College.* Washington, D.C.: The AEI Press, 2004.

Kelley, Stanley. *Interpreting Elections.* Princeton, N.J.: Princeton University Press, 1983.

Lewis, Charles. *The Buying of the President 2004.* New York: HarperCollins, 2004.

Mayer, William G. *The Making of the Presidential Candidates 2004.* Lanham, Md.: Rowman & Littlefield, 2004.

Patterson, Thomas E. *The Vanishing Voter: Public Involvement in an Age of Uncertainty.* New York: Knopf, 2002.

Tenpas, Kathryn Dunn. *Presidents as Candidates: Inside the White House for the Presidential Campaign.* New York: Garland, 1997.

Troy, Gil. *See How They Ran: The Changing Role of the Presidential Candidate.* New York: Free Press, 1991.

Wayne, Stephen J. *Is This Any Way To Run a Democratic Election?* 2nd ed. Boston: Houghton Mifflin, 2003.

Wayne, Stephen J. *The Road to the White House 2004.* Belmont, CA.: Thompson/ Wadsworth, 2004.

West, Darrell M. *Air Wars.* 3rd ed. Washington, D.C.: Congressional Quarterly, 2001.

5

THE EXECUTIVE OFFICE OF THE PRESIDENT: THE PARADOX OF POLITICIZATION

Matthew J. Dickinson

A PRESIDENT'S EFFECTIVENESS AS A LEADER IS OFTEN attributed to his individual qualities—his intelligence, knowledge, temperament, and experiences. Although the presidency is an intensely personal office, how well a president leads is not simply a function of who he (someday she) is. Leadership also depends upon institutional factors, particularly the roles and routines of the almost two thousand men and women working in the Executive Office of the President (EOP). Formally established in 1939, the EOP is not so much a single office as it is an umbrella organization that today shelters more than a dozen presidential staff agencies of varying significance (see Table 1).[1] Because presidents rely on these agencies for administrative support, advice, and expertise, presidential leadership in the modern era is as much an institutional phenomenon as a personal one.

To better understand the institutional side of presidential leadership, this chapter examines the origins and evolution of the most significant EOP staff agencies. These include the White House Office (WHO) and related policy staffs, and the Office of Management and Budget (OMB).[2] These staff agencies are responsible for tasks that are closely linked to the president's daily activities, and thus directly affect the exercise of presidential power. Presidents are keenly aware of the important role these agencies play, and therefore prefer to staff them at the highest levels with individuals who share their political and policy goals. However, personnel hired for their ideological compatibility with the president do not always possess the experience or knowledge necessary to help the presi-

TABLE 1

The Executive Office of the President

Agency	Employees	Year Established
White House Office	406	1939
(Includes Homeland Security Staff)		(2001)
Office of the Vice President	24	1972
Office of Management and Budget	521	1921
Office of Administration	212	1977
Council of Economic Advisers	28	1946
Council on Environmental Quality	22	1969
Office of Policy Development	32	1970
(includes National Economic Council)		(1993)
(includes Domestic Council)		(1993)
Executive Residence at the White House	90	
National Security Council	54	1947
Office of National Drug Control Policy	102	1988
Office of Science and Technology Policy	28	1976
Office of the U.S. Trade Representative	212	1963
Total EOP Employment (as of May 2004)	1,731	

SOURCE: Office of Personnel Management

dent achieve his objectives, particularly if the hires lack government experience at the national level. This dynamic, in which presidents staff the major EOP agencies with politically responsive but administratively inexperienced aides, creates what might be labeled the paradox of politicization: by recruiting presidential aides on the basis of political loyalty, the EOP agencies are often less competent at helping presidents govern. Over time, this lack of administrative effectiveness can erode a president's political support.

Ideally, of course, presidents want staff agencies to exhibit both administrative competence and political responsiveness.[3] That is, they seek politically "neutral" aides who can provide expert advice, analysis, and administrative service free of partisan bias. At the same time, however, they want these advisors to support and, preferably, share the president's political preferences. As this chapter will make clear, however, encompassing both "neutral competence" and political responsiveness within one advisory system has proven difficult. Particularly since the 1970s, the president's need for political loyalty has tended to trump his desire for nonpartisan expertise. The result is a pattern of institutional development in which administrative power within the EOP has gravitated toward the White House Office, the most politically responsive of the presidential staff agencies. At the same time, presidents have increased the number of political appointees at the upper levels of the non–White House EOP agencies, and brought the agencies more tightly under White House staff control. The end result is a more thoroughly politicized, White House–dominated EOP, but one that is short on institutional memory, administrative expertise, and organizational continuity.

This was not the intent of those, particularly President Franklin D. Roosevelt, who created the EOP in 1939. As described more thoroughly below, Roosevelt and his presidential successors, at least through Lyndon B. Johnson, sought to strengthen and protect the EOP's capacity for neutral competence. This meant developing a presidential staff system that, outside the White House proper, was dominated by career civil servants possessing extensive knowledge of government programs and processes. In an era of strong political support for government activism, neutrally competent staffs benefited presidents politically.

It is true that Roosevelt's successors also increased the size and influence of the White House Office. But for the most part, the WHO's political staff remained separate from the career-dominated EOP agencies outside the White House. Presidents thus could draw on two relatively separate sources of staff support, political and institutional, espousing different perspectives and with different skills and expertise.[4]

But developments in the 1960s and 1970s altered the context of presidential leadership. In an era of growing budget deficits, divided government, a more open political process, and a general loss of public faith in "big government," presidents beginning with Richard Nixon no longer saw unalloyed benefits in relying on "neutral" staff agencies. Instead, they sought greater political responsiveness. This meant relying more heavily on aides within the White House Office, and appointing political loyalists to exercise top-down control of the other EOP agencies.

This trend has not been without controversy. Numerous critics in both academia and government argue that a more politicized staff tends to elevate the president's short-term political interest above longer term, more substantive and broad-based concerns. Moreover, they argue, when presidential decisions are evaluated by their likely impact on the president's political standing rather than the presidency as an institution, the leadership capabilities of the executive office actually suffer. The result over time, critics claim, is that presidents lose political influence as well.

To reverse the trend toward a politicized presidency, and to restore some semblance of a more neutrally competent staff system, some reformers advocate significant changes to the EOP. These include reducing White House staff size and, presumably, its influence; revitalizing the traditional presidential Cabinet as a source of administrative support; and restoring the influence of career civil servants within the EOP. Although presidents often voice support for all these proposals, they have as yet shown little inclination to adopt them.

Those who are skeptical of reform argue that presidents' reluctance to embrace administrative change is perfectly understandable. Given increasing demands for—and constraints on—presidential leadership, presidents have no choice but to strengthen those staff agencies, especially the White House, most amenable to their control. From the skeptics' perspective, exhorting presidents to resist politicizing the presidency is naive because it ignores the strategic realities that drive presidents to pursue responsive competence in the first place.

Reformers and skeptics do agree on one thing: simply pinpointing the flaws of the politicized presidency cannot by itself justify reform. Rather, the costs and benefits of politicization must be weighed against those of administrative alternatives. How effective would presidents be without politicized staff support? Moreover, even if reform is desirable, presidents cannot be expected to undertake it singlehandedly, given the deep-seated nature of the forces driving politicization in the first place. Instead, significant and lasting administrative reform will require not only more widespread changes to the American political system, but also the collective action of the nation's major political actors and institutions, especially Congress and leaders in both political parties. Barring such a concerted effort, it is likely that presidents will continue to rely on an EOP that exhibits responsive, and not neutral, competence.

The rest of this chapter, building on this initial framework, is constructed as follows. The first section describes the evolution of the presidential staff system, beginning with a brief history of staffing during the premodern presidential era. This is followed by a close examination of the EOP's origins under Franklin D. Roosevelt. Section two turns to a more detailed examination of the history of the White House Office and the related policy staffs, and the OMB. Section three examines the forces that have compelled presidents, particularly Richard Nixon, to pursue politicization, and analyzes some of the consequences of politicization for presidential leadership. Section four discusses the likelihood and desirability of administrative reform. The chapter concludes by placing the paradox of the politicized EOP within the larger context of the longstanding American ambivalence toward executive leadership.

The Evolution of the Presidential Staff

Historically speaking, the EOP is of relatively recent vintage. Until the early twentieth century, the presidency consisted almost entirely of the president and a handful of aides with clerical functions. Not infrequently, these aides were presidential relatives paid out of the president's salary; Congress did not appropriate separate funds for a presidential staff until 1857. Even then, it remained small in size and influence. On the cusp of the twentieth century, President William

McKinley's staff totaled about a dozen aides, including one political secretary, two assistant secretaries, and two executive clerks. Presidential staffs remained roughly this size during the next three decades.

For policy advice and broader administrative support, presidents in this pre-modern period relied primarily on the traditional Cabinet, an extraconstitutional body consisting of the heads of the major executive branch departments. Additional advice came from informal "kitchen" cabinets, composed of party leaders, other politicos, and even friends. Cabinet members, however, were often the president's chief political rivals, with their allegiance typically divided between the president who appointed them and a Congress that provided departmental funding and implementing legislation. Moreover, as the Cabinet grew larger and more substantively diverse with the addition of new departments, beginning in the mid-nineteenth century, it became less useful as a source of support geared toward the president's broader administrative perspective. Others on whom presidents relied, such as fellow partisans in Congress or local politicians, often found their political allegiance to the president in tension with their institutional loyalties. And acquaintances and friends frequently lacked the access and expertise needed to knowledgeably advise presidents.

Congress took an initial step to provide the president with a truly presidential staff in 1921, when it passed and President Warren Harding signed the Budget and Accounting Act. The legislation established the Bureau of the Budget (BoB) within the Treasury Department to assist the president in developing an executive budget. In addition, the BoB was expected to provide presidents with organizational advice and expertise. During the next decade, the BoB discharged its duties by focusing predominantly on holding down government expenditures and reducing waste and inefficiency. This cost-cutting mentality sufficed during the period of economic growth and balanced budgets, and for the relatively small federal government that characterized the Republican presidencies of Harding, Calvin Coolidge, and Herbert Hoover. But it proved woefully inadequate when Franklin D. Roosevelt took office in 1933 and proceeded to expand the size and scope of the federal government to combat the Great Depression.

Roosevelt, with congressional acquiescence, created a range of New Deal relief and recovery programs designed to resuscitate the nation's free-enterprise system and to help citizens cope with economic dislocation and rising unemployment. By increasing federal spending and expanding the budget deficit, however, FDR rendered the BoB's single-minded focus on cost control and balanced budgets increasingly less relevant. The traditional Cabinet, meanwhile, now swelled by the addition of many new federal agencies, grew more unwieldy and even less useful as a means of coordinating the increasingly complex and interrelated series of New Deal programs.

By the end of FDR's first term, it became clear that, in the famous words of the President's Committee on Administrative Management (better known as the

Brownlow Committee), "the president needs help."[5] Roosevelt appointed the Brownlow Committee in 1936 to draw up a blueprint for reorganizing the executive branch and modernizing the presidential office. The intent was to give FDR a managerial capacity commensurate with his growing responsibilities. Acting on recommendations contained in the Committee's 1937 report, Roosevelt in 1939 formally established the EOP.[6] However, Roosevelt's organizational blueprint for a neutrally competent EOP was gradually superseded by his successors' desire for a more politically responsive staff system. The following section looks more closely at FDR's original plan for the EOP—and why it eventually was discarded.

Establishing the EOP: The Era of Neutral Competence

In his September 10, 1939, press release announcing the EOP's establishment, Roosevelt explained that the "task of general supervision and over-all management . . . rest upon the President as the Constitutional Chief Executive." Citing the growing size and complexity of government and the concomitant increase in presidential responsibilities, he argued that this "particular responsibility of the President requires better organization." The newly created EOP, therefore, "must be molded into a compact organization, with the functions and duties of each unit carefully defined and with systematic procedures developed. . . . Only after this has been accomplished will the President have adequate machinery for the business like handling of his job."[7] As its title—*the* Executive Office of the President—suggests, FDR intended the EOP to be a single institution with a unified purpose.

At the start, it consisted of five staff agencies of varying size and significance. These included the White House Office (WHO), the Bureau of the Budget (BoB), a National Resources Planning Board (NRPB), a Liaison Office for Personnel Management, and an Office of Government Reports.[8] As noted above, Roosevelt's administrative plan was based on recommendations contained in the 1937 Brownlow Committee report. The Committee advocated equipping the president with several presidential staff agencies responsible for the major "managerial" functions of budgeting, personnel, policy planning, reporting, and auditing, as well as a sweeping reorganization of the executive branch. Significantly, under the original Brownlow plan, the White House staff would increase by not more than a half dozen administrative assistants, no larger than what the president could personally supervise. The aides would demonstrate a "passion for anonymity," operating largely behind the scenes without any independent basis of power. They were not to supplant the role of the Cabinet as presidential advisors. The Committee did not recommend—nor would FDR have accepted—a White House staff of the size and level of functional specialization and administrative layering that came to characterize his successors' presidential staffs.

After the report was published in 1937, however, Congress blocked legislative efforts to implement its recommendations for the next two years. This was partly a reaction to FDR's failed attempt in 1937 to "pack" the Supreme Court with sympathetic justices and to his later, largely unsuccessful effort to intervene in his party's 1938 midterm congressional nominating process. It also reflected congressional unease about executive branch reorganization, which threatened existing political relations with key constituency groups.[9] By 1939, Roosevelt realized he could not win legislative approval to reorganize the executive branch. Nor would Congress give him the control over personnel policy and the auditing of governmental expenditures that he sought. He narrowed his focus, therefore, and used his reorganization authority to implement a more limited version of Brownlow's proposals. Pursuant to authority granted by the 1939 Reorganization Act, FDR established the EOP, including the WHO, and transferred several agencies, including the BoB, into it.

By creating the EOP, FDR sought to provide, in Hugh Heclo's words, "a fairly coherent central capability to bring greater unity of purpose and consistency of action to the executive branch."[10] To do so, the EOP was organized on three broad conceptual premises. First, its component staff agencies were responsible for those managerial tasks that were inherently executive and could not be performed elsewhere. Second, the EOP was not to engage in policy making; its primary task was to provide, through the staff agencies' control of the major managerial functions, a means for presidents to better manage the policy-making process. Policy proposals would still primarily emanate from the Cabinet departments and other executive branch agencies. Roosevelt's small corps of White House aides would facilitate this process by developing substantive expertise in particular policy areas, consulting with department officials as needed. But they would not develop their own policy-making capability—they were facilitators, expeditors, and information seekers, backstopped by the staff of the institutional agencies in charge of the major management functions.

Perhaps most importantly, Roosevelt envisioned an EOP that was largely staffed by careerists with extensive governmental experience, rather than by political appointees. Further, he hoped that many would be generalists, rather than specialists, who would broaden their perspective by periodically rotating through the White House Office, giving it a career component as well. In this vein, FDR asked acting BoB director Daniel Bell, a civil servant with eleven years of experience in the Treasury Department, to become the permanent BoB director. When Bell refused because he did not want to lose his civil service status, FDR did not replace him with a Democratic political supporter. Instead, he hired Harold Smith, a registered Republican with extensive management experience at the state level. One other political appointee assisted Smith as assistant director. With these two exceptions, the BoB was staffed entirely by career civil servants.

Roosevelt's creation of the EOP is justly celebrated as a landmark in the evolution of the modern presidency. It is important to remember, however, that Roosevelt's initial staffing arrangements survived his presidency only in altered form. In part, this was due to the onset of World War II, which diverted FDR's attention from the sustained focus needed to see the EOP through its inevitable growing pains. Congress, never enamored of the NRPB planning function, cut its appropriations to nothing in 1943, and the office ceased operations. The Liaison Office for Personnel Management had proved to be of little administrative use to FDR or his successor, Harry Truman; after a period of neglect, its functions were transferred to the Civil Service Commission in 1953. The Office of Government Reports was absorbed by the Office of War Information in 1942 and, after a brief resurrection in 1946, was permanently interred in 1948.

In significant respects, however, the basic structure of FDR's EOP endured beyond his administration. Most notably, the Bureau of the Budget entered its "golden age"—a period that lasted through Truman's presidency—and subsisted in somewhat diminished form through the early part of Lyndon B. Johnson's presidency.[11] During the decade after its transfer into the EOP, the BoB grew in size from less than fifty to six hundred employees, acquired new functions, and broadened old ones. A Division of Fiscal Analysis was established within the agency to analyze the economic impact of the government's tax and spending policies, a response to the growing use of the federal budget in a fiscally compensatory fashion. The BoB's legislative clearance function expanded beyond a narrow focus on enrolled bills (those passed by Congress and awaiting the president's signature or veto) to a broader assessment of whether legislative proposals emanating from the executive branch were in accord with the president's program. This change strengthened the president's legislative agenda–setting power. The BoB's newly established Division of Administrative Management developed into an important source of organizational and management advice, particularly during World War II.[12]

In short, in the decade after the EOP's formal creation, the BoB provided the president with a ready source of institutional input and expanded administrative capacity, much as FDR had intended. Even as the BoB grew larger and more powerful, however, the White House Office retained its intimate character as a personal staff to the president, with its primary responsibilities centered on his daily activities. During FDR's presidency, its budgeted size remained at roughly 40 aides, although this number excludes the 120 or so clerical staff detailed to work in the White House while on the payroll of other agencies. At the senior staff level, Roosevelt's three political secretaries continued to handle relations with the press, Congress, and the public, as well as his correspondence, appointments, and scheduling. The additional half-dozen administrative assistants authorized by the 1939 Reorganization Plan performed largely as FDR had anticipated, gathering intelligence, acquiring some substantive expertise, and engaging in troubleshooting on his behalf. But the WHO did not develop much coordinative capacity, and Roosevelt never bothered to designate an aide to manage the White House Office on his behalf, in large part because the WHO never grew larger than he could personally supervise.[13]

There is evidence that Roosevelt planned additional changes to the EOP. He asked Louis Brownlow in 1943 to submit recommendations for its postwar organization. Brownlow responded with a plan for a series of interdepartmental Cabinet committees that would serve a policy-making function. The president's assistants would manage these committees, and a strengthened BoB would be responsible for monitoring the policies they produced and for reporting back to the president. These Cabinet-level councils seem to foreshadow the subsequent establishment of the national security, domestic, homeland security, and economic policy councils (described more fully below). But Roosevelt rejected Brownlow's plan, saying, "He has not got the answer yet. I don't think anyone has. I am a bumblebee. I am going to keep on bumbling."[14]

Politicizing the EOP: The Growth of the White House Office and the Policy Staffs

Where Roosevelt's "bumbling" would have led will never been known. But it is difficult to believe that he would have countenanced the trend during the next six decades toward a White House–centered, more thoroughly politicized EOP. Figure 1 shows that the EOP personnel more than doubled in number from 1940 through May 2004.[15] During the same period, its budget grew from $2.8 million to $387 million. More importantly, much of that growth was centered in the White House Office—a clear violation of FDR's precept that this personal political staff grow no larger than the president could personally supervise. Figure 2 shows the increase in the WHO budgeted staff from 1940 to 2004.

Figure 2 includes White House political aides and clerical staff. However, it understates the White House staff's actual operating size, because it does not account for presidents' use of detailees (aides working full-time in the White House while on the payroll of other agencies). Nor does it include aides paid out of special funds outside the White House budget. And it excludes most of the aides working on the various policy staffs. Accordingly, a more realistic view of the White House staff size is presented in Figure 3, which includes all aides who work for the White House, the policy staffs, and aides detailed to work in the White House while on different payrolls.

Figure 3 reveals a relatively steady increase in White House staff size, from approximately 225 aides at FDR's death to more than 670 at its peak during Richard Nixon's presidency. Thereafter, staff totals fell somewhat to a bit more than 500 aides by Ronald Reagan's second year in office, and they have remained at roughly this level through George W. Bush's presidency in 2004. Although

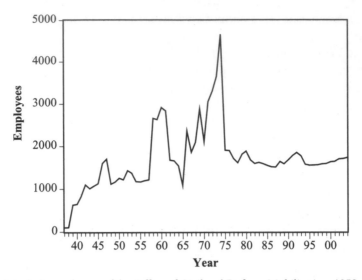

NOTE: Totals include employees of the Office of Civil and Defense Mobilization, 1958–61, and the Office of Emergency Preparedness, 1968–73.

SOURCE: United States budget, successive years.

Figure 1   Total Employment, Executive Office of the President, 1937–2004

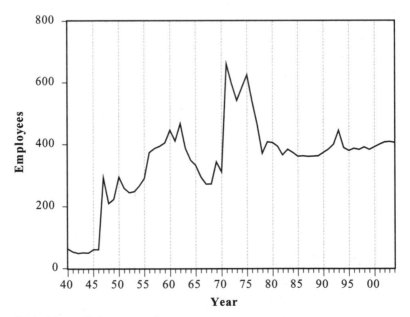

SOURCE: United States Budget, successive years.

Figure 2   Budgeted White House Staff, 1940–2004

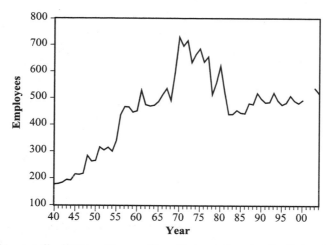

NOTE: Combines staff of White House office, National Security Staff, the Office of Policy Development (including the Domestic and National Economic councils), Special Projects, and detailed aides. (Detailed aides not available for 2001–02.)

SOURCE: Federal Civilian Workplace Statistics, successive years. Detailees, 1979–2004, from White House "Aggregate Report on Personnel Pursuant to Title 3, United States Code, Section 113." Details and Special Projects, 1934–78, from the *Congressional Record* (April 4, 1978), 8643.

Figure 3   "Real" White House Staff Growth, 1940–2004

there is tremendous variation in staff totals from year to year, the largest staff increase took place during Nixon's presidency in the years 1969–1972, when the White House staff added more than 200 aides.[16]

This large jump in total White House staff size mirrors a significant increase in Nixon's "senior" White House staff as well. The annual *United States Government Manual* lists all aides working in the White House Office and, beginning in 1970, in the Domestic Council and its various successor staffs, with titles that include "to the president."[17] The phrase indicates that these aides have received presidential commissions, signifying that they occupy upper-level White House positions that possess significant policy or political functions. Figure 4 shows the annual change in the numbers of these senior White House officials.

Again, there was a significant jump during Nixon's presidency; the number of assistants to the president almost doubled during his first year in office, from 23 to 40, and rose above 50 within the next year. Although there were also substantial increases in the number of senior-level White House staff under Presidents Reagan and Clinton, judging by their staff titles these later increases did not involve the acquisition of new White House staff functions. Instead, they signify a growth in the number of senior staff performing existing functions. The "standard model" of the modern White House staff was essentially

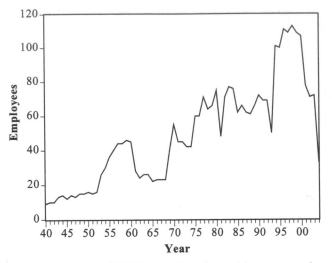

NOTE: Bush White House listing for 2004 does not include special assistants to the president.

SOURCE: United States Government Manual, successive years.

Figure 4   White House Staff Listed in U.S. Government Manual, 1937–2004

established during Nixon's presidency, with his successors largely building on those precedents.

As discussed in the next section, the story is essentially the same when looking at the history of the presidential staffs dealing with national security, domestic, economic and—most recently—homeland security policy. It is Nixon who primarily transformed the National Security Council (NSC) staff into the president's personal foreign policy staff, and who created the Domestic Council and staff. Although Presidents Bill Clinton and George W. Bush later added economic and homeland security councils and staffs, these are largely based on Nixon's domestic staff model. In each instance, the council staffs have come to dominate the councils for which they ostensibly work. Moreover, although formally located outside the White House Office, these policy staffs are all directed by, and largely composed of, the president's White House staff. For all intents and purposes, then, they are extensions of the White House Office.

The National Security Staff

The earliest manifestation of a formal policy-making capability within the EOP took place outside the White House Office. In 1947 Congress created the National Security Council (Public Law 80-253) consisting of the president, the secretaries of State, Defense, Army, Navy, and Air Force, and the chairman of the newly created National Security Resources Board.[18] The Council was charged with advising the president "with respect to the integration of domestic, foreign, and military policies relating to national security."[19] This legislation also unified the military services within a National Military Establishment (renamed the Department of Defense in 1949), established the Joint Chiefs of Staff, and created the Central Intelligence Agency—all part of the post–World War II reorganization of the United States' military and intelligence services. Under a 1949 legislative amendment (P.L. 81-216), the civilian secretaries of the three military branches were removed from membership on the NSC, and it was officially incorporated into the EOP.

Significantly, neither the 1947 statute nor the 1949 amendment speak in any detail about an NSC staff; the only staff position explicitly authorized under either act is that of the executive secretary: "The Council shall have a staff to be headed by a civilian executive secretary who shall be appointed by the President. . . ."[20] Additional organizational details were to be left to the president's discretion. Clearly, however, Congress did not intend to create, nor did President Truman want, an independent national security staff serving the president. Indeed, Truman opposed legislation creating the NSC, which he saw as an attempt to constrain his foreign policy-making role. Congress, however, reacting to FDR's unilateral diplomatic and military leadership during World War II, was determined to force Truman to consult more broadly when making foreign policy.

Although Truman signed legislation creating the NSC into law—the price to be paid for unifying the military services—he refused to even meet with the Council on a regular basis until the Korean War. During his presidency the NSC staff grew no larger than about twenty aides, supplemented by about a dozen more assistants on loan from other departments. These aides performed primarily clerical functions: preparing agendas, circulating papers, and reviewing the implementation of NSC orders. They did not formulate national security policy and were not a presidential staff in any sense of the word.

As with its White House counterpart, however, during the next half century the NSC staff grew significantly larger, and it acquired new functions. More importantly, it became a separate foreign policy staff reporting directly to the president. Figure 5 provides an overview of NSC staff growth, based on monthly budget figures, for the period 1947–2004.[21] Again, as with the White House Office, these official figures probably understate the actual size of the NSC staff. An academic study published in 2000, at the start of George W. Bush's presidency, put the true size of the NSC considerably higher, at about 225 aides, including 100 or so professional staff.[22] Nevertheless, the official numbers do reveal important change points in the evolution of the NSC staff.

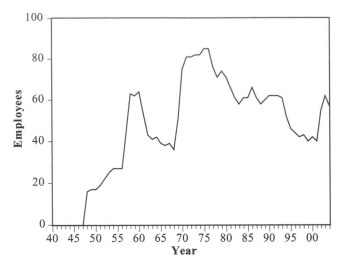

SOURCE: Federal Civilian Workforce, Monthly listings.

Figure 5   National Security Council Staff, 1947–2004

There was an initial steep increase in staff size under Dwight Eisenhower, but these figures are somewhat distorted by the inclusion of the Operations Coordination Board (OCB), which oversaw the development of strategies to implement NSC decisions. Established in 1953, the OCB was not formally incorporated into the NSC staff until 1957, which explains the jump in NSC staff size during that year. (It was later abolished by Kennedy, which largely explains the decrease in NSC staff during his presidency.)[23] Despite the increase in staff size, however, Eisenhower used the NSC staff much as Truman did: as an administrative secretariat responsible for long-term planning and clerical support to the NSC. It did not operate as a policy-making body. For day-to-day management of national security affairs, Eisenhower relied on his staff secretary, Andrew Goodpaster, working in close conjunction with his secretary of state. The NSC staff remained largely a policy planning body.

However, Eisenhower established an important precedent when he created the position of special assistant to the president for national security affairs (hereafter NSA, or national security advisor) within the White House Office in 1953. Although all of Eisenhower's national security advisors operated largely as process managers, their successors, beginning with Kennedy's NSA McGeorge Bundy, increasingly took on a policy advocacy and operational role, in effect merging Goodpaster's role with that of Eisenhower's NSA. They were assisted in this function by increasingly larger and more specialized NSC staffs. Bundy began this transformation when he moved his office from the Old Executive Office Building to the West Wing of the White House, closer to the president. Bundy also oversaw a newly created White House "situation room" that served as a communication center for important national security cable traffic. This gave the NSA independent access to national security information from overseas.

Nixon accelerated the transformation of the NSC staff into an independent advisory body, reporting directly to the president. Under his NSA Henry Kissinger's direction, the NSC staff grew to more than eighty budgeted aides, including more than fifty professionals, with dozens more detailed to the staff. Moreover, Kissinger's aides took on operational duties, including diplomatic negotiations that were formerly the province of the State Department. Indeed, by Nixon's second term, Kissinger had displaced William Rogers as Nixon's Secretary of State while maintaining his position as national security advisor.

No subsequent national security advisor has wielded as much power as Kissinger, or held dual posts as both secretary of state and national security advisor (Congress passed legislation forbidding one person from holding both positions simultaneously). Moreover, looking only at budgeted figures, NSC staffs have actually receded in size somewhat from the peak levels reached under Kissinger, although this may reflect creative bookkeeping rather than an actual reduction in personnel. Nonetheless, Nixon's successors have clearly not tried to return to the era in which the NSC staff served primarily as an administrative secretariat to the full NSC council. Instead, they have adopted the Nixon precedent in which the NSA, supported by the NSC staff, serves as their primary source of national security advice and expertise.

Moreover, presidents have continued to use the NSC staff in an operational capacity, rather than rely on members of executive branch agencies specializing in foreign policy. Thus, it was Kissinger, and not Secretary of State William Rogers, who negotiated Nixon's opening to Communist China. Similarly, Ronald Reagan's NSC advisors Robert McFarlane and John Poindexter masterminded his politically controversial effort to sell arms to Iran for the release of American hostages being held in Lebanon, and to divert excess funds from those sales to support the U.S.-backed contras in Nicaragua. And it was George W. Bush's NSC advisor Condoleezza Rice, not Secretary of State Colin Powell, who in 2003 was placed in charge of managing the administration's strategy for dealing with the post-invasion insurgency movement in Iraq.

In a little more than a half-century, then, the small staff of careerists assigned to serve the National Security Council has developed into an independent presidential foreign policy staff, composed largely of presidential appointees, whose influence now eclipses that of the statutory NSC. This was made abundantly clear during President Bush's deliberations with his key advisors in the aftermath of the attacks of September 11, 2001. In structuring his advisory organization in this period, Bush effectively eliminated any operational distinction between the formal NSC and the NSC staff. Rice, as Bush's NSA, operated as a de facto council member, on par with the council's statutory members. Bush also integrated members of his White House staff into council deliberations, essentially merging portions of the two staffs.

The point was further driven home at the start of Bush's second presidential term in 2005, when he appointed Rice as the new Secretary of State. Although Rice had to give up her NSA role (in contrast to Kissinger under Nixon), it was a clear signal that Bush intended to bring the foreign policy process under tighter White House control. (Rice's deputy, Stephen J. Hadley, became the new national security advisor.) Rice replaced Colin Powell, who had initially opposed the president's decision to invade Iraq, and who was generally viewed as the most moderate and independent member of Bush's foreign policy team. Rice's appointment, then, is entirely consistent with the longer-term trend toward a more White House–dominated foreign policy process.

The Bureau of the Budget, the White House, and the Domestic Policy Staffs

A similar trend toward White House domination has occurred on the domestic (including economic and homeland security) policy side. During the premodern presidential era, most presidents utilized the Cabinet departments as their primary source of policy ideas and legislative proposals. For the most part, however, presidents had very little means for fitting budget or legislative requests from executive branch agencies into an overall economic or policy framework. With the BoB's creation in 1921, presidents acquired greater control over the budgeting process by virtue of putting together an executive budget for congressional consideration. The BoB "cleared" budget requests, as well as related testimony, from executive branch departments; that is, it determined whether they were in accord with the president's overall economic targets. This clearance function expanded under FDR to gradually include all legislative proposals, executive orders, and finally, enrolled bills—legislation that had passed Congress and was awaiting presidential action.[24]

For the most part, this clearance process tended to be reactive, was often ignored, and frequently focused on cost containment. However, several developments beginning during Truman's presidency transformed both the clearance process and the BoB's policy development role. The first was the 1946 Employment Act, which established the three-person Council of Economic Advisers (CEA) within the EOP to provide macroeconomic advice to the president. The act also required the president to prepare an annual economic report recommending policies for maintaining "full" employment. This, in symbol if not in fact, established the president as the "manager of economic prosperity." Because presidents' political fortunes were now tied even closer to the state of the national economy, they had a stronger incentive to control macroeconomic policy making from the White House.

A second development was political. Heading into the 1948 presidential campaign, and facing an uphill battle for reelection, Truman sought to portray the Republican-controlled 80th Congress as a "do nothing" legislative body. Toward this end, Truman developed a comprehensive presidential program and submitted it to Congress, as opposed to using central clearance simply to aggregate departmental requests for legislation (for more on the development of legislative programs by modern presidents, see Andrew Rudalevige in this volume). The idea was to actively use his agenda-setting power to promote legislation and thus cast an unfavorable light on the inaction of the Republican-controlled Congress.

The BoB, under the leadership of James E. Webb, worked closely with Truman's White House staff to develop a presidential program to submit to Congress. This more proactive process of legislative development signified a subtle but important shift in the BoB's relationship to the White House, and in the domestic policy process. Gradually, senior-level White House aides began to take the lead in policy development. However, because they used the BoB as their primary staff support, policy development was subjected to the institutional input of the agency's career staff. This was an important safeguard, because it allowed presidents to balance the BoB's institutional perspective with the more political views of their White House staffs when evaluating the merits of budgetary and legislative proposals.

For the most part, the process of program development and legislative clearance that originated during Truman's administration remained formally in place through Lyndon B. Johnson's presidency. But it came under increasing pressure as both John F. Kennedy and especially LBJ gradually supplemented the normal clearance process with outside task forces in search of new policy ideas. In part, they did so because of concerns that the BoB's institutional procedures were still largely geared to the budgeting process. Moreover, the BoB's management side never provided the program analysis and coordinative capacity that presidents increasingly sought, particularly as federal programs grew larger and more complex. By the time Richard Nixon became president in 1969, momentum, in the form of recommendations by several blue-ribbon commissions for reforming the BoB and the policy development process, was already building.[25]

Nixon capitalized on that momentum by fundamentally restructuring the White House and the BoB. Acting on the recommendations of the Ash Council, a latter-day Brownlow Committee he had appointed to study executive branch organization, Nixon in 1970 created the Domestic Council to serve as a counterpart to the National Security Council.[26] It was composed of the major Cabinet departments involved in domestic policy, supported by a staff headed by a White House assistant for domestic policy.[27] Under the same reorganization act creating the Domestic Council, Nixon also transformed the BoB into the Office of Management and Budget (OMB). Nixon's actions reflected his belief that the government's social and economic programs had expanded without adequate policy planning or analysis. The intent, as Nixon put it, was for the Domestic Council to tell him what to do, and the OMB to explain how to do it. In his statement accompanying the reorganization, Nixon noted: "There does not now exist an organized, institutionally-staffed group charged with advising the Presidents on the total range of domestic policy. The Domestic Council will fill that bill."[28] Moreover, by placing the word "management" into the OMB's title, Nixon sought to emphasize what he hoped would be the agency's renewed focus on providing organizational advice. The twin efforts to get the OMB to focus more heavily on management, as opposed to its budgetary functions, and to create a stronger capacity for policy analysis within the White House, dated back at least to Eisenhower's administration, and had been recommended by two study panels appointed by Johnson, the Price task force and the Heineman task force.[29]

In fact, however, neither innovation succeeded in achieving its purpose. The OMB never developed a substantial managerial capacity. Rather than neutral competence, presidents beginning with Nixon sought to politicize the OMB's upper personnel layer in order to bring its budgeting and regulatory oversight functions under tighter White House control. Nixon added a layer of six politically appointed program associate directors (PADs) to oversee the OMB's budget-examining divisions. As part of the 1970 reorganization, he also moved the newly appointed OMB director George Schultz into the West Wing of the White House, signifying his desire for a more politically responsive budget agency. Jimmy Carter built on Nixon's precedents by adding to the OMB two politically appointed executive associate directors, one for budgeting and one for management issues.

During this period, the agency gradually moved from privately advising the president to serving as a presidential spokesperson to other political actors. David Stockman, who served as Reagan's OMB director, was the most visible example of this trend toward political responsiveness. It was under Stockman, most scholars agree, that the OMB's politicization reached its high-water mark; numerous studies document how Stockman orchestrated Reagan's tax and spending policies through Congress during his first term, and how the OMB's expanded regulatory clearance capacity was used for partisan purposes during the 1980s.[30] Although subsequent OMB directors have tended to lack Stockman's visibility, the agency by all accounts has not reverted to its previous status as a repository of neutral competence.[31] This transformation is reflected in the presidential choices for OMB director in recent years. Rather than experienced administrators like Harold Smith, presidents have looked for individuals who shared their political goals. For example, Mitchell Daniels, George W. Bush's first OMB director, served formerly as a Senate aide to Richard Lugar, and later as the White House political director in the Reagan administration (and has made the full transition to being a politician as the current governor of Indiana). Joshua Bolten, the OMB director who replaced Daniels in 2003, served previously as the deputy chief of staff of policy development in Bush's White House.

Nor did the Domestic Council succeed in institutionalizing a long-term capacity for program analysis. Although every president after Nixon experimented with ways to integrate the Cabinet departments into the policy-making process, inevitably these Cabinet-based councils came to be dominated by the White House–based domestic policy staff. In fact, in 1977 under Reorganization Plan I, Jimmy Carter formally abolished the Domestic Council, replacing it with a White House–based Domestic Policy Staff (DPS).[32] In 1981, Reagan renamed the DPS the Office of Policy Development (OPD), part of his effort to revitalize the role of the Cabinet departments in the policy process. Toward this end he established a number of issue-based Cabinet councils, smaller in size but similar in purpose to the Domestic Council. By the end of his presidency, however, only the two councils dealing with economic and domestic policy remained active.

President Clinton institutionalized this arrangement by formally establishing two Cabinet-level councils: the National Economic Council (Executive Order 12835, January 25, 1993) and the Domestic Policy Council (Executive Order 12859, August 16, 1993). Both councils were located within the Office of Policy Development and were staffed by White House aides and headed by senior-level

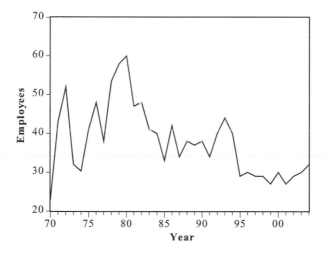

NOTE: Includes staff for Domestic Council (1970–1976, Domestic Policy Staff (1977–81), and Office of Policy Development (1981–2004).

SOURCE: Federal Civilian Workplace Statistics, monthly listings.

Figure 6   Domestic Policy Staff, 1970–2004

White House assistants. As a result, Clinton's White House staff largely directed domestic and economic policy making during his administration.

This has also been the case for Clinton's successor, George W. Bush. Indeed, at the start of Bush's second presidential term, in 2005, Bush appointed his chief political advisor and campaign strategist Karl Rove as deputy White House chief of staff, responsible for coordinating policy development among the Cabinet-level policy councils. Rove's appointment may have simply formally recognized a preexisting situation; many observers believed Rove dominated the policy process during Bush's first term. But it clearly signaled Bush's intent to make certain that policy development remained integrated with political strategy. Moreover, consistent with Rice's appointment as Secretary of State, Bush began his second term by also placing former White House domestic advisor Margaret Spellings and White House legal counsel Alberto Gonzales in charge of the Education and Justice Departments, respectively. Again, the appointments signified Bush's intent to ensure greater White House control over important Cabinet departments and related policy.

Bush's effort to centralize White House control over policy development extended to homeland security in the aftermath of the September 11, 2001, terrorist attacks on targets in New York and Washington, D.C. On October 8, 2001, Bush created a fourth Cabinet-level policy council, the Homeland Security Council (HSC), along with a separate Office of Homeland Security within the EOP (E.O. 13228).[33] A White House aide, the assistant to the president for homeland security, headed the Office of Homeland Security. In this instance, however, the White House assistant was given formal standing on the HSC, eliminating any pretense that the White House homeland security staff served in a supporting capacity to the Council's Cabinet members. Homeland Security Presidential Directive 1, issued by Bush on October 29, 2001, made the White House assistant for homeland security the chair of the HSC "Principals Committee," thus formally recognizing the White House staff's preeminent role in the formulation of homeland security policy. Although Bush succumbed to political pressure from Congress and supported the establishment of the Department of Homeland Security in November 2002 (P.L. 107-296), a Cabinet-level department created by merging some 170,000 government employees across 22 agencies, he still maintains a White House–based Homeland Security staff of about 40 aides, headed by the assistant to the president for homeland security.[34]

Bush's administrative strategy can be seen as the culmination of presidents' efforts, dating back at least to the Nixon administration, to assert White House domination over the domestic, economic, and now the homeland security policy process. Although presidents prior to Nixon certainly utilized the White House staff to expedite and facilitate the policy process, there was no pretense that the White House staff possessed an independent policy-making capability.

Nor did presidents allow White House aides to interpose themselves between the president and his Cabinet advisors; the White House was expected to play a supporting role, providing administrative service to the Cabinet secretaries and their departments. At the same time, outside the White House proper, career-dominated EOP staff agencies—particularly the BoB—discharged their managerial responsibilities from an institutional as opposed to partisan perspective. This is not to suggest that during the pre-Nixon era the BoB was politically neutral. But it was expected to analyze budgetary and legislative policy, and to carry out managerial functions more generally, from the broader perspective of the presidential office, as opposed to the narrow partisan interests of the president himself. In Hugh Heclo's apt phrase, the BoB in the pre-Nixon era provided "partisanship that shifts with the changing partisans."[35] To preserve this institutional perspective, presidents took great pains to see that the EOP agencies, particularly the BoB, were not overtly politicized; they remained largely composed of career civil servants with extensive government experience.

All this changed beginning with Nixon's presidency. Although a degree of White House staff centralization and EOP politicization is evident as early as Eisenhower's administration, it was Nixon who vastly expanded the size of the White House Office, created the first domestic policy staff, and began to transform the OMB into a more politicized agency. These administrative developments paralleled changes on the foreign policy side, where the NSC staff was transformed into an independent policy-making entity with operational capabilities. For the most part, Nixon's presidential successors have continued his pattern of White House policy centralization and EOP politicization, or at least have done nothing to reverse these trends.

What explains the demise of the Roosevelt staff model, as embodied in the Brownlow Report and largely embraced by presidents through at least Johnson? As the next section reveals, the politicized presidency is largely a reaction to a changing political and policy climate that has made it more difficult for presidents to appreciate the virtues of neutral competence.

White House Centralization and EOP Politicization: Causes and Consequences

By the end of the 1970s, Roosevelt's model for the EOP had essentially disappeared. Rather than a tightly knit grouping of institutionally oriented staff agencies that bolstered the president's managerial capacities, the EOP instead was a heavily politicized and organizationally unwieldy holding company, dominated by the White House Office and related policy staffs, and serving a variety of different purposes. Not all EOP agencies were created on presidential initiative. Congress placed some there, such as the CEA in 1946, to illustrate the importance legislators attached to specific issues—in this case, the need for the president to devise policies to reduce unemployment. The EOP also became a repository for functions that Congress did not trust other agencies to perform, as when it pulled the Office of the U.S. Trade Representative (USTR) out of the State Department in 1963 and placed it in the EOP. In addition, presidents used the EOP to shield treasured programs from bureaucratic infighting, as when LBJ placed the Office of Economic Opportunity (OEO) there in 1964 rather than entrust his anti-poverty programs to the departments of Labor; Health, Education and Welfare (HEW, now called Health and Human Services [HHS]); or Housing and Urban Development (HUD). Presidents also utilized the EOP to demonstrate their commitment to particular issues, as with the creation of the Special Action Office for Drug Abuse Prevention in 1971.[36]

The failure to sustain the EOP's original organizational framework was not preordained, but with hindsight it is easy to understand.[37] In the most immediate sense, the politicization of the EOP agencies—particularly the BoB—reflects a confluence of trends that coalesced in the 1970s in ways that caused presidents to rethink their administrative needs. In part, this reflects changing political ideologies; at a simplified level, Roosevelt and his Democratic presidential successors believed that government could help solve public problems, while Nixon and his Republican successors more often viewed government programs as a source of these problems.[38] But contrasting ideologies are only part of the story. Nixon and his successors faced a different strategic environment than did their predecessors. Except for 1947–1948, the party of Democratic presidents held a majority in Congress, and thus the legislative process was a more palatable option for making public policy. In contrast, Nixon and his successors through 2004 faced divided government for 26 of the 36 years they held the Oval Office. Further, during the New Deal era, the permanent government was predominantly staffed with careerists who shared a Democratic outlook. In this context, it served presidents' interests to utilize a legislative clearance process that worked closely with departments and agencies. Nixon and his successors—particularly the Republican presidents—believed, not entirely without reason, that the permanent government was only lukewarm toward their political objectives.[39]

Moreover, Nixon entered the presidency just as the political agenda entered a period dominated by budget deficits, deregulation, and government retrenchment. This changed presidents' administrative needs in ways that made the traditional qualities of continuity, professionalism, and the substantive analysis of policy less important to presidents than the ability to exercise top-down budgeting and regulatory control. Whereas Roosevelt and his New Deal successors sought to empower executive branch departments and agencies, the post-LBJ presidents wanted to control them. In short, the administrative interests of Democratic presidents who sought legislative solutions to societal problems differed significantly from those of predominantly Republican presidents intent on pursuing regulatory reform, covert foreign policies, and de-funding social programs.

A change in strategic realities in the 1970s also explains the centralization of power within the White House staff.[40] In perhaps the most insightful analysis of the sources of presidential power, Richard Neustadt argues that a president's effective influence on policy and political outcomes depends on how well he (someday she) bargains with other political actors. By negotiating transactions that appeal to the interests of other political actors, presidents build the coalitions necessary to achieve their political and policy objectives.[41] And by anticipating the likely impact of those outcomes on their sources of bargaining influence, presidents preserve their sources of bargaining power down the road.

Neustadt first articulated his thesis in 1960, when bargaining took place through interaction with relatively durable "protocoalitions" of party officials, congressional leaders, executive branch officials, and a limited number of interest groups and media figures.[42] Even as he wrote the first edition of his book, however, developments were underway that would eventually fragment these protocoalitions. These included changes to the presidential selection system, the rise of the incumbency advantage in Congress, a proliferation of issue-oriented interest groups, and, most recently, the transformation of the two parties' constituency base. The cumulative impact produced a less insular, more unstable, and politically less predictable bargaining process.

To begin, there was a sharp durable shift in the electoral process in the period 1968–1976 from a relatively closed system dominated by the party elite to a much more permeable and increasingly specialized process.[43] Moreover, this shift takes place against the backdrop of long-term decline in the importance of party and an increase in the influence of issues on electoral outcomes. As described by Steven Wayne in this volume, presidents reacted by developing their own personal campaign staffs with expertise in polling, issue research, advertising, campaign finance, and other skills necessary for coalition building in this new environment.

These changes in the electoral process affected the president's ability to govern. Most noticeably, the mid-1960s witnessed the rise of the incumbency advantage in Congress, fueled in part by a growth in personal staffs with which to engage in casework and constituency service. Presidential "coattails"—never very long to begin with—diminished still more, and legislators felt less electorally indebted to their nominal party leader.[44] And, as the constituency base of each party grew increasingly "pure," the number of party moderates on Capitol Hill who provided a means for bridging party differences decreased. As Presidents Bill Clinton and George W. Bush discovered, the presence of legislative procedures designed to protect minority interests—particularly in the Senate—made it difficult to rely on a partisan majority alone for congressional support. The growth in party unity thus cut both ways; the president became more sure of unified party support, but also of unified opposition.

At the same time, internal reforms that "democratized" Congress weakened the influence of committee chairs on key committees.[45] Moreover, a revived party caucus became a useful tool through which party members in Congress could discipline wayward party members who might have more moderate policy leanings. From the president's perspective, then, coalition building became a more difficult process in part because of the growing number of legislators with increasingly polarized political views, and the inability of party leaders to broker deals on their party's behalf. The development of more unified parties, therefore, did not necessarily brighten a president's legislative prospects even during times of unified government.

In response, presidents tried to pressure recalcitrant lawmakers by taking their case to the public, utilizing new communications technologies, particularly the rise of television, and capitalizing on their standing as the only elected leader in American politics with a national constituency.[46] But members of Congress became increasingly adept at "going public" as well, using media strategies often supported financially by the single-issue interest groups that proliferated in the 1960s and 1970s.[47] The growth of political action committees in the wake of the 1974 campaign finance reforms was only the most obvious manifestation of this fracturing of public discourse into a cacophony of political voices. "Narrowcasting," driven by the advent of cable and twenty-four-hour news services, replaced broadcasting as the primary means of disseminating the news to an increasingly fragmented viewing audience.[48] As a result, as discussed in detail by Lawrence Jacobs in this volume, presidents found it harder to mobilize a national constituency to support their policies, and instead began focusing their message to targeted audiences, depending on the issue at hand.

The upshot of these developments is that, beginning in the 1970s, exercising presidential power became a more politically complicated process. During the pre-1970 era of "institutionalized pluralism," presidents could build coalitions by relying on a party elite who generally shared their political interests. The demands of the new political system in an era of the "permanent campaign," however, forced presidents to use many of the same coalition-building techniques that worked on the campaign trail—and to hire the same people who had wielded those techniques for them. No longer could presidents rely solely on a coterie of leading political actors within Congress, the parties, the media, and major interest groups for information and advice. Instead, they were forced to recruit their own experts. The result was a larger White House staff whose functions were increasingly centered on process of coalition building.

The transformation in staff roles is made plain when comparing the responsibilities of FDR's and Nixon's White House staff. Roosevelt's White House primarily handled five tasks, each linked to his daily activities: appointments, correspondence, press relations, scheduling, and speechwriting. Under Nixon, that number more than doubled; in addition to the five tasks administered by FDR's aides, Nixon's White House devised policy, cultivated interest group support, oversaw public communications strategies, administered Cabinet meetings, handled liaison with the House and Senate, and provided legal advice.[49] These form the core functions of the modern White House staff and have been for the most part adopted by Nixon's successors.

Looking only at senior White House aides, it becomes clear that much of the growth in White House staff during Nixon's presidency was due to his efforts to build political coalitions. In 1969 more than 40 percent of Nixon's White House staff were assigned staff titles related to some form of political outreach. That percentage rose to almost 60 percent by the start of his second term in 1973. In the same period, the proportion of staff devoted primarily to policy development dropped from more than 30 percent of the White House to less than 20 percent (although the raw numbers increase). These percentages remain roughly the same today, with the majority of Bush's senior staff devoted to political coalition building.

A similar political dynamic, albeit at a slower pace, governed staff growth in the national security policy realm. Up through Johnson's presidency, the NSC staff functions were dominated by aides specializing in either geographic areas, such as Latin America, the Middle East, and Southeast Asia, or specific policy areas, such as arms control and nuclear testing. Under Nixon and Ford, however, the NSC staff began to include officials with more politically oriented responsibilities. Ford's NSC staff had aides responsible for congressional relations and press liaison. Zbigniew Brzezinski, Carter's NSA, appointed a personal press spokesman. Reagan added NSC staff responsible for providing legal counsel. By 2004, Bush's NSC was even more specialized, with aides spread across three broad functional categories encompassing some twenty-one separate subdivisions, including staff responsible for relations with Congress, the press, and interest groups.[50] Although not perfectly mirroring the distribution of responsibilities exhibited by the more politically oriented White House staff, the development of a large, functionally specialized NSC staff was driven by much the same forces. Jimmy Carter's NSA Brzezinski succinctly summarizes the presidential rationale:

> . . . [O]n foreign policy matters the President needs someone close to him who shares his larger "presidential" perspective and can rise above narrower bureaucratic concerns. This is why coordination is easier to achieve if attempted from the White House than if it is undertaken from one of the key departments. . . . Moreover, such coordination is manifestly easier to impose if it is openly associated with the shaping of policy as such, for the making of policy inevitably tends to become the coordination of policy.[51]

The evolution of a White House–centered EOP may have been a logical response by presidents to a changing operating environment, particular from 1969 to 1977. But many critics charge that the blurring of the EOP's institutional perspective with the WHO's more political orientation has not been without cost.[52] Roosevelt's division of institutional and personal staff, they argue, served as an important safeguard. By incorporating career-based staff resources into his decision-making process, Roosevelt created an administrative warning device. Institutional input helped him avert decisions that might otherwise erode long-term presidential bargaining leverage for short-term personal political gains. Of course, the two perspectives frequently overlapped—what benefited the presidency usually helped the incumbent president—but the obverse was not always true. Today, however, with institutional and personally oriented staffs merged within a single, White House–dominated EOP, a president's short-term personal political considerations are more likely to drive out long-term institutional concerns. By losing the means to evaluate the likely impact of today's decisions on the presidency's institutional effectiveness tomorrow, presidents risk jeopardizing their sources of power (and, although less important to each incumbent, their successors' sources of power as well).

Moreover, critics contend, the loss of institutional perspective manifests itself in other ways. By merging institutional and political advice, and politicizing the institutional staff agencies, presidential staffs are less likely to anticipate the probable consequences of particular policy decisions.[53] This is partly due to the loss of institutional memory; politicization means there are fewer aides with knowledge of basic governmental administrative processes or the past details of policy proposals. The result are policies that do not achieve stated objectives or that produce unintended consequences.

Less obviously, the politicization of the EOP can actually produce a loss of political sensitivity. Staff enlargement and differentiation pull functions once performed by other political actors into the domain of the White House–centered advising system.[54] Consequently, presidents find themselves relying primarily on the White House staff to gauge the likely impact of presidential choices on a president's sources of influence. But aides clustered within a White House–centered orbit do not necessarily possess the knowledge to adequately advise presidents in this regard. This is partly due to the gradual divorce between a president's political interests and those of his party (see Sidney Milkis in this volume). Prior to the 1960s, presidents relied on party leaders at the local and state levels to gauge the likely impact of presidential choices on the president's party support. But as the ties that bound presidents to parties began dissolving in the 1960s, the White House staff gradually absorbed the functions, but not necessarily the expertise, once possessed by the party hierarchy.[55] The White House staff is beholden primarily to the president, not his party.[56] As the White House staff absorbs political functions, then, a president's contact with other political actors who have independent political bases lessens. So, too, does the likelihood that he will be warned of politically foolish actions.[57]

Critics also point to the dangers of White House staff specialization. As coalition building encompasses more varied interests, they claim, presidents naturally seek additional aides with the expertise and information to conduct liaison with these specialized audiences, including Congress, interest groups, state and local governments, agencies within the federal government, the press corps, and even foreign governments. But in delegating "outreach" activities to specialized staff, they may become special pleaders, serving the interests of the targeted audiences, not the president.[58]

As the White House staff becomes internally differentiated, it also grows bigger, adding to the president's management burdens.[59] He is often less able to ensure that they are working in his interest, and his aides are less able to anticipate his needs.[60] Moreover, the centralization of authority within the White House staff branch has adverse system-wide repercussions. As Joel Aberbach and Bert Rockman observe, it tends "to induce retaliatory behavior" among other governing institutions.[61] Emulating executive branch staff growth, Congress has expanded its own staff capacities. And, as James Pfiffner argues, attempts by the White House staff to politicize the federal bureaucracy may decrease presidential effectiveness. He writes, "The more political appointees there are and the more layers which separate the agency head and career executives, the longer it will take to establish effective control."[62] The end result is political and policy stalemate—not expanded presidential power.

Similar criticisms have been leveled at the centralization of authority within the NSC staff. In particular, critics contend that the growth in NSC staff size and the acquisition of new advising functions reveals a fundamental tension at the heart of the national security advisor's position: should she play a policy advocacy and operational role, or act primarily as a process manager responsible for coordinating foreign policy advice to the President? Over time, for the reasons Brzezinski cites, the policy advocacy and operational role has tended to win out. Critics argue, however, that by taking on this function, supported by an independent staff of national security specialists, the national security advisor often cuts the president off from the expert input of careerists in the relevant departments and agencies. Moreover, a staff focused on policy advocacy and implementation is less likely to objectively engage in the policy analysis and coordination that the president requires. A case in point, some charge, is Bush's decision to invade Iraq in 2003. Critics complain that the NSC staff under Condoleezza Rice mismanaged the decision-making process, largely ignoring warnings from careerists, particularly those working in the State Department and intelligence agencies, which contradicted some of the key premises on which Bush based his decision to go to war. Instead, Bush relied much more on the advice of political appointees, particularly the so-called "neocons" working in the Department of Defense and on Vice President Cheney's staff.

These criticisms are strongly suggestive, but probably not conclusive. The problem is that one cannot know how matters would stand had presidents not politicized the EOP. Consider the measures scholars typically cite to support their claims regarding the adverse consequences of EOP politicization: presidential decisions that fail to achieve desired objectives; more general indicators of declining presidential influence, such as opinion polls, reelection rates, and historical reputations; and the post-1972 presidential reform efforts. It is true that there are several important presidential decisions in recent years that, with hindsight, would have benefited from the input of careerists with the relevant expertise and institutional memory. These include Reagan's 1981 tax and spending cuts, which produced more than a decade of structural budget deficits; the 1985–1986 Iran-contra affair; the Clinton administration's failed effort in 1993 to enact fundamental health care reform; and, most recently, George W. Bush's decision to invade Iraq. In each instance, one could make a persuasive case that insight from career civil servants within government was ignored or not solicited.

Moreover, the staff-related mishaps of Gerald Ford, Jimmy Carter, and George H. W. Bush suggest that the dangers of White House centralization and EOP politicization may manifest itself not only in spectacular instances of staff misjudgment and scandal, but also in a less perceptible erosion of presidential power through time. Recall that Ford, Carter, and Bush were all one-term presidents generally characterized as politically ineffective due in part to poor judgment by their staffs. Although Clinton served two terms, his presidency was severely handicapped, in large part due to staff-related errors made early in his presidency.

The problem is that these and similarly broadly construed measures of weakening presidential leadership cannot be entirely blamed on White House centralization and EOP politicization. Certainly they are influenced by the more difficult bargaining environment described earlier in this chapter.[63] Simply put, there is a strong case to be made that presidential leadership has become more difficult during the last three decades for reasons that include, yet go beyond, a more politicized staff system. Nonetheless, the lack of incontrovertible proof regarding the dangers of a more politicized EOP has not stopped critics from proposing a number of administrative reforms.

Reform?

Beginning with the Brownlow Report's celebrated warning in 1937 that the "president needs help," presidency scholars generally supported the expansion of the presidential staff as a means of providing presidents with the authority to meet their growing obligations. But the revelations regarding the role that White House advisors played in presidential decisions pertaining to Watergate, the Iran-contra affair, the Clintons' health care reform effort, and the recent decision to invade Iraq, not to mention lesser staff-related miscues, has altered some scholars' views. Beginning as early as the 1970s, a number of influential commissions recommended reforms, including reducing White House staff size, making presidential assistants accountable to Congress, regularizing decision procedures, and reinvigorating the traditional presidential Cabinet as the primary locus of presidential administrative support.[64] Implicit within this school of thought was the presumption that if presidents only had the political will, they could implement the suggested reforms. For the most part, however, presidents have not reacted favorably to these proposals.[65]

In 1972 Nixon, concerned that his White House staff had grown too large and unwieldy, resolved to reduce its size and to reallocate administrative power to a few senior aides and Cabinet officials. At the same time, however, he tried to broaden his administrative reach by further politicizing the upper levels of the executive branch agencies.[66] In the wake of Watergate, Gerald Ford also embraced White House staff reductions, in part to end repeated clashes between Nixon holdovers and Ford appointees.[67] Although he trimmed almost one hundred people from the White House Office, these peripheral cuts were not permanent. Carter, who had campaigned in 1977 on a promise to reduce White House staff size, instead largely shifted them from the White House to other executive staff agency payrolls, including the newly created Office of Administration.[68] Reagan reacted to the Iran-contra scandal by opting for more White House staff hierarchy and a reversion to regularized staffing procedures. George H. W. Bush, after a presidential term plagued by the failings of key aides, promised a major overhaul of the White House Office if he won reelection. Clinton also campaigned on a promise to cut his White House staff size, by some 25 percent, but once in office he achieved this goal by eliminating important clerical support staff. To date, George W. Bush has opted to remove key advisors rather than engage in more systematic staff reform, although he did embrace recommendations to revamp oversight of the nation's intelligence agencies.

It appears, then, that with the exception of a few halfhearted attempts to reduce White House staff size, presidents have not been committed to administrative changes of the type advocated by reformers. In John Hart's words, "Presidents and reformers are fundamentally at odds with one another over the very basis on which the reformers have argued their case. There is obviously something about being president that makes one see virtues in politicizing the EOP and centralizing power in the White House."[69]

The reluctance of presidents to do what scholars argue they should do offers a cautionary lesson. A variety of developments in the American political system have collectively made it harder for presidents to construct the coalitions that are critical for achieving policy objectives. They have responded by centralizing staff support within the White House, and politicizing the EOP agencies. Barring some reversion to a previous, more insular era, in which presidential bargaining once again becomes largely the province of political elites with predictable and more moderate policy preferences, it is hard to see why presidents would wish to reverse this administrative pattern. At most, would-be reformers can only hope to, in Hugh Heclo's words, "nurture those tendencies . . . that have the effect of making the EOP an instrument for positively serving a succession of presidents, and not simply catering to the personal entourage of the president of the day. . . ."[70]

Toward this end, Heclo suggests several reforms, including "cross-fertilizing" personnel in the White House policy staffs with the staffs of the CEA and the NSC, in order to cultivate a more generalist outlook, and to accentuate the career components of these staffs. Building on Heclo's suggestion, it might be possible to make greater use of officials in the Senior Executive Service—roughly eight thousand top-level, predominantly careerist executive branch officials (described by Patricia Ingraham in this volume)—by rotating them for tours of duty in the White House. Heclo also suggests making the director of the Office of Administration a career appointee, and generally giving that office greater control over EOP personnel policies, such as authorizing the use of detailees to the White House.[71]

Looking more broadly at the EOP, several recommendations come to mind. First, those agencies that serve largely operational, as opposed to staff, functions ought to be relocated to the executive branch. This would include the USTR's office, and perhaps the "drug czar's" office as well. It is, of course, easy to exhort presidents to quit adding layers of political appointees to the upper levels of the EOP agencies, particularly the OMB, but it is hard to imagine a reversal of this trend, particular when budgets remain so integral to the president's domestic agenda and political standing. Nevertheless, further politicization of the EOP agencies' upper levels ought to be firmly resisted.

But these reforms, even if implemented, will be at best marginal adjustments to the current, politicized presidency. Indeed, one is tempted to argue that the significance of an administrative reform is inversely proportional to the likelihood of its implementation. Urging presidents to think "institutionally"—to adopt a time horizon that extends beyond the life of their administration—is politically impracticable, particularly after passage of the Twenty-second Amendment, which limits presidents to two terms in office. Presidents live in the present, whereas institutional staff agencies must adopt a perspective that stretches decades into the future. Given these clashing incentives, it is perhaps unrealistic to expect presidents to support reforms designed to bolster the presidency as an institution, particularly if those reforms involve reducing the political responsiveness of their staffs. This is not to argue that presidents do not need neutrally competent staff agencies. It is to say, however, that left on their own, presidents cannot be expected to invest much political capital in insuring these agencies' survival in a "neutrally competent" form. As Hart warns in his discussion of the distinction between the president and the presidency, "From the perspective of the president in power, they are one and the same thing."[72]

At a more fundamental level, the debate over the presidential staff system is really a debate regarding competing conceptions of the presidency. Americans have always embraced two somewhat contradictory visions, without fully choosing either one. On the one hand, we fear the centralization of power within a single elected official, and therefore support efforts to circumscribe presidential power. On the other, we want presidents to possess the energy and latitude required to act decisively in times of crisis. In short, we seek both accountability and energy in a single office. At different times in American history, we have tilted toward one or the other of these conceptions, but we have never fully embraced one to the exclusion of the other.

Similarly, I argue, the evolution of the presidential advisory system reflects shifting conceptions of presidential leadership. Interestingly, however, presidents' efforts to politicize the presidency are most likely to occur during times when presidential power is perceived to be "weak," as occurred in the 1970s—a period of economic uncertainty, growing public skepticism of government's ability to solve societal problems, and a sense of foreign policy drift. Conversely, during periods of "strong" presidential leadership, as with FDR during the New Deal and World War II, presidents have less incentive to centralize political control within their own White House office. Stated another way, the search by presidents for political support, administratively speaking, turns inward when they perceive a general lack of backing within the surrounding political environment. If correct, this suggests that the pendulum of administrative reform will only begin to swing back toward neutral competence when—and if—there develops a broad political consensus on the need for strong presidential leadership. Barring that development, however, we may expect presidents to continue to centralize administrative control within the White House and to politicize the remaining EOP staff agencies. Presidents still need help, and—critics notwithstanding—they are determined to get it where they can.

Notes

*This chapter benefited from the helpful comments of Joel Aberbach, Fred Greenstein, Hugh Heclo, Stephen Hess, Mark Peterson, Jeffrey Weinberg and participants at the Annenberg conferences on the Executive Branch.

1. Note that the actual number differs according to the sources consulted and how an EOP agency is defined. Thus the White House's official Web site lists a total of 17 EOP agencies, including the "Cabinet," although the Cabinet has no formal basis in statute, and additional offices for Global Communications, Faith-Based and Community Initiatives, National Aids Policy, and National Drug Control Policy, some of which are actually part of the White House Office. All told, since its formal inception in 1939, the EOP has housed some 55 agencies for varying lengths of tenure. This total does not include the more than a dozen war-related EOP agencies operating during World War II.

2. The WHO consists of the president's closest personal political advisors. They handle the president's scheduling, appointments, and correspondence, and provide political outreach and advice pertaining to core constituencies and key political institutions, including Congress, the media, state and local governments, the executive branch, interest groups, and the public.

   Working closely with the White House Office are four staffs dealing with domestic, homeland security, economic and national security policy, respectively. They provide administrative support to the four cabinet councils: the National Security Council (NSC), the Domestic Council (DC), the National Economic Council (NEC), and the Homeland Security Council (HSC). Each of these four councils is composed of the secretaries of the cabinet departments with responsibilities pertaining to their particular issue areas. The DC and the NEC are subsumed within the Office of Policy Development (OPD). Both the NSC and the OPD are considered separate EOP agencies. The Homeland Security Council, in contrast, is paid out of the White House Office budget and therefore does not have a separate EOP listing. However, because all the council staffs are headed by White House assistants, and are largely composed of White House aides, they are best viewed as extensions of the White House staff, even when listed separately in the EOP entities (see Table 5.1).

   The OMB (formerly the Bureau of the Budget) is headed by a presidential appointee (confirmed by the Senate). The agency is responsible for preparing the president's budget and for providing fiscal analysis, advising on administrative management, and performing legislative and regulatory clearance. All are described more fully below.

3. See Moe "The Politicized Presidency" in Peterson and Chubb, *New Direction in American Politics,* 235–271; and Hugh Heclo, "The Office of Management and Budget and the Presidency: The Problem of Neutral Competence," *The Public Interest* 38 (Winter 1975), 80–98.

4. By "institutional," I mean an agency dominated by career civil servants with a commitment to neutral competence.

5. President's Committee on Administrative Management (hereafter the Brownlow Committee Report), 5.

6. Although the phrase "executive office of the president" was used prior to Roosevelt's presidency, it did not acquire formal status until this time.

7. Press Release, September 10, 1939. Executive Order 8248 formally established the EOP two days earlier, under authority granted the President by Reorganization Plans I and II (July 1, 1939).

8. As part of Reorganization Plan I, Congress authorized FDR to add up to six administrative assistants to his White House staff. The BoB was transferred from the Treasury Department, where it has been located since its inception in 1921. The NRPB, which provided long-term policy planning assistance, was formerly an adjunct to the traditional presidential Cabinet funded from emergency appropriations. To gain greater control over governmental hiring, Roosevelt initially sought to move the Civil Service Commission into the EOP. When rebuffed by Congress, he opted instead for appointing one aide as liaison to the CSC; this was the Liaison Office for Personnel Management. The Office of Government Reports pulled

together several existing public information agencies responsible for disseminating government information to the public. In anticipation of a "national emergency," E.O. 8248 also made provisions for "an office of emergency management as the president shall determine." This was in fact a bookkeeping maneuver created in anticipation of a coming war. On May 25, 1940, FDR formally established the OEM as an umbrella organization housing any temporary defense-related agencies created during the war emergency.

9. Brownlow recommended merging all independent regulatory commissions into existing Cabinet departments headed by secretaries appointed by FDR, replacing the Civil Service Commission with a personnel agency that reported directly to him, creating a central policy planning board that would have overseen a series of regional planning agencies situated across the country, and giving the president control over the auditing of government expenditures. Congress rejected these proposals, forcing FDR to adopt them in modified form.

10. Heclo, "The Executive Office of the President," Occasional Paper, Center for American Political Studies, Harvard University, 1983, 11.

11. Matthew J. Dickinson and Andrew Rudalevige, "Presidents, Responsiveness and Competence: Revisiting the Golden Age at the Bureau of the Budget," *Political Science Quarterly* (Winter 2004), 633–654; Patrick J. Wolf, "Neutral and Responsive Competence: The Bureau of the Budget, 1939-48, Revisited," *Administration and Society* 31 (March 1999), 142–167.

12. At Roosevelt's death in April 1945, Smith was seeking to broaden the BoB's mandate still further, by expanding the duties of the Fiscal Analysis division to include responsibility for macroeconomic analysis and economic reporting. But these tasks were instead assigned to the Council of Economic Advisers (CEA), created by Congress in 1946 as part of the Employment Act.

13. Roosevelt considered making William H. McReynolds, a White House administrative assistant appointed after the 1939 reorganization, who had 25 years of government experience, a de facto "in house" coordinator of the other White House administrative assistants. Instead, he appointed him to fill the position of Liaison to the Office of Personnel Management.

14. The story is recounted in Don K. Price, *America's Unwritten Constitution: Science, Religion and Political Responsibility* (Cambridge, Mass.: Harvard University Press), 120–123.

15. The elevated personnel number during the years 1958–1961 is due to the presence of the Office of the Civil and Defense Mobilization, which was placed in the EOP during this time.

16. There was an increase of roughly 80 aides under Eisenhower in the period 1956–1958. Some of this growth is associated with the acquisition of new functions relating to the cold war, including the appointment of White House assistants for arms control, agricultural trade, and psychological warfare. Recall that Harold Stassen was appointed by Eisenhower as his White House assistant for arms control and acquired a staff of about 50. Smaller staffs served Clarence Randall, who handled agricultural trade, and C. D. Jackson, in charge of public relations aspects of the cold war. Charles E. Walcott and Karen M. Hult, *Governing the White House* (Lawrence: University Press of Kansas, 1995), 65, 171.

17. These listings do not for the most part include those with career status, and those who perform primarily clerical or "operating" tasks, nor do they typically include more than the very senior National Security staff.
18. The National Security Resources Board advised the president regarding civil defense issues, and survived in various forms through 1973, when its functions were absorbed by several cabinet agencies.
19. Public Law 80-253, Title I, Section 101 (a).
20. Title I, Section 101(b), subheading (c) of the 1947 National Security Act (P.L. 80-253).
21. These are professionals and administrative aides paid out of the NSC budget as listed in the monthly Federal Report of Civilian Workforce statistics.
22. Ivo H. Dalder and I. M. Destler, "A New NSC for a New Administration," Policy Brief Number 68 (Washington, D.C.: The Brookings Institution, November 2000). Available online at http://wwww.brookedu/dybdocroot/comm/policybriefs /pb068/pb68.htm.
23. See Executive Order 10700 (February 27, 1957).
24. Richard E. Neustadt, "Presidency and Legislation: The Growth of Central Clearance," *American Political Science Review* 48 (September 1954), 641–671, and Neustadt, "Presidency and Legislation: Planning the President's Program," *American Political Science Review* 49 (December 1955), 980–1021.
25. These include the 1964 Task Force on Government Reorganization (the Price task force), and a second Task Force on Government Reorganization (the Heineman task force) appointed in 1966, and Nixon's transition study team headed by Frank Lindsay.
26. The Domestic Council was established in the EOP by Reorganization Plan 2 (March 12, 1970).
27. The Cabinet departments on the Domestic Council included Treasury; Interior; Agriculture; Commerce; Labor; Health Education and Welfare; Housing and Urban Development; and Transportation.
28. Quoted in Peri Arnold, "Executive Reorganization," in Harold C. Relyea, *The Executive Office of the President* (Westport. Conn.: Greenwood Press, 1997), 431.
29. For details on both, see Arnold, *Making the Managerial Presidency*.
30. Moe, "The Politicized Presidency"; David Stockman, *The Triumph of Politics* (New York: Harper & Row, 1986); David Mathiasen, "The Evolution of the Office of Management and Budget under President Reagan," *Public Budgeting and Finance* 8 (Autumn 1988), 3–14; Peter M. Benda and Charles H. Levine, "Reagan and the Bureaucracy: The Bequest, the Promise and the Legacy," in Charles O. Jones, *The Reagan Legacy: Promises and Performance* (Chatham, N.J.: Chatham House, 1988); and Bruce E. Johnson, "From Analyst to Negotiator: The OMB's New Role," *Journal of Policy Analysis and Management* 3 (Summer 1984), 501–515.
31. For succinct overviews, see James P. Pfiffner, "OMB: Professionalization, Politicization, and the Presidency," in Colin Campbell and Margaret Jane Wyszomirski, eds., *Executive Leadership in Anglo-American Systems* (Pittsburgh, Pa.: University of Pittsburgh Press, 1991), 195–218; Wyszomirski, "The De-Institutionalization of Presidential Staff Agencies," *Public Administration Review* (September–October 1982), 455; and Judith E. Michaels, *The President's Call:*

Executive Leadership from FDR to George Bush (Pittsburgh, Pa.: University of Pittsburgh Press, 1997), 70–77.

32. Carter's plan also established an Office of Administration in the EOP, responsible for providing routine administrative support to the other EOP staff agencies, but without any capacity to provide overall administrative coordination. In fact, the Office of Administration, although legally a separate EOP entity, takes its instructions from the President's White House assistant for management and administration. See Martha J. Kumar and Terry Sullivan, eds., *The White House World* (College Station, Tex.: Texas A&M University Press, 2003), 300.

33. In addition to the assistant to the president for homeland security, the Homeland Security Council consists of the president; vice president; secretaries of the Treasury, Defense, Health and Human Services, and Transportation; the Attorney General, and the directors of the FBI, the CIA, and the Federal Emergency Management Agency (FEMA).

34. Staff estimates are derived from the House hearings on the fiscal year 2005 appropriations requests for the EOP and the White House Office. Note the Homeland Security Council was also formally still in existence.

35. Heclo, "The OMB and the Presidency," 82.

36. Although abolished in 1975, it was reestablished during Reagan's presidency.

37. This discussion draws heavily on Dickinson and Rudalevige (2004).

38. For similar arguments, see Rourke, "Responsiveness and Neutral Competence in American Bureaucracy," and Wyszomirski, "The De-institutionalization of Presidential Staff Agencies."

39. Joel Aberbach and Bert A. Rockman, *In the Web of Politics: Three Decades of the Federal Executive* (Washington, D.C.: The Brookings Institution, 2000); and Richard P. Nathan, *The Plot That Failed: Nixon and the Administrative Presidency* (New York: John Wiley, 1975).

40. This section is based in part on Matthew J. Dickinson, "Explaining the Growth of the Presidential Branch, 1940–2000," in Barry C. Burden, ed., *Uncertainty in American Politics* (New York: Cambridge University Press, 2003).

41. Neustadt, *Presidential Power.*

42. Samuel Kernell uses the phrase "protocoalitions" in his *Going Public*, 16–17.

43. Michael Hagen and William Mayer, "The Modern Politics of Presidential Selection," in Mayer, ed., *In Pursuit of the White House 2000: How We Choose Our Presidential Nominees* (New York: Seven Bridges Press, 2000), 21.

44. Regarding presidential coattails, see Robert S. Erickson and Gerald C. Wright, "Voters, Candidates, and Issues in Congressional Elections," in Lawrence C. Dodd and Bruce I. Oppenheimer, eds., *Congress Reconsidered*, 7th ed. (Washington, D.C.: Congressional Quarterly Press, 2001), 71.

45. See David Rohde, *Parties and Leaders in the Post-Reform House* (Chicago: University of Chicago Press, 1991).

46. See generally Kernell, *Going Public.*

47. Anthony Corrado "Running Backward: The Congressional Money Chase," in Norman Ornstein and Thomas Mann, eds., *The Permanent Campaign and Its Future* (Washington, D.C.: American Enterprise Institute and The Brookings Institution, 2000), 75–107.

48. Stephen Hess, "The Press and the Permanent Campaign," in Ornstein and Mann, *Permanent Campaign*, 38–53.

49. Descriptions of individual staff functions were derived from a number of sources. Most helpful were the finding aids at the various presidential libraries, as well as several secondary sources, including Walcott and Hult, *Governing the White House*, and Patterson, *The White House Staff*.

50. John Hart, "The New National Security Strategy and the Old National Security Council," in George C. Edwards and Philip John Davies, eds., *New Challenges for the American Presidency* (New York: Pearson Longman, 2004), 191; Patterson, *The White House Staff*, 62–73.

51. Zbigniew Brzezinski, *Power and Principle* (New York: Farrar, Straus, Giroux, 1985), 535.

52. For specific criticisms and sources, see my *Bitter Harvest*, especially chapter 2, and Hart, *The Presidential Branch*, 195–233.

53. Walter Williams, *Mismanaging America: The Rise of the Anti-analytic Presidency* (Lawrence: University Press of Kansas, 1990); Heclo, "Office of Management and Budget; Lester G. Seligman and Cary R. Covington, *The Coalitional Presidency* (Chicago: Dorsey Press, 1989); and William Carey, "Presidential Staffing in the Sixties and Seventies," *Public Administration Review* 29 (September–October 1969), 450–458.

54. See generally Seligman and Covington, *The Coalitional Presidency*, 150–158.

55. For details, see Roger G. Brown, "Party and Bureaucracy: from Kennedy to Reagan," *Political Science Quarterly* 97, no. 2 (Summer 1982), 279–294; Godfrey Hodgson, *All Things to All Men: The False Promise of the Modern American Presidency from Franklin D. Roosevelt to Ronald Reagan* (New York: Simon & Schuster, 1980), 161–182; Theodore Lowi, *The Personal Presidency: Power Invested, Promise Unfulfilled* (Ithaca, N.Y.: Cornell University Press, 1985), 67–96; Austin Ranney, "The Political Parties: Reform and Decline" in Anthony King, ed., *The New American Political System* (Washington, D.C.: AEI Press, 1990), 213–248; Sidney M. Milkis, *The President and the Parties: The Transformation of the American Party System since the New Deal* (New York: Oxford University Press, 1993).

56. On this point see Nicole Woolsey Biggart, "A Sociological Analysis of the Presidential Staff," *The Sociological Quarterly* 25 (Winter 1984), 27–43; and Matthew Holden, "Why Entourage Politics Is Volatile," in Pfiffner, *Managerial Presidency*, 61–77.

57. Independent actors include cabinet heads, party officials, congressional leaders and influential state and local politicians. See also Richard E. Neustadt "The Constraining of the President: The Presidency after Watergate," *British Journal of Political Science* 4, no. 4 (1974), 383–397.

58. Hess and Pfiffner, *Organizing the Presidency*, 172–173.

59. For discussions of White House staff size, see generally Cronin, "The Swelling of the Presidency," in Peter Woll, ed., *American Government: Readings and Cases,* 8th ed., (Boston, Little, Brown, 1984), 345–359; Hart, *The Presidential Branch*, 97–109; and Hess and Pfiffner, *Organizing the Presidency*, 225–226.

60. Francis Rourke "Presidentializing the Bureaucracy: From Kennedy to Reagan," in Pfiffner, *Managerial Presidency*, 134; Hess and Pfiffner, *Organizing the Presidency*, 172;

Kernell, *Going Public*; and Jeffrey K. Tulis, *The Rhetorical Presidency* (Princeton, N.J.: Princeton University Press, 1987).

61. Joel D. Aberbach and Bert Rockman, "Mandarins or Mandates? Control and Discretion in the Modern Administrative State," in Pfiffner, *Managerial Presidency*, 165.

62. James P. Pfiffner, "Political Appointees and Career Executives," in Pfiffner, *Managerial Presidency*, 179. See also Aberbach and Rockman, "Mandarins or Mandates?"

63. See generally the articles in King, *The New American Political System*; John E. Chubb and Paul E. Peterson, *The New Direction in American Politics* (Washington, D.C.: The Brookings Institution, 1985); and John E. Chubb and Paul E. Peterson, *Can the Government Govern?* (Washington, D.C.: The Brookings Institution, 1989).

64. For an overview of suggested reforms, see Hart, *The Presidential Branch*, 195–233.

65. For an overview of some of these attempts, see Hart, *The Presidential Branch*; Hess and Pfiffner, *Organizing the Presidency*; Arnold, *Making the Managerial Presidency*; and Seidman and Gilmour, *Politics, Position, and Power*.

66. Seidman and Gilmour, *Politics, Position, and Power*; and Nathan, *The Plot That Failed*.

67. See Robert Hartmann, *Palace Politics: An Inside Account of the Ford Years* (New York: McGraw-Hill Book Co., 1980), 34–36, 272–302.

68. See Dom Bonafede, "White House Reorganization: Separating Smoke from Substance," *The National Journal* 10, no. 46 (1977), 1307–1311.

69. Hart, *The Presidential Branch*, 233.

70. Heclo, "The Executive Office of the President," 31.

71. Heclo, "The Executive Office of the President," 31–32.

72. Hart, *The Presidential Branch*, 216.

Bibliography

Arnold, Peri. *Making the Managerial Presidency: Comprehensive Reorganization Planning, 1905–1996.* 2nd rev. ed. Lawrence: University Press of Kansas, 1998. This presents a comprehensive overview of presidents' efforts, dating back to the nineteenth century, to reorganize the executive branch.

Brownlow, Louis, Harold D. Smith, Charles E. Merriam, William H. McReynolds, Lowell Mellett, and Luther Gulick. "Symposium: The Executive Office of the President." *Public Administration Review* 1, no. 2 (Winter 1941), 101–189. An early assessment of the Executive Office of the President by those who created and served in it during Roosevelt's presidency.

Dickinson, Matthew J. *Bitter Harvest: FDR, Presidential Power and the Growth of the Presidential Branch.* New York: Cambridge University Press, 1997. In-depth examination of President Franklin Roosevelt's intent in creating the Executive Office of the President. Dickinson contrasts the Roosevelt model with the White House–dominated presidential staff system on which presidents rely today, and finds the current system defective in several respects.

George, Alexander. *Presidential Decisionmaking in Foreign Policy.* Boulder, Colo.: Westview Press, 1980. An interesting effort to examine how best to organize presidential advisors for decision making in foreign policy.

Hart, John. 1995. *The Presidential Branch, From Washington to Clinton*. 2nd ed. Chatham, N.J.: Chatham House, 1995. Hart has produced the best analysis of the evolution of the White House staff, and of the Executive Office of the President. He is particularly good at critiquing reform proposals.

Heclo, Hugh. *A Government of Strangers*. Washington, D.C.: The Brookings Institution, 1977. Although now dated, it remains the best single study of the relationship between presidents, their political appointees, and the permanent government. The focus is on the executive branch, rather than the Executive Office of the President, but it addresses important issues of presidential leadership that apply to both.

Hess, Stephen, with James P. Pfiffner. *Organizing the Presidency*. 3rd ed. Washington, D.C.: The Brookings Institution, 2002. A very readable book describing how presidents from Roosevelt through Clinton organized their White House staffs.

Hult, Karen M., and Charles E. Walcott. *Empowering the White House: Governance under Nixon, Ford, and Carter*. Lawrence: University Press of Kansas, 2004. Although some readers may find the theory that frames the chapters somewhat difficult to follow, the actual descriptions of how these three presidents organized their White House staffs are very well done.

Jones, Charles O., ed. *Preparing to Be President: The Memos of Richard E. Neustadt*. Washington, D.C.: American Enterprise Institute, 2000. A wonderful compilation of the confidential advice of the nation's premier presidency scholar to presidents from Kennedy through Clinton.

Kernell, Samuel. *Going Public: New Strategies of Presidential Leadership*. 3rd ed. Washington, D.C.: Congressional Quarterly Press, 1997. Although his thesis is overstated, Kernell presents a useful summary of the changes affecting the exercise of presidential power during the last four decades.

Kumar, Martha J., and Terry Sullivan, eds. *The White House World*. College Station: Texas A&M University Press, 2003. Although limited by the failure to go back in history far enough, this is an interesting overview of some of the major staff elements in the White House Office today.

Moe, Terry M. "The Politicized Presidency." In *New Directions in American Politics,* edited by John Chubb and Paul E. Peterson. Washington, D.C.: The Brookings Institution, 1985. A succinct and powerful critique of "neutral competence."

Neustadt, Richard E. *Presidential Power and the Modern Presidents*. New York: The Free Press, 1990. Now in its fourth edition, it remains the single best book on the American Presidency, written by someone who both served in the White House and advised presidents for more than a half-century.

Patterson, Bradley. *The White House Staff: Inside the West Wing and Beyond*. Washington, D.C.: The Brookings Institution, 2000. An informative overview of the White House staff from someone who admires what they do, and who once served there himself.

Pfiffner, James P. *The Managerial Presidency*. 2nd ed. College Station: Texas A&M Press, 1999. Contains a useful series of articles by scholars analyzing different presidential staff offices, and debating how—and whether—presidents might best manage them.

The President's Committee on Administrative Management. *Report with Special Studies*. Washington, D.C.: Government Printing Office, 1937. The original Brownlow

Committee study used by Franklin Roosevelt to create the Executive Office of the President; it still rewards careful reading today, if only to remind readers how different the present-day presidential staff system is from the vision of the authors of this study.

Relyea, Harold C., ed. *The Executive Office of the President.* Westport, Conn.: Greenwood Press, 1997. A useful anthology containing articles describing the history of the major staff agencies in the Executive Office of the President.

Seidman, Harold, and Robert Gilmore. *Politics, Position, and Power: From the Positive to the Regulatory State.* 4th ed. New York: Oxford University Press, 1986. Examines how presidents attempt to control the executive branch, and why those efforts invariable fail.

6

COMMUNICATING FROM THE WHITE HOUSE: PRESIDENTIAL NARROWCASTING AND THE NATIONAL INTEREST

Lawrence R. Jacobs

President George W. Bush proclaimed in Vienna, Ohio, on October 27, 2004, that he was "working on the people's business, doing what's right for America . . . [and] for everybody who lives in this country." President Bush's presentation of himself as a leader who represents and protects the interests of all Americans is not unusual for American presidents, even if it comes after the trauma of the September 11, 2001 terrorist attacks and in the closing days of a closely contested election. Bill Clinton evoked a similar claim to lead and protect the nation when he promised, in a television interview with Sam Donaldson of ABC, days before the commemoration of D-Day on June 5, 1994, that he would "speak for the American people," or when he portrayed himself as "the symbol of America" at a dinner in Coral Gables, Florida, on April 29, 1996.

Presidents Bush and Clinton have led opposing political parties during a particularly acrimonious period of American history and, yet, both are part of a tradition, stretching back to the nineteenth century, of presidents who publicly portray themselves as "stewards of the people" whose actions serve the country as a whole as well as its greater good.[1] Scott James in this volume reviews the pattern of presidential claims to this mantle of representing the nation as a whole.

Although presidents may publicly present themselves as representing the nation, the reality is that presidents win elections and then govern by assembling a coalition of disparate interests and groups. For all practical purposes, they are inaugurated with no political constituency that can be called "the nation." There is no "whole" for which a president can speak. The support for the president in approval ratings and in elections rests on recruiting and then holding many different segments and factions within the country.[2]

The gap between the public rhetoric of a president who claims to serve the nation and his actual behavior and strategies, which cater to subgroups and narrow interests, reflects and contributes to two traditions in American political development, both of which are supported by large and respected bodies of research. The first tradition emphasizes the self-interest of individuals and factions of citizens and politicians. The American political process, in this view, is little more than a cash register, aggregating up the demands and interests of individuals, organizations, and subgroups. Voters cast their ballots to secure the enactment of policies that help them, pressure groups lobby government on behalf of their membership, and politicians seek to win reelection by adopting policies that secure them votes at the ballot box and campaign contributions from lobbyists. According to this tradition, the "common good" is a fiction, a smokescreen put up by politicians and the well-organized to camouflage from public view the bargaining and deal making that occur among self-interested political factions.[3]

The second tradition insists that citizens and politicians are not autonomous isolates but rather talk and reason together in collective processes—from interpersonal discussions to media-mediated processes of information distribution—in order to identify their shared concerns and promote their common good. In this account, "civic republican" virtue and public-spirited deliberation and decision making are consistent themes in American political development. Research has shown that voters regularly put more emphasis on the national economy than their own "pocketbook"; millions of Americans volunteer and contribute to organizations, even though others "free ride" on their commitments, and they support groups that help minorities, the environment, and children, even though they stand to gain no direct tangible benefit; and many members of Congress bypass high visibility committees and take on policies out of a motivation to advance the country's long-term well-being. According to the civic republican account, it is the firemen who ran into the burning Twin Towers on September 11 who stand for American values and will remain national heroes. In this telling of American political development, the preferences, interests, and identities of individuals are not fixed by objective conditions and irreversible human nature but rather are the product of social interactions and communally shared meanings. This tradition acknowledges that fealty to individual rights and self-interested behavior has gained the upper hand in the United States but insists that this is the product (rather than the cause) of particular institutions and social relations, and that Americans continue to harbor a strong attraction to the idea of promoting the common good.[4]

The framers of the U.S. Constitution incorporated the tension between pursuing self-interest and promoting the enduring permanent interests of the nation.[5] *The Federalist Papers*, which were penned by the lead writers of the Constitution and offer unique insight into its design, famously contrasted "factions," which they described as "united and actuated by some common impulse of passion or of interest," with "the permanent and aggregate interests of the community." According to the Federalists, the challenge facing American government and society was to "secure [both] the public good and private rights."[6] On the one hand, *Federalist Paper* 10 accepted self-interested motivations as "sown in the nature of man" and instead concentrated on harnessing its effects in order to protect individual rights and prevent autocratic government. Allowing "[a]mbition . . . to counteract ambition," *Federalist Paper* 51 explained, would motivate government officials to check and balance each other: "the constant aim is to divide and arrange the several office in such a manner as that each may be a check on the other—that the private interest of every individual may be a sentinel over the public rights."[7]

On the other hand, the Constitution's framers expected citizens and, especially, their representatives to identify and promote "the public good." While they accepted that "the people *commonly intend* the public good,"[8] the framers' primary focus was on the people's representatives "whose wisdom may best discern the true interest of their country and [are] . . . least likely to sacrifice it to temporary or partial considerations."[9] The president is singled out for exerting leadership to advance the country's overall, "aggregate" interests as the government's ceremonial head, commander in chief, and sole occupant of executive branch.[10] *Federalist Papers* 70 and 71 argue that the president is best able to "secure [the nation's] . . . interests" because of his unique ability to lead with energy, secrecy, and dispatch and to "act [on] his own opinion with vigor and decision" in order to defend "the interests of the people" against their momentary passions or the legislature's overreaching.[11] *Federalist Paper* 68 defends the Electoral College for facilitating the selection of "characters pre-eminent for ability and virtue" who would provide "independent" leadership and "good administration" that benefited the nation's enduring interests. The contribution of the Electoral College was to shield the president from the "tempt[ation] to sacrifice his duty" in the face of political pressures to succumb to demagoguery and "intrigue and corruption." Of particular importance, the Constitution's framers did not equate the "public good" with majority opinion; indeed, they repeatedly warned that majoritarian movements that trampled individual liberties (notably, the right to private property) represented a threat to the country's overall interests.

Presidents have managed the dual legacy of American political development by using their public rhetoric to affirm their devotion to the national interest while working behind the scenes to stitch together narrow subgroups into a coalition to support their legislation as well as the election of themselves and their fellow partisans. Presidents reap political benefits from publicly positioning themselves as defenders of the nation against the selfish. Over time, presidents have come to travel more and speak more in public about their crusade for the national interest as they attempt to mobilize the country and use this support as a cudgel against recalcitrant members of Congress and interest groups.[12] For instance, President Bush's drive to enact tax cuts was festooned with barnstorming trips around the country that heralded his proposals as advancing the country's overall interests even as critics pointed to the disproportionate gains of the affluent. Indeed, Bush's appeals over the heads of the Washington establishment to enact tax cuts follow a well-worn path taken by Bill Clinton and other modern presidents. As Stephen Wayne discusses in this volume, these campaigns for policy change amount to a "permanent campaign" that deploys the same tools and strategies as does a candidate for office, blurring the line between governing and running for election.

While presidents have publicly advertised their promotion of the national interest, they have worked hard to win the support of political subgroups by relying on two strategies; both strategies have been used for generations, though the particular techniques for pursuing them have changed dramatically. The first strategy is to collect information—accurate, detailed, and extensive profiles of voters and, especially, critical slices of the electorate. The techniques and sources that presidents have used to gather quality information on political factions have significantly changed, from political parties in the nineteenth century to interest groups in the first half of the twentieth century and private presidential polling since the 1960s. In addition to relying on historical evidence, this chapter goes inside the White House—via archival records, interviews, and other evidence— to trace dramatic changes in how presidents since John F. Kennedy have used private polls (referred to here as "subgroup polling") to routinely track electoral segments. The White House's private polling was consistently designed to measure demographics—such as age, gender, race, and income—as well as other critical descriptive characteristics (e.g., whether the respondents live on a farm or in a city). The Nixon and Reagan White Houses initiated critical changes: they substantially increased polling on demographic subgroups and on overtly political segments of the electorate—namely, partisans, likely voters, and the attentive public. President George W. Bush has expanded on the practices of his predecessors in using subgroup polling to collect voter information.

The second related strategy is communication with the mass public and the president's discrete sets of supporters or potential backers. The tools of communications include grassroots organizing (including political parties, interest groups, and volunteers), promotional trips by presidents and their Cabinet secretaries, under-the-radar communications with specialized audiences, and White House management of media coverage of the president and his statements in press conferences and major speeches such as the annual State of the Union address. The White House's public communications are honed by its extensive information on voters. During the past three decades, presidents have become particularly skilled at using their private polling to calibrate the words, arguments, and symbols that they attempt to convey through grassroots organizing, promotional travel, and the media. The principal purpose of this integrated system of political intelligence gathering and communications is to hold core supporters and to lure a more narrowly drawn group of potential supporters.

The truth is that presidents have long relied on information gathering and calibrated communications to build coalitions made up of parts of the electorate and the political establishment. The efforts of contemporary presidents stand out for the techniques they use and the sharpness of the contrast between their ubiquitous public persona and their intensifying strategies behind the scenes. One of the paradoxes of our time is that as presidents have promoted themselves ever more aggressively and visibly as defenders of the national interests, they and their advisors have devoted more attention to tracking and influencing narrow, discrete segments of the country to support the administration. Their national public visibility belies a sustained and growing dependence on discrete parts of the country to win enactment of legislation in Washington and to woo voters to cast their ballots for themselves and their political party.

This chapter begins by tracing the evolution of presidential techniques for collecting reliable political information from political parties and interest groups to the sophisticated polling that exists today. Particular attention is devoted to examining the rise of private polling by presidents since Kennedy and, in particular, the emergence of "subgroup polling." The next section turns to the White House's public communications and, especially, its relations with the press. The following section reveals that the political information gathered by the White House guides its public communications, relying on archival records, interviews, and other evidence since the Kennedy presidency. The chapter concludes that changes in the White House's intelligence gathering and communications to "narrowcast" presidential coalition building to more finely drawn segments of the electorate have altered political calculations and have had significant consequences for American politics and governance.

The Development of Presidential Techniques
for Collecting Political Information

Faced with the prospect of losing an election or seeing their party defeated, presidents have strong incentives to seek out the most reliable, available gauge of what voters are thinking. Historically, presidents first turned to political parties and then to interest groups as tools for political surveillance.[13]

The United States pioneered the development of political parties as organizations that mobilized the mass of voters. Andrew Jackson, who was denied the nomination for president in 1828, led a movement that used political parties to rally voters and propel him into the White House in 1832. In the following decades, political parties became a mechanism for political elites to reach out to voters but also to size up their support in the electorate. In an era when travel was difficult and communications slow, political parties collected basic information on large blocks of voters—such as whether Democrats or Republicans were most popular in particular neighborhoods.

Toward the end of the nineteenth century, loyalty to political parties began to loosen, and politicians started to search for new mechanisms to gather more detailed and accurate information on voters. Politicians turned, in part, to organized groups that represented major sets of interests, such as business and labor, as a "replace[ment for] political parties as the most reliable media for both ascertaining and responding to the views of segments of voters." Interest groups introduced a capacity for more "specialized intelligence about the electorate" in terms of class, business, occupation, profession, and gender.[14]

One of the political innovations of interest groups—one that scientific polling would later significantly expand upon—was to help "campaigns beg[in] to perceive segments [of the electorate] that had not been transparent during the heyday of partisan politics." Equipped with more detailed information from interest groups, politicians developed a "targeted style" of fashioning policies and messages to appeal to the self-interests of narrower segments of voters. As one historian explains, "Politicians, like marketers in the first two decades of the twentieth century, thrilled to the possibility of national constituencies, only to discover that these national markets could often be reached most successfully by identifying and targeting fragments of the whole—whether defined by gradations in income, functional group representation, or gender."[15]

Interest groups (and political parties) performed two critical functions for presidents: they collected valuable information and they communicated with disparate political groups. Herbert Hoover, for instance, used interest groups to "distinguish between voters by class, occupation, and policy preferences, and . . . [to enable] to reflect their wishes back through these same channels."[16] Although interest groups and, before them, political parties were valued by politicians as tools for tracking voters, and though they continue to be helpful in gathering political intelligence,[17] their value as information sources and communicators was "less than perfect" in the eyes of politicians who sought more precise, frequent, and private sources of information.

The Rise of Presidential Polling and the Focus on Political Subgroups

Scientific polling was embraced by presidents once it had demonstrated its advantages in collecting information that identified and helped win over supportive segments of the electorate. Private polling by presidents has developed in two important respects since the 1960s: it has sharply expanded the scope and amount of information it delivers, and it has increasingly focused on "subgroup polling" of critical slices of the electorate.

More and Better White House Polls

POLLING FROM KENNEDY TO REAGAN. Private presidential polling as a routine part of White House operations starts in earnest with John F. Kennedy and then sharply increases in its amount and quality. The expansion of the White House's public opinion apparatus is most plainly evident in the number of its polls.[18] Figure 1 shows that Louis Harris supplied 15 private polling reports to the Kennedy White House, often by relying upon ad hoc arrangements such as "piggybacking" questions on surveys sponsored by other clients. Oliver Quayle, whom Harris had recommended to replace him when he became a pollster for major media organizations, provided most of the 110 surveys that Lyndon Johnson received. Nixon escalated the number of private surveys to 173, relying on a stable of trustworthy pollsters who had Republican "bona fides" to conduct his research, including established firms like Opinion Research Corporation and new upstarts like Robert Teeter (who later codirected a polling firm that worked for the *Wall Street Journal* and directed George H. W. Bush's 1992 campaign) and Richard Wirthlin (who polled for President Reagan). Wirthlin conducted at least 204 private surveys for Reagan, though more probably remain to be publicly released by the Reagan Presidential Library.

The overall trend in the number of polls and other aspects of the White House's public opinion operation are conditioned by several factors. First, the most significant change is from the Democratic administrations of the 1960s (the Kennedy and Johnson administrations) to the subsequent Republican administrations (the Nixon and Reagan presidencies), which reflect developments in survey technology, political conditions, and political learning.[19] There is a qualitative difference in the quality and political utility of the two eras: the Democrats "piggybacked" their polls on surveys being conducted for other clients and had relatively limited control over their timing and content; the Republicans commissioned their surveys, dictating their content and timing.[20] The implication is that the trend in presidential polling as measured over time may actually underestimate its political importance to Nixon and Reagan, compared to the Kennedy and Johnson administrations. Second, the intensity of Nixon's polling is inflated because of his resignation.[21] In short, the major change is from the Democratic to Republican presidents, and the similarity between Nixon and Reagan is partly an artifact of Nixon's failure to finish his second term.

The increased number of presidential polls coincided with their applications to a widening set of political challenges, from a tool for elections to a valuable instrument used throughout the presidential term. Harris, for instance, conducted three times more polls during Kennedy's election campaign (55) than during his term in office (15). Johnson, Nixon, and Reagan all conduced exten-

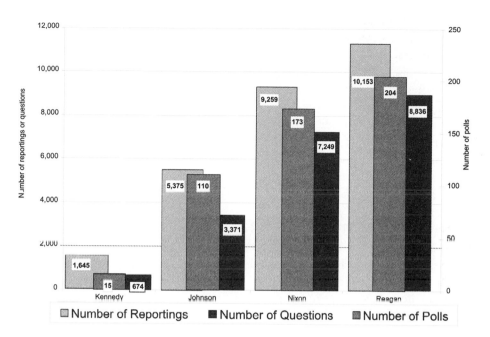

NOTE: These counts are of polls that were regularly conducted (with White House input) and forwarded to the president and his top advisors, who then gave them serious attention. Kennedy's principal pollster was Louis Harris, Johnson's was Oliver Quayle (though Kraft and Napolitan stepped in briefly toward the end of LBJ's term), Nixon's was Opinion Research Corporation, Chilton, and Market Opinion Research (with smaller roles by Becker, Behavioral Research, Central, and Decision Making Information), and Reagan's was Decision Making Information. These counts are from polls conducted after the President was inaugurated. See text for more details.

SOURCE: Presidential Archives.

Figure 1   Growth of Presidential Polling

sive survey research beyond their election campaigns, though obviously the number and intensiveness of surveying increased as elections approached.

The raw count of the number of polls maps the sheer size of the polling operations across nearly three decades; but it does not necessarily convey the changing scope and sophistication of White House polling. This change in content is partly captured by the growing number of discrete polling results that were collected by the White House's private polls (referred to here as "reportings").

Figure 1 shows a dramatic rise in the amount of polling information flowing into the White House. There is an increase from 1,645 reportings under Kennedy to 10,153 under Reagan. This means, for example, that the Reagan White House received 15 discrete pieces of information from a survey that asked respondents to evaluate 15 aspects of the president's personality, from strength to warmth. The rise in the number of discrete reportings to the White House was greater in some cases than indicated by the number of polls. For instance, Nixon conducted about 57 percent more polls than Johnson, and he received 72 percent more discrete bits of information on public opinion than did his predecessor. In other words, each poll delivered more information to Nixon.

The sophistication of presidential polling also improved over time. Early presidential polls often relied upon a relatively small number of questions that used an open-ended format. In effect, these polls were fishing for what they could find. One common question, for instance, was to ask respondents to volunteer what they saw as the problems facing the country; another standard question asked respondents to describe what they liked least and most about the president.

By contrast, Nixon and his advisors developed sophisticated research designs that required a greater number of survey questions and were rooted in cutting-edge research in the academy and in commercial advertising. Figure 1 shows that the number of questions asked by presidents rapidly expanded, rising from 674 questions under Kennedy to 8,836 questions under Reagan. Where Johnson's surveys used an open-ended question to troll for public reactions to the president's personality, Nixon and Reagan used sophisticated methodologies to map out the public's perceptions of the president's personal character, which then fed into discussions of political strategy.[22] Later presidents developed more elaborate surveys by borrowing heavily from scholarly articles in *Public Opinion Quarterly* and from the graduates of the premier survey research centers such as the University of Michigan.

The increased extensiveness, scope, and sophistication of presidential polling were reflected in its widening distribution within the White House. Fearful of criticism and unsure of its compensating benefits, President Kennedy stored his polls in his brother's safe in the attorney general's office. Nixon's chief of staff, H. R. Haldeman, stored the private polls in his office safe, though he selectively shared them with senior aides. Reagan's White House expanded the circulation of polling results to senior staff as well as to those with specializations in foreign and domestic policy.[23] Even as recent presidents have circulated their polling results within the administration, they continue to insist that their advisors keep their polls private and not allow them to circulate outside the White House; private control over the polls allows the White House to examine sensitive topics (such as whether to replace the vice president, as Nixon did) and to keep valuable findings from rivals.

PRESIDENTIAL POLLING SINCE REAGAN. Although a complete appraisal of presidential polling since Reagan must wait for the fuller opening of archival records, early archival evidence and journalistic accounts indicate that it continues and has probably expanded under the last three presidents. President George H. W.

Bush has been portrayed as thoroughly uninterested in polling, with one journalistic review of recent presidents confidently announcing that he "practically eschewed polls altogether."[24] But preliminary reviews of newly opened archival records at the Bush Library suggest that he did conduct considerably more polling than was known publicly, though probably not at the level of his immediate predecessors and successors. On the other hand, interviews and selective reviews of White House documents and financial disclosures indicate that Bill Clinton and George W. Bush have resumed the kind of extensive and sophisticated polling that Nixon and Reagan introduced.

George W. Bush ran against Al Gore in the 2000 presidential election promising to "govern based upon principle and not on polls and focus groups." Bush's rhetorical dismissal of polls was part and parcel of his general rejection of Bill Clinton; it does not, however, describe his actual behavior. Indeed, some estimates suggest that Bush may be doing more polling than Clinton.[25] This disjuncture between rhetorical flourish and actual behavior is not new; Lyndon Johnson's flagrant promotion of favorable private polls prompted Nixon to hide his own, far more extensive private polling operation.

Bush's team of pollsters, focus group conveners, and analysts closely monitored the public's thinking about policy issues, nonpolicy matters, and its perceptions of the president. The White House relied on Jan van Lohuizen, its lead pollster, and also benefited from expert assistance in analyzing survey data (an operation that was led by Fred Steeper, who had previously worked for the Nixon White House). In addition, the President's reelection committee and the national Republican Party developed huge data bases on tens of millions of Americans. These data contain a wide range of politically relevant information, from voter registration to political contributions, based on census reports as well as private and other public sources.[26]

Bush's reelection committee also assembled an extraordinary set of data on the consumer preferences of Americans. Ken Mehlman, manager of Bush's reelection campaign, explained that his team "did what Visa did" to figure out "how [voters] live": "We acquired a lot of consumer data [on such questions as] 'What magazine do you subscribe to? Do you own a gun? How often do the folks go to church? Where do you send your kids to school? Are you married?'"[27]

In short, the search by presidents for political information has evolved from plotting the basic preferences of voters for political parties and their self-interests as deciphered by interest groups to increasingly extensive and sophisticated polls on political attitudes and behavior as well as massive data bases on consumer buying habits. The White House's operations to gather information have expanded from winning election campaigns to equipping presidents to enhance their political standing during the governing phase. Underlying the evolution of different tools for gathering information is a similar motivation: to know more about voters. One of the most important results of this drive has been to widen the White House's information on electoral subgroups.

Subdividing the American Electorate: The Rise of Subgroup Polling

Polling is costly for presidents. It requires significant financial investments and can be a political liability if it becomes a visible part of the White House. Presidents absorb the financial and political costs of polling because they value the information they gather on big political questions: Do voters approve of the president's job performance, and how do voters stack him up against challengers? Media stories on polls largely report the evaluations of the entire country, running a headline, for instance, that the president's approval has dropped below 50 percent (a political litmus test of political weakness). Although the White House welcomes reports on the views of all Americans, practical politics is the business of stitching together many discrete parts of the electorate—the political equivalent of subatomic particles. What the White House craves is accurate and precise information that equips it to write off particular subgroups that are unalterably hostile, to lock down the parts that are loyally devoted, and to concentrate on recruiting the factions and clusters that appear receptive but remain elusive. Although presidents previously turned to political parties and interest groups to help them understand the segments of the electorate, scientific polls introduce an unparalleled advantage: they provide reliable, precise, frequent, and private information that disaggregates the electorate into finely cut slices.

Presidents since Kennedy have enhanced their capacity to pinpoint and recruit electoral segments by collecting two types of information. First, they track political subgroups based on core demographic traits such as income and race. Second, under Nixon and Reagan, the White House expanded its monitoring of subgroups to include political identities (i.e., party affiliation and ideological orientation) and past voting behavior.

DEMOGRAPHIC SUBGROUPS. The demographic characteristics of income, race, and ethnicity define some of the oldest and most enduring cleavages that politicians have used to distinguish friendly from unfriendly voters. Private presidential polling has replaced seat-of-the pants judgments and sweeping conclusions about demographic leanings with laser-guided diagnostics.

Presidential polling on demographic subgroups results from the perennial complaints that presidents and their senior aides directed toward their pollsters: aggregate polling data are not helpful to their practical political work of isolating the pockets of real or potential support. The result is a steady expansion since the Kennedy White House in the polling of the core demographic traits of income, race, age, gender, and education. Figure 2 shows that 7 to about 10 percent of all poll reports to the White House relate to core demographic traits. The total

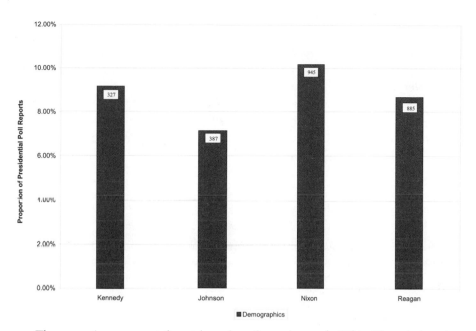

NOTE: The proportions represent the total number of reportings to the White House in its private polls regarding demographic traits (total is superimposed at the top of each bar) in relation to the total number of all private poll reportings to the White House. For information on private White House polling firms see note for Figure 1.

SOURCE: Presidential Archives.

Figure 2   Presidential Polling on Demographic Traits

number of reports to the White House on demographics more than doubled, from 327 under Kennedy to 945 under Nixon and 885 in the Reagan White House.

The White House's tracking of demographic traits has allowed it to investigate approval of the president among specific subgroups, electoral strength as measured against rivals, and competing policy positions. Did the president draw his greatest support from higher as compared to lower income groups, men versus women, and whites versus nonwhites?

Information on the president's standing among different pockets of the electorate was a critical asset. Not surprisingly, the proportional attention to demographics typically ranked as one of most heavily polled areas within the White House and one that was consistently tracked by presidents. The fairly constant attention to demographics contrasts with other areas of heavy White House polling (such as personal image) where there were notable changes due to technical breakthroughs in survey research, turnover in the cast of political personalities, and political disruptions that introduced new political challenges.

ATTITUDINAL AND BEHAVIORAL SUBGROUPS. The growing extent and sophistication of the White House's public opinion apparatus has enhanced its capacity to track political identities beyond demographic traits. In particular, White House polls after Kennedy expanded its tracking of two sets of political identities: attitudinal identities and behavioral identities.

Partisan and Ideological Identities. White House polls tracked enduring identities based on the core political attitudes of party identification (Democratic, Republican, or independent) and political ideology (conservative, liberal, or moderate). They monitored the strength of these political identities, attempting to pinpoint their partisans and ideological allies as well as potential new recruits.

Figure 3 shows the sharp rise in the absolute and proportional polling by the White House of partisan and ideological affinities. While Kennedy did not track these identities and Johnson did so only episodically, Nixon devoted sustained attention to them. The major rise in polling on attitudinal identities came under Reagan, when the absolute and proportional amount of information grew

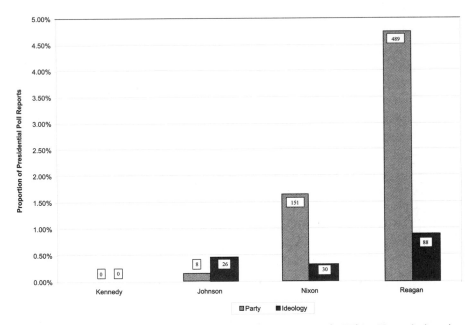

NOTE: The proportions represent the total number of reportings to the White House in its private polls regarding partisan and ideological identifications (total is superimposed at the top of each bar) in relation to the total number of all private poll reportings to the White House. For information on private White House polling firms see note for Figure 1.

SOURCE: Presidential Archives.

Figure 3   Presidential Polling on Political Party and Ideology

threefold over the levels under Nixon. This is a significant development given overall "takeoff" in polling, revealing a determination by the Nixon and Reagan administrations to track conservatives not only in the Republican Party but also in the Democratic Party. The Republican presidents were searching for new recruits for a conservative coalition that would be anchored in longtime Republicans while drawing in disaffected Democrats.

Identities of Political Activists. The White House's polling apparatus also tracked subgroups of Americans who were active in the electoral process and campaigns. These subgroups were defined by their past and likely future turnout to vote as well as their degree of interest, knowledge, and attention to candidates, campaign advertisements, and presidential debates. The purpose of these survey items was to pinpoint the president's supporters who were quite active in the electoral and campaign process, voters who regularly turned out but split their ticket between Democratic and Republican candidates, and citizens who were sympathetic with the president's political philosophy (whether conservative or liberal) but did not turn out regularly to vote.

Figure 4 shows that polling on the political behavior and activity of subgroups rose sharply from Kennedy to Reagan. Research on the subgroups of political activists was not the most extensive form of subgroup polling; it did not account for even 2 percent of White House polling under any of the four presidents, compared to the 7 to 10 percent commitment to polling on demographics. Nonetheless, the attention to political activity and behavior was notable: it was greater than polling on ideological identities under some presidents, and it increased at significant rates. Polling on voting behavior was conducted under both Kennedy and Johnson, but it rose threefold under Nixon and increased another 50 percent in the Reagan White House.

The Nixon White House was particularly interested in "ticket splitters," while the Reagan team targeted voters who were most active in campaigns. One of the most striking features of White House polling on behavioral identities is the surge in attention under Reagan to voter involvement in election campaigns. Under Kennedy, Johnson, and Nixon, the White House gave no or little attention to campaign activists. The Reagan White House, however, sharply expanded its polling on this subgroup, exceeding even its work on voting activists. Reagan and his aides were intent on finding the small cluster of Americans who most closely followed and were involved in campaigns.

These developments reflect a hardheaded adaptation to the reality that the voting universe was shrinking to about half of the eligible electorate and the Democratic Party's majority was splintering as civil rights issues loosened its hold over southern states (especially among white voters). Polling on the behavioral subgroups equipped the White House to cater to individuals within the voting universe, to target irregular voters who were sympathetic, and to ignore Americans who were hostile and tended not to participate.

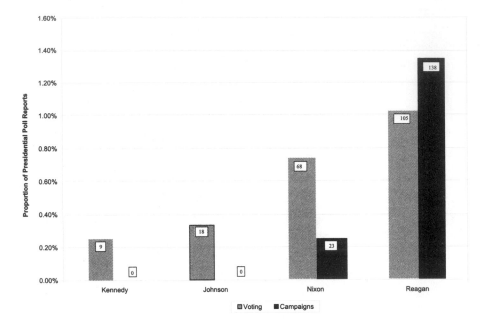

NOTE: The proportions represent the total number of reportings to the White House in its private polls regarding political activists (total is superimposed at the top of each bar) in relation to the total number of all private poll reportings to the White House. Polling on political activism focused on past and likely future turnout to vote as well as degree of interest, knowledge, and attention to candidates, campaign advertisements, and presidential debates. For information on private White House polling firms see note for Figure 1.
SOURCE: Presidential Archives.

Figure 4   Presidential Polling on Political Activists

SUBGROUP POLLING CONTINUES UNDER GEORGE W. BUSH. President Bush continued to the track voters based on age, income, religious affiliation and other subgroup traits.[28] The president and his advisors have devoted particular attention to geographic locations within states and metropolitan areas, separating out voters who live in urban areas from those who reside in rural communities and new and older suburban neighborhoods. In Florida, for instance, his team carefully tracked voters in the corridor along Interstate 4 that lies in the center of the state.

The Bush team shares Nixon's and Reagan's keen interest in collecting information on political behavior. During the president's push for tax cuts, his pollsters monitored not only the view of his loyal base of Republican supporters but also the reactions of voters who moved back and forth between parties or were not regular voters. The president's campaign team devoted a great deal of time and expense in 2004 to tracking conservatives who had often failed to vote. A regional political director for Bush boasted that these voters were the "true target of this campaign." In one of the major advances over the 2000 campaign, the 2004 team identified the actual individuals who were "unmotivated," or, as the campaign described them, "unreliable" and "lazy" because they had voted in only one of the last three or four elections or had just recently registered to vote.

Presidents usually listen before they speak; they closely monitor voters in order to fashion their communications with Americans. The following sections examine the administration's relations with the press (the principal means for reaching the country) and the White House's use of its political intelligence to hone its public communications.

How Presidents Reach Their Audience

Today we are accustomed to getting news reports nearly every day on what the president said or did. Even when President Bush goes on vacation to the desolate town of Crawford, Texas, an army of journalists camp out on a dusty lane to report daily updates, if only to relay whether the chief executive went fishing. With little thought, we accept the statements of the White House's press secretary as expressing the views and even the inner thoughts of the president (such as how he felt about news of a natural tragedy). Cabinet secretaries are also accepted as the president's ambassadors, receiving generous press coverage from local reporters when they land in towns and cities to make announcements touting the president and the administration's policies. Yet the daily press coverage of the president and his administration, and the acceptance and even expectation of presidential spokespersons are—in historical terms—recent developments. The evolution of a commercial press and the strategic drive of presidents to communicate more often and more effectively with the public have produced today's conventions.

Built into the relationship between the White House and the press is a tug of war. The distinctiveness of each institution generates incentives and pressures that in large part transcend the idiosyncrasies of individual presidents and reporters— whether the individuals are the winsome Ronald Reagan or paranoid Richard Nixon, the feisty CBS news anchor Dan Rather or the deferential television interviewer Barbara Walters.

The Constitution makes the president the single most powerful individual in the U.S. government, and yet Congress, the courts, state governments, and a host of nongovernmental organizations all possess the authority and resources to stymie most presidential initiatives. Facing constraints on what presidents see as their responsibility to lead, they attempt to augment their scarce political resources within Washington by mobilizing public support and then wielding it to sway members of Congress to support their initiatives; they go outside Washington to unify elites within Washington. Presidents equate their ability to rally the public and to enhance their influence to their control of the information that flows from their administration to the public. Their principal tactics for mastering this information flow are: to centralize decisions about mass communications within the White House, a process that now consumes an entire division, staffed by over 50 personnel; and to hone the content of that information to most effectively resonate with voters and, especially, targeted subgroups.

The president has unique advantages in managing the press. Within the U.S. government, he is the single most powerful individual with regard to the country's defense and many aspects of its domestic policy. Only the president has the opportunity to command television coverage during prime time to deliver a major speech, such as the annual State of the Union address at the beginning of each year, to make important announcements like Bush's warnings of an imminent invasion of Iraq in the spring of 2003, or to convene a solo press conference. Televised speeches give the president unparalleled power over the policymaking agenda, selecting subjects and policies that will dominate debate in Congress and in the country.

The unrivaled importance and public prominence of the president has convinced media editors to single it out as a "beat" that deserves around-the-clock coverage by their reporters, making the White House the most closely watched and extensively reported government office in the country. For many stories, the White House is the best or only source of information for the press to do its job, giving the president and his staff an opportunity to use that dependency to shape information to put themselves in the best possible light.[29] For instance, press coverage of Saddam Hussein's connection to the September 11 terrorists and weapons of mass destruction relied on administration sources claiming to have exclusive intelligence, which they used to shape the debate about going to war. The White House's determination to use this dependence to manage the press is also illustrated by the advice that Senator Jay Rockefeller and White House aides offered First Lady Hillary Clinton when she was launching President Clinton's health reform initiative in 1993: passing health legislation required the "ability to define the health care reform debate on our own terms" and to incorporate journalists in a "crafted information flow."[30]

In comparison to the White House, the media are driven by two quite different sets of incentives that consistently put them at odds with the administration.[31] First, the media in the United States are privately owned businesses that must generate profits by attracting large audiences. This puts a premium on news stories of the president that feature a "big story" of importance and pack audience-grabbing conflict and suspense. Covering the Iraq War, for instance, was a big story that was made particularly riveting by the administration's decision to allow reporters to "embed" with a military division, which gave viewers and readers an extraordinarily immediate and visceral feel for the operation. Conflicts over the conduct of the Iraq War and the size of the U.S. military deployment among Secretary of Defense Donald Rumsfeld, the military, and

members of Congress added further suspense to the story, creating new opportunities to build audiences.

The media's second incentive is to serve as a neutral "watchdog" that scruti-
nizes government in order to generate accurate and independent information that
allows the public to hold government officials accountable. The decline of political
parties and the emergence of a commercial press that aimed to widen its audience
gave rise to the professional norm of "objectivity," the expectation that journalists
(even as they scrutinize government officials) will present "both" sides of a story, on
the assumption that the truth lies somewhere between competing claims.

The tug of war between the White House and the press often results in
mutual recrimination. White House officials frequently complain that the press
misrepresents their comments and distorts the important issues on the government's agenda by focusing public attention on personal rivalries or disputes with
Congress, at the expense of more important developments like a new report
showing signs of an economic recovery or the president's announcement of a
foreign policy breakthrough. Reporters, on the other hand, suspect that they are
being misled or deceived. David Gergen, who worked for three Republican
presidents and one Democratic president, concedes that in his "experience over
the past thirty years, every White House . . . has on occasion willfully misled or
lied to the press," with the exception of Gerald Ford's presidency.[32] By 2005, a
growing number of reporters concluded that they were deceived by the Bush
White House on Iraq after the administration's most forceful arguments for
invading Iraq (the existence of significant stores of weapons of mass destruction
and Saddam Hussein's connection to the September 11 attacks) proved
unfounded.[33] This tug of war is anchored in the historic evolution of presidential
communications using both the press and direct outreach mechanisms.

The Historic Roots of Presidential Communications with the Mass Public

In the nineteenth century, presidents used political parties to reach out to
voters. Local party organizations not only sized up the thinking of voters but also
organized meetings, put on parades and speeches, and took other steps to communicate with their members and their neighbors. The parties prepared their
own newspapers, which loyally reported the speeches and activities of their
politicians. The policies and public comments of the president were glowingly
recounted in the newspapers controlled by his party and were mercilessly
ridiculed in the publications of the opposing party.[34] In nineteenth-century
America, partisan newspapers enjoyed the largest circulation, and the newspaper
was the principal means through which Americans learned about Washington
politics, as travel and other forms of communications were slow and limited.

By the end of the nineteenth century, presidents had branched out from the
partisan press. They began to replace political parties with interest groups as a
mechanism not only for tracking the sentiments of voters but also for reaching

out to them. Presidents saw interest groups as a "crucial vessel for uniting disparate individuals toward associative ends."[35]

Another significant development was the growing attempt of the White House to manage the media. President William McKinley took several important steps, starting in the second half of the 1890s, to control and centralize information in the White House as part of his efforts to marshal public support for his foreign policy.[36] He attempted to exert greater control over the content of the information flowing from his administration by developing a staff that specialized in working with reporters, foreshadowing the later press office and press secretary. He also initiated the White House's efforts to set the media's agenda by generating a steady supply of information that would keep the administration and its activities constantly before the public. This effort would evolve into "daily feedings" of briefings, press releases, advance copies of speeches that allowed reporters to file stories before their deadlines, and accommodations in the White House that allowed them to set up shop near the president's offices. To evaluate and improve its effectiveness, the McKinley White House monitored newspaper coverage of itself.

Subsequent presidents continued and expanded these innovations. Teddy Roosevelt saw the media as a valuable instrument for appealing to the public to challenge vested interests. Although William Taft was politically pressured to continue the new relations with the press started by his predecessors, it was Woodrow Wilson who vigorously expanded relations with the press and centralized control in the White House. Among Wilson's innovations was to resume the tradition of the president orally delivering his State of the Union address to Congress (a tradition that had been suspended after George Washington) and to develop the White House's capacity to communicate directly with Americans by launching nationwide campaigns, such as its promotions to rally the country during World War I.

In 1929, Herbert Hoover appointed the first press secretary, expanding the White House staff's specialization in press relations. Under Franklin D. Roosevelt in the early 1930s, the press secretary was given greater authority to systematically structure the routines of the press, to structure its contacts in the administration, and to discipline executive branch departments to project the public message that the White House designed. In addition, the Roosevelt White House encouraged ties with a new medium (radio) and strengthened existing ties with others (newspapers and film).[37]

By World War II, the outlines of the contemporary relations between the president and press began to emerge. In the following decades, decisions about the information that would be made public and how it would be presented were further centralized within the White House.

Modern Mass Communications: From Kennedy to Bush

The modern era of public communications by presidents starts with John Kennedy and his calculated use of television. According to one of Kennedy's close aides, the President identified "public communications—educating, persuading, and mobilizing... [public opinion]" as one of his most important jobs.[38] The priority that Kennedy placed on mass communications propelled a series of innovations, including regular televised press conferences, and a concerted effort to integrate executive branch agencies in the feeding and managing of the press. The result was to bring Washington into the living rooms of Americans, making "normal" what had been quite extraordinary only shortly before Kennedy's election.

Kennedy's embrace of modern communications technology launched a consistent effort by subsequent presidents to steadily improve the White House's capacity to manage the press. The White House press secretary and his base of operations, the Press Office, cemented their roles as the nerve center for the administration's relations with the press and the command center for focusing the attention of the press on the president. The press secretary would also continue to corral the executive branch departments to follow the policy positions and messages that the White House developed and to insist that the executive branch agencies "push up" good news to White House so that the president could announce it and thereby take the credit. In addition to continuing to use the media as a way to reach the public, presidents systematically used the Cabinet secretaries as public relations tools, a kind of public lobbyist that could be deployed throughout the country to directly promote the president and the administration's policies.

For instance, the Clinton White House pinned much of its hopes of passing its ambitious health reform plan in 1993 and 1994 on managing the press.[39] The president's aides developed a series of "game plans" to centralize control over the administration's public statement within the White House and to saturate the press with its "message" of introducing "security for all" in the expectation that this would crowd out the opposing messages of reform opponents. The political constraints on presidents can offset even laboriously drawn communications plans; the Clinton initiative utterly failed in the face of harsh attacks by interest groups and Republicans and from divisions among congressional Democrats.

Public Communications under George W. Bush

Ronald Reagan was often described as the "great communicator" for his adept skill in delivering a speech and handling public events. President Bush is, by comparison, uncomfortable in public events covered by the press, mangling English grammar and losing his train of thought. Perhaps as compensation for Bush's personal unease with the press, he has notably strengthened the White House's domination over the flow of information to journalists and the public, expanding the staffing of its communications operation from 39 to 52.[40]

Presidents since the nineteenth century have looked for ways to deliver their messages directly to the public, bypassing (when necessary) the press, which can serve as a "filter," according to President Bush. Until the mid-twentieth century, presidents relied on political parties and interests groups to communicate directly. Presidents since FDR have capitalized on modern transportation, building a sophisticated White House operation for writing speeches and arranging travel, allowing the president to routinely take his message to towns and cities across the country. Like other modern presidents, Bush used this capability to barnstorm the country for his legislative proposals and for his reelection campaign, targeting specific areas and segments of the country. In Florida, for instance, he traveled not only to the most widely known destinations, like Miami and Tampa, but also to new suburbs that were relatively unknown outside the state, like Niceville and New Port Richey.

One of Bush's innovations was to strengthen the president's ability to conduct grassroots organizing for his reelection and for his policy initiatives (from tax cuts to socially conservative legislation and judicial nominees). Although previous administrations solicited the support of interest groups and voluntary associations, the Bush White House was particularly aggressive in building ties to community organizations from churches to small businesses. The president courted (in public and in private) Evangelical, Catholic, and Jewish assemblies as part of a calculated effort to construct a coalition of diverse religious faiths. Although social conservatives were initially a bit suspicious of Bush's commitment to their agenda, they came to accept him (according to one religious leader) as "a man of great, deep faith . . . who didn't just talk about being a religious person, but lives it out."[41] These community ties helped Bush to mobilize an army of volunteers that far surpassed the numbers he was able to rally in 2000. In Florida, for instance, the number of volunteers for Bush rose by more than tenfold, from less than 10,000 to 109,000. The volunteers gave Bush an army on the ground that made phone calls, walked neighborhoods, wrote letters, and provided transportation for voters to the voting booths.

In addition to direct grassroots organizing, the Bush White House has taken a strikingly disciplined and systematic approach to handling the press. The commercial pressure on the press to win audiences puts a premium (as explained by Karl Rove, the political architect of Bush's campaigns and presidency) on "get[ting] a headline or get[ting] a story that will make people pay attention to their magazine, newspaper, or television more." "The nature of the news business," another advisor concludes, "is that conflict is news."[42] The White House has designed a tightly structured approach to controlling the information that flows to the press. The release of information is centralized within the White House and in the hands of a few designated staff: the press secretary and director of its entire communications operations (Dan Bartlett and Nicolle Devenish). Other staff, including the President's chief of staff, Andy Card, rarely talk with reporters, insisting that "[i]t's not our job to be sources."

The White House staff members responsible for public communications are expected to be "automatons" who follow the directions given by the president and senior staff at daily meetings designed to "get everyone on the same song sheet," as Bartlett reports. Armed with their marching orders, the president's press secretary (Ari Fleischer, then Scott McClellan) meets with the mass media every day, first in the informal morning "gaggle," when journalists pose questions without the glare of television cameras, and then at midday, when the cameras are on. The press secretary works all day—beginning early in the morning—anticipating the questions that reporters will pose and formulating answers that reflect the thinking of the president, his top aides, and the specialists in the wider administration such as the Department of Defense. Several times a week, the president himself meets in the Oval Office with a revolving group of about a dozen reporters and photographers who are allowed to ask a few questions.

The most uncommon events are the press conferences when Bush alone takes questions from reporters in front of television cameras. Bush has held fewer solo press conferences than any of his postwar predecessors because of his personal unease and the White House's determination to "control your message," as one aide responsible for communications put it. In addition to tending to the national mass media, the White House caters to out-of-town media, whose representatives tend to be less aggressive and suspicious than the veteran Washington reporters. It also reaches out to more specialized media, from religious publications to the in-house networks operated by private gyms. In addition to the White House's regular contacts with the press, the president's communications staff meets with officials throughout the administration to distribute "talking points" to ensure they stay on the "message" defined by the House and to make it possible for "everyone [to] say exactly the same thing."

From the perspective of the Bush White House, the administration has been remarkably successful both in controlling the press agenda and in locking the press out of the White House, following the president's reported insistence that the administration "tal[k] about what we want to talk about, not what the press want to talk about." The result has been a "funnel of information" from the president to the communications staff to the administration more widely. With remarkable success, the Bush White House has in Bartlett's view created a kind "mind meld" and "the most disciplined White House in history," according to Reagan's communications guru Michael Deaver. This stands in contrast to previous administrations, when officials would set up their own operations to advance themselves and their favored policies. Bill Clinton, for instance, fumed in the wake of books and newspaper stories based on leaks from staff and advisors.

The Bush administration's successful control over the flow of information has complicated the media's job. On the one hand, many reporters bristle at the "fortress" or "wall" that the White House has erected to keep information private and to limit their access to official sources to a minimum. They complain that they are treated with "contempt" and reminisce fondly about the porous administrations of the past, when it was they who were courted by White House officials.

On the other hand, the hunt for the rare and therefore valued high-level source in the Bush White House puts considerable pressure on journalists to pull their punches and favorably portray the administration. According to ABC news anchor Peter Jennings, "There is a feeling among some members of the press corps that you are either favored by the Administration or not, and that will have something to do with your access." Jennings himself reported a "rather naked" warning that one of his stories on a White House official "better be good" if he wanted to be granted continued access to high-level officials. George Stephanopoulos, a former Clinton aide and host of a Sunday television talk show, has had a hard time landing high-level officials because the White House is punishing him for unfavorable coverage. By contrast, Bob Woodward has been rewarded for what the White House sees as favorable coverage; he has been granted interviews with Bush and department secretaries (including Donald Rumsfeld and Colin Powell) that have allowed him to write two best-selling books. Capturing the contradictory pressures on reporters both to land the audience-grabbing story and to serve as a watchdog, CNN's Christiane Amanpour worried during the Iraq War that "the press was muzzled . . . and self-muzzled."

The White House Strategy of Narrowcasting

The effectiveness of White House communications, the president and his aides have calculated, depends on tailoring messages that resonate with Americans and, specifically, with politically important segments of the electorate. Presidents invest tremendous resources into tracking the views of voters in order to hone their outward communications.

Presidents turned to interest groups at the outset of the twentieth century precisely because they provided information on segments of the electorate for fashioning messages that were tailored to appeal to them. The development of private presidential polling as a tool for meticulously monitoring support or potential support of the president among subgroups of voters refined the White House's enduring interest in calibrating its outward communications. The next sections examine the strategic uses of the White House's expansion of public opinion research and subgroup polling from demographic traits to overtly political characteristics, focusing on the presidencies of Richard Nixon, Ronald Reagan, and George W. Bush.

Presidential Polling and the Subgroup Strategies of the Nixon White House

Nixon and his aides began to work earnestly on his 1972 reelection campaign about halfway through his first term. Much of their strategy focused on tracking and recruiting distinct political subgroups or, as one influential advisor put it, "segment[ing] the electorate."[43] Nixon's chief of staff, H. R. Haldeman, instructed his staff to mine the White House's "considerable amount of polling data [on] . . . subgroups within the population" in order to run breakdowns and cross-tabulations on trial heats and Nixon's approval ratings.[44] Reflecting this intense concentration on pinpointing supportive factions, Nixon at one point lashed out at "Teeter's polling [as] a disaster" because it was focusing on "our old constituency in the fashionable suburbs" and was missing some of the new subgroups that were inclined to support him—the "hard hats and blue collar types."[45]

Nixon's appeal to the "silent majority" early in his first term illustrates his wide-ranging commitment to "build our own new coalition."[46] The White House's polls in 1969 tested "public reaction to this concept" and reported that it was well-received, especially among "Republicans, northern voters, conservatives, and high school graduates." Convinced that the concept of the "silent majority" was a "valuable tool for the Nixon administration for generating and maintaining public support," aides recommended "consistent effort to reinforce the identification [in order to] preserv[e] and buil[d] administration support."[47] Nixon closed out 1969 with a memorandum to his chief of staff asking for a report on the administration's efforts to "mobilize the silent majority."[48]

Although the White House's intense concentration on the "silent majority" would fade over time, Nixon's early outreach to this political constellation did reflect a sustained effort to "fin[d] out which groups are shifting [and why]."[49] Archival records confirm the strong interest of the Nixon White House in tracking the demographic subgroups reported in Figure 2. Nixon and Haldeman carefully sifted through the "splits" in White House polls, raising questions about surprising results.[50] For instance, one set of analyses compared presidential approval ratings in four polls in early 1971 to identify which subgroups least liked the President (the educated and youngest) and which liked him best (non-southerners, Catholics, and the older).[51] In a meeting with Nixon that was recorded in Haldeman's meticulous diary, John Ehrlichman, another senior White House official, "pushed hard on the basis of [a White House] poll that [the issue of the environment] is the way to reach new people that now are not for us."[52]

FINDING ATTITUDINAL AND BEHAVIORAL FACTIONS. One of the innovations of the Nixon White House was to substantially expand polling on political attitudes in search of supportive segments of the American electorate. White House polls tracked "significant differences" based on party identification and ideology in trial heats, approval ratings, and concerning policy issues and other areas.

White House polling on partisan and ideological attitudes identified a puzzle: Americans tended to identify themselves both as conservative and as loyal to the Democratic Party.[53] The challenge, in the White House's view, was to build a conservative coalition by peeling off voters from the Democratic Party who considered themselves conservative or moderate and by deemphasizing party identification as a basis of political identity. Haldeman pressed his aides to conduct "breakdowns . . . on Conservative versus Liberal" on trial heats, approval ratings, and other politically important areas.[54] Nixon was alerted of poll results showing that Republicans were "solid" and that "independents plus defecting Democrats will tip the balance." The strategic implication, according to the White House's polling consultant, was that the "campaign strategy should . . . deemphasize the President's role as leader of the Republican Party" and instead "stress the administration's achievements and presidential roles and characteristics already seen in a favorable light."[55]

A second innovation in the Nixon White House's polling was to focus on "behavioral voting groups rather than attitudinal groups." Although partisan and ideological attitudes were important, Nixon and his advisors targeted their polling and outreach efforts in planning the 1972 campaign on "ticket splitters" in the conviction that these differences in political behavior "will be much more useful for the campaign" in targeting the decisive swing voters. Specifically, the director of Nixon's polling during the campaign, Robert Teeter, insisted on "classifying the voters in terms of Republicans, ticket splitters, and Democrats on the basis of their past voting behavior rather than into Republicans, Independents, and Democrats on the basis of their self perception or attitude." The strategic advantage of this behavioral approach was to identify voters who "almost always split their ticket and are, therefore, available to either side in most elections."[56]

This behavioral approach formed the foundation of the White House's "target voter strategy." The value of this kind of subgroup polling, one senior campaign official explained, is that it "assures that concentrations of voters can be identified who will vote for the President in greater proportions."[57] In a familiar refrain, Teeter reported to John Mitchell (attorney general and director of Nixon's reelection campaign) that "past voting behavior is the most important factor affecting the President's vote" and that "demographic bloc voting is . . . *less important* than voting behavior in affecting the election."[58]

SUBGROUP POLLING GUIDES PUBLIC COMMUNICATIONS. The White House's polling on political segments guided its public communications and most important activities. Warning that "it will be difficult for the President to attract the ticket-splitter on the basis of specific issues," Teeter recommended to Mitchell that the campaign "appeal to these swing voters on the basis of a set of well-articulated goals for the country."[59]

Polling information on critical subgroups also influenced the White House's allocation of Nixon's time and the campaign's efforts. Nixon's team developed "measures [of] the amount of ticket-splitting in all the counties of the all 50 states [in order to] . . . *pinpoint those areas where ticket splitting is highest and allocate our resources there.*"[60] The "ticket-splitter data" were also used to shape direct mail efforts and the design of the campaign's organization. They also guided the "scheduling [of] the President and the First Family"—namely, the "priority areas to visit" and the "issues which are of significantly greater concern to the voters of a specific area" for each of these visits.[61] Moreover, information on the political behavior of specific segments of the electorate helped steer efforts to identify, register, and turn out voters most likely to support the president.[62]

Harnessing Subgroup Polling to Message Development: The Reagan White House

Ronald Reagan and his senior aides expanded the Nixon White House's polling on demographic, attitudinal, and behavioral subgroups. The major innovation of the Reagan White House was to use polling on these subgroups to craft and target the presentations of its decisions.

HEIGHTENED MONITORING OF ELECTORAL SUBGROUPS. Compared to previous administrations (especially its Democratic predecessors), the Reagan White House increased the absolute and relative amount of information it received on the "characteristics of voters" in order to monitor the "voters who form Reagan's core and swing support."[63] Part of this effort focused on the "core Reagan support group" as defined by three slices of the electorate: demographic clusters (high income earners, men, whites, and voters who lived in the south and west), political attitudes (conservatives and loyalists of the Republican Party) and political activists (routine voters and energetic advocates). In tracking "Reagan's strongest supporters" after he was inaugurated in 1981, the White House was particularly alert for newer religious Protestant groups—namely, "born again" Christians.[64]

In addition to making sure that Reagan's base was unified, his pollster Richard Wirthlin and advisors fully appreciated that their core supporters "alone do not constitute an electoral majority." They were preoccupied with tracking and wooing the segments of the electorate that "took Reagan over the top in 1980"—voters who were middle-income earners, older (45–64), had some college education, lived in the Midwest, and were weak Democrats and ideologically somewhat conservative or moderate.[65]

The White House's sensitivity to the component parts of Reagan's coalition was reflected in Wirthlin's parsing of what he presented as "aggregate" polling results. He broke down aggregate results into three critical electoral segments: "strength," which included "base Republicans"; "swing," which encompassed white southern Baptists, Catholics, independents, and leaners; and "secondary swing," which included veterans and professionals.[66]

Political attitudes and, especially, party identification were areas of particular interest in the White House as it maneuvered to realign a majority of the electorate toward the Republican Party. (Figure 3 shows a sharp spike in polling on partisan subgroups during the Reagan presidency.) Wirthlin and White House polling analysts persistently tracked the particular "groups that hold the keys to any permanent realignment."[67]

Reagan's team also carefully studied the subgroups who were most likely to vote and to participate in campaigns. For instance, it made special efforts to reach out to "gun groups" because they were identified as "among the top three types of conservative groups in political effectiveness . . . [and in] concentrating [their substantial] resources on specific election contests and specific legislative battles."[68]

More than their predecessors, Reagan and his senior advisors broke down the policy preferences of majorities to study the views of critical segments of the electorate. For instance, when White House polling showed that majorities had shifted toward favoring cuts in defense spending to reduce the federal budget deficit, Reagan's team discounted the findings because "those who are most in favor of [it] . . . (postgraduates, liberals, blacks, Deep South residents, college graduates, and unmarried women) are not our strength constituency *or* the key swing constituencies." Instead, staff focused on "swing and strength constituencies . . . [but especially] swing groups—White Baptists, blue-collar workers, Catholics."[69]

The White House similarly defied aggregate majorities opposed to the administration's positions on social issues in favor of following the preferences of subgroups. Gary Bauer forcefully argued, for instance, that "when we are on the 'wrong' side of . . . issues from a public opinion standpoint . . . [Reagan's position] still may be politically positive." In particular, he pointed to Reagan's opposition to abortion as a critical draw for urban Catholics who had spurned Democrats because they were "associated with abortion on demand."[70] On race, the White House also scrutinized "[poll] responses with a geographic and ethnic breakdown," finding that a substantial portion of southern whites supported, among other potential legislative action, the reauthorization of the 1965 Voting Rights Act.[71]

On other issues, polling of subgroups prompted the White House to consider non-action. For instance, Wirthlin reported that legislation granting amnesty to illegal immigrants "carrie[d] liabilities for the President" because "elements of our key constituents are on both sides of the issue." "[T]he best political solution," the pollster counseled, "is deadlocking the bill in [the] conference committee."[72]

PROGRAMMING THE "GREAT COMMUNICATOR" TO APPEAL TO POLITICAL SEGMENTS. The most innovative aspects of the Reagan White House's subgroup polling were in crafting the words and arguments to publicly communicate its positions.

The regular polling of Reagan's presentations departs from the practice of previous presidents, who generally used neutral wordings to identify the public's preferences toward, for example, policies concerning government spending for job training.

Reagan and his advisors pursued three new directions in using their polling to effectively target public communications on core supporters and swing voters. First, they systematically polled the message by, in effect, test marketing its sales pitches among subpopulations. The purpose was to "test the maneuverability of positions" and to "assess the effectiveness of campaigning."[73] For instance, Wirthlin conducted research in 1982 and 1983 on how to alter the terms of debate about fiscal priorities in order to deflect the growing public unease toward rising budget deficits. His surveys reported that Americans blamed Reagan for not delivering on his campaign theme of balancing the budget. Wirthlin found that they were "giv[ing] [him] low approval ratings on his handling of the deficit" and were now challenging his core policy goals by favoring "reduc[ed] defense spending or [creation of a] contingency tax." Wirthlin responded to these findings not by proposing that the president change policy but by composing an alternative position that the public supported: he reported strong support for a message favoring a constitutional amendment to balance the budget and recommended a "strategy" of promoting a balanced budget through "an aggressive program of presidential events, statements, and surrogate support." The rationale for the president's public campaigning for a balanced budget amendment, Wirthlin candidly acknowledged, was that it would "overcome the perception that [the president] is not fulfilling his campaign promise."[74] Senior White House advisors used Wirthlin's polls to argue for "cut[ting] domestic spending as a means to balance the budget and improve the economy [because it was backed by] . . . the core Reagan support group."[75]

The second new direction in targeted public communications involved using a balanced frame format to compare competing presentations, with an eye to how different demographic, attitudinal, and behavior subgroups responded. In particular, the administration tested its arguments against those of its opponents (using excerpts from their own statements), using two fictitious people, Mr. Smith and Mr. Jones. For instance, Wirthlin used a balanced frame format to study reactions to job-retraining legislation:

Now, I'd like you to try something different. I'm going to read you the positions of two men, Mr. Smith and Mr. Jones. After I read you both statements, please tell me if you . . . strongly like Smith . . . somewhat like Smith . . . somewhat like Jones or strongly like Jones. . . .

Mr. Smith says the Comprehensive Employment and Training Act (CETA) provides make-work government jobs at too high a cost to taxpayers and should be severely reduced in size or eliminated.

Mr. Jones says the Comprehensive Employment and Training Act (CETA) provides opportunities for the disadvantaged to have work and is a wise use of federal money.

Wirthlin analyzed reactions to these alternative public presentations, offering the White House "comparison[s]" across a variety of subgroups defined by income, union membership, and other traits.[76]

The White House used balanced frame questions to anticipate and attempt to defuse negative public reactions among critical electoral subgroups. For example, Wirthlin investigated public reactions to the potentially explosive issue of modifying the Voting Rights Act. He reported that neutral question wordings showed that "the public is split fairly evenly," but that the balanced framed format revealed that "injection of terms like 'rights' and 'abuses' . . . [made] the results change significantly." He was particularly concerned that criticism of the administration's handling of the Voting Rights Act could make it "a leverage issue . . . [that] serves as a signal to other key coalitional elements as to how the Reagan Administration may deal with them." Referring to Hispanic and other subsets of voters, Wirthlin used the balanced frame format to warn that "dealing with this problem has very significant political ramifications that reach far beyond the immediate issue of the Right to Vote."[77]

The third innovation in targeted message development was to monitor the effectiveness of Reagan's speeches and public presentations in State of the Union address and other highly visible comments. Small groups of up to fifty adults were regularly assembled to view major speeches, using handheld devices to record on a five-point scale (from very positive to very negative) their reactions to the president's message, style, and delivery on a line-by-line basis. This "pulse-line" analysis thus provided a detailed evaluation of each section of the President's address.[78] For instance, a "pulseline" analysis of Reagan's nationally televised 1986 address on peace and national security pinpointed his use of the words "declining spending" and a "crisis in recruitment and retention" as producing a decline of interest and support. The "negative reaction," Wirthlin explained, stemmed from "anticipation that Reagan is going to ask for more money for defense" and from suspicion that the military purchases of new fighters reflects "waste and fraud." The peak in positive reaction came as the president heralded "security by building . . . strength," which Wirthlin attributed to his group's "hope of real progress."[79] Chief of Staff Don Regan forwarded Wirthlin's "pulseline" analysis of the president's speech to the White House's senior national security staff and requested that they use it "as a tool in . . . refin[ing] future arguments."[80]

Analyses of small-group reactions to Reagan's speeches supplemented (according to Wirthlin) the White House's tracking of subgroups in large public opinion surveys that were conducted at the same time. Wirthlin reported to the

White House that the participants in the small groups were "stratified to enhance their representativeness." Their most important contribution to the White House's strategizing was that small-group studies "provided an opportunity to probe in depth *why* people responded as they did."[81] This capability equipped Wirthlin to explain (rather than simply describe) the reactions of subgroups.

The recurring loop of subgroup polling and message development that Nixon and Reagan developed was extended by George W. Bush.

George W. Bush Continues the Reagan Legacy

Journalistic accounts suggest that the Bush White House's polling also guided its public communications to critical electoral subgroups. Like the Reagan administration, the Bush White House also attempted to use subgroup polling to hold loyal Republicans while reaching out to swing voters. Bush, however, was less willing than Reagan to let his outreach to swing voters mitigate his efforts to expand his base by targeting religious conservatives and other ideologically sympathetic subgroups. Bush and his advisors honed the president's messages and policy initiatives (especially, his opposition to abortion, same-sex marriage, and embryonic stem cell research) to what they identified as the disaffection and frustration of social conservatives toward permissive or immoral behavior of the wider society.[82]

The strategy of targeting social conservatives in the 2004 election helped Bush (according to exit polls by the National Election Pool) to increase his share of the vote among Protestants, Jews, and Catholics—even though he was running against a Catholic. Indeed, Bush's successful courting of this subgroup left some Republican consultants (like hard-edged Republican consultant Arthur Finkelstein) worrying that it would "strengthe[n] the ability of the Christian right to nominate the next Republican [presidential] nominee" and to block Republicans who more socially moderate.[83]

Bush and his team pursued a variety of strategies during his first term in office and the 2004 campaign to hone the president's messages and policy initiatives. Like Reagan, they used polling on political subgroups to select the wordings of his public statements during his first term in office. For instance, his polling team reported that tax cuts were not popular among swing voters, even though his Republican base strongly supported them. His solution was to redesign the public presentation, not the policy: "slip a conservative agenda past a moderate public."[84] Another illustration of Bush's use of poll-honed presentations is his promotion of Social Security privatization. Although balanced public opinion research has consistently showed significant public opposition to restructuring the program (especially when informed of the transition costs),[85] Bush's polling team carefully designed his presentations to rely on such alluring words as "choice," "control," and "higher returns," tapping into the public's distrust of government to properly invest Social Security money. His second-term effort to enact structural changes in Social Security initially relied on charged words like "crisis" in the hopes of generating support (even though many experts judge the financial shortfall as short of crisis proportions).

The importance that President Bush placed on tracking and appealing to critical segments of the electorate during his first term is strikingly evident in former Treasury Secretary Paul O'Neill's reactions to decision making in the current White House as compared to his service under President Nixon. O'Neill reports that in the Nixon administration, political advisors and their focus on voting niches were largely kept away from policy decisions on taxes and budgets; by contrast, he found these considerations to be decisive influences in shaping policies in the Bush White House. (A similar criticism was made of the Clinton White House.) Satiating the expectations of electoral subgroups took prece- dence over O'Neill's argument that "the national interest" was served by bal- anced budgets, a position that was dismissed as politically naïve and dangerous to the president's reelection.[86]

During the 2004 campaign, Bush and his advisors used polling on critical subgroups to tailor their message, advertising, travel plans, and efforts to turn out voters. Although poll-honed strategy has become a staple of modern campaigns, the Bush campaign improved its sophistication and intensity and carried the techniques over into a permanent campaign that seamlessly crossed from cam- paigning to governing and back again.

In the 2004 campaign, the national Republican Party analyzed vast data files on voter registration, political contributions, and other politically valuable infor- mation in order to target mailings and personal contacts on actual individuals who fit a profile of supporting or potentially supporting Bush's reelection. The campaign also targeted advertisements for in-house networks of private gyms. According to campaign director Ken Mehlman, the campaign went after gym rats after its "demographic studies and analysis [that] showed us that a lot of young families get information not at the 7 o'clock news but at the 7 o'clock workout before they got home."[87]

Subgroup polling also produced efficiencies in voter mobilization efforts. Bush's reelection campaign deliberately decided against the traditional campaign approach of deploying volunteers to knock on doors in neighborhoods that had voted heavily for Republicans in past elections. Instead, it studied the political and even consumer behaviors and attitudes of Americans to predict which par- ticular individuals were most likely to vote for Bush and then targeted its resources on those specific individuals. In particular, the Bush campaign's polling on political subgroups pinpointed its large grass roots efforts on turning out con- servatives who had often failed to vote—a group it referred to as "unreliable" or "lazy" voters. Equipped with reliable information on political attitudes (conser- vatism) and political behavior (non-voting), the campaign's volunteers repeat- edly contacted "lazy" conservative voters in the final weeks of the campaign.

According to one campaign worker, voters who had not regularly turned out in the past and "were a Republican or a likely Republican voter . . . heard from us more than you ever dreamed possible." In the campaign's final three days, volunteers frequently called or visited these selected individuals and, apparently, these kinds of personal contacts contributed to the largest voter turnout since 1968.[88]

Segmented Responsiveness, Factionalism, and the National Interest

The president occupies a unique position. He alone sits atop the executive branch; the legislative and judicial branches are controlled by literally hundreds of elected and appointed officials. The Constitution's framers hailed this "unity" of power in one individual as a distinguishing feature of the chief executive.[89] In a symbolic sense, the president is the government and the representative of the nation; he serves as the ceremonial head of state, as the commander in chief, and as the single most visible face of government for Americans. The president's standing as a symbol of the nation offers a political opportunity and responsibility to articulate the enduring elements of civic republicanism and the tradition of promoting the common good to serve the permanent and aggregate interests of the nation.

Some have argued that the notion of the "common good" is a fiction,[90] while others have suggested that the virtue Americans attach to promoting the "common good" has been ground down by the designs of American institutions that reward the self-interested demands of individuals and subgroups.[91] The reality facing presidents is that winning legislative battles and elections depends on reaching out and holding the support of the disparate elements of American politics. Occasionally, a president is elected (like Jimmy Carter) who insists on serving as a "trustee" of the people, promoting the permanent interests of the nation and opposing narrow sectional interests in Congress and Washington; but these chief executives usually end their terms embattled and defeated.[92]

Politically ambitious presidents who are committed to expanding their power and prestige find themselves in a kind of Kabuki theater. They face strong incentives to mount the public stage to portray themselves as representing the nation as a whole, against the self-interested demands of narrow segments of American society. This speaks to the aspirations of Americans as a community. Meanwhile, off stage and out of the easy view of the broad public, presidents depend on attracting and then holding the support of narrow slices of American society. Presidents may talk about representing the country as a whole, but they come to work thinking about its parts that support them.

Scientific polls that collect extensive and accurate information about subgroups of Americans and that influence decisions about the White House's public communications continue a long-standing pattern in American political development. The question is whether and how targeted polling and narrowcasted communications make a difference to the practice of politics and to the operation of a broadly responsive democracy in America.

Subgroup polling and targeted communications matter for two reasons. First, the increase in reliable, extensive, frequent, and private information on voters and political subgroups (from their basic descriptive demographic traits to their behavioral and attitudinal characteristics) significantly improves the precision and efficiency of presidential communications. The new information has allowed contemporary presidents to shift from communications that carpeted neighborhoods based on their overall party loyalties or interest group affiliations to mailings, phone calls, and other communications that are pinpointed on discrete individuals. When volunteers in the 2004 presidential election traveled to a block of single-unit housing, they had information that allowed them to knock on the first, seventh, and ninth houses while skipping the others.

Subgroup polling also equips the White House to pre-test the precise words and symbols that will resonate with targeted subgroups. The White House often knows how discrete sets of individuals will respond to specific messages before they are actually delivered by the president. The Bush campaign's agenda of restricting gay marriage and abortion was launched with some confidence that it would mobilize social conservatives of diverse religious backgrounds. By contrast, the political parties and interest groups that informed past White Houses exposed presidents to higher risks of inadvertently offending critical voting groups and to absorbing greater costs in terms of volunteers and campaign efforts. In today's competitive elections, failure to operate an efficient and precise campaign constitutes a significant disadvantage.

The second impact of subgroup polling is that it intensifies and expands the incentives to discount the preferences of majorities on a range of issues (from social policy, tax policy, and immigration to foreign policy) in favor of the views of subgroups who harbor intense preferences.[93] It not a new story in America that better organized and financed interests hold the upper hand over the broad public.[94] What is new, however, is that this advantage has solidified and strengthened in recent decades, as a recent task force of the American Political Science Association reports.[95]

The growth and increasing sophistication of subgroup polling is one among a number of new, mutually reinforcing developments that have significantly enlarged the incentives of ambitious politicians to cater to narrow interests. The reforms in the 1970s of each major party's process for selecting its nominees shifted political power to party activists and single-issue campaigners who harbor intense preferences for quite particular ends. Campaign contributions by individuals and groups representing narrow, intensely felt interests further ratcheted up the incentives for politicians and presidents to cater to subgroups. Responding to the views of majorities can expose presidents to the wrath of these subgroups. When forced to choose between the views of subgroups and the majority, the politically safer strategy is to defy majorities that do not harbor intense preferences in favor of supportive subgroups.

Polling that tracks subgroups and test-markets public presentations has increased the confidence of the White House in discounting the views of majority opinion in order to cater to political factions. Its sophisticated capacity to hone presidential communications to change the perceptions of both narrow subgroups and broader publics to favor the president's positions is expected to offset whatever political costs are threatened by passing over the views of majority opinion.

President Bush's focus on expanding his base of support among social conservatives put a premium on promoting policies and messages that satisfied the intense views of particular subgroups, diminishing the White House's attention to policies or compromises that responded to average citizens. For instance, he promoted changes in Social Security, tax cuts, and social issues like abortion and gay marriage that were opposed by majorities or strong pluralities of Americans. Bush won the 2000 and 2004 elections by defying the conventional wisdom that the political center chooses the president; he failed to take a majority of independents unaffiliated with either major party or philosophical moderates.

Presidential polling and its analyses of subgroups did not produce a new-found attentiveness in the White House to segments of the electorate. But it did improve the efficiency and precision of appealing to political subgroups while diminishing the perceived costs of defying the majorities.

Polling subgroups and narrowcasting presidential communications are, in today's system of elections, politically expedient, but do they run against the national interest or democratic principles? After all, America is a diverse country and responding to that pluralism of interests has been heralded as a unique strength of the country, from the nineteenth-century observer Alexis de Tocqueville to more contemporary political observers.[96] President Bush's electoral victories without the center could be justified as fulfilling a requirement of democratic systems by responding to intensely felt preferences.[97] What is wrong with a president rewarding his supporters?

The optimistic interpretation of political catering to subgroups has been persistently challenged, however. A long-standing tradition of civic republicanism has lauded responsiveness to the broad public and leadership that delivers public goods of benefit to the entire. In the 1780s, the framers of the Constitution warned of "factions" in The Federalist Papers and insisted that presidents be "independent" to promote the permanent, aggregate interests of the country by fending off the ravenous special interests. Writing nearly a century later, Woodrow Wilson (who was elected president in 1912 after his years as a scholar) sounded the alarm that government policy was being driven by narrow parochial interests at the expense of wider collective interests.[98] Teddy Roosevelt attacked "trusts" as a threat to the national interest, warning that "local selfishness or . . . wealthy special interests, . . . bring national activities to deadlock."[99] The politics of our own time have been animated by efforts to reign in campaign contributions and by Senator John McCain's crusade against the special interests that have burrowed their way into both political parties. Analyzing the "Washington Establishment," Morris Fiorina concludes that government policy is an "accidental by-product" of a process geared to serve individual incumbents and their allies, at the expense of the comprehensive and long-term interests of the country.[100]

Two concerns have woven their way through the long-standing criticisms of factional politics and extend to the "factional polling" of contemporary presidents. First, the preoccupation with responding to political subgroups and discounting the preferences of majorities leads to underinvestments in critical public goods that serve the entire community. Indeed, funding for inclusive education—a classic collective good identified by generations of economists and political observers since Adam Smith—has become increasingly uneven, with fewer opportunities for lower income groups.[101]

Second, factional politics are systematically biased. They favor the organized and affluent, promoting a form of democracy that offers full political rights in theory while accepting systematic disparities in its actual practice. A large and systematic body of research has now established beyond dispute that voting, participation in interest groups, campaign contributions, and other forms of participation by citizens are systematically exercised more by individuals and groups with higher income and occupational and professional advancement. Recent political developments—including the expanded dominance of corporate and professional pressure groups in Washington and the ever larger amounts of money flowing into politics—have widened the advantage of the already advantaged.[102]

Factional politics rewards the loudest and most articulate in this environment of unequal voices. Even the alternations of Democratic and Republican administrations systematically neglect individuals and groups who are not active or organized.[103] The overall effect of a political system that caters to political factions is to reward the already organized and advantaged at the expense of the larger national interest as well as the interests of the broad public.

Notes

*I would like to acknowledge the stellar research assistance of Melanie Burns and the comments of the editors and participants in several meetings related to this project.

1. Terri Bimes and Quinn Mulroy, "The Rise and Decline of Presidential Populism," *Studies in American Political Development* 18 (Fall 2004), 136–159; John Gerring, *Party Ideologies in America, 1828–1996* (New York: Cambridge University Press, 1998).

2. Peterson, *Legislating Together;* Ceaser, *Presidential Selection;* Conley, *Presidential Mandates.*

3. Individualism and self-interest have been identified as the foundation of American culture; see Louis Hartz, *The Liberal Tradition in America* (New York: Harcourt Brace Jovanovich, 1955). For commentary on the formation and operation of interest groups, see Arthur Bentley, *The Process of Government: A Study of Social Pressures* (Chicago: University of Chicago Press, 1908); and David Truman, *The Governmental Process* (New York: Knopf, 1959). For more recent "rational choice" analysis of political institutions, see Barry Weingast, "Rational Choice Institutionalism," in Ira Katznelson and Helen Milner, eds., *Political Science: The State of the Discipline* (New York: W. W. Norton, 2002), 660–692. This assumption has been strongly challenged on a number of fronts as an exaggeration or misunderstanding of American culture, history, and institutional dynamics. See, for example, Jane Mansbridge, *Beyond Adversarial Democracy* (Chicago: University of Chicago Press, 1980); Mansbridge, "Self-Interest in Political Life," *Political Theory* 18 (February 1990), 132–153; Michael Taylor, "Battering RAMs," *Critical Review* 9 (1995), 223–234; John Dryzek, *Deliberative Democracy and Beyond: Liberals, Critics, Contestations* (New York: Oxford University Press, 2000), chap. 2; Deborah Stone, *Policy Paradox and Political Reason* (Glenview, Ill.: Scott, Foresman, 1988).

4. Over the past half century, a significant body of research has reported that citizens and politicians are "public regarding" and genuinely interested in advancing the collective interests and common good of society. American history is infused with a "civic republicanism"; see, for example, Gordon Wood, *The Creation of the American Republic* (Chapel Hill: University of North Carolina Press, 1969); I. Kramnick, "Republican Revisionism Revisited," *American Historical Review* 87 (1982), 629–664; Craig Calhoun, ed, *Habermas and the Public Sphere* (Cambridge, Mass.: MIT Press, 1992). Individuals are motivated by a desire to achieve solidarity with a group and promote a cause; see James Q. Wilson, *The Amateur Democrat* (Chicago: University of Chicago Press, 1962), and Wilson, *Political Organizations* (New York: Basic Books, 1973). Americans make "sociotropic" evaluations of candidates, see Donald Kinder and Roderick Kiewiet, "Sociotropic Politics," *British Journal of Political Science* 11 (1981), 129–161; Diana Mutz and Jeffery J. Mondak, "Dimensions of Sociotropic Behavior: Group-Based Judgments of Fairness and Well-Being," *American Journal of Political Science* 41 (January 1997), 284–308. Individuals express sympathy with other people and sacrifice their own self-interest to defend a broader principle; see Amartya Sen, "Rational Fools: A Critique of the Behavioral Foundations of Economic Theory," *Philosophy and Public Affairs* 6 (1977), 328–329. And individuals take non-instrumental, value-oriented actions; see Albert Hirschman, "Against Parsimony: Three Easy Ways of Complicating Some Categories of Economic Discovery," *American Economic Review* 74 (May 1984), 89–96. A number of studies report that a significant proportion of members of Congress select congressional committees and promote policies to make what they see as good public policy and serve the country's long-term well-being; see Richard Fenno, *Congressmen in Committees* (Boston: Little, Brown, 1973); John Kingdon, *Congressmen's Voting Decisions*, 3rd ed. (Ann Arbor: University

of Michigan Press, 1989); Arthur Maas, *Congress and the Common Good* (New York: Basic Books, 1983); David Volger and Sidney Waldman, *Congress and Democracy* (Washington, D.C.: Congressional Quarterly, 1985). Within political theory, an influential body of "communitarians" emphasize the collective and social nature of politics and the definition of individual interests and what is seen as rational; see, for example, Michael Sandel, *Democracy's Discontent: America in Search of a Public Philosophy* (Cambridge, Mass.: Harvard University Press, 1996).

5. This discussion of *The Federalist Papers* draws on a significant body of research (e.g., Wood, *Creation of the American Republic*; Kramnick, "Republican Revisionism Revisited"; Mansbridge, "Self-Interest in Political Life").

6. *Federalist Paper* 10 in Cooke, Jacob, ed., *The Federalist* (Middletown, Conn.: Wesleyan University Press, 1961), 57, 61.

7. Ibid., *Federalist Paper* 51, 349.

8. Ibid., *Federalist Paper* 71, 482.

9. Ibid., *Federalist Paper* 10, 62.

10. For a thoughtful discussion of the Federalists' emphasis on the president's independence and on his discretion to pursue the nation's long-term interests (as compared with Congress's parochial interests), see Tulis, *Rhetorical Presidency*, 39–40.

11. Cooke, ed., *Federalist Paper* 70, 471–472, and *Federalist Paper* 71, 482–483.

12. Kernell, *Going Public;* Tulis, *Rhetorical Presidency.*

13. This section is based on Brian Balogh, "'Mirrors of Desire': Interest Groups, Elections, and the Targeted Style in Twentieth-Century America" in Meg Jacobs, William J. Novak, and Julian E. Zelizer, eds., *The Democratic Experiment: New Directions in American Political History* (Princeton, N.J.: Princeton University Press, 2003).

14. Ibid., 222, 224, 242.

15. Ibid., 229, 233.

16. Ibid., 224.

17. Mark Peterson, "The Presidency and Organized Interests: White House Patterns of Interest Group Liaison," *The American Political Science Review* 86 (September 1992), 612–625.

18. This section draws on Jacobs and Jackson, "Presidential Leadership and the Threat to Popular Sovereignty"; Jacobs and Shapiro, *Politicians Don't Pander;* Jacobs and Shapiro, "The Rise of Presidential Polling"; Jacobs and Burns, "The Second Face of the Public Presidency."

19. Among the factors that contributed to the expansion of White House polling under Nixon and Reagan are the lower cost and increased speed and sophistication of public opinion surveys, and the increased electoral competitiveness of the Republican and Democratic parties, as well as the divided government that left each party in control of one of the lawmaking branches. In addition, the Republican presidents learned about the strategic utility of public opinion research from the successes and pitfalls of their predecessors as well as other politicians.

20. Although comparisons across presidents offer a general indication of overall trends, limited control by Kennedy and Johnson over the form of the polling data they

received and their relative lack of sophistication suggests that counts of the numbers of questions and of the discrete reportings of data should not necessarily be equated with similar counts of the Nixon and Reagan survey research. For instance, the Democratic presidents regularly relied on routinized formats in which one series (for instance, one that asked respondents to identify the most important problems facing the country and the president's position on those problems) produced a number of discrete findings. By contrast, each discrete finding in polling under Nixon and Reagan generally came from separate discrete polls, reflecting the greater precision and refinement of the Republican operations.

21. The number of polls, questions, and reportings that were conducted each year that Nixon was in office are all larger than the average annual rates for Reagan. This reflects the fact that presidents conducted a large proportion of their survey work during election years; Nixon and Reagan both conducted extensive polling in preparation for their reelection campaigns. The difference is that Nixon failed to finish his second term, a period when presidential polling has traditionally declined. Put simply, the result is that annual rates of Nixon's polling may appear to be higher than Reagan's due to Nixon's abbreviated term in office.

22. Druckman, Jacobs, and Ostermeier, "Candidate Strategies to Prime Issues and Image."

23. Heith, "Staffing the White House Public Opinion Apparatus: 1969–1988," 165–189.

24. The discussion here and below of recent presidential polling is based on Green, "The Other War Room," 11–16.

25. The section is based on Green, "The Other War Room," and Don Van Natta, Abby Goodnough, Christopher Drew, and William Yardley, "Bush Secured Victory in Florida by Veering from Beaten Path," New York Times, November 7, 2004, A1.

26. Joyce Purnick, "Data Crunchers Try to Pinpoint Voters' Politics," New York Times, April 7, 2004, A1, and "One-Doorbell-One-Vote Tactic Reemerges in Bush-Kerry Race," New York Times, April 6, 2004, A1.

27. Quoted in Adam Nagourney, "Bush Campaign Manager Views the Electoral Divide," New York Times, November 19, 2004, A18.

28. This section is based on Van Natta et al., "Bush Secured Victory."

29. Michael Baruch Grossman and Martha Joynt Kumar, Portraying the President: The White House and the News Media (Baltimore: Johns Hopkins University Press, 1981); Timothy Cook, Governing with the News: The News Media as Political Institution (Chicago: University of Chicago Press, 1998).

30. Memo to First Lady from Jay Rockefeller, May 26, 1993, "Health Care Reform Communications"; "A Winning Strategy for Health Care Reform," presentation to First Lady by Magaziner, and Bob Boorstin, July 1993; memo to First Lady from Mike Lux, "Positioning Ourselves on Health Care," May 3, 1993.

31. Ben Bagdikian, The Media Monopoly, 4th ed. (Boston: Beacon, 1992); George Donohue, Phillip Tichenor, and Clarice Olien, "A Guard Dog Perspective on the Role of the Media," Journal of Communication 45 (Spring 1995): 115–132; Doris Graber, Mass Media and American Politics, 4th ed. (Washington, D.C.: Congressional Quarterly Press, 1993).

32. Unless otherwise noted, the discussion of the relations between the Bush White House and the press is based on Ken Auletta, "Fortress Bush: How the White House Keeps the Press under Control," *New Yorker*, January 19, 2004, 53–65. The Gergen quote is from Auletta, "Fortress Bush," 64.

33. Auletta, "Fortress Bush," 63.

34. Stephen Koss, *The Rise and Fall of the Political Press in Britain: The Nineteenth Century* (Chapel Hill: University of North Carolina Press, 1981).

35. Balogh, "Mirrors of Desire," 230.

36. Unless otherwise noted, the discussion of the history of presidential press relations is based on Robert Hilderbrand, *People and Power: Executive Management of Public Opinion in Foreign Affairs, 1897–1921* (Chapel Hill: University of North Carolina Press, 1981).

37. Richard Steele, *Propaganda in an Open Society: The Roosevelt Administration and the Media, 1933-41* (Westport, Conn.: Greenwood Press, 1985).

38. Theodore Sorensen, *Kennedy* (New York: Bantam Books, 1965), 310.

39. Jacobs and Shapiro, *Politicians Don't Pander*.

40. This section is based on Auletta, "Fortress Bush;" Van Natta et al., "Bush Secured Victory"; Laurie Goodstein and William Yardley, "President Benefits from Efforts to Build a Coalition of Religious Voters," *New York Times*, November 5, 2004, A22.

41. Quoted in Goodstein and Yardley, "President Benefits."

42. Quotes of Bush officials in the remainder of this section are from Auletta, "Fortress Bush," 53–62.

43. Memo from Robert Teeter to H. R. Haldeman, December 6, 1971, Haldeman Papers, Box 368.

44. Memo from Larry Higby to Gordon Strachan and Bruce Kehrli, September 6, 1971, Haldeman Papers, Box 335.

45. Diary of Nixon's chief of staff, H. R. Haldeman, entry for October 10, 1972.

46. Haldeman Diary, entry for January 8, 1970.

47. "The Public Appraises the Nixon Administration and Key Issues." Confidential Survey. Conducted for the RNC in consultation with David R. Derge by ORC, December 1969. Haldeman Papers, Box 406.

48. Memo to Haldeman from Nixon, December 30, 1969, Personal Presidential Files, Box 1.

49. Memo from Larry Higby to Gordon Strachan, May 21, 1971, Haldeman Papers, Box 356.

50. Memo from Haldeman to Strachan, January 31, 1971, Haldeman Papers, Box 335.

51. Memo from Strachan to Haldeman, February 4, 1972. Haldeman Papers, Box 335.

52. Haldeman Diary, entry for June 9, 1971.

53. "The Public Appraises the Nixon Administration and Key Issues." Confidential Survey. Conducted for the RNC in consultation with David R. Derge by ORC, December 1969. Haldeman Papers, Box 406.

54. Memo from Larry Higby to Gordon Strachan and Bruce Kehrli, September 6, 1971, Haldeman Papers, Box 335.

55. Memo to Nixon from David Derge, July 4, 1971, Haldeman Papers, Box 343.

56. Memo from Robert Teeter to H. R. Haldeman, December 6, 1971, Haldeman

Papers, Box 368. (All archival records from the Nixon presidency are from the holdings maintained by the National Archives and Records Administration.)

57. Memo to Mitchell from Peter Flanigan, September 30, 1971, Haldeman Papers, Box 368.

58. Memo to Mitchell from Teeter, "Interim Analysis Report," April 17, 1972, Haldeman Papers, Box 362.

59. Memo to Mitchell from Teeter, April 12, 1972.

60. Memo from Teeter to Mitchell, May 11, 1972, Haldeman Papers, Box 362.

61. Memo to Chapin from Teeter, July 25, 1972 (marked "Confidential"), Haldeman Papers, Box 363; memo to Mitchell from Teeter, "Interim Analysis Report," April 17, 1972, Haldeman Papers, Box 362.

62. "Ten Days after Victory," An Interim Report by the Committee for the Re-election of the President, Clark MacGregor, November 17, 1972, Haldeman Papers, Box 349.

63. Memo to James Baker, Michael Deaver, Frank Fahrenkopf, Paul Laxalt, Ed Rollins, and Stuart Spencer from Wirthlin, July 26, 1984, Deaver Files (#UA 115586); Wirthlin to Fahrenkopf and Regan, February 7, 1985; memo from Wirthlin to Richard Allen re Mideast, August 21, 1981, PR15 (#043822).

64. Memo to Meese, Baker, and Deaver from Wirthlin re "Reagan Performance," February 2, 1982; memo from Richard Beal to Edwin Meese, James Baker, Michael Deaver, and William Clark, March 12, 1982.

65. Memo from Richard Beal to Edwin Meese, James Baker, Michael Deaver, and William Clark, March 12, 1982.

66. Memo to Baker, Deaver, Fahrenkopf, Laxalt, Rollins, and Spencer from Wirthlin, July 26, 1984. Deaver Files (#UA 115586).

67. Memo from Wirthlin to Fahrenkopf and Regan, February 7, 1985; memo from Wirthlin to Dick Richards, March 11, 1981, Elizabeth Dole Papers, Box 6391; memo from Ed Rollins to Don Regan, July 9, 1985, PR15 (#317420); William Lacy to Regan, October 23, 1985; Wirthlin to Regan, February 12, 1986; letter from Roger Porter to Wirthlin, November 14, 1984.

68. "Gun Control Issue Forecast," September 21, 1981 (Elizabeth Dole Files, OA 5455).

69. Untitled memo, PR15, document #213994; Decision/Making/Information, "National Benchmark Survey of Public Attitudes," for the Republican National Committee, November 1983, Chapman Files, Box 29.

70. Memo from Gary Bauer from Edwin Harper re "Polls on the Social Issues," March 29, 1982, PR15 (#093915).

71. Memo from Wirthlin to Baker, Deaver, and Meese, July 17, 1981.

72. Memo to Baker, Deaver, Fahrenkopf, Laxalt, Rollins, and Spencer from Wirthlin, July 26, 1984, Deaver Files (#UA 115586).

73. Memo from Walter Raymond to Rodney McDaniel re "FOR A (Public Opinion Surveys)," April 9, 1986 (N5C#8602875).

74. Untitled memo, PR15, document #213994.

75. Memo from Richard Beal to Edwin Meese, James Baker, Michael Deaver, and William Clark, March 12, 1982.

76. Respondents split between the two alternatives, tilting slightly toward Mr. Jones's supportive view of CETA (50 percent to 46 percent). Decision/Making/ Information, "National Survey of Public Attitudes," for the Republican National Committee, January 1981.

77. Memo to Richard Richards from Wirthlin re "Attitudes toward Voting Rights Act," June 18, 1981.

78. Analyses of Reagan speeches by Wirthlin's firm (Decision/Making/ Information or DMI) include the following: Wirthlin to President Ronald Reagan, "Analysis of 1987 State of the Union Address," February 2, 1987, CF PR15 attached to cover note from David Chew to President, February 3, 1987 (#45915455); "Analysis of the President's Peace and National Security Address," March 1986 attached to cover note from David Chew to President, March 4, 1986; "Results of analysis of UN Address on October 31, 1985," Chew Paper (Wirthlin, folder 1) (#14145); Wirthlin to Regan and Buchanan, "Analysis of Presidential Speech to Congress following Summit Meeting with Soviets," November 11, 1985.

79. Reagan Library, PR15, "Analysis of the President's Peace and National Security Address," DMI, March 1986 attached to cover note from David Chew to president, March 4, 1986.

80. Memo from David Chew to Admiral Poindexter, Dennis Thomas, and Pat Buchanan forwarding Regan's request for a meeting with Wirthlin (meeting held on March 10. 1986), March 5, 1986 (CF PR15, CF FR15, #37774155).

81. For instance, Wirthlin to Regan and Buchanan, Analysis of Presidential Speech to Congress following Summit Meeting with Soviets, 11/22/85.

82. This section is based on Goodstein and Yardley, "President Benefits"; Van Natta et al., "Bush Secured Victory in Florida"; Nagourney, "Bush Campaign Manager Views the Electoral Divide"; Purnick, "Data Crunchers" and "One-Doorbell-One-Vote Tactic."

83. Michael Janofsky, "G.O.P. Adviser Says Bush's Evangelical Strategy Split Country," *New York Times*, November 11, 2004, A25.

84. Green, "The Other War Room," 14.

85. Fay Lomax Cook and Lawrence R. Jacobs, "Assessing Assumptions about Attitudes toward Social Security: Popular Claims Meet Hard Data," in Peter Edelman, Dallas Salisbury, and Pamela Larson, eds., *The Future of Social Insurance: Incremental Action or Fundamental Reform* (Washington, D.C.: Brookings Institution, 2002), 82–118.

86. Ron Suskind, *The Price of Loyalty: George W. Bush, the White House, and the Education of Paul O'Neill* (New York: Simon & Schuster, 2004).

87. Quoted in Nagourney, "Bush Campaign Manager."

88. Vanishing Voter Project, 2004.

89. *Federalist Paper* 70.

90. Joseph Schumpeter, *Capitalism, Socialism, and Democracy* (New York: Harper, 1950).

91. For example, Mansbridge, "Self-Interest in Political Life."

92. Charles O. Jones, *The Trusteeship Presidency: Jimmy Carter and the United States Congress* (Baton Rouge: Louisiana State University Press, 1988).

93. Lawrence R. Jacobs and Benjamin I. Page, "Who Influences U.S. Foreign Policy?" *American Political Science Review* 99 (February 2005), 107–124; Jacobs and Shapiro, *Politicians Don't Pander*; Morris P. Fiorina, "Extreme Voices: A Dark Side of Civic Engagement," in Theda Skocpol and Morris P. Fiorina, eds., *Civic Engagement in American Democracy* (Washington, D.C., and New York: The Brookings Institution Press and Russell Sage Foundation, 1999), 396–425; American Political Science Association, Task Force on "Inequality and American Democracy" (www.apsanet .org/inequality).

94. The concern with the disproportionate influence of special interests is a consistent theme that stretches from *The Federalist Papers* and Charles Beard's analysis of the economic forces that shaped the Constitution to better serve the "anti-pluralists" of the 1960s. Charles Beard, *An Economic Interpretation of the Constitution of the United States* (New York: Macmillan Company, 1913); E. E. Schattschneider, *The Semisovereign People: A Realist's View of Democracy in America* (New York: Holt, Rinehart and Winston, 1960).

95. American Political Science Association, Task Force on Inequality and American Democracy, "American Democracy in an Age of Rising Inequality" (Washington, D.C.: American Political Science Association, and *Perspectives on Politics* 2 [December 2004]), 651–666.

96. Truman, *The Governmental Process*.

97. William H. Riker, *Democracy in the United States* (New York: Macmillan, 1965) and *Liberalism against Populism: A Confrontation between the Theory of Democracy and the Theory of Social Choice* (Prospect Heights, Ill.: Waveland Press, 1988).

98. Wilson, *Congressional Government*.

99. Quoted in Sidney Milkis and Daniel Tichenor, "'Direct Democracy' and Social Justice: The Progressive Party Campaign of 1912," *Studies in American Political Development* 8 (Fall 1994), 289.

100. Morris P. Fiorina, *Congress, Keystone of the Washington Establishment*, 2nd ed. (New Haven: Yale University Press, 1989).

101. Jennifer L. Hochschild and Nathan Scovronick, *The American Dream and the Public Schools* (Oxford University Press 2003), 9–76; National Center for Public Policy and Higher Education, *Losing Ground: A National Status Report on the Affordability of American Higher Education* (San Jose, Calif., 2002).

102. This research is reviewed in the report on political voice compiled by the American Political Science Association Task Force on Inequality and American Democracy and *Perspectives on Politics* 2 (December 2004), 651–666.

103. One possible rejoinder is to point to polls that show the similarity in the views of voters and non-voters, lessening the danger of participatory inequalities. Evidence has now emerged, however, that polls systematically underrepresent groups who participate less in American politics and that voters and political representatives deliver messages to government officials that neglect the perspectives of these groups. Adam J. Berinsky, "Silent Voices: Social Welfare Policy Opinions and Political Equality in America," *American Journal of Political Science* 46 (2002), 276–287; Sidney Verba, Kay Lehman Schlozman, and Henry E. Brady, *Voice and Equality: Civic Voluntarism in American Politics* (Cambridge, Mass.: Harvard University Press, 1995).

Bibliography

Burke, Edmund. "Speech to the Electors of Bristol." In *Burke's Politics, Selected Writings and Speeches,* edited by R. Hoffmann and P. Levack. New York: Knopf, 1949.

Ceaser, James W. *Presidential Selection: Theory and Development.* Princeton, N.J.: Princeton University Press, 1979.

Conley, Patricia Heidotting. *Presidential Mandates: How Elections Shape the National Agenda.* Chicago: University of Chicago Press, 2001.

Druckman, James, Lawrence Jacobs, and Eric Ostermeier. "Candidate Strategies to Prime Issues and Image." *Journal of Politics* (December 2004), 1205–1227.

Edwards, George C., III. *The Public Presidency: The Pursuit of Popular Support.* New York: St. Martin's Press, 1983.

Gallup, George, and Saul Rae. *The Pulse of Democracy.* New York: Simon and Schuster, 1940.

Green, Joshua. "The Other War Room: President Bush Doesn't Believe in Polling—Just Ask His Pollsters." *Washington Monthly* 34 (April 2002), 11–16.

Heith, Diane. "Staffing the White House Public Opinion Apparatus: 1969–1988." *Public Opinion Quarterly* 62 (1998), 165–189.

Jacobs, Lawrence R. *The Health of Nations: Public Opinion and the Making of Health Policy in the U.S. and Britain.* Ithaca, N.Y.: Cornell University Press, 1993.

Jacobs, Lawrence R. "Institutions and Culture: Health Policy and Public Opinion in the U.S. and Britain." *World Politics* 44 (January 1992), 179–209.

Jacobs, Lawrence R. "The Recoil Effect: Public Opinion and Policymaking in the U.S. and Britain." *Comparative Politics* 24 (January 1992), 199–217.

Jacobs, Lawrence R., and Melanie Burns. "The Second Face of the Public Presidency: Presidential Polling and the Shift from Policy to Personality Polling." *Presidential Studies Quarterly* 34 (Fall 2004), 536–556.

Jacobs, Lawrence R., and Melinda Jackson. "Presidential Leadership and the Threat to Popular Sovereignty: Building an Appealing Image to Dodge Unpopular Policy Issues in the Nixon White House." In *Polls, Politics, and the Dilemmas of Democracy,* edited by Matt Streb. Albany: State University of New York Press, 2004.

Jacobs, Lawrence R., and Robert Y. Shapiro. *Politicians Don't Pander: Political Manipulation and the Loss of Democratic Responsiveness.* Chicago: University of Chicago Press, 2000.

Jacobs, Lawrence R., and Robert Y. Shapiro. "The Rise of Presidential Polling: The Nixon White House in Historical Perspective." *Public Opinion Quarterly* 59 (Summer 1995), 163–195.

Kernell, Samuel. *Going Public: New Strategies of Presidential Leadership.* 2nd ed. Washington, D.C.: Congressional Quarterly Press, 1993.

Neustadt, Richard E. *Presidential Power: The Politics of Leadership from FDR to Carter.* New York: Wiley, 1980.

Page, Benjamin, and Robert Shapiro. *The Rational Public.* Chicago: University of Chicago Press, 1992.

Peterson, Mark. *Legislating Together: The White House and Capitol Hill from Eisenhower to Reagen.* Cambridge, Mass.: Harvard University Press, 1990.

Tulis, Jeffrey. *The Rhetorical Presidency.* Princeton, N.J.: Princeton University Press, 1987.

Wilson, Woodrow. *Congressional Government*. Boston: Houghton Mifflin, 1885.

Wilson, Woodrow. *Constitutional Government in the United States*. New York: Columbia University Press, 1908.

Wilson, Woodrow. *Leaders of Men*. Princeton, N.J.: Princeton University Press, 1952.

7

THE PERSON OF THE PRESIDENT, LEADERSHIP, AND GREATNESS

Fred I. Greenstein

I F ONE SET OUT TO DESIGN A DEMOCRACY IN WHICH THE personal qualities of the top leader could be expected to have an impact on political outcomes, the result might well resemble the political system of the United States. The separation of powers and the Constitutional provision of a president with such autonomous powers as the veto have enabled chief executives to place a personal stamp on the nation's policies since the founding of the Republic, but until the 1930s Congress typically took the lead in policy making, and the activities of the federal government had little impact on the nation and world.

Then arose what has come to be called the modern presidency. Under the stimulus of the administrative imperatives of the New Deal and World War II, and the entrepreneurial leadership of Franklin D. Roosevelt, there was a dramatic increase in the scope and influence of the federal government and therefore its chief executive. The president's capacity to make a difference was further magnified by the emergence of the United States as a world power with a growing arsenal of nuclear weapons. Meanwhile, presidents began to make an increasing amount of policy independent of the legislature, drawing on their sweeping administrative powers, and the Executive Office of the President was created, providing chief executives with the organizational support needed to carry out their expanded obligations. (For a related discussion of the advent of the modern presidency, see the observations of Scott James in this volume.)

The question of who occupies the Oval Office is most critical in decisions of war and peace, a domain in which the president has the status of commander in chief. There is no more telling illustration of the significance of the person of the president than the Cuban Missile Crisis of October 1962. In that month, President John F. Kennedy and his senior staff learned that the Soviet Union was secretly installing in Cuba a complex of ballistic missiles capable of obliterating much of the United States. This, Kennedy concluded, could not be allowed to stand. His advisors were split between those who favored finding a nonviolent means of inducing the Soviets to withdraw their missiles and those who called for an immediate air strike on the missile sites, a course of action that we now know would have been likely to trigger a devastating nuclear exchange. Kennedy decided on the more cautious option, even privately acceding to a Soviet demand that the United States withdraw its missiles from Turkey in exchange for the removal of the Soviet missiles in Cuba.

Despite his (and someday her) life-or-death power in international affairs, the American president is far from all-powerful. Presidents are constrained by other forces in society and the political system. Of the presidents since World War II, Gerald Ford, Jimmy Carter, and George H.W. Bush were defeated at the polls, Harry S. Truman and Lyndon B. Johnson chose not to seek reelection at times when they were deeply unpopular, Richard M. Nixon resigned, and Kennedy was assassinated. Moreover, even popular chief executives are sometimes blocked or forced to modify their goals by the other powers-that-be in the political system, especially in the domestic sphere. Nevertheless, the personal qualities of the individual who happens to be president at a particular point in American history can have as great an impact as the impersonal forces and structures that command the bulk of attention in the scholarly literature on American government.

Qualities That Shape Presidential Performance

How can the concerned citizen assess the quality of a president's job performance? There are two broad ways of doing so. One is by asking whether and to what extent the president's policies comport with the citizen's own values and convictions. In this fundamentally personal realm, the specialized knowledge of the presidential scholar has little to contribute, although valuable insight can be derived from the study of ethics and political philosophy. The other is by evaluating the strengths and weaknesses that a president brings to his responsibilities. Here the presidential specialist *can* make a contribution.

This chapter will examine the president's performance in terms of six qualities that bear on the job of the chief executive.[1] The first relates to what might be thought of as the outer face of presidential leadership: the president's ability as a public communicator. The second pertains to its inner face: the president's organizational capacity. The third and fourth apply to the president as a political operator: his political skill and the degree to which it is harnessed to a workable policy vision. The fifth and sixth bear on the cognitive style with which the president processes the torrent of communications directed to him, and the president's emotional intelligence, the degree to which he is the master of his emotions, rather than permitting them to intrude into his conduct in office.[2]

Effectiveness as a Public Communicator

The technology of contemporary mass communication makes the president a constant presence in the nation and the world, but for an office that places a premium on the bully pulpit, the presidency has been surprisingly lacking in accomplished public communicators. The most conspicuous exceptions are Franklin D. Roosevelt, John F. Kennedy, and Ronald Reagan. Other presidents who were less consistently effective in their public communications sometimes hit rhetorical home runs, for example, George W. Bush in the immediate aftermath of the terrorist attacks of September 11, 2001, and Bill Clinton when he was at his best.

Chief executives who are daunted by the eloquence of Roosevelt, Kennedy, and Reagan should be relieved to learn that their rhetorical powers were arrived at by dint of experience and effort—they were not inborn. When FDR was a political novice, his wife, Eleanor, heard him give a speech and was taken aback by his long pauses and slow delivery. "I was worried for fear that he would never go on," she recalled.[3] When the twenty-nine-year-old Kennedy entered the House of Representatives, he was a soft-spoken, halting public speaker; his rhetorical panache evolved in the course of years of collaboration with his speechwriter and alter ego, Theodore Sorensen.[4] Despite Reagan's extensive experience as a radio announcer and movie actor, he did not perfect the polished podium manner of his political years until the 1950s, when he spent much of the decade on the public-speaking circuit as a representative of the General Electric corporation.[5]

Organizational Capacity

A president's proficiency as an organizer of his administration includes his ability to select well-qualified aides and mold them into an effective team. It also includes his capacity to devise organizational procedures that ensure him a rich flow of advice and information, while minimizing the tendency of subordinates to tell their boss what they sense he wants to hear. FDR sought to foster diversity in the recommendations that reached him by pitting his assistants against one another. Kennedy charged his brother Robert with scrutinizing the proposals of his other advisors for potential pitfalls.

Political Skill

The notion that a political leader needs to be skilled might seem too obvious for commentary, were it not that the American political system places exceptional political demands on its chief executive. The Constitution, which was framed in the eighteenth century with a view to making it difficult for the government to act, remains in force in an era in which the government is called upon to take on innumerable politically demanding initiatives. If there was ever a need to demonstrate the importance of a president's political skill, it was put to rest by the difficulties encountered by Jimmy Carter, who was impressively effective in pursuing the presidency, but was reluctant to engage in political give-and-take once in the White House. As a result, he had limited success in winning the support of other key political actors, particularly the legislators whose backing he needed to advance his ambitious program.

Lyndon Johnson, by way of contrast, was one of the most masterful politicians in the nation's history. Within hours after Kennedy's assassination, Johnson had begun to muster support for major policy departures, including the first civil rights bill with enforcement provisions since Reconstruction. Nonetheless, Johnson embarked on an open-ended U.S. military intervention in Vietnam in 1965, without establishing its probable duration, troop requirements, and political feasibility, using his skill to downplay its magnitude in order not to impede the enactment of his domestic program. By 1968, a half-million American troops were enmeshed in Southeast Asia, and the nation was wracked with antiwar protest. In the absence of a viable policy, Johnson's political prowess proved to be counterproductive.[6] This brings us to the matter of the ends toward which a president's skill is directed—his policy vision.

Policy Vision

When we say that a president exhibits "vision," we may be pointing to his use of rhetoric that stirs the imagination and evokes intense feeling. For present purposes, however, the term is here employed to address the less lofty matter of whether and to what extent a president's actions are grounded in explicitly enunciated policies, particularly ones capable of accomplishing his goals. The presidents whose actions were most clearly guided by an overarching set of objectives were Dwight Eisenhower, Richard Nixon, Ronald Reagan, and George W. Bush. The absence of a sense of direction can lead a president to drift from one policy to another; a defective policy vision can lead him to take actions that are ineffective or have undesirable consequences.

Cognitive Style

Presidents vary in their intellectual endowments. Jimmy Carter had an engineer's proclivity to reduce issues to their component parts, a mind-set that failed to provide his administration with an overall sense of direction. Such a narrow cognitive style is in contrast to a broader, more strategic intelligence that cuts to the heart of problems and identifies their policy implications. A noteworthy illustration of strategic intelligence is provided by Richard Nixon. Two years before becoming president, Nixon published an article in which he called for ending the American military involvement in Vietnam, establishing an amicable relationship with the People's Republic of China, and stabilizing U.S. relations with the Soviet Union, and implied that the U.S. military involvement in Vietnam was out of proportion to the American stake in the situation in Southeast Asia.[7] By the final year of his first term, Nixon had presided over an opening to China, secured an accommodation with the Soviet Union, and ended the U.S. combat role in Vietnam.

Emotional Intelligence

Just as Richard Nixon provides a positive model in the realm of strategic intelligence, he is a distinctly negative exemplar as far as emotional intelligence is concerned. Nixon's emotional flaws negated his impressive strengths. During the same four years in which he made his international breakthroughs, Nixon embarked on what one of his aides referred to as the "Watergate horrors"—the covert campaign of espionage and sabotage against his perceived enemies that had fatal consequences for his presidency.

No chief executive has excelled in every one of the capacities just reviewed. Strength in one may compensate for weakness in another, however. Thus JFK presided over a rather disorganized White House, but his actions in the Cuban missile crisis were clear-headed and wise. Jimmy Carter was almost willfully resistant to political give-and-take, but he was pragmatic and deft in brokering a peace agreement between Israel and Egypt. George H. W. Bush was deficient in what he deprecated as "the vision thing," but he was highly effective in the diplomatic prelude to the 1991 Gulf War. There is, however, one presidential quality that should be indispensable—emotional intelligence. There can be few more profound risks in the nuclear age than an emotionally challenged commander in chief, particularly one with hostile impulses and defective impulse control.

Chief Executives in Action: Two Cases

In order to put flesh on the bones of this formulation, this chapter presents case studies of the two most recent modern presidents as of this writing: Bill Clinton and George W. Bush.

The Undisciplined Political Style of Bill Clinton

No one who is indifferent to politics becomes president of the United States, but some chief executives stand out as political in every fiber of their being. Bill Clinton was such a figure. In addition, Clinton was notable for his intelligence, energy, and eloquence, as well as a lack of self-discipline that led him into difficulties and a resiliency that enabled him to extricate himself from many of them.

BEFORE THE PRESIDENCY. William Jefferson Clinton was born on August 19, 1946, in a southwest Arkansas hamlet with the politically valuable name of

Hope. His father died in an automobile accident three months before Bill's birth. His mother was a nurse whose optimistic outlook and ability to rebound from the deaths of three husbands was a prototype for her son's capacity for political regeneration. When Bill was four, she married a car salesman who proved to be an alcoholic. Clinton possesses a number of traits associated with children from families in which there is alcohol abuse. As he once put it, growing up in a such family left him with "much greater empathy for other people's problems than the average person" and provided him with "skills about how to keep people together and try to work things out." But as he acknowledged, such an upbringing "causes you to want to avoid trouble, you tend to try to keep the peace at all costs."[8]

Clinton was president of his high school freshman and sophomore classes, a National Merit scholar, and an avid participant in extracurricular activities. At age sixteen, he attended a White House event in which he shook hands with President Kennedy, an experience that reinforced his captivation with politics. He chose to attend college at Georgetown University in Washington, D.C., where he stood out academically, was active in campus politics, and worked for Arkansas Senator William Fulbright. He became an anti–Vietnam War activist and won admission to the Rhodes program, studying at Oxford between 1968 and 1970. He then attended Yale Law School, where he met his wife-to-be, the equally high-achieving Hillary Rodham.

After law school, Clinton returned to Arkansas and was elected governor in 1978, becoming the nation's youngest state chief executive in four decades. Two years later, however, he was defeated for reelection by a little-known Republican. The consensus in Arkansas was that he had brought this reversal on himself by advancing a host of policies with little regard for their political feasibility and by instituting a steep increase in automobile license fees.

Clinton was stunned by his defeat, but he bounced back and mounted a drive to regain the governorship. He taped a television commercial apologizing for the shortcomings of his governorship, and recast himself as a pragmatic moderate. In 1982, he was again elected governor and went on to win reelection three times. In October 1991, Clinton announced his presidential candidacy, billing himself as a new-style Democrat who combined sympathy for the underprivileged with a hardheaded emphasis on individual responsibility.

The presidential primary season had barely begun when Clinton was dealt a pair of body blows. One was a report in the press of his tangled efforts to avoid military service during the Vietnam War.[9] The other was the assertion of an Arkansas nightclub singer that she and Clinton had been lovers for the past decade. Clinton explained his efforts to avoid the draft by saying that, like other loyal young men at the time, he had been torn between his love of country and abhorrence of what he regarded as an immoral conflict. He dealt with the sexual accusation by appearing on national television with Hillary and acknowledging that he had "caused pain" in their marriage, but that they had resolved their problems.[10] He went on to win the nomination and the general election, defeating President George H. W. Bush; Clinton received 43 percent of the vote, Bush received 38 percent, and 19 percent of the vote went to Independent candidate H. Ross Perot.

PRESIDENTIAL PERFORMANCE. The standard advice to new presidents is to "hit the ground running." That entails making good use of the transition between the election and inauguration by selecting a strong team, choosing it early, focusing on a few major goals, and skillfully advancing them immediately after taking office. Bill Clinton's presidency hit the ground stumbling. Clinton selected an inexperienced White House staff. He ran behind schedule in selecting Cabinet nominees. His candidate for the key post of attorney general had to withdraw when it was revealed that she had broken the law by employing two illegal aliens as domestic servants and had failed to pay their Social Security taxes. Moreover, having declared that on taking office he would focus on stimulating the economy "like a laser," one of his first acts was to issue an executive order instructing the military not to bar homosexuals from service, triggering a barrage of protests from, among others, Joint Chiefs of Staff Chairman Colin Powell. Clinton then backed off, and adopted the awkward "don't ask, don't tell" policy of forbidding the military to inquire about sexual orientation, but permitting it to discharge self-professed gays.

The difficulties continued throughout the hundred-day period that has come to be a marker of the promise of a new presidency. Most damaging was the failure of Congress to enact Clinton's signature economic stimulus bill, but there were a number of lesser problems, many of which stemmed from the lack of experience of Clinton's staff. By June, Clinton's approval rating had plunged by 20 points from its initial 58 percent. Then, just as the political world began to write him off, Clinton displayed the capacity for self-correction that has been his hallmark. He added a number of Washington-wise professionals to his White House staff, which he had initially populated with Arkansans and former campaign aides. By year's end, he had given a dazzling presentation of his proposed reform of the health care system to a joint session of Congress, brokered passage of the landmark North American Free Trade Agreement (NAFTA), and presided over a ceremony on the White House lawn in which Israeli premier Yitzhak Rabin and Palestinian Liberation Organization chairman Yasir Arafat signed a peace accord.

In January 1994, Clinton's approval level was back to 58 percent, but the new year proved to be trouble laden. In January, in a move he would later have cause to regret, Clinton requested the attorney general to appoint an independent counsel to investigate charges that he and Hillary had engaged in fraud in connection with a 1980s Arkansas real estate venture called the Whitewater

Development Corporation. Several months later, the judicial panel supervising the inquiry replaced the original appointee with the zealous Kenneth W. Starr, who made it his mission to search for wrongdoing on Clinton's part.

The most damaging blow of the year for Clinton was the failure of his most ambitious policy initiative, a bill guaranteeing health care to all Americans. Clinton had entrusted its drafting to an administration task force under the direction of the First Lady. The task force drew fire for convening in secret, and came forth with a highly complex bill, which it reported late, enabling the opposition to mobilize. The proposal died in committee not long before the 1994 congressional election. The election was a stinging rebuke to Clinton. The Republicans seized control of Congress in a massive sweep, gaining fifty-two seats in the House and eight in the Senate.

The mastermind of the triumph was the abrasively entrepreneurial Georgia congressman Newt Gingrich, who had persuaded the Republican House candidates to commit themselves to a ten-point conservative legislative program called the Contract with America. In January 1995, Gingrich, now Speaker of the House, convened the newly elected House of Representatives with all of the fanfare of a presidential inauguration. The House passed nine of the ten measures in the Republican contract, and on April 7, Gingrich declared victory in a prime-time television address. Clinton was reduced to asserting lamely that he had not become politically superfluous, because "the Constitution makes me relevant."

Circumstances soon demonstrated that the bully pulpit could make him more than merely relevant. On April 19, 1995, a massive bomb was detonated at the Alfred P. Murrah Federal Building in Oklahoma City, killing 163 people. Clinton delivered a moving address on April 23 at a memorial service for the victims at the site of the destruction. A *Time* magazine poll conducted immediately after his remarks found that his approval level had soared from 49 percent a month earlier to 60 percent.[11]

Then it became Gingrich's turn to miscalculate. The Speaker pushed through severe spending reductions on education, the environment, and Medicare. Clinton presented himself as the defender of those programs, but added that he also favored a balanced budget. When Clinton vetoed the bills mandating the spending cuts, there was an impasse that led to a pair of shutdowns of the federal government. Deprived of needed services, the public sided with Clinton, and Gingrich became deeply unpopular. As the 1996 election approached, Clinton focused on traditionally Republican issues, calling for more police officers on the streets, stiffer sentences for criminals, and policies designed to reduce teen pregnancy. In a final act of repositioning, Clinton signed a sweeping welfare reform act, offending many liberal Democrats, but following through on his 1992 promise to "end welfare as we know it."

Clinton was reelected with 49 percent of the popular vote; Republican Bob Dole received 40 percent and Perot 9 percent. In January 1997, Clinton launched his second term with a call for a government that "lives within its means, and does more with less."[12] In the weeks that followed, he spelled out an extensive list of low-price-tag legislative initiatives relating to such matters as education, crime, the environment, and welfare. With a booming economy and appealing proposals, Clinton's approval levels over the course of 1997 reached the highest levels to date of his presidency, but the following year was consumed by scandal and impeachment.

Clinton's troubles in 1998 went back to the period three years earlier, when he allowed the government to shut down rather than countenance GOP budget cuts. The White House relied on unpaid volunteers to do the work of furloughed government employees during the shutdowns, among them a twenty-one-year-old intern named Monica Lewinsky. In an act of breathtaking recklessness, Clinton invited Lewinsky into his office, where she performed oral sex on him for the first of ten times over an eighteen-month period.

As might have been predicted, she did not keep the encounters secret. She discussed them with (among others) an older coworker, who secretly made tape recordings of their conversations, providing them to independent council Kenneth Starr, who expanded his investigation to Clinton's relationship with Lewinsky. His concern, Starr insisted, was not with Clinton's personal morality, but whether he had perjured himself by denying that he had been sexually involved with Lewinsky. Starr's office took testimony from Clinton's closest aides, his personal secretary, and even his Secret Service bodyguards. When it became Clinton's time to testify, he confessed to his relationship with Lewinsky, calling it "a critical lapse in judgment" and acknowledging that in his effort to conceal the affair he had "misled people, including even my wife."[13]

On September 9, Starr submitted his report to Congress, stating eleven possible grounds for impeaching Clinton. Although the balance of forces in the Senate made it evident that Clinton could not be convicted, the House Republicans were undeterred. On December 19, following highly partisan hearings, the House voted along party lines to adopt two articles of impeachment, charging Clinton with perjury and obstruction of justice.

If ever there were a Pyrrhic victory, it was the Republican success in impeaching Clinton. In the first public opinion poll after the House vote, Clinton's approval level soared to 73 percent, the highest rating of his presidency. By then, the astonishing outcome of the midterm election was known. The Democrats gained five seats in the House of Representatives—the first seat gain by a party in control of the White House since 1934. The House Republicans turned against Gingrich, who announced that he would resign from Congress. In early 1998, the nation witnessed the spectacle of the chief justice of the United States presiding over a Senate trial of the president of the United States, the second such trial in the nation's history. Neither article of impeachment received majority support, much less the two-thirds report that would have been required to convict Clinton.

In January 1999, with the Senate trial still in progress, Clinton delivered a bravura State of the Union address, proposing a spate of attractive initiatives. In an allusion to his impeachment, he called on Congress to put aside their divisions and join him in constructive policy making. But the final two years in office of a lame-duck president are not a propitious time for policy breakthroughs, and the new session of Congress produced only routine measures. Presidential politics dominated the final year of the Clinton presidency.

Remaining engaged to the end, but blocked domestically, Clinton turned his prodigious energy and political skill to international peacemaking. He made an impressive effort to broker a peace agreement in the Middle East. A success would have added impressively to the rather limited legacy of his presidency. At the eleventh hour, however, the negotiations failed. In the final month of his presidency, Clinton went into high gear, denying himself sleep, giving numerous farewell speeches, and issuing a spate of executive orders and pardons of criminal offenders, short-circuiting the review process of such actions. In short, the messiness of the end of his presidency paralleled that of its beginning.

BOTTOM LINE. At his best, Clinton was superb at public communication. He was at the top of his form when on the defensive or when the context evoked his Southern Baptist heritage, as in his 1995 address in Oklahoma City. At his worst, he was long-winded, unfocused, and "off message," which is to say that his rhetoric mirrored the rest of his leadership. He was anything but a natural in the case of organizational capacity. The organization of Clinton's White House was likened to that of a child's soccer team in which there are no assigned positions and each player chases the ball. Especially in the early period of his presidency, Clinton and his aides moved freely from issue to issue without a clear division of labor; participation in presidential meetings was often a function of who showed up. After the chaotic opening months of his presidency, however, Clinton found aides who were able to channel his centrifugal tendencies. Still, he never established a principle of organization that conserved his energy and channeled his energies to good effect.

As one might expect of someone who had devoted his adult life to politics, Clinton has been capable of impressive displays of political skill. He was also capable of astonishing missteps and miscalculations. The unevenness of his performance was a function of his readiness to change his policies in response to political exigencies and to overreach himself under favorable circumstances. No president has exceeded Clinton in his grasp of policy specifics, but that mastery did not translate into a clearly defined policy vision. Several factors seem to have been at work. Clinton's intelligence enabled him to envisage complexity; his verbal facility enabled him to dwell on that complexity; and his intensely political nature led him to modify his positions in response to the political context.

Clinton's cognitive style was driven by his exceptional intellectual facility. He read omnivorously, alternating his fare between fiction and demanding works on public policy. He was a sponge for facts and could easily synthesize complex material. As a law student, he was famed for skipping classes, reading other students' lecture notes, and doing better on examinations than the note takers.[14] There is a less positive side to such a cognitive style, however. Rather than cutting to the core of problems, making balanced assessments of them in the manner of Eisenhower, he was capable of behaving like the stereotypical lawyer who masters issues with the speed of oil covering water, but does so at the same depth.

The politically gifted, emotionally challenged William Jefferson Clinton provides a reminder of the fundamental importance of emotional intelligence in the presidency. His political gifts enabled him to thwart the Republican effort to remove him from office, but his psychic shortcomings were debilitating. He did preside over an extended period of economic prosperity, and his presidential achievements include the passage of NAFTA and welfare reform. Yet he is likely to be remembered as a politically talented underachiever. Clinton's undisciplined presidency provides a reminder that in the absence of emotional soundness, the American presidency is a problematic instrument of governance.

George W. Bush and the Politics of Preemption

The American presidency is said to be an office in which some incumbents grow and others merely swell up. If ever there was a chief executive to whom the first applies it is George W. Bush. Arriving in the White House with only modest governmental experience, Bush took a minimalist approach to his responsibilities before the terrorist attacks of September 11, 2001. Rising to the challenge, he went on to preside over the nation with far greater authority and assertiveness. Bush has gone to great lengths to put his stamp on national and international policy, but in doing so has advanced policies that have been intensely controversial in the United States and abroad.

BEFORE THE PRESIDENCY. George W. Bush was born on July 6, 1946, in New Haven, Connecticut, where his war veteran father, George H. W. Bush, was a Yale undergraduate. In contrast to his father, who moved to Texas as an adult but retained the outward signs of a New England transplant, the younger Bush is very much a product of the Lone Star State. Whereas the elder Bush attended a private day school in Greenwich, Connecticut, his son went to public school in Midland, Texas, where oil is the dominant economic force and the ambience is that of tract houses, Little League baseball, and easy informality. After elementary school, Bush followed in his father's path by attending the exclusive Philips Academy in Andover, Massachusetts, and then Yale, but he was more conspicuous for his social skills than his classroom performance, retaining the brash demeanor of a stereotypical Texan.

Although Bush's pre-presidential governmental service consisted only of six years as governor of Texas, he was no political Johnny-come-lately. His paternal grandfather served in the Senate, and his father had a long and varied political career, including two campaigns for the Senate, two terms in the House, eight years as vice president, and four years as president. The younger Bush participated in his father's many election campaigns, managed the campaigns of two GOP Senate candidates, and ran a strong race for Congress himself in his home district.

Two aspects of Bush's pre-presidential years are significant for his presidential leadership. One relates to his personal comportment and spiritual life. For many years, Bush stood out as the under-achieving son of a super-achieving father. Whereas George H. W. Bush had been a war hero, a self-made millionaire, and the holder of a succession of high-profile political positions, the young George W. Bush was a heavy drinker with a devil-may-care lifestyle. In early middle age, however, his life came together. He married the level-headed librarian Laura Welch, became the father of twin girls, experienced a spiritual awakening, and became a regular reader of the Bible. On the morning of his fortieth birthday, he awoke with an intense hangover and swore off alcohol, anchoring his resolve in his Christian faith.

The other is his career as a corporate executive and his business-oriented conservative ethos. After completing college and fulfilling his military obligation in the Texas Air National Guard, Bush attended Harvard Business School, graduating with a master's degree in business administration. He then returned to Texas and founded an oil exploration company. When oil prices plunged in the 1980s, the company foundered, but the tax laws of the time enabled Bush to sell it at a substantial profit. He then became the managing partner of the Texas Rangers, a major league baseball team. In the course of traveling the state to promote the team and appearing on television during its games, Bush became highly visible and was able to win the Texas Republican gubernatorial nomination, defeating the state's popular Democratic governor.

Both facets of Bush's experience were manifested in the formula he invoked to justify his gubernatorial and presidential programs—"compassionate conservatism." By this he meant to suggest that he was hard-headed, but not hard-hearted—that he favored not only such traditional conservative policies as major tax cuts, but also such reforms as a measure that tests the achievement of children in the nation's schools, with a view to identifying schools that are failing to provide disadvantaged children with adequate reading and mathematical skills.

Bush ran for governor on a small number of explicitly stated issues—education and welfare reform, stiffer penalties for juvenile offenders, and limitations on the right to litigate against businesses. He campaigned vigorously, stayed on message, and won with 53 percent of the vote. By the end of the first legislative session, all four measures had been enacted, and in 1998, he was reelected with a resounding 69 percent of the two-party vote.

This success, coupled with name recognition, made Bush the front-runner for the 2000 Republican presidential nomination, which he secured despite being defeated in the New Hampshire primary by Arizona senator John McCain. By March, Bush had won enough delegate support to be sure of the nomination. In the same month, Vice President Al Gore locked in the Democratic nomination. In his presidential campaign, Bush again focused on a handful of clearly delineated issues, including tax reduction; reforms in education, health care, and Social Security; and an initiative designed to channel federal welfare funds through the church-sponsored organizations that deliver much of the charity that reaches high-poverty areas. Nothing in his campaign presaged his administration's military involvements in Afghanistan and Iraq. Indeed, he declared his opposition to a globally expansive foreign policy.

The 2000 election could scarcely have been closer or more controversial. There was a near tie in the popular vote, with a slight edge for Gore. The all-important electoral vote outcome hinged on the state of Florida, where the voters were evenly divided and there was a bewildering number of controversies about the adequacy of the vote count. After a thirty-six day impasse, the U.S. Supreme Court issued a ruling that made Bush the winner.

BUSH AS PRESIDENT. From its very first day, the Bush presidency was off to a less than impressive start. As he took the oath of office, Bush seemed composed and unperturbed by the controversy that attended his election, but he read his inaugural address in a rote and plodding manner, pausing in mid-sentence and stumbling over words. Bush's halting presentation set the tone for his early addresses. He was more fluent on unscripted occasions, but there was a potential problem when he spoke without a text. His lack of national experience placed him at risk of making an error, as when he remarked to an interviewer that the United States was committed to do "whatever it takes" to defend Taiwan from attack by the People's Republic of China.[15] In fact, it was a long-standing American policy to be deliberately vague about how the nation would respond to such a contingency, and Bush had not intended to signal a policy departure. Still another problem with Bush's early public communications was their infrequency. He never addressed the nation from the Oval Office until the night of September 11, 2001. He never convened a major prime-time press conference until a month after that date. And he rarely addressed the nation in his capacity as its symbolic leader.

Despite Bush's shortcomings as a public communicator and his imperfect command of policy specifics, his early leadership was marked by successes in two realms, those of staffing his presidency and promoting his policies. Bush made his single most important personnel choice before he won the nomination, when he selected a highly experienced running mate in the person of Dick Cheney. With Cheney as a source of advice, Bush went on to name an experienced Cabinet and White House staff, not waiting for the resolution of the Florida electoral dispute to make preparations for taking office.

Bush's appointees included many veterans of the Nixon, Ford, Reagan, and George H. W. Bush presidencies, as well two of his own longtime Texas aides, communications advisor Karen Hughes and political strategist Karl Rove. Bush's national security team was particularly well seasoned: Secretary of State Colin Powell had been chairman of the Joint Chiefs of Staff and national security advisor, Secretary of Defense Donald Rumsfeld had previously held the same position, and national security advisor Condoleezza Rice had been a member of his father's National Security Council (NSC) staff.

One of Bush's early legislative successes, his educational reform measure, was very much a bipartisan effort. In his early weeks in office, Bush had put great effort into wooing the Senate's leading liberal Democrat, Edward Kennedy, who helped draft a bill that commanded broad-based support. But bipartisanship was not the norm. Instead, the pattern was set by the way the administration won the enactment of its tax cut, relying almost exclusively on the narrow Republican Congressional majority and a handful of Democratic defectors.

As of the first week of September, even many of Bush's supporters would have agreed with the earlier assertion of the *Washington Post*'s David Broder that the new president had not provided the American people with a "clear definition" of himself.[16] Indeed, when the Gallup organization fielded a presidential support poll that week, it found that public approval of the new president was at its lowest level of the seven months of his presidency: 51 percent. Bush learned that the nation was under attack while he was reading to school children in Booker Elementary School in Sarasota, Florida, in an event intended to publicize his administration's education program. Before leaving the school, he read a statement declaring that "terrorism against our nation will not stand." Because of concern that he would be targeted by terrorists, Bush was flown to the control center of the Strategic Air Command in Nebraska, where he presided by electronic means over a meeting of the National Security Council. At the meeting, the director of the Central Intelligence Agency reported that the attacks were almost certainly the work of al Qaeda, an Afghanistan-based terrorist organization that had been behind other acts of terrorism directed at the United States. Bush then returned to the White House, where he addressed the nation from the Oval Office, asserting that the attacks were "acts of war," that there "would be a monumental struggle between good and evil" in which good would prevail, and that the United States would "make no distinction between the terrorists who committed these acts and those who harbor them."

In the chaotic first day of the episode, Bush came across as less than self-assured. He then underwent a transformation. On September 14, he delivered a moving tribute to the victims of the terrorist attacks in Washington and flew to New York City, where he inspected the wreckage of the World Trade Center and addressed the rescue workers. When they shouted that they could not hear him, he replied, "I can hear you. The rest of the world hears you, and the people who knocked these buildings down will hear all of us soon!" In the weeks that followed, he became a compelling public presence. On September 20, he made a forceful presentation to Congress in which he gave the regime in Afghanistan an ultimatum: turn the al Qaeda leadership over to the United States and close down its terrorist camps. Three weeks later, he delivered a highly effective address to the United Nations. Most impressive was his October 11 prime-time news conference in the East Room of the White House. Responding in depth to questions, Bush radiated a sense of composure and made evident his detailed mastery of his administration's anti-terrorism policies.

Just as Bush's conduct of his responsibilities improved dramatically, the public's ratings of his performance surged to 90 percent, the record high in Gallup presidential approval ratings. Members of the political community also formed markedly more positive views of Bush's leadership qualities. Even many of his critics concluded that he had been underestimated, a view that extended to other nations. On October 20, for example, a columnist for the influential *Frankfurter Allgemeine* commented that Bush had grown into his job "before our eyes," comparing him to another president who rose to the demands of his times following an unpromising start, Harry S. Truman.[17]

In early October, the Afghan regime let it be known that it would not surrender the al Qaeda leadership, and the United States and its ally Great Britain began an intensive bombing campaign. Later in the month, U.S. Special Forces entered Afghanistan and began to provide military support to the anti-Taliban Northern Alliance. By November 13, the Northern Alliance had occupied the Afghan capital of Kabul, and in early December, the last major Taliban stronghold surrendered. When the Gallup organization polled the public at the end of December, Bush's approval level was at 86 percent.

Bush had postponed a decision on whether to target Iraq in the "war on terror" in a September NSC meeting in which Defense Secretary Rumsfeld raised that possibility, but Iraq came into his crosshairs in his January 2002 State of the Union address. Anticipating the doctrine of preemption that his administration would formally promulgate later in the year, Bush declared that he would not "wait on events" while "the world's most dangerous weapons" were acquired by "the world's most dangerous regimes." One such regime, he specified, was Iraq, which he grouped with Iran and North Korea in what he described as an "axis of evil."[18]

Bush's speech sent out shock waves. Whereas his response to September 11 had been favorably received, there was widespread criticism at home and abroad of his "axis of evil" locution. Some of it was prompted by a belief that Bush had lumped together nations that were very different in terms of whether and to what extent they posed threats; some was directed at the usage of "evil," which led critics to worry about whether the president's intense personal commitment to evangelical Christianity was leading him to advance an inappropriately moralistic foreign policy.

Bush's address presaged a preoccupation of the remainder of his first term that continued into his second term: his efforts to come to terms with Iraq. Bush's reference to Iraq in his 2002 State of the Union address was the prelude to a procession of actions directed at Saddam Hussein's regime. Diplomacy prevailed in the fall of 2002, when the administration persuaded the United Nations Security Council to enact a resolution insisting that Iraq destroy any weapons of mass destruction it might have and to admit United Nations inspectors to establish that it had done so. Early the following year, the administration turned to military action, attempting without success to persuade the Security Council to authorize the use of force on the grounds that Iraq had failed to comply with the UN demand. Then, in the face of substantial opposition at home and abroad, it launched an invasion of Iraq, proceeding with Great Britain as its principal ally.

The assault on Iraq began on March 20, 2003, and American troops took control of Baghdad on April 6. Bush announced the end of "major combat operations" on May 2, but the situation on the ground remained unsettled well into Bush's second term. As American troop losses mounted, increasing numbers of Americans expressed doubt about whether it had been wise for the United States to intervene in Iraq, and Bush's approval level sank dangerously low for a president seeking reelection. Seemingly unfazed, Bush fought a vigorous campaign against the 2004 Democratic nominee, Massachusetts senator John Kerry. Despite last-minute polls that projected Kerry as the winner, Bush won by 34 electoral votes. His popular vote edge over Kerry was 2.5 percent, the smallest margin for a sitting president in the nation's history. He nevertheless declared the election to have been a "mandate" and went on to propose a highly ambitious program for a second-term chief executive.

BOTTOM LINE. Early in his presidency, Bush seemed not to recognize the importance of the presidential public communication. Following the September 11 attacks, however, he began to address the public regularly, forcefully, even eloquently. He was not uniformly effective thereafter, but when he rehearsed he was effective in his public addresses, and he developed a personable stump style that served him well in the 2004 campaign. On January 20, 2005, he delivered his second-term inaugural address with fluency and confidence. The contrast with his inaugural remarks four years earlier was conspicuous.

Organizational capacity is one the strengths of the nation's first "MBA" president. Bush has chosen strong associates. He also excels at rallying his subordinates. Because avoiding public disagreement is a watchword of his presidency, its internal dynamics are not well documented, but clues are provided by Bob Woodward's reconstructions of the Bush administration's military interventions in Afghanistan and Iraq. Woodward's accounts suggest that in some instances Bush's deliberative processes leave something to be desired. He reports, for example, that Secretary of State Powell and Secretary of Defense Rumsfeld expressed their differences more sharply in meetings that Bush did not attend than ones in which he was present, which suggests that he may sometimes be shielded from potentially valuable debate. Woodward also describes an instance in which Powell met privately with Bush and National Security Advisor Rice in order to register his disagreement with the hawkish proposals of Rumsfeld and Vice President Cheney.[19] When subordinates make end runs around their colleagues, the advice the president gets may be more a function of their bureaucratic skill than the merit of their recommendations.

The congenitally gregarious George W. Bush resembles his fellow Texan Lyndon Johnson in his political skill. As he did in Texas, Bush sometimes has worked effectively on both sides of the aisle. However, there has been a hard edge to his leadership as president that was not evident in Texas. This was evident internationally as well as domestically, most notably in the lead-up to the Iraq war, when his administration failed to make a persuasive case for the urgency of immediate military action and went to war in the face of the opposition of a number of the nation's traditional allies.

Late-night television comedy notwithstanding, Bush has ample native intelligence. He has a cognitive style that seems not to be marked by intellectual curiosity, however, and shows little interest in the play of ideas. Moreover, he favors a corporate leadership model in which he relies on his subordinates to structure his options. After September 11, however, there was a dramatic increase in his mastery of the content of his administration's policies. As a member of Congress who is in regular contact with Bush put it, "He's as smart as he wants to be."[20]

What is critical for a president's emotional intelligence is that his public actions not be distorted by uncontrolled passions. He need not be a paragon of mental health in his private life. By this litmus, the heavy-drinking, young George W. Bush was too volatile to be a promising prospect for a responsible public position. It would not be surprising if a man who abused alcohol until early middle age proved to be an emotional tinder box, but Bush's performance as a private sector executive and as governor of Texas were not marred by emotional excesses. Moreover, he weathered the 2000 and 2004 presidential campaigns with equanimity, and whatever the merits of his administration's military ventures, there is no sign that they were the result of out-of-control emotions.

The topic of policy vision suggests an unlikely parallel between George W. Bush and George H. W. Bush. The first President Bush was famously indifferent to what he was said to have dismissed as "the vision thing." The second President Bush has faulted his father for failing to enunciate clear goals for his presidency and thereby failing to rack up domestic accomplishments on which to campaign for reelection. George W. Bush goes out of his way to evince a policy vision. He holds that if a president does not set his own goals, others will set them for him. However, if his vision that the regime of Saddam Hussein needed to be removed and Iraq proves to be a quagmire, Bush's second term may falter. His presidency may suffer from having a vision, just as his father's suffered for lacking one.

Contextual Effects on Presidential Leadership: The Times and the Public

As the preceding cases illustrate, the capacity of the president to make a difference is a function not only of his personal attributes, but also the political environment in which they are brought to bear. A president who is well-suited to serve in one setting may be ill-suited for another. The most celebrated modern chief executive, Franklin Delano Roosevelt, had been a presence on the national political scene for two decades before entering the White House. He had established himself as a talented politician and eloquent orator, but was viewed as something of a lightweight because he lacked a well-developed policy vision. If FDR had served in an uneventful period, he might have left little in the way of a historical legacy. As it happened, the circumstances of the Great Depression and World War II placed a premium on Roosevelt's inspirational and political gifts. In the absence of those contexts, it is possible that his presidency would be of modest historical interest.

One contextual determinant of the president's ability to make a difference is the extent of his public backing. Congress was deferential to Roosevelt in the early months of his presidency in large part because its members were convinced that he had overwhelming public support. In Roosevelt's time, politicians relied on personal impressions to assess the president's public standing. During the Truman years, a more reliable means of gauging presidential approval came into use: public opinion polls, in which statistically representative cross sections of the public are asked to evaluate the president's handling of his duties. Presidential approval polls have become a force in their own right. High levels of approval can be much to the president's advantage, and low public approval can be a prescription for failure.

The elected term of President Harry Truman provides an example of how a president can be hamstrung by lack of public support. In 1948, Truman won election in his own right in a campaign in which he proposed an ambitious domestic program, including a landmark civil rights proposal and universal health insurance. Before the first year of his second term was over, however, his administration was the recipient of a pair of body blows. In September 1949, the Soviet Union was revealed to have developed nuclear weapons. The next month, mainland China came under Communist control, fueling a venomous public debate over whether the administration had "lost China" and was "soft on communism."

On June 25, 1950, there was yet another politically costly development. American-supported South Korea was invaded by communist North Korea, and Truman and his associates concluded that it would be necessary to employ American troops to prevent a Communist takeover. The war evolved into a politically costly stalemate, in which the United States and its allies were arrayed against not only North Korea, but also the almost limitless manpower of Communist China. For the final two years of Truman's presidency, his approval level was in the 20 to 30 percent approval range, among the lowest in the modern presidency. Not surprisingly, Congress showed no interest in enacting his program.

Public response to the president is conditioned by an important background consideration. In most democracies, executive leadership is divided between a political leader, such as a prime minister, and a head of state, such as a constitutional monarch or a politically neutral president. In the United States, the two roles are combined. As head of state, the president is expected to represent all Americans, but in his political capacity he must engage in the divisive process of advancing his administration's policies. Being more than a "mere" political leader can enhance the president's effectiveness by enabling him to tap the intense loyalty Americans have for their nation.

The feelings bound up in the presidency are prominently displayed on the occasion of the death of a sitting president. There were spontaneous displays of public grief and mourning following the assassination of Kennedy, the death of natural causes of FDR, and even the death of the lackluster Warren Harding. A less grim manifestation of the public bond to the chief executive is the upsurge in presidential approval that commonly follows the outbreak of national crisis, an example being the spike in public evaluations of George W. Bush after the terrorist attacks of September 11, 2001. The depth of emotion invested in the chief executive helps account for the continuing interest in the related matter of presidential greatness.

The Question of Presidential Greatness

The faces of George Washington, Thomas Jefferson, Abraham Lincoln, and Theodore Roosevelt were not chiseled into Mount Rushmore because these men were thought to have been merely competent. They were deemed to have been truly great. But how is greatness to be determined, and can it be ascertained with any degree of objectivity?

The changing assessments of Thomas Jefferson illustrate the uncertainty of such judgments. For much of the nineteenth century, Jefferson was dismissed as an impractical idealist whose vision of a nation of small farmers was irrelevant to an age of urban growth and industrialization. In the Progressive Era and the period of the New Deal, however, he acquired the status of a democratic icon. The Jefferson Memorial was erected in the nation's capital, and a five-cent coin bearing his portrait was issued. But by the final decade of the twentieth century, Jefferson had gone into eclipse as attention shifted to his status as a slave owner and the probable father of several slave children.[21]

Should we conclude from such fluctuations that presidential greatness is merely in the eye of the beholder? There clearly is more to the story. Consider a pair of presidents whose reputations have remained towering despite changes in political climate: George Washington and Abraham Lincoln. At first glance, the two men seem poles apart. Washington was a Virginia aristocrat who comported himself with studied dignity. Lincoln was born into rural poverty, and his manner was droll and homespun. Yet they had two things in common. They held office in periods of national peril and are widely viewed as having risen to the challenge of their times. Washington's challenge was to legitimize the new nation and set it on a firm footing; Lincoln's was to win the war that erupted just after he took office and to restore the Union. Washington brought his good sense and monumental prestige to bear in his efforts, and Lincoln presided over the Civil War with shrewdness and tenacity, going on to seek reconciliation with the South. In both cases the accomplishment was monumental.

There has been a continuing interest in rating and ranking American presidents. A recent volume entitled *The Uses and Abuses of Presidential Ratings* lists the results of ten such efforts in the period from 1948 to 2000.[22] These typically are polls of historians and others who are deemed to be authoritative, and most of them sort the chief executives into five categories: "great," "near great," "above average," "average," "below average," and "failure." The criteria for the ratings are ordinarily left up to the raters, who therefore must decide whether to assess the way in which a president did his job, the merits of his policies, or some combination of both. Because the ratings are overall judgments, they cannot account for the mixed performance of a president such as Richard Nixon, who had major foreign policy accomplishments but was forced to resign in disgrace over Watergate. (Nixon was judged to be a failure in six of the seven surveys in which he was rated and below average in the seventh.)

In spite of the imperfect methodology of such studies, there is striking similarity in their findings. Every study placed Washington and Lincoln in the great category. FDR was also consistently ranked as great, even in a survey commissioned by the *Wall Street Journal* in 2000, which was designed to remedy the alleged liberal bias in earlier studies. Other presidents who were deemed to be great or near great include Thomas Jefferson, Andrew Jackson, Theodore

Roosevelt, Woodrow Wilson, Harry Truman, and Ronald Reagan. Eisenhower registered the greatest change over the years, rising from average in 1962 to above average or near great beginning in the 1980s, when scholarship based on the declassified record of his presidency began to appear in print. (There is a standard list of failures, which, in addition to Nixon, includes James Buchanan, Andrew Johnson, Ulysses S. Grant, and Warren G. Harding.) If there is a common denominator in presidential assessments, it is a bias toward activism, unless the activism is viewed as misplaced, as in the instances of Lyndon Johnson and Vietnam, and Nixon and Watergate.

There are pros and cons to the concern with presidential greatness. The presidents who have been viewed as great provide the nation with unifying symbols, in much the manner of the flag and national anthem. They also serve as role models and sources of lessons. The negative of such ratings is that they divert attention from the full range of presidential experience. The reasons that presidents fail can be as instructive as the reasons they succeed. And the performance of most presidents has been mixed, therefore providing both positive lessons and warnings.

Whatever the merits of the quest for presidential greatness, one thing is certain. The occupant of 1600 Pennsylvania Avenue deserves the closest of scrutiny.

Notes

1. The most influential works on the impact of individual presidents are Richard E. Neustadt, *Presidential Power: The Politics of Leadership* (New York: Norton, 1960), and James David Barber, *The Presidential Character: Predicting Performance in the White House* (Englewood Cliffs, N.J.: 1972), both of which have gone through later editions without a change in theme. The first emphasizes political skill; the second, emotional fitness. My own formulation, which combines and expands on those of Neustadt and Barber, is set forth in Fred I. Greenstein, *The Presidential Difference: Leadership Style from FDR to George W. Bush* (Princeton, N.J.: Princeton University Press, 2004).

2. Daniel Goleman, *Emotional Intelligence* (New York: Bantam Books, 1995).

3. Eleanor Roosevelt, *This Is My Story* (New York: Harper, 1937), 167.

4. Vito N. Silvestri, *Becoming JFK: A Profile in Communication* (Westport, Conn.: Praeger, 2000).

5. Lou Cannon, *Reagan* (New York: G.P. Putnam's Sons, 1982), 94.

6. On the American military intervention in Vietnam, see John P. Burke and Fred I. Greenstein, with the collaboration of Larry Berman and Richard Immerman, *How Presidents Test Reality: Decisions on Vietnam , 1954 and 1965* (New York: Russell Sage, 1989), 118–254.

7. Richard M. Nixon, "Asia after Vietnam," *Foreign Affairs* 46 (October 1967), 111–125.

8. Donald Baer, Matthew Cooper, and David Gergen, "Bill Clinton's Hidden Life," *U.S. News and World Report,* July 20, 1992.

9. Jeffrey H. Birnbaum, "Clinton Received a Vietnam Draft Deferment for an ROTC Program That He Never Joined," *Wall Street Journal*, February 6, 1992.

10. Howard Kurtz, "Clintons Agree To Do '60 Minutes,'" *Washington Post,* January 25, 1992.

11. Richard Lacayo, "A Moment of Silence," *Time*, May 8, 1995, 46.

12. Inaugural Address, January 20, 1997, in *Public Papers of the Presidents: William Jefferson Clinton, 1997* (Washington, D.C.: U.S. Government Printing Office, 1998).

13. "Address to the Nation on Testimony Before the Independent Counsel's Grand Jury," August 17, 1998, *Weekly Compilation of Presidential Documents*, week ending August 24, 1998, online via GPO Access.

14. David Maranis, *First in His Class: The Biography of Bill Clinton* (New York: Simon & Schuster, 1995), 138–139, 234–235.

15. "Bush Pledges to Do Whatever It Takes to Defend Taiwan," CNN, April 25, 2001.

16. David S. Broder, "The Reticent President," *Washington Post,* April 22, 2001.

17. Leo Weiland, "Bush's New Image," *Frankfurter Allgemeine* (English language edition), October 20, 2001.

18. "State of the Union Address," January 29, 2002.

19. Bob Woodward, *Bush at War* (New York: Simon & Schuster, 2002), 177, 332–334. Also see Bob Woodward, *Plan of Attack* (New York: Simon & Schuster, 2004).

20. Stephen Thomma, "Growing on the Job," *Miami Herald*, December 9, 2001.

21. For reviews rankings of presidents see Tom H. Blessing and Robert K. Murray, *Greatness in the White House: Washington through Reagan*, 2nd ed. (University Park, Pa.: Penn State Press, 1994), and Meena Bose and Mark Landis, eds., *The Uses and Abuses of Presidential Ratings* (New York: Nova Science Publishers, 2003). For a reasoned effort to identify a handful of great presidents, see Marc Landy and Sidney M. Milkis, *Presidential Greatness* (Lawrence: University Press of Kansas, 2000). Jefferson's shifting reputation is discussed by R. B. Bernstein in *Thomas Jefferson* (New York: Oxford University Press, 2003), 191–198.

22. Bose and Landis, *Uses and Abuses*, 18–22.

Bibliography

Barber, James David. *The Presidential Character: Predicting Performance in the White House.* 4th ed. Englewood Cliffs, N.J.: Prentice Hall, 1992.

Burke, John P. *The Institutional Presidency*. Baltimore, Md.: Johns Hopkins University Press, 1992.

Graff, Henry F., ed. *The Presidents: A Reference History*. 2nd ed. New York: Scribner's, 1996.

Greenstein, Fred I. *The Presidential Difference: Leadership Style from FDR to George W. Bush.* 2nd ed. Princeton, N.J.: Princeton University Press, 2004.

Hargrove, Erwin C. *The President as Leader: Appealing to the Better Angels of Our Nature.* Lawrence: University Press of Kansas, 1998.

Herring, Pendleton. *Presidential Leadership: The Political Relations of Congress and the Chief Executive*. 2nd ed. Westport, Conn.: Greenwood, 1972.

Jones, Charles O. *The Presidency in a Separated System*. Washington, D.C.: The Brookings Institution, 1994.

Neustadt, Richard E. *Presidential Power and the Modern Presidents: The Politics of Leadership from Roosevelt to Reagan.* New York: Free Press, 1990.

Rossiter, Clinton, L. *The American Presidency.* 2nd ed. New York: Harcourt Brace, 1960.

Skowronek, Stephen. *The Politics Presidents Make: Leadership from John Adams to George Bush.* Cambridge, Mass.: Harvard University Press, 1993.

THE PEOPLE AND POLITICS
OF THE EXECUTIVE AGENCIES

8

THE COMPLEX ORGANIZATION
OF THE EXECUTIVE BRANCH:
THE LEGACIES OF COMPETING
APPROACHES TO ADMINISTRATION

Colin Campbell

WHEN MOST AMERICANS THINK ABOUT THE FEDERAL "bureaucracy," they are likely to conjure up a fairly simple image of a big organization with myriad layers and rules. It is difficult for them to understand why government is not easier to run, more effective, and better at finding common-sense solutions to everyday problems. Much of this volume analyzes the various historical, social, and political factors that complicate the task of governance in the contemporary United States and that make it so difficult to assuage the public's deep reservations about, even contempt for, bureaucracy. For many specialists in public administration and the political authorities who have listened to them, the quest for efficient and effective public management serves as a rally call. However, to many observers—ranging from the deeply attentive to the mildly interested—reform efforts appear simply as the governance equivalent to the search for the Holy Grail.

This chapter will examine three basic approaches, or models, that have been employed to enhance the administration of the federal government. Although they took hold at different times in the twentieth century, each one has left a significant legacy in the structure and procedures of the U.S. federal executive branch. These approaches employ three different conceptions of public management.

First, the "scientific management" model, which emphasizes operational efficiency and is based on notions of how private businesses are run, dominated in the first third of the past century. It still asserts itself substantially in contemporary reform efforts, such as attempts to define managerial objectives and to strengthen the monitoring of performance in relation to them.

Second, the "policy management" model, which asserted itself most clearly in the middle part of the previous century, stressed the partnering of political executives and career officials in devising policy options and monitoring performance. A core theme was to create comprehensive feedback mechanisms that would guide programmatically based adjustments to policy and associated funding. The spread of the Planning, Programming and Budgeting System (PPBS) in the 1960s reflected most clearly the salience of the model (whether real or aspirational) at its apogee. The Pentagon still follows PPBS. Recently the U.S. Air Force has engaged in two strenuous efforts to greatly improve planning and its functional relationship to programming and budgeting.

Third, a "public choice" model, based on theories drawn from microeconomics and the economic analysis of organizations, emerged in the 1960s. Essentially, the model viewed the relationship between politicians and public servants as a subset of economic transactions. It advocated the constriction of government agencies and the roles of their officials within the confines of express provision of goods and services explicitly "purchased" by the public through their representatives, the politicians. Styled by some "new public management," it spread rapidly among Anglo-American nations and was influential as well in international organizations, such as the Organization for Economic Cooperation and Development (OECD) and the World Bank, advancing "best practices" in public management. The model started with the premise that career officials often press personal and institutional agendas that do not comport with the objectives sought by political executives and/or legislators. Frequently taking an adversarial stance vis-à-vis career civil servants, it stressed approaches that would reign in what was viewed as dysfunctional, self-aggrandizing entrepreneurship among permanent bureaucrats.

Each of these models has had clear effects on the organization of the U.S. executive branch. The scientific management model led to the proliferation of specialized offices within departments. As these grew in size, gained legitimacy as players within the executive-bureaucratic arena, and achieved a degree of autonomy, especially in administrative matters, they frequently spun off as agencies operating with a high degree of independence from political executives. The policy management model spawned both efforts in the center of the executive branch—such as placing the Bureau of the Budget in the Executive Office of the President—and within departments—such as the creation and expansion of planning and policy units—to promote the analysis of the policies and programs of agencies from the standpoint of how they advance outcomes important to society.

The more recent public choice model has operated to a very substantial degree in reaction to the policy management approach as a naive attempt to establish synergy between political executives and career officials. It defines the attainment of public value as dependent upon a division of labor whereby political executives alone establish desirable outcomes and specify for career officials the outputs required to fulfill these. The approach has had several organizational consequences. For instance, it favors center-driven, top-down approaches to budgeting (for instance, across-the-board cuts) that circumvent detailed program analysis. In turn, the decline of the salience of analysis has led to reduced capacity in the central coordinating and line agencies alike for policy and program evaluation. Adherents of public choice have also used the layering of the political executive and central control of appointments to impose clearer discipline on both departments and agencies. This chapter will outline in detail the connections between the three models and the current variegation in the organization of the executive branch.

A significant paradox frames any assessment of the effects that these three models have had on the organization of the executive branch. No other nation has developed as immense and powerful a state apparatus—the military establishment, for instance—as has the United States. However, the gargantuan complex of governmental capabilities has emerged in a cultural context in which, with the clear exception of national security, the notion of the interventionist state historically has provoked deep skepticism, if not resentment.

Ambivalence toward the state apparatus and the many shapes it has taken runs through the executive branch. However, officials operating the executive branch of the U.S. government, both appointees and career officials, probably bring to their tasks unrivaled expertise and administrative acuity. Many educated Americans harbor great admiration for many aspects of the British governmental system. This includes the perception among many that the United Kingdom retains a more established and better functioning public service than does the U.S. federal government. Yet, even the most ardent admirers of the British system would find it ludicrous to assert that the U.K. bureaucracy (known as Whitehall) can deploy greater governmental capability than Washington. However, U.S. officials—appointees and career officials alike—face myriad impediments not only to policy entrepreneurship but to administrative innovation as well. Policy entrepreneurship, of course, evokes considerable contention, whereas administrative innovation should fit quintessentially in the executive branch but still proves elusive. In most other advanced democracies, the political executive devises and implements changes in the machinery of government and programs for administrative reform. In the United States, both the administration and Congress compete at what often turns into a low-scoring contact sport—with lengthy impasses, like soccer, but relentless checking, like hockey.

Other systems of government certainly develop and implement policies with complex systems of departments, agencies, independent regulatory agencies and commissions, state and local government, nonprofit organizations, and private commercial contractors. The United States, however, differs in the degree to which the factors mentioned above make coherent meshing of the contributions of these various elements exponentially more difficult than in most other advanced democracies. We will face, thus, the core question of this chapter—how do you achieve coherence within what often appears to be a crazy quilt?

The Models

This section will examine in detail the three models that informed efforts to enhance administration of the federal government through the twentieth century. These are scientific management, policy management, and public choice.

Scientific Management

A deep skepticism of entrusting too much latitude to a permanent state apparatus has accompanied the development of the United States as a nation since the American Revolution. Indeed, the notion of a dichotomy between policy and administration that held such sway in the first third of the last century (until the New Deal) in many respects served as a legitimization of state building, notwithstanding the aversion during this period toward interventionist governance. Frank J. Goodnow immortalized the notion of a role dichotomy between the political executive and permanent officials by arguing that administration should operate as autonomously as possible from politics.[1] Woodrow Wilson and Luther Gullick both pressed the view that management science as practiced in business could easily find many fruitful applications in public administration.[2] Wilson stated the position especially starkly: "The field of administration is a field of business. It is removed from the hurry and strife of politics. . . . It is part of political life only as the methods of the counting-house are part of the life of society; only as machinery is part of the manufactured product."[3]

The purported dichotomy often provides a veil of legitimacy for officials astute at cloaking substantive inputs to decision making. For instance, argumentation focused on efficiency in the face of the tendency among political executives toward profligacy often will trump the political appeal of a program. General C. G. Dawes, the first director of the Bureau of the Budget, captured this while reflecting upon his role in the early 1920s:

> . . . no Cabinet officer on the bridge with the President, advising as to what direction the ship of state should sail . . . will properly serve the captain of the ship or its passengers, the public, if he resents the call of the Director of the Budget from the stoke-hole, put there by the captain to see that coal is not wasted.[4]

The approach's implicit trust in the attainability of the degree of administrative efficiency found in U.S. corporations during the height of the industrial revolution took on near-mythical proportions.

Policy Management

Daniel Carpenter's work reminds us that the scientific management approach—including a degree of deference to expertise in technical areas—proved eminently serviceable during the first half of the last century.[5] And, as noted above, it continues to have an effect on the way the federal bureaucracy is organized and operated.[6] However, the explosion of interventionist government programs under Franklin Delano Roosevelt meant that career officials would have to step outside the bounds of the policy/administration dichotomy. For instance, transfer of the Bureau of the Budget (BoB—since 1970 the Office of Management and Budget, OMB) to the newly created Executive Office of the President in 1939 reflected this trend. Under the activist director Harold Smith, BoB greatly widened the compass of budget examination.[7] It would now as a matter of course consider how secretaries' policy and expenditure proposals fit the president's legislative program and fiscal priorities. Smith, indeed, undertook to revamp the expertise of BoB staff by seeking recruits who had broad training in the social sciences and were strongly oriented toward planning approaches to public policy. Meanwhile, line departments took on board cadres of professionals committed to implementing different elements of the New Deal. In addition, they tended to shadow developments in the center of the executive branch both in pursuing greater rigor in program development and implementation, and in more intense efforts to align policy and budget appeals with the priorities of the administration.

The expansion of the welfare state in developed nations fostered similar patterns in other advanced democracies. By the 1960s and 1970s, students of public administration in advanced liberal democracies began to give great attention to the roles of senior public servants in the executive-bureaucratic arena. Interest heightened notably in the degree to which permanent officials influence the development of policy and do not simply administer its implementation.[8] The concept that career officials bring to the policy process a specific collection of competences not readily available from political executives or their appointees attained wide currency. Indeed, a literature emerged in the late 1970s that saw the involvement of senior permanent officials in policy making as a natural consequence of the leverage they enjoy through their expertise—be it strategic (mastery of how to pursue or thwart change within the system), technical, or a mix of both.[9]

The trend in the literature toward acknowledging the policy and—by extension—political roles of career officials reached its height in 1981. In that year, a work—*Bureaucrats and Politicians in Western Democracies*—appeared that soon became a classic within its genre.[10] The book argued that senior officials rarely confine themselves merely to administration. Minimally, they involve themselves in policy making but restrict themselves to imparting relevant facts and knowledge to decision makers. However, officials close to the apex of power more typically engage in political calculation and manipulation—but in response to narrower bands of concerns than political executives and with less passion or ideology. Significantly, Joel D. Aberbach, Robert H. Putnam, and Bert A. Rockman did argue that some officials—styled "Image IV"—with exceptionally strategic positions develop and employ a full range of behind-the-scenes political skills and passionately commit themselves to assuring specific policy outcomes.[11]

The existing literature revealed fairly substantial evidence of Image IV behavior.[12] It might occur in positions requiring the type of crosscutting gamesmanship that prevails in central coordinating agencies and departments (for instance, the Office of Management and Budget and the Department of the Treasury) and among top officials in line agencies. Further, reactive career officials attempting to maintain the status quo, proactive change agents in the permanent civil service, and political appointees given coordinative or line responsibilities might all reveal Image IV traits to some degree. The evidence contradicted the putative dichotomy between realms of policy and administration that saw the politicians prevailing within the former realm and officials centering their activities in the latter.

Some researchers and practitioners in the early 1980s might have concluded that—with the clear signs of policy roles for career officials—academics and public managers would move on to crafting a positive theory and administrative science for dealing with what appeared obvious. However, they would have come out wide of the mark. Indeed, the last two decades of the past century witnessed a major backlash against the role of senior career public servants in policy making.

Initially, the groundswell appeared the strongest in the United States. Liberals were impatient with the slow expansion of the welfare state and concerned with the acquisitiveness of the so-called military-industrial complex. They frequently registered frustration with obstructionism in government agencies. Those wanting greater responsiveness to societal needs within the public service often spoke of "iron triangles"—intractable alliances of special interests, key bureaucrats, and congressional patrons that, at best, allowed only incremental decision making and, in its worst forms, maintenance of the status quo. Conservatives, on the other hand, viewed career officials as promoters of the "nanny state" who sought only to feather their own nests through "budget maximization."

Public Choice

We cannot assess what has taken place over the past thirty years in terms of the shifts in paradigms for the roles of officials without considering dramatic changes in the prevalent view of accountability in advanced democracies. The nub of the issue rests with how accountability runs through the political process.

First, the theoretical framework for accountability that prevails in the United States differs sharply from that at play in most other advanced democracies, including the so-called Westminster systems—that is, the United Kingdom, Canada, Australia, and New Zealand. In the classic Westminster paradigm, discussed with greater elaboration in this volume by Richard Rose, the public elects a parliament in which one party gains sufficient control to form a government (whether majority, minority, or in coalition). The government, under the leadership of the prime minister, assumes collective responsibility—most immediately, to Parliament, but, ultimately, back to the public, who might not renew its mandate in the next general election. In addition, each minister is individually responsible to Parliament—the theory being that parliamentary displeasure with certain policies or actions might force him or her to resign. Most ministers' "portfolios" involve oversight of all or part of a government department. In the Westminster tradition, career public servants overwhelmingly staffed these organizations in which hierarchical accountability functioned as glue. In exchange for their loyalty and, in instances of policy or managerial failure, silence, ministers imparted to career civil servants a high degree of control over management of their cadre and security of tenure.

Of course, practice has never correlated perfectly with theory. The rise of strong party discipline in the latter part of the nineteenth century meant that during the twentieth century parliamentary backbenchers exerted only limited control over cabinets. The process by which parties garner electoral support through the appeal of their leaders has often given prime ministers sufficient leverage to run command-oriented rather than consultative cabinet government. Career officials, a cadre that traces its ancestry to the royal household, frequently have pursued their own agendas. In the United Kingdom, this took the form of a long-term perspective that often clashed with the immediacy of political exigency. But certainly we have seen failures even of the contractual core of the Westminster system—ministers who have refused to take blame and officials who have not remained silent. And, in any case, Westminster-style accountability becomes multifaceted with officials having to juggle responsibilities to such diverse objects as their minister, their departmental superiors, the prime minister, Parliament, clients, professional standards, and the national interest. Thus, the iterative chain of accountability postulated by the Westminster model rarely pertains in reality. In fact, laments of its passing might well amount to nostalgia for something that never actually existed.

Regarding the presidential-congressional system of the United States, the founders largely construed the arrogance of Britain toward the thirteen colonies as resulting from the autocracy of the executive, as embodied in the monarch. They thus embraced the concept of separation of powers as protection against autocratic rule. Herein, both the executive and legislative branches find themselves on independent mandates. This places the career bureaucracy in the position of serving two masters—the president and Congress. It also makes Cabinet government extremely difficult, as career bureaucrats, ever mindful of the likely responses of their patrons in Congress, often divert Cabinet secretaries from an administration's agenda to one emanating from Congress or from the iron-triangles of congressional committees, interest groups, and bureaucratic officials mentioned above.

If the Westminster tradition has erred on the side of career officials who develop and ply their own views of the national interest, the U.S. tradition has displayed a tendency toward short-term, politics-driven policy making that is capable, other than under extraordinary circumstances, of only incremental change. As we saw in the preceding section, reformers in the United States have struggled to define both the relationship between Cabinet secretaries and their officials and the degree of latitude that permanent public servants should have in devising policy. However, the system did seem to attain a certain degree of equilibrium in the middle part of the last century—notwithstanding perennial angst from both the left and the right over the ability of officials to advocate or obstruct policies.

The two energy shocks of the 1970s, along with increased vulnerability to Asian economic competition, thrust Anglo-American countries into a decline neurosis that swung the popular pendulum against permanent officials' latitude for influencing policy. Indeed, the public became highly susceptible to arguments in favor of constraining public service. Public choice theory increasingly provided the theoretical streetcar for those wanting to "build down" government. It based its appeal upon the notion that politicians could reign in policy entrepreneurship among officials by severely constricting their resources and by becoming highly prescriptive about which goods and services they could purvey. However, its principal advocates betrayed a decidedly American view of the political process. Public choice theory stressed the immense leverage of the career public service in exploiting their expertise and positional advantage to play the political leadership, legislators, and interest groups against one another in order to maximize budgets. Within the public choice framework, other values such as professionalism, service of the public, equity, and ethics would take a back seat to controlling officials so as to minimize budgetary bottom lines.

Public choice theorists reserved special contempt for those who believed that analysis and comprehensive approaches to budgeting would bring government spending into line. That expectation simply took politicians off the scent and led them further into the clutches of budget maximizers.[13] In practice, the separation of powers made the desired constriction of budgets in the United States as elusive as the achievement of comprehensive rationality within and between social welfare programs proved to be in the 1960s. This did not prevent reformers in Westminster systems from attempting to adapt public choice theory to their own circumstances. The consequences went well beyond center-driven, top-down budgeting to mighty impingements of every sort of discretionary authority, including individual ministerial discretion beyond the narrow confines of specific outputs.

A main thrust of public choice in the United States has taken the form of the "administrative presidency."[14] Here, incumbents deploy strategies focused on placing the state apparatus more at their disposal in achieving what Terry Moe has termed "responsive competence." This involves very strong emphasis on the part of presidents and their appointees at channeling the bureaucracy in directions that advance an administration's electoral support and legacy.[15] To Moe, responsive competence contrasts with the tendency for some presidents—for instance, Jimmy Carter—to focus excessively upon the discernment of which options best withstand the scrutiny of the "neutral competence" of the career bureaucracy. Such an emphasis, Moe argued, draws the president and his advisors' attention from the main games—keeping political capital high and enshrining an administration's legacy.

Strategies focused upon responsive competence include increasing the layers of appointees overseeing the work of career officials in departments and agencies, tightening the screening of potential political executives from the standpoint of their likely adherence to the president's agenda, and drawing policy preparation and monitoring of implementation into units operating within the White House Office or the Executive Office of the President. Moe stipulated in 1985 a linear progression whereby presidents relentlessly increase their institutional leverage vis-à-vis both the permanent bureaucracy and Congress's efforts to confound incumbents' policy initiatives and executive decisions.

Ironically, some of the outstanding research outputs inspired by Moe's hypotheses temper claims of a linear progression toward presidential aggrandizement. For instance, William G. Howell at least allows for ebbs and flows in the secular trend. He notes that, "the president's freedom to act unilaterally is defined by Congress's ability, and the judiciary's willingness, to subsequently overturn him."[16] Andrew Rudalevige has found that presidents' embrace of centralized policy formulation operates in response to different arrays of contingencies, not to a monotonic reflex; that centralization helps the president get his way in the executive branch but can undercut his relations with Congress and, therefore, can backfire; and that drawing matters into the White House or the Executive Office of the President ultimately encounters case load limits.[17]

David E. Lewis focuses on the other side of the centralization coin.[18] He examines Congress's efforts to insulate government agencies from presidential influence. He identifies a wide range of factors at play in such dynamics. These include, *inter alia*, evidence that crises with systemwide significance—such as the Great Depression, World War II, and the terrorist attacks of September 11,

2001—make it easier for presidents to centralize, that Republican congresses seem more inclined to insulation than those controlled by the Democrats, that divided government lends itself to greater concern for insulation, that the obvious "public good" nature of national security seems to give the president a wide remit for "aggrandizement," that either the president or Congress can preempt the other in responding to a public concern—and whoever prevails in this way will affect the degree of centralization or insulation—and that the president will take a keener interest in centralization when he or a Cabinet secretary bears statutory obligations of accountability.[19]

Because of the legacies of the three approaches used to organize it, the U.S. executive branch presents a "crazy quilt" of departments and agencies. The use of centralization to bring greater order within the executive branch or of insulation to make entities less beholden to the president operates under a complex system of contingencies and a dizzying array of incentives and constraints that defy imputation of a linear progression. The next section will outline the immense variegation of the far from seamless framework in which the executive branch operates.

The Crosscutting Footprints of Three Traditions

Having established the contours of the three models of public management, we can now analyze the resulting structure of the U.S. executive branch that they have so heavily influenced. First, I examine the current departments headed by members of the Cabinet with consideration of the year in which they were created, their aggregate and discretionary budgets, and, within their policy and management leadership, the respective numbers of presidential appointees requiring Senate confirmation (presidential appointees not requiring Senate confirmation were excluded since, for the most part, they serve part-time on various advisory boards and commissions). Within that leadership, this analysis will also include the number of Senior Executive Service (SES) personnel. The SES figures differentiate between incumbents from the ranks of the career public service and those who have received an appointment as a noncareer official—that is, somebody serving at the pleasure of the administration and subject to removal without right of appeal. (See Appendix for a complete discussion of the sources used for this section.) Second, we will review the structures of these departments from the standpoint of units dedicated to the support of the department secretaries as chief executive officers, units overseeing large policy or programmatic domains, and units supporting general operations within the department but not reporting directly to the secretary. Third, we will examine each agency functioning outside the aegis of a Cabinet-level department with regard to the period in which it was created, its independence (or lack thereof) from direct control by the president, and the mix of appointees and members of the SES (career and noncareer).

Departments

Table 1 summarizes the data concerning departments headed by members of the Cabinet. The departments of the Treasury, State, Justice, and Defense all trace their lineage to 1789. However, only the former two existed from then as Cabinet-level departments under their current name. Defense became in 1949 the umbrella for the departments of War (created in 1789), Navy (1798), and Air (1947). Justice became a Cabinet-level department in 1870 although its head, the attorney general, had belonged to the Cabinet since the ratification of the Constitution.

A significant cluster of departments emerged during the expansion of state intervention that began to take root by the mid-1800s. Generally, administrations justified the creation of these new bureaucratic entities on the grounds that they would bring greater coherence to government's efforts to give direction within major sectors of activity. The first of these, Interior (1849), expressly encompassed functions previously performed by the initial departments that focused on domestic issues. Then called the Home Department, the new agency consolidated under one roof a wide range of organizations, including the General Land Office (from Treasury), the Patent Office (State), the Indian Affairs Office (War), and the military pension offices (War and Navy). Similarly, the Department of Agriculture (1862) initially became viewed as the "people's department" in that it promoted more systematic pursuit of the sector that served as the backbone of the economy at the time. The creation of the Department of Commerce and Labor (1903)—which bifurcated into the current separate departments under the respective names in 1913—reflected the industrialization of the economy during the latter part of the nineteenth century.

Notwithstanding the expansion of the executive branch beginning with the Roosevelt administration, departments enshrining the greatly augmented state lagged behind the addition of functions. All of the departments within this group emerged since 1950. And, administrations used ever more managerial rhetoric to justify the reorganizations on the grounds that bringing disparate units into big tents would enhance policy and implementation within major sectors of government activity. Health and Human Services (1980) owes its origins to the Department of Health, Education and Welfare (1953), which, in turn, clustered under one department the numerous agencies operating in these areas whose accretion had become especially intensified during the New Deal.

A spate of agencies followed upon the coattails of a more interventionist view of governance during the 1960s and 1970s. Housing and Urban Development (1965) attempted to bring about greater integration within and between the fields of housing, community development, and urban affairs. Transportation (1966) principally oversees the operation of several administrations responsible for various elements of the transportation sector. Indeed, with a

TABLE 1

Departments vary greatly in their staff numbers, budgets, and types of officials in senior-level positions.

Department	Employees	Budget	Year Created	Pres. Appt. (w/ Sen.)	SES (Career)	SES (Noncareer)
Department of Agriculture	109,832	$72.185 billion (2003 outlays), $21.99 billion (2003 discretionary outlays)	1889	16	155	41
Department of Commerce	36,000	$5.656 billion ($5.553 billion)	1913	25	152	42
Department of Defense	3,000,000	$388.101 billion	1949	52	351	88
Department of Education	4,487	$57.4 billion ($48.708 billion)	1979	13	66	20
Department of Energy	16,100	$19.832 billion ($21.628 billion)	1977	20	340	34
Department of Health and Human Services	67,000	$501.839 billion ($59.615 billion)	1953	19	284	54
Department of Homeland Security	138,000	$26.355 billion ($27.477 billion)	2002	18	91	53
Department of Housing and Urban Development	10,600	$37.474 billion ($37.221 billion)	1965	15	61	18
Department of the Interior	71,436	$7.96 billion ($10.820 billion)	1849	18	192	31
Department of Justice	112,557	$21.216 billion ($19.251 billion)	1870	222	210	59
Department of Labor	17,347	$69.553 billion ($12.501 billion)	1913	19	71	27
Department of State	30,266	$20.921 billion ($8.585 billion)	1789	193	921	40
Department of Transportation	58,622	$50.809 billion ($49.121 billion)	1966	23	172	31
Department of the Treasury	115,897	$54.448 billion ($10.517 billion)	1789	32	81	23
Department of Veterans Affairs	218,323	$56.887 billion ($25.678 billion)	1989	14	296	13

SOURCES: The data under the headings "Employees" and "Budget" come from *Budget of the United States: Fiscal Year 2005* (Washington, D.C.: Office of Management and Budget, February 2, 2004) and represent actual staff levels and expenditure during fiscal year 2003, which ended on September 30, 2003. The figures concerning presidential appointees confirmed by the Senate, SES (Career), and SES (Noncareer) come from *The Plum Book* [*United States Government Policy and Supporting Positions*], Committee on Government Reform, U.S. House of Representatives, 108th Congress, 2nd Session (Washington, D.C.: U.S. Government Printing Office, November 22, 2004). For a fuller discussion of the *Plum Book* data consult the Appendix to this chapter.

Types of Officials: Pres. Appt (w/ Sen.) includes presidential appointees filling positions requiring Senate confirmation; SES (Career) includes members of the Senior Executive Service who are career officials in the general category, that is, they occupy positions not requiring Senate confirmation but could have been assigned had the administration chosen to do so; and SES (Noncareer) includes appointees occupying positions in the Senior Executive Service.

view to focusing their attention on policy issues rather than day-to-day management, the assistant secretaries advising the secretary on transportation issues
emerging from these areas bear no line authority over the administrations themselves. Education (1979) began as a sub-Cabinet agency (1867) and then a
bureau within Interior (1868) and eventually an office in the Department of
Health, Education and Welfare (1953). The current Cabinet-level department
shoulders responsibility for federal programs directed toward equal access to
education and excellence but also must coordinate with several other departments and agencies with significant roles in the field. The elevation of the
Veterans Administration (1930) to a Cabinet-level department in 1989 heightened the profile of a critical segment of the electorate and their agency, which by
fiscal year 2003 employed a workforce second only to that of Defense.

Crises in fields in which government coordination appeared inadequate
spawned the final two departments—Energy (1977) and Homeland Security
(2002). Energy (1977) came into being between the 1973 and 1979 energy
shocks. However, the development of atomic energy—beginning with the
Manhattan Project in 1942—also provides an important thread to the department's genesis. It houses several formerly independent agencies within the
energy field as well as units from the departments of Commerce, Housing and
Urban Development, the Navy, and the Interior. Policy and implementation
integration within the area of homeland security became a political football after
September 11, 2001. Initially, the Bush administration resisted congressional
pressures for the creation of an umbrella department in this area. However, it co-
opted the idea in the summer of 2002 and, in the process, managed to score
points for appearing more decisive than Congress. As well, on the grounds that
the nation faced a dire emergency, the legislation creating the department placed
protocols over the twenty-two agencies that Homeland Security absorbed,
bringing them under tighter political control and subjecting their employees to
terms and conditions with greater flexibilities—from the standpoint of the polit
ical executive—than those prevailing in the rest of the civil service.

In scanning Table 1, we find a huge range between the budgets of departments and their staff numbers. Aggregate budgets stretch between $5.656 billion
for Commerce and $501.839 billion for Health and Human Services. Leaving
aside the Pentagon, discretionary funding—that is, budget lines beyond the entitlement programs administered by a department—ranges between $5.553 bil-
lion for Commerce (that is, nearly its entire budget) to $59.615 billion for
Health and Human Services (or just 12 percent of the aggregate). In terms of
staff numbers, Defense's three million personnel equal 669 times Education's staff
of 4,487.

We can readily spot departments that stress policy over actual programmatic
operations. On the side of policy, 4,487 employees in Education assist the secretary in dispersion of $57.4 billion—largely to entities outside the department

and, usually, the federal government. On the side of service delivery, 218,000 employees in Veterans Affairs spend $56.887 billion—which is just short of the aggregate available in Education. Budgets, thus, telegraph mixed signals about the position of a department within the executive branch constellation. Some operations like Education, Energy, Housing and Urban Development, and Labor function with relatively modest employee numbers but oversee fairly substantial funding. These departments tend more to channel funds to operational entities beyond their walls rather than administer programs directly. Some, like Commerce, Homeland Security, Interior, Justice, and Veterans Affairs, operate with huge staffs and relatively modest budgets. While these departments all include cerebral units concerned with policy, they also run directly substantial operational components. Significantly, several of the departments responsible for activities that acquired a high degree of legitimacy during the New Deal and World War II—Agriculture, Defense, and Health and Human Services—have attained both high staff levels and control over very large segments of the federal budget. Indeed, both Agriculture and Health and Human Services distribute a substantial amount of funding elsewhere but consume a great deal internally through their own programmatic operations. The departments of State and Transportation perhaps contend in this realm as well, but on a more modest scale.

The various ways in which departments mix presidential appointees and members of the senior executive service suggest some layering—accretions of separate legacies and often conflicting approaches—according to the legacies of scientific management, policy management, and public choice (see Table 1). As noted above, the figures regarding presidential appointees exclude those not requiring Senate confirmation, as such officials, for the most part, serve part-time on various advisory boards and commissions. Regarding SES officials, the Civil Service Reform Act of 1978 mandated creation of the Senior Executive Service (the SES and its origins are described in some detail in the chapter by Patricia Ingraham in this volume.) The advocates of SES envisioned a tier of policy and management professionals who would help bridge the gap between political appointees and department-bound career officials.[20] In this regard, the new cadre attempted to foster the standard of policy management as an executive discipline that maneuvers with ease between policy development and implementation. The 2004 *Plum Book*—the U.S. House of Representatives Committee on Government Reform's inventory of "government policy and supporting positions"—tallied a total of 7,815 SES positions. Of these, the "general" category consists of 4,555 career officials working in policy, supervisory, and managerial positions at the "top level" of the executive branch. Table 1 excludes from the figures the "career reserved" members of the SES—totaling around 3,300 officials—because this group consists of career officials, such as law enforcement officials and auditors, whose legitimacy rests upon clear detachment from the political executive. Table 1 includes members of the State Department who, though not formally inscribed as career members of the SES, occupy comparable positions in the "senior foreign service."

The figures in Table 1 might suggest a tilt among some departments toward a strong emphasis on policy management. On the other hand, in some instances, large numbers of SES officials in relation to relatively small complements of political appointees might suggest a tendency toward scientific management. While members of the SES ostensibly bridge relatively easily to wider policy management issues, the Office of Personnel Management (OPM) still categorizes the professional credentials of the cadre in ways that relate to scientific management—with an emphasis upon specialized credentials. In 2002, OPM classified the occupations of 44 percent of the cadre as "administration," with the remainder divided between "legal" (12 percent), "science/mathematics" (10 percent), "engineering" (10 percent), "financial" (6 percent), "medical/veterinary" (4 percent), and "other" (14 percent).[21] The *Plum Book* is mute on this issue, providing no statistics on the specialties of SES members.

As Table 1 suggests, a high number of career SES officials usually does not imply larger complements of presidential appointees requiring Senate confirmation than those found in other departments. Indeed, all of the departments listing over 280 career SES members (the upper third of the cohort) in the *Plum Book*—Defense, Energy, Health and Human Services, State, and Veterans Affairs—claim numbers of political appointees requiring Senate confirmation that range only between 5 and 21 percent of the numbers of career SES personnel. In this respect, the largest proportion—193 appointees requiring Senate confirmation as against 921 career members of the Senior Foreign Service—captures two practices. First, all ambassadors must receive Senate confirmation regardless of their status as appointees or career officials. Second, administrations increasingly fill ambassadorships with appointees. Each of the five organizations with career SES cadres above 280 relies upon considerable expertise within its policy area. It thus appears that the large complements of career SES members in departments reflect high degrees of reliance upon permanent officials with long-term experience within fairly specialized policy development and implementation domains. Similarly, these departments range between 4 and 25 percent in the ratio of non-career SES to career SES positions. Here, the figure for the Department of State is 4 percent, while those for Defense and Health and Human Services are 25 and 19 percent, respectively. The requirement that even career ambassadors receive Senate confirmation probably plays a role in State's relatively limited use of appointees in SES-level positions.

Two departments, Justice and Treasury, retain substantially stronger complements of political appointees requiring Senate confirmation in relation to career SES members—in the former a 222/210 split, and in the latter a 32/81 differential. Clearly, this suggests the sensitivity of the policy issues that each department encounters and the delicacy of the implementation of these. Ironically, in light of the exclusion discussed above of the "career reserved" category with reference to impartiality, the requirement of Senate approval of nominations as U.S. attorneys and marshals in Justice drives the buoyancy of this department's appointee numbers. Such posts remain critical to patronage and an administration's influence over prosecution and enforcement and suggest the limits to which the system actually seeks to attain and preserve impartiality. In the case of Treasury, notwithstanding its extensive operational responsibilities, the department has also served historically as a powerhouse for economic analysis and advice. The Treasury leadership thus usually includes numerous appointees who have distinguished themselves as advocates within various departmental policy-sensitive domains, such as macroeconomic analysis and forecasting, taxation, international economics, and financial institutions and markets.

We find three departments hosting relatively small proportions of noncareer SES appointees in relation to career incumbents of positions at this level. In each instance—State and Veterans Affairs (4 percent each) and Energy (10 percent)—the domains consist very substantially of highly specialized professionals (respectively, diplomats, health and social service specialists, and natural scientists) who might prove especially immune to direction by "outsiders." Conversely, the departments utilizing high proportions of noncareer officials within their SES complement—Education, Homeland Security, Housing and Urban Development (HUD), and Labor (30, 58, 30, and 38 percent, respectively)—involve policy fields less dominated by professionals with specific types of training and career development experience. As well, Education, Homeland Security, and Labor encompass fields in which the Bush administration has been pursuing several high-priority initiatives, while HUD historically has proven especially porous in respect to politicized leadership. We should take special note of the proportionately huge noncareer SES cadre—58 percent as large as the career SES group—in Homeland Security. This should serve as a barometer of the administration's determination to impose in Homeland Security personnel policies that deviate from those prevailing in other departments. It has justified this approach on the grounds that the department must display a higher degree of responsiveness to political direction than do other public service organizations. This suggests that the administration has used the SES flexibilities to promote a public choice approach in this area—not policy management and certainly not scientific management.

Complexity within Departments

The accretion of levels of political appointees within departments distinguishes the U.S. executive branch from those of other advanced democracies more than any other feature. In U.S. departments, one has to bore down four levels below the secretary before reaching strata populated almost entirely by career officials. No other advanced democracies allow anywhere near this magnitude of occupation of the top leadership positions in bureaucratic departments and agencies by political appointees. In addition, departmental secretaries and agency heads increasingly retain chiefs of staff and personal offices that bring substantial resources to the task of making sure that the policy positions developed in these bureaucratic organizations comport with the priorities of the political leadership.

In the case of department secretaries, such capacity at their fingertips has emerged in parallel with full-fledged policy, analytic, and oversight units working directly with them in their roles as the federal government equivalent of chief executive officers (CEOs). As an example, both the undersecretary for intelligence and the undersecretary for policy in the Office of the Secretary of Defense during the first term of the current administration pressed strenuously Donald H. Rumsfeld's commitment to "transform" the military and have worked intently at keeping the rest of the Pentagon and the services focused on the administration's neoconservative agenda. Indeed, observers regularly attribute to the department's deputy secretary at the time—Paul Wolfowitz—persistent maneuvering in the advancement of neoconservative positions.

The layering of appointees deeply into line units within departments—along with the increasing political thrust of offices supporting the secretary as CEO—bring two especially significant consequences. First, career officials find themselves, at best, remote from the apex. Few would ever interact on a regular basis with their assistant secretary, let alone the secretary. Indeed, career civil servants do not develop a very strong *esprit de corps* beyond their specialized units. Second, even political appointees filling line positions in departments—for instance, most certainly deputy assistant secretaries—can find that they gain only sporadic exposure to the secretary. To make matters worse, they frequently bump up against fellow appointees who enjoy the luxury of reporting directly to the secretary—often because of idiosyncratic reasons, such as the urgency of a policy question or a personal link. The connectivity of such officials can readily trump line appointees when questions arise as to the secretary's preferences.

We encounter three clusters of offices when scanning for differences in the organization of departments. Importantly, however, departments vary greatly in the numbers of units operating under each cluster. In the first cluster, "CEO Support" in Table 2, we find the units whose heads report directly to the secretary. These offices ply disciplines that secretaries *might* deem central to their roles as chief executive officers of major governmental organizations—strategic planning, policy development, budgeting, legal counsel, congressional liaison, White House liaison, intergovernmental affairs, information, public affairs, and financial and management probity (inspectors general). The emphasis here is on "might" because some departments do not enshrine all of these functions in special units. For example, Agriculture seems to have no unit that encompasses strategic planning, whereas Commerce maintains an office of Policy and Strategic Planning that reports to the secretary. Some secretaries relegate some of these roles and the

TABLE 2

The number of units for each department assigned to Chief Executive Officer (CEO) support, policy and programmatic development and management, and Chief Operating Officers (COO) support.

Department	Year Created	CEO Support	Policy and Programmatic	COO Support
Agriculture	1889	6	6	3
Commerce	1913	9	5	4
Defense	1949	16	2	7
Education	1979	6	8	5
Energy	1977	6	10	8
Health and Human Services	1953	9	12	0
Homeland Security	2002	13	7	2
Housing and Urban Development	1965	5	5	7
Interior	1849	5	11	3
Justice	1870	7	22	9
Labor	1913	7	17	2
State	1789	10	5	8
Transportation	1966	15	10	2
Treasury	1789	6	8	7
Veterans Affairs	1989	6	3	10

SOURCES: *The Federal Staff Directory* (Washington, D.C.: Congressional Quarterly, Summer 2004) served as the main source for the figures in this chart. It was augmented, however, with consultation of department and agency Web sites.

units performing them to a cluster in their departments once-removed from their direct management—as we will see below, this is the case with Education.

The second cluster of departmental structures, "Policy and Programmatic," consists of the substantive policy and administrative units that execute the organizations' core missions. In some cases, these units tend to focus on implementation more than policy development, although they shoulder some responsibility for advice concerning the latter. Also, they usually enjoy considerable latitude over their subject area by virtue of specific mandates from Congress, including the earmarking of budget resources that may depart from an administration's expressed priorities. As noted above, assistant-secretary level appointees in the Department of Transportation perform "staff" functions that do not extend to line responsibility for the policy delivery operations within the department. These latter units—responsible for motor carrier safety, highways, highway traffic safety, Saint Lawrence Seaway development, research and special programs, aviation, railroads, transit, maritime transportation, and transportation statistics—function under the organizational moniker of "administration," "corporation," or "bureau." Agriculture presents a similarly granular array of units styled as "service," "agency," or "center." On the other hand, Education, which executes few policies directly, populates its second cluster with what effectively constitute advocacy units, covering such areas as postsecondary education, innovation and improvement, and safe and drug-free schools. Justice and the Treasury provide examples of departments with an almost even blend of policy advisory units and executive bureaus dedicated to substantive fields in their second clusters.

The third cluster, "Operational Support," developed when departments began to construe the function of their deputy secretary—that is, the political appointee immediately under the secretary—as chief operating officer (COO). This moniker became very popular during the Clinton administration. It derived from the corporate model, whereby CEOs delegate a great deal of budgeting and management responsibility to a single officer immediately beneath them. As noted above, Education serves as an example of a department that clearly has followed this template. There the cluster of units reporting directly to the secretary includes the general counsel, inspector general, intergovernmental and interagency affairs, legislation and congressional affairs, public affairs, and educational technology. Meanwhile, the chief financial officer, management, chief information officer, civil rights, and student assistance all come under the direct responsibility of the deputy secretary.

Table 2 reports the number of units belonging to each of the clusters in each department of the Cabinet. In order to be included, units had to report to either the secretary ("CEO Support" or "Policy and Programmatic") or the deputy secretary ("Operational Support"). This categorization was determined by examining the departmental organization charts and the material available on their roles. Some of the older departments—specifically, Justice, Labor, and Interior—seem to have limited the accretion of CEO and/or operational support units. Aside from Defense (from which the numbers for the three armed services departments have been excluded), Homeland Security, Commerce, and Transportation clearly have placed the strongest emphasis on CEO-oriented support units. The fact that Homeland Security—newly created in response to the events of September 11—follows as clearly as it does the CEO support model suggests that the Clinton COO emphasis may have seen its apogee. Minimally, the CEO focus of units with department-wide responsibilities probably reflects the determination of the Bush administration to craft the new agency in a way that would insure responsiveness to the political leadership's priorities in a context of national crisis. In any case, Table 2 reveals the extent to which layering has entailed the introduction of disciplines that secretaries and their deputies tap in the process of trying to give direction to the policy and programmatic elements of their departments.

Agencies

Tables 3 to 7 summarize data concerning agencies that do not operate within departments. We have seen above that many organizations with a degree of administrative autonomy and significant mandates from Congress operate from departments. However, many entities—some exceedingly important and others much less so—function as agencies in the Executive Office of the President (EOP), as independent administrations, under the aegis of a commission, or as a government corporation.[22] This treatment does not include agencies reporting directly to Congress. These include the Architect of the Capitol, the Congressional Budget Office, the Government Accounting Office, the Government Printing Office, the Library of Congress, and the U.S. Tax Court. All of these organizations, with the exception of the Congressional Budget Office, claim at least one presidential appointee requiring Senate confirmation. Tables 3 to 7 do not include organizations located in departments. However, they capture for five substantial epochs in government five things: when the agency was created, its location on a continuum of insulation from presidential control (with positioning in the EOP the most subject to direction and status as a government corporation or other arm's-length organization the least), and the numbers of presidential appointees, career members of the SES, and noncareer SES in the agency. Regarding the date of agency creation, we should remember that some organizations as currently constituted operated previously in different frameworks. The figures, however, simply examine the agencies from the standpoint of their current position in respect to presidential direction. The tables use the current names of agencies; in some cases, these differ from their original names, though their position in relation to presidential control has remained the same. For instance, the Office of Management and Budget was originally the Bureau of the Budget and was located in the Treasury. It moved to the Executive Office of the President in 1939 and assumed its current name in 1970.

The five time periods defined by the tables are: 1789 to 1932 (that is, before the advent of the New Deal); 1933 to 1960 (encompassing the New Deal, World War II, and the beginning of the cold war); 1961 to 1972 (including the New Frontier, the War on Poverty expansion, and Richard Nixon's first attempts at restraining the growth of the state); 1973 to 1980 (the administrative presidency and other strenuous efforts to limit the state, including Jimmy Carter's "President's Reorganization Project"); and 1980 to the present (the onset of public choice under Reagan, extending to attempts by Bill Clinton and George W. Bush to "build-down" government, especially through extensive use of outsourcing.

If our expectations for signs of the layering of bureaucratic traditions hold up, we can anticipate two trends through the five time frames. In the earlier periods, we should see a tendency toward providing agencies a degree of insulation from direct presidential control, as this would comport with the scientific management doctrines of the time. In addition, the agencies created in earlier time frames would rely less than those emerging in later epochs on presidential appointees in relation to members of the SES. As policy management and, eventually, public choice assert themselves, we should witness trends toward less insulation and heftier contingents of presidential appointees in relation to SES-level officials.

Table 3 reveals that the preferred structural venue for agencies still surviving but created before 1933 is under an independent commission (five out of seven agencies in this group). With the exception of the Federal Trade Commission (29 career and 3 noncareer SES), the agencies in this group claim relatively small numbers of SES members. To be sure, the Federal Reserve System—with fully seven presidential appointees confirmed by the Senate—staffs itself with numerous officials at levels equivalent to those of the SES. However, these officials fall outside the compass of SES per se.

Table 4—covering the period that should have witnessed the heyday of scientific management—shows a strong partiality to independent agencies and commissions (14 agencies in the two categories combined, out of 21 created in this time frame). Further, several of these agencies retain large complements of career SES officials in relation to presidential appointees requiring Senate confirmation—with the Social Security Administration (118 to 3), the General Services Administration (26 to 2), the National Aeronautics and Space Administration (115 to 4), and the National Science Foundation (41 to 2) registering especially strong ratios. Seven of the independent agencies or commissions report noncareer SES members. However, we cannot say that the figures

TABLE 3

Agencies Created Pre–New Deal (1789–1932)

Agency	Year Created	Degree of Insulation	Pres. Appt. (w/ Sen.)	SES (Career)	SES (Noncareer)
Armed Forces Retirement Homes	1811	Independent Agency	0	0	0
Federal Reserve System	1913	Independent Agency	7	0	0
U.S. Merit Systems Protection Board	1883	Independent Commission	3	4	2
Commission of Fine Arts	1910	Independent Commission	0	1	0
Federal Trade Commission (FTC)	1914	Independent Commission	5	29	3
U.S. International Trade Commission	1916	Independent Commission	6	6	0
American Battle Monuments Commission	1923	Independent Commission	0	0	0

SOURCE: The figures concerning presidential appointees confirmed by the Senate, SES (Career), and SES (Noncareer) come from *The Plum Book [United States Government Policy and Supporting Positions]*, Committee on Government Reform, U.S. House of Representatives, 108th Congress, 2nd Session (Washington, D.C.: U.S. Government Printing Office, November 22, 2004). For a fuller discussion of the *Plum Book* data consult the Appendix to this chapter.

Types of Officials: See notation at bottom of Table 1.

TABLE 4

Agencies Created during the New Deal, World War II, the Beginning of the Cold War (1933–1960)

Agency	Year Created	Degree of Insulation	Pres. Appt. (w/ Sen.)	SES (Career)	SES (Noncareer)
Office of Management and Budget (OMB)	1939	Exec. Office of the President	6	37	15
Council of Economic Advisors	1946	Exec. Office of the President	3	1	0
National Security Council (NSC)	1947	Exec. Office of the President	0	0	0
Central Intelligence Agency (CIA)	1947	Exec. Office of the President	8	0	0
U.S. Advisory Commission for Public Diplomacy	1948	Exec. Office of the President	0	0	0
Tennessee Valley Authority (TVA)	1933	Independent Agency	4	0	0
Social Security Administration	1946	Independent Agency	3	118	10
General Services Administration (GSA)	1949	Independent Agency	2	26	17
Small Business Administration (SBA)	1953	Independent Agency	4	14	14
National Aeronautics and Space Administration (NASA)	1958	Independent Agency	4	115	4
Securities & Exchange Commission (SEC)	1933	Independent Commission	5	0	0
Federal Communications Commission (FCC)	1934	Independent Commission	5	37	6
National Mediation Board	1934	Independent Commission	3	2	0
National Labor Relations Board (NLRB)	1935	Independent Commission	6	13	4
Selective Service System	1940	Independent Commission	0	1	0
Federal Mediation and Conciliation Service	1947	Independent Commission	1	2	0
National Science Foundation (NSF)	1950	Independent Commission	2	41	0
National Capital Planning Commission	1952	Independent Commission	0	0	0
Commission on Civil Rights	1957	Independent Commission	0	4	1
Export-Import Bank of the United States	1945	Government Corporation	5	0	0
Federal Deposit Insurance Corporation (FDIC)	1950	Government Corporation	4	0	0

SOURCES: See Table 3. Regarding the Office of Management and Budget, Table 4 displays figures from the *Yellow Book* (New York: Leadership Directories, January 2005) due to the incompleteness of SES reporting in OMB by the *Plum Book*.

Types of Officials: See notation at bottom of Table 1.

reach high proportions, except in the cases of the General Services Administration (17 to 26) and the Small Business Administration (14 in each group). Thus, the agencies created in the second time frame seem to maintain SES cadres somewhat less permeable to noncareer SES incumbents than proved the case with departments, as reflected by the data in Table 1. In other words, agencies created between 1933 and 1960 seem to maintain a fairly strong scientific management bent.

Of course, the Office of Management and Budget—which moved to the Executive Office of the President in 1939—originally fit within the scientific management tradition. However, the introduction of associate directors during the Nixon administration created a layer of appointees not requiring Senate confirmation that ultimately folded into the ranks of the noncareer SES after the Civil Service Reform Act of 1978. Currently, presidential appointees requiring Senate confirmation (6) and noncareer SES members (15) constitute more than a third of the senior leadership of the department (58 officials, including career SES). This seems to suggest a migration of the agency during the Nixon administration to public choice, without first passing through policy management. The other Executive Office of the Presidency agencies operate without either career or noncareer SES officials, with the exception of the Council of Economic Advisors, for which the director of macroeconomic forecasting belongs to the career SES.

Table 5—summarizing agencies created between 1961 and 1972—reveals that all but 4 of the 25 agencies emerging in this period serve as either independent agencies or commissions, with the latter prevailing (fully 15 agencies). This reflects a preference for independent commissions, which surfaced in the two previous time frames as well. The data in the 1961–1972 time frame also indicate that just a few agencies account for the bulk of SES positions. Indeed, the 313 career SES working in the Agency for International Development and the 109 located in the Environmental Protection Agency far exceed the total number of SES members operating in the other agencies.

These data prompt an echo from our discussion concerning Table 1, as neither agency has high numbers of noncareer SES in relation to career. The two clearly involve huge areas of activity requiring not just large complements of SES officials but ones with considerable governmental experience as well. Two other agencies warrant mention here. The Equal Employment Opportunity Commission, a smaller agency, hosts 5 presidential appointees requiring Senate confirmation. However, while it runs with the support of 20 career SES, it includes no noncareer SES. Similarly, the Office of the U.S. Trade Representative—an Executive Office of the President agency with 5 appointees requiring confirmation—operates with 18 career SES but only 2 noncareer SES. Agencies created in the 1961–1972 time frame seem to fit the scientific management mold more than that of policy management, much less public choice.

TABLE 5

Agencies Created During the New-Frontier, War-on-Poverty Expansion (1961–1972)

Agency	Year Created	Degree of Insulation	Pres. Appt. (w/ Sen.)	SES (Career)	SES (Noncareer)
Office of the U.S. Trade Representative	1963	Exec. Office of the President	5	18	2
President's Commission on White House Fellowships	1964	Exec. Office of the President	0	0	1
Advisory Council on Historic Preservation	1966	Exec. Office of the President	0	0	0
Council on Environmental Quality	1969	Exec. Office of the President	1	0	0
Agency for International Development	1961	Independent Agency	13	313	1
Peace Corps	1961	Independent Agency	2	3	0
Environmental Protection Agency	1970	Independent Agency	14	109	20
National Credit Union Administration	1970	Independent Agency	3	0	0
United States Postal Service	1970	Independent Agency	9	0	0
Farm Credit Administration	1971	Independent Agency	3	0	0
Delaware River Basin Commission	1961	Independent Commission	0	0	0
Federal Maritime Commission	1961	Independent Commission	5	2	0
Equal Employment Opportunity Commission	1964	Independent Commission	5	20	0
Appalachian Regional Commission	1965	Independent Commission	2	0	0
National Foundation on the Arts and Humanities	1965	Independent Commission	3	9	6
Inter-American Foundation	1969	Independent Commission	0	0	0
National Commission on Libraries and Information Science	1970	Independent Commission	2	0	1
Occupational S&H Review Commission	1970	Independent Commission	3	3	1
Postal Rate Commission	1970	Independent Commission	5	0	0
Susquehanna River Basin Commission	1970	Independent Commission	0	0	0
Committee for Purchase from Blind/Disabled	1971	Independent Commission	0	1	0
Farm Credit System Ins. Corp.	1971	Independent Commission	0	0	0
Federal Election Commission	1971	Independent Commission	6	0	0
Consumer Product Safety Commission	1972	Independent Commission	5	9	1
Marine Mammal Commission	1972	Independent Commission	3	0	0

SOURCE: See Table 3.

Types of Officials: See notation at bottom of Table 1.

Tables 6 and 7 portray similar breakdowns regarding the degree of insulation of agencies, with the emphasis on independent agencies and commissions. This finding flies in the face of our expectations for policy management and public choice approaches to make inroads in the agencies similar to those evident in the departments. Indeed, cumulatively the tables capture a shift away from independent agencies to independent commissions. During 1973–1980 (Table 6), 19 new agencies emerged, with over half (11) operating as independent commissions. This table includes the beginnings of the "administrative presidency," during which Nixon attempted to centralize policy making and the selection of appointees. As noted, he also inserted a new layer of political appointees below those requiring Senate confirmation. Carter formalized this process through the provision of the Civil Reform Act whereby noncareer officials could occupy up to 10 percent of SES positions.

The administrative presidency period thus stood at a midpoint between policy management and public choice. It promoted the former through the notion of potential synergies achieved through managing appointed policy professionals and senior career officials in the same cadre. However, it marked the beginning of intensified White House screening of all political appointees. This ultimately occurred even under Carter, when the disarray of the administration led in 1979 to wholesale purges and a highly centralized process for choosing replacements. Developments related to emerging agencies in the 1973–1980 time frame seem to reveal a congressional strategy of curbing the administrative presidency by distancing newly crafted agency frameworks from direct presidential oversight. As noted, the period witnessed a clear bias toward greater independence. In addition, the agencies now hosting the largest complements of SES officials—the Nuclear Regulatory Commission (69) and the Federal Energy Regulatory Commission (42)—encompass fields placing a premium on scientific knowledge. They each function with almost no noncareer SES officials, the single such individual assigned to the Nuclear Regulatory Commission being the exception.

Table 7, which displays data concerning agencies created from 1981 to 2005, reveals a further swing to the side of independent commissions—15 out of 23 new organizations. Only two of these most recently created agencies function with significant numbers of career SES: the Office of National Drug Control Policy (14), which operates from the Executive Office of the President, and the Broadcasting Board of Governors (15). In the entire list of 23 agencies, we find only 8 noncareer SES members. The table thus offers further evidence of a congressional bias for greater insulation from presidential oversight. In the face of this, administrations—insofar as they pursue public choice or reinvention, the two motifs of executive-bureaucratic politics over the past twenty-five years—have elected to backfill department and older agencies with appointees, rather than venturing into newly crafted organizations. Homeland Security, an amalgam of 22 preexisting administrations and agencies, reflects most clearly this apparent inclination.

TABLE 6

Agencies Created during the Nixon Administrative Presidency and Carter Presidency (1973–1980)

Agency	Year Created	Degree of Insulation	Pres. Appt. (w/ Sen.)	SES (Career)	SES (Noncareer)
Office of Science and Technology Policy	1976	Exec. Office of the President	3	1	4
National Intelligence Council	1978	Exec. Office of the President	0	0	0
Office of Personnel Management	1978	Independent Agency	3	34	5
Office of the Special Counsel	1978	Independent Agency	1	0	1
Architectural and Transportation Barriers Compliance Board	1973	Independent Commission	0	2	0
National Council on Disability	1973	Independent Commission	15	0	0
Commodity Futures Trading Commission	1974	Independent Commission	5	0	0
Nuclear Regulatory Commission	1974	Independent Commission	6	69	1
Railroad Retirement Board	1974	Independent Commission	4	0	0
Japan–U.S. Friendship Commission	1975	Independent Commission	0	1	0
National Transportation Safety Board	1975	Independent Commission	5	1	1
Federal Mine S&H Commission	1977	Independent Commission	5	2	0
Federal Energy Regulatory Commission	1977	Independent Commission	5	42	0
Federal Labor Relations Authority	1978	Independent Commission	4	0	0
Panama Canal Commission	1979	Independent Commission	0	0	0
Overseas Private Investment Corporation	1971	Government Corporation	10	0	0
Pension Benefit Guaranty Corporation	1974	Government Corporation	0	0	0
Harry Truman Scholarship Foundation	1975	Government Corporation	0	0	1
Neighborhood Reinvestment Corporation	1978	Government Corporation	0	0	0

SOURCE: See Table 3.

Types of Officials: See notation at bottom of Table 1.

TABLE 7

Agencies Created during the Public Choice/Reinvention Period (1981–2005)

Agency	Year Created	Degree of Insulation	Pres. Appt. (w/ Sen.)	SES (Career)	SES (Noncareer)
Office of National Drug Control Policy	1988	Exec. Office of the President	5	14	2
Homeland Security Council	2001	Exec. Office of the President	0	0	0
Interagency Council on the Homeless	2002	Exec. Office of the President	0	0	1
National Archives & Records Admin.	1984	Independent Agency	1	6	0
Court Services & Offender Supervision Agency (D.C.)	2001	Independent Agency	1	0	0
Trade and Development Agency	1980	Independent Commission	1	3	0
African Development Foundation	1984	Independent Commission	0	0	0
Arctic Research Commission	1984	Independent Commission	0	1	0
U.S. Sentencing Commission	1984	Independent Commission	0	0	0
Federal Retirement Thrift Inv. Board	1986	Independent Commission	0	2	0
Defense Nuclear Facilities Safety Board	1988	Independent Commission	5	2	0
Navajo and Hopi Indian Relocation Office	1988	Independent Commission	1	2	0
Federal Housing Finance Board	1989	Independent Commission	5	0	0
Office of Government Ethics	1989	Independent Commission	1	0	0
U.S. Chemical S&H Investigation Board	1990	Independent Commission	0	1	0
Broadcasting Board of Governors	1999	Independent Commission	4	15	4
Delta Regional Authority	2001	Independent Commission	1	0	0
United States Election Assistance Commission	2002	Independent Commission	4	0	0
Office of National Counterintelligence Executive	2002	Independent Commission	0	0	0
9-11 Commission	2003	Independent Commission	0	0	0
Barry Goldwater Scholarship Foundation	1986	Government Corporation	0	0	1
Corporation for National & Community Service	1993	Government Corporation	3	1	0
Millennium Challenge Corporation	2004	Government Corporation	1	0	0

SOURCE: See Table 3.

Types of Officials: See notation at bottom of Table 1.

Toward Blending the Traditions

The preceding section reflects the complexity of the U.S. executive branch. Much of this owes to the distinctive character of the U.S. Constitution, whereby both president and Congress play substantial roles in sculpting the contours of the executive branch—not only the organizational structures but their mandates as well. However, we have also seen that the layering of three different models for public management exacerbates the problem.

Each of the three core models that prevailed in thinking about public administration during different segments of the last century maintains a strong presence in current structures. The U.S. executive branch, thus, appears more like a Mediterranean city—with anthropological accretions from ancient, medieval, and modern eras—than a contemporary metropolis crafted from a single, coherent plan. Efforts toward attaining greater cohesion in the system might most profitably start with the assumption that the accumulated structures and cultures have long revealed a Byzantine character. Rather than attempting to override this reality, reformers perhaps should concentrate more on potentially complementary elements of the three traditions.

Pressing Public Choice Too Far

It is instructive that public choice has focused to the degree that it has on the relationship between the political leadership and career officials. However, it is naive in the extreme for those who are concerned that career officials might be manipulating political appointees to believe that a "principal/agent" straightjacket would put things right. This concept cast political authorities as purchasers of specified governmental goods and services. This approach attempted to force public servants into limiting their activities to producing such prescribed "outputs" rather than participating as well in assessment of the likely outcomes of policies and programs embraced by politicians. Notwithstanding this caveat, public choice has tried to tackle an issue that could only have emerged in the twentieth century. Previously, political leaders plied their trade as oligarchs, at best, rather than pluralists, and imparted to like-minded officials huge discretion so that, one might say, they themselves did not have to keep track of where the bodies were buried. Those who studied the relationship between political leaders and officials in the nineteenth century did not anticipate pluralism as it has developed in advanced democracies.

We can thus understand why, in the oligarchic democracies or authoritarian regimes of the nineteenth century, theorists tended to assume that the folkways marking a separate estate would prevail in bureaucracy. Most notably, Max Weber—perhaps the most influential student of bureaucracy—considered a firmly established bureaucracy as a status group whose positions and actions basked in the glory of institutional cogency based on discipline. In this regard,

Weber maintained that strong affective mutual attachments on the part of members of a bureaucracy served as its glue, just as the spiritual commitment of the priest did for the religious order.[23] Weber also revealed considerable skepticism about the ability of either politicians or the public generally to sway a determined bureaucracy. He styled the former as dilettantes pitted against the expert and considered the latter relatively powerless, owing to the difficulty of penetrating a culture bent on maximizing the leverage gained through secrecy.[24]

A mutual respect between politicians and bureaucrats for each other's contributions in the policy arena better serves the interests of the public. However, it acknowledges that such mutuality stands as a tall order—even in oligarchic regimes, much less under the centrifugal pressures of pluralistic democracy. Indeed, the imposition of the strictures of public choice arguably makes equilibrium between the roles of political executives and senior officials more, rather than less, difficult to attain as oligarchy loses sway in advanced democracies.

The New Zealand experience proves instructive in this respect. Before the onset of public choice, the state apparatus of a country with around the population of Kentucky or South Carolina (just over 4 million) indulged itself with the luxury of upward of forty departments that tended to function as fiefdoms narrowly focused on specialized policy domains.[25] After twenty years of public choice, it still does. However, the new managerial doctrine attempted to establish the iterative process inferred in classic views of democratic accountability.[26] As noted, officials would produce only those outputs specifically requested by political authorities who, in turn, would focus on whether the goods and services that they purchase from bureaucrats align with social goals like wealth, justice, and the relief of suffering.

Assessments of the New Zealand reforms have isolated in great detail dysfunctions stemming from construing democratic accountability as bilateral principal/agent relationships between the public and politicians, and then between politicians and bureaucrats. Among these, Robert Gregory has made perhaps the most direct assault on the resultant reemphasis of the policy/administration dichotomy. Indeed, Gregory details how the purchaser/provider, or principal/agent, framework clouded rather than clarified responsibility.[27]

Allen Schick's comprehensive assessment of the New Zealand reforms reached similar conclusions. Schick made his clearest contribution by underscoring the need for shifting the focus of ministers' relations with their departments from purchaser/provider more to that of ownership, shared with officials. This would enshrine mutuality in ministers' and officials' responsibility for achieving overarching social and economic objectives that go beyond the parameters of departmental outputs. In a very pointed passage, Schick inferred that the public choice format has not given sufficient focus to the fact that ministers must serve as *trustees* [my term] of the long-range viability of departments as well as getting increased output at reduced cost: ". . . they should forbear from demanding so much by way of outputs and from pushing the purchase price down so far as to jeopardize the department's long-term capacity to perform."[28] In other words, they should restrain themselves from running the state apparatus into the ground, much like a car owner who neglects the maintenance of his vehicle to the point where it retains virtually none of its value.

Trusteeship and Attaining Policy Competence

Regarding the concept that senior officials share with the political executive an element of trusteeship, a great deal of research during the 1970s equally suggested that top bureaucrats found themselves operating with a degree of autonomy within the executive-bureaucratic arena. This empirical work perhaps did not go so far as to sustain Norton C. Long's assertion in the 1950s that legislators had become less representative, responsive, and responsible than bureaucrats.[29] However, the evidence from several studies suggested that officials saw themselves as playing significant integrative roles within the policy arena.[30] To be sure, subsequent research has suggested that public choice approaches that emerged in the 1980s tempered, if not reversed, this reflex.[31]

Such reeling in of public servants has produced ambiguous results. Wholesale efforts to constrict the strategic perspectives of officials inevitably diminished policy integration. As well, when matters fell between the cracks, it became increasingly difficult to apportion responsibility between and among political leaders and senior officials.

Further, when advanced systems entered into the politics of budgetary surplus—from which the United States soon lapsed—they lost the imperative of fiscal stringency as a justification for command leadership. Surpluses necessitated relearning how to manage choice. And this, in turn, called for a more interactive dialogue between politicians and bureaucrats about strategic objectives. The trusteeship of both cadres concerns the future. Under the politics of constraint, the imperative of addressing the building fiscal crises sharply proscribed deliberations about future programmatic options. The encouragement of wide strategic perspectives among officials struck neoliberals, perhaps with some justification, as a luxury. Under the politics of surplus, strategic choice about future programmatic opportunities becomes a possibility and requires a strong analytic base with regard to both options and implementation. This is the core competency of the senior civil service. Only the United States chose to dodge entirely this set of choices by ceding budgetary surpluses in a flash with myriad tax cuts.

Trusteeship and the Provision of Latitude for Public Service Initiative

The emphasis on the encouragement of trustee cultures in public service dovetails substantially with an emerging consensus among students of public service innovation. This approach argues that fostering conditions that allow spontaneous adaptation on the part of organizations might, in the long run, prove more productive in the quest for innovative public services than pressing controls and guidelines from the center. In addition, both scholars and practitioners embracing this view seem to recognize one thing above all else: when senior career officials enjoy some degree of latitude for autonomous engagement in policy development and deliberations over resource commitments, this, in turn, greatly increases the chances of spontaneous adaptation to future opportunities and challenges.

The potential contribution of reasonable autonomy can be discussed only briefly here.[32] Notionally, executive leaders (both elected officials and their appointees) benefit in the long run by seeking the optimal blend of fiscal, responsive, and strategic competence. By doing so, they optimize policy competence as an integrative element to governance. In the middle part of the last century, advanced democracies—even the United States—accorded significant deference to career officials, especially for their contributions both to fiscal competence (such as macroeconomic analysis and budget assessment) and strategic competence (including evaluating outcomes and long-term effects).

Nonetheless, a perennial issue arose in the United States, even in this era. The separation of powers in the U.S. governmental system does not lend itself to comprehensive coherence in the development and implementation of agencies' long-term strategies. At best, U.S. agencies might be able to deploy "mixed scanning," whereby they engage in some review of their operations and identify selected incremental adjustments that are necessary to assure ongoing political support and to obtain the resources needed to remain viable.[33] However, Barzelay and Campbell have found that even a strenuous, seven-year-long effort in the U.S. Air Force has at best achieved "guided incrementalism," or the capacity at key decision points to reposition the service so that it can move opportunistically when departures from the status quo gain political momentum.[34] This finding fits the mounting evidence that, in the United States, the gods of institutional innovation help those who help themselves.[35]

Significantly, the U.S. public administration literature increasingly advocates a higher degree of spontaneity and inventiveness on the parts of agencies in coping with fiscal stringency and the fragmentation of governance. This advice runs counter to the trend over the past thirty years in advanced democracies. As we have seen above, economic conditions and skepticism about the public-spiritedness of career bureaucrats have led to an emphasis on the standards of budgetary constraint and responsiveness to detailed political direction in efforts to resolve both policy and administrative issues. This reached the point, by the 1980s, at which long-range strategic issues often received little or no weight in debates between players in the executive-bureaucratic complex. As a consequence, political executives now run the risk of routinely settling on dysfunctionally suboptimal policies, from the standpoint of long-term efficacy, as they seek to identify and pursue solutions to many of the greatest challenges faced by their governments.

Students of public service organizations often register alarm about this trend. Martha Derthick's exhaustive work on the U.S. Social Security Administration (SSA) pointed up the potential effectiveness of internally generated strategic planning on the part of agencies.[36] When Derthick revisited the SSA in the late 1980s, she found an agency that had lost its capacity to keep ahead of the curve regarding adaptation of policy and administration to shifting requirements due to the combined effects of fiscal stringency and the proliferation of specific mandates from political authorities.[37] Several studies have echoed such concerns as they pertain more broadly in the U.S. public service.[38]

In response to the discerned malaise in agencies associated with fiscal stringency and constricted mandating, a body of thought has begun to emerge around the view that political executives would gain much more value from standing bureaucracies if they gave more coherent guidance to officials.[39] However, in order to accomplish true symbiosis, they would have to provide bureaucrats with the resources necessary to accomplish stated objectives. More fundamentally, political authorities would have to foster an atmosphere in which officials might function more autonomously.[40] This would facilitate contributions by public servants of creativity, public-spiritedness, and value, to both policy making and administration.[41]

A profound problem emerges here. The agenda toward encouraging greater spontaneity in agencies, although strongly emergent in the United States, will still ring like public administration homilies to many analysts and the bulk of political leaders. Scholars cannot simply praise such efforts and achievements as manifest in the case of the U.S. Air Force in the hope that these will incite entrepreneurial leaders to act more courageously and organizations to work more coherently. We have to find more cogent evidence of the instrumental utility of such approaches more broadly within public services in advanced democracies. Donald F. Kettl recently underscored the necessity of this sort of reflection. He argues that, while spontaneous adaptation served as an ideal during the mid-twentieth century pre-managerial era, it has become a necessity in our current time, in which fiscal stringency and constricted mandating preordain that "the real task of administration is coordination—weaving together separate programs into a sensible policy."[42] How do we move from such theoretical justifications to a systematic body of knowledge that can guide future efforts toward spontaneous adaptation in government departments and agencies? We clearly need a framework that will assist the political and permanent leaders of departments and agencies to diagnose whether their organizations might profitably initiate major strategic adaptation and, if so, to knowledgeably select smart practices for proceeding, given various arrays of circumstances that they might meet. We also must address the concerns of those who have become skeptical of the overload and hollow lip service of innovation exercises imposed from the center.[43] In this respect, the circumstances that prevail in the line agency come to the fore. Most specifically, can the culture of an organization sustain a high level of discourse throughout its executive leadership—including both key political appointees and senior permanent officials—about future strategies, yet at the same time negotiate the inevitable ambiguity as it moves from an agreed vision to specific programmatic commitments? Do the executive-bureaucratic contexts surrounding the issues of greatest importance to the organization lend themselves to "position for opportunities"?[44] That is, do future opportunities and challenges coalesce in compelling ways? If so, the agency's leadership may devise a case whose cogency will immediately galvanize support, once the need for strategic adaptation has captured the attention of stakeholders in the wider policy arena.

While political appointees, White House Office units, and Executive Office of the President agencies can foster conditions that would prove conducive to organizations' pursuing spontaneous adaptation in practice, we must look at individual departments and agencies from the perspective of their potential for releasing and rechanneling inventiveness and creativity in public services. Broadly, recent literature provides increasingly robust guidance for such a perspective. Paul Light, for instance, stresses the importance of the degree of professionalization within an agency workforce—a standard under which the U.S. Air Force would score very high indeed.[45] Presumably, professionalization conveys not just subject-matter expertise but knowledge about how to achieve desired ends as well. Sandford Borins and Daniel P. Carpenter separately identify what we might term the sharpness of an organization's apex as highly relevant to the latitude that career officials might enjoy in pursuing relatively free advocacy for a new organizational vision and associated resource commitments.[46] If organizations have relatively few layers of political appointees between the department or agency head and the top permanent officials, then they seem more likely to engage in creative efforts to revamp themselves.

My own research with Michael Barzelay on the U.S. Air Force uncovered how officials might proceed in insuring that their competencies receive due attention by the political executive.[47] First, they can stake out their credibility in strategic competence. This includes discerning future opportunities and challenges from the standpoint of pursuing the long-term public interest. Second, they can partner constructively with political executives in efforts to optimize the attainment of such enduring public value. That is, they can involve themselves in the type of creative dialogue that will further the attainment of the highest level of policy competence possible, given the immediate exigencies associated with achieving and maintaining a tenable fiscal framework, and servicing the political executives' obvious interests in continued electoral support.

We can relate the findings from such research to the advancement of the type of balance between political responsiveness and long-term strategic issues that we would associate with multifaceted policy competence. Regarding the United States, Joel D. Aberbach has consistently argued that the type of competent public-spiritedness identified in some governmental organizations persists, notwithstanding the tendency for successive administrations since Nixon to assume that officials will remain intractable without considerable prodding.[48] Here a paradox enters the equation. Aberbach has found, in the aftermath of reforms designed to enhance responsiveness, that officials have become significantly more attuned to the exigencies faced by their political masters and less inclined to serve special interests. However, they believe that they have experienced a substantial slippage in the influence they exert over policy.

As we saw earlier, public choice theory emerged in the United States over disgruntlement with the level of autonomy enjoyed during the middle part of the last century by departments and agencies. The reader might find it ironic, thus, that bureaucratic organizations in the U.S. federal government have proven relatively immune to the ripples that have swept through other Anglo-American systems. To be sure, they have endured successive budget cuts. However, many agencies operate with legislated insulation from presidential fiat or direction.[49] Even offices within departments frequently operate within frameworks with significant immunity from direction by the president and/or Cabinet secretaries that Congress has mandated. Principal-agent relations, thus, operate in the United States in connection with the separation of powers and ebbs and flows in relation to such factors as whether the same party controls both the presidency and Congress, the size of congressional majorities, and presidential approval ratings.

Barzelay and Campbell argue that those seeking connectivity between missions, objectives, performance, and resource allocation perhaps set themselves up for failure if they expect one-to-one fits along the way.[50] They studied in depth two massive exercises that took place in the U.S. Air Force during the 1990s. These exercises attempted to improve the effectiveness of long-range future projections as well as programming and budgeting within that organization. The authors found that—as the Air Force learned about the innate difficulty of attaining both goals—approaches such as positioning for opportunities and guided incrementalism, discussed above, while suboptimal in terms of comprehensive transformation, nevertheless proved relatively effective in improving the Air Force's ability to differentiate between critical capabilities and those that were simply desirable.

Several factors came together toward fostering such innovation. First, the Air Force has prided itself in maintaining during its short history a capacity for spontaneous adaptation lacking in the other services. Second, two successive chiefs, beginning in 1994, gave high priority to long-term strategic planning and followed through with attention to intraservice deliberative bodies dedicated to improving the connections among missions, objectives, performance, and budgets. Third, the service learned, as it proceeded through its two major exercises, the importance of engaging the participation and support of the political executive and the major commands who own segments of operations and support. It also gained sophistication in pursuing dialogue with stakeholders—attentive senators and congressmen as well as interest groups. This involved an increased focus on future challenges, requisite critical capabilities for the service to rise to these, and identification of "forks-in-the-road" at which the service had either to make tough resource decisions or resign itself to losing windows of opportunity.

The convergence of these elements—a culture that prized spontaneous adaptation, leadership, the commitment of institutional resources to sustaining strategic planning, and an aptitude for gleaning lessons and applying them rapidly to decisional processes—presents itself in the Air Force case as a rarity. Unfortunately, the center cannot infuse such convergence by fiat. Nor will it likely emerge if political executives have disaggregated organizational structures. One-size-fits-all approaches involving either center-driven aggregation or compartmentalization of governance into output-fixated executive agencies seems to overlook a simple reality about public service: departments must do most of the heavy lifting for the discernment and analysis of policy issues necessary to attain a high degree of rigor and to ensure that implementation across operational units achieves strong coherence.

If departments serve as the connecting points between central guidance and implementation, it follows that the political executives and career officials providing leadership in departments must coordinate with their opposite numbers not only in central coordination agencies but in other pertinent line organizations throughout the governmental system. Very few outcomes fall neatly within the compass of a single agency. The more complex the multiplicity of outputs required to attain an outcome, the more intense and rigorous consultations between the political heads of departments and/or top officials must become. This applies not just to implementation of policies but as well to the development of the intellectual architecture that specifies desired outcomes and prescribes how exactly outputs will come together to realize these. This point might strike the reader as obvious. However, participants in the design and implementation of policy and programs often forget it.

Conclusion

Three models of public management have been significant in the development of the U.S. executive branch, especially over the past century. The layering of these traditions exacerbated the tendency for fragmentation naturally associated with the separation of powers—even within discrete policy fields where organizations might otherwise be able to identify and pursue potential synergies. Indeed, the separation of powers adds to the systemic hurdles that would allow reform models to prevail in their attempts to overtake the status quo. Thus, the remnants of reform efforts continue to assert themselves much like glacial ages etch their legacies indelibly on landscapes.

The purpose of this chapter has been to investigate the existing character of the federal executive branch from the standpoint of the range of departmental formats, the multiplicity of organizational approaches, and the added element of nondepartmental agencies, which themselves have varying degrees of connection to the president or insulation from his influence. Rather than attempting to revamp the executive branch from top to bottom, reformers should focus on fostering greater spontaneous adaptation at departmental and agency levels. Much greater attention should also be given to structures in which appointees and career officials can mediate their competing policy perspectives and agendas.

Appendix

Researchers trying to array the elements and functions of U.S. federal government departments and agencies and the positions of their senior staff members face a number of obstacles. Individual departmental and agency Web sites usually provide useful information about the history, structure, and roles of these various organizations. The *Federal Staff Directory* (Washington, D.C.: Congressional Quarterly Press) offers a single volume with detailed information on individual departments and agencies. Although this source also provides extensive lists of officials working within federal organizations, these often prove incomplete. For instance, the *Federal Staff Directory* will not assign the designation "SES" (Senior Executive Service) unless the department or agency itself reports this information. As a result, the researcher often would have to interpolate the standing of incumbents to positions on the basis of whether occupants of similar posts belonged to the SES. In addition, the *Federal Staff Directory* does not differentiate between career and noncareer SES members.

The *Yellow Book* (New York: Leadership Directories) essentially performs this interpolative function for the researcher. It also differentiates between career and noncareer SES officials. However, it divides its coverage of the federal executive branch between two volumes: one includes only those working in the Washington area, and the other covers those based elsewhere in the country. Further, the latter volume does not include officials assigned outside the United States.

Fortunately, there is one official source for data on political appointments requiring Senate confirmation and career and noncareer members of the SES. Every four years, immediately after presidential elections, the Committee on Government Reform of the U.S. House of Representatives or the Senate Governmental Affairs Committee issues a comprehensive catalogue of senior positions whose incumbents work at the "top level" of policy, supervision, and/or management—including the levels of interest in this chapter. Close comparison of this source—referred to as the *Plum Book* (www.gpoaccess.gov /plumbook/2004)—with the *Federal Staff Directory* and the *Yellow Book* suggests that it does not suffer the undercounting problems of the former but, on the other hand, includes all officials regardless of their location.

Two glitches remain. First, the *Plum Book* listings for the SES do not include "reserved" positions. This problem does not present as significant a difficulty as those encountered with the other sources, precisely because exclusion from the "general" category means that the position cannot be held by a political appointee. General positions are those with a premium on impartiality, such as required in law enforcement and audit positions. Insofar as membership in the SES avails career incumbents of an opportunity to participate in the cut and thrust of executive-bureaucratic politics, the reserved category demarcates positions whose sensitivity regarding neutrality should trump other criteria for performance. The 2004 *Plum Book* reports a total of 7,815 SES positions allocated to departments and agencies. Of these, just over 4,500 are allotted to the "general" category, which includes some 701 noncareer incumbents. This suggests that upwards of 3,300 SES positions are "career reserved."

The second difficulty relates to the Office of Management and Budget. I checked, with regard to every department and agency, to see if the *Plum Book* inclusion of positions tallied roughly with those found in the *Yellow Book*. The Office of Management and Budget (OMB) proved the only agency that yielded substantial discrepancies not explained by the exclusion of non–Washington based officials from the *Yellow Book*—for some reason, the *Plum Book* listings for OMB cut off about a third of the way through the agency. I felt comfortable using the *Yellow Book* in the case of OMB, especially because in this instance I could apply previous knowledge of the agency from prior research projects.

Notes

* I wish to thank Jamie Gillies, a Ph.D. student in political science at the University of British Columbia, for his assistance in the research for this chapter. I am grateful as well for the helpful comments of several colleagues, including the editors of this volume— Joel D. Aberbach and Mark A. Peterson—as well as Matthew Holden, Patricia Ingraham, and James Pfiffner.

1. Frank J. Goodnow, *Politics and Administration* (New York: Macmillan, 1900), 92–93.
2. Woodrow Wilson, "The Study of Administration," *Political Science Quarterly* 16 (1941, reprint); Luther Gulick and L. Urwick, *Papers in the Science of Administration* (New York: Institute of Public Administration, 1937), 10.
3. Wilson, "Study of Administration," 493.
4. C. G. Dawes, *The First Year of the Budget of the United States* (New York: Harper and Brothers, 1923) as cited by Larry Berman, *The Office of Management and Budget and the Presidency, 1921–1979* (Princeton, N.J.: Princeton University Press, 1979), 6.
5. Carpenter, *Forging of Bureaucratic Autonomy*.

6. Paul C. Light, *Tides of Reform: Making Government Work, 1945–1995* (New Haven, Conn.: Yale University Press, 1997).

7. Berman, *Office of Management and Budget*, 18–23.

8. Martin Landau, "The Concept of Decision-Making in the Field of Public Administration," in *Concepts and Issues in Administrative Behavior*, ed. Sidney Mailick and Edward Van Ness (Englewood Cliffs, N.J.: Prentice-Hall, 1962), 10; Robert D. Putnam, "The Political Attitudes of Senior Civil Servants in Western Europe: A Preliminary Report," *British Journal of Political Science* 3 (1973), 277; Joel D. Aberbach and Bert A. Rockman, "The Overlapping Worlds of American Federal Executives and Congressmen," *British Journal of Political Science* 7 (1977).

9. Ezra Suleiman, *Politics, Power, and Bureaucracy in France: The Administrative Elite* (Princeton, N.J.: Princeton University Press, 1974); Colin Campbell and George J. Szablowski, *The Superbureaucrats: Structure and Behavior in Central Agencies* (Toronto: Macmillan, 1979).

10. Aberbach, Putnam, and Rockman, *Bureaucrats and Politicians*.

11. Ibid., 2–20.

12. Colin Campbell, "Review Article: The Political Roles of Senior Government Officials in Advanced Democracies," *British Journal of Political Science* 18 (1988).

13. William A. Niskanen, *Structural Reform of the Federal Budget Process* (Washington, D.C.: American Enterprise Institute, 1973), 6–8.

14. Richard P. Nathan, *The Administrative Presidency* (New York: Wiley, 1983).

15. Moe, "The Politicized Presidency."

16. William G. Howell, *Power Without Persuasion: The Politics of Direct Presidential Action* (Princeton, N.J.: Princeton University Press, 2003), xv.

17. Andrew Rudalevige, *Managing the President's Program: Presidential Leadership and Legislative Policy Formulation* (Princeton, N.J.: Princeton University Press, 2002), 5, 16, 164.

18. David E. Lewis, *Presidents and the Politics of Agency Design: Political Insulation in the United States Government Bureaucracy, 1946–1997* (Stanford, Calif.: Stanford University Press, 2003).

19. Lewis, *Presidents*, 43, 55, 58, 74, 77, 107.

20. Heclo, *Government of Strangers*.

21. See http://www.opm.gov/ses/d02chart2.asp.

22. These categories derive from Lewis, *Presidents*, 44–49.

23. Max Weber, *From Max Weber: Essays in Sociology*, ed. H. H. Gerth and C. Wright Mills (London: Routledge & Kegan Paul, 1948), 253–254.

24. Ibid., 232–233.

25. Jonathan Boston, "The Problems of Coordination: The New Zealand Experience," *Governance* 5 (1992), 91.

26. Graham Scott and Peter Gorringe, "Reform of the Core Public Sector: The New Zealand Experience," *Australian Journal of Public Administration* 48 (1989).

27. Robert Gregory, "Political Responsibility for Bureaucratic Incompetence: Tragedy at Cave Creek," *Public Administration* 76 (1998), 522–523.

28. Allen Schick, *The Spirit of Reform: Managing the New Zealand State Sector in a Time of Change*, a report prepared for the State Services Commission and the Treasury, Wellington, New Zealand, 1996, 43, 44.

29. Norton C. Long, "Bureaucracy and Constitutionalism," *American Political Science Review* 46 (1952), 810.
30. Suleiman, *Political*; Putnam, "Political Attitudes"; Aberbach and Rockman, "Overlapping Worlds"; Robert Presthus, *Elite Accommodation in Canadian Politics* (Toronto: Macmillan, 1973), 60–63; Campbell and Szablowski, *Superbureaucrats*; Aberbach, Putnam, and Rockman, *Bureaucrats*.
31. Joel D. Aberbach, "The President and the Executive Branch," in Colin Campbell and Bert A. Rockman, eds., *The Bush Administration: First Appraisals* (Chatham, N.J.: Chatham House, 1991); Colin Campbell and John Halligan, *Leadership in an Age of Constraint: The Australian Experience* (Sydney: Allen & Unwin, 1992); Colin Campbell and Graham K. Wilson, *The End of Whitehall: Death of a Paradigm?* (Oxford: Blackwell, 1995).
32. Colin Campbell, "Juggling Inputs, Outputs and Outcomes in the Search for Policy Competence: Recent Experience in Australia," *Governance* 14 (2001).
33. Amitai Etzioni, *The Active Society: A Theory of Societal and Political Processes* (New York: Free Press, 1968), 283–288.
34. Michael Barzelay and Colin Campbell, *Preparing for the Future: Strategic Planning in the U.S. Air Force* (Washington, D.C.: The Brookings Institution, 2003), 144–146.
35. Patrick J. Wolf, "Why Must We Reinvent the Federal Government? Putting Historical Development Claims to the Test," *Journal of Public Administration Research and Theory* 7 (1997); Carpenter, *Forging of Bureaucratic Autonomy*.
36. Martha Derthick, *Policymaking for Social Security* (Washington, D.C.: The Brookings Institution, 1979).
37. Martha Derthick, *Agency under Stress: The Social Security Administration in American Government* (Washington, D.C.: The Brookings Institution, 1990), 213–216.
38. William T. Gormley, Jr., *Taming the Bureaucracy: Muscles, Prayers, and Other Strategies* (Washington, D.C.: The Brookings Institution, 1989); Martha Feldman, *Order without Design: Information Production and Policy Making* (Stanford, Calif.: Stanford University Press, 1989).
39. Aberbach and Rockman, *In the Web of Politics*.
40. Carpenter, *Forging of Bureaucratic Autonomy*.
41. Mark H. Moore, *Creating Public Value: Strategic Management in Government* (Cambridge, Mass.: Harvard University Press, 1995); Eugene Bardach, *Getting Agencies to Work Together: The Practice and Theory of Managerial Craftsmanship* (Washington, D.C.: The Brookings Institution, 1998).
42. Kettl, *Transformation of Governance*, 166.
43. Derthick, *Agency under Stress*; Light, *Tides of Reform*.
44. Barzelay and Campbell, *Preparing for the Future*, 8–9.
45. Light, *Tides of Reform*, 221.
46. Sandford Borins, *Innovating with Integrity: How Local Heroes Are Transforming American Government* (Washington, D.C.: Georgetown University Press, 1998), 290–291; Carpenter, *Forging of Bureaucratic Autonomy*, 365–366.
47. Barzelay and Campbell, *Preparing for the Future*.
48. Joel D. Aberbach, "The Federal Executive in an Era of Change," *Governance* 16 (2003).

49. Lewis, *Presidents.*
50. Barzelay and Campbell, *Preparing for the Future.*

Bibliography

Aberbach, Joel D., Robert D. Putnam, and Bert A. Rockman. *Bureaucrats and Politicians in Western Democracies.* Cambridge, Mass.: Harvard University Press, 1981. A seminal work that sets the political roles of senior public servants in the United States within the wider context of the comparative study of bureaucracy.

Aberbach, Joel D., and Bert A. Rockman. *In the Web of Politics: Three Decades of the U.S. Federal Executive.* Washington, D.C.: The Brookings Institution, 2000. Compares executive politics under three administrations: Nixon, Reagan, and George H. W. Bush.

Boston, Jonathan. "The Problems of Coordination: The New Zealand Experience." *Governance* 5 (1992). An excellent treatment of public management reform in New Zealand.

Carpenter, Daniel P. *The Forging of Bureaucratic Autonomy: Reputations, Networks and Policy Innovation in Executive Agencies.* Princeton, N.J.: Princeton University Press, 2001. A crucial examination of spontaneous innovation on the part of government agencies.

Heclo, Hugh. *A Government of Strangers: Executive Politics in Washington.* Washington, D.C.: The Brookings Institution, 1977. States the case for integration of the roles of political appointees and senior career officials.

Kettl, Donald F. *The Transformation of Governance: Public Administration for Twenty-First Century America.* Baltimore, Md.: Johns Hopkins University Press, 2000. Portrays the difficulty of integration within the diverse frameworks of modern executive politics.

Moe, Terry M. "The Politicized Presidency." In *The New Directions in American Politics,* edited by John E. Chubb and Paul E. Peterson. Washington, D.C.: The Brookings Institution, 1985. Has exerted a huge impact on the received wisdom regarding the relations between administrations and the career public service.

9

THE FEDERAL PUBLIC SERVICE:
THE PEOPLE AND THE CHALLENGE

Patricia W. Ingraham

T HE AMERICAN PUBLIC SERVICE IS A PIVOTAL AND
powerful institution in American democracy. Members of the public
service are the immediate connections between the president, the
Congress, the courts, and the citizens they all exist to serve. Citizens see some
members of the public service every day—delivering mail, providing health care
and police protection, fighting fires. Yet most citizens never see the many others
who work behind the scenes to provide social security benefits, air traffic safety,
and a plethora of other services and support. And many citizens fail to understand the critical role that members of the public service play in translating the
promises of public policy and legislation into the realities of daily life. Public servants are not "bloodless bureaucrats," they are people—the heart of government,
fundamental to the quality of life that nations and governments provide to their
citizens. In fairness, many public servants do perform routine tasks in stereotypi-
cally characterless buildings. But many others—most, in fact—are at the "street
level," interacting with citizens frequently, making on-the-spot decisions that
affect citizens' lives and security, and fulfilling the promise that the public service
makes to good government: to act as "stewards of democracy." This is graphically
illustrated by a recent example from the Coast Guard, a small but very important
federal agency whose members work with a many-faceted mission: drug inter-
diction, protection from terrorist attacks in coastal waters and harbors, water
safety education, and rescue on the high seas. Vice Admiral Thad Allen recently
described the "daily activities" of one of his commands to a group of students:
"In South Florida, when there is a boat coming through the channel," he said,
"you see a boat. It might be a pleasure boat. But you don't know if that boat car-

ries drugs, illegal immigrants, or weapons. The Coast Guard doesn't know until they board that boat. And at that moment, they decide the appropriate response and how to act. . . . Our success depends on making the right decision at that moment. That's the reality of daily life in the Coast Guard."[1] For citizens, that simple ability—to make the right decision at the right time—is the reality of expectations for the public service.

This chapter will examine the origins and the nature of the American federal service, as well as some of the "tensions" that surround its daily operations. These tensions include: a fundamental disagreement about the proper role of bureaucracy in American government—a disagreement that dates from the founding days of the republic; disagreement about the extent to which government ought to operate like a business, or whether its basic lack of a "bottom line" renders it unable to utilize private sector business models; debate about the extent to which a public bureaucracy has the responsibility to be a representative bureaucracy and to "look like" the citizens it represents; and about the extent to which efficiency or effectiveness, or both, should be the underlying values of bureaucratic operations. It will be argued here that part of the daily work of the federal service is juggling these tensions and different expectations, while still performing necessary work; I conclude that, although the tensions make the work of the federal service more complex, they are a part of the fabric of government. Efforts at change and reform must necessarily recognize them, and must work with the difficult conditions they create.

The Public Service and Democracy

Understanding that members of the public service live with the paradoxes described in this volume—indeed, that the public service *embodies* some of these tensions—is basic to understanding American government. Over two hundred years into our history, citizens and elected officials want public bureaucracy to be responsive to their needs—essentially on demand—but do not want its members to be wasteful or inefficient in responding to the demands of others. Americans steadfastly refuse to accord public servants the elite or highly respected status so often conferred on their counterparts in other nations, but at the same time demand that those in public service be expert, have cutting edge skills, and offer the best possible services and protections. Congress and the president debate about to whom and to what the public service should be responsive, but agree that the public service is a neutral bystander. Elected officials and the public demand that public employees act more like their private sector counterparts and yet complain when they do; in the rhetorically fueled performance reform period of the late 1990s, for example, employees of the Internal Revenue Service were disciplined when they were perceived to be too aggressive in collecting taxes. Members of Congress accused them of "harassing citizens," but the IRS employees were, in fact, following an earlier congressional directive: to improve the bottom line of the IRS by increasing tax collections. The federal bureaucracy is, in short, precisely as Daniel Carpenter describes it in this volume: born in revolt and distrust to a nation profoundly antibureaucratic to this day, and thus still searching for basic legitimacy.

Paradoxically, the federal service is also fundamental to the articulation and implementation of what Hugh Heclo has termed the "enormous American hopes for the future," the expectation that government can and will provide for ever increasing opportunities and better lives. These conflicts are well considered throughout this volume. The first two chapters provide careful discussions of why, at the founding of the federal government, administration and its role in democratic governance were considered only briefly.[2] Colin Campbell and Donald Kettl (Chapters 8 and 11 in this volume) describe the nearly constant reforms and changes that have attempted to reshape and redirect the federal bureaucracy.

At its founding, the framers' concern with balance of power, checks and balances, and legitimate authority in the new system outweighed consideration of other elements of the emerging state. Bureaucracy, as Carpenter notes in Chapter 2, was to be feared and controlled, not given a formative influence in the nature of the government. Yet the concern did exist for some founders: Alexander Hamilton's ringing proclamation that ". . . we may safely pronounce that the true test of a good government is its aptitude and tendency to produce a good administration" certainly demonstrated an awareness of how central the public service could be.[3]

The core responsibilities that the new government undertook immediately outlined the need for administrative support: national defense, postal service, and the building of roads require large numbers of workers. Still, the limited scope of needs and the relatively small size of the young nation permitted an essentially informal pattern of growth. The fledgling public service was an assemblage of friends, relatives, and acquaintances of officeholders. It can be safely said that the appointment of public employees was essentially viewed as a "right of office" by early officeholders and appointees in the United States[4] and that this right was not seriously challenged for several decades—although it must also be noted that Thomas Jefferson commented on the lack of representativeness of "administration" during his presidency.[5]

The sea change came with the election of Andrew Jackson in 1828. While previous presidents and appointees had operated with a limited definition of citizenship and eligibility for public service that included male, educated land owners but essentially no one else, Andrew Jackson had a somewhat different view of citizenship and patronage. Indeed, he had quite a different view of public service. "The duties of all public offices are, or at least admit of being made, so plain and simple that men of intelligence may readily qualify themselves for their performance; and all can not but believe that more is lost by the long continuance of men in office than is generally gained by their experience."[6] .

The view of public office not only as nothing special, but as simple and inevitably subject to abuse, was epitomized by Jackson's appointment to public positions of partisan supporters who at best fit—in the language of the day—the definition of "simple folk." Jackson did not begin the practice of patronage in the public service, nor did it end with the end of his presidency, but he changed the nature of agreement about how the public service should "look" and how membership in its ranks should be attained and viewed by the broader society. This perspective grew so rapidly that by the time of Abraham Lincoln's presidency it was common to offer bribes for a public job.

Political Thorns in the Path of Merit

This changing nature of the public service, along with the growing opportunities that public service offered, was an important influence on the debate about the proper role of public bureaucracy in government. Patronage was constantly expanding. So were the debilitating effects that its lack of emphasis on qualifications and skills, as well as the nearly constant flux that it introduced into the public service, had on the public service. As the nation developed, as industry emerged, and as perceptions of the needs for stability and expertise in government increased, patronage became more dysfunctional. Presidents and members of Congress—though merrily continuing to appoint large numbers of patronage employees—deplored the overall effect of the practice on the quality of government.

But therein lay a constitutional problem regarding the public service that continues to this day. The problem, briefly, is this: patronage employees are responsive to elected officials—perhaps to a fault. Members of the public service appointed by other means (such as neutral testing) will more likely possess required skills and competencies, but will lack guaranteed responsiveness. This problem, which Frederick Mosher (1968) characterized as a public service "thrice removed" from democratic processes, is uniquely American in many respects.[7] Mosher referred to the practice of "merit," or of admitting members to the public service not by election or by appointment, but by neutral testing, free from partisan influence. Thus, the federal service is not directly responsible through popular election to either the president or Congress, responding to both through the political appointment process, the budget, and oversight. The neutral examination process also provides protection from direct citizen demands and influence for the public bureaucracy. Thus, it is "thrice removed" in an effort to provide it neutral legitimacy and stability. Other democratic nations also rely on such a test- or expertise-based admission system. But with well-developed concepts of the state in place as the administrative apparatus of the state developed, these nations found a neutral, expertise-based public service to be a legitimate and broadly accepted part of government. The United States, lacking that tradition and, in fact, rejecting much of the European model, struggled to develop a replacement that recognized the increasing influence of administration and public service in the American democracy, but also curbed its power and guaranteed its legitimacy by clearly placing responsibility for it with elected officials (see Scott James in this volume for a more in-depth discussion of the "tensions" thus encountered). This process essentially guaranteed, in Woodrow Wilson's terms, a "thorny path" for the development of the public service.[8]

The academic—and political—debates that ensued, most often termed the politics/administration dichotomy and discussed in other chapters of this volume as well—continue to mark both the analysis and the practice of the public service. The American distrust of administrative/bureaucratic institutions that underpins this debate runs very deep. It was graphically summarized by Norton Long: "Because bureaucracy is often viewed as tainted with an ineradicable lust for power, it is alleged that, like fire, it needs constant control to prevent its erupting from beneficent servitude into dangerous and tyrannical mastery."[9] The politics/administration "dichotomy" provided a tidy answer to this need for mastery: politics and policy was the realm of elected and politically appointed officials. Carrying out the directives of elected officials—that is, implementing public policy—was the responsibility of career administrators. And in the ideal version of the dichotomy, the twain would never meet. The reality, of course, is that modern government and policy are much too complex to be forced into neat boxes. Indeed, Woodrow Wilson, often called the "father" of the dichotomy, acknowledged as much in his early description of the "proper" relationship, noting that it would be the continuing responsibility of (neutral) administration to "straighten the path" of government (i.e., of elected and appointed officials).[10]

In 1883 the Pendleton Act formally created a career public service with admission based on neutral testing and free from political influence in hiring and promotion. This would seem to have been a step away from the dilemmas created by one of the paradoxes of American democracy: the response of patronage to every election cycle and the concomitant failure to provide for a fully qualified and stable public service. It was not. There are several explanations, not the least of which was the incremental nature of the act's implementation. It provided that 10 percent of the federal workforce would be covered by the new admission standards; coverage would expand by presidential order, and a limited number of patronage appointments would continue to exist to guide the career service. In practice this meant, of course, that the service grew as presidents decreed; they chose to "blanket in" political appointees at the end of their terms in office. The new emphasis on neutral competence and merit was created, but was irretrievably blended with politics and political responsiveness. A new conundrum was born.

The political responsiveness component of this messy equation has taken many forms over the life of the federal government. Sparring between the executive branch and Congress over the appropriate control of the bureaucracy, several variations of the "administrative presidency," the creation of the Senior Executive Service as an effort to bridge administration and politics, and a prolonged debate about "steering" versus "rowing" in the reinvention debates (these and other issues related to "strengthening the president's hand" are described in more detail by Matthew Dickinson, Colin Campbell, and Donald Kettl in this volume) have all been a part of the controversy.

Efforts by presidents, as the leaders of the executive branch, have sometimes been dramatic. From the time of the Brownlow Commission, which in Franklin Roosevelt's second term declared that the president should be the "center of energy" of the administration, virtually every president has engaged the debate with a specific management strategy. The twentieth century ended with a sharp focus on reinventing government and improved performance; the twenty-first began with George W. Bush's emphasis on the "presidential management agenda." James Pfiffner summarizes the energizing theme:

> The balance between presidential appointees and career executives in governing the United States is a fundamental question of who should rule. But it is also a question of governmental and organizational mechanics. The democratic principle that the president along with political appointees ought to direct policy in the executive branch is not in question, but judgments about the most effective way to organize that control have been changing.[11]

Administrative presidency strategies contain other elements, such as budget cuts, structural reorganizations, and substantive policy reconfigurations. They revert in very important ways to the politics/administration dichotomy; by emphasizing presidential *control* of administration, they also emphasize the civil service as a tool of political leaders. Richard Nixon's management strategy was one of the most sweeping. Jimmy Carter's Civil Service Reform Act in 1978 was the first substantive reorganization of the nation's civil service since its creation in 1883. The Reagan strategy was more about flat-out political control through careful placement of political appointees in executive agencies.[12] Reinventing government, described by Donald Kettl in this volume, turned out to be more about downsizing government in the Clinton years. George Bush's management agenda emphasized specific standards for performance and success and found many government agencies failing.

Why are these developments so important to the public service? Because, as Matthew Holden has noted, "It is a democratic *necessity* for public service to be effective."[13] They are important because, as government grew in size and complexity, the role of the public service increased exponentially. The public sector assumed greatly expanded responsibilities for the social welfare of American citizens in the twentieth century. World Wars I and II contributed to government's overall growth. The exploration of space, increased efforts to achieve medical and other scientific breakthroughs, and the enormous impact of technology on government created demand not just for neutrality in the public service, but for unparalleled expertise. At the same time, the American political system was becoming more diffuse—interest groups were playing larger roles though in the interest of increasingly narrow objectives, political parties were declining in importance as arbiters of national values (although the 2004 presidential election may have altered that trend), and voters' perceptions of issues were increasingly shaped by media influences. Dwight Waldo observed that public administration was "proscribed" from being political, but came to operate increasingly within political interstices.[14] When a decision was not made or was left unclear by political decision makers, it was likely to be made or clarified by members of the public bureaucracy in the implementation process.

Even as public bureaucracy drew on its natural proclivity to clarify, however, the nature of the problems it was called upon to solve grew increasingly complex. The Department of Defense (DoD) provides one example. The largest employer in the federal government, DoD had a clear mission and set of objectives for a number of years; the need to provide for the common defense and to wage war in the pursuit of that defense was a very explicit purpose. At the end of World War II, the cold war created another dimension of that purpose but also provided relatively clear direction. But the end of the cold war eroded that clarity. What kind of force did the military need if the cold war was no longer the threat? The end of large-scale, long-term ground actions and prolonged military presence—such as that of the military in Europe after World War II—and the move to short-term, flexible actions—such as those in Bosnia—meant a nearly complete redefinition of logistical support and jobs. The terrorist actions of September 11, 2001, and subsequent events heightened the uncertainty. New demands for expertise in language skills, in crafting new communities with construction, engineering, and massive public works skills, and—indeed—in nation building have fallen to the contemporary Department of Defense. Other major federal agencies have undergone similar transformations.

The Character of the Contemporary Public Service

Who are the members of the public service who carry out these tasks? How do they come to government? Are they the right people for the new demands? We begin by considering how members of the career civil service have come to their jobs in the years since patronage was no longer the only path.

Entering the Public Service

In September 2004 the total size of the civilian workforce in the federal government was 2,713,229. This number includes Department of Defense civilian personnel (668,227) and employees of the U.S. Postal Service (767, 616), which operates as a corporate entity, separate from other federal agencies. It also includes employees of all three branches of government.[15] This total represents a reduction in total employment over a ten-year period, from 2,991,373 in 1994.[16] Beneath the numbers exist the realities of new kinds of jobs and a variety of paths to federal service. As noted, the Postal Service operates as a separate corporate entity, with its own hiring authority. The State Department also has a personnel system separate from the general classified system. For most executive branch agencies, employees enter the lower levels of the organization through a series of standardized (though sometimes now decentralized) tests. It is also important to note that, despite its apparent size, the federal workforce is actually the smallest of the government workforces in the United States. Generally speaking, state workforces are about twice the size of the federal workforce, while total local government employment is nearly five times the total of federal employment numbers.

At the midlevels of the organizations, applicants for professional and administrative careers entered through examinations, which considered education and experience, but also looked for a series of skills and/or competencies that were standardized across government. One of these examinations, the Federal Service Entrance Exam (FSEE), existed for the twenty-year period from 1954 to 1974. This period was characterized by a sustained effort to regularize federal hiring after the rapid buildup during World War II. The exam was targeted squarely at college graduates who were considering a long-term federal career. The FSEE was replaced by the PACE (Professional and Administrative Careers Examination) in 1974. That examination was abolished in the early 1980s, after it was determined to be discriminatory against minority groups in its screening processes.[17] Though this exam was eventually replaced by the Administrative Careers With America examination, the idea of centralized standardization for professional entry to the civil service was falling out of favor.

Even before that time, however, standardized examinations were accompanied by a series of "excepted authorities" that have allowed hiring based on special skills, education, or other specialized testing. Thus, for example, Schedule A permits the hiring of attorneys and accountants without requiring a federal test, because such applicants have been tested and accredited by their professions. Schedule B permits hiring without standard testing of persons in hard-to-hire areas or of those with very limited employment pools. Since the Eisenhower Administration, Schedule C has permitted the hiring for "policy sensitive" positions that can range from personal secretary to chauffeur to midlevel manager.

There are also large numbers of Excepted Authorities that allow more flexible hiring for generally hard-to-hire occupations (doctors and nurses), for those with special service to the country (Peace Corps Volunteers), for those with excellent academic records (Outstanding Scholars), and for many others. The numbers of special and excepted authorities are so large, in fact, that they are virtually impossible to count accurately. Further, since its inception, the civil service system has awarded special points in both hiring and promotion to veterans through Veterans' Preference, so this group has historically been treated as an excepted or special group as well.

Composition of the Federal Service

Although the hiring record of the federal government in its early years was stark testimony to some of the prejudices imbedded in the society, since the early 1940s, the federal government has been perceived to be an employer more friendly to women than was the market in general. World War II contributed to this; with so many men in the military, positions they had previously held were filled by women. The civil rights movement in the 1960s emphasized the need to hire minorities and persons of color. The Civil Rights Act of 1964, the Equal Pay Act of 1963, and the Equal Opportunity Employment Act of 1973 gave a statutory base to these commitments. Nonetheless, one of the impacts of previous hiring practices, and most notably of the Veterans' Preference provisions noted above,

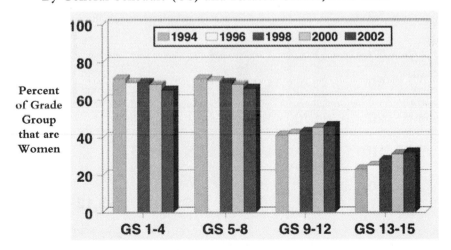

Employment of Women
By General Schedule (GS) and Related Grades, 1994–2002

SOURCE: U.S. Office of Personnel Management, Office of Executive Personnel, "The Senior Executive Service Annual Report," October 2003.

Figure 1   Employment of Women in the Federal Government

is that the federal government admitted and promoted disproportionate numbers of white males for many years. At the lower or entry levels of the bureaucracy, representation of the general population is greatest. It diminishes as one moves up the ranks. The people of the public service are diverse, therefore, but not completely representative throughout all levels of federal public organizations.

At the same time, the composition of the public service has changed in the past twenty-five years and continues to do so. Early characterizations of the civil service as largely unrepresentative of the general population are no longer fully accurate, because the number of women throughout federal agencies, and particularly in the Senior Executive Service (SES), has increased substantially. The SES is the top career executive cadre in the federal government and is discussed in more detail in a later section of this chapter. In an analysis of the Senior Executive Service, for example, the General Accounting Office (now the Government Accountability Office) noted that "The proportion of women went from about 10 percent in 1990 to about 22 percent in 1999."[18]

Total numbers of persons of color at the top levels of federal organizations have also increased, but not as dramatically. In management and supervisory levels, about 12 percent of federal employees were African American in 2003.

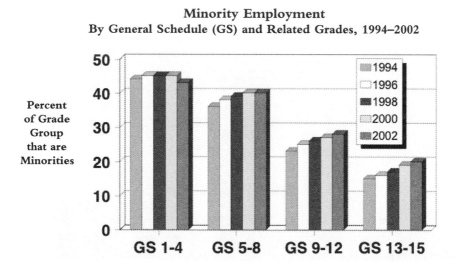

**Minority Employment
By General Schedule (GS) and Related Grades, 1994–2002**

"Minorities" include the following Race/National Origin categories: Black, Hispanic, Asian/Pacific Islander, and American Indian/Alaska Native.

SOURCE: U.S. Office of Personnel Management, Federal Civilian Workforce Statistics, October 2003.

Figure 2   Employment of Minorities in the Federal Government

Comparable figures for Asian American employees and for Native Americans were 3.2 percent and 1.9 percent. Hispanics are now about 5.8 percent of federal mangers and supervisors. In the SES, the percentage of minority members grew from about 7 percent to 13 percent in the decade of the 1990s.[19] In a nutshell, representativeness of the federal bureaucracy has improved—most notably for women—but full representation has not been achieved. Further, because the very top levels of many organizations are the least representative, the challenges of moving diversity "up the ladder" of career opportunity continue to loom large for the federal government.

The Retirement Factor

Increasingly, diversity efforts also focus on achieving age diversity. Downsizing and hiring freezes in the 1990s contributed to an overall aging of the federal workforce. In some agencies, a potential retirement rate of nearly 70 percent (among members of the SES) in the next five years will create very significant skill and expertise gaps.

The potential size of the projected retirements from federal service could shape the demographics of the service as well. Several factors converged to shape this possibility. First, the Veterans' Preference provisions of entry and promotion have enhanced the hiring and promotion prospects of white males simply because they were, for many years, the preponderant group in the military. This

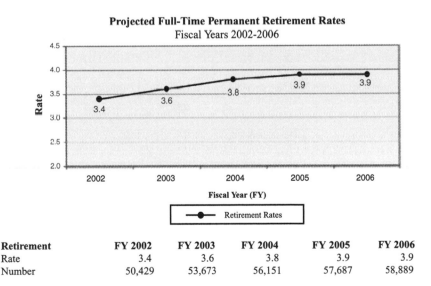

Projected Full-Time Permanent Retirement Rates
Fiscal Years 2002-2006

Retirement	FY 2002	FY 2003	FY 2004	FY 2005	FY 2006
Rate	3.4	3.6	3.8	3.9	3.9
Number	50,429	53,673	56,151	57,687	58,889

SOURCE: National Academy of Public Administration "The Twenty-first Century Manager: Final Report," May 2004.

Figure 3   Projected Retirement Rates

has, as noted above, created a top level at federal agencies that is less representative than lower levels of the organization, but this group is also more likely to be at or near retirement age. If a large-scale retirement exodus does occur in the next ten years, this top level will be reshaped by the members of the feeder pools, who will replace them.

How that feeder group might look and how it might be created are matters of some debate for two reasons. First, as the very upper levels of the agencies were aging but essentially staying in place, middle and lower levels of the organizations were subject to the downsizing and hiring freezes of the Clinton presidency and the "reinventing government" initiatives. These influences were exacerbated by efforts called "strategic buyouts," whose intentions were to hasten the downsizing process by offering incentives to leave federal service. Many of those who chose this option were part of the natural feeder pool for the positions created by the expected retirements. As a result, there are two potential "gaps" in the federal service in the next ten years: that created by an exit at the top by retirement, and that created by the early exit through buyouts of many talented younger members of the civil service. The potential to reshape the composition of the service is great, but the challenge is also evident.

Some observers are sanguine about the prospects. In testimony before Congress, a top official of the Office of Personnel Management argued that, even though only 14 percent of the likely feeder pool are minorities (the likely feeder pool is defined as persons at grades 14 and 15 already in government), nearly one-third are women. Since the top ranks of the service—the Senior Executive Service—number less than 7,000 government-wide, the potential pool of women and minorities, nearly 32,000, could have a sizable impact on reshaping composition.[20] As noted above, however, this can occur only if the government is more aggressive about increasing diversity at top of its organizations. In this regard, the Senior Executive Service will be crucial.[21]

The Senior Executive Service

The Senior Executive Service is a potentially critical component of the federal government. When it was created by the Civil Service Reform Act of 1978, its approximately 7,000 members were intended to create a formal link between the career civil service and the political appointees who provide policy leadership and direction within federal agencies. It was intended, in other words, to breach the traditional politics/administration divide. It was to do this in several ways: first, its members were "de-linked" from many formal civil service protections and were employed instead by performance-based contracts. Members of the SES who receive unsatisfactory performance ratings from their superiors— usually political appointees—three years in a row are subject to dismissal or demotion. Pay and performance bonuses are also based on annual performance reviews. The internal composition of the SES is purposely mixed; 10 percent of its membership government-wide can be political appointees. External (to the agency) recruitment into the SES is encouraged. Current reform discussions are considering whether two separate groups of the Senior Executive Service should be created: one scientific and technical, and one purely executive. Recent changes have mandated annual assessments of suitability of both positions and those who hold them for SES-level jobs. Technically and legally, the cumulative provisions of the SES *should* create a top-level cadre in the public bureaucracy that is more responsive to political direction—if not flat-out control.

But the SES has not been a completely successful effort. The differences it sought to bridge—those between policy making, policy advising, and implementation—are deeply imbedded in the history of the U.S. federal government. Further, the real differences between the members of the SES and the political appointees who direct and lead them are substantial. Members of the federal service most commonly stay with one program or agency throughout their careers. They often have fifteen to eighteen years of experience with that program when they come to the SES position. Members of the political appointee cadre, on the other hand, are explicitly chosen to be outsiders: that is, to bring a new perspective and impetus for change to the organization. In addition, they generally do not stay in one position—or even one agency—very long. Hugh Heclo called this group "a government of strangers," even to one another.[22] In organizational terms, therefore, federal agencies have two groups of leaders: the political appointees and the career members of the SES. Political appointees have been mentioned in this chapter in the context of providing presidential direction and impetus for policy change. The nature of the political appointment process, however, as well as the relationship between appointees and the career civil service is not without contentious debate. Virtually no observer believes that it completely fulfills the task of injecting popular wishes, as summarized by elections, into public bureaucracy.

Political Appointees

Why is the political appointment process considered fundamentally dysfunctional? There are numerous arguments that support the idea that least some level of dysfunction exists. Some have noted, for example, that the bifurcated leadership structure creates instability and inconsistency that is detrimental to effective organizational performance.[23] The Volcker Commission summarized one aspect of the problem in this way:

> When a new administration takes office or a new agency head is appointed, it often seems too politically difficult, or the time horizon too short, to reshape the top ranks or to improve accountability. So more

leadership posts are created to help agency heads and presidents work around old leadership posts they cannot control or remove. Compounded over the decades, this pattern has yielded a federal management structure that is top heavy, cumbersome, and contrary to the goals of effective leadership and meaningful accountability.[24]

This "thickening" of the appointee ranks of government has significant implications for career civil servants in the SES or in other top ranks of the permanent civil service. The members of the SES are the top civil servants below political executives; they are the most likely to interact with them. They are the "first line" of the public service in terms of responsiveness to political direction. A great deal of the pressure created by frequent turnover and change of priorities falls on them. Second, their own career opportunities are limited or "topped out" by the presence of political appointees at the top of the organizational authority structure. While there is good evidence that longer-term political appointees forge relatively good working relationships with career members of the public service, the ongoing problem of short tenure in political positions makes this difficult. High levels of distrust and negative political rhetoric frequently accompany elections and the subsequent changing of political appointees in the executive agencies.

Further, while political appointees can make a difference if they stay in place long enough, that difference may be primarily to the president; Congress figures much less prominently in this debate. The Senate approves only a relatively small percentage (a little less than 25 percent) of the total number of political appointees. The Executive Office of the President is the main decision maker for the rest. The constitutional tug of war is not resolved, and it is clear that some problems exist in the process. The features of split leadership, unclear responsiveness and accountability chains, and troubled communications and lack of trust between career public servants and political appointees remain the defining characteristics of the Senior Executive Service and the public service more broadly.

Are Members of the Public Service Different?

How do the members of the public service look when compared to their private sector or nonprofit counterparts? Are substantial differences obvious? The answers to these questions must begin with a caveat: it is increasingly difficult to draw a definitive line between what is public, what is private, and what is not for profit. Privatization and contracting out have put many previously public jobs into other sectors. There is also substantial evidence that young people entering the job market consider nonprofit employment to be public service, which of course it may be, because many nonprofit agencies are government contractors or otherwise serve the public good.[25]

Given that, some differences do emerge if a strictly "civil service" definition of public service is employed. To begin, management and leadership levels of the federal service are, overall, slightly better educated than the workforce in general. The prototypical "forty-five-year-old white male with a master's degree," though declining somewhat in gender accuracy, continues to render a fairly good picture of the upper levels of the federal service.[26] The federal workforce is older than the workforce in general. As noted earlier, this is due largely to two events in the 1990s: a downsizing of middle manager ranks and a concomitant freeze in hiring. The oldest employees, those nearest to retirement and its benefits, stayed. The "young" middle managers left, as did other such personnel who were eligible for buyouts (incentives for retiring early). No new employees were hired for several years. The result is a demographic gap in a number of federal agencies. The modal age for federal supervisors and managers in 1991 was forty-four; in 2003 it was fifty-four. In that same year over 71 percent of federal managers were forty-five and above.[27]

Still, generally speaking, the federal workforce is very slightly better paid than the U.S. workforce in general. This is not true for the executive levels of the federal service, however, which most estimates place substantially behind private sector counterparts. Except for a very limited number of federal employees government-wide (appointed under special authorities), the total compensation of federal executives cannot exceed $192,600, the salary of the vice president.[28] Without question, this is below the salary of many midlevel executives in the private sector. At lower levels of the organization, however, this disparity is not as clear. The average entry-level federal salary for persons with a bachelor's degree in 2002 was $33,746.[29] According to Bureau of Labor Standards statistics, the roughly comparable private sector professional salary level was just slightly less, about $33,000. Salary levels for contract employees are generally not known, but are often believed to be above those of similar positions in the civil service. There is some evidence to bear this out.[30]

These salary numbers are only part of the story, however. Two other factors are significant in the federal service: benefits and job security. For some time, there was general agreement that the federal benefits and retirement package was superior to that available to many private sector employees. Recent experience with private sector companies that invested employee retirement benefits in company stocks only to later declare bankruptcy has demonstrated that stability and guarantees in a retirement system may be as important as overall amounts. Federal employees enjoy such stability. Generally speaking, they also enjoy greater job security than many of their private sector counterparts. Protections against dismissal and termination are extensive in the federal government. In 2003 the Bureau of Labor Statistics (BLS) reported that about 31 percent of the federal workforce were union members.[31] Agencies or organizations with a notable union presence include the Department of Defense, the Internal

Revenue Service, and several of the legacy agencies in the Department of Homeland Security, such as Customs and Immigration. The level of unionization is one marked difference between the public and private sectors; while one in every four federal employees is a member of a union, BLS data indicate that only slightly over 8 percent of private sector employees are union members.[32] Certainly the pattern found in some federal agencies, such as the Patent and Trademark Office, where over two-thirds of the employees are union members and highly professional positions such as patent examiners and attorneys are unionized, is not found in the private sector.

Although it is often lamented that collective bargaining protections in public agencies are so extensive as to preclude firing incompetent employees, data to support the assertion are limited and difficult to assess. Without any doubt, multiple grievance layers in the federal government make termination of employees for cause or for poor performance tedious and lengthy. In a recent poll, only 27 percent of federal employees agreed that necessary steps were taken to deal with poor performers, and a substantial number translated this failure to a lack of overall confidence in the organization.[33] At the same time, the Merit Systems Protection Board reported that managers' willingness to discipline and terminate employees still in their probationary period with government increased slightly in the 1990s.[34] Recent reforms in Department of Homeland Security agencies, aimed at streamlining and simplifying the appeals process, and provisions in the Department of Defense's civilian personnel reforms will streamline it even more. Though dealing with poor performers is difficult in both public and private sectors, the perception remains strong that it is a more serious problem in public agencies.

Some of these issues translate to a growing unease in the federal service. The quality of leadership, so fundamental to organizational performance, is questioned by many federal employees; nearly half responding to an Office of Personnel Management (OPM) survey in 2003 indicated that leadership and management in their agency was unsatisfactory. Less than half would recommend the federal government as a place to work. But—perhaps perversely—well over 70 percent of federal respondents said that their work was meaningful and important. This quality of public service—a strong commitment to the nature of the job and its challenges—is often cited by organization theorists as a defining characteristic of public service.[35]

Hiring

Hiring in the federal government has long had a reputation for being tedious and lengthy, partly as a result of the testing procedures described earlier. Federal hiring differences are particularly acute for highly technical or scientific jobs or professions. The public sector does not have the ability to match the private sector in "paying the going price" for highly skilled talent or to quickly hire talent when it is available. Title V of the U.S. Code, which serves as an umbrella for many civil service provisions and most certainly for the standardized and centralized model of human resource management in the federal government, is largely responsible. It was designed to cover sets of relatively routine jobs, and the processes and procedures that it instigated operated with the assumption that a steady supply of labor would always be readily available. Some critical components of that assumption are no longer true. Although many clerical, processing, and relatively routine jobs remain in the federal government, there are many new and emerging demands for specialized skills and talents. Indeed, for some organizations, these are the critical occupations. Persons to fill the necessary jobs are in short supply or are not interested in federal employment.

Both Volcker Commissions (1989; 2003) recommended that new flexibilities be created to meet and reward these new needs. Indeed, the second report, issued in 2003, recommended that the General Schedule, the mother stone of classification and compensation practices in the federal government, be abolished.[36] While this is heresy to some, who fear that greater flexibility necessarily suggests renewed political intrusion into the public service, reforms in the Department of Defense, the Department of Homeland Security, NASA, the Government Accountability Office, and other agencies demonstrate that this movement to hire quickly, if necessary, and to tailor hiring practices to critical staffing needs is well underway. Again, the recent experience of one agency provides a potent example. At the 2004 annual meeting of the American Academy of Public Administration, Dr. Julie Geberding talked about the anthrax scare and the response of the Centers for Disease Control, which she directs: "In a matter of days, I went from knowing next to nothing about anthrax to being one of the world's experts on the subject. So did many other CDC staff." This describes the need for an organizational and scientific nimbleness that is not present in many federal agencies at this time: the need to hire technically qualified persons with broad interests and great flexibility and to do so quickly, when the agency need is clear and when expert talent is available. Experts of the kind Dr. Geberding described have many employment opportunities; the six- to eight-month waiting period for a federal job is not likely to result in their hire. So, setting constitutional and other issues aside for the moment, it is useful to ask: What are the current challenges for the public service? Does the contemporary public service really have the ability to meet them? A good starting point is the changing nature of jobs and the shifting organizational challenges that are now part of every federal agency's daily life.

The Changing Nature of Public Work

Public employment in the United States responds to major political, social, and economic events: wars, economic downturns, and major public policy initiatives, such as provision of social security benefits or the "war on poverty." Woodrow Wilson, for example, nearly doubled the federal workforce—to about one million—during World War I. At the end of World War II, the combined impact of Franklin Roosevelt's New Deal and the war had elevated employment to nearly four million.[37] For each such event, the public service assumes new tasks and responsibilities and learns or hires new skills. And inevitably, subsequent federal employment then contracts or remains steady until it receives another jolt of some sort.

The nature of federal jobs increased in complexity with each of these jolts. The impact of technology and the demand for technological expertise is one example of a rapid catapulting of the federal workforce into new terrain and expertise. The system did not always meet such demands effectively. The example of the Internal Revenue Service's initial efforts to modernize its technology, for example, is often cited as a clear example of organizational failure—one of several that led Congress to reform the agency in 1998.[38]

The occupational composition of the entire workforce has changed in response. In 1950 more than half of the classified civil service was in lower level clerical jobs, GS-4 or below. (It is important to note, however, that FDR appointed many employees, sometimes entire agencies, as "excepted" employees outside the classified civil service requirements. Such positions are not necessarily advertised broadly, and standardized tests are not required, since skills are assumed to be policy based.) By the year 2000 their total was only about 15 percent.[39] The percentage of professional and technical positions (GS-7 to GS-13), particularly at the upper ranges of these grades, exploded. These shifts are dramatically demonstrated in Figure 4.

Further, data from OPM demonstrate that at the end of 2000, about 10 percent of the total full-time permanent federal workforce was employed in engineer and scientist positions.[40] The second Volcker Commission summarizes the shift in this way:

> A space program . . . became a significant federal activity. Foreign aid and foreign trade became important components of foreign relations. Ensuring the safety of food and drugs, of travel, and the workplace loomed larger. . . . Science and technology research, complex litigation, rigorous analysis, and innovation in service delivery became critical responsibilities in agency after agency. Financial regulators became hard pressed by the competitiveness of capital markets.[41]

The commission did not include, but could have, the demands that globalization, multinational corporations, constantly emerging environmental problems, a pressing need for cultural awareness and linguistic skills, and the war on terror have placed on the crusty old structures that surround the public service and its operations. And these do not begin to consider the seismic impact that privatization and contracting out have had on the federal workforce.

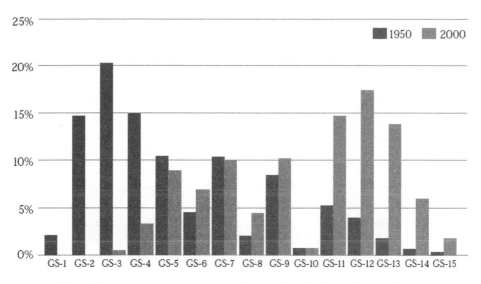

SOURCE: Office of Personnel Management, *A Fresh Start for Federal Pay. The Case for Modernization* (April 2002), p. 5.

Figure 4   The Changing Federal Workforce, 1950–2000.

Contracting Out Government Work

Contracting with the private or nonprofit sectors for government work has a long history at all levels of government. Contractors are used for many purposes: simple service provision, such as laundry or dining facilities, but also research and design of weapons systems, information technology systems, and others, and provision of educational services at all levels of education. Contractors have been used to oversee and conduct nuclear cleanups, to build and maintain space shuttles, and to provide support for (or actual provision of) basic administrative tasks such as payroll administration. For the past decade, some government agencies have become contractors to other government agencies, providing personnel or financial management assistance on a contracted basis. Also in the past decade, contractors have served as intelligence analysts, linguists, and critical logistical support for the military in Bosnia, Afghanistan, and Iraq. Thus, to an increasing, but essentially unknown, extent, "government work" is being performed by people who are not government employees. Daniel Carpenter in this volume argues that some components of the "contracting state" are reaching—or will soon reach—a plateau. But the extent to which contracting has already altered the nature of government and of "government work" will continue to be an important dimension of the contemporary public service.

As early as 1962, the Bell Commission appointed by President John F. Kennedy identified two qualities of contracting that were troublesome. First, contractors were not necessarily subject to and guided by principles of protecting citizen rights and avoiding conflict of interest, as are members of the career service. Second, the panel observed that reliance on contractors for critical expertise and knowledge did not retain that knowledge long term for government, unless the contractors themselves were retained for long periods.[42]

Both concerns were prescient and are of even greater proportions in contemporary government. In fact, the practice of contracting out has grown so substantially that its actual extent is now difficult to know. One analyst argues that the full extent of employment outside the core public service should include employees of other levels of government who are employed or paid by intergovernmental grants.[43] Most observers agree that this is a problematic counting formula. Finding a more accurate estimate is complicated, however, by the fact that government agencies themselves cannot always provide an accurate account of the total numbers of contract employees and their cost to the agency.

Defense agencies are one example. The Pentagon's own internal estimates of contractor workforce size and cost differ. In 2000 Pentagon analysts reported that 230,000 contractors served one component of Defense—the army—in the previous year. They arrived at that figure by dividing the total dollar value of all service contracts by an estimate of the cost of paying a contractor employee (at roughly the level of a career civil servant). Subsequent analyses, however, demonstrated that while less than 230,000 contractors were employed by the army, they cost more per employee. The differences were quite dramatic.[44] In a 2001 analysis, covering only 40 percent of army contract employees, the cost was determined to be $9.2 billion for about 30,000 employees, a figure that would put contracting costs substantially above those of maintaining or creating the jobs in the civil service.[45] In 2002 the Army told Congress that its service support contract estimates ranged from 100,000 to 600,000 employees.[46]

NASA and the Department of Homeland Security also provide examples of the scope and potential consequences of the increasing reliance on contracting. NASA has historically relied upon contractors to carry out some of its core functions. The General Accounting Office noted in 2003 that NASA spends over $12 billion per year on contracted activities.[47] Initially an agency with broad public support and a dazzling mission—to send man into space—NASA became less visible and less widely supported as it moved on to new goals. The agency was subject to significant budget cuts and severe personnel cutbacks. The loss of the space shuttle *Challenger* in 1986 and the *Columbia* tragedy in 2003 were very public failures. Mel Dubnick and Barbara Romzek carefully trace the disconnects that developed within NASA as a result of downsizing, extreme decentralization of operating units, and heavy reliance on contractors. They note that, since the agency's high water mark in the late 1960s and early 1970s, NASA's budget has been cut in half. The staff was cut by at least 40 percent—safety and quality control personnel by over 70 percent—by the time of the *Challenger* disaster.[48] Development of the space shuttle program, of which *Columbia* was a part, was a response to the need to create a new mission with fewer resources, less staff, and less technological expertise within the agency. Increased reliance on contractors was one natural outcome. But since 1990, the General Accounting Office has placed NASA on its "high risk" list for contract management capacity, observing in its most recent report that NASA lacked "accurate and reliable financial and management information on contract spending."[49] NASA's example demonstrates the heavy toll that contract management places on increasingly limited numbers of permanent employees. At the same time, NASA continues to exemplify one paradox of the public service: a strong commitment to agency mission and goals even in the face of adversity. In 2003 the Partnership for Public Service reported that NASA employees considered the agency the best place to work in the federal government.[50]

Reforms at Homeland Security

The Department of Homeland Security (DHS) provides another example of extensive contracting, but also provides some perspective on a different question: Does such contracting lead to the quality that the American public demands of its public service? When it was created, DHS provided one of the most complex reorganization efforts ever to confront the federal government, merging twenty-two existing agencies into a new organization. The logistics alone were formidable; internal politics and management issues were legion. In creating the new organization, Congress also sent a signal about how it views the workforce of the future, giving DHS broad management discretion and flexibility that differed markedly from the traditional civil service systems. Operating in an atmosphere of perceived crisis, DHS had to fly in the face of accepted theories of effective organizational change and accomplish the massive transformation quickly. What did DHS do to respond to these demands? It turned to private sector contractors. One large consultant company managed the planning and consultation stages of specifying the new flexibilities. Another was hired to oversee the implementation of the flexibilities and to consolidate multiple information technology systems. There are also many, many contracts relating to department mission and objectives.

But this is only the tip of the iceberg at the Department of Homeland Security. Each of its legacy agencies is also going through internal changes and significant alterations to mission, and contractors and consultants are playing a large role in that process. In some cases, DHS is still trying to figure out what its mission is: How, for example, does it establish the international communications networks necessary to stay abreast of terrorist threats? How does it work with the states of North Dakota and Montana to ensure that the extensive borders both share with Canada are protected? Contractors and consultants are part of the problem solving activity. These dramatic challenges typify many federal agencies in the twenty-first century. There are others. Despite the difficulties in obtaining hard numbers about the specific size and location of the contractor workforce, therefore, there is no question that the large practice of contracting out has changed the scope and nature of federal work. Donald Kettl notes that becoming a "smart buyer" (of contract services) is one of the largest problems facing the federal government of the future.[51]

Reforming the Public Service

These and other challenges were profoundly amplified by the events of September 11, 2001, and their aftermath. The need to move away from the "business as usual" template for government work and government jobs became starkly clear. The shocks also moved the federal government away from its traditional model of reform—incrementalism.

The incremental pattern of reform for the civil service started early, with the passage of the legislation (the Pendleton Act) that created it but that covered only 10 percent of the existing service. That pattern continued through civil service growth, contraction, and change for over one hundred years. In 1978 the Civil Service Reform Act introduced some major changes—such as merit pay and the creation of the Senior Executive Service, the Office of Personnel Management, and the Merit Systems Protection board —but continued to operate from a base model of standardization, centralization, and very substantial control of both individual agency and individual employee action. By this time, however, the "whole cloth" of a single merit system had frayed badly and continued to do so. Throughout the 1980s, federal agencies with strong ties to Capitol Hill— Defense agencies are the notable example—negotiated and received special pay rates, special hiring authorities, and other flexibilities not enjoyed by federal agencies generally. The 1990s were years of "reinvention" (see Donald Kettl in this volume) and of efforts to move toward "high performance" government.

There were calls for broader and more comprehensive reforms prior to the DHS reforms, particularly in the early years of the Clinton administration. It was determined, however, that comprehensive civil service reform did not have the clout to grab congressional attention; President Jimmy Carter once called the subject "eye-glazing." Congress focused instead on individual agencies with performance problems. Special legislation exempted the Federal Aviation Administration from most provisions of Title V in 1996. Reorganization legislation for the IRS in 1998 provided that agency with new personnel flexibilities.[52] An ever larger percentage of the federal workforce was operating under hiring and pay authorities that were exceptions to traditional civil service law. In addition, entire organizations—the Foreign Service, the Postal Service, the General Accounting Office, for example—operated with different pay and personnel systems. A single merit system was the symbolic rhetoric; the reality was far more complex.

Then came September 11. Management and civil service reforms that had been "back burner" became high priorities. The essentially overnight staffing of the Transportation Safety Administration, the creation of the Department of Homeland Security, and the extensive buildup and deployment at the Department of Defense presented dramatic arguments for reform. One veteran member of the Senior Executive Service summarized the process this way: "When a house of cards falls, it falls fast."[53]

Together, the management reform provisions of the Homeland Security Act and the creation of the National Security Personnel System (as part of a fiscal 2004 defense bill signed by President Bush in November 2003) cover nearly half of federal personnel. DoD alone has 746,000 civilian employees that will be covered by new management provisions.[54] Other agencies are lined up to come on board. President Bush and the Office of Management and Budget are moving forward with plans for government-wide reforms based on the DHS and DoD model.

Why are the new systems so different? Do they—*can* they—create the necessary framework for a quality public service for the future? First, a key point is that the systems do not reconcile the fundamental question of public service accountability. They strongly emphasize improved performance at the individual level and move toward consideration of organizational performance as well. They do not assist in clarifying whether it is the expectations of the president, Congress, citizens, or all of the above that will serve as the basis for performance considerations. As in the case of the IRS agents noted earlier, it is clear that the likelihood for differences in this respect should be considered.

In purely management terms, however, the changes have some common characteristics. They move away from the strong role that collective bargaining has played in workplace conditions, performance rewards, and discipline. In that sense, they suggest that the values of standardization and stability that unions had come to typify no longer serve the interests of public bureaucracies. Similarly, both systems simplify and streamline disciplinary processes, keeping them internal to the agency to a much greater extent and giving managers more discretion in dealing with poor performers in a timely way. Both systems place central emphasis on performance. Both promote simplified and faster hiring. Both systems emphasize—to a much greater degree than before—workforce planning, with an eye toward workforce restructuring and potential downsizing (and additional contracting out). Both increase managerial discretion in these matters very substantially. Collectively, the reforms decisively move away from the perceived equation of merit and civil service with protection and procedure to a new equation of merit with performance. They appear, in short, to move away from standardized control toward greater autonomy for the public service, thus squarely engaging traditional paradoxes: to what or to whom is the public service responsive, and how? Can a theoretically "neutral" service, which is not trusted to engage in policy decisions, is expected to be fully responsive to political direction, and must continue to meet external (and government-wide) standards of fair and equal treatment of employees be given such autonomy?

Most observers agree that the federal public service is being substantially redefined. The long-term transformation will be difficult both for the organizations and for political relations and support. The unions have launched major efforts opposing both packages, arguing that the federal government has responsibility as an employer to guarantee employee protections. Congress is divided on the issue, as, it appears, are substantial portions of the American public. In the face of war, economic uncertainty, very broad international problems, and unceasing demands for performance, employment security guarantees for members of the public service do not appear to be a high priority. Transforming itself, therefore, will be one major challenge for the future of the federal public service. There are others.

The Future: Seeking Legitimacy and Balance

In some ways, members of the public service are now, more than ever, democracy's critical stewards. The tasks and jobs for which they are responsible are more difficult and less predictable than at any point in our nation's history. The ways in which their jobs are carried out—through partnerships, contracts, interorganizational and international agreements—are increasingly multidimensional. And some problems loom large: members of the career service retain final accountability for the contract employees that their organizations have difficulty even counting. Technology poses continuing challenges: it must be adopted expeditiously and wisely, but federal agencies and employees must never allow information technology and data collection to compromise the rights and privacy of citizens. Information management for government necessarily treads the tough line between accessibility and the protection of information about citizens.

Managing the public service of the future will occur in the newly reformed setting of flexibility and discretion. This management is an enterprise in which decisions—which one hopes would be objective and well-reasoned—will be made about workplace conditions and rewards, benefits, successes and failures of the public service. In the best of all possible worlds, these decisions will be fair and equitable. Even so, not everyone will be happy.

The reforms described above, and those certain to follow, address the operational aspects of the public service's challenges: they are technical and, to many, not completely compelling. But the ability to hire quickly, to discipline and reward effectively, to support or limit unionization, to develop and encourage strong leadership are fundamentally political issues. In a democratic setting, the issue of how a government manages its employees is one not only of operational effectiveness, but of accountability to the broader public. The real extent to which overhead controls can be loosened and flexibilities valued is not a management, but a political, question. Simplification and flexibility imply risk. Management, public or private, involves people with different perceptions of fair treatment for them and others. Flexibility, discretion, and accountability in reformed systems occur together only when there is agreement about the expectations and objectives of the reforms. The new reforms may well provide the organizational conditions necessary for quality and effectiveness. They do not and cannot address the broad constitutional paradoxes that have confronted American government and its executive branch since their inception: the fundamental legitimacy of the public bureaucracy; the ways in which it can be held accountable; and the balance between performance in simple efficiency terms and the need for broader effectiveness in democratic terms. The margin of error for success or failure of the federal service will always be determined in the political environment of public organizations and will always depend on the extent to which there is consensus about the legitimacy and authority of bureaucratic action. Absent such consensus, the effectiveness and success of the public service—reformed or not—will be challenged.

And therein lies the rub for the public service in the American federal government. This public service has moved beyond Mosher's description of being "thrice removed" from voters and citizens. The contemporary public service is much more than thrice removed. The force of contracting out has created an additional nebulous network of responsibility and authority—indeed, even of size. Decreased overhead controls and increased flexibility may lead to one kind of performance for the federal service, but the reality of flexibility in an environment historically characterized by low levels of trust and risk aversion remains.

Thus, the debate surrounding the public service has yet to address the problem of reconciling traditional constitutional tensions with more contemporary demands and expectations. Indeed, the most recent reforms were not really about the public service at all; they were about national security. Nor, for that matter, did the reforms address the reality of the total public service. They did not address the cadre of political appointees who direct the service, though the leadership of this group will be crucial to future success. They did not address the contract workforce, although many estimates would place the size of that workforce as larger than that of the civil service and its work as perhaps more sensitive. Fundamentally, they did not address traditional political concerns of accountability and authority. In 1936, John Gaus wrote that "The responsibility of an individual civil servant—to the legislature, to the courts, to citizens generally—is confused."[55] The intervening seventy years have not resolved the confusion. And this continuing confusion creates the major challenge for both current and future members of the federal service and for those who govern them. Charting a clear path through Woodrow Wilson's "thorns" is as central to the public service in the twenty-first century as it was one hundred years ago. But it is also more complex, with less clear direction, less obvious "right" courses of action, and dramatically increased uncertainty. Navigating effectively in this changing and turbulent world was the challenge of the past; it will be the challenge of the future as well.

Notes

1. Lecture by Vice Admiral Thad Allen, The Maxwell School of Citizenship and Public Affairs, Syracuse University, Syracuse, NY. November 11, 2004.

2. John Rohr, *To Run a Constitution: The Legitimacy of the Administrative State* (Lawrence: University Press of Kansas, 1986); see also Charles Goodsell, *The Case For Bureaucracy*, 2nd ed. (Chatham, N.J.: Chatham House Publishers), also comments by Hugh Heclo, second meeting of the Commission on the Executive Branch, University of Pennsylvania, October, 2004.

3. *Federalist Paper* 68. Reprinted in David H. Rosenbloom, Deborah Goldman, and Patricia Ingraham, eds., *Contemporary Public Administration* (New York: McGraw Hill, 1994), 62–65.

4. Stephen Skowronek, *Building a New American State: The Expansion of Administrative Capacities, 1877–1920* (New York: Cambridge University Press, 1982).

5. See the discussion in Ingraham, *Foundation of Merit,* chap. 2.

6. Quoted in Ingraham, *Foundation of Merit,* 20.

7. Frederick Mosher, *Democracy and the Public Service* (New York: Oxford University Press, 1968).

8. See Ezra Suleiman, ed., *Bureaucrats and Policy Making: A Comparative Overview* (New York: Holmes & Meier, 1985). See also Richard Stillman, *Preface to Public Administration: A Search for Themes and Direction* (New York: St. Martin's Press, 1991).

9. Norton E. Long, " Bureaucracy and Constitutionalism," *American Political Science Review* 46 (September 1952), 808-818. Reprinted in Rosenbloom, Goldman, and Ingraham, eds., *Contemporary Public Administration,* 70.

10. See Woodrow Wilson, "The Study of Administration," *Political Science Quarterly* 2 (June 1887), 200. For a more contemporary discussion, see Jameson Doig "If I See a Murderous Fellow Sharpening a Knife Cleverly . . . The Wilsonian Dichotomy and the Public Authority Tradition," *Public Administration Review* 43 (March–April 1983), 292–304.

11. James P. Pfiffner quoted in the "Report of the Task Force on Recruitment and Retention to the National Commission on the Public Service," in *Leadership for America: Rebuilding the Public Service* (Washington, D.C.: The Commission, 1989), 2:81.

12. For a more complete discussion of these strategies and of the relationship between the president and the career bureaucracy, see Ingraham, *Foundation of Merit,* chap. 6; and Aberbach and Rockman, *In the Web of Politics.*

13. Matthew Holden, quoted from notes of the Annenberg Commission meeting for the Institutions of American Democracy project, Philadelphia, March 2004.

14. Waldo, *Administrative State.*

15. U.S. Office of Personnel Management, *Federal Civilian Workforce Statistics as of September 2004.* Table 1, at http://www.opm.gov.feddata/Sept./04 (accessed March 2005).

16. U.S. Office of Personnel Management, *Federal Civilian Workforce Statistics Employment and Trends as of January 2004*. Table 2, at http://www.opm.gov /feddata/html/2004/january/jan04.pdf (accessed July 2004) and *Biography of an Ideal*.

17. All of these changes and others are discussed in Ingraham, *Foundation of Merit*.

18. U.S. General Accounting Office, *Senior Executive Service: Diversity Increased in the Past Decade* (Washington, D.C.: GAO, 2001).

19. Ibid.

20. National Academy of Public Administration, *The Twenty-first Century Federal Manager: A Study of Changing Roles and Competencies* (Washington, D.C.: NAPA, 2004), 39.

21. U.S. General Accounting Office, *Senior Executive Service*.

22. Heclo, *Government of Strangers*.

23. See Carolyn Ban and Patricia Ingraham, "Short-timers: Political appointees in the Reagan Administration," *Administration and Society* (Spring 1990), 106-124; and Patricia Ingraham, "Building Bridges or Burning Them? Political Appointees and the Career Bureaucracy," *Public Administration Review* 47 (September– October), 425-435. In 1989 and 2003, Blue Ribbon panels led by Paul Volcker examined the federal civil service and both recommended reform to the political management system. See National Commission on the Public Service (The Second Volcker Commission), *Urgent Business for America: Revitalizing the Federal Government for the 21st Century* (Washington, D.C.: The Brookings Institution, January 2003), and National Commission on the Public Service, *Leadership for America: Revitalizing the Public Service* (Washington, D.C.: National Commission, 1989).

24. The National Commission on the Public Service, 2003, p. 20.

25. Paul C. Light, *The New Public Service* (Washington, D.C.: The Brookings Institution, 2001).

26. U.S. Office of Personnel Management, *Biography of an Ideal*, 163–165.

27. National Academy of Public Administration, *The 21st Century Federal Manager: Final Report and Recommendations* (Washington, D.C.: NAPA, 2004), 27.

28. Ibid.

29. Partnership for Public Service, "Working for the Public," online at http//www .ourpublicservice.org (accessed January 27, 2004).

30. Jason Peckenpaugh "Army Contractors Earn Higher Salaries" at http://www .govexec.com.dailyfed/0701/072601p.1.htm (accessed August, 2004)

31. U.S. Bureau of Labor Statistics, *Union Membership* (2004), Table 3, union affiliation of employed wage and salary workers by occupation at http://stats.bls.gov/news .release/union2.t03.htm (accessed July 2004).

32. Ibid.

33. U.S. Office of Personnel Management, *What Do Federal Employees Say? Results from the Federal Human Capital Survey (2003)* at http://www.fhcs.opm.gov/fhcs_Report .txt. (accessed July, 2004).

34. U.S. Merit Systems Protection Board, *Issues of Merit* (Washington, D.C.: MSPB, May 2001), 3.

35. See, for example, Hal G. Rainey, *Understanding and Managing Public Organizations*, 3rd ed. (San Francisco: Jossey Bass, 2003), chap. 9.

36. The National Commission on the Public Service, *Urgent Business for America*.

37. From Ingraham, *Foundation of Merit*, 31–32.

38. James Thompson and Hal G. Rainey, *Modernizing Human Resource Management in the Federal Government: The IRS Model*, (Arlington, Va.: IBM Endowment for the Business of Government, 2003).

39. U.S. Office of Personnel Management, *Biography of an Ideal*.

40. U.S. Office of Personnel Management, *Federal Civilian Workforce Statistics Demographic Profile of the Federal Workforce as of September 2002*, at http://www.opm .gov/feddata/demograp/02demo.pdf (accessed July 2004).

41. The National Commission on the Public Service (the Second Volcker Commission) *Urgent Business for America: Revitalizing the Federal Government for the 21st Century* (Washington, D.C.: The Brookings Institution), 2003, p. 34.

42. Ibid.; see also U.S. Bureau of the Budget, *Report to the President on Government Contracting for Research and Development* (May 1962).

43. Paul C. Light, *The True Size of Government* (Washington, D.C.: The Brookings Institution, 1999).

44. Daily Briefing, *Government Executive* (Washington, D.C.: July 17 and July 26, 2001).

45. Daily Briefing, *Government Executive* (July 26, 2001).

46. Dan Guttman, "Governance by Contract: Constitutional Visions; Time for Reflection and Choice." *Public Contract Law Journal* 33 (Winter 2004), 321-360.

47. U.S. General Accounting Office, *Performance and Accountability Series. National Aeronautics and Space Administration* (January 2003), at http://www.gao.gov/pas /2003/d03114.pdf (accessed July 2004).

48. Barbara S. Romzek, and Melvin J. Dubnick, "Accountability in the Public Sector: Lessons from the Challenger Tragedy." *Public Administration Review* 47 (May–June 1987), 227-239.

49. U.S. Government Accountability Office, *Performance and Accountability*.

50. Partnership for Public Service, "Best Places to Work in the Federal Government, 2003," at www.bestplacestowork.org, November (accessed July 2004).

51. Kettl, Donald F. *The Transformation of Governance* (Washington, D.C.: The Brookings Institution, 2000).

52. James R. Thompson and Hal G. Rainey, *Modernizing Human Resource Management in the Federal Government: The IRS Model* (Washington, D.C.: The IBM Endowment for the Business of Government, April 2003).

53. Patricia W. Ingraham, "Striving for Balance: Reforms in Human Resource Management," in Ewan Ferlie, Christopher Pollitt, and Laurence Lynn, Jr., eds., *Handbook of Comparative Public Administration and Policy* (Oxford: Oxford University Press, forthcoming).

54. Patricia W. Ingraham and Heather Getha Taylor, "Lessons Learned from the Federal Demonstration Projects," manuscript under review.

55. John M. Gaus, Leonard D. White, and Marshall E. Dimock, eds. *The Frontiers of Public Administration* (Chicago: University of Chicago Press, 1936), 31.

Bibliography

Aberbach, Joel D., and Bert A. Rockman. *In the Web of Politics.* Washington, D.C.: The Brookings Institution, 2001.

Heclo, Hugh. *A Government of Strangers: Executive Politics in Washington.* Washington, D.C.: The Brookings Institution, 1977.

Ingraham, Patricia W. *The Foundation of Merit: Public Service in American Democracy.* Baltimore: The Johns Hopkins University Press, 1995.

U.S. Office of Personnel Management. *Biography of an Ideal: A History of the Federal Civil Service.* Washington, D.C.: U.S. Office of Personnel Management, 2003.

U.S. Office of Personnel Management. *A Fresh Start for Federal Pay: The Case for Modernization.* Washington, D.C.: Office of Personnel Management, 2002.

Van Riper, Paul. *A History of the United States Civil Service.* Evanston, Ill.: Row Peterson, 1958.

Waldo, Dwight. *The Administrative State.* New York: Ronald Press, 1948.

10

CAUGHT IN THE MIDDLE:
THE PRESIDENT, CONGRESS, AND
THE POLITICAL-BUREAUCRATIC SYSTEM

Barry R. Weingast

AMERICA IS GOVERNED BY A VAST FEDERAL BUREAU-cracy that makes policy decisions across a remarkable range of policy issues, including clean air, consumer protection, worker rights, social security, foreign policy, and protection from terrorism. The rise of the administrative state—government by bureaucracy—poses many questions for a democracy. How can 536 elected officials hope to influence tens of thousands of programs, each with many options, run by over a million bureaucrats supported by many million more contract workers? Are bureaucratic policy decisions in any sense responsive to the interests of the public?

Many provide negative answers to these questions, for example, arguing that bureaucrats are "unelected representatives" who make policy without being responsive to citizens or their political principals, Congress and the president. Others argue that the bureaucracy is uncontrollable and runaway.[1] Dodd and Schott, for example, argue that in many respects, the federal bureaucracy is, "a prodigal child. Although born of congressional intent, it has taken on a life of its own and has matured to a point where its muscle and brawn can be turned against its creator."[2]

Further, multiple and contradictory public perceptions exist about the bureaucracy. Perhaps the most common is that the bureaucracy is an overblown source of fat, living off the people that the agencies are nominally charged with serving. A second is that the president, qua chief executive, controls the bureaucracy.

The federal bureaucracy is embedded in the American separation of powers system, implying a complex set of political relationships that I call the political-bureaucratic system. This system shapes bureaucratic behavior and policy making. In a real sense, the bureaucracy is "caught in the middle" between Congress and the president. Although the executive departments and agencies are lodged within the executive branch, they are not under the full control of the president. They are also influenced by Congress, through the legislative, appropriations, and the oversight processes. While the agencies are largely created and funded by Congress, they are not handmaidens of the legislature. In short, the bureaucracy has multiple principals (or masters), and the architecture of America's political institutions explains why this is so. In the words of Aberbach and Rockman, bureaucrats are lodged "in the web of politics."[3]

The purpose of this chapter is to explain the logic of the political-bureaucratic system, including why the bureaucracy chooses one policy instead of another. In the process, it answers the above questions, explaining the sense in which elected officials control the bureaucracy. It will also explore various normative questions, such as how well this system works and what are its biases.

To begin, it is useful to ask why elected officials find it at all necessary to delegate authority to the executive agencies to make and carry out policy (the two often occur together, since operations and policy are, in practice, commonly intertwined). Delegation occurs because citizen demands on the government are so large and varied that elected officials alone cannot address them all. First and foremost, delegation economizes on the resources, time, and effort of elected officials. Additionally, many policy decisions require the development of expertise and specialized knowledge. Elected officials cannot develop these capabilities across so many different areas, and so they delegate these tasks to administrative agencies. All modern governments delegate to bureaucracies, whether the communist government of the former Soviet Union, a wide array of past and present authoritarian governments, or democratic governments. Bureaucracies are simply necessary to get done the wide range of the modern state's activities.

Still, not all policies are delegated. Historically, Congress has decided the projects built by the Corps of Engineers,[4] yet it does not decide the acceptable level of impurities in drinking water. What determines the degree of delegation? The literature about delegation provides an important principle about delegation: political officials know something about what they want to achieve—say clean air or a safe workplace—but they do not know the details of how to implement those goals. The uncertainty principle holds that, as the political officials' uncertainty increases relative to that of experts, they will delegate more discretion to the bureaucracy.[5]

Yet this reason for delegation—when elected officials do not have the expertise to make the desired policy decisions—creates a potential problem: delegation creates the risk of decisions that are unresponsive to elected officials' interests and thus to interests of the publics they represent. This problem is known as the political "control problem": how do elected officials in a democratic system delegate authority to a bureaucracy while ensuring that it remains responsive to them and, more generally, to the public?[6] This defines the control problem.

Delegation raises three separate impediments to bureaucratic control by elected officials. First, delegation creates the information problem noted above: that bureaucrats become the experts in their policy domain and can potentially use their information to serve their own goals rather than those of elected officials. Second, the "multiple principal" problem arises because bureaucrats serve not one master, but several in the form of the president, the House of Representatives, and the Senate; therefore, control of bureaucrats is problematic. These different actors typically have conflicting goals, implying that corrective legislation is difficult to the extent that the agency deviates from its legislative mandate in a way desired by one of these principals. Third, today's elected officials face the political turnover problem, the notion that others are likely to hold power in the future who will have different goals and who will attempt to alter an agency's policy. The risk of turnover means that today's officials will seek ways of locking in their policies by placing impediments to future policy changes.

Each of these problems is difficult, and in combination, they seem almost insurmountable. Yet, over the two centuries of the republic, elected officials have evolved a complex system for mitigating these control problems. Indeed, officials possess a range of tools for dealing with agencies, including using structure and process to constrain agency decision making and to bias it in favor of certain outcomes. In addition, elected officials possess a range of *ex post* reactions (those that occur after an agency has acted). Because bureaucrats seek to avoid adverse *ex post* reactions, these reactions provide bureaucrats with *ex ante* incentives (that is, those in place before an agency has acted) to serve the interests of elected officials.

In important respects, we get exactly the bureaucracy that elected officials desire.[7] These officials have resolved the control problem to a considerable extent. And yet the result is a peculiar political-bureaucratic system with considerable biases and problems. As a product of the American constitutional system, bureaucratic policy making reflects the flaws of the larger system.

This chapter will first build the tools to understand the political logic of the administrative state and then will turn to the larger questions about what type of system this is. The essay proceeds as follows. Section 2 discusses the importance of compromise for the goals of legislation. Section 3 explores the three problems of bureaucratic control. Section 4 explains the logic of the administrative state. Section 5 briefly mentions the evolution of this system over the past few decades. Section 6 then turns to the implications of this perspective for the larger issues.

Legislation Qua Compromise: Inconsistent Objectives

All legislation is the product of compromise among competing interests. Per the framers' design, members of Congress and the president rarely think with one mind about a given problem. Moreover, by design, legislation is hard to pass. Not only must legislation attain majorities in both Houses of Congress as well as the president's signature (subject to the veto-override provisions), but congressional rules and procedures imply a number of other veto gates that must be opened for legislation to pass, including relevant committees with policy jurisdiction, the Senate filibuster (granting a minority the ability to hold up legislation), the House Rules Committee, and so on. These rules and procedures imply that the president and many different legislators can hold up policy, and many use this to force compromise from others.

The fact of multiple-veto opportunities implies that the national government often faces "gridlock"; for large numbers of policy areas, no legislation can be passed.[8] Further, it implies that no single person in the legislative process can control the design of legislation; attempting to do so will just maintain the status quo as other players simply hold up the legislation. Multiple veto opportunities, then, mean that a wide variety of provisions must be added in order to get so many different legislators and the president to go along. Too often, players who possess the opportunity to veto legislation hold out for provisions that satisfy a narrow constituency, often in a manner that is inconsistent with the overall act's purpose.

This form of political compromise means that few major acts pursue an objective—such as clean air, consumer safety, occupational health, or homeland security—with a consistent purpose and with an efficient bureaucracy designed to pursue it. Instead, agencies are typically given vague mandates, required to follow complex procedures, and subjected to a considerable range of restrictions whose logic is not determined by the policy objective.

The savings and loan bailout in 1989 provides an illustration.[9] Prior to this legislation, savings and loans (S&Ls) were a separate category of banks that differed from institutions officially called banks.[10] A flawed regulatory system, combined with financial problems among savings and loans, led to exploding S&L debt. In most other industries, these firms would have been forced out of business. But banking is special in several senses, largely because of the complex web of regulatory mechanisms, one piece of which is deposit insurance. Because so many people lost their savings when banks failed during the Great Depression, the government created deposit insurance, guaranteeing that it would bail out ailing banks and insure bank deposits. This system worked fine when only a few banks failed at any given time; the regulators used their funds to take over the bank, infuse cash, and find another bank to purchase or merge with the ailing bank. When many banks have problems simultaneously, this can become quite expensive.

The huge rise in interest rates created immense problems for the savings and loan industry in the mid-1980s. Because their deposits were short-term, they rose with interest rates; but because interest on their assets—by design, disproportionately home loans—rose only slowly, a great many S&Ls faced financial problems simultaneously. These financial problems would continue to mount quickly unless ailing banks were closed or taken over by the regulators and infused with new cash. Economists in 1985 estimated the problem at $12 billion. Too many ailing banks caused the system to run out of funds. Lack of funds implied that the problem was that the regulatory system could not take over ailing banks, allowing ailing savings and loans to keep their doors open despite losing more and more money.[11]

Members of Congress first proposed legislation in 1986 to infuse the system with cash and stop its mounting losses. But representatives of constituency interests that sought other goals held up the legislation in both the House and the Senate. Representatives in the House used this legislation to pass new housing benefits, while senators used it to pass new banking regulations having nothing to do with the savings and loan problem. Although the House and Senate each passed a version of the legislation to resolve the growing S&L crisis, they failed to pass legislation because they could not reconcile their differences on the issues added on. This failure delayed the first infusion of new cash into the industry by a year, allowing losses to mount.

In 1987 Congress did pass legislation. But it was not until the problem got considerably larger—then estimated to be over $100 billion—that Congress passed a serious bailout bill in 1989. Amazingly, despite the immense expense, here too congressional interests used this bill to pursue other goals—such as housing and urban development—thereby significantly increasing the bailout's cost. Because Congress failed to deal swiftly with this problem, it mushroomed to 30 times the figure in 1985, well over $300 billion.

Environmental laws provide another illustration.[12] The overall purpose of the Clean Air Act of 1970 was to provide the basis for achieving and maintaining clean air by regulating sources of pollution, such as businesses and motor vehicles. One issue on which the House, Senate, and president differed was whether areas that were above the minimal regulatory levels would have to remain at those high levels—that is, prevent significant deterioration in air quality—or if they would be allowed to increase pollution levels as long as they remained above the minimum standards. In the end, the latter view won out. Although the legislation provided for some elements of clean air, it allowed significant deterioration in regions above the minimal standards.

As another illustration, consider the landmark 1964 Civil Rights Act.[13] The principal purpose was redressing racial discrimination, especially in the South, where racism was institutionalized through the so-called "Jim Crow" system. White southerners in Congress sought to protect their system by fighting the legislation with every means available. In previous years, southerners had long used various congressional procedures, such as the Senate filibuster, to prevent any significant civil rights legislation. Often called the "longest debate," the filibuster and the struggle to overcome it were the principal political event in passing the 1964 Act;[14] it remains one of the central dramas in all of congressional history.

To break the filibuster—at that time, requiring two-thirds of all Senators—necessitated that civil rights supporters among northern Democrats gain the support of most Republicans. Although in 1964 there were some liberal and moderate Republicans, most were conservative and opposed increasing national government regulation of the economy. Interestingly, their support was in part garnered by mitigating the impact of the act on the North, clearly inconsistent with the overall goals of eliminating racial discrimination. Through a large series of small amendments, the Republicans slowly focused the legislation on the official, *de jure* system of discrimination throughout the South.

Finally, consider homeland security.[15] The overall purpose of these measures passed in the wake of the attacks of September 11, 2001, is to protect the country against terrorism. The legislation pursuing this objective also adds considerable new pork barrel spending, much of which is only peripherally related to security. Moreover, by casting the homeland security net as widely as possible, the president has used the umbrella of security to centralize and reorganize a remarkably wide range of agencies whose mandates only tangentially deal with security.[16] The president has been able to reorient many of these agencies away from their social mandates (which he disapproves) in favor of providing tasks related to security. And as with the savings and loan example, this legislation contains several provisions having little to do with homeland security. For example, the legislation contained retroactive liability protection for the pharmaceutical industry, effectively disrupting a series of recent class action suits. It also extended liability protection to the companies that provide airport screening. Finally, the legislation establishes a new homeland security research center, designating fifteen criteria, for which the only qualifying institution is Texas A&M University.

Conclusion

To summarize, the complexities of the legislative process means that the policy goals of each agency are complex and not straightforward. The multiple vetoes inherent in the legislative process empower representatives favoring a wide range of interest groups and constituencies, and they use their legislative power to insist that the legislation contain benefits for them, often at the expense of the legislation's overall goals. Because no one interest can prevail, legislation typically includes pieces attempting to pursue different and often inconsistent goals.

Three Impediments to Bureaucratic Control

Three fundamental problems plague political officials in their attempts to control the bureaucracy: the information problem, the multiple principal problem, and the political turnover problem.

The Information Problem

The sheer size and complexity of modern governmental bureaucracy make it difficult for political officials to have a command of what the bureaucracy is doing, let alone have the ability to guide each bureaucracy in its various policy choices. Thousands of different agencies exist, most of which deal with multiple problems, each with a wide range of policy options. Most of these problems are complex, requiring expertise just to understand what options are available, let alone which is best for America. Many scholars have concluded that the sheer complexity alone makes oversight and control impossible.[17] Clarkson and Muris, for example, argue with respect to the Federal Trade Commission (FTC):

> The ability of Congress to monitor individual FTC activities is effectively limited. Yet . . . even with its most effective tools, Congress can redirect resources into or away from specific programs only after detailed analysis at the level beyond the institutional competence of Congress except on an, at most, occasional project. . . . Oversight and ad hoc monitoring seldom influence Commission activities.[18]

The scope of the bureaucracy and its complex tasks make it difficult for political officials and their staffs to master all that government agencies are doing.

Scope and complexity alone are not the sole aspects of the information problem. These problems combine with another. The agents (political appointees and career bureaucrats who run the agency) may have preferences about the policies within their jurisdiction that differ significantly from those of their political principals. Agency expertise combines with the agency's potentially different preferences to create massive problems for political officials who are, by definition, not experts in these policies. Put simply, experts can potentially use their knowledge to bias policy decisions in ways that are difficult for their political principals to monitor.

For example, suppose bureaucrats at the Environmental Protection Agency (EPA) are pro-environment. This policy bias might lead them to avoid evaluating certain options not favored by environmentalists, such as incentive-based or market-based policies; or, such evaluations may be conducted in a way that biases choice away from these options, which are branded as unworkable or too expensive.

The very task of the bureaucracy to become experts makes an agency's strategic use of its expertise difficult to combat. Worse still, students of bureaucracy argue that elected officials are more likely to delegate the greater the uncertainty over policy.[19] Greater policy uncertainty implies greater returns to expertise, making delegation more attractive to elected officials who cannot make such investments. This motivation for delegation, however, necessarily implies that the information problem is inherent in delegation.

The Multiple Principal Problem

The president and members of Congress typically disagree about policy. This implies they also differ in their evaluation of an agency's performance and hence in the directions they would like to see the agency alter its policy.

As noted in the previous section, the legislation that creates a new bureaucracy, delegates a new task to a bureaucracy, or modifies an existing mandate is necessarily a compromise among the House, the Senate, and the president. In general, each sought something different for this bureaucracy, and none got its way. The legislation instead represents a compromise among the goals of these three sets of actors. Each agency therefore has multiple principals, each with its own preferences.

The policy disagreements among a bureaucracy's political principals create another control problem. Suppose the agency decides to deviate from the policy mandated in the legislation, for example, by moving in the direction preferred by the president. In principle, political officials could pass a new law forcing the agent to move back to the original mandate, but the president has no incentive to agree to it since the agency's deviation makes him or her better off. Moreover, this same logic holds if the agency moves in the direction preferred by Congress and away from that of the president.

The difficulty with passing new legislation creates the possibility of agency drift—the ability of the agency to move policy away from the original legislation.[20] As long as the agency moves in a way that makes at least one of these principal actors—the House, the Senate, or the president—better off, then corrective legislation cannot take place.

Agency drift creates a dilemma for political officials, for it means that the agency, not they, picks the policy. Although one principal is better off *ex post*, it is the bureaucracy, not political officials, who choose which. All three sets of actors are therefore better off if they can devise a way to prevent agency drift.

The multiple principal problem varies with political circumstances. Divided government (when each of the two parties holds at least one of the House, Senate, and presidency) generally implies large divergence of policy preferences, and hence greater potential for agency drift. United government (when one party holds all three) generally means less disagreement. Yet even with united government, the degree of disagreement varies with administrations. At present, for example, there seems to be a relatively high degree of common interest between President Bush and the Republican-dominated Congress, but there was much less during the Carter administration, when Democrats controlled the presidency and the Congress.

The Political Turnover Problem

No group of politicians has a lock on political power.[21] Elections, changing public opinion, and changing political fortunes imply political change. With these changes come political turnover, which brings to power new political officials whose preferences diverge from those of their predecessors (studies show that preference change among members of Congress arises far more from membership turnover than from existing members changing their minds).[22]

New political officials with policy preferences that differ from their predecessors will use all available tools to influence bureaucratic policy in directions they prefer. By definition, this implies moving policy away from that of their predecessors. Political turnover therefore raises the problem of political drift, the notion that political officials with new preferences will seek to move agency policies away from those set by their predecessors.[23]

Political drift creates a problem for today's political officials who want to insulate their policies from it. This problem means that today's political officials will seek ways to raise the costs to future politicians of meddling with the bureaucracy so as to change its course.[24] In particular, they will seek ways to lock in their policies and insulate them from the influence of future political officials.

Implications

Political officials seeking to control the bureaucracy face three separate problems. Each one alone is difficult, but in combination, they imply massive problems for monitoring and control of agency policy making by political officials. Without solutions to these problems, elected officials cannot ensure that the bureaucracy implements the policies they design.

The Political-Bureaucratic System's Solution to the Control Problems

Although elected officials face multiple impediments to control of the bureaucracy, all is not hopeless. Before examining how elected officials mitigate or solve the control problem, some general theoretical propositions are in order.

First, as Banks and I theorize, in areas where elected officials view control over policy as critical, yet they cannot expect to control an agency, they are far less likely to create it in the first place: after all, if control is critical but problematic, the enacting coalition cannot ensure the agency will implement the desired policies.[25]

This principle has two implications. First, Congress will fail to address some policies because members of Congress cannot solve the control problem. Second, if elected officials could not in general solve the control problem, the federal bureaucracy and hence the national government would be considerably smaller. Put another way, a necessary condition for the growth of the national government in the twentieth century, and especially since the early 1960s, is that elected officials devised means to control the bureaucracy.

The second and more important proposition is that political officials have a number of tools and procedures with which they can influence bureaucratic agency choice. Consider the problem of agency drift. Agency drift is especially problematic when an agency is able to conspire with a set of constituents or interest groups to present a movement in policy as a fait accompli, with the interest groups helping to prevent elected officials from reacting.

My third proposition is that underlying the multiple principal problem is the notion that coalitions in American politics are ephemeral; they are difficult if not impossible to form again in the future. The key for the enacting coalition, then, is to create a set of *ex ante* procedures that make it difficult for an agency to drift away from the desired policy. We have already discussed the uncertainty principle; often, elected officials do not know the precise policies they want. Yet they typically do know what mix of interest groups and constituents they seek to benefit. The decision of what mix of interests to foster underlies the passage of all legislation.

Political Tools for the Control Problem

Ideally, elected officials seek means of control that do not require their own time, effort, and resources. They do so through a mix of incentives and constraints. Consider first the problem of incentives. To the extent that political officials create an incentive system based on *ex post* consequences, they provide agency decision makers with *ex ante* incentives to follow the interests of political officials.

"Fire alarm" oversight is oversight triggered in response to a constituent sounding an alarm to members of Congress that something is going wrong with some bureaucracy. This type of oversight differs from "police patrol" oversight in which congressional committees plan in advance to investigate an agency. Fire alarm oversight is an important aspect of bureaucratic control.[26] I have emphasized the problem of thousands of agencies, each with dozens or more decisions, with each decision complex and with multiple options. Viewed from this perspective, the task of overseeing and controlling the bureaucracy seems impossible—even with 10,000 staff, Congress simply cannot do it. In one sense, this is correct. Members of Congress simply cannot effectively monitor *all* that happens in the bureaucracy. Even so, studies of oversight emphasize that members of Congress do develop expertise in the areas of their committee's jurisdiction and, further, that they do conduct considerable oversight.[27]

But in another sense, the question of whether elected officials actively oversee the bureaucracy is not the key question: to some extent, they do not have to know. Elected officials need not be the principal monitors of agencies, if their constituencies are. Constituencies have the biggest incentives to monitor an agency, and they typically have close ties to their elected officials.

The success of *ex post* incentives for agencies depends critically on fire alarm oversight. Political officials simply cannot investigate all agencies each year, let alone solve the information problem that led to delegation in the first place. They therefore rely critically on their constituents to sound fire alarms when something is going wrong. These alarms bring the attention and action of political officials when needed. Of course, something going "wrong" here has a deep political meaning rather than an objective one—it is "wrong" in the sense of whom elected officials seek to benefit. The main conclusion is this: if the consequences of fire alarm–triggered reactions are sufficient, then agency decision makers will seek to avoid them, and hence do the bidding of political officials.

Another avenue of influence concerns unilateral action by the president, for example, through issuing executive orders, national security directives, and executive agreements.[28] Executive orders allow the president to issue directives to particular agencies and to all agencies at once. Moreover, these orders have become more common over time. Executive orders can reorganize an agency or policy area, including subjugating bureaus to others. These orders can also force the entire bureaucracy to take certain actions. They have been used to affect policies as diverse as ordering nondiscrimination by the government, the handling of national emergencies, wetlands regulation, government-owned corporations, and government procurement. Moreover, every president since Richard Nixon has used executive orders as a means of forcing agencies to consider additional aspects of their proposed regulations, thus slowing down the process of new regulations. In perhaps one of the more dramatic bureaucratic moves by a president, Nixon used an executive order to create the Environmental Protection Agency (EPA). Unilateral action provides the president with a means of forcing agencies to adjust both their procedures and their policy choices.

The political tools available to elected officials for mitigating agency drift fall into two categories. *Ex ante* constraints are those in place at the time of an agency's creation or that were put in place in the agency's enabling legislation. These constraints affect an agency's decisions in predictable ways, for example, by preventing it from taking certain actions or making some types of actions more difficult for the agency than others. *Ex post* controls are those actions and reactions that occur after an agency makes its decision. To the extent that agency officials anticipate likely reactions, they affect agency decisions.

Ex Ante Constraints

When formulated properly, *ex ante* constraints influence an agency's decision making in ways desired by the enacted coalition. These constraints make it less likely that an agency will deviate from the policies desired by that coalition.

The Administrative Procedure Act (APA) of 1946, as amended by other legislation and interpreted in a wide range of court cases, lays out a set of general procedures by which agencies must make their decisions.[29] These procedures are designed to satisfy the due process clauses of the Fifth and Fourteenth Amendments to the Constitution and require that agency actions be neither "arbitrary" nor "capricious."

Specifically, the APA (as amended and interpreted) requires:

- An agency cannot simply announce a new policy without warning. Instead, it must give "notice" that it will consider an issue.
- The agency must solicit "comments," allowing all interested parties to communicate their views.
- Agencies must allow "participation" in the decision-making processes.
- The agency must explicitly deal with all the evidence presented to it and must provide a rational link between the evidence and its decisions.
- The agency must execute these procedures without prejudice or bias in favor of any policy.
- *Ex parte* contacts (those outside official procedures) between the agency and any interested parties are prohibited.
- Agency procedures and decisions are subject to the Freedom of Information Act (FOIA) and the Government in the Sunshine Act (GITSA), which require that all agency evidence and procedures be open and available.

Each of these procedures has a direct rationale in due process rights of individuals and satisfies basic fairness criteria. If an agency exhibits prejudice before hearing the evidence, then this is evidence that the official proceedings are a charade. If an agency cannot provide a rationale for its decisions based on all the evidence, then its decisions are arbitrary and capricious. If it prohibits participation of interested parties, it both denies basic rights of interested parties and risks failing to collect information of direct relevance to its decisions.

Each of these procedures also has a profound political implication relevant for the control problem. First and foremost, procedural due process of this sort ensures that all major policy decisions are conducted in the open and, further, that they take time, sometimes a long time. Openness and deliberateness (if not outright delay) prevent agencies from presenting political officials with fait accompli policy changes that are engineered in secret between the agency and a set of interests that differs from those that political officials sought to benefit. These procedures ensure advance warning of important policy changes, both to political officials and to their constituents. This allows constituents to monitor agency proceedings and to activate fire alarms if necessary.

Second, the constraints on participation ensure that the agency collects all the politically relevant information necessary for political officials should their attention be required: Who are the interested parties? How are they affected? How do they feel about the proposed agency decisions? What are the alternatives that the agency failed to consider or choose?

These procedures have several political advantages for elected officials. They ensure that agencies collect all this information in the normal course of their operation. By making this information publicly available, these procedures ensure that the constituents of elected officials have all the information they need, and can pull fire alarms or take an agency to court when necessary. Finally, they ensure that, should the time and energy of political officials be necessary, these officials and their staffs have all the relevant information.

Third, the entire set of procedures—notice, comment, participation, rational decision making—provide elected officials with numerous opportunities along the way to signal dissatisfaction to an agency if agency proceedings appear to be going in a direction not favored by these officials. This allows agency decision makers to gauge the likely political reaction to their decisions, in particular, letting them know when to expect a costly political reaction.

Fourth, these procedures work as a gauge of political interest and controversiality, providing elected officials with the political information they need to know before intervening. Finally, the courts play a central role in enforcing these procedures. For example, any evidence of *ex parte* contact between an agency and an interested party provides courts with easy grounds for reversing an agency decision. The same outcome is inevitable if an agency fails to observe the procedures prescribed for it in the laws it administers or that it has created for itself. Because this reversal forces an agency to start the proceeding over, it is very costly. Of course, enfranchising the courts allows them to exercise a degree of policy discretion.[30]

For example, reflecting the Reagan administration's antigovernment, anti–economic regulation views, new administrators in several agencies simply announced that they were rescinding a regulation recently promulgated by their predecessors. This change in policy, announced by new agency leaders, failed to follow the agency procedures and was thus reversed by the courts as arbitrary and capricious.[31]

In short, these procedures greatly reduce an agency's information advantage over its political sponsors and constituents. Further, these procedures greatly increase the efficacy of *ex post* sanctions. The incentive effect of swifter and more accurately applied sanctions causes bureaucrats to be more reluctant to deviate from the policy preferences of their political overseers. In short, administrative procedures have political implications aimed at mitigating the control problem.[32]

In addition to the general procedural prescriptions imposed by the APA (as amended and interpreted) on virtually all administrative agencies, enabling legislation for new agencies or new mandates for existing agencies have often imposed a wide range of procedures in specific policy areas designed to have political effects.

"DECK STACKING." Political officials design many specific procedures to "stack the deck" in favor of specific constituents who are the intended beneficiaries of the bargain struck by the coalition that created the agency. For example, legislation often assigns the burden of proof. This allocation dramatically affects decisions by biasing decisions against the party that bears the burden. Under the original regulation of airline competition by the Civil Aeronautics Board (CAB), the agency protected incumbent firms from competitive entry by firms wishing to charge lower prices. Potential entrants held the burden of proof that their entry would not harm existing air carriers. Since they sought entry to charge lower prices as a means of capturing business, entry provided direct proof of intent to harm, thus making it impossible to gain permission to enter. The Airline Deregulation Act of 1978, seeking to increase competition in the airline industry, reversed this burden by requiring the CAB to authorize entry unless it was not consistent "with public convenience and necessity," benefiting new entrants and consumers.

The Toxic Substance Control Act (TSCA) provides another illustration. As originally proposed in 1971, this bill would have created a regulatory mechanism for chemicals paralleling that of the Food and Drug Administration's (FDA) regulation of drugs. Before marketing a new drug, pharmaceutical manufacturers must first prove that it is both safe and efficacious: the burden of proof lies with the manufacturer. The original proposal of TSCA assigned the burden of proof on chemical firms, requiring that they prove their product safe prior to introduction in the market. This proposal would not pass, so the proponents weakened the regulatory mechanism to allow firms to market a new chemical unless, during a brief notification period, the EPA moved to promulgate a test rule or to ban or restrict the chemical. Vastly fewer new chemicals would have been introduced had manufacturers been assigned the burden to prove their products safe.

Various regulatory areas provide for subsidized participation of groups likely to be underrepresented in the process. Small businesses and consumers often fall in this category. A great many regulatory agencies, for example, have special provisions to ease the regulatory burden and ease the cost of participation of small businesses. Similarly, at one time, eleven different agencies had funds for representation of consumer groups, including the Federal Trade Commission, the National Highway Traffic Safety Administration, the EPA, the Consumer Produce Safety Commission, the CAB, and the Nuclear Regulatory Commission.[33]

The advent of Environmental Impact Statements (EISs) provides another illustration. As a political force, the environmental movement gained ground only slowly in the mid- to late 1960s, then growing enormously in 1969 and

1970. These years witnessed the creation of the Environmental Protection Agency (EPA) as well as the National Environmental Protection Act (NEPA) and the Clean Air Act. A major problem for environmentalists concerned how to improve the quality of the government's decisions concerning the environment. NEPA provided one answer, by forcing all governmental agencies whose decisions affected the environment to fill out EISs. Along with EISs came a range of procedures of how to do them, including the notice, comment, and participation.

NEPA therefore enfranchised new environmental interests to participate in a wide range of agency proceedings, affording them opportunities not only to have their views heard, but also to impose costs on agencies through delay. Because delay is costly, the new EIS affected many agencies' strategy: one way to avoid long delays imposed by environmentalist suits was to take greater account of their interests in agency decisions.

Nuclear power regulation illustrates the effect of the new EIS procedures. NEPA granted environmentalists important new procedural tools with which to influence agency decision making.[34] Before building a nuclear power plant—that is, a plant using nuclear power to generate electricity—electric power providers had first to gain approval to construct and then to operate a nuclear power plant. The complexities and dangers of nuclear power combined with a complex regulatory process to make this process very expensive and time consuming. The environmentalists intervened in many proposed plants, seeking to improve the environmental quality of the design and operation or to halt the process altogether. Linda R. Cohen shows that, although the environmentalists lost virtually all their contentions, they were able to impose substantial delay, which raised the costs of nuclear power sufficiently that utilities simply stopped ordering these types of plants.[35] The EIS process gave environmentalists an important new forum in which to raise more questions about the design and therefore to impose further delays. The nuclear power case illustrates how Congress successfully used the EIS procedure to afford environmentalists a range of regulatory proceedings.

Another form of procedure commonly used in legislation concerns agenda control, that is, affecting an agency's ability to control what policies it considers. If the coalition producing a statute reflects a diversity of conflicting interests, then the statute will often seek to mirror these pressures before the agency. Thus, the enabling legislation may charge an agency with benefiting a constituency, but subject to constraints that are influenced by another constituency. For example, Congress charged the Occupational Safety and Health Administration (OSHA) with regulating the workplace to benefit labor. Yet it also placed constraints on OSHA that limited the agency's ability to control its agenda: prior to writing a health regulation, OSHA needed what the legislation termed a "criteria document." These documents were to be produced by another new agency, the National Institute of Occupational Safety and Health (NIOSH), that was to be located in another Cabinet department altogether (Congress put OSHA in the Department of Labor and NIOSH in what was then the Department of Health, Education, and Welfare). This separation made NIOSH subject to a different set of political pressures, implying far less influence from organized labor than if it were simply a bureau located within OSHA.

Jonathan Macey observes that elected officials can influence the subsequent politics in their design decisions about whether to combine several tasks within a single agency or to separate these tasks into different agencies.[36] In the case of regulation of various financial markets, Congress both segmented the markets (e.g., strictly separating banks from securities firms from insurance firms) and designed separate agencies for each of the major elements. Insurance firms, banks, savings and loan, and securities firms all faced major prohibitions on conducting business in any of these other categories. Further, each market segment was regulated by an agency devoted solely to that industry. In contrast, with the rise of trucks as an important factor in surface transportation, Congress combined their regulation with railroad regulation by the Interstate Commerce Commission (ICC).

As Macey argues, the difference in political behavior of these regulatory agencies was entirely predictable. Firms in each of the financial markets, regulated by its own agency, came to be a dominant political force in their regulatory agency's decisions and hence the principal beneficiary of regulation. In contrast, trucking and railroad interests both had influence with the ICC, and these two different segments of the industry were forced to compromise on regulatory mechanisms. By controlling the structure and scope of the regulatory plan, elected officials can directly affect the distribution of regulatory benefits.

INSTITUTIONALIZED PRESIDENCY. Many of the processes of control are biased in favor of Congress; this institution predominates both in the appropriations process and in the oversight process.[37] Presidents are not without their own resources, however. As Terry Moe argues, presidents face a mismatch of expectations and capabilities.[38] Citizens look to the president as the national leader, as the person in charge; and yet the president's resources simply cannot match these expectations, in large part because presidents must share power with Congress and because the bureaucracy is so vast. (See Matthew Dickinson in this volume for a more detailed discussion of this point.)

In the face of this mismatch, all modern presidents have attempted to enhance their power, in part through institutionalizing their office and expanding those parts of the federal structure most closely allied with them, including the White House Office, the Executive Office of the President, and the Office of Management and Budget.

Moe has questioned why the president relies more on close advisors, say in the White House, than on the government's experts in the bureaucracy. After all, the latter are the policy experts, while the former are generalists, typically without a level of policy expertise that matches that of the bureaucracy. Moe's answer fits with the information problem above: the bureaucracy may have greater expertise, but it lacks loyalty to the president. Regarding the information problem: because most bureaucrats' goals differ from those of the president, they have a strategic incentive to manipulate the information provided to the chief executive. Presidents end up relying on those close to them because those advisors are loyal; in particular, their preferences closely match those of the president they serve, so the president does not have to worry about manipulation. According to Moe, presidents willingly trade off knowledge and expertise for action that is compatible with their goals.

The main implication is that modern presidents, though in varying degrees, have sought, through use of the White House–controlled offices and a strategy of placing loyalist political appointees in key agencies (see below), to build up the institutional portion of the bureaucracy most loyal to them, allowing them to develop policy independent of the career bureaucracy and to guide it to implement this policy.

APPOINTMENTS. Finally, another category of *ex ante* controls is the appointment of senior agency officials. The president is clearly the most visible actor in the appointments process, but recent studies show the significant influence of Congress.[39] The Senate, which must approve the president's nominees, is particularly influential. Because a nomination rejection is very costly to the nominee, it becomes costly to the president. Not only is a rejection a source of embarrassment, it makes many potential nominees for future positions more reluctant to let their names be put forward.

We should also distinguish between the president's appointees to the White House Office (WHO) and those to the executive branch more generally. Loyalty to the president is far more characteristic of members of the WHO. The Congress has much less influence here: these are the president's people, and most of these appointments do not require Senate confirmation. The president's influence is less certain over appointments to the executive branch beyond the White House. First, the Senate must confirm hundreds of these appointments. Second, many political appointees to agencies reflect a political exchange, whether explicit or implicit. The electoral support of particular interest groups may be assured when the president appoints an agency leader sympathetic to their interests. Practically, the role of Congress and interest groups means that, although leaders of agencies reflect the president's overall priorities, a great many may diverge from the president in their policy concerns. (A main component of the "administrative presidency strategy," described by Richard Nathan and by several authors in this volume, is the appointment of administration "loyalists" to top positions in the agencies and is part of an effort by several recent presidents to counter this tendency for appointees to diverge from the president's priorities.)[40]

This divergence of interest between the president and many agency heads also hinders unity and policy coordination within the executive branch and especially with the president. The lack of unity also opens the executive branch to congressional influence.

Ex Post *Controls*

Ex post controls are means by which elected officials react after the fact to bureaucratic decisions. As noted above, to the extent that these reactions are predictable, they set up an *ex ante* incentive system. A wide variety of reactions are important for agency decision making.

LEGISLATION. Legislation can dramatically modify an agency's mandate and decision-making procedures. If an agency moves in a direction not desired by elected officials, legislation can correct this problem. Moreover, legislative redirection typically adversely affects the agency, so agencies seek to avoid situations that put them at risk of legislative correction.

The force of new legislation makes it a powerful tool. Yet, as noted, the circumstances under which it is feasible are rare. Legislation is therefore used only occasionally. Nonetheless, as John Ferejohn and Charles Shipan show, the threat of legislation is sometimes sufficient to force an agency to adjust.[41] This occurs because no one knows in advance how hard members of Congress will push the legislation. Because there is some chance that legislation will pass, many agencies will take corrective action to forestall action.

OVERSIGHT. An important means available to both Congress and the president is official oversight—investigations into agency process and decision making. Oversight includes many types, including periodic audit-like investigations that occur every few years; and oversight in response to a political problem or fire alarm.[42] Moreover, Congress conducts oversight directly through hearings, while both the Office of Management and Budget (OMB) and the Government Accountability Office (GAO, formerly called the General Accounting Office) oversee, investigate, and otherwise watch agencies for the president and Congress respectively. Studies show that oversight is not random, but most common in areas in which members of Congress have policies they seek to advocate or in which their policy preferences directly conflict with those of the executive branch.[43]

The existence of periodic audit-like oversight means that bureaucrats in every agency know that, every few years, they will be subject to public scrutiny and evaluation. This process typically includes the ability of affected parties and various political constituencies to provide their input and signal problems as they see it. Moreover, as Aberbach emphasizes, members of Congress holding oversight hearings is a signal of interest.[44] Not only does this force the agency to defend its actions in public, but the signal suggests that congressional meddling might follow if the agency fails to take account of congressional interests. This forum gives political officials the opportunity to make life difficult for the agency. Corrective legislation may be impossible, but sustained, intense hearings and accompanying tasks (such as answering in great detail a series of questions about actions) impose immense burdens on agencies and their leaders.[45]

The typical political appointee to an agency serves on the order of two years. Many come from the private sector, seeking to enhance their reputations and their professional standing. Successful public service allows an appointee to move up both the private and public employment hierarchies. The intense political scrutiny of prolonged oversight can be quite dangerous for political appointees because it attracts political attention, often quite negative and therefore associating the appointee with trouble rather than success. Further, sustained oversight takes an appointee away from policy duties, making the appointee much less likely to succeed in accomplishing his or her political goals. A prolonged congressional investigation may prevent an appointee from accomplishing any goals while in Washington. Aberbach and Rockman report for example, that political appointees report considerable "micromanagement" by both the OMB and Congress.[46]

Seen as a form of harassment, *ex post* oversight provides political appointees with incentives to avoid actions that trigger the close scrutiny of fire-alarm oversight. This in turn implies that agency leaders will seek to avoid decisions that cause constituents to pull fire alarms. Put differently, the best way for political appointees to avoid harassment from prolonged investigations is to serve constituents of elected officials.

APPROPRIATIONS. Agency budgets are formulated through a complex congressional appropriations process that has long been a source of influence on bureaucratic decision making.[47] Congress and the president regularly reward programs that they favor with expanding budgets and punish those they dislike with contracting or slowly expanding budgets. Similarly, presidents use the OMB to cut programs they do not favor.

Elected officials can also earmark funds for specific activities; they can also insert provisions that prevent an agency from spending any money on other activities. For example, as Congress turned more conservative regarding the consumer protection activities of the Federal Trade Commission (FTC) in the late 1970s and 1980s, it used the appropriations process to prohibit the commission from spending any funds on several of its ongoing investigations.

Here too, anticipated budgetary reactions provide *ex ante* incentives. Ambitious agency leaders who seek to make a name for themselves as successful innovators must not only avoid the disfavor that impels elected officials to block their initiatives, but also must garner their active support through budget increases. Because elected officials reward those agencies that serve their political interests, systematic budgetary increases and decreases provide leaders with incentives to serve elected officials' constituents.

Of course, all this works best when Congress and the president have a working compromise concerning which interests they seek to benefit. When they are at loggerheads, seeking to benefit different constituencies in an agency's environment, this process works less well. Yet even there, the process is not as crippling as it is with the gridlock implied by the difficulty of passing new legislation. Budgets must be passed every year, and this has forced Congress and the president to arrive at working compromises for budgetary decisions when they disagree. One aspect of the process of compromise is that the president and Congress engage in negotiation and exchange, whereby they each agree to give up something in areas they care less about in exchange for greater control in areas they care more about.

To summarize, the force of this subsection is that *ex post* reactions provide a powerful set of tools for elected officials to control agency decision making and what agencies do. By definition of the delegation motivation, elected officials cannot know in sufficient detail how to direct bureaucratic decisions and hence to specify in advance what bureaucrats should do to serve their interests.

Conclusions

Because problems of bureaucratic compliance are ubiquitous, elected officials have evolved a complex political-bureaucratic system to help them control bureaucratic policy making. Elected officials utilize a range of *ex ante* controls, including general procedures (such as those contained in the APA) and specific procedures in enabling legislation. Often times, this legislation is designed to stack the deck in favor of particular interests and against others. A variety of *ex post* controls are also useful. These include traditional oversight, fire alarm oversight, the appropriations process, and unilateral presidential action. In a real sense, bureaucratic policy choice is responsive to the interests of elected officials.[48]

This section has emphasized political control in the context of regulatory policy. Other types of agencies exist, including service agencies, such as the Social Security Administration, and procurement agencies, such as those within the Department of Defense. Different agency settings have different types of politics, yet in each case, elected officials face a similar control problem. The mix of political tools used in these contexts often differs from regulation, but the goals and outcomes are similar.

Evolution of the Political-Bureaucratic System, 1980–Present

This section will briefly explore the evolution of two aspects of the political-bureaucratic system: the rise of extremists in politics, and the rise of a more partisan and polarized Congress.

Extremists

A major change in American politics over the last several decades is the rise of increasingly special interests, focused on a single issue. When V. O. Key and others wrote during the mid-twentieth century about interest groups, they had three main chapters: one each on business, labor, and agriculture.[49] These groups were large and encompassing, and therefore required compromise in order to advocate particular policies. In modern America, most issues have several interest groups, sometimes competing, sometimes cooperating. As the government has come to deal with a great many more issues over the last fifty years, active interests have become on average more extreme, meaning that many come from the end of the distribution of political opinion rather than the center.

At the same time, money has become more important in politics and political campaigns, and the money tends to be generated by interests who feel strongest about an issue. Here too, those interests tend to be toward the end of the political distribution rather than the middle.

Both changes have made elite politics, especially that of elected officials, more polarized and extreme. Active interests who debate particular issues tend now to come from extremes—black hats and white hats, as Morris Fiorina terms them.[50] Indeed, one of the principal observations in the so-called "culture wars" is the notion that America can be divided into two hostile political camps without a political center.[51]

As discussed above, the political-bureaucratic system rewards active interests. These interests have the ability to monitor agencies; to develop close connections with members of Congress, president, and the parties; and to sound fire alarms. Because active interests are more likely to be influential in politics, the growing polarization implies that the bureaucratic system will serve the extremes more over time.

A More Polarized and Partisan Congress

A range of congressional scholars demonstrate the increasing polarization in Congress.[52] In comparison with Congress at the mid-twentieth century, parties in today's Congress are significantly more homogeneous. Congress may today be described as two armed, hostile camps, forced to interact (if not get along) within the institution.

In addition to this congressional polarization and homogenization, there appears under President George W. Bush to be more coordination between the Republican majority in Congress and the president. For the political-bureaucratic system, this translates into greater influence of the president. This appears to have an influence with the Department of Homeland Security, where Bush and Republican majorities have engineered a major reorganization of the government, reorienting a great many programs away from their traditional mandates toward homeland security. Similarly, Bush seems reasonably successful in his faith-based initiative, having a surprisingly wide range of agencies reach out to church-related groups.

Implications

While exploring these two issues in detail is beyond the scope of this chapter, they both indicate some changes in the nature of the performance of the political-bureaucratic system. Both seem to be related, and to indicate that there are fewer moderates among elected officials and the active interests. To the extent that active groups and elected officials have become more extreme relative to the population, it means that policies are less likely to serve the average citizen.

Conclusions and Broader Implications

Elected officials delegate authority for two reasons: delegation allows them to economize their own time and resources, and many policy areas require the development of specialized knowledge, expertise, and information collection that is simply beyond the officials' reach. Both motivations for delegation, but especially the second, mean that elected officials cannot know in sufficient detail how to direct bureaucratic decisions and hence to specify in advance what an agency should do to serve their interests. If elected officials had to direct bureaucrats to get what they wanted, the task would be hopeless.

Instead, elected officials have created a political-bureaucratic system that controls agency decision making through other means. First, the committee system implies that members of Congress specialize by subject area, and many gain considerable policy expertise over the years; so, too, do the relevant congressional staff. Periodic oversight hearings provide a means for the official assessment of agency performance, including the reauthorization process.[53]

Second, elected officials shift much of the effort and resources involved in monitoring agencies to constituents and the courts. Constituents have both the incentives and the means to monitor agency proceedings. Courts ensure that agencies follow prescribed procedures and constraints required by due process, the APA, and in various enabling statutes.

Third, structure and process, enforced by the courts, provide each agency with a range of *ex ante* constraints and incentives. Elected officials use these tools to stack the deck in favor of some interests and against others.

Fourth, the fire-alarm mechanism holds the threat of bringing intense congressional scrutiny of an agency. This attention has two separate effects. It typically conveys information to the agency about the direction officials would like the agency to take. More importantly, most bureaucrats seek to avoid this form of scrutiny and harassment, and the best way to do this is to serve the interests who hold the power to direct Congress's attention.

Fifth, the budgetary process rewards agencies that serve elected officials' constituencies. Agencies that devise creative ways of serving elected officials' constituents tend to flourish in comparison with those that do not. *Ex post* reactions, including fire alarms and budgets, provide a powerful set of tools for elected officials to control agency decision making.

The political logic of bureaucratic decision making is that these tools combine to provide an effective system for controlling a vast array of different programs across thousands of agencies and tens of thousands of policy areas. Agencies that fail to serve elected officials' political interests do not prosper.

Does Control Imply Good Policy?

This approach to understanding the logic of the political-bureaucratic system allows us to address the larger questions with which this chapter opened. The first question concerns the definition of those whom the bureaucracy serves. Are bureaucracies runaway and uncontrollable?

The approach discussed here argues that the bureaucracies are not uncontrollable or runaway; elected officials possess a range of tools to reign in agencies of this type. Although many argue that the informational advantage established by delegating policy to an administrative agency greatly advantages the bureaucracy over elected officials,[54] we have seen that these officials possess a range of means to help mitigate the informational advantage established by delegating policy to an administrative agency.

Indeed, *ex ante* constraints and *ex post* reactions combine to address all three problems raised by delegation. Consider the problem of agency drift and the prevention of bureaucratic *faits accompli* that present elected officials with policy changes that are difficult to reverse. *Ex ante* procedures in the APA and in various enabling statutes require that all agency proceedings must be open, and that they take many steps. These procedures at once prevent agency surprise attacks and enable elected officials' constituents to monitor all agency activity. If an agency appears to be pursuing an undesirable direction, fire alarm oversight holds the threat of a series of *ex post* reactions that harass and punish those agencies that fail to serve important political constituencies. Anticipation of this reaction provides agencies with *ex ante* incentives to cater to important political constituents.

Similarly, this system addresses the "multiple principal actor" problem that typically prevents Congress and the president from using corrective legislation to steer an errant agency back on track. Because these officials often disagree about desired policy, an agency may potentially manipulate them. As long as the agency's policy drift favors one of the actors (the House, the Senate, or the president), corrective legislation cannot be used to move the agency back to the status quo. Yet elected officials anticipate this possibility at the time of creating the agency. To make this type of bureaucratic manipulation less likely, officials use a combination of *ex ante* constraints and *ex post* incentives to create an expected balance among competing interests that members of the enacting coalition seek to benefit. *Ex ante* constraints are designed to mirror the political environment facing the enacting coalition and to stack the deck in favor of particular interests and to disadvantage others.

Third, these tools also address the political turnover problem by blunting the influence of future officials. Again, structure and process enacted into legislation advantage some constituents over others and raise the costs to future officials of using pressure to alter an agency's policies. Because political officials of previous eras have used structure and process to prevent agency drift, they also reduce the flexibility of future elected officials. Indeed, today's officials are likely to feel frustrated at their lack of control over the bureaucracy.

In short, bureaucracies are not out of control. Although bureaucrats "pull the levers" of policy making, they are not solely or even primarily responsible for choosing which levers to pull. The political-bureaucratic system ensures that agencies are responsive to the interests of elected officials.

But this responsiveness to elected officials raises a deeper question: What type of control does this system imply? In particular, does the political-bureaucratic system result in good public policy? This question is harder to answer—the system has both positive and negative aspects. On the positive side, we have seen that the administrative state is not a collection of runaway, uncontrollable bureaucracies. The political-bureaucratic system allows the government to deal with thousands of different policy issues every day, and with a notable degree of responsiveness to elected officials' interests and hence to their constituents. The bureaucracy provides America with the type of policies negotiated by elected officials acting within the American constitutional system.

Nonetheless, all is not well with the bureaucracy—the system exhibits a range of serious flaws. For one, the bureaucracy produces policy piecemeal rather than in a coordinated fashion. Both Fiorina and Moe make similar arguments about this problem, which Fiorina calls the "mismatch of incentives and capabilities."[55] The president has the incentive to create coordinated control over the bureaucracy, but lacks the means. Congress has the means of coordinated control, but not the incentive. The goals of the presidents, based on the incentive to serve national constituencies, imply that they prefer centralized control of the bureaucracy, a bureaucracy they can direct and shape according to their policy interests. Members of Congress, elected from small constituencies within the nation, prefer decentralized control by committee and subcommittee. Yet even the president's incentive to coordinate the bureaucracy has limits. The need to assemble electoral coalitions push the president to serve a wide range of constituencies, many of which are as narrow as those served by members of Congress.

Moe also observes that in some areas, interest groups are so dominant that they can affect the fate of many elected officials.[56] In such cases, elected officials are likely to use their power to ensure that the relevant bureaucratic agency is highly focused on serving that organized group's interest. He offers the example of teachers' unions. More broadly, the system is clearly designed to favor active and organized interests. In some cases, these interests may be diffuse, as in Social Security recipients. But in a great many cases in modern American, this means that narrowly defined special interest groups have more influence than the general public.

The result is a set of policy decisions that, area by area, focus on a balance of political constituencies, many emphasizing more narrow congressional constituencies, others emphasizing larger presidential ones. Fire-alarm oversight reflects active monitoring of agencies by constituents. Unfortunately, this process necessarily biases policy in favor of active groups and away from the public who, even when the total stakes are large, typically have low per capita stakes and therefore do not pay attention. Indeed, studies of regulatory agency policy have, for over half a century, emphasized their service to various interest groups, often the interests they nominally regulate for the benefit of the public.[57]

In a real sense, bureaucracies are caught in the middle of a complex political system, with a tug of war between Congress and the president. The logic of the political-bureaucratic system forces agencies to pay attention to their masters, and that often means serving narrow constituencies with the capability of monitoring agencies at the expense of ignoring larger constituencies—such as the public at large—who do not have the incentive of capabilities of monitoring an agency and sounding fire alarms. As Fiorina concludes:

> When we see a public agency spending inordinate amounts of public funds to pave over certain congressional districts, we are not observing an out of control agency. We are observing an agency that is paying off the members of Congress who nurture it. The federal agencies exist in a symbiotic relationship with the congressional committees and subcommittees to which they report. Of course, not everything an agency does is of concern to its set of relevant members. It purchases freedom in such areas by playing ball in the areas that are of concern. So part of the agency may be genuinely out of control, but Congress wants it that way. It is a necessary cost of maintaining a bureaucracy sufficiently unconstrained (in law and by its nominal leaders) that it is permeable to congressional influence.[58]

In a similar vein, Aberbach and Rockman argue that if the bureaucracy is full of contradictions and inconsistencies, the fault lies with its masters.[59] The separation of powers system, the congressional committee system, and a fragmented system of active interest groups all push toward a bureaucratic system that serves political constituencies, often quite narrow ones and often at the public's expense.

An important aspect of being caught in the middle is that the legislative system is simply not capable of solving problems efficiently. The system of multiple vetoes and holdups implies that too many different interests are involved in producing legislation. Many of these interests care solely about a narrow portion of the legislation that affects their constituents rather than the larger whole. The result is that virtually all legislation fails to address problems directly and that most legislation contains provisions that are inconsistent with the overall legislative purpose or that seriously compromise the ability of the legislation to address the problems it seeks to solve.

Moe takes this argument further by arguing that the bureaucracy is not merely inefficient but in fact is designed to fail. "American public bureaucracy is not designed to be effective. The bureaucracy arises out of politics, and its design reflects the interests, strategies, and compromises of those who exercise political power."[60] As we have seen, the political compromises necessary to produce legislation often cripple the agency's ability to address its goals.

For example, consider the problem of regulating occupational health and safety by OSHA.[61] Organized labor sought a powerful, streamlined agency with a broad mandate, unconstrained by procedures, and located within the Department of Labor (where organized labor has significant influence). Yet such an agency had insufficient support within Congress to pass. In order to gain greater support, proponents had to compromise this vision. Moreover, President Richard Nixon, a proponent of a constrained OSHA, sought to place limits on the agency through a structure and process that placed significant burdens on the agency. As noted above, the agency was burdened with dealing with NIOSH, which set part of its agenda. Enforcement was to be federalized in the sense that each state could create its own agency to enforce the national law, thus taking many aspects of enforcement out of OSHA's hands. In many areas, the legislation forced OSHA to adopt a range of industry consensus standards rather than devise its own regulations. As Moe concludes, structural constraints combined with divided authority to "create confusion, lack of coordination, and multiple veto points. No one was in charge, and the secretary of labor, in particular, was kept weak."[62] Economists studying OSHA consistently show that its regulation is costly and burdensome. It does produce benefits for labor, but at a much higher costs than necessary.[63]

Another aspect of inefficiency arises out of the political-bureaucratic system's strategies to mitigate the problems of agency drift and of multiple principals. By design, administrative procedures make bureaucratic decision making slow and ponderous. The political advantage of this system to elected officials is that it prevents agency *faits accompli* by ensuring that constituents have adequate time to monitor agencies, sound fire alarms, and engage the attention of political officials if the need arises. Yet it also means that bureaucracies have difficulty addressing problems that need immediate attention.

337

All these arguments point to a flawed system. The bureaucracy is not out of control, but the type of control it creates reflects the nature of the American political system, with divided powers, multiple centers of power, and a lack of centralized coordination. The president is nominally the chief executive, but is not in charge of the bureaucracy. Congress plays an ongoing direct and indirect role in administration. The political-bureaucratic system may ensure that bureaucracies are responsive, but this implies responsiveness to active political constituencies. Bureaucracies are caught in the middle of this system, forced to respond to the incentives they face.

This system often, perhaps typically, neglects the larger national interests of the broad public. Because active interests are far more likely to monitor agencies, communicate with members of Congress, pull fire alarms, and make campaign donations, the political-bureaucratic system serves their interests more effectively than it does those of the public. The president has the greatest incentive to represent national constituencies, yet as we have seen, the mismatch of incentives and capabilities means that Congress often frustrates the president's ability to pursue these interests (and, of course, presidents often pursue most vigorously the interests of their own electoral constituencies).

Bureaucracy is a pejorative term in modern America, and rightly so. The approach developed here helps explain why. The political compromises necessitated by the American constitutional system mean that legislation rarely attacks problems in a straightforward manner, but typically through political compromise that combines multiple and conflicting goals, that adds complex procedures, and that often includes mechanisms designed to prevent the agency from attaining its goals. Political officials find cumbersome procedures necessary both to facility monitoring and control, but also to place constraints on agency drift and to mitigate the problems of political turnover.

Notes

*The author gratefully acknowledges Joel Aberbach, Daniel Carpenter, Dara Cohen, Mariano-Florentino Cuellar, Terry Moe, and Bert Rockman for helpful conversations.

1. Clarkson and Muris, *Federal Trace Commission since 1970*; Dodd and Shott, *Congress and the Administrative State*; and Wilson, *Politics of Regulation*.
2. Dodd and Shott, *Congress and the Administrative State*, 2.
3. Joel D. Aberbach and Bert A. Rockman, *In the Web of Politics: Three Decades of the U.S. Federal Executive* (Washington, D.C.: The Brookings Institution, 2000.)
4. John A. Ferejohn, *Pork Barrel Politics* (Stanford: Stanford University Press, 1974.)
5. Kathleen Bawn, "Political Control versus Expertise: Congressional Choices about Administrative Procedures," *American Journal of Political Science* (1995), 89, 62–73; Epstein and O'Halloran, *Delegating Powers*; and Huber and Shipan, *Deliberate Discretion*.

6. Weingast, "Congressional Bureaucratic System."

7. See Aberbach and Rockman, *Web of Politics*, especially chap. 5; and Fiorina, "Congressional Control of the Bureaucracy."

8. Brady and Volden, *Revolving Gridlock*; and Krehbiel, *Pivotal Politics.*

9. This illustration draws on Romer and Weingast, "Political Foundations of the Thrift Debacle."

10. Banks and savings and loans differed in a variety of technical ways, for example, the types of loans they could make, the interest rates they could charge; and banks had the right to issue checks.

11. One reason these ailing banks could keep their doors open was that, in the absence of supervision, they raised interest rates on deposits. This attracted more cash in the short run, but increased the S&L's long-term liabilities in a way that could not be sustained.

12. See McNollgast, "Structure and Process, Politics and Policy."

13. This section draws on Rodriguez and Weingast, "Positive Political Theory of Legislative History."

14. Eskridge, Jr., Frickey, and Garrett, *Legislation*; and Whalen and Whalen, *The Longest Debate.*

15. Dara Cohen provided input for this paragraph.

16. Indeed, the homeland security reorganizations is one of the biggest administrative reorganizations in modern times.

17. Wilson, *Politics of Regulation.*

18. Clarkson and Muris, *Federal Trade Commission*, 34.

19. Bawn, "Political Control versus Expertise; Epstein and O'Halloran. *Delegating Powers*; and Huber and Shipan, *Deliberate Discretion.*

20. William N. Eskridge, Jr., and John Ferejohn, "Making the Deal Stick: Enforcing the Original Constitutional Understanding in the Modern Regulatory State," *Journal of Law, Economics and Organization* 8, no. 1 (March 1992); Horn, *Political Economy of Public Administration*; McNollgast, "Administrative Procedures as Instruments of Political Control"; and Murray J. Horn and Kenneth A. Shipley, "Commentary on 'Administrative Arrangements and the Political Control of Agencies': Administrative Process and Organizational Form as Legislative Responses to Agency Costs," *Virginia Law Review* (March 1989), 75, 499–508.

21. Terry M. Moe, "The Politics of Bureaucratic Structure," in John E. Chubb and Paul E. Peterson, eds., *Can the Government Govern?* (Washington, D.C.: The Brookings Institution, 1989).

22. David Brady and Barbara Sinclair, "Building Majorities for Policy Changes in the House of Representatives," *Journal of Politics* 46 (Nov. 1984), 1033–1060.

23. Ibid.

24. Moe, "Politics of Bureaucratic Structure,"; and Rui J. P. de Figueiredo, Jr., and Richard G. Vanden Bergh, "The Political Economy of State Level Administrative Procedure Acts," *Journal of Law and Economics* 47, no. 2 (2004), 569–588.

25. Banks and Weingast, "Political Control of Bureaucracies."

26. Mathew D. McCubbins and Thomas Schwartz, "Congressional Oversight Overlooked: Police Patrols vs. Fire Alarms," *American Journal of Political Science* 28 (1984), 165–179; and Aberbach, *Keeping a Watchful Eye.*

27. Aberbach, *Keeping a Watchful Eye*; and Fenno, *Power of the Purse*.

28. Terry M. Moe and William Howell, "The Presidential Power of Unilateral Action," *Journal of Law, Economics and Organizations* 15, no. 1 (1999), 132–179; and William Howell. *Power without Persuasion: The Politics of Direct Presidential Action* (Princeton, N.J.: Princeton University Press, 2003).

29. McNollgast, "Administrative Procedures as Instruments of Political Control," and "The Political Origins of the Administrative Procedure Act."

30. Studying this problem is beyond the scope of this chapter. See, however, Brian A. Marks, "A Model of Judicial Influence on Congressional Policymaking: *Grove City College v. Bell,*" Working Papers in Political Science P-88-7, Hoover Institution; McNollgast, "Structure and Process"; Ferejohn and Shipan, "Congressional Influence on Administrative Agencies."

31. See, for example, *State Farm Mut. Auto Ins. v. Department of Transportation*, 680 F.2d 206 (D.C. Cir. 1982).

32. McNollgast, "Administrative Procedures"; and McNollgast, "Political Origins."

33. McNollgast, "Administrative Procedures."

34. Linda R. Cohen, "Innovation and Atomic Energy: Nuclear Power Regulation, 1966–Present," *Law and Contemporary Problems* 43 (1979), 67–97; and McNollgast, "Positive and Normative Models of Due Process."

35. Ibid.

36. Jonathan R. Macey, "Organizational Design and Political Control of Administrative Agencies," *Journal of Law, Economics, and Organization* 8 (1992), 93–119.

37. See Kiewiet and McCubbins, *Logic of Delegation,* on the appropriations process. See Aberbach, *Keeping a Watchful Eye*; Fiorina, "Congressional Control of the Bureaucracy"; McCubbins and Schwartz, "Congressional Oversight"; and Weingast and Moran, "Bureaucratic Discretion," on oversight.

38. Moe, "Politicized Presidency."

39. See, for example, Nolan McCarty, "The Appointments Dilemma," *American Journal of Political Science*, 48, no. 3 (2004), 413–428; and Susan K. Snyder and Barry R. Weingast. "The American System of Shared Powers: The President, Congress, and the NLRB," *Journal of Law, Economics, and Organization* 16 (November 2000), 269–305.

40. Richard Nathan, *The Administrative Presidency* (New York: Macmillan, 1983).

41. Ferejohn and Shipan, "Congressional Influence on Administrative Agencies"; and Ferejohn, John A., and Charles R. Shipan, "Congressional Influence on Bureaucracy," *Journal of Law, Economics, and Organization* 6 (1990), 1–20.

42. Aberbach, *Keeping a Watchful Eye*.

43. Ibid.

44. Ibid., chap. 9.

45. Studies of this process emphasize how bureaucrats dread this type of congressional scrutiny (see Aberbach, *Keeping a Watchful Eye*, and Fenno, *Power of the Purse*).

46. Aberbach and Rockman, *Web of Politics,* 120–121.

47. Fenno. *Power of the Purse;* Kiewiet and McCubbins. *Logic of Delegation*; Weingast, "Congressional Bureaucratic System."

48. Aberbach and Rockman, *Web of Politics*.

49. See Key, *Politics, Parties, and Pressure Groups*, part I.
50. Fiorina, *Culture War*.
51. Fiorina, *Culture War*, forcefully argues that this is a myth. Although elites can be divided into two very different camps, this is not true for voters. Fiorina presents considerable evidence that, although elites are more polarized, citizens are no more so now than in 1970.
52. See, e.g., Fiorina, *Culture War*, and Gary W. Cox and Keith Poole "On Measuring Partisanship in Roll Call Voting: The U.S. House of Representatives, 1877-1999." *American Journal of Political Science* 46 (2002), 477–489.
53. Joel D. Aberbach, "What's Happened to the Watchful Eye?" *Congress and the Presidency* 29 (Spring 2002), 3–24, shows that the reauthorization process seems to be breaking down. Far fewer reauthorization hearings are being held, implying less scrutiny and evaluation of this type.
54. Dodd and Shott, *Congress and the Administrative State*; Niskanen. *Bureaucracy and Representative Government;* Wilson. *Politics of Regulation;* and Wilson, *Bureaucracy*.
55. Fiorina, "Congressional Control of the Bureaucracy"; Moe, "Politicized Presidency."
56. Terry M. Moe, "Political Control and the Power of the Agent," Working Paper, Hoover Institution (Stanford University, 2005).
57. See for example, Bernstein. *Regulating Business*; Edelman. *Symbolic Uses of Power;* and McConnell. *Private Power and American Democracy*. Modern students of the political economy of regulation have refined this approach, though the general conclusion remains valid (see, e.g., Noll, "Economic Perspectives on the Politics of Regulation")
58. Fiorina, "Congressional Control of the Bureaucracy," 337.
59. Aberbach and Rockman, *Web of Politics*.
60. Moe, "Politics of Bureaucratic Structure," 267.
61. McNollgast, "Administrative Procedures as Instruments of Political Control"; and Moe, "Politics of Bureaucratic Structure."
62. Moe, "Politics of Bureaucratic Structure," 298–299.
63. Ann Bartel and Lacy Glen Thomas, "Direct and Indirect Effects of Regulation: A New Look at OSHA's Impact," *Journal of Law and Economics* 28, no. 1 (1985), 1–26.

Bibliography

Aberbach, Joel. *Keeping a Watchful Eye*. Washington, D.C.: The Brookings Institution, 1990.

Banks, Jeffrey, and Barry R. Weingast. "The Political Control of Bureaucracies under Asymmetric Information." *American Journal of Political Science* 36 (1992), 509–524.

Bernstein, Marver. *Regulating Business by Independent Commission*. Princeton, N.J.: Princeton University Press, 1955.

Brady, David W., and Craig Volden. *Revolving Gridlock*. Boulder, Colo.: Westview, 1998.

Clarkson, Kenneth W., and Timothy J. Muris. *The Federal Trace Commission since 1970: Economic Regulation and Bureaucratic Behavior*. New York: Cambridge University Press, 1981.

Dodd, Lawrence C., and Richard L. Shott. *Congress and the Administrative State*. New York: Wiley, 1979.

Edelman, Murray. *The Symbolic Uses of Power*. Urbana: University of Illinois Press, 1964.

Epstein, David, and Sharyn O'Halloran. *Delegating Powers: A Transaction Cost Politics Approach to Policy Making under Separate Powers*. New York: Cambridge University Press, 1999.

Eskridge, William, N., Jr., Philip P. Frickey, and Elizabeth Garrett. *Legislation: Statutes and the Creation of Public Policy*. 3rd ed. St. Paul: West Publishing, 2001.

Fenno, Richard F. *Power of the Purse*. Boston: Little, Brown, 1966.

Ferejohn, John A., and Charles R. Shipan. "Congressional Influence on Administrative Agencies: A Case Study of Telecommunications Policy." In *Congress Reconsidered*, edited by Lawrence C. Dodd and Bruce I. Oppenheimer. 4th ed. Washington, D.C.: Congressional Quarterly Press, 1989.

Fiorina, Morris P. "Congressional Control of the Bureaucracy." In *Congress Reconsidered*, edited by Lawrence C. Dodd and Bruce I. Oppenheimer. 4th ed. Washington, D.C.: Congressional Quarterly Press, 1989.

Fiorina, Morris P. *Culture War? The Myth of a Polarized America*. New York: Pearson Longman, 2005.

Horn, Murray J. *The Political Economy of Public Administration*. New York: Cambridge University Press, 1995.

Huber, John D., and Charles R. Shipan. *Deliberate Discretion: The Institutional Foundations of Bureaucratic Autonomy*. New York: Cambridge University Press, 2002.

Key, V. O., Jr. *Politics, Parties, and Pressure Groups*. 5th ed. New York: Thomas Y. Crowell, 1964.

Kiewiet, D. Roderick, and Mathew D. McCubbins. *The Logic of Delegation: Congressional Parties and the Appropriations Process*. Berkeley: University of California Press, 1991.

Krehbiel, Keith. *Pivotal Politics*. Chicago: University of Chicago Press, 1998.

Lewis, David E. "The Adverse Consequences of the Politics of Agency Design for Presidential Management in the United States: The Relative Durability of Insulated Agencies." *British Journal of Political Science* 34 (2004), 377–404.

Malbin, Michael J. *Unelected Representatives*. New York: Basic Books, 1980

McConnell, Grant. *Private Power and American Democracy*. New York: Vintage, 1966.

McNollgast (Mathew D. McCubbins, Roger G. Noll, and Barry R. Weingast). "Administrative Procedures as Instruments of Political Control." *Journal of Law, Economics, and Organization* 3 (Fall 1987), 243–277.

McNollgast (Mathew D. McCubbins, Roger G. Noll, and Barry R. Weingast). "Structure and Process, Politics and Policy: Administrative Arrangements and the Political Control of Agencies." *Virginia Law Review* 75 (March 1989), 431–482.

McNollgast (Mathew D. McCubbins, Roger G. Noll, and Barry R. Weingast). "Positive and Normative Models of Due Process: An Integrative Approach to Administrative Procedures." *Journal of Law, Economics, and Organization* 6 (1990), 307–332.

McNollgast (Mathew D. McCubbins, Roger G. Noll, and Barry R. Weingast). "The Political Origins of the Administrative Procedure Act." *Journal of Law, Economics, and Organization* 15 (April 1999), 180–217.

Moe, Terry M. "The Politicized Presidency." In *The New Direction in American Politics*, edited by John E. Chubb and Paul E. Peterson. Washington, D.C.: The Brookings Institution, 1985.

Moe, Terry M. "The Political Structure of Agencies." In *Can the Government Govern?* edited by John E. Chubb and Paul E. Peterson. Washington, D.C.: The Brookings Institution, 1989.

Noll, Roger G. "Economic Perspectives on the Politics of Regulation." In *Handbook of Industrial Organization*, edited by Richard Schmalense and Robert D. Willig, vol. II. Amsterdam: North-Holland, 1989.

Niskanen, William. *Bureaucracy and Representative Government*. Chicago: Aldine, 1971.

Pashigian, B. Peter. "The Effect of Environmental Regulation on Optimal Plant Size and Factor Shares." *Journal of Law and Economics* 27 (1984), 1–28.

Rodriguez, Daniel, and Barry R. Weingast. "The Positive Political Theory of Legislative History: New Perspectives on the 1964 Civil Rights Act and Its Interpretation." *University of Pennsylvania Law Review* 151, no. 4 (April 2003), 1417–1542.

Romer, Thomas, and Barry R. Weingast. "Political Foundations of the Thrift Debacle." In *Politics and Economics in the 1980s*, edited by Alberto Alesina and Geoffrey Carliner. National Bureau of Economic Research Conference Series. Chicago: University of Chicago Press, 1991.

Shepsle, Kenneth A. "The Changing Textbook Congress." In *Can the Government Govern?* edited by John E. Chubb and Paul E. Peterson. Washington, D.C.: The Brookings Institution, 1989.

Weingast, Barry R. "The Congressional Bureaucratic System: A Principal Agent Perspective (with applications to the SEC)." In "Carnegie Papers on Political Economy," edited by Alan Meltzer, Thomas Romer, and Howard Rosenthal, special supplement to *Public Choice* 44 (1984), 147–191.

Weingast, Barry R., and Mark J. Moran. "Bureaucratic Discretion or Congressional Control: Regulatory Policymaking by the FTC." *Journal of Political Economy* 91 (October 1983), 765–800.

Whalen, Charles, and Barbara Whalen. *The Longest Debate: A Legislative History of the 1964 Civil Rights Act*. Cabin John, Md.: Seven Locks Press, 1985.

Wilson, James Q. *The Politics of Regulation*. New York: Basic Books, 1980.

Wilson, James Q. *Bureaucracy: What Government Agencies Do and Why They Do It*. New York: Basic Books, 1989.

11

REFORMING THE EXECUTIVE BRANCH
OF THE U.S. GOVERNMENT

Donald F. Kettl

AMERICA HAS LONG BEEN A NATION OF PRAGMATIC reorganizers, especially when it comes to public institutions. Even as he tinkered with stoves and lightning rods, Benjamin Franklin also created a lending library, fire brigade, night watchmen unit, hospital, militia, and university. In his stimulating biography of Franklin, Walter Isaacson quotes the sage of Pennsylvania as writing, "The good men may do separately is small compared with what they may do collectively."[1] He and his fellow founders took this lesson to heart. In struggling to balance the vastly complex political issues that threatened to tear the new nation apart before it was even born, they created modern federalism, they transformed Montesquieu's notion of separation of powers into reality, and they framed an intricately balanced three-part national government that has stood the test of time.

The mark of the genius of America's founders is not so much in the institutions they created, although the structure of American government remains one of the world's most prominent and fascinating models. Rather, it is in the system's remarkable ability to stretch, change, and adapt—without breaking—as new problems present themselves. America is built on a powerful system of values expressed in the Constitution and the Bill of Rights. But just as much, it is built on the premise that the nation must constantly modify its institutions to fit them to new puzzles. Its success requires a focus on making things work and a constant effort to make things work better. Indeed, compared with nations elsewhere in the world, Americans have long been among the most enthusiastic reformers.

Toward the end of the twentieth century, however, the reform movement, in the United States and around the world, began to change. Other nations, especially the so-called Westminster nations of Australia, Canada, New Zealand, and the United Kingdom, dramatically picked up the pace of reform. And compared with American reforms, they pursued strategies that were more comprehensive, more aggressive, and more ideologically focused. This movement, christened "the new public management," set up a stark contrast. Americans continued their reform efforts, as we shall see. But American reforms proved more ad hoc, more narrowly focused, and more pragmatic. They provide a fascinating window into the puzzle of American exceptionalism that Richard Rose touches on in Chapter 3 of this volume and that has fascinated many able scholars over the years.[2]

Reform efforts around the world have always been focused in part on efficiency and effectiveness—improving the government's ability to produce better services for less money—and in part on politics—tweaking the bureaucracy to connect better with citizens and to reflect more closely the values of elected officials. The "new public management" reformers believed that improvements in administrative efficiency would provide leverage for political gain. By contrast, Americans have tended more to use administrative reforms as political symbols, and to leverage those symbols for political gain. This fundamental distinction—reform as efficiency versus reform as symbol—flows from the complex pluralism of American politics (which makes it important to serve a wide array of political interests) and the highly diffuse nature of American political institutions (which makes it more difficult than in Westminster nations for any single player to shape policy results).

Thus, the story of reform in American government is in part a study of how the United States compares with other major democracies. And it is also a guide to the nation's linkages between political decisions and policy results.

The Stages of Government Reform

Starting with the Progressive era of the late nineteenth century, American reform has rarely paused for more than a short time. Reform commissions examining the basic structure and function of government were a recurring fixture of American politics (see Table 1). The basic fabric of American government has proven remarkably durable, but Americans have never stopped trying to stretch it into new shapes.

The Evolution of American Reforms

Throughout American history, new problems have arisen for which existing policies, processes, and institutions seemed a poor answer. One of the great strengths of American democracy has been that, when these strains have occurred, Americans have been pragmatic in seeking new ways of solving the problem. Instead of falling back on ideology or adhering to rigid principles, Americans have sometimes tinkered with their systems—and periodically have

TABLE 1

Major Commissions to Improve the Executive Branch, 1905–2000.

1. Keep Commission (1905–1909)
   - Personnel management, government contracting, information management
2. President's Commission on Economy and Efficiency (1910–1913)
   - The case for a national executive budget
3. Joint Committee on Reorganization (1921–1924)
   - Methods of redistributing executive functions among the departments
4. President's Committee on Administrative Management (Brownlow Committee, 1936–1937)
   - Recommended creation of the Executive Office of the President
5. First Hoover Commission (1947–1949)
   - Comprehensive review of the organization and function of the executive branch; built on task force reports
6. Second Hoover Commission (1953–1955)
   - Follow-up to first Hoover Commission; focused more on policy problems than organizational structure
7. Study commissions on executive reorganization (1953–1968)
   - Series of low-key reforms that produced quiet but important changes
8. Ash Council (1969–1971)
   - Proposals for a fundamental restructuring of the executive branch, including merging existing departments into four new super-departments
9. Carter reorganization effort (1977–1979)
   - Bottom-up, process-based effort to reorganize government; ended up mostly in failure; new Cabinet departments created independently of effort
10. Grace Commission (1982–1984)
    - Large-scale effort to determine how government could be operated for less money; heavy focus on privatization
11. National Performance Review (1993)
    - Effort to "reinvent" government to improve its performance

SOURCE: Derived from Ronald C. Moe, *Reorganizing the Executive Branch in the Twentieth Century: Landmark Commissions*, report 92-293 GOV (Congressional Research Service, March 1992).

developed reforms both dramatic and sweeping. The government faced a series of new problems during the twentieth century, which provoked three substantial periods of reform: an era of *structural* innovation, which carried over from the late nineteenth century and saw remarkable innovation in the form of government; an era of *policy* innovation, which began in the New Deal and was capped by the Great Society in the 1960s; and an era of *procedural* innovation, which started in the late 1970s and provided a bridge into the twenty-first century.

STRUCTURAL INNOVATION. When government reformers surveyed the political landscape toward the end of the nineteenth century, they came to a simple conclusion: government's challenges had grown more quickly than government's ability to meet them. Large corporate trusts overwhelmed many citizens' sense of fairness. Railroad barons were accused of muscling smaller businesses and communities. Big swings in interest rates and the money supply fueled economic boom-bust cycles, especially in rural America. Investigators found unsanitary conditions in meat-packing plants and the use of poisonous dyes and preservatives in foods. Itinerant merchants peddled worthless, and sometimes dangerous, patent medicines. After the 1929 stock market crash helped spark the Depression, reformers worried about the stability of the banking system and the ability of the government to help put the economy back on its feet and to put food into the hands of hungry Americans.

As each big issue arose, reformers met it with a common response: to create a new governmental structure to solve the problem. Congress created the Interstate Commerce Commission (1887) to regulate the railroads and the Federal Trade Commission (1914) to help bust the trusts. The Federal Reserve

TABLE 2
The Federal Executive Departments

Department	Year created
State	1789
War*	1789
Treasury	1789
Navy*	1798
Interior	1849
Justice	1870
Post Office**	1872
Agriculture	1889
Commerce***	1903
Labor***	1913
Defense	1947
Health, Education, and Welfare#	1953
Housing and Urban Development	1965
Transportation	1966
Energy	1977
Education#	1979
Veterans Affairs	1988
Homeland Security	2002

*Combined into Department of Defense in 1947.
**Transformed into U.S. Postal Service, an independent establishment in 1971, and its Cabinet status ended.
***Originally named Commerce and Labor.
#Originally named Health, Education, and Welfare. Separated in 1979 into Health and Human Services, and Education.

Board (1913) managed the money supply and the Food and Drug Administration (1906) worked to make the food supply safer. The Securities and Exchange Commission (1934) sought to restabilize the trading of stocks and bonds. To strengthen the president's ability to manage the federal government by managing the budget, Congress established the Bureau of the Budget (1921). New departmental-level organizations came into being for Justice (1870), Post Office (1872), Agriculture (1889), Commerce (1903), and Labor (1913). It was as lively and energetic a time of institution building as the nation had seen since its infancy, and federal reformers have not matched the pace since.[3]

As diverse as the policy problems and governmental responses were, a core strategy lay behind this structural movement. Reformers viewed these problems as a sign of a government that was too weak to cope with rapid social and economic change. Private institutions, especially big corporations, had grown more quickly than government's ability to oversee them—and to ensure that private competition served the public interest. Solving the problems required a stronger government, and that required new governmental organizations. The structural era was quite remarkable in several respects: for its concentrated and energetic action, its focused diagnosis of government's problems and its straightforward response, and its commitment to organizational responses to tough problems. From the New Deal to the war on terrorism, Americans have often looked to restructuring as a solution to pressing policy and political problems. But never was the linkage between problem solving and structural change so clear.

POLICY INNOVATION. As the nation moved more deeply into the twentieth century, reformers' belief in structural solutions to government's problems began to erode as the New Deal took root. In part, this was because the hectic Progressive reform era had created the most obvious of new bureaucracies. It was also because restructuring seemed a poor fit for tough new problems. Reformers wanted a stronger government, but they saw the problem of strength in a very different way. The Progressives diagnosed government's problem as one of weak coordination, which required the creation of new organizations. The New Dealers saw the problem as one of inadequate resources, which required the creation of new programs financed with more money. To be sure, Franklin D. Roosevelt created an alphabet soup of new government agencies, but unlike the Progressives' regulatory agencies, which aimed to strengthen government's coordination muscles, the central mission of New Deal agencies was to move money.

And move money they did. In just a decade, federal spending as a share of the gross domestic product (the federal government's share of the domestic economy) nearly quadrupled from 1930 to 1941, just before the outbreak of World War II (see Figure 1). The New Deal proved a remarkably fertile greenhouse for growing new government programs. The federal government funded work relief

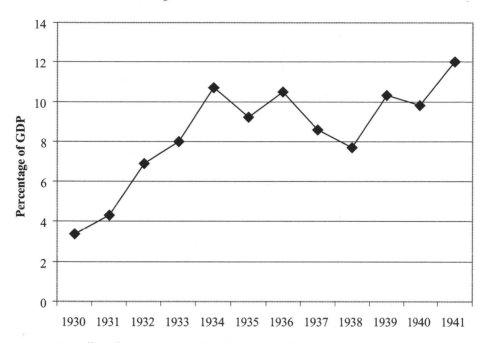

SOURCE: U.S. Office of Management and Budget, *Budget of the United States Government, Fiscal Year 2005: Historical Tables* (2004), Table 1.2, at http://www.whitehouse.gov/omb/budget/fy2005/sheets /hist01z2.xls.

Figure 1   Federal Spending as a Share of the Domestic Economy, 1930–1941

and public works projects. In many public buildings around the country, New Deal–financed murals still decorate the walls. The federal government created a new era of partnerships with state and local governments through grant programs. Moreover, Roosevelt led the passage of the Social Security Act (1935), which established what was to become the federal government's largest program within just two generations.[4]

To be sure, some structural changes accompanied the era of policy innovation. In the New Deal, new agencies proliferated (although many of them did not have a long life). The Social Security Administration became large and powerful, cycling into and later out of the Department of Health, Education, and Welfare (later the Department of Health and Human Services). But unlike the agencies created in the structural era, which focused on strengthening government's power, the agencies created in the era of policy innovation tended to have a primary mission of spending money. Their power came not from their regulatory muscle but from the budget dollars they distributed. And as government spending rose after World War II, so did the size and power of government agencies charged with distributing the money.

349

PROCEDURAL INNOVATION. As spending rose, government officials and their critics struggled with new puzzles. How could the nation ensure that the programs worked? How could the programs be made both effective and accountable? After World War II, two commissions headed by former president Herbert Hoover tackled the problems. The Hoover Commissions had enormous impact on thinking about how best to do government's work. And they marked an important transition in that thinking. The first Hoover Commission concentrated on government's structure. The second Hoover Commission shifted to a focus on government's processes. That transition guided most of the governmental reform movement for the rest of the twentieth century.

In the academic world, the questions about government performance proved so tough that they provoked a new subfield of political science, "implementation," rooted in public policy and dedicated to the puzzle of why so many programs seemed to work so poorly. As the discursive subtitle of a book by Jeffrey L. Pressman and Aaron Wildavsky soberly wondered, "How Great Expectations in Washington Are Dashed in Oakland; Or, Why It's Amazing That Federal Programs Work at All, This Being a Saga of the Economic Development Administration as Told by Two Sympathetic Observers Who Seek to Build Morals on a Foundation of Ruined Hopes."[5] Reformers worried that the federal grant programs to state and local governments had produced inflexible approaches that poorly matched local problems and that gave too little power to those in the areas most affected by the programs, especially in poor and minority neighborhoods. In the eyes of some critics, however, the efforts to remedy the problems had transformed the federal government's promise of "maximum feasible participation" in the programs into "maximum feasible misunderstanding," as Daniel Patrick Moynihan put it during his academic days.[6] Critics contended that government programs had grown so large that they worked poorly and that they were unresponsive to the very people they were designed to serve.

On an even broader plane, worries arose that American government was becoming too centered at the national level and, in Washington, was becoming too concentrated in the White House, creating an "imperial presidency."[7] The revelations of Richard Nixon's Watergate scandal only underlined the concern that power in the American system had become far too concentrated.

In struggling with these issues, reformers discovered that the nation had little taste for cutting back on the growth of government spending or for profound structural change. Hardening of Washington's organizational arteries, both in the capital's bureaucracy and especially in the jurisdictions of congressional subcommittees, made it difficult to consider reversing the course of structural innovation. Reformers in the 1970s therefore turned to procedural innovation. Instead of cutting back on spending or trying to restructure public agencies, reformers worked to shift governmental power by changing its procedures. To give state and local governments more power over federal money, first Nixon and then

Gerald Ford worked with Congress to combine existing categorical programs into block grants. These new programs broadened the categories in which state and local governments could spend federal cash; reduced planning, paperwork, and approval; and encouraged subnational governments to focus the money on problems they viewed as most important. And then, in a sharp rebuke to Nixon, Congress sought to rebalance spending power by creating a new congressional budget process. Instead of dealing with spending bills one at a time, with appropriations set simply by the total of programs Congress approved, Congress committed itself to setting overall targets for revenue and expenditures and then enforcing those targets on its own committees.

After forty years of virtually uninterrupted accretion of power to Washington and, within Washington, to the executive branch, the reforms of the 1970s—during the Nixon and Ford administrations—marked a turning point. In both political rhetoric and policy process, the early 1970s marked a high point of "slouching toward Washington," as David B. Walker described the evolution of federalism.[8] And as Congress flexed at least limited muscle, the period also marked a plateau in the accretion of national power in the White House. State and local governments continued to tussle with Washington over the balance of power, and rules in programs like Medicaid and environmental protection continued to spark complaints about excessive federal control. For its part, members of Congress regularly bristled at the exercise of presidential power, regardless of which party controlled the White House. But, on both fronts, the rise of procedural innovations helped stem the concentration of political power.

When the Reagan administration took office, its officials took a different procedural tack. They began with the ideological conclusion that government, especially in Washington, had gotten too big and too powerful. They recognized that a frontal assault on the New Deal and Great Society welfare state would meet insurmountable opposition, in both Congress and the nation at large. So they pursued a privatization strategy trying to turn as much as possible of the government's work over to the private sector, especially through contracting out. The Reagan administration bolstered the strategy with yet another presidential commission, headed by businessman J. Peter Grace. Unlike most previous twentieth century commissions, which sought to strengthen government's power to manage its programs, the Grace Commission aimed at cutting government and spinning the administration of as many government programs as possible into the private sector.

Neither Reagan nor his commission had much success on the first front. Federal spending as a share of the gross domestic product (the government's contribution to the domestic economy) nudged down slightly, from 22.2 percent in fiscal year 1981 to 21.2 percent in 1989. But government contracting rose substantially. Just how much is difficult to determine, since the federal government does not measure contracting in a clear and consistent way. The anecdotal evidence, however, is huge and substantial, with aggressive contracting out for everything from cafeteria service in federal office buildings to maintenance services on military bases. In a 1999 study, Paul C. Light estimated that the federal government had a "shadow" workforce consisting of 12.7 million full-time equivalent jobs—compared with the federal government's 1.9 million civilian executive-branch employees. For every federal employee, Light determined, there are 6.7 "shadow" employees helping produce the government's goods and services. In some departments, the ratio is even larger. Light calculates that the Department of Energy has 35 contractor employees for every federal worker.[9]

In the last half of the twentieth century, government reformers took a distinctly different approach from those of the first half. To be sure, structural reforms continued, including the creation of the Environmental Protection Agency, the Department of Energy, the Department of Education, and the Department of Veterans Affairs to coordinate programs in their respective realms. Most of these efforts were more cosmetic than substantial. The creation of the Department of Homeland Security in 2002 was more typical of the early structural reforms, but such efforts were more the exception than the rule. Likewise, the federal government continued policy innovation, most notably with the establishment of the Medicare and Medicaid programs, which had an enormous reach across the levels and sectors of American government. The most substantial and long-lasting reforms, however, focused on procedural shifts: changing the government's rules and tactics to make government work better and, in the case of the Reagan efforts, to try to make it smaller and cheaper as well.

The Era of Reinvention

These issues came into sharp focus during the 1992 presidential campaign. Maverick businessman H. Ross Perot challenged both parties to deal with the harsh realities of the federal government's rising deficits. His plain-speaking style and common-sense arguments, supplemented by charts showing the country's rising economic problems, tapped into the deep-seated concern of many Americans. He won a surprising 19 percent of the popular vote and stunned Republican and Democratic leaders. Bill Clinton won the presidency by just a 5 percent margin over George H. W. Bush, and as he took office, he and his advisors were already looking down the road to the 1996 election. They calculated that whoever captured the Perot voters would have an overwhelming advantage, and they set out to win them over.

CLINTON AND "REINVENTING GOVERNMENT." A key element in the strategy was Clinton's March 1993 promise to "reinvent" American government. He put Vice President Al Gore in charge of the effort, and Gore enlisted hundreds of federal employees in a six-month effort to scour the government from top to bottom for money-saving ideas. The September reinvention report contained 384 recommendations that promised $108 billion in savings and a 12 percent reduction in the federal workforce within five years. The goal was simple: "creating a government that works better and costs less."[10]

The reinvention campaign was more than just a quick response to the political heat that Perot generated. David Osborne and Ted Gaebler—a journalist and a former city manager—had captured the Clinton campaign's interest with a best-seller, *Reinventing Government*.[11] (Osborne already had an inside track to Clinton. His 1988 book, *Laboratories of Democracy*, described a little-known governor as a fast-rising leader—Bill Clinton.)[12] Osborne and Gaebler argued that government could work better if it empowered its employees to do what they knew best—by sweeping away the rules and procedures that disabled the innate entrepreneurial spirit of its workers, by providing stronger incentives for high performance, and by focusing more on citizens as customers. Osborne wrote a short version of the argument for the Progressive Policy Institute's campaign manifesto, which in turn was the policy map for the Clinton campaign and the new administration.[13]

The recommendations ran from old saws, like ending the federal government's subsidy for mohair production, to the cutting-edge, like creating a performance management system for the federal government. It created great energy, through its army of employees from across the government who generated the ideas. And it created great publicity, as Gore himself put his personal reputation behind the effort. He appeared on network television, from newsmagazines exploring government purchasing rules for floor wax to a spot on *Late Night with David Letterman*, where he shattered an ashtray to demonstrate the arcane procurement procedures for many government products.

The "works better, costs less" formula certainly had great appeal. It promised a more productive, more efficient government—a better government that would shrink the deficit. That was a theme that embodied the "new Democrat" approach Clinton promoted and that went right to the heart of Perot's campaign. However, the theme embodied a profound tension. The "works better" piece envisioned a government in which reformers swept away the barriers—obsolete structures, archaic processes, and inadequate leadership—that kept government employees from doing their work as they knew how to do it. The proponents of reinvention suggested replacing top-down rule-based government with bottom-up customer-driven entrepreneurial government. The "costs less" piece saw a government encrusted with waste that had to be scraped away: obsolete programs to be eliminated, excessive layers of management to be trimmed, redundant employees to be eliminated.

The "works better" approach envisioned motivating and "empowering" employees to do a better job. The "costs less" approach sought to slash away unneeded programs and people. The reinvention strategists and White House political operatives calculated that their credibility depended on producing large savings. Producing large savings required tough words and tougher cuts. Getting quick results meant making large, rapid cuts in the number of federal employees, which the Clinton administration did in concert with Congress. The political realities, including the need for quick victories, and the harsh administrative facts, including how hard it was to change deep-seated rules and cultures, emphasized the "costs less" side of the equation. That, in turn, made it that much harder to accomplish the "works better" side. Indeed, with their jobs at risk, federal employees balked at taking the big risks that the "works better" side of the reinvention equation demanded.

The "works better" campaign undoubtedly produced big impacts, especially in the spread of improved customer service and "e-government" and in a fundamental reform of the federal procurement system. But it did little to stave off a determined Republican assault on the Clinton administration through the party's "Contract with America," which promised a radical rollback in government programs and a dramatic cut in Democratic programs. The Republican effort put the reinvention campaign back on its heels. It led Gore to shift the reinvention effort from making government work better to asking what government ought to do to begin with—even asking federal managers to consider the implications if their agencies were eliminated. In their 1995 report, Gore and his collaborators even included sections on "Why We Have a Federal Government"—and "How Things Got Out of Hand."[14] The Republican assault also led the reinvention strategists to ratchet up their target for downsizing the federal bureaucracy, to 273,000 employees.

In the reinvention effort's last years, Gore focused more on strengthening e-government and in making substantial improvements at thirty-two "high-impact agencies," where fundamental reforms had the best chance of making the biggest difference. The effort did indeed produce some significant accomplishments, especially e-government improvements at agencies like the Social Security Administration and the Internal Revenue Service. For better or worse, however, the reinvention effort became firmly fixed to Gore and became most identified with the downsizing campaign. On that score, the administration delivered on its promise. From 1993 to 2001, the number of federal civilian employees declined by 365,000 (17 percent), to the lowest level since the Kennedy administration. The Defense Department accounted for two-thirds of the downsizing. There was little strategic workforce planning that went behind the downsizing, and the workforce reductions left the federal government with a mismatch of employees and responsibilities. The downsizing occurred haphazardly, as a result of buyouts and other incentives for employees to leave the federal workforce, leaving behind a major workforce challenge. Nevertheless, the administration did indeed hit the target it promised.

The irony of Gore's close identification with reinventing government, however, is that he got very little political credit for the very effort that had helped to

define "new Democrats." In fact, he barely mentioned the reinventing government effort during the 2000 presidential campaign, and the effort attracted little
attention or discussion. The Clinton administration left behind a smaller government, measured at least by the number of federal employees, as well as significant
improvements in procurement, e-government, and the operation of several
important agencies. The intensive reinvention campaign, however, produced little political impact.

THE BUSH MANAGEMENT AGENDA. It was scarcely surprising that one of the
George W. Bush administration's first steps was to close down the Clinton reinventing government office and the program it ran. But following the Reagan
privatization effort and the Clinton reinventing government campaign, management reform had become firmly established at the top levels of American government. Bush came into office with his own different plan. Unlike the massive
Clinton effort, with hundreds of items scattered throughout government and
managed from a small office up 17th Street from the White House, Bush developed an effort tightly focused on results and managed from the Office of
Management and Budget. In his management plan, Bush said.

> Government likes to begin things—to declare grand new programs and
> causes and national objectives. But good beginnings are not the measure
> of success. What matters in the end is completion. Performance. Results.
> Not just making promises, but making good on promises. In my
> Administration, that will be the standard from the farthest regional
> office of government to the highest office of the land.[15]

The five-point management agenda began with attention to the strategic
management of human capital. It sought to expand significantly the government's contracting out of services and it pledged improved financial management. It expanded the federal government's e-government initiatives. Finally and
most importantly, it sought to measure the performance of federal programs and
to integrate performance information into budget decisions.

The effort to integrate performance with the budget was a massive step.
Over a five-year period, the Bush administration ordered the managers of all federal programs to define strategic goals and to devise performance measures for
assessing their achievement of those goals. The federal government had long
sought to link budgeting with performance, especially with the famous reforms
(including the Planning Programming Budgeting System, or PPBS for short)
introduced by Robert McNamara into the Pentagon. Bush's effort marked the
broadest and most aggressive performance measurement effort in the nation's
history. Congress in 1993 had already mandated that federal agencies measure
the performance of their programs, so the legislative mandate provided little
room for backsliding.

Of course, determining what to do with the performance numbers proved a major challenge. Did a low grade suggest problems that more money could solve? Or would more money simply be funding more of what had already been shown not to work? Cynics sometimes suggested that the Bush performance measurement system did little more than provide a rationalization for ideological decisions the administration had already determined to make. But despite the debate, it is clear that by tying the performance measures to budgets and by backing them up with the muscle of the Office of Management and Budget (OMB), the Bush administration produced more movement on performance measurement than the federal government had previously seen.

A keystone of the effort was a "traffic light" scoreboard for each federal department, with red lights for unsatisfactory performance, yellow for mixed results, and green for success. OMB proved a tough grader. After almost two years, federal agencies earned just four green lights out of a total of 130. Two-thirds of the grades were red lights. OMB launched a major initiative to try to help more agencies "get to green," and the capital region's vast network of contractors sprang to work helping agency managers improve their performance scores.[16] The traffic-light system proved a marvelously simple and powerful tool for attracting attention to the president's management agenda, for creating lively news stories for the press, and for making it difficult for top department mangers to escape the pressure to improve results.

Unlike the Clinton effort, there were few simple "costs less" targets like downsizing. However, the traffic-light system, coupled with a limited agenda, created a focus on the "works better" targets, and Bush budget officials used the performance scores to indicate budget cuts. Though critics of the Bush system continued to suspect that the scores merely provided analytical justification for cuts the administration wanted to make on ideological grounds, virtually everyone agreed that moving to a system more focused on measuring results and integrating that system with OMB's budget process were both big steps forward.

The ultimate test of the Bush management agenda will depend on its staying power. But it did make several important points. A strategy for government reform has become increasingly central to the presidency. Focused management strategies integrated with the budgetary process, and supervised through top-level agencies like OMB, are more likely to get sustained attention from top government officials.

Finally, getting long-term results depends ultimately on gaining attention to management issues from Congress—and that is something with which the Clinton and Bush administrations alike struggled. Management—the focus on results instead of the creation of policy—simply did not engage many members of Congress. Agency officials thus constantly faced cross-pressures from Congress on the matters of their traditional concerns: how money was distributed, how program problems created opportunities for attracting the press to oversight hearings, and how they could intervene in agency activities to help constituents. For presidential reformers, that meant a constant struggle to get and keep the focus of agency officials on the reform agenda.

Reform in Defense and Homeland Security

One additional element of reform deserves careful attention. Especially since the end of World War II, the American federal government has periodically reformed its defense and foreign affairs establishment. Defense reform has sometimes been out of sync with reform on the domestic side of American government. For example, as the domestic side was engaged in policy innovation, the defense side underwent substantial structural innovation. In response to coordination problems that emerged during World War II and the need for a new defense establishment to fight the cold war, Congress and the president restructured the defense establishment. In 1947 the Air Corps was separated from the Army, and the two services were combined with the Navy and Marine Corps into a new Department of Defense, under the unified command of a secretary. The restructuring certainly did not resolve the traditional interservice rivalries, but it did strengthen the president's ability to shape and implement defense policy.

The defense establishment caught up with domestic reforms in the 1960s with a round of procedural innovations. Defense Secretary Robert McNamara brought private-sector management strategies from his previous position as president of Ford, and he introduced an aggressive Planning-Programming-Budgeting System into Pentagon financial management. His goal was to force the services to focus on the broad strategies they were seeking to accomplish, to determine what weapons systems they needed in order to do so, and to account for the full purchase price of their program decisions as they made them. McNamara sought to prevent the steady escalation of prices in weapons development. And by focusing on strategic needs, he hoped to wring out some of the rivalries that often led the armed services to purchase similar but competing equipment, like similar fighters for both the Navy and the Air Force.

President Johnson liked the system so much that in 1965 he ordered all federal agencies to use PPBS for their budgets. The paperwork burden of the system soon caused it to collapse. As critics pointed out, the system had substantial problems with hard weapons systems in the Pentagon and broke down under the political cross-pressures and fuzzy goals of domestic agencies.[17] The Nixon administration abandoned PPBS and replaced it with its own "management by objectives" budgeting process. But the underlying logic of PPBS—understanding a weapon as a system and trying to account for its full costs—remained so powerful in the Pentagon that the department's budgeters continue to use variations of the system, including aggressive efforts at strategic planning.[18]

The September 11, 2001, terrorist attacks led to a round of even deeper thinking about how best to defend the nation. After first strongly opposing congressional proposals for a new Department of Homeland Security, President George W. Bush not only agreed with the need to create the department but ensured that it matched his own vision of what it ought to do. The new department brought together twenty-two different federal agencies in what was the largest restructuring of the federal government since the creation of the Department of Defense in 1947. Indeed, given the vast range of agencies (from the Secret Service to agencies dealing with bioterrorism) and given the huge shift in missions (each of the agencies was expected to continue doing what it had been doing in addition to taking on a new homeland security mission), it was probably the most difficult organizational restructuring in the nation's history.

But the national commission impaneled to examine the attacks and how the nation ought to respond argued that the federal government needed to go much further. It documented the problem of "connecting the dots" among intelligence findings and operational responses, and it concluded that the nation needed a new cabinet-level intelligence czar to oversee and coordinate the nation's vast range of intelligence agencies, including the Central Intelligence Agency, the Federal Bureau of Investigation, and the National Security Agency.[19] The debate proved to be highly charged, both emotionally and politically. Most of all, it underlined the continuing and basic American impulse: to respond to fundamental problems through organizational restructuring, in part to try to solve the underlying issues, in part to demonstrate political resolve, and in part to create organizational symbols of the government's ongoing commitment. The implementation of the homeland security restructuring, however, shapes an ongoing management problem that will preoccupy top government officials for years.

The New Public Management

American presidents were not the world's only reformers. Indeed, through the 1980s and 1990s, top officials in other parts of the world proved far more aggressive in trying to reform their governments than was the case in the United States. Especially in the Westminster-style countries of Australia, Canada, New Zealand, and the United Kingdom, the reforms were especially far-ranging.

The New Zealand Reforms

Nowhere were management reforms more broad or aggressive than in New Zealand. The country was struggling with twin economic problems—rising costs for an expansive welfare state, and a declining economy that was failing to keep pace with the growth of regional economies. As Allen Schick concluded, "Economic conditions were not sustainable in New Zealand." Faced with political roadblocks in rolling back the welfare state, the nation's leaders therefore turned to governmental reform as a solution.[20] The New Zealand reforms, which were launched in 1984 and which later shaped the key elements of a movement christened "the new public management" (or NPM for short), began with a simple premise: government work cannot be efficient unless managers have the freedom to act; it cannot be held accountable unless managers have clear goals and specific targets against which their performance can be measured. The New Zealand approach to the NPM drew heavily on institutional economics, transaction cost analysis, and agency theory. Unlike America's more limited and pragmatic reforms, the New Zealand reforms had a clear theoretical provenance, dating to Ronald Coase's famous 1937 article, work by Oliver Williamson, and the theories developed by the Chicago school of economics.[21]

The New Zealand reforms, at their core, sought to define a clear line between government policy and the manager's responsibility for carrying it out. The government split its administrative apparatus into a relatively large number (more than 35) agencies reporting to the prime minister and cabinet. The logic: a larger number of agencies made it possible to create smaller and more precise areas of responsibility for top administrative officials. The government set clear production targets for its programs (from the number of miles of highway to be paved to the number of vaccinations to be administered). It would purchase these outputs from government agencies, with specified production at an agreed-upon price. The government would measure the performance of managers against these targets. Top managers would be hired by contract, instead of through the civil service system or political appointment, and would have substantial managerial flexibility in deciding how best to produce the outputs.

According to Allen Schick's remarkably comprehensive evaluation of the reforms, the NPM produced results that were "bold and unprecedented":

> . . . the reforms have lived up to most of the lofty expectations held for them. The organizational cocoon of the old State sector has been broken open and structures reshaped through the application of the reforms' overriding principles. The State sector is more efficient, productive, and responsive, and there generally has been significant improvement in the quality of services provided to New Zealanders.

The result, in Schick's view, was nothing less than "the transformation of public management through the ground breaking development and application of new methods of managerial accountability."[22] Since then, New Zealand has retreated somewhat from its aggressive reforms. It has broadened the focus of its performance measures to encompass the social impact of its management decisions, and the system's top official have worried that the strategy of defining administrative responsibility narrowly has led to problems slipping through the cracks between agencies.

Nevertheless, the general New Zealand strategy has continued to influence reformers around the world. It has spilled over to Australia, Canada, and the United Kingdom, which all adopted variations of the NPM. At the core was an economic model, which held that government would be more efficient and responsive if it were subjected to more marketlike incentives. That meant putting the jobs of public employees at risk, providing government managers with more flexibility but holding them accountable through aggressive performance measurement, giving citizens more choice and treating them more like "customers," and wherever possible shedding state-owned industries. In all four countries, it led to widespread privatization of government-owned companies, like the airlines and telecommunications, as the reformers worked to replace public organizations with private enterprises.

The NPM continued to spread and develop. Most European nations adopted some version of the reforms. British Prime Minister Margaret Thatcher implemented a variation on New Zealand's strategy with her 1988 "Next Steps" approach, which created independent agencies, gave managers more flexibility, and held them accountable for performance. Prime Minister Tony Blair introduced "joined-up government," a strategy aimed at improving the coordination of government programs. Its core was stronger e-government, and it aimed among other things at creating a "no wrong door" approach. Tired of "not my job" complaints, Blair launched an aggressive technology-based system that would help link citizens to the services they needed, regardless of the office at which they began their search. (Therefore, there was "no wrong door" into government.) Meanwhile, within the international development community, a pitched battle arose over whether the NPM could accelerate the pace of economic growth or whether it demanded such extensive management capacity that it would send development strategies in the wrong direction.[23]

The "New Public Management" and Reform in America

That drew a sharp distinction with American reforms, which did not have the same strong ideological framework, which were not as broad or comprehensive, and which did not seek to transform the fundamental relationship between citizens and government. Moreover, privatization was very different in the United States, which had very few state-owned enterprises to sell off to begin with. In the United States, by contrast, "privatization" became a strategy of a rapid expansion in contracting out. Indeed, American "privatization" was principally a strategy of pushing as much service delivery into the private sector as possible; service provision remained public, but their delivery did not. The philosophy was similar. The NPM held that marketlike incentives could improve the efficiency and responsiveness of public officials. U.S. conservatives pushed the argument one step further and held that government should turn over as much responsibility as possible to private markets.

In fact, the worldwide reform movement was remarkable for its concentrated energy, shared ideas, and concentrated action. But American reforms differed systematically from many of those championed in the NPM. Consider the basic differences. (This analysis, summarized in Table 3, is based on some of the common themes. Practices in the countries often varied widely.)

- *Model.* American reformers borrowed heavily from private-sector analysts, who made the case for downsizing and for more emphasis on customer service. The NPM, by contrast, grew from the theoretical arguments of institutional economics.
- *Focus of reform.* In addition to downsizing, American reformers concentrated on reforming government's basic processes, like procurement. The NPM focused on broader structural reforms.
- *Goals.* The NPM had sharp, well defined goals. By contrast, American reformers had relatively vague goals revolving around the "works better/costs less" paradox.
- *Top leaders.* Top government officials took strong leadership roles in the NPM. Leadership of American reforms was relatively weak and less consistent in contrast.
- *Legislative role.* The NPM grew out of parliamentary democracies. Because the prime minister was the leader of the parliamentary majority, there was stronger support for the NPM within the legislature than in the United States, where few members of Congress had much interest in management.
- *Measurement of results.* American reforms (in both the Clinton and Bush administrations) sought to measure outcomes, or the impact of government programs. NPM reformers, by contrast, focused at first on narrower outputs, or the activity produced by a government program. Outcomes tended to be far more difficult to measure, so the NPM reformers made greater progress with their measures. But the real political interest lay with what impact government programs actually had, so even NPM reformers tended over time to attempt to measure outcomes more effectively.
- *Accountability.* The NPM sought accountability through a managerial process, especially formal contracts between the government and its top managers. The NPM sought to create a new, far more explicit system of accountability through written standards. The Americans, by contrast, depended on the existing (and often troubled) political relationships between senior executives and elected officials.
- *Risks.* NPM reforms tended to be high-risk. Managers who did not perform well could lose their jobs, and the transparency of the contract and output measurement systems focused sharp public attention on performance. In the United States, because measures were mushy and political attention was far more diffuse, the risks for performance problems tended to be lower.

TABLE 3
American reforms and the "new public management."

	New Public Management	American Reforms
Model	New economics	Business
Focus of reform	Transformation of structure	Reform of process
Goals	Precise	Fuzzy
Role of top leadership	Relatively strong	Relatively weak
Role of legislature	Relatively strong	Relatively weak
Measurement of results	Outputs	Outcomes
Accountability process	Managerial: through contracts	Political: through existing systems
Risks for success/failure	High stakes	Low stakes

Starting in the 1980s, government reformers produced a remarkable global movement.[24] There were strong core elements: a commitment to move past what reformers viewed as the pathologies of big government programs and too-powerful bureaucracies; a strong focus on performance and service; and an effort to integrate government management with political leadership. Indeed, the reformers shared a unusually strong belief in the notion that good management would be good politics—and that strong political leadership could refashion what government did and how government did it.

But there were also fundamental distinctions between American reforms and the leading efforts taking place elsewhere in the world. American reforms tended to be less intense, less sharply focused, and supported by less-aggressive political leadership. And even compared with the intense effort made by the Clinton reinvention campaign to downsize the federal workforce, efforts to shrink the size of government were even more aggressive in the NPM reforms. On the other hand, even though American reformers came later to the game, they were more ambitious in some key respects: a broader array of reform ideas (ranging from e-government to employee empowerment), and a more ambitious effort to measure the outcomes of government programs (even if the results were highly uneven).

The Impact of Reform

Few nations have America's undying impulse for fundamental reform and itinerary tinkering with government. What effects have these changes produced? And how do American reforms compare with those in other nations?

362

Costs Less

A major goal of government reform, in the United States and around the world, was shrinking government's size to reduce its cost. "Costs less" is, after all, half of the reinvention equation. Conservatives had become convinced that government had grown too large and too powerful. Liberals, even those committed to a stronger government, found that making the case for bigger government had become ever more difficult. The ideological battles have produced a profound and lasting tug of war over how big government ought to be.

NUMBER OF AGENCIES. Deciding what "big government" meant, however, let alone determining how best to measure it, proved a daunting job. How "big" is the federal government? One approach is to count the number of major agencies. Cabinet-level departments have been created throughout American history, most recently with the Department of Homeland Security (2002). With the notable exception of the federalization of airport screeners with the creation of DHS, however, the creation of most new cabinet departments has not been accompanied by a vast increase in governmental employees or functions. Cabinet status has far more to do with symbols than substance. As long as symbols are themselves important to key political players as an indicator of size, the number of cabinet-level agencies (and their subunits) will be a rough measure of the size of government, but not its reach or power.

NUMBER OF EMPLOYEES. A second measure of government's size is the number of employees. Federal employment grew rapidly during World War II, as government expanded for the war effort. When the war ended, however, federal civilian employment quickly settled to about 2 million employees, where it remained remarkably stable for decades. The Clinton reinvention effort downsized the federal workforce significantly, but the numbers began creeping back up again with the growth of the government's homeland security effort (see Figure 2). The message from the data is that, as measured by the number of employees, the federal government is certainly not significantly bigger than it was at the end of World War II. To be sure, the federal government has relied increasingly on nongovernmental proxies for service delivery, so counting just government employees does not give a good sense of the number of people actually doing its work.[25] But since World War II, the federal government has not increased its own size, measured by the number of its employees.

GOVERNMENT SPENDING. A third indicator, government spending, likewise gives surprising results. Government spending increased from $111 billion in 1963 to $2.2 trillion in 2003. But if spending is measured as a share of the economy, to take account both of economic growth and inflation, the trend falls in a far more narrow range. Federal spending gradually increased through the mid-

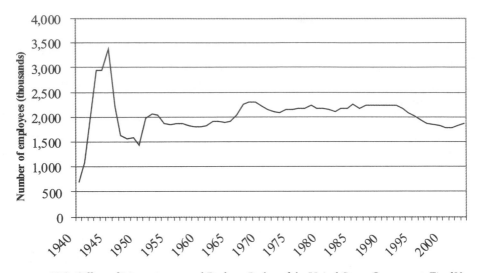

SOURCE: U.S. Office of Management and Budget, *Budget of the United States Government, Fiscal Year 2005: Historical Tables* (2004), Table 17.1, at http://www.whitehouse.gov/omb/budget/fy2005 /sheets/hist17z1.xls.

Figure 2   Federal Civilian Employment

1980s—including the Reagan administration, as the president led a major defense buildup. Federal spending fell back during the 1990s until spiking again in the early 2000s, because of the costs of homeland security and the war in Iraq (see Figure 3). The data do not show a steady upward growth of federal spending.

Even these figures are deceptive, however. Federal discretionary spending—for domestic programs like national parks and air traffic control as well as for foreign affairs and defense—over this period shrank 40 percent. In contrast, federal spending for entitlements—for programs like Social Security, Medicare, and Medicaid—nearly doubled. The vague and imprecise sense that many Americans have of a rapid growth in the federal government—and, especially, in government spending—does not match reality. Federal spending has in fact grown significantly, but for the programs shaped by automatic formulas and other features beyond the control of budget makers. Moreover, these entitlement programs are among those most strongly and fervently supported by citizens. By contrast, for the federal programs that decision makers control through the annual budget process, government has actually shrunken significantly. This is not, in sum, a picture of big growth of the federal government.

A comparison with the impact of NPM reforms on the size of government is instructive. The government sector was a far larger share of the national economy in the NPM nations than in the United States. As reformers sought to shrink the size of government spending and employment, NPM reformers were

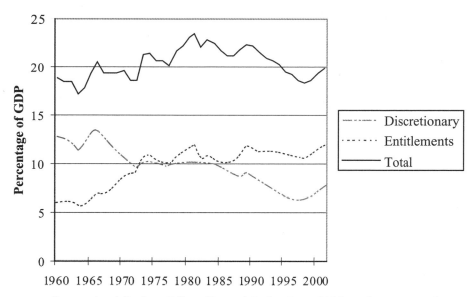

SOURCE: Congressional Budget Office, *Historical Budget Data* (2004), at http://www.cbo.gov/showdoc.cfm?index=1821&sequence=0#table5.

Figure 3   Trends in Federal Government Spending

aiming at making their governments more the size of American government. Since the American public sector never was as large as in the NPM nations, Americans put their energy elsewhere. For example, in 1985 public employment in the United States was 14.8 percent of total employment. In the United Kingdom, it was 21.6. By 1999 the two nations were more nearly even: 14.6 in the United States, and 12.6 percent in the United Kingdom.[26]

In spending, the principal—and perhaps surprising—effect was to narrow the differences in spending among the NPM nations and the United States. Over time, the NPM nations have used the reforms to bring their government outlays closer to those in the United States, while American reforms in contrast have remained relatively stable. American governmental spending (at all levels of government, which is how the Organization for Economic Cooperation and Development tabulates government outlays), dropped slightly, from 36.7 to 35.2 percent of the gross domestic product (GDP, the measure of the size of the economy) from 1987 to 2005. In New Zealand, by contrast, government spending dropped from 53.6 to 38.5 percent of GDP over the same period, a decline of more than one-fourth (see Figure 4).[27]

GOVERNMENT'S REACH. In addition to the number of organizational units, governmental employees, and government spending, there is a fourth way of assessing the size of government: its reach. This is a more amorphous indicator for which

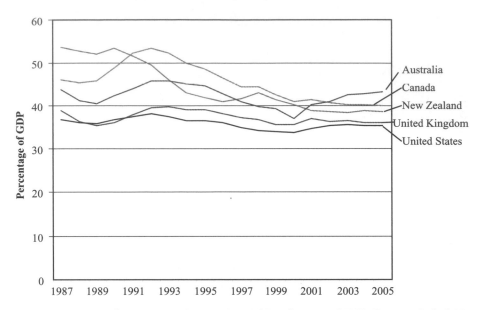

SOURCE: Organization for Economic Cooperation and Development, *OECD Economic Outlook No. 75* (2004), at 374

Figure 4   Trends in Government Spending

there are few good data. In part, it is a fuzzy sense of how deeply government seems to reach into people's lives. More rigorously, it is a concept about how much private and nonprofit sector activity the government leverages through its spending, taxing, lending, and regulatory programs.[28] While the concept is quite real, it is an extremely difficult one to measure. We know how much money government spends, but we can only approximate how much public money flows through private and nonprofit organizations and how many jobs it generates there. We know how much money government collects in taxes, and we have good approximations for the revenue the government foregoes through special tax incentives (like deductions and credits), but how much private and nonprofit activity this supports is difficult to determine precisely. The same is true for government's vast lending portfolio, including loans for everything from agricultural production and recovery to natural disasters to college aid. The government's regulatory reach is even more difficult to assess. We can count the number of volumes in the federal government's compendium, the Code of Federal Regulations (although this basic source is now most widely consulted on the World Wide Web).[29] Conservatives hold that there are far too many regulations. Liberals disagree. But everyone does concur that the reach of federal rules is substantial and growing.

The reach of federal power is unquestionably large, and it is quite certainly larger than a generation ago. Medicare and Medicaid, even though the two programs cover only a fraction of the nation's population (the elderly and the poor), have come to shape the entire health care system. Federal environmental, health, and safety regulations govern the top-to-bottom operation of most businesses. Federal loans subsidize half of all college students,[30] and government corporations have created an enormous secondary mortgage market that has made housing loans cheaper and more plentiful. Consumers count on federal rules to safeguard the food we eat, the cars we drive, and the planes in which we fly.

In this vast, unquestionably large, but largely uncharted reach of the federal government lies an important paradox. As we have seen, by most common measures of size, the federal government has not grown significantly in the last fifty years. Its reach, however, is vastly greater. That is because the real growth of the federal government has come through complex strategies and tactics whose real impact is not in the federal government's activity, but in how its activity shapes the behavior of for-profit and non-profit organizations. The federal government's role has become much more one of moving money than of managing people. Its impact has come much more through its leverage of markets. Its reach has become vastly larger even though, by most measures of size, it has not grown.

The American reinvention effort had indeed shrunken the size of the federal government, by most ways of measuring it. But at the same time, government's reach had paradoxically increased. How can we assess the "costs less" promise of reinvention? As national problems, from homeland security to health care, have become larger and more complex, government has faced a dilemma: finding ways to respond to pressing public concern without increasing government's size. American government officials have cleverly done so by relying on indirect government strategies and tactics—including especially contracting out, regulations, and tax programs—in which the government expands programs without expanding the size of government (at least according to the measures that most citizens and public officials typically use). The American government has thus expanded its reach without increasing its size, and many nations around the world—including the NPM reformers—have begun following the American lead, for the same reasons.

Works Better

The other half of the reinvention equation—making the government work better—is far harder to assess. In part, it is because problems multiply faster than the reforms, so it is difficult for reinvention to keep up. In part, it is because getting good measures of results is so tremendously difficult. The methodological problems are enormous, especially since reformers in the United States focused on measuring outcomes instead of outputs. (Outcomes are harder to measure because they require clear definition of goals, assessment of outputs, and broader measures of how these outputs affect social conditions, and a comparison of these impacts with program goals. This is a very tall order.)

Moreover, the "works better" half of the equation often has less political salience. Government policy makers tend to focus more on spending and distributing money than they do on producing results. The president is less chief executive than national spokesman and political leader. Members of Congress have stronger incentives for focusing on spending over results.

It is easier to track the measures of size than the indicators of performance. There have unquestionably been efficiency improvements. Anyone who once struggled to collect the forms needed to file income taxes will marvel at how much easier it is to get the needed forms and instructions from the Internal Revenue Service Web site. But there have been no broad-scope evaluations, and the limited assessments of academics and the Government Accountability Office suggest a mixed record. In general, as two of the foremost international observers of government reform, Christopher Pollitt and Geert Bouckaert, found, "Despite the existence of a flourishing evaluation culture in the U.S. public service, it is extremely difficult to come to any sure assessment of the impact of the reforms since 1980."[31] If we ask whether America's reforms have made government "work better," it is hard to come to a conclusion other than "probably—but it is hard to know for sure where, and by how much."

The same is true for assessing many of the reforms around the world. Much of the rhetoric surrounding reforms is utopian, and elected officials have been eager to tell citizens (and voters) about how much they have accomplished. The biggest change has often been a "changed climate," with a stronger focus on performance, more deregulation, and more reliance on privatization strategies. But tracking the impact is difficult. There is a great deal of data, but much of the data are not very systematic, especially evaluating achievements. Assessing changes in the culture of government bureaucracies is much harder, and evidence about increasing trust in government is difficult to assess. Ultimately, evidence about reforms around the world, according to Pollitt and Bouckaert, "is both sparse and ambiguous. This is partly because most governments do not seem to have looked very hard for this type of information, but partly also because such information is difficult and expensive to collect, and then hard to interpret."[32]

Nevertheless, even though clear evidence for improvements in the performance of American government is slim, there is substantial evidence that Americans—especially top officials—are paying more attention to it. Performance was a major theme for the Clinton and George W. Bush administrations. Moreover, the Bush reforms had as a central theme the effort to hard-wire performance measurement into the budgetary process, and to integrate that process into OMB's decision making, so that it would remain after the administration left. It remains to be seen just how permanent this performance measurement process will be, what political impact it might produce, and what additional leverage it might give the president in controlling the bureaucracy and steering relationships with Congress. But, regardless of its short-term impact, the recent emphasis on performance is an important shift in American executive life.

Reforming American Government

As a nation founded on both pragmatism and revolution, Americans have been at the government reform business for a very long time. Its founders invented modern federalism and translated the concept of separation of powers into reality. They created a remarkably resilient system characterized less by powerful institutions than by their ability to flex and adapt to changing social, economic, and political problems. Especially in the twentieth century, there was scarcely a period when the national government was not in the midst of major reforms.

America is hardly alone in the instinct for reform. In the last two decades of the twentieth century, a widespread reform movement focused on improving government performance swept through much of the industrialized, and even the developing, world. Some nations, especially among the Westminster countries, moved more aggressively than the United States on a broader front. They privatized some government-owned industries, shrank the size of government, introduced contract-driven agencies, and developed output-based accountability systems. A major round of American reforms began later, with the "reinventing government" initiative of the Clinton administration and the management agenda of the Bush administration. The Clinton reforms were broad, ambitious, and outcome-driven, but they had less aggressive leadership from the top and uneven penetration to the bottom of the bureaucracy. The Bush reforms were far more narrow, focused on increasing contracting out and linking outcome measures to budget decisions. In one sense, American reforms lagged behind those in some other parts of the world. In another sense, American reforms set a new framework for citizen-centered, outcome-driven government that many other nations began to explore themselves. And the contagion of ideas—from the private sector to the public sector, from other nations to the United States (and vice versa)—continues to fuel reform.

The American impulse toward reform thus had a distinctively different character from reform movements in other parts of the world, especially because the United States had not created as large a welfare state as many other nations. Indeed, many other nations worked for two decades to shrink the size of their government (measured as government's share of the GDP) to the size of the American government *before* its reforms.

The American system of separated powers made it impossible to create a precise output-based system or to hold public managers accountable through a contract-based system. In the United States, the cross-pressures exerted by the executive, legislative, and judicial branches make the policy goals of public programs inevitably vague, changing, and sometimes conflicting. These cross-pressures make it difficult to create a consistent audience for performance measures—and for political officials to decide what to do with them (beyond sometimes using them as weapons in the larger political battle, which creates strong disincentives for public managers to produce evidence that could be used against them). Moreover, the American political system is not only multi-branch. Public policy is more multi-layer (federal, state, and local) and multi-sector (public, private, and nonprofit) than anywhere else in the world.

That makes it even more difficult to assign precise responsibilities for results, since government (especially at the federal level) increasingly shares those responsibilities with partners whose actions are often under uneven control. Federal agencies operate in a hierarchical structure created by Congress and managed (more or less) by the president and his executive office. Federal partners operate through grants, contracts, regulations, loans, tax incentives, and other tools that defy hierarchical control or clear outcome standards. This does not mean that accountability is impossible. Rather, it means that the government must devise new and innovative tools of accountability that match the rapid advancement of the tools of government. For the most part, the tools have advanced more quickly than have the systems to manage them—ensuring a demand for continuing reinvention within American government.

This steady march of government reform can easily promote cynicism. Through the constant reform movement, does anything ever really change? Does the process swing back and forth through endless cycles, which put heavy emphasis on one set of values (like efficiency and effectiveness) only to have new problems build up and shift the emphasis to different values (like responsiveness and accountability)?[33] In short, do we ever truly make progress? A careful look at American administrative history over the twentieth century says that the answer unquestionably is "yes." The nation has new agencies for managing the money supply and air safety, for protecting food and the environment, for increasing homeland security and intelligence integration. To be sure, none works as well as their founders intended or the way that many Americans expect. And to be sure, some Americans resist the idea that government ought to have a powerful role in some of these functions to begin with. Moreover, the processes of government, from improved technology to stronger budget control systems, are unquestionably better. The performance management systems introduced in the Clinton and George W. Bush administrations, while much criticized, have certainly strengthened the ability of top officials to track what federal agencies do and how well they do it.

Of course, the federal government is not really built for top-down management. The separation of powers ensures that administrative agencies pay as much attention to Congress and, especially, to its committees as to the president and his staff. The multiplicity of interest groups, and the multiple arenas in which they seek leverage over public policy, only multiplies the centrifugal forces on government management. Presidents inevitably find themselves focusing on a hand-ful of the really big issues, and they have little time and less interest in trying to "manage" the government. The analysts on the White House staff and in the Office of Management and Budget find themselves stretched and, often, out-gunned on all but the biggest managerial issues. The deck is therefore stacked against presidential reforms. Presidential efforts to strengthen top-down mana-gerial control over federal agencies, let alone over the vast network of contractors and grantees who actually deliver most federal programs, can never be more than modestly successful.

Why, then, do presidents continue to insist on doing things that so often seem destined to fail? After all, new presidents and, especially, their advisors know the history well indeed.

The answer is complex, but the complexities yield rich insights into the workings of executive branch politics. Management reforms, in fact, often suc-ceed, at least in part, in ways that have value for the president. First, presidents typically are eager to establish their distinctive mark on the presidency and, espe-cially, to signal the bureaucracy that a new person is in charge. The announce-ment of new reform initiatives conveys strong signals. When Bush took over from Clinton, for example, he immediately shut down Gore's "reinventing gov-ernment" office and announced his management reforms. This signaled stronger top-level attention to management and a stronger link to the budgetary process. But the reform process focuses sharp attention on the fourth paradox we have identified in this book: the need for a bureaucracy responsive to elected offi-cials—especially the president—and our expectation of a stable, expert bureau-cracy whose capacity stretches beyond that of any particular administration.

Second, these signals do more than create symbols. They provide a counter-balance to the powerful pull of Congress on executive branch agencies. New presidents not only need to separate themselves from their predecessors. They also need to fight the continuing battle between the White House and Capitol Hill over who shapes bureaucratic behavior. As Barry Weingast points out in Chapter 10 of this volume, executive departments often find themselves caught in the middle of a tug of war between the president and Congress, and presidents have used managerial reforms to try to tip the balance in their favor.

Third, in an era when more and more of the federal budget is "uncontrol-lable," driven by entitlements and long-term commitments over which presidents have little control, any tool that offers even modest leverage is welcome. Even if their public statements rarely reflect the fact, presidents seldom have sweeping expectations about large-scale reforms, and any additional influence is welcome. Moreover, as Colin Campbell explains in Chapter 8 of this volume, presidents face an executive branch structure that is increasingly complex. Reforms have been increasingly attractive as ways to increase the president's ability to influence this structure. Indeed, coupled with the centrifugal forces on the bureaucracy, this tension echoes the third paradox identified in this book, the expectation of strong presidential leadership and the fear of excessive presidential power.

Finally, the typical perspective on presidential management reforms—big announcements with little effect and subsequent erosion of interest, only to follow the same cycle in the next presidency—is inaccurate. In fact, many reforms have had lasting impact behind the headlines. The much-maligned "planning-programming-budgeting system" introduced by Robert McNamara and his Kennedy administration "whiz kids" continues to influence Pentagon budgets. Gore's customer-service initiatives have transformed everything from the way the IRS communicates with taxpayers to the Social Security Administration's efforts to strengthen its telephone service. Although each president begins by publicly sweeping away the reforms of his predecessor, in reality many of them endure, and some have had long-term impact.

In sum, the reform process works more like a ratchet than a pendulum, with government's capacity increased a step at a time. Sometimes the ratchet slips back, and sometimes reformers struggle over who controls how big the steps are and in what direction they ought to move. But it is difficult to dispute the proposition that American government is more efficient and effective because of the efforts of its reformers.

Big problems remain to be solved, however. Even though American government is relatively small in comparison with the rest of the world, many Americans believe it is too large. That is especially true because of government's expansive and growing reach, which has continued to increase even though by other measures of size government has barely grown at all (or, in some cases, has even shrunk). America's constant debate over reforming government has often focused on its structure, policies, and processes. Much of it has been about how to make it work better. But much of the debate—even about the issue of reform—has also been about what government *should* do.

Thus the partisan battles over reform, even if couched in seemingly narrow management terms, are often about much bigger questions that revolve around important, changing emphases of key political values. Many reforms seemingly directed at improving performance are therefore also about creating political symbols and resolving political conflict. That is true in other nations as well, of course, but the very nature of American political institutions makes the pressures for transforming administrative reform into political struggle especially large and lasting.

It also is part of the engine driving America's relentless reform movement. Everyone talks about government and reforming it. Yet the nation has a long history of hostility to government and the public service, even as its reformers seek to improve it. New policy problems present government with new management challenges, but they also present new venues in which to struggle over the enduring political questions at the core of American society.

Notes

1. Walter Isaacson, *Benjamin Franklin: An American Life* (New York: Simon and Schuster, 2003), 102.

2. For example, see Graham K. Wilson, *Only in America? American Politics in Comparative Perspective* (Chatham, N.J.: Chatham House, 1998); and John W. Kingdon, *America the Unusual* (Belmont, Calif.: Wadsworth, 1998).

3. For an outstanding history and analysis of this period, see Daniel P. Carpenter, *The Forging of Bureaucratic Autonomy: Reputations, Networks, and Policy Innovation in Executive Agencies, 1862–1928* (Princeton, N.J.: Princeton University Press, 2001).

4. The definitive study of the Social Security program is Martha Derthick, *Policy Making for Social Security* (Washington, D.C.: The Brookings Institution, 1979).

5. Jeffrey L. Pressman and Aaron Wildavsky, *Implementation: How Great Expectations in Washington Are Dashed in Oakland; Or, Why It's Amazing That Federal Programs Work at All, This Being a Saga of the Economic Development Administration as Told by Two Sympathetic Observers Who Seek to Build Morals on a Foundation of Ruined Hopes* (Berkeley: University of California Press, 1973).

6. Daniel Patrick Moynihan, *Maximum Feasible Misunderstanding: Community Action in the War on Poverty* (New York: Macmillan, 1970).

7. Arthur M. Schlesinger, Jr., *The Imperial Presidency* (Boston: Houghton Mifflin, 1973).

8. David B. Walker, *The Rebirth of Federalism: Slouching toward Washington*, 2nd ed. (Washington, D.C.: CQ Press, 1999).

9. Paul C. Light, *The True Size of Government* (Washington, D.C.: The Brookings Institution, 1999), pp. 1, 22–25.

10. Al Gore, *From Red Tape to Results: Creating a Government That Works Better and Costs Less* (Washington, D.C.: National Performance Review, September 7, 1993). For an assessment of this effort, see Donald F. Kettl, *Reinventing Government: A Fifth Year Report Card* (Washington, D.C.: The Brookings Institution, 1998).

11. Osborne and Gaebler, *Reinventing Government*.

12. David Osborne, *Laboratories of Democracy* (Cambridge: Harvard Business School Press, 1988).

13. David Osborne, "Reinventing Government: Creating an Entrepreneurial Federal Establishment," in Will Marshall and Martin Schram, eds., *Mandate for Change* (New York: Berkeley Books, 1993), 237–261.

14. Al Gore, *Common Sense Government: Works Better and Costs Less* (Washington, D.C.: U.S. GPO, 1995), 14–16.

15. U.S. Office of Management and Budget, *President's Management Agenda* (GPO, 2001), 4, at http://www.whitehouse.gov/omb/budget/fy2002/mgmt.pdf.

16. Amelia Gruber, "Nine Agencies Earn Higher Management Grades," Govexec.com (July 14, 2003), at http://www.govexec.com/dailyfed/0703/071403a1.htm (accessed July 18, 2003).

17. For an examination of the issues and the case for PPBS, see Charles J. Hitch and Roland McKean, *The Economics of Defense in the Nuclear Age* (Cambridge, Mass.: Harvard University Press, 1967). Charles L. Schultze has an enthusiastic endorsement of the approach in *The Politics and Economics of Public Spending* (Washington,

D.C.: The Brookings Institution, 1968). Finally, for a history of the development of PPBS, see Robert D. Lee, Jr., and Ronald W. Johnson, *Public Budgeting Systems* (Baltimore, Md.: University Park Press, 1983).

18. See Barzelay and Campbell, *Preparing for the Future.*
19. National Commission on Terrorist Attacks upon the United States, *The 9/11 Commission Report* (New York: W. W. Norton, 2004).
20. Schick, *The Spirit of Reform,* 11.
21. See R. H. Coase, "The Nature of the Firm," *Economica* 4 (1937), 386–405; and Oliver E. Williamson, *Markets and Hierarchies: Analysis and Antitrust Implications* (New York: Free Press, 1975).
22. Schick, *The Spirit of Reform,* Executive Summary. Available at: http://www.ssc .govt.nz/display/document.asp?docid=2845&pageno=1#P1_0.
23. See, for example, Allen Schick, "Why Most Developing Countries Should Not Try New Zealand Reforms," *The World Bank Research Observer* 13 (February 1998), 123–131.
24. See Donald F. Kettl, *The Global Public Management Revolution: A Report on the Transformation of Governance* (Washington, D.C.: The Brookings Institution, 2000).
25. See Donald F. Kettl, *Government by Proxy: (Mis)Managing Federal Programs* (Washington, D.C.: CQ Press, 1988); and Lester M. Salamon, ed., *The Tools of Government: A Public Management Handbook for the Era of Third-Party Government* (New York: Oxford University Press, 2002).
26. Organization for Economic Cooperation and Development, OECD Public Management Service (2001), at http://www.oecd.org/dataoecd/37/43/1849079.xls.
27. For a discussion of American exceptionalism, see Wilson, *Only in America.*
28. For a discussion of the policy and politics of these tools, see Salamon, ed., *The Tools of Government.*
29. See http://www.gpoaccess.gov/cfr/index.html.
30. June Kronholz, "Student Loans Take Political Stage," *Wall Street Journal* (May 3, 2004), A4.
31. Pollitt and Bouckaert, *Public Management Reform,* 284.
32. Ibid., 131. More generally, see chapter 5. On the problem of assessing management reforms, see George A. Boyne, Catherine Farrell, Jennifer Law, Martin Powell, and Richard M. Walker, *Evaluating Public Management Reforms* (Buckingham, U.K.: Open University Press, 2003).
33. On the issue of shifting values, see Arthur Okun, *Equality and Efficiency: The Big Tradeoff* (Washington, D.C.: The Brookings Institution, 1975). Paul Light has explored the historical trends of government reinvention in *The Tides of Reform.*

Bibliography

Barzelay, Michael, and Colin Campbell. *Preparing for the Future: Strategic Planning in the U.S. Air Force.* Washington, D.C.: The Brookings Institution, 2003. A keenly insightful book about how management reforms have transformed the Air Force. It is the best work on the implications of reform at the operating levels of the bureaucracy.

Kettl, Donald F. *The Global Public Management Revolution.* Washington, D.C.: The Brookings Institution, 2005. A concise review of the trends in government reform in the United States and around the world.

Kettl, Donald F., ed., with John J. DiIulio, Jr. *Inside the Reinvention Machine: Appraising Governmental Reform.* Washington, D.C.: The Brookings Institution, 1995. An analysis of the implementation of the Clinton "reinventing government" initiative.

Light, Paul C. *The Tides of Reform: Making Government Work, 1945–1995.* New Haven: Yale University Press, 1997. An excellent history of government reform in the second half of the twentieth century.

Osborne, David, and Ted Gaebler. *Reinventing Government: How the Entrepreneurial Spirit Is Transforming the Public Sector.* Reading, Mass.: Addison-Wesley, 1992. The highly influential book that helped shape the Clinton administration's reform initiative.

Pollitt, Christopher, and Geert Bouckaert. *Public Management Reform: A Comparative Analysis.* Oxford: Oxford University Press, 2000. An excellent study of reforms around the world, which places the American reforms in a broad, comparative perspective.

Schick, Allen. *The Spirit of Reform: Managing the New Zealand State Sector in a Time of Change.* Wellington: New Zealand State Services Commission and the Treasury, 1996. The definitive analysis of the New Zealand government reforms.

U.S. Office of Management and Budget. *President's Management Agenda.* Government Printing Office, 2001, available at: http://www.whitehouse.gov/omb/budget /fy2002/mgmt.pdf. This document lays out the Bush administration's management reform strategy.

THE PRESIDENT, EXECUTIVE AGENCIES, AND THE INSTITUTIONS OF POLICY MAKING

12

EXECUTIVE POWER AND POLITICAL PARTIES: THE DILEMMAS OF SCALE IN AMERICAN DEMOCRACY

Sidney M. Milkis

THE RELATIONSHIP BETWEEN THE EXECUTIVE BRANCH and the American party system has never been easy. The architects of the Constitution established a nonpartisan president who, with the support of the judiciary and Senate, was intended to play the leading institutional role in checking and controlling "the violence of faction" that the framers feared would rend the fabric of representative government. Even after the presidency became a more partisan office during the early nineteenth century—a development tied to holding the executive office accountable to Congress as well as state and local interests—its authority continued to depend on an ability to remain independent of party politics, especially during national emergencies, such as the Civil War and the Spanish-American War.

Deliberately welded to the Constitution by Jeffersonian and Jacksonian reformers to thwart Hamiltonian nationalism and to keep power close enough to the people for representative government to prevail, parties were rooted in the states and localities; they penetrated deeply into American society between the 1830s and 1890s. During the twentieth century, however, the "Constitution-against-Parties," as Richard Hofstadter called it, would become newly relevant.[1] Localized parties represented a formidable obstacle to Progressive reformers who considered the expansion of national administrative power essential to economic and political reform. Aroused by antiparty sentiment, the Progressive movement tended to discredit rather than reform partisanship. Given the constitutional and political difficulties involved in establishing a national programmatic, let alone social democratic, party in the United States, most Progressives looked to revive the antipartyism of the original Constitution as an agent of reform. Progressives hoped, as Herbert Croly put it, "to give democratic meaning and purpose to the Hamiltonian tradition and method."[2] Progressive democracy glimpsed a national community, in which new political institutions such as the direct primary, initiative, and referendum would forge a direct link between public opinion and government representatives. It rested on the possibility of creating a "modern," independent executive who might become, as Theodore Roosevelt put it, "the steward of the public welfare."[3]

The inherent tension between the presidency and the party system reached a critical point during the 1930s. With Franklin D. Roosevelt and the New Deal, the modern presidency became an enduring part of American political life. The "institutionalization" of the modern executive office, arguably the most significant constitutional legacy of FDR's New Deal, ruptured the limited but critical bond that linked presidents and parties. The modern executive branch embodied the reform aspirations of Progressive reformers; it was crafted with the intention of reducing the influence of the two-party system on American politics. An extraordinary party leader, Roosevelt gave rise to a critical partisan realignment that established the Democrats as the majority party in the country. At the same time, the New Deal transformed the Democratic Party into a way station on the road to a more administrative Constitution, to a more centralized and bureaucratic form of democracy that focused American political life on the president and administrative agencies.

Roosevelt's extraordinary party leadership thus contributed to the decline of the American party system. This decline continued—even accelerated—under the administrations of subsequent presidents, notably Lyndon B. Johnson and Richard Nixon. Yet as became clear during the presidency of Ronald Reagan, the erosion of old-style partisan politics had allowed a more national and issue-based party system to develop, forging new links between presidents and parties. Just as traditional parties were formed to constrain presidential ambition, so the "new" American party system seems better suited to serve the political and programmatic ambitions of the modern executive. George W. Bush further advanced and benefited from the more national programmatic party that arose with the resurgence and transformation of conservatism during the Reagan presidency. It remains to be seen, however, whether the national programmatic parties can perform the parties' historic function of moderating presidential ambition and mobilizing public support for political values and government policies.

Presidents, Parties, and the Constitution

The critical and uneasy relationship between the American presidency and political parties sheds light on the central question of the American experiment:

whether it is possible to realize self-government on a grand scale. This was the question that divided the Federalists and the Antifederalists; and it was revisited in the constitutional struggles between the Jeffersonian Republicans and the Hamiltonian Federalists. As formed during the first three decades of the nineteenth century, political parties reflected the concern first expressed by the Antifederalists, and later revised by Jefferson, that the Constitution provided inadequately for the cultivation of an active and competent citizenry. The Antifederalists were not fond of partisanship, but like their Jeffersonian descendants they viewed political parties as the most practical remedy for the corrosion of confidence between rulers and ruled, indeed among citizens themselves, in a large political system. Formed during the early part of the nineteenth century, political parties were conceived as bulwarks of decentralization, as localized political associations that could provide a vital link between constitutional offices, especially the executive, and the people; they would do so by balancing state and local communities, championed by the Antifederalists as the true guardians of the people's rights, and the national government, strengthened by the Constitution of 1787.

Significantly, Madison, the principal architect of the "Constitution-against-Parties," became a defender of parties and local self-government during the critical partisan battles between the Republicans and Federalists. Alexander Hamilton's success as secretary of the treasury in the Washington administration in strengthening the executive led Madison to rethink his understanding of republican government, to recognize that the Antifederalists might have been more correct in their criticisms of the Constitution than he previously had thought. By the early 1790s, he joined Jefferson in opposition to the Federalists, in the formulation of a party program of government decentralization, which renewed the conflicts that had divided the Federalists and Antifederalists and, consequently, gave birth to the American party system.[4]

Those who played the leading parts in legitimizing and building parties, in making them part of the "living Constitution" by the 1830s, were not "antifederalists." Even the Jacksonians, who embraced a more militant states' rights position than their Jeffersonian forebears, supported the idea that the Constitution beheld "a more perfect union." Jacksonian parties, in fact, found their strength principally in the political combat of presidential elections—a battleground that encouraged Democratic and Whig partisans to overlook their differences in the interest of victory. Moreover, the positions espoused during these campaigns were not words to be ignored but, as one Whig representative put it, "worth fighting for . . . the rules of our action." The national quality and strength of the two parties were demonstrated by the impressive party cohesion that shaped the work of the federal government during the 1830s and 1840s.[5] Paradoxically, the Jacksonian party system established a national framework of principles and behavior that defied local differences even as it transformed the doctrine of local self-government into a national idea. The Jacksonian presidency, celebrated as the "tribune" of the people, embodied the rising spirit of democratic nationalism, which sustained and strengthened the Union in the face of serious conflicts over the tariff law and slavery.

Still, no less than the Jeffersonian Republicans, Jacksonian Democrats feared that the institutional dynamics of the original Constitution tended toward "consolidation," undermining the formation of local self-government, which they sought to strengthen as the sentinels of liberty in American constitutional democracy. The Jeffersonians and Jacksonsonians sought a remedy for this political disease in partisan principles and practices that valued the decentralization of power.

Modern party politics in Great Britain and Europe began at the end of the nineteenth century with the effort to reform a state that presumed the existence of strong national controls; in contrast, American political parties matured as the cornerstone of a political order that celebrated democratic individualism and presumed the absence of centralized administrative authority.[6] The form of party organization that was legitimized during the Jeffersonian and Jacksonian eras endured well into the twentieth century. Even the rise of the Republican Party during the 1850s, as a result of the slavery controversy, and the subsequent demise of the Whigs, did not alter the essential characteristics of the party system in the United States, and these characteristics—decentralized organization and hostility to administrative centralization—restrained rather than facilitated executive power.

The decentralized party system did not always constrain presidential ambition. Indeed, Washington apart, America's greatest presidents were all either founders or re-founders of political parties. In important respects, all of America's "reconstructive leaders," to use Stephen Skowronek's phrase, have used parties to remake American politics in their own image, to "reset the very terms of constitutional government."[7] But such extraordinary party leadership has highlighted the collective nature of great political transformations in the United States. Political parties have kept presidents faithful to broader interests, even as, episodically, during periods of partisan realignment, they have given presidents the political strength to embark on ambitious projects of national reform. Moreover, prior to the New Deal, none of the programs to which the electorate had subscribed during a partisan realignment had called for a substantial exercise of executive power.

Progressive Democracy and the Decline of the Party State

Progressives championed a new national order that could not abide the localized democracy of the nineteenth century. Their reform zeal aimed, above all else, at the concentration of wealth that arose with the industrialization revolution, specifically at the giant corporations—the "Trusts"—which, according to Progressive reformers, constituted uncontrolled and irresponsible units of power in American society. These industrial combinations created the perception that opportunity had become less equal in the United States, that growing corporate power threatened the freedom of individuals to earn a living. This threat to equal opportunity posed a severe challenge to the doctrine of local self-government, as reformers had good reason to believe that the great business interests, represented by newly formed associations such as the National Civic Federation, had captured and corrupted local officials for their own profit. By the end of the nineteenth century, party leaders—both Democrats and Republicans—were scorned as irresponsible "bosses" who did the bidding of special interests.

Viewing parties as the linchpin of corruption and injustice, Progressives championed, as one reformer put it, "government at first-hand: government of the People directly *by* the People."[8] Indeed, in their attack on intermediate associations such as political parties and interest groups, reformers of the early twentieth century issued a battle cry that enlisted popular support not only for women's suffrage, primaries, and direct election of senators but also for methods of "pure democracy," such as initiative, referendum, and recall. Especially controversial was the Progressives' program to subject constitutional questions to direct popular control, including proposals for an easier method to amend the Constitution and referenda on laws that the state courts declared unconstitutional. This commitment to direct democracy became the centerpiece of the Progressive Party campaign of 1912, which was sanctified as a "covenant with the people," a deep and abiding pledge to make the people "masters of their Constitution."

The brief, but significant, experience of the Progressive Party underscores the powerful centrifugal force of progressive democracy. With the celebrated former president Theodore Roosevelt as its candidate, the Bull Moose Party won 27.4 percent of the popular vote and eighty-eight electoral votes from six states in 1912. This was extraordinary for a third party: in fact, no third-party candidate for the presidency—before or after 1912—has received so large a percentage of the popular vote or as many electoral votes as did Theodore Roosevelt. Despite its remarkable showing in 1912, however, the Progressive Party was dead four years later, its fate inseparable from the dynamic leader who embodied its cause. The old saw of historical literature is that the Progressive Party was essentially a personal vehicle for Theodore Roosevelt, an organization relegated to serving his ambition to return to the White House. Consequently, the Progressive Party was not invested with a collective mission and organization that could survive his return to the Republican Party in 1916.

Yet the Progressive Party lies at the very heart of fundamental changes in American politics—changes that were initially, if only partially, negotiated during the Progressive Era. The personalistic quality of Roosevelt's campaign was part and parcel of these changes, but they went much deeper than his desire to regain past political mastery. The Progressive Party, with its leader-centered organization, accommodated and embodied an array of reformers—insurgent Republican officeholders, disaffected Democrats, crusading journalists, academics, social workers, and other activists—who hoped that the new party coalition would realize their common goal of expanding the responsibilities of the federal government and making it more responsive to popular economic, social, and political demands.[9]

The Progressive pledge to rescue the government from the throes of corporate capitalism resembled the Jacksonians' hatred of the "monster bank"; however, most Progressives were avowedly hostile to Jacksonian democracy, dubbed derisively by Croly as "pioneer democracy." As Martin Shefter has written,

> For each of the major institutional reforms in the Jacksonian era, the Progressives sponsored an equal and opposite reform. The Jacksonians had increased the number of executive offices subject to popular election; the Progressives sought to reduce that number and to create the position of chief executive through such reforms as the short ballot and the strong mayor plan of municipal government. . . . The Jacksonians extended the franchise; the Progressives contracted it through registration, literacy, and citizenship requirements. The Jacksonians established party conventions to nominate candidates for elective office; the Progressives replaced them with primary elections. The Jacksonians created a hierarchical structure of party committees to manage the electorate; the Progressives sought to destroy these party organizations or at least render their tasks more difficult through such reforms as the nonpartisan municipal government, and the separation of local, state, and national elections. Finally, the Jacksonians established a party press and accorded influence to the political editor; the Progressive movement was linked to the emergence of a self-consciously independent press (magazines as well as newspapers) and with muckraking journalists.[10]

In condemning reformers for lacking a coherent set of principles, contemporary scholars point to the apparent contradiction between Progressives' celebration of direct democracy and their hope to achieve more disinterested government, which seemed to demand a more powerful and independent bureaucracy.[11] Certainly, the Progressive faith in public opinion was far from complete. Most Progressives celebrated an idea of national community that did not include immigrants and African Americans.[12] Moreover, the commitment of Progressive reformers to forming an independent executive led to support for technical expertise that insulated government decisions from the vagaries of public opinion and elections.

Progressives did not celebrate expertise for its own sake, however. Rather, they sought to strengthen national administrative power as an arm of presidential responsibility. "At present our administration is organized chiefly upon the principle that the executive shall not be permitted to do much good for fear that he will do harm," Croly lamented. "It ought to be organized on the principle that he shall have full power to do either well or ill, but that if he does ill, he will have no defense against punishment."[13] As Roosevelt described this concept of executive power, the president was "a steward of the people bound actively and affirmatively to do all he could for the people, and not content himself with the negative merit of keeping his talents undamaged in a napkin."[14] Significantly, TR's presidency (1901–1909) marked the dividing line between the old commitment to party patronage in public affairs and the modern recognition that nonpolitical administration was a principal tool of governance. A civil service reform bill, the Pendleton Act, had been enacted in 1883, in response to the assassination of President James A. Garfield by a disappointed office seeker. The Pendleton Act, which created a bipartisan Civil Service Commission, provided for competitive (merit-based) examinations for federal jobs, and authorized the president to expand the bounds of civil service coverage by executive order, had a limited effect on the executive branch until Roosevelt occupied the White House. TR pushed the coverage of the merit system for hiring, promotion, and tenure almost to the limit. By the end of his incumbency, approximately 60 percent of the civil service was included in the merit system, even as the federal workforce expanded from approximately 250,000 in 1901 to around 365,000 in 1909.

Americans have never carried the idea of nonpolitical service to the same lengths as the British; indeed, Progressives' celebration of the "people" testified to their diffident approach to building a professional civil service when compared to the state-building efforts in other representative democracies. But by the time of Roosevelt's term in office, merit had begun to supplant spoils. Presidential leadership, previously dependent on patronage-seeking state and local party machines, now required careful attention to administrative management, some times to foster economy and efficiency and sometimes to bolster the power of the increasingly active federal government. The new challenge for the president was to take charge of the large and disparate administrative apparatus. As Skowronek has written, "A state building sequence that began with Roosevelt's determination to forge 'a more orderly system of control,' ended with the consolidation of a new governmental order defiant of all attempts at control."[15]

Without denying that the Progressive movement was weakened by a tension between reforms that diminished democracy and those that sought to make democracy more direct, its central thrust was an attack on political parties and the creation of a more direct, programmatic link between the executive branch and the people. Progressives argued that the expansion of social welfare programs and "pure democracy" were inextricably connected. Reforms such as the direct primary, as well as the initiative and referendum, were designed to overthrow the localized two-party system in the United States, which bestowed on the separated institutions of the federal government a certain unity of control, while at the same time it restrained programmatic ambition and prevented the development of a stable and energetic administration of social policy. By the same token, the triumph of "progressive" over "pioneer" democracy, as Croly framed it, would put the American people directly in touch with the councils of power, thus strengthening the demand for government support and would allow, indeed, require, administrative agencies to play their proper role in the realization of progressive social welfare policy.[16] "So our nascent, insurgent, still unfolded democracy, which unites many men in a common hostility to certain broad economic and political developments, is now passing over to a definite program," the Progressive thinker Walter Weyl wrote hopefully in 1912. "It is becoming positive . . . and seeks to test its motives and ideals in relation to American history and conditions."[17]

For Progressives, public opinion would reach fulfillment with the formation of an independent executive power, freed from the provincial, special, and corrupt influence of political parties. Dedicated to Jeffersonian and Jacksonian principles, political parties in the United States were wedded to constitutional arrangements that impeded the expansion of national administrative power in the name of the people's economic welfare. The origins and organizing principles of the American party system established it as a force against the creation of a "modern state." The Progressive reformers' commitment to building such a state—that is, to the creation of a national political power with expansive programmatic responsibilities—meant that the party system had to be either weakened or reconstructed. As Barry Karl has noted, the Progressive Party campaign of 1912 was as much "an attack on the whole concept of political parties as it was an effort to create a single party whose doctrinal clarity and moral purity would represent the true interest of the nation as a whole."[18]

New Deal Liberalism and the American Party System

The decisive break with the American tradition of limited government anticipated by Theodore Roosevelt's Progressive Party campaign of 1912 came with Franklin D. Roosevelt in the 1930s and his deft reinterpretation of the "liberal tradition" in the United States. Liberalism had always been associated with Jeffersonian principles and the natural rights tradition of limited government drawn from John Locke's *Second Treatise of Government* and the Declaration of Independence. Roosevelt pronounced a new liberalism in which constitutional government and the natural rights tradition were not abandoned but were linked to programmatic expansion and an activist national government. As the public philosophy of the New Deal, this new liberalism, in its programmatic form, required a rethinking of the idea of natural rights in American politics.

Roosevelt first spoke of the need to modernize elements of the old faith in his Commonwealth Club address, delivered during the 1932 campaign and appropriately understood as the New Deal manifesto. The theme was that the time had come—indeed, had come three decades earlier—to recognize the "new terms of the old social contract." It was necessary to rewrite the social contract to take account of the national economy and the concentration of economic power. With the adoption of a new compact, the American people would establish a countervailing power—a stronger national state—lest the United States steer a "steady course toward economic oligarchy." Protection of the national welfare must shift from the private citizen to the government; the guarantee of equal opportunity required that individual initiative be restrained and directed by national administration:

> Clearly all this calls for a reappraisal of values. Our task now is not discovery or exploitation of natural resources or necessarily producing new goods. It is the soberer and less dramatic business of administering resources and plants already in hand, of seeking to reestablish foreign markets for our surplus production, of meeting the problems of under-consumption, of adjusting production to consumption, of distributing wealth and products more equitably, of adapting existing economic organizations to the service of the people. The day of enlightened administration has come.[19]

The creation of a national state with expansive supervisory powers would be a "long, slow task." The Commonwealth Club address was sensitive to the uneasy fit between energetic central government and constitutional principles in the United States. It was imperative, therefore, that the New Deal be informed by a public philosophy in which the new concept of state power would be carefully interwoven with earlier conceptions of American government. The task of modern government, FDR announced, was "to assist the development of an economic declaration of rights, an economic constitutional order." The traditional emphasis in American politics on individual self-reliance should therefore give way to a new understanding of individualism, in which the government acted as a regulating and unifying agency, guaranteeing individual men and women protection from the uncertainties of the marketplace. Thus, the most significant aspect of the departure from natural to programmatic liberalism was the association of constitutional rights with the extension, rather than the restriction, of the role of the national government.

The need to construct an economic constitutional order, first articulated in the Commonwealth Club address, was a consistent theme of Roosevelt's long presidency. The 1936 platform was, at FDR's insistence, written as a pastiche of the Declaration and emphasized the need for a fundamental reexamination of rights; if the national government was to meet its obligations, the natural rights tradition had to be enlarged to include programmatic rights. With respect to the 1935 Social Security legislation, the platform claims:

We hold this truth to be self-evident—that the test of representative government is its ability to promote the safety and happiness of the people. . . . We have built foundations for the security of those who are faced with the hazards of unemployment and old age; for the orphaned, the crippled and the blind. On the foundation of the Social Security Act we are determined to erect a structure of economic security for all our people, making sure that this benefit shall keep step with the ever-increasing capacity of America to provide a high standard of living for all its citizens.[20]

As FDR would later detail in his 1944 State of the Union address, constructing a foundation for economic security meant that the inalienable rights protected by the Constitution—speech, press, worship, due process—had to be "supplemented" by a new bill of rights "under which a new basis of security and property can be established for all—regardless of station, race, or creed." Included in the second bill of rights were the right to a useful and remunerative job; the right to own enough to provide adequate food, clothing, and recreation; the right to adequate protection from the economic fears of old age, sickness, accident, and unemployment; and the right to a good education.[21]

These new rights were never formally ratified as part of the Constitution, but they became the foundation of political dialogue, redefining the role of the national government. In the wake of the Roosevelt revolution, nearly every public policy was propounded as a right, attempting to confer constitutional status on programs like Social Security, Medicare, welfare, and food stamps. With the advent of the New Deal political order, an understanding of rights dedicated to limiting government gradually gave way to a more expansive understanding of rights, a transformation in the governing philosophy of the United States that required major changes in American political institutions.

The defense of Progressive reforms in terms of extending the rights of the Constitution was a critical development in the advent of a positive understanding of government responsibility. The distinction between Progressives and Conservatives, as boldly set forth by the Progressive Party campaign of 1912, all too visibly challenged the prevailing principles of constitutional government and the self-interested basis of American politics. The Progressive dream of national community portended an unvarnished majoritarianism that threatened the Constitution's promise to protect individual freedom from the vagaries of mass opinion. The New Deal understanding of reform, however, appealed more directly to the American constitutional tradition by asserting a connection between nationalism and rights, albeit rights that looked beyond the original social contract. Roosevelt gave legitimacy to Progressive principles by imbedding them in the language of constitutionalism and interpreting them as an expansion rather than a subversion of the natural rights tradition.

FDR's reappraisal of values is important to understanding the New Deal, but it is also important in understanding his influence on political parties and the separation of powers. The new understanding of the Declaration of Independence required an assault on the established party system, which had long been allied with constitutional arrangements that favored a decentralization of power. This effort to weaken traditional party organizations, which presupposed either a transformation or decline of partisanship, began during the Progressive era, but it fell to FDR and the architects of the New Deal to make progressive democracy an enduring part of American politics. Paradoxically, the New Deal both strengthened the national resolve of political parties and attenuated partisan loyalties in the electorate.

Party Responsibility and the Creation of the Modern Presidency

In part, Roosevelt undertook an assault on the party system to make it more national and principled in character. He wanted to overcome the state and local orientation of the party system, which was suited to congressional primacy and was poorly organized for progressive action by the national government, and to establish a national, executive-centered party, which would be more suitably organized for the expression of national purposes. With such a task in mind, the Roosevelt administration modified traditional partisan practices in an effort to make the Democratic Party, as FDR put it, one of "militant liberalism."[22] This, in turn, would bring about a structural transformation of the party system, pitting a reformed Democratic party against a conservative Republican party. As Roosevelt wrote in the introduction to the seventh volume of his presidential papers, "Generally speaking in a representative form of government there are generally two schools of political belief—liberal and conservative. The system of party responsibility in American politics requires that one of his parties become the liberal party and the other the conservative party."[23]

The most dramatic moment in Roosevelt's challenge to traditional party practices was the so-called purge campaign of 1938. This involved FDR directly in one gubernatorial and several congressional primary campaigns (twelve contests in all) in a bold effort to replace conservative Democrats with candidates who were "100 percent New Dealers." The special concern of this campaign was the South (southern Democracy), a Democratic stronghold since the Civil War, but, given the commitment to states' rights in that region, one that also represented, as a prominent journalist of the time, Thomas Stokes, put it, "the ball and chain which hobbled the party's forward march."[24]

As the press noted frequently after the 1938 purge campaign, no president had ever gone as far as Roosevelt in striving to stamp his policies on his party.[25] In the context of American politics, where presidential dominance over the decentralized party system was a cardinal vice, this was an extraordinary effort. With the purge and other initiatives, such as the elimination of the "two-thirds" rule (requiring a candidate to receive two-thirds of the convention delegate votes in order to win the party's nomination), the Roosevelt administration initiated a process whereby, increasingly, the party system evolved from predominantly local to national and programmatic organizations.[26]

At the same time, the New Deal made partisanship less important. Roosevelt's partisan leadership, although it effected important changes in the Democratic Party, and, eventually the Republican Party as well, envisioned a personal link with the public that would enable the president to govern from his position as leader of the nation, not just of that party that governed the nation.[27] For example, in all but one of the 1938 primary campaigns in which he participated personally, Roosevelt chose to make a direct appeal to public opinion rather than attempt to work through or to reform the regular party apparatus. This strategy was encouraged by earlier reforms, especially the direct primary, which had begun to weaken the grip of party organizations on the voters. Radio broadcasting also made direct presidential appeals an enticing strategy, especially for as popular a president with as fine a radio presence as Roosevelt.

In the final analysis, the "benign dictatorship" Roosevelt sought to impose on the Democratic Party was more conducive to corroding the American party system than to reforming it. The emphasis FDR placed on forging a direct link between himself and the public reflected a lack of faith in party politics and a deliberate attempt to supplant collective responsibility (based on give-and-take between the president and Congress) with executive responsibility. Building on the actions of his Progressive predecessors, Roosevelt broke traditions that buttressed collective partisan responsibility. Following the example TR set at the Progressive Party convention, FDR accepted the 1932 Democratic nomination of his party in person; thereafter, this became settled practice within the two-party system and signaled the emergence of presidential campaigns conducted less by parties than by individual candidates. Roosevelt also rejected the Jeffersonian tradition that prohibited presidents from delivering State of the Union and other important messages before Congress. Woodrow Wilson first revived the practice, abandoned by Jefferson, of addressing Congress in person. But not until FDR's 1933 State of the Union address did this practice become an enduring routine— an annual ritual that, with the rise of the mass media, encouraged presidents to make direct appeals to public opinion.

Roosevelt and most New Dealers believed that a full revamping of partisan politics was impractical, given the obstacles to party government that were so deeply ingrained in the American political experience. The immense failure of the purge campaign reinforced this view: in the dozen states in which the president acted against entrenched incumbents, he was successful in only two—Oregon and New York. Moreover, Roosevelt and his political allies did not view the welfare state as a partisan issue. The reform program of the 1930s was conceived as a "second bill of rights" that should be established as much as possible in permanent programs beyond the uncertainties of public opinion and elections.

The most important of these new programmatic rights was Social Security. FDR carefully nurtured Social Security to appear as a right, an entitlement. He insisted that it be financed by a payroll tax rather than by general revenues: "We put those payroll contributions there so to give the contributors a legal, moral, and political right to collect their pensions. . . . With those taxes in there, no damn politician can scrap my social security program."[28] The development of the Social Security program thus illustrates how the New Deal became the cornerstone of an executive establishment—and administrative constitution—that was shielded from the uncertainties of public opinion, political parties, and elections. By the 1950s, Social Security was the "third rail" of American politics, and those who challenged it risked humiliating political defeat. By European standards, the Social Security program was quite limited. It did not include any support for health care, and its levels of welfare spending and unemployment compensation were low. Unlike old age insurance, the administration of these parts of the program left considerable discretion and funding responsibility to the states, which dealt out justice unevenly. Nevertheless, Social Security marked a watershed in the national government's assumption of the responsibility to protect individuals from the vagaries of the market. Its benefits, especially old age pensions, grew over the years, so that Social Security became the largest of all federal programs. As Martha Derthick has written, FDR and the architects of the Social Security program "sought to foreclose the options of future generations by committing them irrevocably to a program that promises benefits by right as well as those particular benefits that have been incorporated into an ever expanding law. In that sense, they designed social security to be uncontrollable."[29]

Given the programmatic ambitions of FDR and his fellow New Dealers, the most significant institutional reforms of the New Deal did not promote party government but fostered a program that would establish the president as the guardian of an expanding welfare state. This program, as embodied in the 1937 executive reorganization bill, would have greatly extended presidential authority over the executive branch, including the independent regulatory commissions. The president and executive agencies would also be delegated extensive authority to govern, making unnecessary the constant cooperation of party members in Congress. As the Brownlow Committee report put it, with the strengthening of the executive, the "brief exultant commitment" to progressive reform that was expressed in 1932, and especially 1936, would now be more firmly established in "persistent, determined, competent, day by day administration of what the Nation has decided to do."[30]

It is interesting to note that the administrative reform bill, which was intended to make parties less important, became, at Roosevelt's urging, a party government–style "vote of confidence" for the administration in Congress.

Roosevelt initially lost this vote in 1938, when the reorganization bill was defeated in the House of Representatives, but he did manage to keep administrative reform sufficiently prominent in the party councils that a compromise version passed in 1939. Although considerably weaker than Roosevelt's original proposal, the 1939 Executive Reorganization Act was, in effect, the organic statute of the "modern presidency." Roosevelt's extraordinary crisis leadership was, so to speak, institutionalized, by the administrative reform bill, for this statute ratified a process whereby public expectations and institutional arrangements established the president, rather than Congress or political parties, as the center of government activity. As Matthew Dickinson's chapter in this volume shows, it not only provided authority for the creation of the Executive Office of the President, which included the newly formed White House Office and a strengthened and refurbished Bureau of the Budget, but also enhanced the president's control of the expanding activities of the executive branch. As such, the reorganization act represents the genesis of the institutional presidency, which was equipped to govern independently of the constraints imposed by the regular political process.

The civil service reform carried out by the Roosevelt administration was another important part of the effort to replace partisan politics with executive administration. The original reorganization proposal of 1937 contained provisions to make the administration of civil service more effective and to expand the merit system. The reorganization bill passed in 1939 was shorn of this controversial feature; but Roosevelt found it possible to accomplish extensive civil service reform through executive action and legislation. He extended merit protection to personnel appointed by the administration during its first term, four-fifths of whom had been brought into government outside of merit channels.[31] Since the Progressive era, the choice was posed as one between politics and spoils, on the one hand, and nonpartisan, nonpolitical administration, on the other. The New Deal celebrated an administrative politics that denied nourishment to the regular party apparatus but fed instead an executive department oriented toward expanding liberal programs. As the administrative historian Paul Van Riper has noted, the new practices created a new kind of patronage, "a sort of intellectual and ideological patronage rather than the more traditional partisan type."[32]

The rise of the modern presidency transformed the executive office dramatically, with profound consequences for American democracy. Before FDR, the presidency was a simple office; the "West Wing," now the subject of a popular television show, did not exist. But in the wake of the "Roosevelt revolution," people in that wing of the White House came to form the nerve center of the Executive Office of the President. There is a real sense in which presidents no longer run for office and govern as the head of a party; instead, they campaign and seek to enact programs as the head of a personal organization they have created in their own image. These organizations now carry out tasks party leaders and organizations once performed, such as staffing the executive branch, connecting the president to interest groups, formulating public policy, and directing campaigns. Perhaps most important, as Lawrence Jacobs's chapter in this volume illustrates, the presidential staff plays a critical part in enabling the president to communicate with the people. Significantly, Roosevelt was not only the first president to make effective use of the radio, he also was the first president to make extensive use of surveys and pollsters, giving the president a direct source of information about what the people were thinking, and how they were responding to his program. With the help of the respected pollster Hadley Cantril, the Roosevelt administration learned that the American people viewed the idea of a "second bill of rights" favorably. These polls, no doubt, encouraged Roosevelt to make the economic bill of rights the centerpiece of his 1944 State of the Union address, his most important wartime speech.[33]

The Administrative State and the "New" Party System

Presidential leadership during the New Deal prepared the executive branch to be a government unto itself and established the presidency rather than the party as the locus of political responsibility. This shift was greatly augmented by World War II and the cold war. With the Great Depression giving way to war, another expansion of presidential power took place, as part of the national security state, further weakening the executive's ties with the party system. As the New Deal prepared for war, Roosevelt spoke not only of the government's obligation to guarantee "freedom from want" but also of its responsibility to provide "freedom from fear"—to protect the American people, and the world, against foreign aggression. This obligation to uphold "human rights" became a new guarantee of security, which presupposed a further expansion of national administrative power.[34] The forces of internationalism allowed Harry Truman to persuade Congress to carry out additional administrative reform in 1947, which increased the powers of, and centralized control over, the National Security State. Dubbed the National Security Act, it created the National Security Council, the Central Intelligence Agency, and the Department of Defense.[35]

Although the war and its aftermath were important, the modern presidency was created to chart the course for, and direct the voyage to, a more liberal America. Roosevelt's pronouncement of a "second bill of rights" proclaimed and began that task, but it fell to Lyndon Johnson, as one journalist noted, to "codify the New Deal vision of a good society."[36] This program entailed expanding the economic constitutional order with such policy innovations as Medicare and Medicaid, and, even more important, extending these benefits to African Americans.

Johnson's attempt to create the Great Society marked a significant extension of programmatic liberalism and accelerated the effort to transcend partisan politics. Roosevelt's ill-fated efforts to guide the affairs of his party were well remembered by Johnson, who came to Congress in 1937 in a special House election as an enthusiastic supporter of the New Deal. He took Roosevelt's experience to be the best example of the generally ephemeral nature of party government in the United States, and he fully expected the cohesive Democratic support he received from Congress after the 1964 election to be temporary. Moreover, Johnson's greatest programmatic achievement, the enactment of the 1964 and 1965 Civil Rights bills, created considerable friction between the White House and local party organizations, especially, but not exclusively, in the South. Thus, Johnson, like Roosevelt, looked beyond the party system toward the politics of "enlightened administration."[37]

With the enactment of the 1965 Civil Rights Act (the Voting Rights Act), Johnson ensured the transformation of southern Democracy that had eluded FDR. Civil rights reform emancipated the Democratic Party from its most conservative wing—the ball and chain that had hobbled its forward march. But this gain in doctrinal consistency came at the price of weakening the New Deal coalition. During the ascendancy of the New Deal coalition, southern whites identified with, and voted consistently for, the Democratic Party. Since the enactment of civil rights legislation, a majority of the white southern electorate has not voted for a Democratic presidential candidate. The new party system in the South also dramatically affected congressional elections. In the 75th Congress that balked at FDR's court-"packing" and executive reorganizations plans, there were 120 House seats in the thirteen southern states (the old Confederacy, plus Kentucky and Oklahoma). A full 117 of those 120 were in Democratic hands. By the end of the 1980s, those same states had 124 seats. But only 85 of them were Democratic; more than a quarter had migrated to the Republican side of the aisle. Moreover, the 1965 Voting Rights Act substantially increased the number of black voters in the South, thus tending to transform the legislative behavior of those southern representatives who remained on the Democratic side of the aisle. It was a sign of the times in 1983 when southern Democrats voted 78 to 12 in favor of a holiday honoring Martin Luther King.[38]

The transformation of southern politics would dramatically change the New Deal party system, preparing the ground for the rise of more national and programmatic parties during the 1980s. In the short term, however, Johnson's civil rights reforms further aggrandized executive administration. The enactment of these reforms signaled a dramatic reinvigoration of the modern presidency. Indeed, the early years of the Johnson presidency marked the historical height of presidential government. The White House Office and the Executive Office of the President had been increasingly active in formulating programs since the administration of Franklin Roosevelt. Under Johnson, however, political and policy responsibility was concentrated in the presidency to an unprecedented extent. Equally important, the civil rights acts enlisted the president and several executive agencies in an ongoing effort to ban racial discrimination. These laws empowered the federal bureaucracy—especially the Department of Justice, the Department of Health, Education, and Welfare, and the newly formed Equal Employment Opportunity Commission—to assist the courts in creating enforcement mechanisms for civil rights. These proved to be effective, greatly abetting the desegregation of southern schools and the registration of black voters below the Mason-Dixon line.

Republican Presidents and the Conservative Administrative Presidency

As a party of administration, the Democrats established the conditions for the end of parties, unless or until a party sprang up that was anti-administration. Although no such party has emerged in American politics, the Republicans under Richard Nixon and especially Ronald Reagan embraced programs, such as new federalism and regulatory relief, that challenged the institutional legacy of the New Deal. This bolder conservative posture coincided with the construction of a formidable national Republican organization with strength at the federal level that is unprecedented in American politics. After 1976, the Republican National Committee and the two other Republican bodies, the National Republican Senatorial Committee and the National Republican Congressional (House) Committee, greatly expanded their efforts to raise funds and provide services at the national level for state and local candidates. The Democrats lagged behind party-building efforts, but the losses they suffered in the 1980 election encouraged them to modernize the national political machinery, openly imitating some of the devices employed by the Republicans. Arguably, a party system had finally evolved that was compatible with the national polity forged on the anvil of the New Deal.[39]

Nonetheless, the new party system was shaped, and in important respects overshadowed, by the modern presidency. Nixon and Reagan presumed to challenge the New Deal by embracing its institutional legacy. Conceiving of the modern presidency as, ideologically, a two-edged sword, they emphasized popular appeals and administrative politics that undermined "collective responsibility." Given that the New Deal was based on a party strategy to replace traditional politics with administration, it is not surprising that the Republican challenge to liberal policies produced a conservative "administrative presidency." For a time, at least, this development retarded the revival of partisanship. Nixon and Reagan centralized power in the White House, thus preempting the Republican party organization's political responsibilities; and they pursued their programs with acts of administrative discretion that weakened efforts to carry out broad-based party policies.

The administrative reforms initiated by Republican presidents were encouraged by and, in turn, helped perpetuate the condition of divided government that prevailed virtually without interruption between 1968 and 1992. Prior to 1994, the challenge to programmatic liberalism never extended beyond the presidency, leaving Congress, as well as states and localities, under Democratic control. Republican presidents, facing hostility not only in the bureaucracy, but also in Congress and the States, were, even more than Democrats, encouraged to pursue policy goals by seeking to concentrate executive power in the White House. Moreover, the Reagan administration frequently expressed common cause with a modern conservative movement whose advocates did not so clearly want to limit the national state; indeed, modern conservatives championed certain causes that presupposed exploiting national administrative power in the service of conservative principles. Considering a strong national state necessary to foster economic growth, nurture family values, and, especially, oppose communism, the Reagan administration tended to honor "new federalism" and regulatory relief in the breach more than in the observance.

Ironically, Reagan's greatest accomplishment involved an act of perpetuation. Attempting to finish what Truman had begun, he prosecuted the cold war to a successful conclusion. The Reagan administration expanded on the military buildup that started in the Carter Administration in response to the war in Afghanistan; and Reagan's tough talk about the Soviet Union—the "Evil Empire"—steered American policy away from Nixon's detour toward détente, which fit the post-Vietnam malaise, and back to the main route of containment pursued by Truman, Eisenhower, Kennedy, and Johnson. Just as Reagan deserves some credit for the triumphant end of the cold war, so his militant anticommunism reinforced, even advanced, executive aggrandizement. The Iran-contra scandal, for example, was not simply a matter of the president being asleep on his watch; rather, it also revealed the Reagan administration's determination to assume a more forceful anticommunist posture in Central America in the face of a recalcitrant Congress and bureaucracy.[40]

A close examination of policy making during the Reagan years provides numerous examples of the administration's resorting to unilateral executive action. Not only was policy centered in the White House and other support agencies in the Executive Office of the President, but much care was taken to plant White House loyalists in the departments and agencies—people who could be relied on to ride herd on civil servants and carry forth programs. Most important, a wide range of policies to deregulate business were pursued, not through legislative change, but by administrative action, delay, and repeal. President Reagan's Executive Orders 12291 and 12498 mandated a comprehensive review of proposed agency regulations and centralized the review process in the Office of Management and Budget. Reagan also appointed a Task Force on Regulatory Relief, headed by Vice President George H. W. Bush, to apply cost-benefit analyses to existing rules.[41] In this light, the Iran–contra scandal may be seen not as an aberration but, rather, as an extreme example of how the Reagan administration reacted when it anticipated or was confronted with congressional resistance to its proposals. This pursuit of conservative policy options through the administrative presidency continued with George H. W. Bush's elevation to the White House. The burden of curbing environmental, consumer, and civil rights regulations fell on the Competitiveness Council, chaired by Vice President Dan Quayle, which like its predecessor, the Task Force of Regulatory Relief, required administrative agencies to justify the costs of existing and proposed regulations.

The conservative administrative presidency did not go unchallenged. As designed by the Democrats, the modern presidency was conceived as an ally of programmatic rights. When this view was seemingly violated by Vietnam and its aftermath, reformers set out to protect liberal programs from unfriendly executives. By the time Lyndon Johnson left the White House, support for unilateral executive action had begun to erode, occasioned by the controversial use of presidential power in Vietnam; it virtually disappeared under the strain of divided government. The result was a "reformation" of New Deal administrative politics, which brought Congress and the courts into the details of administration. The institutional reforms in Congress during the 1970s, which devolved policy responsibility to subcommittees and increased the number of congressional staff support members, were compatible with the attention being paid by legislators to policy specialization, which increased congressional oversight of the administrative state while making Congress more administrative in its structure and activities. Similarly, the Judiciary's decreasing reliance on constitutional decisions in its rulings affecting the political economy and its emphasis on interpreting statutes to determine the responsibilities of executive agencies were symptomatic of its post–New Deal role as "managing partner of the administrative state."[42] Consequently, the efforts of Republicans to compensate for their inability to control Congress by seeking to circumvent legislative restrictions on presidential conduct were matched by Democratic initiatives to burden the executive with smothering legislative and judicial oversight.[43] The opposition to liberal reform, then, did not end in a challenge to national administrative power but in a raw and disruptive battle to control its services.

A major, if not main, forum for partisan conflict during the Reagan and Bush years was a sequence of investigations in which Democrats and Republicans sought to discredit one another. The legal scrutiny of public officials was in part a logical response to the Watergate scandal. To prevent another Nixon-style "Saturday Night Massacre," Congress passed the Ethics in Government Act of 1978, which provided for the appointment of independent counsels to investigate allegations of criminal activity. Not surprisingly, divided government encouraged the exploitation of the act for partisan purposes. In the 1980s congressional Democrats found themselves in a position to demand criminal investigations and possible jail sentences for their political opponents. When Bill Clinton became president in 1993, congressional Republicans turned the tide with a vengeance. As a consequence, political disagreements were readily transformed into criminal charges. Moreover, investigation under the special prosecutor statute tended to deflect attention from legitimate constitutional and policy differences and to focus the attention of Congress, the press, and citizens alike on scandals. Disgrace, imprisonment, and, most dramatically, presidential impeachment thus joined electoral defeat as a risk of political combat in the United States.

The Democratic and Republican parties had raised large campaign war chests and fostered party discipline in Washington, yet they risked losing their connection to the American people. Indeed, as fierce partisan battles were waged within the "beltway," the influence of Democrats and Republicans on the perceptions and habits of the American people continued to decline. For example, in the 27 states (plus Washington, D.C.) that register voters by party, the number of voters who chose not to identify with either of the major parties rose significantly during the 1980s and 1990s; just as important, with the exception of 1992, when a number of voters were drawn to the polls by H. Ross Perot's independent campaign, turnout in elections during these decades was chronically low, rivaling the ennui of the 1920s, when many women, newly enfranchised by the Nineteenth Amendment, were unfamiliar with voting and many states had registration laws that discriminated against recent immigrants and African Americans.[44]

George W. Bush, Party Polarization, and the Ratification of the Modern Presidency

The 2000 election testified to the estrangement between the parties and the electorate. Neither the Democratic nominee, Vice President Al Gore, nor the Republican, Governor George Bush of Texas, took positions that offered a way out of the fractious state of American politics. Both candidates adopted a centrist pragmatic stance during the general election campaign that was designed to shore up the principal programs of the welfare state. The activist core of the Democratic and Republican parties differed starkly on issues such as abortion and the environment, reflecting their fundamental disagreements about the role of government and the relationship between church and state. But the two candidates sought to distance themselves from their parties, each of them seeking a strategic center between Democratic liberalism and Republican conservatism. The election ended in a virtual tie, a deadlock ultimately resolved by the Supreme Court. The controversial conclusion to the election bitterly divided policy activists and loyal partisans, but not the American people, many of whom, consistent with the recent pattern of low turnout and public indifference toward politics, had stayed away from the polls.

Like his predecessor, Bill Clinton, candidate Bush sought to forge a "third way," signifying the modern presidency's dominant but uneasy place in contemporary American politics. The disjuncture between the bitter partisanship within the Capitol and the weakening of partisan affiliation outside it—along with his skill in combining doctrines—won Clinton a certain following in the country. At its best, Clinton's third way sought consensus for a limited but energetic national government. All too often, however, this approach degenerated into a politics of expediency that substituted polls and focus groups for leadership.[45] Bush's "compassionate conservatism" seemed to have the same strengths and weakness as Clinton's "new covenant." Indeed, Bush's campaign speeches bore a striking resemblance to Clinton's rhetoric during the 1992 and 1996 elections. And the Bush administration programs that embodied these values—especially his reform proposals for education, social services, and welfare—invoked many of the ideas incubated at the Democratic Leadership Council (DLC), a centrist political group, that gave rise to Clinton's policy initiatives.

Important differences marked Bush's and Clinton's stance toward partisanship, however. Clinton never made clear how his "third way" politics would serve the core principles of the Democratic Party; in fact, he and the DLC were highly ambivalent, if not avowedly hostile, to partisanship. But Bush embraced "compassionate conservatism" as a doctrine that he and his close advisors hoped would strengthen the appeal of the Republican Party. Bush's rhetoric and policy proposals, his top political strategist, Karl Rove, claimed, were a deliberate attempt to play to conservative values without being reflexively antigovernment.[46] Bush's call for substantial tax cuts appealed to the right's hostility to government. But the president also acknowledged, columnist E. J. Dionne observed, "that most people do not draw meaning from the marketplace alone, and that the marketplace is not the sole test or most important source of virtue."[47] "The invisible hand works many miracles," Bush said in July 1999. "But it cannot touch the human heart. . . . We are a nation of rugged individuals. But we are also the country of the second chance—tied together by bonds of friendship and community and solidarity."[48]

In part, the moral commitment Bush envisioned would be served by empowering nonprofit institutions that worked outside government. For example, he proposed changes in federal and state regulations that would allow private "faith-based" charitable organizations to play a larger role in providing government social services to the poor. The national government would have an important role in sustaining moral values as well. As Michael Gerson, Bush's principal speech writer, argued, the president's rhetoric did not try to "split the difference between liberalism and conservatism." Rather, Bush's speeches sought to convey how "activist government could be used for conservative ends."[49] The Reagan presidency had also made use of national administrative power; but the Bush administration was prepared to take big government conservatism much further.

Although Reagan and his conservative allies once talked of eliminating the Department of Education, Bush proposed to make the nation's public schools more accountable to the department by linking federal aid to national standards of learning. Social conservatives had long sought to advance morality by opposing abortion. Bush professed to be staunchly "pro-life," but he called for a more "incremental" attack on abortion. More important, he proposed to buttress conservative religious values with affirmative government efforts to help the poor, promote marriage, and ensure that "every child will be educated."[50]

Bush's ambition to redefine Republican conservatism entailed a difficult balancing act between partisanship and bipartisan cooperation. This task was made all the more difficult by the tenuous hold the Republicans had on government. The Senate was evenly split between Democrats and Republicans when Bush took office, with Vice President Richard Cheney breaking the tie. In the beginning of his presidency, Bush chose to identify with his party's strong ideological leaders in Congress, hoping to solidify his base support before reaching out to independent voters. He reaped both the benefits and costs of this early strategy of partisan conservatism. The president persuaded Congress to enact the leading conservative plank in his 2000 platform, a ten-year, $1.5 trillion tax cut. At the same time, his emphasis on traditional conservative issues such as tax cuts, regulatory relief, energy production, and missile defense risked alienating moderate Republicans, a dwindling but pivotal group in the closely divided House and Senate. The president and his party paid dearly for this approach in May 2001, when Senator James Jeffords of Vermont announced that he was transferring his allegiance from the Republican to the Democratic caucus, giving control of the Senate to the Democrats.[51] Within days, every Senate committee and subcommittee chairmanship was transferred into Democratic hands.

Facing the prospect of partisan obstruction by Senate Democrats, the Bush administration intensified its efforts to consolidate political and policy responsibility within the White House. The first President Bush's top political strategist, Lee Atwater, had worked at the Republican National Committee (RNC) rather than at the White House, helping to sustain for a time the status and independence of the national party organization. In contrast, Karl Rove, an Atwater protégé, became a top White House advisor. He staffed a new Office of Strategic Initiatives that oversaw a nearly complete melding of presidential and partisan politics. Rove granted that the national parties that had emerged since the 1980s "were of great importance in the tactical and mechanical aspects of electing a president." But they were "less important in developing a political and policy strategy for the White House." In effect, he said, parties served as a critical "means to the president's end." The emergence of the modern executive office presupposed that "the White House had to determine the administration's objectives" and, by implication, those of the party.[52] Rove assumed political responsibilities that undercut the power of the RNC chair, James S. Gillmore III, who was replaced with the more compliant Mark Raciot. Politics was joined to policy as Rove sought to position the president as a nontraditional Republican. By the end of his first summer in the White House, Bush was beginning to stress education and values, not taxes and defense.[53]

Bush-style "compassionate conservatism" promised to soften the Republican party's harsh antigovernment edge. It also gave the president a platform to act independently of his party. Programs such as faith-based initiatives and educational reform were not pursued within Republican councils. Rather, as had been the custom since the development of the modern presidency, the White House advanced these objectives through executive orders and bipartisan cooperation. The education bill in particular seemed less a use of government to serve conservative principles than an uneasy compromise between liberal demands for spending and conservative insistence on standards. Bush trumpeted his alliance with the liberal Democratic icon, Sen. Edward M. Kennedy of Massachusetts, in passing education reform legislation in 2001.[54]

No less than the "third way," then, "compassionate conservatism" promised to transcend the long-standing contest in American politics between the rights-based claims of entitlement and the virtues of individual responsibility. As Bush noted in February 2001, in his first major address to Congress and the nation, "Our new governing vision says government should be active, but limited, engaged but not overbearing." Bush's rhetorical but vague pragmatism showed the same tendency as Clinton's to deflect the country's attention from hard choices. Bush denied, for instance, that the American people needed to choose between a $1.5 trillion tax cut and a laundry list of programs, including the middle-class entitlements that Democrats championed.[55]

September 11 and the War on Terrorism

The President's attention shifted dramatically away from matters such as faith-based initiatives and educational reform when the United States was struck by terrorists of the al Qaeda network on September 11, 2001. In the aftermath of the first attack on the American continent since the War of 1812, and the most deadly in the nation's history, the country appeared to unite overnight. Citizens gave generously to relief funds to aid the families of those who lost their lives. The American flag was unfurled everywhere, and patriotic hymns, especially, "God Bless America," were sung repeatedly. Polls showed a remarkable and immediate jump in support for Bush, from 51 percent approval of the job he was doing as president to 90 percent approval, within days of the September 11 attack. A strong consensus quickly formed in support of his military response to the terrorist assault.

In the short term, the war on terrorism strengthened the modern presidency and greatly tempered the polarized partisanship that had plagued it during the previous three decades. Hardly a discouraging word was heard when the Bush administration created an Office of Homeland Security, imposed tighter restrictions on airports, and embraced deficit spending to help the economy and fight a war in Afghanistan, which harbored the al Qaeda leaders. Highlighting the need for bipartisanship in a time of national crisis, Bush justified the war on terrorism in words that echoed Franklin Roosevelt. "Freedom and fear are at war," he told a joint session of Congress on September 20. "The advance of human freedom—the great achievement of our time, and great hope of every time—now depends on us. Our nation—this generation—will lift a dark threat of violence from our people and our future. We will rally around the world to this cause by our efforts, by our courage."[56]

As the president prepared the nation for new responsibilities at home and abroad, presidential scholars and public officials dusted off concerns from the 1960s and 1970s about an imperial presidency. Already executive-centered in its approach to politics and policy, the Bush White House became even more insulated from Congress and the Republican Party as it planned and fought the war against terrorism. Both Democrats and Republicans complained when Homeland Security Director Tom Ridge refused to testify before Congress about the president's homeland defense budget. The administration claimed that Ridge's office was akin to the National Security Council, a presidential agency whose officials did not have to appear before Congress. Similarly, Attorney General John Ashcroft encountered bipartisan criticism when the administration unilaterally put some measures in place to crack down on terrorism at home, including military tribunals to try suspected foreign terrorists and a rule allowing investigators to listen in on some lawyer-client conversations.[57]

For a time these complaints failed to penetrate the aura of invincibility that Bush had enjoyed since September 11. But the roots of congressional resentment ran deep. Beginning in the spring of 2002, Bush administration officials, and then the president himself, openly pursued the possibility of another military venture: an invasion of Iraq that, unlike the Persian Gulf War of 1991, would involve a "preemptive" attack and have as its mission the removal of Saddam Hussein from power. Recognizing the country's obsession with homeland security and reluctant to thwart a popular president as the midterm elections approached, Congress passed a resolution in October 2002, authorizing the president to use military force against Iraq "as he determines to be necessary." In doing so, legislators sustained the Bush administration's revival of the cold war–era belief that an overriding cause—the containment of communism then, the war against terrorism now—justified the expansive use of presidential power around the globe.

Risking the bipartisan support that accrued in the aftermath of the September 11 attacks, Bush threw himself into the 2002 midterm election campaign earlier and more energetically than any president in history. Unlike his predecessors, Bush had experienced both united and divided government during his first two years in office. He was convinced long before the 2002 election campaign began that his best strategy for leading Congress was to regain control of the Senate for the Republican Party.

In seeking a Republican Senate, Bush faced a daunting challenge: the average loss for the president's party in post–World War II midterms elections was four Senate seats. Even worse from the Republicans' standpoint, their party was more "exposed" in 2002 than the Democrats: twenty Republican seats were at stake in the election, compared with fourteen Democratic seats. Finally, the president's party had not taken control of the Senate away from the other party in a midterm election since 1882.

Bush, following Rove's advice, decided well in advance of the elections to become actively involved in the campaign for a Republican majority in Congress. He and Rove recruited strong Republican challengers to incumbent Democratic senators, even to the point of intervening in state party politics to do so. The president's strenuous efforts to raise a campaign war chest and his numerous campaign appearances for GOP candidates strengthened his influence over his party: Bush was the featured attraction at sixty-seven fund-raising events that raised a record $141 million in campaign contributions for the Republican Party and its candidates. Several of these appearances were in states where the Republican candidate was trailing and where, if the Democrats had won, Bush risked being blamed for defeat. The results of the election vindicated Bush's decision to take this risk. The Republicans gained two seats in the Senate, transforming them from minority to majority status, and increased their majority in the House of Representatives. An election eve poll indicated that 50 percent of the voters were basing their decision on their opinion of the president, many more than the 34 percent who had done so in 1990 or the 37 percent who had done so in 1998. Of these 50 percent, 31 percent were pro-Bush and only 19 percent opposed him.[58]

Political analysts were quick to describe the historic nature of the Republican victory and to credit Bush as the most successful party-building president since Franklin Roosevelt.[59] Not only did the 2002 elections mark the first time in more than a century that the president's party had regained control of the Senate at midterm, it also represented the first time since FDR that a president saw his party gain seats in both houses of Congress in a first-term midterm election. The GOP also emerged from the elections with more state legislative seats than the Democrats for the first time in half a century; and even though the number of Republican governors declined from 29 to 27 during Bush's first term, Arnold Schwarzenegger's victory in the 2003 California recall election gave the Republican Party control of the governorships of the four most populous states: California, Texas, New York, and Florida.

Bush could not take all the credit for the Republican gains. Since the late 1970s, the Republican Party had been developing into a formidable national organization, in which the Republican National Committee, rather than state and local organizations, became the principal agent of party building activities. This top-down approach to party building appeared to many critics to be too centralized and too dependent on television advertising to perform the parties' traditional role of mobilizing voters and popular support; but the Republican Party, believing that it had been out-organized "on the ground" by Democrats in the 2000 election, began to put together a massive grassroots mobilizing strategy in 2002. Democrats since the New Deal had relied on auxiliary party organizations like labor unions to get out the vote. But the GOP created its own national organization to mobilize supporters. Depending on volunteers, albeit closely monitored ones, and face-to-face appeals to voters, the Republicans built on their 2002 success to mount the most ambitious national grassroots campaign in the party's history for the 2004 elections.[60]

Bush not only benefited from the development of what might be considered the first national party machine in history, he played a critical role in strengthening it. The White House recruited candidates, raised money to fund their campaigns, and helped to attract volunteers to identify Republican voters and get them out to vote. Just as Ronald Reagan had played a critical part in laying a philosophical and political foundation that enabled the Republican Party to become a solidly conservative and electorally competitive party by 1984, so did Bush make an important contribution in enlarging the core supporters of the party. During his first term, Bush broke Reagan's record for attracting first-time contributors to the Republican Party: under Reagan, 853,595 people donated to the Republican Party for the first time; by the time Bush stood for reelection, he had already attracted more than one million new donors to the GOP.[61] More important, although Reagan never converted his personal popularity into Republican control of Congress or the states, Bush approached reelection in 2004 with his party in charge of the House, the Senate, and most governorships. Indeed, the Republican Party had more political control than at any time since the 1920s.

Nevertheless, the centrality of the Bush White House in mobilizing support and framing the issues in both the 2002 and 2004 elections suggests that modern presidential politics continues to subordinate partisan to executive responsibility. Held in the aftermath of the September 11 attacks and the launch of the "war on terrorism," the midterm elections celebrated executive power. The elections turned on issues of domestic and international security, not on the social and economic concerns that traditionally drive the parties. The president's "compassionate conservatism" obscured somewhat the choice between liberalism and conservatism. Bush strayed from conservatives' visceral dislike of government not only in his commitment to faith-based initiatives and education reform, but also in his support for adding an expensive prescription drug benefit to Medicare.[62] Bush's blitzkrieg in the final days of the campaign trumpeted his proposal for a new Department of Homeland Security, attacking Democratic senators who had resisted his insistence that the president be authorized to suspend collective bargaining rules for departmental employees. Claiming that every president since John F. Kennedy had been granted the authority to override such rules when the national security was at stake, Bush charged that the Democrats were putting "special interests" ahead of the interests of the American people. That charge, reinforced by negative television ads, proved especially important in defeating incumbent Democratic senators in Georgia and Missouri. In a post-election session of Congress, the Democrats relented, joining with Republicans to create the Department of Homeland Security and granting Bush authority to establish flexible work rules for the new department's employees.[63]

Although the Iraq War, which began in March 2003, further aggravated the partisan rancor aroused by Bush's aggressive campaigning in the midterm elections, Republicans and Democrats both subscribed to the idea that the president, rather than Congress or the political parties, should assume principal responsibility for the war against terrorism. When Congress took up the question of Iraq in October 2002, Democrats had been divided about whether the country should go to war. But facing a popular president and elections in November, they were anxious to get the war issue behind them and change the subject to the flagging economy. Many justified their vote by claiming that the Iraqi resolution did not declare war but, instead, delegated to the president authority to go to war and determine its scope and duration. Senator John Kerry, who would become the Democratic nominee for president in 2004, raised substantial arguments against going to war with Iraq, but he voted for the Iraqi resolution because he accepted presidential superiority over Congress, and presidential independence from party politics, in foreign affairs. "We are affirming a president's right and responsibility to keep the American people safe," Kerry said, "and the president must take that grant of responsibility seriously."[64]

The controversy over Bush's Iraq War policy shaped the politics of the 2004 presidential campaign, which aroused intense partisan activity and, in comparison to recent elections, the rapt attention of the American people.[65] But the contest was not so much about Republican and Democratic principles as whether George Bush or John Kerry was more likely to manage the Herculean tasks of economic and homeland security effectively and justly. Consequently, although both the Republicans and Democrats engaged in innovative and effective practices to raise campaign funds, get their message out, and mobilize voters, nothing guaranteed that these incipient national machines would endure beyond the election.[66] As one leading Bush campaign strategist put it, "both parties' organizing force has focused on President Bush—the Republicans in defense of his leadership; the Democrats in opposition—hostility—to it. After the election, both parties will be challenged to sustain a collective commitment independently of their devotion to or hatred of Bush."[67] Similarly, a prominent figure in the Kerry campaign acknowledged that the Democratic campaign did not emphasize party principles, but focused instead on presenting the Democratic senator as a "plausible alternative" to the incumbent president, one who displayed the "strength required of a leader in post-9/11 America."[68]

The 2004 election, widely regarded as a referendum on the Bush presidency, appeared to sanction Bush's approach to homeland security and war on terrorism. Bush won 51 percent of the popular vote to Kerry's 48 percent, and the Republicans gained three seats in the House and four in the Senate. The gains in Congress were built on Bush's narrow but solid victory. In all the key Senate races, such as the five open southern seats, which the Republicans swept, Bush did better at the polls than the GOP's candidate, winning by an average of 18 percentage points to their 6.[69] Democrats did better in the House; indeed, the Republican gains were due to the ability of Bush's Texas allies, most notably, GOP House majority leader, Tom Delay, to push through a controversial redistricting plan that led to the defeat of four Democratic incumbents and a pickup of five seats in all. Nonetheless, the failure of the Democrats to make gains, let alone retake the House, also followed from their inability to make significant electoral advances anywhere in the country. (Outside Texas, the Democrats gained two seats.) Democrats acknowledged, for example, that they failed to take away two vulnerable seats in Connecticut, partly because Bush did much better in the state than they had expected.[70]

Besides the Republican victory, the 2004 election was notable for ending nearly four decades of desultory participation in presidential campaigns: slightly more than 60 percent of the eligible electorate voted, the largest turnout in a presidential election since 1968.[71] The results indicated that the country remained divided. Indeed, the divisions between Republicans and Democrats appeared to have deepened and become more widespread since 2000. But the rough parity between the parties had clearly given way to a Republican edge. Rove interpreted this tilt toward Bush and the Republicans as another critical advance in the "rolling realignment" that since the 1980s had been slowly but surely establishing the GOP as a governing majority.[72]

The changes in southern politics born of the civil rights revolution appeared to support this interpretation. White southerners had been rebelling against national Democratic politics for a generation; but beginning with the Reagan presidency, the Republicans expanded their appeal with conservative positions on such issues as taxes, national defense, and moral values. The growing GOP support in the South—reaching moderate as well as conservative voters—culminated with the 1994 elections, in which a large majority of southern whites began to support Republican candidates in congressional and state campaigns. After the 1994 elections, which gave Republicans control of the House and Senate for the first time in forty years, southern Republicans commanded a majority of governorships, a majority of seats in the Senate, and a majority of seats in the House. The Republicans had not been so well positioned below the

Mason Dixon line since the nineteenth century. The 2004 election dramatically reinforced this trend: Bush won every southern state, dominating so completely that he carried nearly 85 percent of all the counties across the region—and more than 90 percent of the counties where whites form a majority of the population. Moreover, Bush's support during the 2002 and 2004 campaigns helped Republicans stretch their southern advantage in both the House and Senate. White southerners' long memories of the Civil War and Reconstruction had allowed the Democrats to control Congress for most of the post–New Deal era, even as the South became estranged from the national Democratic Party. The 2004 election capped a partisan realignment in the South that may signal the full development of a national party system and the emergence of an enduring Republican majority.[73]

In light of the dominant role the White House played in mobilizing religious fundamentalists and framing the issues, however, Bush's win may have been as much a personal victory (of a limited sort, given the narrow margin) as a partisan achievement. The referendum on his presidency electrified the national party organizations, but it subordinated partisan to executive responsibility.[74] The question remains, therefore, whether the profound revival of the modern executive's governing authority in the wake of September 11 has brought to fruition a national party system or continued the long-term development of a modern presidency that renders collective partisanship impractical.

Conclusion: The Modern Presidency, Political Parties, and American Democracy

Given the domestic and international challenges posed by the twentieth and twenty-first centuries, the development of the modern presidency as the principal agent of American democracy seems justified. A new sense of executive responsibility was needed, one that the contemporary presidency fulfills rather admirably. Indeed, extraordinary presidential leadership played a critical part in the two greatest triumphs of recent American history: the end of forced segregation in the South and the triumphant conclusion to the cold war. Still, the expansion of national administrative power that followed the New Deal realignment did not result in the form of national state envisioned by Roosevelt and the architects of the modern presidency—one that established regulation and social welfare policy that could be expressions of national unity and commitment. As Karl has argued, Americans continue to abhor, even as they embrace, national administrative power.[75] The American public supports executive action in the name of the greater security that New Dealers championed—in defense of the new rights that FDR celebrated as "freedom from want" and "freedom from fear." But this support for domestic entitlements such as Social Security and Medicare, and for protection from threats abroad such as international terrorism, has not translated into the firm acceptance of executive dominion. Charged with the stewardship of this "uneasy state," as Karl calls it, presidents have attempted to use the tools of the modern presidency, rhetoric and administration, to form new, more personal ties with the public. But the rhetorical and administrative presidencies—the two pillars of modern executive leadership—are not merely two sides of the same coin. Although the Brownlow Committee, which developed the blueprint for the modern executive, envisioned presidents overseeing the "persistent, determined, competent day-by-day administration of what the nation has decided to do," the connection between popular support and national administrative power has always been fragile in American politics. Roosevelt himself was somewhat diffident in his support of unilateral executive power. Indeed, the New Deal order created new obstacles to statist ambitions. Once viewed as entitlements, New Deal programs became autonomous islands of power that would constrain presidents no less than had localized parties. In the wake of his victory in the 2004 election, President Bush proposed to further diminish the national government's authority to administer the Social Security program. He proposed allowing workers under age fifty-five to divert some of their Social Security payroll taxes into personal retirement accounts. This reform, the White House claimed, would yield a better rate of return on funds dedicated to Social Security benefits; equally important, the personal retirement accounts would recast the core New Deal entitlement as a vehicle by which individuals would assume greater responsibility to plan for their own retirement. The money in personal accounts, Bush promised, would belong to individuals, not the government.[76]

It is a truism of American politics that the president has prerogatives in foreign policy that are not available in domestic affairs. As James Madison warned, "War is the true nurse of executive aggrandizement."[77] Still, the modern executive's responsibility to uphold "freedom from fear" has brought obligations to international organizations and allies and spawned an expansive bureaucracy that constrains as much as it empowers presidents. George W. Bush's willingness to pursue a policy of preemption without the sanction of the United Nations and the support of America's European allies has exposed him to hard challenges from moderate Republicans and Democrats, who charge, as John Kerry put it in his acceptance speech at the Democratic Convention, that America must have "a president who has the credibility to bring our allies to our side and share the burden, reduce the cost to American taxpayers, reduce the risk to American soldiers."[78] Moreover, the bipartisan 9/11 Commission's report, issued in July 2004, roiled the presidential campaign and threatened to diminish Bush's command of the war on terrorism. Responding to the popular support for the 9/11 Commission, Bush, who initially opposed creation of the commission, was pressured to drop his opposition to two of its most prominent recommendations: creation of a national director of intelligence and of a federal intelligence clearinghouse.[79]

Caught between the Scylla of bureaucratic indifference and the Charybdis of the public's demand for new rights, the modern presidency has evolved, or degenerated, into a plebiscitary form of politics that mocks the New Deal concept of "enlightened administration" and exposes citizens to the sort of public figures who will exploit their impatience with the difficult tasks of sustaining a healthy constitutional democracy. As the shifting fortunes of the Clinton and Bush presidencies have dramatically illustrated, the New Deal freed the executive from the local party politics of the nineteenth-century polity, but at the cost of subjecting it to fractious politics within the Washington beltway and volatile public opinion outside it.

Perhaps the national parties will bridge more effectively the traditions of republican government in the United States and the exigencies of national administrative power. The current Republican Party and president seem more committed and better equipped to coordinate campaigns and collaborate on policy than were the Democrats under Bill Clinton. The 2002 and 2004 elections gave dramatic testimony to ways that the relationship between the modern president and the party can be mutually beneficial. Just as Bush played a critical part in drawing campaign funds and loyalists to his party, so did he benefit from the steadfast backing of his party members in Congress and party loyalists in the electorate. Without this rock-solid support from his fellow Republicans, Bush's pursuit of controversial tax cuts and the polarizing Iraq War would have been far more treacherous politically. The traditional decentralized parties, nourished by the patronage system, acted as a gravitational pull on presidential ambition; the new national parties, sustained not only by the national party committees, but also by advocacy groups, think tanks, and the mass media, encourage presidents to advance bold programs and policies. The rise of more national and programmatic parties deprives partisanship in the United States of some of the tolerance that hitherto has made party loyalty so compatible with the pluralistic traditions in American politics. It may be, however, as A. James Reichley has written, "that a politics tied more clearly to principles and ideals is more appropriate to the current stage of our national life."[80]

At this point, however, the prospects for a "new party system" are very uncertain. The establishment of the president as the "steward of the public welfare" has put a premium on candidate-centered campaigns and organization. More important, given the nature of the modern executive office, it summons individuals whose ambition is best served by acting outside party politics; only then, as Hamilton wrote in *Federalist 72*, can they pursue "extensive and arduous benefits for the public benefit."[81] Presidents can be strong, indeed, can best display their personal qualities, "above party," Wilson Carey McWilliams has written. By contrast, "Congress cannot be effective, let alone powerful, without the institution of party. . . . A legislature can rival the executive's claim to public confidence only to the extent that it is accountable, which presumes a principle of *collective* responsibility."[82] The rise of the modern presidency, then, encourages each occupant of the White House to exploit the full splendor of the executive office at the expense of public debate and resolution that best take place in Congress and the state legislatures.

The relationship between the president and political parties thus invites us to consider a dilemma as old as the Republic. How can a state that is expansive and powerful enough to protect our rights provide for an active and competent citizenry? In the nineteenth century, Americans sought answers to this dilemma in a natural rights version of liberalism that celebrated localism. Traditional party organizations and newspapers rectified the Constitution's insufficient attention to civic matters. But there was no "golden age" of parties. Progressive and New Deal reformers had good reasons to view localized parties and the provincial liberties they upheld as an obstacle to economic, racial, and political justice. By the same token, the modern executive establishment, born of New Deal "programmatic liberalism," has weakened political parties and has fostered a more active and better equipped state—the national resolve to tackle such problems as forced segregation at home as well as communism and terrorism abroad—but one without adequate means of common deliberation and public judgment, without the means to sustain the vitality of its civic culture. This is the modern dilemma of America's "extended republic"—this is the central challenge for American democracy at the dawn of a new century.

Notes

1. Richard Hofstadter, *The Idea of a Party System: The Rise of Legitimate Opposition in the United States, 1780–1840* (Berkeley: University of California Press, 1969).
2. Herbert Croly, *The Promise of American Life* (New York: Macmillan, 1909; New York: Dutton, 1963), 169.
3. Theodore Roosevelt, "The New Nationalism," speech at Osawatomie, Kansas, August 31, 1910, printed in Robert V. Friedenberg, *Theodore Roosevelt and the Rhetoric of Militant Decency* (New York: Greenwood Press, 1990), 158.
4. For a more complete development of this argument, see Sidney M. Milkis, *Political Parties and Constitutional Government: Remaking American Democracy* (Baltimore, Md.: Johns Hopkins University Press, 1999), chap. 2.
5. Joel Silbey, *The Partisan Imperative* (New York: Oxford University Press, 1985), 36.
6. Stephen Skowronek, *Building a New American State: The Expansion of National Administrative Capacities, 1877–1920* (Cambridge: Cambridge University Press, 1982).
7. Skowronek, *The Politics Presidents Make,* 38–39. On the relationship between "great" presidents and party politics, see Landy and Milkis, *Presidential Greatness.*
8. Charles Merz, "Progressivism: Old and New," *Atlantic Monthly* 132 (July 1923), 106 (emphasis in original).
9. For a more complete discussion of the Progressive Party and its legacy, see Sidney M. Milkis and Daniel J. Tichenor, "'Direct Democracy' and Social Justice: The

Progressive Party Campaign of 1912," *Studies in American Political Development* 8 (Fall 1994), 282–340.

10. Shefter, *Political Parties and the State,* 77. Also see Eldon Eisenach, *The Lost Promise of Progressivism* (Lawrence: University Press of Kansas, 1994), chaps. 1, 4.

11. For example, see Daniel T. Rogers, "In Search of Progressivism," *Review of American History* 10 (December 1982), 114–123.

12. On the limits of progressive democracy, see Robert Wiebe, *Self-Rule: A Cultural History of American Democracy* (Chicago: University of Chicago Press, 1995), chap. 7; and Rogers Smith, *Civic Ideals: Conflicting Visions of Citizenship in the United States* (New Haven, Ct.: Yale University Press, 1999), especially chap. 12.

13. Croly, *Promise of American Life,* 338. On the progressive's commitment to strengthening executive administration, see Peri Arnold, *Making the Managerial Presidency* (Princeton, N.J.: Princeton University Press, 1986), chap. 2.

14. Theodore Roosevelt, *The Works of Theodore Roosevelt,* 20 vols. (New York: Scribner's, 1926), vol. 20, 317.

15. Skowronek, *Building a New American State,* 176.

16. Croly, *Progressive Democracy,* chaps. 2, 16.

17. Walter Weyl, *The New Democracy* (New York: Macmillan, 1912), 5.

18. Barry Karl, *The Uneasy State: The United States from 1915 to 1945* (Chicago: University of Chicago Press, 1993), 234–235.

19. Franklin D. Roosevelt, *Public Papers and Addresses,* 13 vols., ed. Samuel I. Rosenman (New York: Random House, 1938–1950), vol. 1, 751–752.

20. "Democratic Platform of 1936," in *National Party Platforms,* ed. Donald Bruce Johnson (Urbana: University of Illinois Press, 1978), 360.

21. Roosevelt, *Public Papers and Addresses,* vol. 13, 40.

22. Roosevelt, *Public Papers and Addresses,* vol. 7, xxxi.

23. Roosevelt, introduction to *Public Papers and Addresses,* vol. 7, xxix.

24. Thomas Stokes, *Chip Off My Shoulder* (Princeton, N.J.: Princeton University Press, 1940), 503.

25. For example, see Raymond Clapper, "Roosevelt Tries the Primaries," *Current History,* October 1938, 16.

26. On the elimination of the two-thirds rule, see Milkis, *President and the Parties,* 69–74. For a primary account of the debate over the two-thirds rule as it took shape during the 1930s, see Frank Clarkin, "Two-Thirds Rule Facing Abolition," *New York Times,* January 5, 1936, sec. 6.

27. Morton J. Frisch, *Franklin D. Roosevelt: The Contribution of the New Deal to American Political Thought and Practice* (Boston: St. Wayne, 1975), 79.

28. FDR quoted in Martha Derthick, *Policymaking for Social Security* (Washington, D.C.: The Brookings Institution, 1983), 230.

29. Ibid., 417.

30. *Report of the President's Committee on Administrative Management* (Washington, D.C.: U.S. Government Printing Office, 1937), 53. The committee, headed by Louis Brownlow, played a critical role in the planning and politics of executive reorganization from 1936 to 1940. For a splendid and thorough analysis of the committee, see Barry Karl, *Executive Reorganization and Reform in the New Deal* (Cambridge, Mass.:

Harvard University Press, 1963). See also, Milkis, *President and the Parties*, chaps. 4 and 5.

31. Memorandum, "Extending the Competitive Classified Civil Service," Herbert Emmerich to Louis Brownlow, June 29, 1938; and Civil Service Commission, statement, regarding executive order of June 24, 1938, extending the merit system; both in *Papers of the President's Committee on Administrative Management*, Franklin D. Roosevelt Library, Hyde Park, New York. With the passage of the Ramspeck Act in 1940, this convulsive movement to reshape the civil service was virtually completed. The Ramspeck Act authorized the president to extend the merit system to nearly 200,000 positions previously exempted by law, many of them occupied by supporters of the New Deal. Roosevelt took early advantage of this authorization in 1941. By executive order he extended the coverage of the civil service protection to include about 95 percent of the permanent service. Leonard White, "Franklin Roosevelt and the Public Service," *Public Personal Review* 6 (July 1945), 142.

32. Paul Van Riper, *History of the United States Civil Service* (Evanston, Ill.: Row, Peterson, 1958), 327. The merging of politics and administration took a critical turn as a result of the 1939 Hatch Act. Until passage of this bill, which barred most federal employees from participating in campaigns, the Roosevelt administration made use of the growing army of federal workers in state and local political activity, including some of the purge campaigns. Even though the Hatch Act curtailed Roosevelt's ability to continue these activities, the president signed the legislation. He was more interested in orienting the executive branch as an instrument of programmatic reform than he was in developing a national political machine, and the insulation of federal officials from party politics was not incompatible with such a task.

33. Oscar Cox to Hadley Cantril, May 3, 1943; Hadley Cantril to Oscar Cox, April 30, 1943; Memorandum, Hadley Cantril to David Niles, James Barnes, and Oscar Ewing, April 30, 1943; "Public Opinion: The NRPB Report and Social Security, Office of Public Opinion Research," April 28, 1943. Roosevelt Library, Oscar Cox Papers, Box 100, Lend-Lease Files. On the Roosevelt administration's use of polls, see Robert Eisenger and Jeremy Brown, "Polling as a Means toward Presidential Autonomy: Emil Hurja, Hadley Cantril, and the Roosevelt Administration," *International Journal of Public Opinion Research* 10 (1998), 239–256; and Lowi, *Personal President*, 62–66.

34. Roosevelt, *Public Papers and Addresses*, vol. 9, 671–672.

35. Martin Shefter, "War, Trade, and U.S. Party Politics," in Ira Katznelson and Martin Shefter, eds., *Shaped by War and Trade* (Princeton, N.J.: Princeton University Press, 2002), 123.

36. Richard A. Rovere, "A Man for This Age Too," *New York Times Magazine*, April 11, 1965, 118.

37. On Johnson and the Democratic party, see Milkis, *President and the Parties,* chaps. 7 and 8. On Johnson and civil rights reform, see Milkis, "The Modern Presidency, Social Movements, and the Administrative State: Lyndon Johnson and the Civil Rights Movement," paper prepared for conference, "Political Action and Change: Leaders, Entrepreneurs, and Agents in American Political Development," Yale University, New Haven, Connecticut, October 22–23, 2004.

38. Alan Ehrenhalt, "Changing South Perils Conservative Coalition," *Congressional Quarterly Weekly Report*, August 1, 1987, 1704. On the transformation of the New Deal party system that followed from civil rights reform, see Edward G. Carmines and Harold W. Stanley, "The Transformation of the New Deal Party System: Social Groups, Political Ideology, and Changing Partisanship among Northern Whites, 1972–1998," *Political Behavior* 14, no. 3 (1992), 213–237; and Earle Black and Merle Black, *The Rise of Southern Republicans* (Cambridge, Mass.: Harvard University Press, 2002), especially chap. 8.

39. A. James Reichley, "The Rise of National Parties," in *New Direction in American Politics*, ed. John E. Chubb and Paul Peterson (Washington, D.C.: The Brookings Institution, 1985), 191–195. By the end of the 1980s, Reichley was less hopeful that the emergent parties were well suited to perform the parties' historic function of mobilizing public support for political values and government policies. See his richly detailed study, *The Life of the Parties: A History of American Political Parties* (New York: Free Press, 1992), esp. chaps. 18–21.

40. As the minority report of the congressional committees investigating the Iran-contra affair acknowledged, "President Reagan gave his subordinates strong, clear, and consistent guidance about the basic thrust of his policies he wanted them to pursue toward Nicaragua. There is some question and dispute about *precisely* the level at which he chose to follow the operational details. There is no doubt, however, . . . [that] the President set the U.S. policy toward Nicaragua, with few if any ambiguities, and then left subordinates more or less free to implement it." *Report of the Congressional Committees Investigating the Iran-Contra Affair*, 100th Congress, 1st session, House Report 100-433, Senate Report 100-216 (Washington, D.C.: U.S. Government Printing Office, 1987), 501 (emphasis in original).

41. On Reagan's regulatory program, see Richard A. Harris and Sidney M. Milkis, *The Politics of Regulatory Change: A Tale of Two Agencies*, 2nd ed. (New York: Oxford University Press, 1996).

42. See, for example, Jeremy Rabkin, *Judicial Compulsions* (New York: Basic Books, 1989).

43. Benjamin Ginsberg and Martin Shefter, *Politics by Other Means: The Declining Importance of Elections in America* (New York: Basic Books, 1990); and R. Shep Melnick, *Between the Lines* (Washington, D.C.: The Brookings Institution, 1994).

44. On the rising number of independents in the electorate, see Rhodes Cook, "More Voters Are Steering Away from Party Labels," *The Washington Post*, June 27, 2004, B1.

45. Clinton's "third way" politics is carefully analyzed and placed in historical perspective by Skowronek, *The Politics Presidents Make*, 447–464.

46. Personal interview with Karl Rove, November 15, 2001.

47. E. J. Dionne Jr., "Conservatism Recast," *Washington Post*, January 27, 2002, B1.

48. George W. Bush, "Duty of Hope," speech, Indianapolis, Ind., July 22, 1999, at www.georgewbush.com.

49. Personal interview with Michael Gerson, November 15, 2001.

50. Rove interview; remarks by Governor Bush, June 12, 1999, Cedar Rapids, Iowa, at www.georgewbush.com.

51. Tish Durkin, "The Scene: The Jeffords Defection and the Risk of Snap Judgments," *National Journal*, May 26, 2001. Available at http://nationaljournal.com.

52. Rove interview. Rove believed that Atwater, his friend of twenty years, had made a mistake in going to the RNC. Political power fell into the hands of White House Chief of Staff John Sununu. A leading conservative in Washington who worked in the Bush administration had strongly urged Rove to work at the White House, not the RNC, "where organizational frustrations were rampant." Interview with conservative journalist, not for attribution, November 13, 2001.

53. Fred Barnes, "The Impresario: Karl Rove, Orchestrator of the Bush White House," *Weekly Standard*, August 20, 2001. Available at http://weeklystandard.com.

54. On January 21, 2001, Bush created a faith-based office and charged it to "eliminate unnecessary legislative, regulatory, and other bureaucratic barriers that impede faith-based and other community efforts to solve social problems"; Executive Order 13199, Establishment of Faith-Based and Community Initiatives. He also ordered the Department of Labor, Education, Health and Human Services, and Housing and Urban Development, as well as the Attorney General's Office, to establish Centers for Faith-Based and Community Initiatives within their departments. These centers were to perform internal audits, identify barriers to the participation of faith-based organizations in providing social services, and devise plans to remove these barriers; Executive Order 13198, Agency Responsibilities with Respect to Faith-Based and Community Initiatives, January 29, 2001. The education bill involved a compromise between the White House, which wanted accountability, and liberal Democrats in the Senate, such as Kennedy, who wanted increased spending. The president referred to this rapprochement with Kennedy in his State of the Union address, joking about how the folks back in the Crawford, Texas, Coffee House would be shocked when they heard him praise the Senate's leading liberal; George W. Bush, State of the Union address, January 22, 2002, at www.whitehouse.gov.

55. George W. Bush, "Address to Joint Session of Congress," February 27, 2001, *Washington Post*, February 28, 2001, A10.

56. George W. Bush, address to the joint session of Congess and the nation, January 20, 2002, at www.whitehouse.gov.

57. David Nather and Jill Barshay, "Hill Warning: Respect Level from White House Too Low," *CQ Weekly*, March 9, 2002. Available at http://library.cqpress.com /cqweekly.

58. Adam Nagourney and Jane Elder, "In Poll, Americans Say Both Parties Lack Vision, *New York Times*, November 3, 2002, sec. 1. An election-eve Gallup Poll reported that 53 percent would be using their vote "in order to send a message that you support [or oppose] George W. Bush." Of these, 35 percent said they would vote to support him and 18 percent said they would vote to express their opposition. David W. Moore and Jeffrey M. Jones, "Late Shift toward Republicans in Congressional Vote," November 4, 2002, at www.gallup.com.

59. Rhodes Cook, "Bush, the Democrats, and 'Red' and 'Blue' America," Rhodes Cook Newsletter, October, 2003, at www.rhodescook.com.

60. Personal interview with Matthew Dowd, political strategist for the Bush-Cheney Campaign, July 8, 2004; see also, Matt Bai, "The Multilevel Marketing of the President," *New York Times Magazine*, April 25, 2004, 43. Dowd insisted that a centralized grassroots campaign was not an oxymoron. The "ground war" was built with

community volunteers, but "once they volunteer, we ask them to do certain things. A national organization has to have a consistent message and mechanics. If the message is not consistent, if tasks are not systematically assigned, the campaign will implode. This was the message of the [failed Howard] Dean campaign: letting people loose can get the candidate in trouble. The message and organization must be relatively disciplined." The centralized grassroots campaign was not without spontaneity, however. "The campaign headquarters gave people tasks, but volunteers on the ground had some flexibility in determining how to carry out those tasks. It was local volunteers, for example, who learned that model homes in subdivisions was a good place to register new voters."

61. The average contribution of the new donors was less than $30. Republican National Committee press release, October 1, 2003. Personal interview with Christine Iverson, press secretary, Republican National Committee, July 7, 2004.

62. The Bush White House, with the support of Republican leaders in the House and Senate, pushed the prescription-drug benefit through Congress in November 2003, overcoming strong resistance from militant conservatives, who objected to a costly expansion of an entitlement program, and ardent liberals, who feared that the program would restructure, not expand Medicare, because it included provisions and incentives that would "privatize" the program. As House majority leader, Tom Delay (R-Texas), put it, the prescription drug legislation contained initiatives like Health Savings Accounts, a tax benefit that would encourage individuals to shelter income for a variety of health-related expenses, that presented Republicans with "a historic opportunity to put a conservative imprint on a major entitlement program." Delay cited in Theda Skocpol, "A Bad Senior Moment: The GOP Won This Medicare Fight. Now Democrats Must Keep Seniors (and Themselves) United," *The American Prospect*, January 2004. Available at www.prospect.org.

63. John Mintz, "Homeland Security Agency Launched," *Washington Post*, November 26, 2002, A1.

64. Kerry cited in Louis Fisher, "The Way We Go to War: The Iraq Resolution," in Gary L. Gregg II and Mark J. Rozell, eds., *Considering the Bush Presidency* (New York: Oxford University Press, 2004), 119.

65. William Schneider, "Super-Charged Electorate," *National Journal*, June 5, 2004. Available at http://nationaljournal.com.

66. A number of progressive groups, so-called "527 groups," which were formed outside the regular party organization in order to circumvent campaign finance regulations, formed an alliance to build an impressive media and ground campaign to match the efforts of the Republican Party. The task, as Simon Rosenfeld, president of the New Democratic Network, framed it, was to build a progressive "information-age political machine" to counter the conservative movement's partisan infrastructure. Personal interview, August 9, 2004; see also Matt Bai, "Wiring the Vast Left-Wing Conspiracy," *New York Times Magazine*, July 25, 2004, 30.

67. Personal interview with Bush-Cheney campaign official, not for attribution, July 8, 2004.

68. Personal interview with Kerry-Edwards campaign official (not for attribution), August 4, 2004.

69. James Ceaser and Andrew Busch, *Red over Blue* (Lanham, Md.: Rowman and Littlefield, 2005), chap. 5.

70. Peter E. Harrell, "House Now a Slightly Redder Hue," *CQ Weekly Report*, November 6, 2004, 2621.

71. Brian Faler, "Election Turnout in 2004 Was Highest since 1968," *Washington Post*, January 15, 2005, A5.

72. Dan Balz and Mike Allen, "Four More Years Attributed to Rove's Strategy," *The Washington Post*, November 7, 2004, A1.

73. Ronald Brownstein, "GOP Has Lock on South, and Democrats Can't Find Key," *Los Angeles Times,* December 15, 2004, A1.

74. The conventional wisdom after the election claimed that moral values, especially as they applied to the gay marriage controversy, tipped the election to Bush and the Republican Party. Clearly, cultural values played an important part in the election. But close analysis reveals that the war on terrorism made more of a difference. The Rasmussen Poll, which proved to be the most accurate survey throughout the election season, showed that the most important issue to voters was "national security," not "cultural" values. "Election Night Rasmussen Poll," at www.rasmussenreports .com. See also Paul Freedman, "The Gay Marriage Myth: Terrorism Not Values Drove Bush's Re-election," *Slate,* November 5, 2004. Available at www.slate.com/id /2109275. For a convincing critique of the view that American politics is roiled by a "culture war," see Morris P. Fiorina, *Culture War? The Myth of a Polarized America* (New York: Longman, 2005).

75. Karl, *Uneasy State*, 225–239.

76. Stephen Mufson, "FDR's Deal, in Bush's Terms," *The Washington Post*, February 20, 2005, B3. There are limits to how much Bush's plan would "privatize" Social Security. It would transfer a substantial portion of tax revenues from the control of government to individual accounts, but government would still force people to save, control the investment choices they make, and regulate the rate of withdrawals.

77. James Madison, "Helvidius Letters, Number 4," in *The Writings of James Madison*, ed. Gaillard Hunt (New York: G. P. Putnam's, 1906), vol. 6, 174.

78. Sen. John Kerry's speech accepting the presidential nomination of the Democratic Party at the Democratic National Convention at the Fleet Center in Boston, Mass., July 29. 2004, at www.washingtonpost.com.

79. Jim VandeHei, "9/11 Panel Roiling Campaign Platforms," *The Washington Post*, August 9, 2004, A1.

80. Reichley, "The Rise of National Parties," 199.

81. Alexander Hamilton, James Madison, and John Jay, *The Federalist Papers*, ed. Clinton Rossiter (New York: New American Library, 1961), Number 72, 437.

82. Wilson Carey McWilliams, "The Anti-Federalists, Representation and Party," *Northwestern University Law Review* 84, no. 1 (Fall 1989), 35 (emphasis in original).

Bibliography

Ceaser, James. *Presidential Selection: Theory and Development.* Princeton, N.J.: Princeton University Press, 1979. A penetrating analysis of the presidential selection process that spans the founding, the rise of the partisan presidency in the early part of the nineteenth century, and the emergence of the modern candidate-centered campaign during the twentieth century.

Croly, Herbert, *Progressive Democracy* (1914). Somerset, N.J.: Transaction Publishers, 1998. This new edition, with an introduction by Sidney A. Pearson, shows how this influential progressive thinker and editor anticipated and helped legitimate the rise of an administrative state that would transform the relationship between the presidency and political parties.

Cotter, Cornelius P., James L. Gibson, John F. Bibby, and Robert L. Huckshorn. *Party Organizations in American Politics.* New York: Praeger, 1984. A carefully researched study of a "new" American party system, in which national and programmatic party organizations arose from the ashes of the traditional decentralized and patronage based party organizations.

Ellis, Richard, ed. *Speaking to the People: The Rhetorical Presidency in Historical Perspective.* Amherst: University of Massachusetts Press, 1998. This volume on the historical development of the relationship between the presidency and public opinion includes many essays that shed light on the complex interplay between the presidency, party politics, and popular leadership

Harmel, Robert, ed. *Presidents and Their Parties: Leadership or Neglect?* New York: Praeger, 1984. Includes a number of essays that examine the uneasy relationship between the presidency and the party system.

James, Scott. *Presidents, Parties, and the State: A Party System Perspective on Democratic Regulatory Choice, 1884–1936.* New York: Cambridge University Press, 2000. Shows how the Democratic Party suspended its commitment to states rights and invested in national regulatory power in order to strengthen its electoral position in the nation.

Ketcham, Ralph. *Presidents above Parties: The First American Presidency, 1789–1829.* Chapel Hill: University of North Carolina Press, 1984. The best source on the early presidents and how the constitutional obligation in which they believed obligated the executive to stand apart from and to moderate partisanship.

Korzi, Michael. *A Seat of Popular Leadership: The Presidency, Political Parties and Democratic Government.* Amherst: University of Massachusetts Press, 2004. This book views the formation of a mass party system, and its capture of the presidency, as a critical constitutional transformation that made the rule of "We the People" practical.

Landy, Marc, and Sidney M. Milkis. *Presidential Greatness.* Lawrence: University Press of Kansas, 2001. All presidents considered great leaders, this book reveals, took party politics very seriously; indeed, Washington apart, America's greatest presidents either founded or refounded a political party that proved to be a critical agent of their political achievement.

Lowi, Theodore. *The Personal President: Power Invested, Promise Unfulfilled.* Ithaca, N.Y.: Cornell University Press, 1986. A study that examines how presidents have neglected party leadership to build a direct, yet fragile relationship with public opinion.

McWilliams, Wilson Carey. *Beyond the Politics of Disappointment: American Elections, 1980–1998.* New York: Seven Bridges Press, 1999. Taking account of recent presidential elections, one of the most distinguished analysts of American politics laments how mass culture and advanced technology have weakened political parties and American democracy.

Milkis, Sidney M., *The President and the Parties: The Transformation of the American Party System since the New Deal.* New York: Oxford University Press, 1993. Shows how the New Deal and the rise of the modern presidency led to the subordination of party politics to an executive establishment.

Shefter, Martin. *Political Parties and the State: The American Historical Experience.* Princeton, N.J.: Princeton University Press, 1993. A superb, historically rich analysis of the relationship between party politics and the bureaucracy.

Skowronek, Stephen. *The Politics Presidents Make: Leadership from John Adams to Bill Clinton.* Cambridge, Mass.: Harvard University Press, 1997. The best study of the role presidents play in periodically remaking American politics and government. Partisanship, this book shows, has sometimes helped to fulfill and other times thwarted the presidents' ambition to shape the politics of their time.

Wilson, Woodrow. *Constitutional Government in the United States* (1908). Somerset, N.J.: Transaction Publishers, 2002. A new edition, with an introduction by Sidney A. Pearson, this book reveals Wilson's thoughts on the relationship between progressive reform, the executive, and the party system.

13

THE EXECUTIVE BRANCH
AND THE LEGISLATIVE PROCESS

Andrew Rudalevige

THE IMAGE STILL LINGERS IN THE MIND'S EYE—LYNDON Baines Johnson, his gaze intense, his tall frame leaning forward to invade the space of a cornered member of Congress whose vote he needs to extract. Moving from inspiration to analysis, from flattering to bullying, Johnson radiates presidential power over the legislative branch. "This is not me, this is your country," he is telling a recalcitrant Senate icon, Richard Russell of Georgia. "Your future is your country and you're going to do everything you can to serve America." Russell holds out, but not for long: "I'm at your command." To which Johnson replies, "You damned sure are . . ."[1]

The "Johnson Treatment" exemplifies popular views of what skilled presidents can achieve when dealing with Congress. But, in fact, presidents' relations with Capitol Hill are far more complicated. Rarely do they involve a Congress obediently at presidential command. Further, a president's interactions with the legislative branch are themselves only part of those undertaken by the executive branch as a whole. For much of American history, presidents themselves rarely played a direct role in the legislative process, despite the Constitution's demand that they propose measures to Congress and its grant of veto power over congressional enactments.

Over time, however, both instruments have become important strategic tools. The notion of a comprehensive presidential legislative program—distinct from proposals arising from the wider bureaucracy—has become an institution, a fundamental expectation of executive leadership. From a rarely used power aimed at preventing unconstitutional measures from becoming law, the veto has become one way for presidents to bargain over policy outcomes and to stymie unwanted congressional initiatives. Legislative involvement anchors the very definition of the "modern" presidency, coming fully to the fore with the Roosevelt administration in 1933, as described by Scott James in this volume. Before that, as one leading scholar writes, there was "at best a grudging acceptance that the President would be 'interested' in the doings of Congress." Now "it has come to be taken for granted that he should regularly initiate and seek to win support for legislative action as part of his continuing responsibilities."[2]

Indeed, modern presidents have found that their capacity for leadership, even their competence, is judged on the basis of their program and its reception. A 1973 memo to Richard Nixon from his budget director crystallizes the point:

> . . . [L]egislating is perceived as governing and governing is perceived as legislating. Legislation—conceiving it, proposing it, fighting over it, winning or losing, making the proper proclamation when passed or signed—not only is the main "action" seen in Washington but is the key political currency in dealing with the voting public. . . . Therefore . . . the President must necessarily consider legislative initiatives and actions as central to his own interest and his own leadership efforts.[3]

The decades since have merely reinforced that conclusion. In 2001, for example, as George W. Bush prepared to take office, his ability to gain support for his legislative agenda in the wake of a bitterly contested election was considered vital to establishing his very legitimacy as president. Bush himself soon argued he had passed that test: Washington was "headed for a year of strong, meaningful legislative achievement," thanks to his administration's "new tone, clear agenda, and active leadership. . . . Beginning in September," he added, "I'll be proposing creative ways to tackle some of the toughest problems in our society."[4] By that September, of course, the substantive focus of the legislative agenda would change dramatically—but the call for legislative leadership would not.

This chapter explores the reality of the "legislative presidency."[5] It traces the linkages between the executive and legislative branches, culminating in the creation of a presidential legislative program. It examines contemporary interbranch relations, focusing on how presidents bargain with Congress, both as and after a bill becomes a law. Finally, it asks whether presidents have become the "chief legislators" in the American system of government—and whether, if so, this is a healthy development.

Separated Institutions Sharing Power

The U.S. Constitution begins with a clear claim: "all legislative powers herein granted shall be vested in a Congress of the United States." Yet as Richard Neustadt famously commented, American government is made up of "separated institutions sharing power," and legislative powers likewise bridge rather than divide the branches.[6]

In some cases, presidents must call on legislators in order to exercise their own executive powers. High-level appointments to the executive and judicial branches must be confirmed by the Senate, for instance; treaties require the vote of two-thirds of senators in order to take effect. Further, the Constitution directly interposes presidents in the lawmaking process by urging them to recommend measures they deem "necessary and expedient" for legislative consideration and by granting them the power to veto congressional enactments.

Most presidents in the early republic did not seek to intervene in legislative affairs beyond their explicit constitutional duties. Even the clearest of those—the power inherent in the veto—lay largely dormant. George Washington, worried the veto would become a dead letter if he did not use it at all, did so twice during his eight years in office. But only eight vetoes followed in the next twenty-eight years. Presidents rejected only those statutes they deemed unconstitutional, believing that policy differences with Congress were not legitimate cause for the veto pen.

This philosophy began to shift as the nineteenth century progressed (as James's chapter details). Andrew Jackson set a precedent for policy-based vetoes, rejecting twelve measures in all, most notably congressional attempts to renew the Bank of the United States. John Tyler, who became president when William Henry Harrison died in 1841, vetoed two more bank bills and two tariff measures. To be sure, these exceptions provoked notable hostility. Jackson was censured by the Senate; and the "perfidious" Tyler's vetoes prompted Whig Party members in Congress to call for both his impeachment and a constitutional amendment restricting the veto power. Still, while largely without legislative support for the rest of his term, Tyler had shown that even politically weak presidents could often utilize their constitutional tools to manage policy outcomes. Future presidents would pick up that mantle. By the 1930s, vetoes had become a routine part of the legislative bargaining process discussed below.

On the positive side of the legislative process—formulation—presidents were also mostly tacit. There were exceptions. Washington's Treasury secretary, Alexander Hamilton, helped craft statutes governing the new republic's economic policy, and Thomas Jefferson also worked closely, if more subtly, with congressional leaders. But those precedents did not take hold. Instead, presidents tended merely to highlight major issues for congressional consideration and left it at that. Defending his passivity as the Civil War loomed, James Buchanan insisted he had "called the attention of Congress to th[e] subject" of Southern secession but that "it was the imperative duty of Congress," not the president, to go on from there. During Reconstruction, one congressman noted that if senators "visited the White House, it was to give, not to receive, advice." By the time William McKinley took office in 1897, a contemporary scholar observed that the president's copartisans in Congress were not even called the "administration party," since "the President has . . . so slight a share in initiating the legislative policy. His message to Congress is really an address to the country, and has no direct influence upon Congress."[7]

As the twentieth century dawned, then, presidential leadership in the legislative arena was of relatively minor import. This was true even in the substantive area arguably most critical to carrying out national policy—the annual federal budget—where departments and agencies submitted their requests directly to Congress.

Indeed, most contact between the departments and the legislative branch was unmediated by the White House. Keep in mind that, aside from the presidency itself, the executive branch is a congressional creation. Grounded in laws and funded by budgets passed by Congress, bureaus and bureaucrats have long maintained a close relationship with legislators and especially with legislative committees. Departments lobby on behalf of their programmatic initiatives, all the while providing information and occasional advice to members of Congress; legislators try to direct departmental behavior through statute, oversight hearings, and the budget process. The scope of official interactions is suggested by the two to three thousand executive communications to Congress (testimony, letters, draft legislation) coordinated and cleared each year through the president's staff.[8] There is also extensive, less formal, contact between legislative staff and agency personnel over constituent "casework," as lawmakers seek to fix (and take credit for fixing) local problems ranging from missing benefit checks to military base closures.

These interactions became more frequent, and more necessary, as the national government expanded in size and scope. At the same time, however, expectations of presidential leadership rose as well. Progressive Era management doctrine urged policy makers to centralize authority in executive hands, portraying the president as chief officer of a burgeoning business. After World War I, such arguments succeeded in rationalizing the budget process under the president's authority: the 1921 Budget and Accounting Act gave presidents responsibility for overseeing individual agencies' budget requests and producing a unified, coordinated executive budget. A new organization, the Bureau of the Budget (BoB), was created within the Treasury Department to serve as the administration's staff arm in this endeavor.

The BoB's founding doctrine was to cut costs, and to be "impartial, impersonal, and non-political" in so doing.[9] But during the 1930s, President Franklin Roosevelt settled on the Bureau as a mechanism for reviewing not only fiscal measures but the full range of legislative proposals that departments wanted to send to Congress. Eventually, "central clearance" through BoB encompassed not only legislation but proposed departmental testimony before Congress, executive orders, and enrolled bills awaiting presidential signature. (In the 1980s, President Reagan would add the review of major regulations to the list.)

As discussed in more detail in Matthew Dickinson's chapter in this volume, in 1939 FDR also spearheaded the creation of the Executive Office of the President (EOP), which included BoB. The shift from Treasury established the Bureau as a truly presidential agency and helped formalize the clearance process. By the late 1940s, legislative clearance was no longer simply a reactive process of monitoring departmental proposals and avowing or disavowing their "presidential" nature. Items were still designated as "in accord," or not, with the presidential program. But the nature of the program was quickly evolving.

The President's Program: From Insult to Institution

As we have seen, for many years the president's constitutional power to suggest measures to Congress was rarely activated. In the early twentieth century, forays into the legislative arena by Theodore Roosevelt, William Howard Taft, and Woodrow Wilson began to change this. Wilson, notably, had broad ideas of presidential party leadership and presented his program in person to Congress. Still, legislators routinely denounced such executive involvement as encroachment that insulted their institutional prerogatives—until the Great Depression left Americans searching for answers and leadership. Immediately after taking office, Franklin Roosevelt called Congress into special session to consider his new banking legislation, which was passed in hours without having even been formally printed. So began the famous "hundred days" (March to June 1933), which have become the inevitable benchmark for Roosevelt's successors. During this time a flood of proposals rolled out of the executive branch and into law.

A dozen years later, at Roosevelt's death, the president's involvement in legislation was no longer insult, but not yet institution. But FDR's successor, Harry Truman, changed this. Truman realized that if the Republican "do nothing" Congress was to be made a successful electoral foil in 1948, the president needed an affirmative alternative. Throughout that year, special messages urging a wide range of legislation were sent to Congress nearly weekly. After Truman's surprise win, this systematic packaging of presidential requests became routine under the watchful eye of the Budget Bureau and its Legislative Reference Division. Proposals came from varied sources: they were solicited from the departments, developed in the BoB itself, and crafted by the growing White House staff. There had always been a presidential program in the sense that presidents were expected to take positions on the major concerns of their time. But now the program had developed from a sporadic stab at passing issues into "a comprehensive and coordinated inventory of the nation's current legislative needs, reflecting the President's own judgments, choices, and priorities in every major area of Federal action."[10]

The president's program soon became a regular part of interbranch relations, and for a simple reason: it met the needs of governance, and of many actors in government. After the New Deal and World War II, American government was permanently enlarged in size and scope, with an accompanying need for policy innovation. From the president's vantage, a program had potential policy and electoral benefit, and was a means to make a mark on history. For the rest of the executive branch, it provided a regular means of elevating select departmental initiatives onto a much more salient stage. From Congress's point of view, it provided a ready guide to administrative desires and national needs.

Thus, by the time Dwight Eisenhower took office, legislators not only accepted but demanded a presidential agenda. When the new administration was slow in providing one in 1953, a House committee chair angrily admonished Ike: "Don't expect us to start from scratch on what you people want. That's not the way we do things here—*you* draft the bills, and *we* work them over."[11] Eisenhower complied. All subsequent presidents have done likewise.

Formulating the Program

Having institutionalized a legislative program, presidents needed a way to create one, year to year. Early attempts consisted largely of choosing the best of whatever proposals bubbled up from a survey of the bureaucracy. Circular A-19, first issued by the Budget Bureau in 1946 and still in effect, requires agencies to lay out their proposed legislative program for White House consideration and clearance. Thus departments and agencies were the first—and still crucial—piece of the formulation puzzle.

This is natural enough, given statutory grants of authority to the departments and the wealth of resources housed there. Their substantive expertise is especially hard to duplicate: the thousand or so policy analysts in the White House and EOP constitute a drop in the bucket compared to the 2.7 million civilians in the wider federal service. Even when presidents have sought to shut out bureaucratic input, as with a series of task forces in the 1960s, they have often found themselves reliant upon it for translating outsiders' ideas into legislative substance.

However, the executive branch does not answer only to the chief executive. Beyond their extensive ties to Congress, bureaus are also linked to the interest groups whose constituencies they were created to serve and are bound by their statutorily defined duties. Departments and agencies remain an important source of policy development, as Daniel Carpenter's chapter in this volume makes clear. But from the presidential vantage, their ongoing agendas make them reluctant to produce new, large-scale policy reforms that disadvantage existing programs, clientele, or committees of jurisdiction. One Nixon aide commented that "nothing ever comes from the bureaucracy that hasn't been hashed and re-hashed for years." Jimmy Carter, putting a bipartisan stamp on the sentiment, complained that bureaucracy was "an anchor," too often devoid of "a single exciting or innovative idea . . ."[12]

Presidents wanted proposals that matched their own policy preferences, not those of legislators or interest groups; they wanted new, innovative bills that met their political needs and their campaign platform. Thus, as a presidential program became an annual necessity, so did an institutional response. That response took the form of centralized advisory mechanisms that could affirmatively coordinate the bureaus and even formulate policy without them.

As Dickinson shows elsewhere in this volume, as early as the 1940s the makings of a presidential policy staff took shape, housed both in the White House and the Budget Bureau (reorganized in 1970 to become the Office of Management and Budget [OMB]). Congress abetted this development by creating the Council of Economic Advisers (1946) and the National Security Council (1947) within the EOP; the staff support to these councils, if not always the councils themselves, soon became important presidential resources. Dwight Eisenhower added to the White House staff a large number of functionally specific posts that doubled Cabinet portfolios, from public works planning to foreign economic policy. John Kennedy utilized outside task forces from academia and elsewhere to develop ideas, an idea amplified by Lyndon Johnson, who also enhanced the role of the White House–based domestic policy staff. Richard Nixon expanded and formalized the latter by creating the cabinet-level Domestic Council, staffed, like the NSC, by White House personnel. Presidents since have sometimes discarded the council, but they have kept the staff, joined in 1993 by aides to a new National Economic Council designed to oversee "inter-mestic" economic concerns and in 2002 to a Homeland Security Council. A White House Office of Public Liaison came on the scene in the 1970s, institutionalizing a means for organized interests to communicate their concerns, legislative and otherwise, to the president.

These staffs, along with the OMB, serve to develop and seek out new ideas from sources ranging from freelancing civil servants to policy think tanks. They also ride herd on departments and agencies by representing the president on interdepartmental working groups and Cabinet councils. As such, they provide a means of tapping bureaucratic expertise while ensuring that presidential preferences remain front and center as policy is developed. Centralization has costs, though, as well as benefits, since the growth of the executive office staff runs the risks of replicating the bureaucratic pathologies it was created to defuse and of shutting out diverse views from the formulation process. It is a balancing act that some presidents, and staffs, have pulled off better than others.[13]

Several other aspects of formulation should be mentioned. First is the importance of cyclic mechanisms to policy development. The drafting of the State of the Union address, for example, marks an annual effort by political policy entrepreneurs to convert their ideas into the president's. The budget process, and to a lesser extent the preparation of the Economic Report, provide additional opportunities to present the president's priorities early each calendar year.

So does a regular rotation of expiring legislation. The need to periodically reauthorize various programs gives presidents an excellent opportunity to achieve desired change: the 106th Congress's failure to reauthorize the Elementary and Secondary Education Act in 1999–2000, for example, gave President Bush's No Child Left Behind Act a clear opening in 2001. On the flip side, of course, an administration that would just as soon avoid a given issue may be compelled to address it.

Budgeting is a special example of a recurring obligation. The Budget and Accounting Act requirement for a unified executive branch budget went far beyond providing for efficient accounting, given the critical role of fiscal policy in determining national priorities and policies. Harry Truman went so far as to combine his State of the Union and Budget messages in 1946, arguing "it is clear that the budgetary program and the general program of the government are actually inseparable."[14] This fact, along with the action-forcing nature of the budget cycle, has greatly empowered the OMB, which over time has itself become more politicized. The dynamic of large budget deficits, nearly constant since the early 1980s, places fiscal issues at the center of legislative formulation and thus make the OMB a more potent player in policy formulation. That trend is reinforced when presidents (e.g., Eisenhower, Reagan, G. W. Bush) seek to police the wider executive branch using the budget as enforcement mechanism.

Picturing the Program

How extensive is the president's program? One comprehensive study identified nearly 3,200 messages and 7,800 proposals propounded by presidents between 1949 and 2002.[15] Of these, about two-thirds are largely domestic in nature and about one-fifth foreign, with the rest dealing with budget or reorganization issues cutting across both domains. Note, though, that foreign policy is less often legislated, and that treaties are not included in these figures. If they were, the foreign/domestic weighting would be much closer to 50-50.[16]

A snapshot view of the past five decades is presented in Figure 1. The figure shows two measures for the years 1949-2002: the number of messages sent to Congress by each president each session, and the number of specific proposals those messages comprised. Note that the number of messages and proposals sent by presidents varies not only across administrations, but within them, depending on how (and when) presidents choose to package their agendas.

Again, the executive branch's involvement in the legislative process goes well beyond the activities channeled by the White House. But by now the presidential program itself is both well-established and extensive. While annual programs have ranged from the carefully limited to the immense, presidents have clearly engaged the legislative presidency. In the postwar era they sent an average of 58 messages per year to Congress, ranging from George H. W.

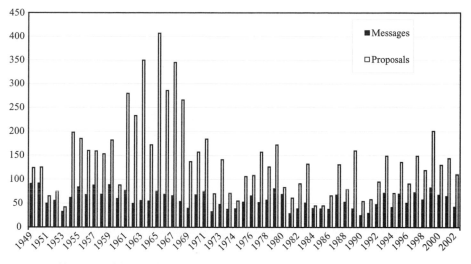

SOURCE. *Public Papers of the Presidents.* There are two entries for 1974, representing both Presidents Nixon and Ford.

Figure 1   Presidential Messages and Proposals, 1949–2002

Bush's low of 36 to Truman's high of 70. The average number of proposals included in those messages each year was 141, peaking in the activist New Frontier and Great Society years at nearly 300. Even the least active president on this score, Reagan, averaged over 80 proposals per year. And these are conservative estimates, for they do not represent the entirety of presidents' involvement in legislative politics. Presidents must consider appointments, treaties, vetoes, and legislative demands for information and testimony; they must react as well as act. For the executive program is far from the whole of the overall congressional agenda.

CHIEF LEGISLATOR? That last point has sometimes been forgotten. In the mid-1960s, for example, Samuel Huntington wrote that "the President now determines the legislative agenda of Congress almost as thoroughly as the British Cabinet sets the legislative agenda of Parliament." His observation arose from the experience of the Great Depression and World War II, reinforced by Lyndon Johnson's sweeping legislative enactments after the Kennedy assassination. But scholars had tagged the president as "chief legislator" long before the Great Society.[17]

Certainly the president's role in legislative formulation vis-à-vis Congress has increased dramatically over time. A landmark 1946 study showed that as early as the years 1933–1940, just two of twenty-four major enactments were formulated mostly by Congress. However, as author Lawrence Chamberlain argued then, "the widespread belief that the White House is the source of most modern legislation is exaggerated." Instead, the trend was toward processes that blended executive and legislative initiative; even "presidential" proposals often had a long history on Capitol Hill before being adopted and refined by the administration.[18]

That model of cooperative—or at least conjoined—legislative development remains the template today. While their findings depend on the time frame and methodology they use, scholars report that around half of major bills are jointly developed, with the remainder split roughly evenly between president and Congress. One study concluded that, contrary to Huntington's claim, a full two-thirds of 825 important pieces of legislation between 1953 and 1996 were congressional, not presidential. It seems premature to declare that the legislative branch is no longer in the business of legislating.[19]

After all, Congress is not truly an "it" but a "they," and the hundreds of members who constitute that plural have their own political needs and substantive agendas. Presidents and their staffs must track and react to thousands of individual legislative initiatives each session, seeking to forestall, co-opt, modify or squelch them. Proactive legislators can drive the president's own agenda by making certain topics salient—for example, through oversight hearings of administration activities and policy implementation, or by creating outside investigatory bodies (such as the two Hoover Commissions of the 1940s and 1950s, or the 9/11 Commission of 2002–2004) that spur changes to the list of executive priorities. Further, appointments requiring Senate confirmation, while not programmatic per se, take up space on the legislative calendar and can tax presidential capital.

It is nonetheless fair to conclude that presidents maintain an outsize ability to spotlight the policy stage. If, as the old saw goes, the president can't tell legislators what to think, he can often tell them what to think about. In the contemporary media age, presidents have a reserved slot in the news cycle, with the continuing capacity to focus the nation's—and thus Congress's—attention on the issues they choose to highlight. The annual State of the Union address has become a pivotal event, its presentation of presidential priorities parsed by and then parceled out to legislators. The president's initiatives almost invariably receive congressional attention and agenda space, especially in periods of unified government or in times of crisis. Overall, presidents get at least a committee hearing on nine of every ten bills they push and serious consideration of over 80 percent of their most important proposals, a real advantage given the huge number of pending items and limited time available each legislative session. Consider by contrast the fate of most bills in the 108th Congress (2003–2004): over 8,600 were filed; but only a little over a thousand were ever reported from committee and just 454 became law.[20]

Thus, active presidents may indeed dominate the legislative agenda. Whether they dominate its outcomes as well is another question.

Selling the Program: Legislative Bargaining and Legislative Success

"Those kids . . . don't have any idea of how to get along" with Congress, Vice President Johnson complained of the Kennedy staff. The White House, he griped, can't "start yelling 'frog' at everybody and expect 'em to jump."[21]

In other words, if by now presidents have little choice but to propose, Congress still has the power to dispose—and in its own way. Unlike prime ministers in parliamentary systems, presidents have no built-in legislative majority whose own electoral fate is directly tied to the executive's success. Nor do presidents have power to command obedience across the branches. They possess no formal authority over legislators, who control the national purse strings and are neither selected for nor removed from office by the White House. Senator Russell's obeisance to President Johnson, related at the start of this chapter, had more to do with long friendship and the compelling need for national unity after the Kennedy assassination than with any constitutional dictates. As Senate stalwart Robert C. Byrd told his new colleagues in January 1999, "Remember, you don't serve *under* any president. You serve *with* a president."[22]

Legislative success is nevertheless a critical component in overall evaluations of presidential success. The president's tasks "as leader of Congress are difficult and delicate, yet he must bend to them steadily or be judged a failure," Clinton Rossiter concluded a half-century ago. Or, as Carter and Clinton administration official Stu Eizenstat put it: "People judge strong presidents versus weak presidents on the basis of whether they perceive that the president is able to get the Congress to do what he wants. And brother, if you have the perception that you cannot, then regardless of how competent you may be you are not going to be judged competent in the office."[23]

How, then, can a president "get the Congress to do what he wants," or something approximating it? Since presidents cannot command, they must persuade. And they have used a wide range of bargaining tools to try to persuade members of Congress that supporting the president's legislative desires is in their own best interest as well. The remainder of this section, after discussing what legislative success itself might mean, examines the tools presidents possess and the challenges they face in obtaining that success.

Measuring Success

Though presidents are assessed on the basis of legislative success, there is no "industry standard" measure of that success. Presidents themselves are strategic in using ways of evaluating their proposals that maximize their claims to legislative leadership. A 1962 memo to John F. Kennedy pondered the desirability of adding "other bills we expect to pass" to the list of presidential program items, so as to "fatten our 'batting average.'" Not surprisingly, a Nixon aide later assigned to compare Nixon's legislative track record to Kennedy's could only conclude that "it will take more study to determine what they included in their figures. They must have counted more items as 'bills' than we have. . . . We could be accused of comparing apples and avocados."[24]

Scholars have proposed a variety of more systematic measures, some of which are tracked over time in Table 1. Still, the problem of apples and avocados remains. Should one count the overall level of congressional support for the president? Or should the focus be on whether the president "wins" specific roll calls? If the latter, which roll calls: all those on which the president has taken a position, or just some set of key votes?

Such measures enable observers to infer how much influence presidents have had on the decisions of individual or aggregated legislators. But roll call votes make up just a small portion of congressional action. Items may be passed by voice vote, or as part of an omnibus package. The key decision may come in committee, or through negotiation of a rule or unanimous consent agreement governing debate, or in conference committee, without ever coming to a recorded vote. Further, even when votes occur they may be misleading. When George W. Bush "lost" a series of roll calls on riders to the fiscal 2005 budget, his success score went down—but few of those riders, thanks to sympathetic conferees, ever became law. On the other hand, as the Kennedy memo suggests, votes can be gamed: holding all else constant, more ambitious presidents—because they ask for more—will have lower success rates, and presidents who ask for things that will pass anyway will boost their "batting average."

Perhaps then the relevant measure is the fate of various presidential proposals. Here we can examine both the fate of individual items and the overall proportion of the president's program that becomes law. These are both useful indicators. Yet they too have drawbacks, since some proposals do presidents more good politically by *not* being enacted. As the 2004 campaign approached, for instance, President Bush's failure to gain approval for a constitutional amendment banning same-sex marriage probably helped his electoral cause by galvanizing conservatives to vote. He could not pass the highway funding bill he wanted, but forestalled a much more expensive version, raising another query: from the president's perspective, might success be judged instead by how much bad legislation he can stop? But here a problem common to all these measures arises: they cannot distinguish between easy and hard, significant and transient "success." A president who passes much legislation in some areas may founder in others. It would be nice to weigh, as well as count, votes, vetoes, or enacted laws. This is hard to do, and rarely systematically attempted. Further, absolute scores do not control well for variance: the summary statistics reported here may hide large differences between members of Congress or large shifts within a given presidency (as when, for example, an incumbent loses his party majorities during his term.)

Nonetheless, as long as their potential weaknesses are kept in mind, all of these indicators are useful. As one would expect, as a group they are positively

TABLE 1

Alternate Measures of Presidential Success in Congress.

President	All Votes	Contested Votes	Important Votes	Average Annual Member Support		% Portion of Program Enacted (0–3 scale)	% Presidential Initiatives That Became Law	% Vetoes Sustained
	(a)	(b)	(c)	(d)	(d)	(e)	(f)	(g)
				House	Senate			
Truman	—	—	—	—	—	1.45	—	93
Eisenhower	71.7	61.5	62.7	58	58	1.65	50	97
Kennedy	84.6	79.5	70.5	60	59	1.30	49	100
Johnson	82.6	75.5	72.2	58	58	1.74	61	100
Nixon	67.0	56.7	58.7	55	53	1.07	26	73
Ford	57.7	46.0	56	44	53	0.85	13	75
Carter	76.4	69.2	69.3	56	60	1.59	44	85
Reagan	61.8	53.9	69.9	46	57	1.29	18	78
G.H.W. Bush	51.7	44.2	52	45	57	1.16	50	97
Clinton	57.6	47.9	58	52	61	1.53 ('93–96)	60 ('93–'96)	95
G.W. Bush (2001–04)	81.5	73.4	61	58	77	—	—	No vetoes

(a) Percent of recorded votes in House and Senate on which the president took a public position and prevailed. Source: *CQ Weekly* (December 11, 2004), 2946.

(b) Percent of contested votes in House and Senate on which the president's position prevailed Source: Jon R. Bond and Richard Fleisher, *The President in the Legislative Arena* (Chicago: University of Chicago Press, 1990), Table 3.2, as updated and corrected by Bond and generously provided to author.

(c) Percent of important votes on which the president's position prevailed. Source: Bond and Fleisher, *Legislative Arena*, Table 3.4; updated by author using key votes from Congressional Quarterly's *Congress and the Nation* series.

(d) Annual average percentage of member support: that is, how often the average member of each chamber sided with the president on votes on which he took a position. Source: George C. Edwards, III, *At the Margins: Presidential Leadership of Congress* (New Haven, CT:Yale University Press), Table 2.2, updated by author.

(e) Average success of presidential proposals, scaled zero through three. A score of three would indicate that the president got largely all he wanted; two, that he got over half; one, less than half; zero, none. Source: Andrew Rudalevige, *Managing the President's Program: Presidential Leadership and Legislative Policy Formulation* (Princeton, NJ: Princeton University Press, 2002), Table 7.2.

(f) Source: George C. Edwards, III, and Andrew Barrett, "Presidential Agenda Setting in Congress," in Jon R. Bond and Richard Fleisher, eds., *Polarized Politics: Congress and the President in a Partisan Era* (Washington, DC: CQ Press, 2000), Table 6.6, adapted by author. Because of the way data are presented, Kennedy includes 1964 and Nixon includes 1974.

(g) Vetoes do not include "pocket vetoes" that cannot be overridden. Source: Office of the House Clerk, U.S. House of Representatives.

correlated—as one rises, so do the others, all else equal—but each points to a distinct aspect of presidential success in Congress. Their utility depends on the question being asked. For example, a president with relatively low support scores may still prove successful in winning critical decisions on the issues he really cares about and changing a given policy outcome. President Clinton's second-term bargaining over appropriations (see below) is an apt example. A president with a relatively low batting average on "key" votes, like George W. Bush, might find that the bulk of his program nonetheless became law.

Or the obverse could be true: a president might prevail on most roll calls, but nonetheless see little translation of his program into statute. Some scholars argue this was John F. Kennedy and Jimmy Carter's fate. A president with little affirmative legislative success, such as Gerald Ford, may still be successful in preventing the enactment of legislation from which he strongly dissents.

Given a definition of power as influence over governmental outcomes—a president's substantive impact on the polity—tracking the nature of what actually becomes law is probably the most convincing measure of success. On this score, aggregate studies of presidential success show the president to be an important, but hardly dominant—a necessary, but not sufficient—figure in legislative policy making. In the parliamentary systems described by Richard Rose's chapter in this volume, prime ministers can expect to succeed with nearly all of their major legislation; otherwise, the majority party risks dissolving the government and forcing new elections.[25] In the United States, across the second half of the twentieth century, presidents got basically what they wanted in a little less than 30 percent of cases, garnering substantial victories on another 20 percent. Thus, about half the time presidents got all or most of what they wanted.[26] This is better than we might think. Still, as Table 1 shows, presidents have a more difficult time winning support on important issues or initiatives. Further, the fact that half of presidential proposals are scorned or ignored also highlights the temptation that presidents feel to go around the legislative process via unilateral action. Such action itself then digs new channels through which future legislative relations run, or run aground.

Contexts of Bargaining and Success

Why does presidential success vary? Why are some presidents successful and others less so? One possibility is that some presidents are simply better at legislative relations than others. As Fred Greenstein shows in his chapter of this volume, presidents have brought to the office quite different personal qualities, which have affected their capacity for influence on Capitol Hill. Certainly pundits and scholars alike frequently judge presidents on everything from the heights scaled by their rhetoric to their ability to schmooze lawmakers via some combination of substance and self-interest. The "Johnson Treatment" and Reagan's image as the "Great Communicator" are often contrasted with Richard Nixon's insularity and Jimmy Carter's malaise, with other presidents ranging between those extremes.

Still, legislative wins cannot be reduced solely to a winning personality, skillfully wielded. Such an approach cannot sum up the wide differences across the presidencies shown in Table 1, nor especially the intra-administration variance the averages presented there disguise. That is, it cannot take into account why less talented presidents often did better than the more talented, or why supposedly talented and less talented presidents alike sometimes achieved and sometimes failed to achieve. Presumably by 1968 Lyndon Johnson had not lost whatever personal attributes he possessed in 1965—but by 1968, according to one aide, "he couldn't get [a resolution honoring] Mother's Day through" Congress. Indeed, "not one study of presidential-congressional relationships that has systematically examined several presidencies and numerous legislative events over an extended period of time has found presidential legislative skills to be a potent explanation for variations in congressional responses to the president."[27]

In considering the resources that shape presidential relations with Congress, then, it is important to start by emphasizing that only some of them are dependent upon the president himself. Many are contextual, grounded in the national mood, in ongoing events, and in the results of the last election.

POLITICAL PARTY AND IDEOLOGY. Most prominently, the president's ability to bargain with a given Congress is bounded by the partisan makeup of that Congress. Party seats are the "gold standard" of presidential influence; simply put, the more copartisans of the president holding legislative office, the better the president's chances of success.[28] This makes sense: the party label serves as a proxy for a set of common policy preferences across different issue areas. Further, since members of the president's party have a vested interest in seeing "their" president succeed—lest his failure rub off on their own electoral efforts—presidents should have an easier time convincing them of both the substantive and political merits of administration proposals. Indeed, more than half of presidential initiatives offered under unified government become law, but just over a quarter when party control is divided. As we have seen, Lyndon Johnson was a skilled bargainer, but his ability to "get 'em to jump" correlated closely with his majority in Congress: it soared after the 1964 Democratic landslide, and plummeted when the 1966 midterms saw the loss of some four dozen Democratic members. Likewise, Bill Clinton's overall success on contested roll call votes in the 103rd Congress (with a Democratic majority) was 83 percent, but in the three subsequent Congresses (after the Republicans took control) less than half that; the proportion of his proposals passed, meanwhile, dropped by more than 40 percent after 1994. The average GOP House member voted with George W. Bush more than 80 percent of the time during his first term, but the average Democrat just 30 percent of the time.[29]

Even the narrowest majority allows a party to organize the chamber and thereby control the committee and floor agenda. But unified government is no panacea for presidents; it raises expectations for success but cannot, in itself, meet them. Given the need to build multiple majorities in different places as the legislative process progresses, a simple majority may not be enough. While George W. Bush won many House votes because of party leaders' willingness to limit debate and twist arms in favor of his policies, he had less success in the Senate, where a supermajority of sixty votes is needed to break filibusters holding up legislation or appointments. Bicameralism matters: representatives and senators represent different electoral constituencies, and play by different rules, forcing presidents to forge a strategy that solves two equations, sometimes in sequence, sometimes at once.

Further, not every member of the president's party will always support the president. Some may vote "off" because of concerns specific to their congressional district. Others may share a party label but diverge on various policy matters. The cohort of conservative southern Democrats in Congress into the 1990s meant that Democratic presidents could count on less support for their policies than a simple partisan tally suggested. As Johnson once commented of his 258 House copartisans, "We've only got 150 Democrats. The rest of 'em are Southerners."[30] Likewise, moderate Republicans, especially from the Northeast, were an important part of the Republican caucus for many years. Such members were described as "cross-pressured"; scholars often found it useful to model the impact of intraparty nuances on presidential bargaining by acting as if there were four parties in Congress, not two.[31]

Over time, and especially since the 1980s, party unity has increased significantly. Cross-pressured members became harder to find as the parties grew simultaneously more ideologically cohesive and farther apart from one another. This development tended to make legislative behavior more predictable, especially since at the same time legislators made internal changes that strengthened their leaders' ability to enforce party loyalty. That in turn helped presidents like George W. Bush; as one House member commented in 2004, "the similarities of the policy approaches on Capitol Hill and in the White House let him pick his fights, because most of the time there's no need to have a fight."[32] But it hurt presidents ideologically distant from the swing voters in each chamber, or from the relevant subject-matter committee with jurisdiction over a given proposal.

ELECTORAL MANDATES. Beyond determining the makeup of Congress, elections are often said to invest a president with a mandate—with the moral authority to pursue his agenda. Popular presidents are also said to have "coattails" on which underdog congressional candidates of the president's party can be pulled into office, with debts to repay. After the 1980 election, Ronald Reagan said that Congress should enact his economic platform, since "it is what the American people told us with their votes they wanted." Even George W. Bush played down notions that his popular vote loss in 2000 would require him to compromise his legislative program. "I believe I'm standing here because I campaigned on issues that people heard," Bush said after the election. After 2004 he was even more direct about claiming a mandate: "I earned capital in the campaign, political capital—and now I intend to spend it."[33]

Few agreed with Bush either time, but then voters choose candidates for many reasons that do not constitute an endorsement of a particular policy change. Perceptions are important nonetheless. Academic analysis of exit polls suggested that Reagan's relatively narrow victory in 1980 (he won just 51 percent of the popular vote) was driven largely by voters' desire to get rid of Jimmy Carter, not by a longing for the policies Reagan espoused. Yet Reagan, the media, and (most importantly) members of Congress accepted the contrary case, and Reagan won impressive victories on budget and tax bills in 1981.[34]

In this sense, mandates are asserted and negotiated, rather than declared by voters. "Real" coattails likewise are relatively rare. Since incumbent members of Congress have increasingly been provided with districts that minimize electoral competition, they rarely run behind the president in their constituencies. Still, where coattails occur, or members believe they occur, they are a resource presidents can call on. President Reagan's assurance he would not campaign against Democrats who supported his tax and budget program brought a number of lawmakers onboard his bandwagon. President Bush's success in stumping against recalcitrant Democrats in the 2002 midterm elections likewise helped shape subsequent legislative perceptions of his clout.

CRISIS. In times of national crisis, legislators are far more likely to defer to presidential initiative. The Congress, like the public as a whole, tends to "rally 'round the flag" in wartime, and to respond readily to natural or manmade disasters. The September 11, 2001, terrorist attacks are of course the most prominent recent example. Just three days later, Congress granted President Bush wide authority to retaliate. Other legislation, from $40 billion in supplemental funding to the wide-ranging Patriot Act, quickly followed.

Even far less dramatic events that focus attention on a given policy need tend to elicit sympathetic legislative responses to presidential initiatives. For example, oil spills have driven proposals strengthening tanker hulls; well-publicized crimes have driven eponymous shifts in federal criminal law.[35]

PUBLIC APPROVAL. Nearly every week, pollsters ask the American public if they approve of the job the president is doing. The higher his overall approval, the more "juice" a president is posited to have in his legislative dealings. Presidents, their staffs, legislators, and pundits all argue that presidential leverage is linked to his public popularity.[36] As discussed later, presidents try to use that popularity as a tool. But it also serves as a broader backdrop to executive-legislative interaction, since public approval varies predictably as the other contexts described here change. Presidents nearly always suffer when the nation's economy goes south, or when scandal strikes. Conversely, they benefit from an inaugural "honeymoon" at the start of their term, and from the post-crisis rally phenomenon noted above. Most dramatically, George W. Bush saw his approval ratings skyrocket from 51 percent on September 10, 2001, to almost 90 percent by September 14. While many rallies are followed by quick slumps, Bush's approval hovered over 70 percent for a full year, and rose again after the Iraq War began in the spring of 2003. That context provided him with opportunities for legislative success that less popular presidents did not possess.

THE BROADER POLITICAL FRAMEWORK. A number of other, broader contexts also shape the political regime within which presidents must operate. National expectations of government (is it a solution, or a problem?), the strength of centralized leadership in Congress, the relative unity of the presidents' coalition of supporters, the size and disposition of the interest group universe, the types of campaigns driven by a given configuration of the media and the campaign finance framework, and even, as noted, the state of the national economy are all things over which the president has little direct control. In recent years, for example, the fragmentation of cohesive media, interest groups, and party coalitions has made presidents' bargaining environments much more complex.[37] In short, where presidents fall in "political time," and their ability to discern the tenor of that time, gives them a better or worse chance of achieving policy change. "History," as Bush aide Karl Rove mused in early 2005, "has a way of intruding on you."[38]

Tools of Bargaining and Success

Within the contextual framework sketched above, presidents must still make strategic and tactical decisions about how to achieve their legislative goals. The mechanism is bargaining, but bargaining writ broadly.

The traditional notion of bargaining is simple exchange—in this context, the trade of benefits, from district parks to desired nominations, for votes. Narratives of President Johnson's hammering out civil rights legislation in 1964, President Clinton's efforts to win his budget's passage in 1993, or President Bush's hard sell on a prescription drug program for senior citizens in 2003 provide multiple examples. But bargaining is really about setting up a framework of alternatives that favor acceptance of one's offer. Explicit deals are only part of the story. Limiting lawmakers' options, the tactical use of public pressure, and the use (and threatened use) of the veto are all also important strategies.

Over time, presidents have expanded their staff resources to manage all of these aspects of bargaining. Much early congressional liaison was through the Bureau of the Budget or the White House counsel's office. In 1953, Dwight

Eisenhower created a specialized congressional relations office in the White House to formalize those dealings, and each president since has followed his lead. These days the legislative affairs office has about a dozen members, assigned to House and Senate. Press aides and presidential surrogates take to the airwaves to shape the agenda; "statements of administration policy" (SAPs) are issued by the OMB to let legislators know how the White House wants them to vote on a given measure. Presidents have also utilized ongoing or temporary centralized staff groups to manage legislative affairs. An example of the former is Reagan's Legislative Strategy Group, chaired by staff chief James Baker; the latter is epitomized by the "Intensive Care Unit" created to push Clinton's health care reform package. These staffs collectively provide a way to communicate presidential needs to members of Congress, and also the reverse—beyond policy feedback, requests for appointments, presidential visits to the district, even Kennedy Center tickets or quick constituent "meet-and-greets," are channeled through them.[39]

Departments have their own legislative liaison offices as well, which work on departmental policy items not part of the president's program proper, as well as on more salient proposals within their jurisdiction. Departments occasionally utilize their direct ties to Congress to evade presidential preferences, but presidents have worked hard to keep "everyone" (as one G. W. Bush staffer put it) "on the same sheet of music" as the White House. As a result, successive administrations have successfully reduced civil servants' contacts with Congress, while increasing their ties to the White House.[40]

DEFINING THE ALTERNATIVES. The outcomes of any collective decision are strongly dependent on the rules and alternatives that guide them. Since the preferences of any legislative majority are fluid, within a given range, presidents have the opportunity to steer those majorities toward their own preferred option. Substance, timing, and presentation (even the titling) matter for building a majority in each chamber in favor of the president's proposal instead of some other. Thus bargaining starts with agenda setting and policy formulation: choosing a particular policy agenda and packaging it attractively are vital to presidential success.[41] For instance, George W. Bush framed the 2002 resolution authorizing him to use force against Saddam Hussein's Iraq not only as a measure crucial to national security but as a way of empowering the United Nations, giving multilateralist lawmakers additional reason to buy in.

As far as timing goes, early in a term is usually better than later: "move it or lose it," one scholar has advised. The expectations for immediate action in the first "hundred days" may be unfair, given the substantive and logistical difficulties of complicated policy making, but legislative sessions go by quickly and presidential political capital depletes rapidly as the post-inaugural honeymoon ends.[42]

That is not to say that presidents can do everything at once. Too few priorities may be better than too many; usually, presidents should choose the targeted "rifle" approach over firing a less focused "shotgun" blast of legislative proposals at Congress. There is only so much that a given set of lawmakers can handle, a problem exacerbated when presidents clog the pipeline with multiple, complex proposals. As Lyndon Johnson memorably claimed, "Congress is a whiskey drinker." After all, "You can put an awful lot of whiskey into a man if you just let him sip it. But if you try to force the whole bottle down his throat at one time, he'll throw it up."[43]

How the "whiskey drinkers" are handled during the formulation process may matter as well. Centralized processes that exclude departmental and/or congressional input may fail to take into account substantive and political dimensions of a measure and damage its chances for legislative approval. So may the level of detail in a given draft proposal—whether too little, or too much. Specificity sets detailed parameters, and makes ownership clear. But in some cases, simple outlines are equally valuable, allowing broad claims of victory after Congress has wrestled with the devils in the details. This latter strategy has been increasingly common in recent years.

CHOOSING ISSUES. The biggest choice facing presidents regarding substance—when they have a choice—is the issue area itself. Some issues are "dead on arrival," while others are congruent with the tenor of the times.[44] Identifying and leading on resonant issues augments legislative success.

In general, presidents have tended to be more successful in foreign policy than on domestic matters. Some argue that there are "two presidencies," reflecting congressional deference in foreign policy and national security concerns and a distinct lack of deference on the domestic front.[45]

To be sure, politics no longer stops at the water's edge. The end of the cold war, the broader rise of polarizing partisanship, and the growth of interest groups focused on international affairs have all contributed to new levels of divisiveness over foreign affairs. Further, after Vietnam and Watergate, Congress sought to build institutional safeguards against presidential excess, passing among other measures the War Powers Resolution and Intelligence Oversight Act.

Yet despite occasional high-salience setbacks, modern presidents have generally had their way in foreign affairs. Treaties, of course, represent an area where a legislative role is mandated, but presidents have rarely lost the ratification battles they have chosen to press to the end. Just twenty-one treaties have been defeated on the Senate floor since 1789. Nonetheless, presidents have frequently skirted that battlefield altogether by negotiating international executive agreements that have the force of a treaty but do not require Senate approval. Unilateral action has also marked military policy, even after Vietnam. The 1973 War Powers Resolution was supposed to reinforce the Constitutional mandate that Congress, not the president, declare war; but presidents have never conceded the measure's constitutionality, and its wording leaves gaping loopholes for presidential initiative. Presidents have used American armed forces without legislative sanction in a wide array of military operations since 1973, most notably in the bombing of Serbia and Kosovo in 1999.

In any case, Congress has chosen not to press the point too hard. The War Powers Resolution may have helped pressure both George H. W. Bush and George W. Bush to seek legislative authorization for the 1991 and 2003 wars against Iraq. But the recent tendency toward granting presidents "blank checks" of military authority represents congressional blame avoidance more than legislative partnership and oversight in military affairs. Foreign policy remains a presidential strength, and is likely to remain so if only because of the office's structural unity and its command over the informational and administrative resources governing diplomacy and warfare.[46]

CHOOSING PEOPLE. For presidents, people are another kind of issue. Presidential nominations are a subset of formulation: individuals may make an important substantive difference to their assigned jobs, and some attract much more conflict to their confirmation processes than others. Furthermore, the sheer numbers of individuals involved is striking; some eleven hundred executive slots require senatorial "advice and consent," even before judicial vacancies are considered. When faced with this, JFK moaned that he didn't know any people—only voters.

To meet Kennedy's complaint, presidents have centralized institutional resources for the consideration of nominees in the White House personnel office and (for judicial nominees) in the office of the White House Counsel. Departmental secretaries and Supreme Court justices attract the most attention, and here the stakes are high and the opposition often fierce. Controversial nominees may be defeated (as with Supreme Court nominee Robert Bork in 1987) or withdrawn (as with putative attorney general Zoë Baird in 1993 or homeland security secretary Bernard Kerik in 2005).

Still, if presidents get a lot of advice, they also get a lot of consent. Those rejected become oft-repeated by virtue of their relative rarity: only nine individuals have been formally rejected by the Senate, even at the Cabinet level. Judicial nominees, because of their life tenure, tend to receive less deference from Congress than do the departmental nominees that make up the president's administrative team. But even here, presidents normally place hundreds of people on the bench. Bill Clinton, for example, made nearly four hundred judicial appointments and George W. Bush slightly over two hundred in his first term alone; each was successful in getting more than 80 percent of his nominees confirmed.[47]

Choosing nominees is like choosing legislation. As in the legislative arena, presidents must reconcile their policy preferences with what might fly in Congress; they must consider the explosion of media outlets and interest group involvement; they must consider issues of framing and timing; they must consider whether to act unilaterally (through "recess appointments") to achieve, at least for a time, what they could not in the Senate. Presidents make different strategic choices along these lines. At some cost to the judicial entrenchment of his ideology, President Clinton largely tried to avoid confrontation with a Republican Senate by selecting moderate judges for the bench. His successor, however, courted controversy (but also his political base) by sending the Senate several high-profile judicial nominees that many Democratic members found unacceptably ideological. When those nominees were filibustered, Bush used his recess appointment power to appoint two of them anyway, scoring political points if not a permanent victory. The battle rejoined in 2005.[48]

USING THE "BULLY PULPIT." A president's public standing provides a context for legislative success, as discussed above, but it is also instrumental. Not surprisingly, presidents seek to improve their public standing to raise support both for their administration generally and for specific policy proposals. Such tactics even made their way into popular culture when the 1995 film *The American President* depicted a presidential advisor urging his boss to trade some of his poll numbers for votes on a controversial environmental bill.

As Lawrence Jacobs discusses in his chapter of this volume, real-world presidents do attempt to utilize a "going public" strategy through both broad and targeted communications with the public as a means of rallying pressure on reluctant members of Congress.[49] What Theodore Roosevelt called the "bully pulpit" does allow presidents to influence the policy agenda, and sometimes to shape the terms of key debates—no mean feats. Bill Clinton staved off the appeal of tax cuts by demanding Congress "save Social Security first"; the estate tax was later repealed when it became the "death tax." Presidents who choose and frame their issues carefully may be able to expand the field of conflict to publicly highlight legislative recalcitrance and attract support. They may mobilize existing public sentiment into a forceful voice that propels their legislative preferences. And they may also be able to "spin" outcomes in a way that favors their side, no matter the substantive reality.

It is decidedly less clear that presidents have generally succeeded by these means in systematically swaying legislative opinion, or even public opinion, where latent support for presidential policies is lacking. One recent study concluded flatly that "presidents are rarely able to move the public to support their policies. Nor is the bully pulpit much help to chief executives in increasing their own approval ratings."[50] The context of approval thus matters both for the strategy chosen and for its impact.

Further, while some research has found consistent links between approval ratings and legislative success, most has not. Hollywood aside, poll ratings are not hard currency. Most likely, the impact of approval is conditional, not linear, and anything that hardens legislative preferences will limit the impact of fluctuations in approval. For example, as partisanship in Congress intensifies, the effect of public approval fades, since typically sized shifts in approval ratings are not large enough to change minds already made up. Even a large upward swing might not help the president if the reasons for the change can be isolated. George H. W. Bush's sky-high approval after the Gulf War, notably, did not carry over to his domestic agenda.[51]

Another reason for the lack of systematic findings may be a question of variance, or lack of variance, in rhetorical skill. While some presidents are certainly more articulate than others, a candidate who cannot communicate at all is unlikely to make it through the grind of a contemporary campaign. The marginal value of having communication skills above this rather high baseline may not be sufficient to overcome other constraints on legislative choice.

GETTING TO "NO." "Find me something I can veto," Franklin Roosevelt instructed his staff, when he felt that Congress was taking him for granted. In all he found 635 somethings over twelve years, 138 of them public bills (as opposed to private relief measures).

Presidents in far weaker political positions than FDR have found the veto an invaluable part of their legislative repertoire. Preventing bad law from enactment, while a negative feat, nonetheless keeps ongoing policy within the range of presidential preference. Since two-thirds of each chamber must be mustered to override a veto, overrides are rare, occurring on fewer than five percent of vetoed bills. Only nine of Roosevelt's vetoes—1.4% of the total—were ever overridden. More impressively, even a president like Gerald Ford, facing huge opposition majorities and unable to press much of a positive agenda, was overridden less than 20 percent of the time.[52]

It is worth stressing that vetoes themselves remain relatively rare events. Over time, fewer than 3 percent of the public bills reaching the president's desk have been vetoed. President George W. Bush did not issue a single veto during his first term. Yet Bush commented that "the best tool I have besides persuasion is to veto." As this statement suggests, "veto bargaining" is nearly constant: the threat of the veto is often more important than carrying it out. Because overrides are so difficult; because something is usually better than nothing; and because nothing is so often the outcome of the legislative process, members of Congress usually prefer to pass a bill that will avoid veto, even if it means coming more than halfway toward the president's ideal policy. Presidents can use sequences of demands, backed by veto threats, to give Congress a more exact sense of where those preferences are.[53] Sometimes, of course, legislators don't care. Occasionally the majority may even want to provoke a veto, despite the impossibility of an override, so as to create a campaign issue (as the Democratic caucus did during the 1992 debate over family and medical leave).

Veto strategies gain special power during the budget process, when failure to pass appropriations bills can lead to the shutdown of government functions. In 1995–1996, the battle between President Clinton and the Republican majority in Congress came to just this end, and legislators took the brunt of the public's anger. Clinton successfully used a veto strategy to paint conservative Republicans as extremists as he aimed toward reelection in 1996. In his second term, despite dealing with a hostile Congress that had gone so far as to impeach him, Clinton remained extremely successful in extracting funding for his policy priorities. He so adroitly used veto threats to manipulate the budget endgame that one Republican senator complained in 2000 of "a dictatorial system of the president saying what is acceptable, and the Congress being held hostage . . ., concerned about being blamed for shutting down the government."[54]

AFTER A BILL BECOMES A LAW. Presidential-congressional relations do not stop when a bill makes it through the legislative gauntlet. The battle over the bureaucracy is treated in depth elsewhere in this volume (see especially the chapter by Barry Weingast), but it is worth noting here that presidents have administrative resources to shape the way initiatives are implemented by the executive branch even after enactment. This begins as the bill is signed into law. Presidential "signing statements," while constitutionally dubious, have successfully directed executive agencies in their interpretation of the law as they make decisions about implementation—including whether to do so in the first place. One recent example set aside requirements that the Department of Homeland Security forward to Congress and its Government Accountability Office (GAO) certain information withheld from the public.

Such statements are part of a broad array of presidential directives, also including executive orders, presidential memoranda, and proclamations, that seek to shape how a law is made effective. The impact of these mechanisms has increased dramatically in recent years. Recent examples include the Clinton setaside, by proclamation, of nearly two million acres of land in Utah as a national monument, and the Bush initiative to expand the provision of social services by faith-based organizations. Classified national security directives also serve to shape American foreign policy in ways rarely reviewed by the legislative branch.[55]

Sometimes presidential orders merely put into motion actions specified in statute. But when legislation is vague or silent on a particular matter, they may move policy in directions lawmakers did not contemplate. The usual vehicle is the rule-making process. While discussion of the Code of Federal Regulation puts normal people to sleep—indeed, this is part of its advantage as a quiet vehicle for policy redirection—the substance of any law is in many ways determined by the regulations issued in its name. The No Child Left Behind Act passed in 2002 provides a good example: the effect of its testing and accountability requirements on schools and students was not clear until the Department of Education had issued rules governing what kind of tests were required and how state standards for measuring pupil proficiency could be defined. The 1981 addition of regulatory review to the central clearance process housed in the Office of Management and Budget thus gave presidents a useful tool of coordination and control. Presidents have also paid careful attention to the people overseeing rule making, with an expanded White House personnel office seeking to ensure that even lower-level appointees are in tune with administration policy preferences. To continue the example above, it is no accident that the Department of Education is one of the most politicized agencies in the federal government.

Of course, even as presidents seek to control the agencies, legislators do the same—sometimes abetted by the agencies themselves, who may want statutory sanction to evade presidential directive. In 1996, for instance, Congress fought back on the regulatory front by giving itself power to delay and block major rules changes. Legislators can also choose to write extraordinarily detailed legislation that limits agency, and White House, discretion over regulatory interpretation of the statute's intent. Increasingly, too, they place earmarks or "riders" in budget bills that target appropriations to specific projects; one study found that the number of earmarks more than doubled between 1994 and 2004. And Congress routinely weighs in on appointments. Nomination hearings often explore past departmental decisions and lay down markers for what is expected in the future. The 2005 hearings over George W. Bush's nominations for attorney general and secretary of state raised issues ranging from the use of torture to the AIDS epidemic.[56]

Such efforts highlight the latent power of Congress. Its ability to probe executive branch behavior is potentially vast, ranging from investigative hearings to the impeachment and removal of the president. Long-term change requires legislative sanction, and presidents who seek to "win" their point through administrative end-runs even after losing in the legislative arena may find their fortunes rudely, and loudly, reversed. Still, the difficulties of collective action frequently enfeeble Congressional oversight. Presidents will often be tempted to try their luck and go it alone.

Summary

The preceding discussion suggests that the question of presidents' legislative success should be reframed. Rather than ask whether presidents got all they wanted, we should ask instead how well, controlling for resources and obstacles, presidents exploited their opportunities for leadership. The presidential talents brought to bear on legislative bargaining must be considered within the historical, political, and electoral contexts facing each administration: the upper and lower bounds of success are drawn by factors outside a president's direct control. A compelling personality or a soaring speech make their marks in the margins of legislative success, but the size and coherence of the congressional majority, or the presence of crisis, make more systematic differences.

Still, if presidential skill works mostly at the margins, in any individual close call—and in a 50-50 nation, most calls are close—the most interesting play might be in those margins. Through adroitly framing issues, presidents may even be able to structure where the margins are drawn. It is here that the attributes Fred Greenstein explores in his chapter have the greatest consequence. In any individual case, it matters who is president.

The Executive Branch, Congress, and Legislation

The framers of the Constitution created separate branches that could not function separately. And so the executive branch has always been intertwined in the legislative process. From appointments to vetoes, from programmatic initiatives to the intricacies of the budget process, the branches are bound inextricably in a system that must work in tandem if it is to work at all.

Even today, the "president's program" represents just a fraction of the interactions between Congress and the executive, much of it driven by legislators and agency personnel. As this chapter has emphasized, dealings with Congress are widely dispersed across the entire executive establishment: departments remain important players in patterning policy for legislative perusal and maintain tight linkages to appropriations and authorizing committees.

However, the immense growth of the American state has made presidential leadership more central to that process, and more critical. The demands of the modern presidency did not make the president "chief legislator," but they did make attention to legislating one of his chief jobs. The presidency has become a positive source of policy development and political leadership rather than merely a negative check on legislative usurpation. Doing so has left a permanent institutional mark. Unmediated contacts between Congress and the bureaucracy have become less common. White House efforts to come to grips with, and get astride, the process of policy formulation across the wider bureaucracy have led to the creation and utilization of centralized staff resources enabling presidents to use the legislative process to set down markers for both the next election, and for history.

What sort of presidential leadership is possible in this area? Certainly presidents face no easy task. To be successful, by their own lights and the public's, they must try to keep departments responsive to the White House, not the Capitol. They must utilize departmental expertise while fashioning a program that meets their own policy preferences and political needs. They must then bargain with legislators—in House and Senate, committee and caucus, public and private—to gain acceptance of their proposals. Through those labyrinths leadership lies, achieved only in the course of crafting a series of hard choices among a myriad of competing concerns. Every decision has positive managerial, political, and policy costs as well as the loss of opportunities forgone.

Presidents often rail against this reality, and against the American government's bias toward the status quo. They argue that they alone represent the national interest against legislative fealty to local, special interests. Many observers have agreed; Clinton Rossiter, summing up conventional wisdom at midcentury, argued that "since Congress is no longer minded or organized to guide itself, the refusal or inability of the President to serve as leader results in weak and disorganized government."[57] That argument still has resonance, especially as hugely complex global issues, from terrorism to trade, become part of the permanent context facing American political leaders. In substantive areas ranging from budgeting to war powers, Congress has indeed ceded much ground to presidential authority.

Yet most of the time, as we have seen, presidents are facilitators, rather than directors, of change.[58] That is just as well. American democracy, it has been said, is a system for people who are not too sure they are right—but few unsure individuals attain the presidency. As a result, presidents' claims to personify the national interest are overblown and often overbearing, as the Jacobs chapter in this volume makes clear. Certainly the framers expected that "the genius of republican liberty" rested in vesting political power and trust "not in a few, but a number of hands."[59]

Put another way, presidential power, however great, is meant to be conditional, one part of a complex, interactive system producing policy outputs. Those outputs, to be legitimate, require debate and deliberation; they require the construction of multiple majorities out of diverse constituencies with distinct interests—and these are legislative functions, not executive. Presidential direction is efficient, but efficiency is not always the primary value of government. Direction is not the same as debate, indeed does not brook debate. Thus, even in the world after September 11, ours is not—and must not become—a government centered on the president alone.[60]

Yet facilitation is no mean function. In a system of separated powers, separated further by polarization and particularism, it is in fact a crucial task. Even where it is exercised, gridlock threatens. Without it, gridlock rules. "Energy in the executive," Alexander Hamilton famously argued, "is a leading character in the definition of good government."[61] The key is to marry energetic presidential leadership to the accountability enforced by the vigorous debate of legislators—and voters—living out their own assigned roles in the American constitutional structure.

Notes

*The author would like to thank those whose comments helped refine this chapter, including Paul Baker, George Edwards, Fred Greenstein, Jim Pfiffner, Steve Wayne, and

Barry Weingast, and give special acknowledgment to the extensive and constructive feedback provided by Mark Peterson, Joel Aberbach, and Jeffrey Weinberg.

1. This conversation, which took place on November 29, 1963, is transcribed at http://americanradioworks.publicradio.org/features/prestapes/lbj_rr_092963 .html (accessed January 13, 2005).
2. Fred Greenstein, "Change and Continuity in the Modern Presidency," in Anthony King, ed., *The New American Political System* (Washington, D.C.: American Enterprise Institute Press, 1978), 45–46.
3. Roy Ash to President, "Strengthening the Presidency," memo of August 24, 1973, White House Central Files: Staff Member and Office Files, Roy Ash, *Ash Memos to the President, February 1973 to December 1973,* Nixon Presidential Materials Staff, College Park, Md.
4. Alison Mitchell, "Winning: Now He Must Convince the Voters," *New York Times* (December 17, 2000): IV-1; Bush, "Remarks Following a Cabinet Meeting on the Legislative Agenda," August 3, *Public Papers of the Presidents, 2001.*
5. Wayne, *The Legislative Presidency.*
6. Richard E. Neustadt, *Presidential Power and the Modern Presidents* (New York: Free Press, 1990), 29.
7. Binkley, *President and Congress,* 185; James Buchanan, *Mr. Buchanan's Administration on the Eve of the Rebellion* (New York: D. Appleton and Co., 1866), 153–154; Mary Parker Follett, *The Speaker of the House of Representatives* (New York: Longmans, Green, 1896), 325. Note that Buchanan's successor, Abraham Lincoln, was an active leader, but much of his leadership was executive in nature (or framed that way), not legislative.
8. This figure is drawn from recent clearance totals for the 107th and 108th Congresses generously provided by the Legislative Reference Division, Office of Management and Budget.
9. Charles A. Dawes, Budget Director, "The Basic Principles of Budget Operation in the United States," June 29, 1921, Record Group 51, Records of the Bureau of the Budget: General Subject Files (Series 21.1), *Budget Bureau—General, 1-6,* National Archives, College Park, Md.
10. Richard E. Neustadt, "Presidency and Legislation: Planning the President's Program," *American Political Science Review* 49 (December 1955), 980; James Sundquist, *The Decline and Resurgence of Congress* (Washington, D.C.: The Brookings Institution, 1981), chap. 6.
11. Neustadt, "Presidency and Legislation," 1000, 1014–1015.
12. Light, *The President's Agenda,* 82; Kenneth W. Thompson, eds., *Portraits of American Presidents,* vol. 8, *The Carter Presidency* (Lanham, Md.: University Press of America, 1990), 6.
13. Rudalevige, *Managing the President's Program,* chaps. 3 and 8.
14. *Public Papers of the Presidents, 1946,* January 21.
15. A message is defined as a communication from the president to both chambers of Congress on a single topic on a single day (thus by this measure a State of the Union address normally contains multiple messages.) Data are drawn from the annual *Public Papers of the Presidents,* as compiled for 1949–1996 in Rudalevige, *Managing the President's*

Program, Ch. 4. More detailed definitions of "message" and "proposal" are provided there. Data for 1997–2002 have been updated by the author using those definitions.

16. Rudalevige, *Managing the President's Program*, 72. The two-chamber rule (again, only proposals requiring consideration by both House and Senate are included in the count) excludes treaties. Further, treaty requests are not consistently listed in the *Public Papers*. However, presidents have submitted well over 1,000 treaties to the Senate since 1953.

17. Samuel Huntington, "Congressional Responses to the Twentieth Century," in David B. Truman, ed., *The Congress and America's Future*, 2nd ed. (Englewood Cliffs, N.J.: Prentice-Hall, 1973 [1965]), 28. For "chief legislator," see Howard Lee McBain, *The Living Constitution* (New York: Macmillan, 1939 [1927]), chap. 4; Clinton Rossiter, *The American Presidency* (New York: Harcourt, Brace, and World, 1956), chap. 1.

18. Lawrence H. Chamberlain, *The President, Congress, and Legislation* (New York: Columbia University Press, 1946), 19, 450ff.

19. William M. Goldsmith, *The Growth of Presidential Power: A Documented History*, vol. 3 (New York: Chelsea House, 1974), 1390–1406; Jones, *The Presidency in a Separated System*, chap. 7; George C. Edwards, III, and Andrew Barrett, "Presidential Agenda Setting in Congress," in Jon R. Bond and Richard Fleisher, eds., *Polarized Politics: Congress and the President in a Partisan Era* (Washington, D.C.: Congressional Quarterly Press, 2000), 128.

20. Figures from Edwards and Barrett, "Presidential Agenda Setting" and (on important bills) Peterson, *Legislating Together*, table 5.3, though Edwards and Barrett, using a different definition of importance, find that hearings, at least, were held on 98% of those proposals. On divided government and crisis, see Andrew J. Taylor, "Domestic Agenda Setting, 1947–1994," *Legislative Studies Quarterly* 23 (August 1998), 380. Figures on the 108th Congress are from the "Resumé of Congressional Activity" at http://thomas.loc.gov/ (accessed January 19, 2005); they do not include resolutions not requiring presidential signature to take effect.

21. Jeff Shesol, *Mutual Contempt: Lyndon Johnson, Robert Kennedy, and the Feud That Defined a Decade* (New York: W. W. Norton, 1997), 100.

22. Quoted in Joel Achenbach, "The Proud Compromisers," *Washington Post* (January 9, 1999), A1.

23. Rossiter, *The American Presidency*, 15; Eizenstat, Miller Center Interviews, Carter Presidency Project, vol. 13, January 1982, Jimmy Carter Library, 105.

24. Quoted in Rudalevige, *Managing the President's Program*, 63.

25. A major proposal backed by the prime minister but opposed by her party may prompt a vote of "no confidence" in the government—which removes the prime minister but also forces new elections for all seats in the parliament.

26. Rudalevige, *Managing the President's Program*, table 7.1. Other recent studies have come to similar conclusions. One, covering 1953–1984, found that presidents won on about 35% of their proposals and compromised on another 19%. Another, covering 1953–1996, found that presidential program items succeed about 40% of the time overall, with a large divergence between periods of divided and unified government. See Peterson, *Legislating Together*, table 3.1; Edwards and Barrett, "Presidential Agenda Setting," table 6-6.

27. Kenneth O'Donnell, oral history of July 23, 1969, Lyndon B. Johnson Library, 91; Mark A. Peterson, "The President and Congress," in Michael Nelson, ed., *The Presidency and the Political System*, 6th ed. (Washington, D.C.: Congressional Quarterly Press, 2000), 490.

28. Light, *President's Agenda*, 281; see also Edwards, *At the Margins,* 172–173; Jon R. Bond and Richard Fleisher, *The President in the Legislative Arena* (Chicago: University of Chicago Press, 1990), chap. 4; Steven A. Shull and Thomas C. Shaw, *Explaining Congressional-Presidential Relations: A Multiple Perspective Approach* (Albany: State University of New York Press, 1999), 84ff.

29. Edwards and Barrett, "Presidential Agenda Setting," 128; and see the sources in Table 1.

30. Quoted in a 1963 conversation with *Washington Post* publisher Katherine Graham in Michael R. Beschloss, ed., *Taking Charge: The Johnson White House Tapes, 1963–1964* (New York: Simon & Schuster, 1997), 84. LBJ slightly overestimated the number of geographical southerners in the caucus, but perhaps not the number of presidential loyalists.

31. See Bond and Fleisher, *President in the Legislative Arena*, 87; Richard Fleisher and Jon R. Bond, "Partisanship and the President's Quest for Votes on the Floor of Congress," in Bond and Fleisher, eds., *Polarized Politics: Congress and the President in a Partisan Era* (Washington, D.C.: Congressional Quarterly Press, 2000).

32. Rep. Christopher Cox (R-Calif.), quoted in Joseph J. Schatz, "With a Deft and Light Touch, Bush Finds Ways to Win," *CQ Weekly* (December 11, 2004), 2900.

33. Patricia Heidotting Conley, *Presidential Mandates: How Elections Shape the National Agenda* (Chicago: University of Chicago Press, 2001), 3; Mike Allen, "Bush to Forge Ahead with Agenda," *Washington Post* (December 14, 2000), A1; Bush, press conference of November 4, 2004, Office of the White House Press Secretary; Jim VandeHei and Michael A. Fletcher, "Bush Says Election Ratified Iraq Policy," *Washington Post* (January 16, 2005), A1.

34. On coattails, see Edwards, *At the Margins*, chap. 8.

35. See "Laci's Law," "Megan's Law," and the like. For a discussion of the role of "focusing events" in legislative decision making, see John W. Kingdon, *Agendas, Alternatives, and Public Policies*, 2nd ed. (New York: HarperCollins, 1995).

36. See, e.g., the quotes in George C. Edwards, III, "Aligning Tests with Theory: Presidential Approval as a Source of Influence on Congress," *Congress and the Presidency* 24 (Fall 1997): 113–130.

37. See the Dickinson chapter in this volume for a more extensive discussion of this point, described by Samuel Kernell as a shift from "institutionalized" to "individualized" pluralism.

38. Rove quoted in Dan Balz and Michael Fletcher, "Looking to Apply Lessons Learned," *Washington Post* (January 20, 2005), A1. See also Stephen Skowronek, *The Politics Presidents Make* (Cambridge, Mass.: Harvard University Press, 1994); Peterson, *Legislating Together*, chap. 4, provides an excellent discussion of the "pure" and "malleable" contexts presidents face, and shape.

39. Balz and Fletcher, "Lessons Learned"; Collier, *Between the Branches,* 244; David Nather, "President's New Hill Lobbyist Is Big on Favors, Not Threats," *CQ Weekly*

(January 25, 2003), 182; Wayne, *Legislative Presidency*. SAPs for the current administration can be accessed on the OMB website, http://www.whitehouse.gov
/omb/legislative/sap/index.html (accessed January 19, 2005).

40. Nather, "President's New Hill Lobbyist," 182; Joel D. Aberbach and Bert A.
Rockman, *In the Web of Politics: Three Decades of the U.S. Federal Executive*
(Washington, D.C.: The Brookings Institution, 2000), 114–119.

41. See Paul J. Quirk, "What Do We Know?" in William Crotty, ed., *Political Science:
Looking toward the Future*, vol. 4 (Evanston, Ill.: Northwestern University Press, 1991),
47; Bond and Fleisher, *Legislative Arena*, 230; Rudalevige, *Managing*, 113.

42. Light, *President's Agenda*, 218.

43. James P. Pfiffner, *The Strategic Presidency*, 2nd rev. ed. (Lawrence: University Press of
Kansas, 1996); Joseph A. Califano, Jr., *The Triumph and Tragedy of Lyndon Johnson* (New
York: Simon & Schuster, 1991), 142.

44. Kingdon, *Agendas*; Jones, *Separated System*, 201–202.

45. Empirical studies of the topic have been mixed, generally showing that any divergence has faded somewhat over time. See Shull and Shaw, *Explaining*, 85–86.

46. Rudalevige, *The New Imperial Presidency*.

47. See Denis Steven Rutkus and Mitchel A. Sollenberger, *Judicial Nomination Statistics:
U.S. District and Circuit Courts, 1977-2003: CRS Report RL31635* (Washington, D.C.:
Congressional Research Service, 2004), table 2(b), updated by author using statistics
from the White House and U.S. Senate Committee on the Judiciary websites.

48. Recess appointments are made when the Senate is not in session and allow the
appointee to serve until the end of the next Senate session (thus, for an appointment
made in 2005, to the end of 2006.) Recess appointees may be confirmed to fill their
post permanently during or after this time. In late 2004 the Supreme Court was
asked to rule that Bush had overstepped the bounds of the recess appointment
power, but declined to do so. In 2005, the GOP leadership threatened to change
Senate rules to abolish filibusters on judicial nominees, a "nuclear option" forestalled
in May by bipartisan compromise but that may reappear when the next Supreme
Court vacancy opens.

49. Samuel Kernell, *Going Public: New Strategies of Presidential Leadership*, 3rd ed.
(Washington, D.C.: CQ Press, 1997).

50. George C. Edwards, III, *On Deaf Ears: The Limits of the Bully Pulpit* (New Haven: Yale
University Press, 2003), 79. See also Brandice Canes-Wrone, "The President's
Legislative Influence from Public Appeals," *American Journal of Political Science* 45
(April 2001): 313–329; for an intriguing discussion of "spin," see Collier, *Between the
Branches*, 210.

51. Jon R. Bond, Richard Fleisher, and B. Dan Wood, "The Marginal and Time-Varying
Effect of Public Approval on Presidential Success in Congress," *Journal of Politics* 65
(February 2003): 92–110; Richard J. Powell and Dean Schloyer, "Public Presidential
Appeals and Congressional Floor Votes," *Congress and the Presidency* 30 (Autumn
2003): 123–138; Peterson, "President and Congress," 493f; and Neustadt, *Presidential
Power*, chap. 5.

52. Richard E. Neustadt, "Presidency and Legislation: The Growth of Central Clearance,"
American Political Science Review 48 (September 1954), 656. Ford's total here includes

pocket vetoes. For veto and override totals for all presidents see the Office of the House Clerk, http://clerk.house.gov/histHigh/Congressional_History/vetoes.html.

53. Bush, "Remarks to Reporters," *Weekly Compilation of Presidential Documents* (April 26, 2002), 692; Cameron, *Veto Bargaining,* 8–9.

54. Sen. Arlen Specter (R.-Pa.) quoted in Victoria Allred, "Versatility with the Veto," *CQ Weekly* (January 20, 2001), 176.

55. See, e.g., Phillip J. Cooper, *By Order of the President: The Use and Abuse of Executive Direct Action* (Lawrence: University Press of Kansas, 2002).

56. The earmarking study was conducted by the Congressional Research Service and described in Joseph J. Schatz, "Difficulty in Distinguishing the Earmarks from the 'Pork,'" *CQ Weekly* (February 7, 2004), 328. Transcripts for the Alberto Gonzales and Condoleeza Rice hearings may be found on the websites maintained by the Senate Judiciary and Foreign Relations committees, respectively.

57. Rossiter, *American Presidency,* 14. Likewise Samuel Huntington concluded in the 1960s that "legislation has become much too complex politically to be effectively handled by a representative assembly," and that Congress should largely get out of the lawmaking business in favor of serving as an up-or-down arbiter of presidential proposals. See "Congressional Responses," 37–38.

58. Edwards, *At the Margins,* 4ff.

59. E. E. Schattschneider, *Two Hundred Million Americans in Search of a Government* (New York: Holt, Rinehart, and Winston, 1969), 53; James Madison, "Federalist 37," in Clinton Rossiter, ed., *The Federalist Papers* (New York: Mentor, 1961), 227.

60. Jones, *Separated System.*

61. Hamilton, "Federalist 70," in Rossiter, *The Federalist Papers,* 423.

Bibliography

Binkley, Wilfred. *President and Congress,* 3rd rev. ed. New York: Vintage, 1962. Classic historical account of executive-legislative relations from the framing of the Constitution to the 1950s.

Bond, Jon R., and Richard Fleisher, eds. *Polarized Politics: Congress and the President in a Partisan Era.* Washington, D.C.: CQ Press, 2000. A collection of essays updating inter-branch relations in light of the fierce partisanship of the 1990s and 2000s.

Bond, Jon R., Richard Fleisher, and B. Dan Wood. "The Marginal and Time-Varying Effect of Public Approval on Presidential Success in Congress," *Journal of Politics* 65 (February 2003), 92–110. Provides a useful bibliography and new findings on this much-studied topic.

Cameron, Charles M. *Veto Bargaining: Presidents and the Politics of Negative Power.* New York: Cambridge University Press, 2000. The most systematic study of vetoes as a sequential negotiation between presidents and Congress.

Collier, Kenneth E. *Between the Branches: The White House Office of Legislative Affairs.* Pittsburgh: University of Pittsburgh Press, 1997. The history and effects of the president's staff of congressional lobbyists.

Conley, Richard. *The Presidency, Congress, and Divided Government.* College Station: Texas A&M Press, 2002. The long-term effects of partisan divisions on presidential legislative success.

Edwards, George C., III. *At the Margins: Presidential Leadership of Congress.* New Haven, Conn:Yale University Press, 1989. Systematic attempt to study the effects of personality and leadership skill, as opposed to broader political contexts, on legislative success.

Jacobson, Gary C. "Partisan Polarization in Presidential Support: The Electoral Connection," *Congress and the Presidency* 30 (Spring 2003): 1–36.A good overview of how increased polarization in Congress affects presidential bargaining with legislators.

Jones, Charles O. *The Presidency in a Separated System.* Washington, D.C.: The Brookings Institution, 1994. Detailed study of postwar policy formulation process, emphasizing the necessity of cooperation between presidents and Congress.

Kaufman, Herbert. *The Administrative Behavior of Federal Bureau Chiefs.* Washington, D.C.: Brookings Institution Press, 1982. A look at how the wider executive branch interacts with Congress, and with the White House.

Kearns, Doris. *Lyndon Johnson and the American Dream.* New York: Harper & Row, 1976. A compelling study of the president most often held up as a paragon of legislative bargaining skill.

Light, Paul C. *The President's Agenda: Domestic Policy Choice from Kennedy to Clinton,* 3rd ed. Baltimore: Johns Hopkins University Press, 1999. Rich account of how presidents choose the policies that comprise their agenda.

Neustadt, Richard E. *Presidential Power and the Modern Presidents.* New York: Free Press, 1990. Classic account of the necessity for and constraints on presidential bargaining, first published in 1960 and updated to include the Reagan administration.

Peterson, Mark A. *Legislating Together: The White House and Capitol Hill from Eisenhower to Reagan.* Cambridge, Mass.: Harvard University Press, 1990. Valuable study of the contexts and conflicts between the "tandem institutions" of American government.

Rudalevige, Andrew. *Managing the President's Program: Presidential Leadership and Legislative Policy Formulation.* Princeton, N.J.: Princeton University Press, 2002. Detailed treatment of what items have comprised the presidential program, presidents' managerial strategies for formulating them, and the impact of those strategies on legislative success.

Rudalevige, Andrew. *The New Imperial Presidency? Renewing Presidential Power after Watergate.* Ann Arbor: University of Michigan Press, 2005. A sequel of sorts to Sundquist (see below), stressing inter-branch relations from the 1970s through the 2004 election.

Sundquist, James. *The Decline and Resurgence of Congress.* Washington, D.C.: The Brookings Institution, 1981. Traces the structural weaknesses of Congress and the resultant rise of presidential authority vis-à-vis legislature, followed by the legislative resurgence of the 1970s.

Thurber, James A., ed. *Rivals for Power,* 3rd ed. Washington, D.C.: CQ Press, 2005. A collection of essays by scholars and policymakers familiar with presidential-legislative interaction.

Waldman, Steven. *The Bill: How Legislation Really Becomes Law.* New York: Penguin, 1996. A very readable case study of the actors and interests involved in a presidential attempt to translate his campaign agenda into law.

Wayne, Stephen J. *The Legislative Presidency.* New York: Harper & Row, 1978. The first, and still vital, detailed study of how the presidential branch has been organized to deal with legislative affairs.

14

THE COURTS, JURISPRUDENCE, AND THE EXECUTIVE BRANCH

R. Shep Melnick

A MERICAN HISTORY IS LITTERED WITH DRAMATIC confrontations between the president and the federal courts. Soon after the pivotal election of 1800, the Jeffersonians launched a full-scale assault on the Federalist-dominated judiciary. They repealed a law passed by the lame-duck Federalist Congress that had allowed lame-duck President John Adams to appoint sixteen new judges. Jefferson's party then tried to remove the most intemperate and partisan Federalist judges through impeachment.[1] Franklin Roosevelt fought an equally bitter but ultimately more successful battle with the Supreme Court. When a number of Court rulings threatened the New Deal in 1934–36, Roosevelt proposed legislation that would allow him to appoint enough new justices to swing the Court to his side. Although FDR's court-packing bill died in Congress, Supreme Court retirements allowed him to create a Court that warmly embraced the New Deal's conception of the Constitution. Presidents Jackson and Lincoln responded to judicial defeats by ignoring court orders. During the Korean War, President Truman cursed the Court for ordering him to return the nation's steel mills to private owners, but he complied. Ronald Reagan and George H. W. Bush tried for years to convince the Court to overturn *Roe v. Wade*. They failed. No president lost as many court battles as Richard Nixon, whose fate was sealed when the Court ordered him to turn over the Watergate tapes to the Special Prosecutor's office. The Supreme Court's 1997 decision allowing private suits to proceed against a sitting president set in motion a chain of events that eventually led to the impeachment of President Clinton. In the summer of 2004 the Supreme Court ordered the administration of President George W. Bush to make fundamental changes in its treatment of enemy combatants.

It would not be unreasonable to assume that these conflicts between the courts and the executive arise from divergent views of the powers of the president. From *Marbury v. Madison* in the early nineteenth century to *Hamdi v. Rumsfeld* in the early years of the twenty-first century, the Supreme Court has insisted that ours is "a government of laws, not of men," that the president is "subject to the same laws that apply to all other members of society," and that "it is emphatically the province and duty of the Judicial Department to say what the law is."[2] As Scott James points out in his chapter in this volume, most presidents—including all our great presidents and virtually all the presidents of the twentieth century—have staked out a much different position, claiming a broad prerogative power, which John Locke famously defined as "the power to act according to discretion for the public good without the prescription of the Law and sometimes even against it."[3] In Thomas Jefferson's words, "To lose our country by a scrupulous adherence to written law, would be to lose the law itself, with life, liberty, property, and all those who are enjoying them with us; thus absurdly sacrificing the end to the means."[4] At the beginning of the Civil War, Abraham Lincoln asked, "Are all the laws but one to go unexecuted, and the Government itself go to pieces, lest that one be violated?" In *Ex Parte Milligan* the Supreme Court responded to such assertions of presidential power by warning that this "doctrine of necessity" leads "directly to anarchy or despotism." The Constitution must be "a law for ruler and people, equally in war and in peace . . . in *all* times and under *all* circumstances."[5]

Given the contrasting perspective of judges and chief executives, it is remarkable how rarely the federal courts have ruled that the president has exceeded his constitutional powers. In times of war and national emergency the Supreme Court has almost always either adopted an extremely broad reading of presidential power or prudently found a way to avoid hearing cases that challenge the president's ability to deal with ugly necessities. Despite its tough talk in *Ex Parte Milligan*, the Court did nothing to stop Lincoln's assertion of emergency power while the Civil War raged. In 1944 the Court approved President Roosevelt's decision to place thousands of Japanese Americans in internment camps. The Supreme Court has scrupulously avoided hearing cases challenging the president's ability to commit troops to combat without a congressional declaration of war. "Taking American history as a whole," Robert Scigliano wrote in 1988, "the court has not been very hard on the office of the president."[6]

Struggles between the president and the courts have almost always centered not on the inherent constitutional powers of the executive, but on the important substantive political issues of the day. For the Marshall Court and Jeffersonian presidents, this was the division of authority between the states and the national government. For presidents from Theodore Roosevelt to his cousin Franklin, it was the power of the federal government to regulate private enterprise and to create a rudimentary welfare state. More recently it has been the so-called "social issues," above all race, religion, and sexuality. Since in America, as Tocqueville noted, "there is almost no political question in the United States that is not resolved sooner or later into a judicial question,"[7] both the president and the Court frequently stake out contrasting positions on controversial political issues. As we will see later in this chapter, presidents have not had much success in using appointments to bend the Court to their will. Elections often resolve similar disagreements between the president and Congress. But since judges have life tenure, struggles between the president and the courts can continue for years—even decades.

When courts disagree with the executive, they frequently claim to act on behalf of the third branch, Congress. For example, when the Supreme Court invalidated President Truman's seizure of the steel mills—one of the rare instances of the Court opposing an assertion of executive power in wartime—it argued that Congress had explicitly rejected this remedy and had authorized suitable alternatives. When the Court blocked FDR's attempt to fire a member of the Federal Trade Commission, it insisted that Congress had established specific and exclusive procedures for removing the official in question. In 2000 the Supreme Court invalidated restrictions on tobacco advertising and distribution announced by the Food and Drug Administration with the full support of President Clinton. The Court's majority found that "Congress has directly spoken to the issue here and precluded the FDA's jurisdiction to regulate tobacco products."[8] Hundreds of times each year, lower court judges interpret federal statutes in ways that substantially reduce the discretion of the White House and political executives appointed by the president. However often we repeat the mantra that "the judiciary interprets the law and the executive enforces it," the plain truth is that judges and administrators are *both* in the business of interpreting and enforcing laws passed by Congress. They frequently disagree about what the words of these statutes mean and what the Congress that passed them had intended.

In general, judges are most likely to defer to the executive (a) on matters of foreign policy, (b) in times of war and national emergency, (c) when Congress has remained silent, and (d) when the president himself has taken decisive action. Conversely, (a) on domestic matters, (b) in normal times, (c) when Congress has legislated with some specificity, and (d) when action was taken by administrators other than the president, judges are more likely to limit executive authority and second-guess administrative decisions. Consequently, looking exclusively at the best-known constitutional decisions, which focus on the former, will not provide an adequate guide to the huge number of more mundane cases that fall into the latter category. This chapter first examines the major Supreme Court decisions that lay out the general contours of executive power under Article II of the Constitution. It then reviews the federal courts' shifting doctrines on the authority of administrative agencies. It closes with an examination of the president's capacity to influence the judiciary through appointments and control over the federal government's litigational strategies.

The Executive Power from Marbury *to* Youngstown

Chief Justice John Marshall's opinion in *Marbury v. Madison* is best known for establishing judicial review, that is, the authority of the Court to invalidate laws passed by Congress when the Court finds they conflict with the Constitution. Just as important, though, was the Court's assertion that the judicial branch can order executive officials to perform duties mandated by statute, in this instance the delivery of a commission to a justice of the peace:

> [W]hen the legislature proceeds to impose on that [executive] officer other duties; when he is directed peremptorily to perform such actions; when the rights of individuals are dependent on the performance of those acts; he is so far the officer of the law; is amenable to the law for his conduct; and cannot sport away the vested rights of others. . . . [I]t seems equally clear that the individual who considers himself injured has a right to resort to the law of his country for a remedy.[9]

With one stroke, Marshall in effect established the federal judiciary as the president's rival for control of the federal bureaucracy.

After finding that Marbury had a right to his commission and that the judiciary had the power to command Secretary of State James Madison to deliver it, Marshall prudently pulled back from a confrontation with the Jefferson administration. Given the new administration's hostility to the Federalist-dominated judiciary, it is highly likely that Jefferson and Madison would have refused to comply, thus weakening, perhaps fatally, the authority of the Court. The brilliance of Marshall's opinion lay in the way it used the controversial power of judicial review to avoid a potentially debilitating struggle with the executive. Having delivered his lecture on the authority of the judicial branch, Marshall suddenly discovered that the Marbury's case was not properly before the Supreme Court. Relying on a strained reading of Article III's grant of jurisdiction (an interpretation Marshall himself later repudiated), the chief justice found that Congress had exceeded its authority by granting the Supreme Court original jurisdiction in cases such as this. Consequently, that section of the Judiciary Act of 1789 was unconstitutional. Marbury would need to start again in another court. Like judicial review, the idea that the court could issue a direct order to the president and his subordinates was highly controversial at the time, but eventually became a cornerstone of American constitutional law. Like many subsequent Supreme Court decisions on presidential power, *Marbury v. Madison* was a skillful combination of legal principle and political prudence.

Given the decades of animosity between the Marshall Court and the administrations of Presidents Jefferson, Madison, Monroe, and Jackson, it is remarkable how seldom the Court ordered executive officers to perform what are today called "nondiscretionary duties." Not until 1838 did the Supreme Court issue a direct command to an executive officer, and that was in a minor case involving payments due to a contractor hired by the postmaster general.[10] The paucity of such legal action was due in part to the miniscule size of the executive branch in the early republic. (As hard as it is to believe today, in the early 1800s there were as many legislators making the law in Washington as there were executive officials carrying it out. Before the Civil War, the Post Office was the only civilian agency of any size.)[11] Moreover, Congress quickly developed the habit of keeping a tight rein on administrators, reducing the likelihood of significant disparities between legal duties and administrative behavior. Neither the Marshall Court nor the Taney Court was inclined to take a narrow view of the powers of the president. Washington's Neutrality Proclamation, Jefferson's Louisiana Purchase, the Monroe Doctrine, Jackson's removal of deposits from the Bank of the United States—all of these fateful assertions of unilateral presidential power proceeded without judicial resistance.

The most significant struggle between nineteenth-century presidents and the Supreme Court over executive power came in the wake of President Lincoln's extraordinary exercise of prerogative power at the beginning of the Civil War. Without waiting for congressional approval, Lincoln called up new troops, ordered construction of warships, established a blockade of Southern ports (at the time considered an act of war), and seized rail and telegraph lines. Most seriously, on six occasions Lincoln suspended the privilege of the writ of habeas corpus without the congressional authorization explicitly required by the Constitution. Lincoln told Congress, "These measures, whether strictly legal or not, were ventured upon, under what appeared to be popular demand and a public necessity, trusting that Congress would readily ratify them."[12] Congress eventually did. The Supreme Court approved some of these emergency measures as a valid exercise of executive authority.[13] It remained silent on most of the others.

In two cases, though, the judicial branch found that the president had violated the Constitution when he unilaterally suspended the writ of habeas corpus. In *Ex Parte Merryman,*[14] Chief Justice Roger Taney ordered the immediate release of a civilian held by the Union army. President Lincoln and the army simply ignored the Court. In 1866, a full year after the end of hostilities and Lincoln's death, the Court ordered the release of another civilian.[15] This time the military complied. It is important to note that for all its brave talk about placing constitutional limits on the president and the military, the full Court waited until the war had been won before issuing such a decision. It could hardly ignore the fact that in times of crisis it cannot count on the executive branch to obey its commands.

As the United States expanded its power in the international realm, the Court regularly accepted presidents' claims to direct the nation's military and diplomatic affairs with minimal authorization from Congress. The broadest statement of the president's inherent power in foreign affairs came in Justice George Sutherland's frequently cited 1936 *Curtiss-Wright* opinion.[16] In domestic affairs, the Court explained, the president and Congress may exercise only the power delegated to them by the Constitution:

> In that field, the primary purpose of the Constitution was to carve from the general mass of legislative power then possessed by the states such power as it was thought desirable to vest in the federal government, leaving those not included in the enumeration still to the states.

In contrast, "the power of external sovereignty passed from the Crown not to the colonies severally, but to the colonies in their collective and corporate capacity as the United States of America." It was this extensive power   "the very delicate, plenary and exclusive power of the President as sole organ of the federal government in the field of international relations"—that was placed in the hands of the president by Article II. Not only can the president act without congressional authorization in external affairs, but the nature of the enterprise requires the president to be accorded "a degree of discretion and freedom from statutory restriction which would not be admissible were domestic affairs alone involved." No grudging acceptance of presidential power here; the Court went out of its way to expand the constitutional prerogatives of the president.

Justice Sutherland's opinion in *Curtiss-Wright* was not empty rhetoric. The Court has repeatedly placed its stamp of approval on executive agreements negotiated by the president but not submitted to Congress for its approval (as the Constitution requires for treaties). Some of these judicially sanctioned agreements have extinguished extremely valuable property rights and suspended cases pending before federal and international tribunals.[17] The Court has also allowed the president to terminate agreements previously ratified by the Senate.[18] It has studiously avoided hearing cases on the president's authority to commit troops to battle without a declaration of war. As Louis Fisher has pointed out, in these areas the Court's "meaning was clear: If Congress wants to confront the president, it must do so by exerting legislative powers, not by turning to the courts. . . . If Congress fails to defend its prerogatives, it cannot expect to be bailed out by the courts."[19] Despite the judicial activism of the post-*Brown* era, the federal courts have continued to treat most foreign policy disputes as "political questions" unsuitable for judicial resolution. This has usually left the president in charge.

In the late nineteenth century the Supreme Court began to recognize inherent presidential power in domestic affairs as well. For example, the Court upheld President Grover Cleveland's use of federal troops to break the Pullman strike of 1895 despite the absence of authorizing legislation.[20] It later allowed President William H. Taft to withdraw from sale of land that Congress had explicitly opened to purchase by U.S. citizens.[21] In an 1890 case the Court pondered whether the president's duty to "take care that the laws be faithfully executed" is

> limited to the enforcement of acts of Congress or of treaties of the United States according to their express terms, or does it include the rights, duties, and obligations growing out of the Constitution itself, our international relations, and all the protections implied by the nature of the government under the Constitution?[22]

Since the turn of the last century, its answer has been the latter.

Paradoxically, many of the opinions recognizing an expansive presidential power were authored by conservative justices who opposed the modern welfare and regulatory state and who frequently infuriated activist presidents such as Theodore Roosevelt, Woodrow Wilson, and Franklin Roosevelt. It is probably not surprising that the same Court that restricted the authority of Congress and state legislatures to enact minimum wage and maximum hour laws also found implicit in Article II the power to use troops to break a labor strike. Less expected is the fact that during the 1920s and 1930s, Justice Sutherland and Chief Justice Taft were the most vigorous defenders of executive authority in foreign policy and of the president's authority to remove executive branch officials. In contrast, the leading liberal justices of the era, Louis Brandeis and Oliver Wendell Holmes, endorsed a more limited understanding of executive power—as did the most obstreperous conservatives, Justices James McReynolds and Willis Van Devanter.[23] This was not an issue that produced typical left-right divisions.

The Court's acquiescence to presidential power reached its apogee during World War II. It all but abandoned the nondelegation principles announced in 1935, allowing the Roosevelt administration to impose nationwide price and wage controls on the basis of legislation that provided only the vaguest of legislative standards.[24] It tolerated Roosevelt's extensive use of executive agreements, even when these agreements clearly conflicted with the congressional policy of neutrality.[25] The Court gave its imprimatur to the use of military tribunals to try those accused of sabotage on American soil.[26] Most remarkable of all was the Court's decision in *Korematsu v. U.S.,* condoning the use of a naked racial classification to imprison a large number of American citizens.[27]

Never again would the Supreme Court be so willing to defer to the authority of the president and the military. Eight years after upholding the internment of Japanese Americans, the Court's decision in *Youngstown Sheet and Tube Co. v. Sawyer* denied President Truman the power to seize steel mills threatened by labor strikes during the Korean War. Despite the fact that a shutdown of the steel industry posed a much graver risk to the American war effort than did the

Japanese Americans who lived on the West Coast during World War II, the Court ordered the president to return the steel mills to their private owners. Truman complied, and a long strike ensued. The six-member Court majority included five Roosevelt appointees, along with one of Truman's (Tom Clark, whom the irate President called "my biggest mistake" and "about the dumbest man that I have ever run across").[28]

In both *Korematsu* and *Youngstown*, it was the concurring opinion of Justice Robert Jackson that shed most light on the Court's role in coping with hard cases such as these. In *Korematsu,* Jackson presented a compelling argument for what Alexander Bickel later called "the passive virtues," that is, finding ways to avoid an unwinnable confrontation with another branch of government without giving a judicial imprimatur to a practice that threatens fundamental rights.[29] Internment of Japanese citizens, Jackson pointed out, was as clear a violation of the Constitution as one could ever find. Yet

> It would be impracticable and dangerous idealism to expect or insist that each specific military command in an area of probable operations will conform to conventional tests of constitutionality. When an area is so beset that it must be put under military control at all, the paramount consideration is that its measures be successful, rather than legal. The armed services must protect a society, not merely its Constitution. . . . No court can require such a commander in such circumstances to act as a reasonable man; he may be unreasonably cautious and exacting.

The Supreme Court sitting in Washington has neither the raw power to compel the military to desist nor the intelligence to know whether this expedient is truly necessary. "In the very nature of things military decisions are not susceptible to intelligent judicial appraisal." This does not mean, however, that in such instances the Court must find that the executive has acted within the bounds of the Constitutions:

> [I]f we cannot confine military expedients by the Constitution, neither would I distort the Constitution to approve all that the military may deem expedient. . . . I cannot say, from any evidence before me, that the orders of General DeWitt were not reasonably expedient military precautions, nor could I say that they were. But even if they were permissible military procedures, I deny that it follows that they are constitutional.

The gravest danger created by a finding of constitutionality is that it allows the extraordinary to become ordinary. In Jackson's words,

> a judicial construction of the due process clause that will sustain this order is a far more subtle blow to liberty than the promulgation of the

order itself. A military order, however unconstitutional, is not apt to last longer than the military emergency. . . . But once a judicial opinion rationalizes such an order to show that it conforms to the Constitution, or rather rationalizes the Constitution to show that the Constitution sanctions such an order, the Court for all time has validated the principle of racial discrimination in criminal procedure and of transplanting American citizens. The principle then lies about like a loaded weapon ready for the hand of any authority that can bring forward a plausible claim of an urgent need. Every repetition imbeds that principle more deeply in our law and thinking and expands it to new purposes. . . . There it has a generative power of its own, and all that it creates will be in its own image.

While the Supreme Court should not engage in a potentially futile effort to order the military to close the internment camps, neither should it allow the judiciary to participate in such an unconstitutional venture.

If Jackson's analysis in *Korematsu* has often guided the Court's prudential inaction, his famous concurrence in *Youngstown* has formed the framework for most of the Court's subsequent rulings on presidential power. Nearly thirty years later, Chief Justice William Rehnquist noted that Jackson's frequently quoted opinion "brings together as much combination of analysis and common sense as there is in this area."[30] The heart of Jackson's argument—and the rule of thumb the Court has applied ever since—is that the reach of the president's implied powers depends in large part on whether and how Congress has acted: "Presidential powers are not fixed but fluctuate, depending upon their disjunction or conjunction with those of Congress." Thus, "When the President acts pursuant to an express or implied authorization of Congress, his authority is at its maximum, for it includes all that he possesses in his own right plus all that Congress can delegate." In contrast, "When the President takes measures incompatible with the expressed or implied will of Congress, his power is at its lowest ebb, for then he can rely only upon his own constitutional powers minus any constitutional powers of Congress over the matter." Most ambiguous is the middle ground, where the president "acts in absence of either a congressional grant or denial of authority." Here

> he can only rely upon his own independent powers, but here is a zone of twilight in which he and Congress may have concurrent authority, or in which its distribution is uncertain. . . . In this area, any actual test of power is likely to depend on the imperatives of events and contemporary imponderables rather than on abstract theories of law.

Justice Jackson resolved this particular dispute by making the debatable finding that Congress had passed legislation specifically denying the president power to act as Truman had done. Sensible as this approach may be, it places in the hands of judges enormous discretion to establish not only what the Constitution means, but what Congress has said in particular statutes.[31]

Since Youngstown: More Decisions, Less Clarity

In the half century since *Youngstown*, the Supreme Court has issued a number of rulings on the extent and limits presidential power. Yet what Jackson wrote in 1952 remains true today: "[A] judge . . . may be surprised at the poverty of really useful and unambiguous authority applicable to concrete problems of executive power as they actually present themselves."[32] This is partly by design: in difficult cases, Chief Justice Rehnquist has explained, the Court is "acutely aware of the necessity to rest decision on the narrowest possible ground capable of deciding the case."[33] Moreover, as Louis Fisher has noted, over the past twenty-five years the Court has offered "limited help in resolving the basic disputes of separation of powers" because "it has bounced back and forth, sometimes embracing a functional, pragmatic approach, sometimes adopting a doctrinaire, formalist model."[34]

The Court's motley post-*Youngstown* case law reflects four important features of recent American politics. First and most obvious is America's role as the world's leading superpower. After World War II, the United States for the first time in its history maintained a large permanent military establishment, one that was frequently deployed without a formal declaration of war. During the cold war and the war on terrorism, the line between the home front and theaters of battle—and thus between foreign and domestic policy—grew fuzzier and fuzzier. Given the weight the Court has always placed on this distinction, the number of hard cases confronting the Court was bound to multiply.

Second, as the size and scope of the American welfare and regulatory state grew, so did presidential efforts to control bureaucratic discretion. Presidents expanded the Executive Office of the President, issued more executive orders, and insisted upon more White House control over political executives. In the 1970s Congress responded to these presidential moves by devising new methods for overseeing the administration of the programs it had authorized. Many of the resulting policy conflicts turned up in court.

Third, this rivalry between Congress and the executive was heightened by the prevalence of divided government. Before 1952, divided government was an exception; usually the same party controlled both houses of Congress and the White House. For the past half century, divided government has been the norm: in the fifty years stretching from 1952 to 2002, the same party controlled the House, the Senate, and the presidency for only seventeen years. Congress has often tried to enlist the courts in its battle with the executive by expanding opportunities for judicial review of agency action.

Finally, with its seminal *Brown v. Board of Education* decision in 1954, the Supreme Court inaugurated an unprecedented era of judicial activism. The Court's newfound interest in protecting civil rights and civil liberties has at times conflicted with the policies and priorities of presidents. At other times, though, the Court has been eager to delegate to the executive branch the authority to expand and enforce rights of national citizenship.

It would take an entire book (and a long, tedious one at that) to review the separation of powers decisions of the Warren, Burger, and Rehnquist Courts. For present purposes it will suffice to establish five major themes of post-*Youngstown* jurisprudence. First, the Court has remained reluctant to become entangled in disputes over the use of military forces or agreements with foreign powers, describing these as "political questions" fit for resolution by Congress and the president, not the courts. For example, it refused to rule on the legality of the war in Vietnam or subsequent military action in El Salvador, Grenada, Nicaragua, Panama, and Kuwait. It gave the executive branch a virtual blank check to carry out the deal that freed the hostages held by Iran in 1979–1981. It refused to hear a suit filed by Senator Barry Goldwater challenging the president's authority to terminate our formal treaty with Taiwan.[35]

Second, in recent years the federal courts have become bolder in exercising review over executive and congressional determination on matters that fall in the gray area between foreign and domestic policy. One example of this is immigration policy. As Peter Schuck has shown, before the 1980s "judges had upheld almost all federal immigration policies, viewing them as expressions of U.S. sovereignty to which ordinary constitutional principles simply did not apply."[36] Under the so-called "plenary power doctrine," immigration policy was a branch of national security policy, and immigration officials had been entrusted by Congress to act as "sole and exclusive judge" of deportation and exclusion.[37] The federal courts abandoned the "plenary power" doctrine in the 1980s, reviewing executive action to see if it was in accord with congressional intent and at times striking down legislative provisions as contrary to the Constitution.[38]

Another major example is the Court's recent insistence that enemy combatants held either in the United States or in territory under the jurisdiction of the United States retain their right to challenge their confinement in federal court.[39] Although most of these prisoners were held by the military, they had for many months remained outside any war zone. In *Hamdi v. Rumsfeld* the Court announced that an American citizen held as an enemy combatant "must receive notice of the factual basis for his classification, and a fair opportunity to rebut the government's factual assertions before a neutral decision maker."[40] But the Court did not demand that the prisoners be accorded all the rights of the accused that the Court has found implicit in the Bill of Rights. The proceedings may be tailored to alleviate their uncommon potential to burden the Executive at a time of ongoing military conflict. Hearsay, for example, may need to be accepted as the most reliable available evidence from the Government in such a proceeding. Likewise the Constitution would not be offended by a presumption in favor of the Government's evidence, so long as that presumption remained a rebuttable one and fair opportunity for rebuttal was provided.[41]

In *Rasul v. Bush* the court determined that the federal courts have jurisdiction over habeas corpus petitions filed by foreign nationals held by the military in "territories over which the United States exercises exclusive jurisdiction and control"—which includes the U.S. military base at Guantanamo. The Court did not want to give the military a blank check to hold enemy combatants indefinitely, but it left the executive branch with broad discretion to devise appropriate procedures. How far the Court will go in restricting the discretion of the military and the president remains to be seen.

Third, the Court has for all intents and purposes thrown in the towel on the nondelegation doctrine. Although the Court has continued to demand that Congress provide administrators with "intelligible standards" to guide their discretion, since 1935 it has never found a statute lacking such standards. In practice, anything goes.[42] At least in the absence of congressional directives to the contrary, the Court has also given the president broad authority to control the extensive discretion exercised by federal administrators. It has recognized the president's authority to issue sweeping executive orders and to use the Office of Management and Budget and other arms of the Executive Office of the President to supervise the bureaucracy. As we will see in the next section, in recent decades the central legal issue has not been the constitutional authority of the president to direct lower-level administrators, but the extent to which Congress has specifically precluded a policy advocated by the president or has mandated a policy he opposes.

Fourth, the Supreme Court has been highly suspicious of institutional innovations that seem to mix legislative and executive power. In *INS v. Chadha*[43] the Court ruled that legislative vetoes violate the requirement in Article I that all legislation be "presented" to the president for his signature or veto. For many years prior to *Chadha,* Congress had passed legislation authorizing presidents to take a particular action (e.g., an executive reorganization or an arms sale), but reserving to itself the option of blocking this action by passing a veto resolution in one or both houses. Presidents had long welcomed the new powers granted by these statutes, but insisted that the veto provisions were unconstitutional—a classic example of trying to take the sweet without the bitter. In 1983 the Supreme Court agreed, invalidating in one fell swoop two hundred federal statutes—more than it had struck down in the previous 180 years combined.

Although the Court presented its decision as protecting executive power, it is far from evident that this has been the effect. Most obviously, with legislative veto provisions legally unenforceable, Congress is less likely to delegate extensive new powers to the president. Remarkably, Congress has continued to include legislative veto provisions in legislation. Indeed, since 1983 it enacted well over four hundred legislative vetoes. The Court's finding of unconstitutionality makes these statutory provisions legally unenforceable. But the fact that legislative vetoes are not *legally* enforceable does not mean that they are *politically* unenforceable. Presidents know that if they ignore congressional vetoes they will face retaliation, perhaps in the form of repeal of the initial grant of authority.[44] This is almost always enough to force the president to back off.

In another high-visibility case, *Bowsher v. Synar*, the Court struck down the provision of the Gram-Rudman-Hollings budget control law that gave the comptroller general the authority to trigger the automatic, across-the-board budget cuts known as "sequestration." The Court held that since the comptroller general can be removed from office only by Congress and not by the president, he cannot be assigned tasks that are executive in nature.[45] In 1998 the Court also struck down legislation providing the president with a line-item veto.[46] In these cases the Court has adopted a highly formal understanding of separation of powers that leaves little room for new institutional arrangements, even when they represent a bipartisan and cross-institutional effort to deal with serious national problems.

Finally, in marked contrast to its refusal to tolerate congressional infringement of executive prerogatives, the Court has been quite willing to subject the president to *judicial* controls and procedures. For example, in *Morrison v. Olsen*[47] the Court upheld the independent prosecutor statute, which created a powerful, high-ranking executive officer appointed by federal judges rather than by the president. Why the special prosecutor can exercise executive power but the comptroller general—who is in fact appointed by the president—cannot remains a legal mystery. Similarly, in *U.S. v. Nixon* the Court justified the limits it placed on executive privilege by emphasizing the importance of the evidence sought (the Watergate tapes) in the judicial process: "The impediment that an absolute, unqualified [executive] privilege would place in the way of the primary constitutional duty of the Judicial Branch to do justice in criminal prosecutions would plainly conflict with the function of the courts under Article III."[48] Years later, in *Clinton v. Jones,* the Court allowed civil suits to proceed against a sitting president. Justice Stevens responded to the president's claim that such litigation "may impose an unacceptable burden on the President's time and energy, and therefore impair the effective performance of his office" with the calm reassurance that "if properly managed by the District Court" civil litigation such as this "appears to us highly unlikely to occupy any substantial amount of [President Clinton's] time"[49]—a prediction that turned out to be spectacularly wrong.

A large number of the federal court's post–World War II rulings on executive power—ranging from executive privilege to impoundment, from official immunity to the investigative powers of Congress—have grown out of the bitter partisan feuds that characterized the period of divided government stretching from 1968 to 2000. Neither side was able to win a convincing victory in the electoral arena; both sides looked for unorthodox (and at times surreptitious) methods for prevailing; and each searched for scandals that would discredit its opponent. Responding to the Watergate scandals of the Nixon Administration, Congress institutionalized this process by creating "special prosecutors" and "independent counsels" specifically designed to move such disputes out of the political arena and into a legal one. Lengthy investigation and litigation by special prosecutors has focused on everything from the highly significant foreign policy and constitutional issues at stake in the Reagan Administration's Iran-Contra scandal to the personal peccadilloes of the president himself (the Monica Lewinsky affair), the president's family (e.g., the Whitewater investigation during the Clinton administration and "Billygate" during the Carter administration), and the president's senior staff (e.g., Hamilton Jordan in the late 1970s and Edwin Meese in the mid-1980s). As a result, most presidents since Nixon have spent an enormous amount of time and political capital defending themselves and their advisors against charges of perjury and other forms of illegal behavior. Rarely have these extensive investigations culminated in convictions in a court of law. The process, as they say, is the punishment.

Those looking for clear, consistent themes in these Supreme Court decisions search in vain. Chief Justice Rehnquist observed that "it is doubtless both futile and perhaps dangerous to find any epigrammatical explanation of how this country has been governed."[50] The Court has generally (but not always) been circumspect in intervening in foreign policy and military matters. It has been wary of congressional usurpation of executive authority, but quite happy to authorize judicial supervision of presidential activity. The Supreme Court handles only a tiny fraction of the federal cases involving executive authority, usually offering broad generalizations rather than clear rules and leaving the lower courts with the job of specifying the extent of presidential power, administrative discretion, and judicial supervision required by a particular federal statute. The contours of executive power, therefore, are determined at least as much in the trenches of "administrative law" as in the rarified air of constitutional interpretation.

Judicial Review of Administrative Action

Article II of the Constitution states that "the executive power shall be vested in a president of the United States of America," but then gives Congress the authority to establish executive departments and to "vest the appointment of such inferior officers, as they think proper, in the president alone, in the courts of law, or in the head of departments." Although there is general agreement that the president must retain the power to appoint "major" officers—subject, of course, to the "advice and consent of the Senate"—there is no clear dividing line between major and "inferior" officers. Today about three thousand political executives are subject to Senate confirmation.[51] Almost all of the remaining three million federal employees are both selected and subject to removal according to rules established by Congress. Congress not only specifies the qualifications of these officers, but frequently mandates "nondiscretionary duties" for major and inferior officers alike. Congress regularly uses its many other powers, especially the power of the purse, to enforce these commands. As John Marshall established in *Marbury v. Madison*, these legislative demands can also be enforced by the federal courts. In other words, the Constitution subjects the federal bureaucracy to three masters: the president, Congress, and reviewing courts.

A central, undeniable feature of the modern administrative state is that the bulk of interpretation of federal law is done by administrators, not judges. Each year federal administrators produce volumes of formal rules, interpretive memos, administrative guidelines, and the like. Facing this reality, the Supreme Court has frequently repeated that "this Court shows great deference to the interpretation given the statute by the officers or agency charged with its administration."[52] In *Chevron v. NRDC*, one of the most important decisions of the 1980s, the Court announced that when "the statute is silent or ambiguous with respect to the specific issue," the sole question before a reviewing court is whether the agency adopted a "permissible construction of the statute." The court "may not substitute its own construction of a statutory provision for a reasonable interpretation made by the administrator of an agency."[53]

This long line of Supreme Court cases coexists uneasily with another set of precedents, which insist that "it is emphatically the province and duty of the *judicial department* to say what the law is."[54] As the Court stated more recently, "A pure question of statutory construction is for the court to decide."[55] When anointing themselves as the authoritative interpreter of federal statutes, judges usually claim to protect congressional policies from executive branch distortion. Judge Skelly Wright echoed a common theme when he wrote that the duty of the judiciary is "to see that the important legislative purposes heralded in the halls of Congress are not lost or misdirected in the vast hallways of the federal bureaucracy."[56] In short, the combination of American separation of powers and the modern administrative state produces two rival interpreters of federal law, only one of which is subject to some control by the president.

Over the past century, the federal courts have swung back and forth between the deferential approach set forth in the *Chevron* decision and the more searching review advocated first by conservatives in the 1920s and 1930s and later by liberals in the 1970s and 1980s. More deference usually translates into more opportunities for presidents and their aides to influence administrative discretion. Stricter judicial review usually assumes that administrative decisions should be made on the basis of congressional intent and scientific fact-finding rather than the political judgments of presidents and their appointees.[57]

In the early decades of the twentieth century, federal judges tended to adopt a narrow reading of federal regulatory statutes and to be wary of leaving administrators with significant discretion. Distrust of administrative discretion was closely linked with judicial distaste for government regulation of the economy. To make administrative agencies palatable to the courts, Congress often designed them to look like appellate courts. Thus early regulatory bodies were multi-member commissions, such as the Interstate Commerce Commission, the Federal Trade Commission, and the Federal Maritime Commission, which operated through time-consuming formal adjudication, slowly developing case law rather than issuing general rules. They were often labeled "independent" commissions, which meant formally independent of the president and informally dependent on Congress and the courts.

The New Deal challenged this cramped understanding of the authority of administrative agencies, and largely prevailed. The constitutional revolution of 1937 ushered in a new era of judicial deference to administrative expertise and presidential leadership. In Congress a multi-year battle between liberals (led by Presidents Roosevelt and Truman) and conservatives (egged on by the American Bar Association) culminated in a compromise, the Administrative Procedures Act of 1946 (APA). The APA essentially codified existing administrative and judicial review practices. Congress left itself free to choose on a case-by-case basis whether to give agencies broad rule-making power subject to minimal judicial review or to require administrators to operate through formal adjudication subject to more rigorous judicial review. Or Congress could (and often did) invent hybrid procedures and standards of judicial review. In designing new agencies, presidents tended to favor the rule-making model, while Congress preferred a somewhat more elaborate process. Meanwhile, reviewing courts created extensive case law on the requirements for adjudication, but gave agencies broad latitude in their interpretation of substantive statutory requirements. If administrative law was a battlefield between New Dealers and advocates of laissez-faire in the 1920s and 1930s, by the 1950s it had become a backwater dominated by those interests that had regular dealings with the regulatory commissions.[58]

In the late 1960s and early 1970s, what Richard Stewart has called the "reformation of American administrative law" again altered relations among agencies, reviewing courts, Congress, and the presidency.[59] At the heart of this "reformation" lay three key changes. First, reviewing courts insisted that agencies open their doors to a wide array of interests, not just traditional business groups, but environmentalists, consumer advocates, civil rights organizations, welfare recipients, and a variety of ideologically oriented "public interest" groups. In Stewart's words, federal courts changed the focus of judicial review (in the process expanding and transforming traditional procedural devices) so that its dominant purpose is no longer the prevention of unauthorized intrusions on private autonomy, but the assurance of fair representation for all affected interests in the exercise of the legislative power delegated to the agencies.[60]

Second, the courts insisted upon taking what they called a "hard look" at both the evidence supporting administrative action and the agency's interpretation of its statutory mandate. In an era of divided government and unusually hostile legislative-executive relations, the federal courts presented themselves as the champions of *congressional* intent, which they often equated with the intent of the agency's authorizing committees in the House and Senate.[61] Third, while administrative law had traditionally focused on claims that agencies' *actions* exceeded their statutory authority, the "new administrative law" was even more concerned about administrative lethargy and omission. Courts told administrators to initiate significant new programs, to expand eligibility for entitlement programs, to regulate new pollutants and health risks, to take more vigorous enforcement action, to expand legal protections to new groups, and to spend more money more quickly.[62] In order to take on this new role, the courts relaxed traditional standing requirements and allowed what have become known as "private attorneys general" to play an important role in the setting of agency priorities.

In one of the most famous administrative law decisions of the 1970s, David Bazelon, chief judge of the D.C. Circuit, announced that in this "new era in the long and fruitful collaboration of administrative agencies and reviewing courts" the "fundamental personal interests in life, health, and liberty" would have a "special claim to judicial protection, in comparison with the economic interests at stake in a ratemaking or licensing procedure."[63] The fact that health had replaced property in the pantheon of judicially protected rights showed that the courts were often more interested in helping the potential beneficiaries of government programs than in protecting the vested interests of those who would bear their costs.

These new administrative law doctrines significantly reduced the ability of the White House and the Office of Management and Budget to control policy making within the agencies. This was particularly true during the presidencies of Richard Nixon, Gerald Ford, and Ronald Reagan, when the "new administrative law" was at its height and these presidents were fighting pitched battles with Congress over regulation and spending. Nixon lost numerous battles over environmental policy, civil rights, and entitlements as a result of court rulings. Reagan was similarly defeated in a particularly prolonged and nasty dispute over disability benefits.[64] By making agency rule-making procedures ever more elaborate, the courts made the president and his lieutenants look like uninformed, politically motivated interlopers in a thorough, courtlike proceeding. By adopting the heroic assumption that legislation enacted by Congress contains clear policy mandates, they made agency receptivity to the political preferences of the White House seem illegitimate. The president, Martin Shapiro writes, "now faces courts which are his rivals in agenda setting and in the formulation of public goals and values."[65]

The "reformation" of administrative law was the work not of the Supreme Court, but of the lower federal courts, particularly the D.C. Circuit, which hears far more administrative law cases than any other tribunal. As then-professor Antonin Scalia so colorfully put it, in administrative law "the D.C. Circuit is something of a resident manager, and the Supreme Court an absentee landlord."[66] In the late 1970s the Supreme Court indicated that it was uneasy with some of the D.C. Circuit's more innovative rulings.[67] The Supreme Court's 1984 *Chevron* decision stated in very clear terms that a reviewing court should defer to an agency decision unless that decision is clearly inconsistent with the language of the statute. Empirical studies of the lower courts' response to the *Chevron* decision indicate that for a few years district and circuit court judges did become more deferential. But as early as 1988 the effects of *Chevron* seemed to be wearing off.[68] Part of the reason for this is that the Supreme Court simply does not pay much attention to administrative law issues; it has neither the capacity nor the will to monitor the multitude of highly complex cases resolved by the courts below. Just as important is the fact that the Supreme Court itself frequently departs from the norm of deference announced in *Chevron*. Just the year before, for example, the Court had held that the Reagan administration could not reverse a controversial seatbelt rule previously announced by the Carter administration. Once a policy had been established by one administration, little judicial deference was due to a subsequent administration with a different set of policy preferences.[69] In recent years the Court has held that *Chevron* deference does not apply to agency policies announced outside the rule-making process.[70] Similarly, while the Supreme Court has on several occasions emphasized the importance of protecting agencies' prosecutorial discretion and capacity to set their own agendas, it has failed to take aggressive action to quash citizen suits that in effect allow interest groups to dictate agency priorities.[71]

An important feature of administrative law is that seemingly routine district and circuit court decisions on administrative procedures and the meaning of particular federal statutes are more important for determining the extent of presidential control over the bureaucracy than are the Supreme Court's occasional constitutional pronouncements on that subject. In recent decades presidents have therefore paid increased attention to lower court nominations—particularly those of the D.C. Circuit—and the Senate has subjected these nominees to close scrutiny.

The (Usually) Disappointing Power of Appointment

Although courts can constrain the exercise of executive power, they can also serve as important *instruments* of presidential power. All federal judges are nominated by the president, and the vast majority of these nominees are approved by the Senate. A president's judicial appointees remain in office for years—even decades—after he leaves office. As Attorney General Ed Meese once candidly admitted, the Reagan Administration saw judicial selection as a way "to institutionalize the Reagan Revolution so it can't be set aside no matter what happens in future presidential elections."[72] It is hard to think of another way in which a president can have such a long-lasting effect on institutional arrangements and public policy.

Yet very few presidents have managed to mold the federal courts to their liking. Indeed, only twice in the nation's history could one say that presidents have transformed the judiciary. Presidents Washington and Adams created a Federalist bench that survived for decades despite the Jeffersonians' strenuous efforts to displace it. FDR vanquished the conservative Supreme Court and created a progressive replacement. Washington and Adams had the advantage of appointing every member of the new judicial branch. Roosevelt's unrivaled tenure in office allowed him to appoint eight justices to the Supreme Court and a substantial portion of the lower courts as well. No president since Washington has had so many Supreme Court appointments or used them so well.

Presidents frequently lament their inability to reshape the Supreme Court. Harry Truman was characteristically plainspoken on this: "Packing the Supreme Court simply can't be done . . . I've tried it and it won't work. . . . Whenever you put a man on the Supreme Court he ceases to be your friend. I'm sure of that."[73] James Madison ignored Thomas Jefferson's advice that Joseph Storey would become a vigorous ally of John Marshall, and lived to regret that nomination. Woodrow Wilson placed his attorney general, James McReynolds, on the Court only to find that McReynolds voted against the administration at virtually every turn—and was so rabidly anti-Semitic that he would not even behave civilly around Wilson's most famous nominee, Louis Brandeis. When asked if he had made any mistakes as president, Eisenhower replied, "Yes, and they are both sitting on the Supreme Court." He was obviously referring to Chief Justice Earl Warren and Justice William Brennan. If George H. W. Bush had been asked the same question, it is likely that his answer would have been, "Yes, two, raising taxes and nominating David Souter." One out of every four or five presidential nominees seriously disappoints the president who placed him on the bench.[74]

How a nominee will vote once he is on the Court is hardly the only consideration presidents take into account when making their selections. Presidents use nominations to pay off political debts (e.g., Earl Warren, who helped deliver California to Eisenhower during the 1952 Republican convention) or to placate

TABLE 1

President	Number of Supreme Court Appointments*
Washington	10
F. D. Roosevelt	8
Jackson	6
Lincoln, Taft, Eisenhower	5
Cleveland, Harrison, Harding, Truman, Nixon, Reagan	4
All others 3 or fewer	

*Does not include sitting associate justices elevated to chief justice.

SOURCE: Henry Abraham, *Justices, Presidents, and Senators.*

a regional, ethnic, or religious constituency (e.g., FDR and the southerner James Byrnes; Eisenhower and the Catholic William Brennan). This was particularly true during the nineteenth century, when the limited jurisdiction of the federal courts made appointments less significant from a policy point of view. Both Jackson and Lincoln appointed politically ambitious members of their Cabinet in hopes that they would stop making trouble once they were on the bench.[75]

Of even greater significance is the fact that the Senate must confirm all judicial nominations. Of the nearly 150 Supreme Court nominations submitted by presidents, the Senate has rejected 30 and refused to act upon another 11.[76] Presidents face the greatest difficulty getting their nominees approved when the opposition party controls the Senate and when they are in their final year in office. Informal norms of "senatorial courtesy" also allow senators to veto candidates from their own state whom they oppose.

Since the late 1960s the scrutiny given to Supreme Court nominations by the Senate and the White House has increased significantly. This is a product of both divided government and the large number of controversial issues handed by the modern Court. Congress how holds hearings on all nominations (something it did not do before 1930), expects the nominee to testify in person (which they generally did not do before 1955), televises the proceedings (since 1981), tries to engage the nominee in an extensive discussion of controversial issues (which usually draws the disingenuous response that the nominee does not want to "prejudge" issues that might come before the Court), and conducts extensive staff investigations of the nominee's background, writing, and judicial record. In 1981 President Reagan created the Office of Legal Policy within the Department of Justice to screen candidates for judicial posts. This was part of a concerted effort to place more conservative justices on the bench and to reduce the power of senators over circuit court nominations. Both Presidents Bush retained this practice. Meanwhile, a wide array of interest groups has regularly been engaged in supporting and opposing judicial nominations. For example, over three hundred advocacy groups voiced their opposition to the nomination of Robert Bork in 1987, employing "a wide variety of tactics including advertising, grass roots events, focus groups and polling."[77] This confirmation process provided us with a new political verb: "to bork" now means to respond to a presidential nomination with immediate, unrelenting, at times scurrilous, and ultimately successful opposition.

Not surprisingly, confirmation battles have grown increasingly contentious and often nasty. Republicans blocked LBJ's nomination of Abe Fortas to be chief justice in 1968, initiating an investigation of his personal finances that eventually led to his resignation. Democrats retaliated by rejecting two of President Nixon's nominations in 1970. Not only did the Senate reject Reagan's nomination of Robert Bork in 1987, but the president was forced to withdraw his second nomination, Douglas Ginsburg, as well. The Senate approved President Bush's nomination of Clarence Thomas by the narrow vote of 52–48 after several days of extraordinarily contentious televised hearings and unprecedented *ad hominem* attacks. When Republicans took control of Congress in 1994, they were slow in acting upon President Clinton's lower court nominations. Indeed, in 1996 the Senate did not confirm a single one of Clinton's circuit court nominees.[78] As soon as Democrats regained their Senate majority in 2002, they returned the favor. After 2003, Senate Democrats used the threat of filibuster to kill a number of Bush nominations and to slow most of the rest. In 2004, President Bush took the provocative step of granting two of the nominees whose confirmation had been stalled brief recess appointments on the court of appeals. (Article II of the Constitution allows the president to fill vacancies while the Senate is in recess, but provides that these appointments will expire at the end of the next session of Congress.) Since the two parties are sharply divided on many issues handled by the Supreme Court—abortion, affirmative action, gay rights, tort reform, and many others—both sides are determined to prevent the other from getting a permanent majority on the Court.

Presidents almost always claim to nominate men and women with "fine legal minds," and in the twentieth century professional groups, most notably the American Bar Association (ABA) and assorted groups of law professors, have claimed the right to evaluate their assessments. Since 1945 a committee of the ABA has rated Supreme Court nominees for the Senate Judiciary Committee. Some presidents have allowed the ABA to examine and rate candidates under consideration by the White House. Intense pressure from the legal profession forced President Hoover to appoint Benjamin Cardozo, a New York State judge with a particularly sterling reputation.[79] In contrast, the low ratings the ABA's evaluation committee gave to Nixon nominee Harold Carswell in 1970 contributed to his defeat. One sign of the professionalization of judicial selection is the fact that in recent decades almost all Supreme Court justices have had previous judicial experience, usually on the federal bench. Of the thirteen justices appointed since 1967, only two (Powell and Rehnquist) had not served as judges, and only one of the remaining eleven (O'Connor) had not been a federal judge. In contrast, fewer than half of the justices appointed between 1937 and 1967 had any prior judicial experience.[80] The influence of the ABA, though, has been in decline in recent years, especially when Republicans hold the White House. Conservatives were incensed when four members of the ABA committee gave Robert Bork, one of the most eminent law professors of his generation, an "unqualified" rating. Like many Democratic senators, these members of the ABA committee believed that Bork's opposition to a number of Warren Court precedents placed him "out of the legal mainstream." In 2001 the Bush White House announced that it would not submit any names to the ABA for evaluation.[81]

Most presidents are astute enough to realize that some "fine legal minds" support their policies and their understanding of the Constitution and many other "fine legal minds" do not. As Theodore Roosevelt wrote to Henry Cabot Lodge after he left office, "I should hold myself as guilty of an irreparable wrong to the nation if I should put [on the Court] any man who was not absolutely sane and sound on the great national policies for which we stand in public life."[82] Attorney General Robert Kennedy offered this summary of how the Kennedy administration chose its Supreme Court nominees:

> You want someone who generally agreed with you on what role government should play in American life, what role the individual in society should have. You didn't think how he would vote in an apportionment case or in a criminal case. You wanted someone who, in the long run, you could believe would be best. You wanted someone who agreed generally with your views of the country.[83]

Lyndon Johnson's trusted aide Joseph Califano reported that Johnson "viewed the court as a means both of perpetuating his social reforms and of upholding various legislative compromises he had reached on controversial issues."[84] A task force established by the Reagan Department of Justice to evaluate judicial nominees listed among the required qualifications the following:[85]

- refusal to create new constitutional rights for the individual
- deference to states in their spheres
- appropriate deference to agencies
- disposition towards less government rather than more
- appreciation for the role of the free market in our society
- respect for traditional values

While presidents routinely deny that they are establishing a "litmus test" for nominees, it is hard to believe that any of them would knowingly appoint a justice who disagrees with them on a key policy or constitutional issue.

Why, then, do presidents so frequently get it wrong? In recent years, part of the problem facing presidents is that the norm of legal professionalism has forced them to appoint people that they do not know well, and at the same time the contentiousness of confirmation hearings creates incentives for picking nominees without an extensive "paper trail." It is highly likely that no one in the Bush White House knew what "stealth nominee" David Souter really thought about *Roe v. Wade.* Just as importantly, the thinking of Supreme Court justices frequently evolves over their many long years on the bench, as the journeys of Harry Blackmun and John Paul Stevens from moderate conservatives to staunch liberals vividly demonstrate.

The biggest challenge presidents face in selecting justices is not predicting how they will vote on the key issues of the current day, but how they will vote on the central issues of subsequent decades. Lincoln, for example, placed on the Court men who upheld almost all the powers he asserted during the Civil War. But after the War his appointees adopted very narrow readings of the Thirteenth, Fourteenth, and Fifteenth Amendments. The "strict constructionists" Nixon appointed did narrow somewhat the rights of the accused, a hotly debated issue during the 1968 presidential campaign, but they also supported abortion rights and affirmative action, issues that were hardly on the administration's radar screen when it made its four Supreme Court appointments.

Almost all studies of the president's judicial appointments focus on the Supreme Court. Yet as we have seen, the power to appoint district and circuit court judges is hardly insignificant. As Table 2 shows, the number of federal judges appointed by each president has grown substantially since the 1930s. In a little over twelve years in office, FDR appointed 133 district court judges and 50 circuit court judges. Jimmy Carter outdid Roosevelt in his single term. After eight years in office, Ronald Reagan managed to break Carter's record.

Presidents differ markedly in the amount of attention they pay to lower court appointments. At one extreme lie FDR and Ronald Reagan. Sheldon Goldman's meticulously researched book on presidential appointment of district and circuit court judges found that "both Reagan and Roosevelt sought to change the direction of government, and both saw the federal courts as frustrating their policy agenda. Both sought to use the power of judicial appointments to place on the bench judges who shared their general philosophy."[86] Although FDR had initially viewed judgeships primarily as patronage, he changed his tune after lower court judges issued "about 1600 injunctions against enforcement of various New Deal programs" in 1935–1936.[87] After that, he actively recruited nominees, speaking openly about the need to place "liberal" and "progressive" judges on the federal bench. Selecting judges was "an activity that Roosevelt apparently relished."[88] Reagan came into office promising to change the orientation of the federal judiciary. Not only did he establish a new office in the Department of Justice to screen candidates for judgeships, but "the highest levels of the White House staff . . .

played an ongoing, active role in the selection of judges."[89] The Reagan administration asked senators to supply more than one name for each position in order to ensure that only judicial conservatives were appointed.

At the other extreme lie Dwight Eisenhower and, surprisingly, Richard Nixon. Neither of them had much interest in judicial appointments; neither saw judges as affecting the policy arenas about which they cared most. Both delegated the task of picking judges to the Department of Justice, which favored relatively moderate, establishment Republicans.[90] Democratic presidents Truman, Kennedy, and Johnson fell between these two extremes. They tended to see judgeships in terms of patronage, not policy making. For JFK and LBJ the appointment of southern judges presented a vexing problem: Democratic senators from the deep South tended to favor segregationists, but both presidents were intent on placing pro–civil rights judges on the federal bench. When they succeeded, they antagonized powerful members of Congress.[91]

On judicial appointments, as on so many other matters, Jimmy Carter stands awkwardly apart. As one of those rare presidents who seem to hate politics, Carter insisted that senators establish "merit selection" panels rather than use judicial appointments as patronage. At the same time, he gave high priority to appointing more women and minorities to the bench. Carter's Department of Justice stressed merit selection; his White House staff emphasized affirmative action. When the two came into conflict, the latter usually prevailed. Although Carter claimed not to consider ideology in his appointments, his appointees have proven to be the most liberal of any recent president, including fellow Democrat Bill Clinton.[92]

TABLE 2

President	Circuit Court Judges		District Court Judges	
Roosevelt	50	(55)	133	(183)
Truman	26	(64)	97	(219)
Eisenhower	45	(66)	126	(237)
Kennedy	20	(74)	103	(293)
Johnson	41	(83)	126	(324)
Nixon	45	(95)	179	(382)
Ford	12	(95)	52	(383)
Carter	56	(120)	202	(456)
Bush, George H.W.	37	(150)	148	(565)
Clinton	49		246	(649)

Figure in parentheses is total number of judges at each level during president's last year in office.

SOURCE: David O'Brien, "Judicial Legacies: The Clinton Presidency and the Courts"; and Sheldon Goldman, *Picking Federal Judges.*

For most of American history, senators of the president's party have exerted predominant influence over the selection of district court judges—thus the well-known definition of a federal judge as "a lawyer who knows a senator." Senatorial privilege declined under Presidents Carter and Reagan, and has yet to rebound.[93] Because the jurisdiction of each circuit court of appeal includes several states, individual senators have less influence in the selection of appellate judges. Presidents have even greater control over nominees to the D.C. Circuit which (conveniently for the White House) does not include the geographic territory of any member of the Senate. Given its importance for administrative law, the D.C. Circuit is also one of the country's most powerful courts. It also faces fewer divisive social issues (such as abortion) than most of the circuit courts. For all these reasons, the D.C. Circuit has become a breeding ground and launching pad for Supreme Court justices. Among its alumni are Justices Antonin Scalia, Clarence Thomas, Ruth Bader Ginsburg, and Warren Burger, as well as unsuccessful nominees Robert Bork and Douglas Ginsburg. The president's nominations for the D.C. Circuit have therefore been particularly controversial in Congress in recent years. For example, two of George W. Bush's nominees, John G. Roberts, Jr., and Miguel Estrada, were blocked by Senate Democrats. As David O'Brien puts it, "both Roberts and Estrada have impressive academic and professional qualifications, along with well-established connections to the D.C. conservative legal community. And that is precisely why Bush nominated them and why liberals vigorously oppose holding hearings on their nominations."[94]

To what extent can presidents use lower court appointments to affect the evolution of legal doctrine? The truth is that we really do not know the answer to this question. Until the 1980s most presidents (with the conspicuous exception of FDR) did not view these appointments as a way to change legal policy. Recent studies of voting patterns on circuit courts reveal some differences between judges appointed by Carter and Clinton on the one hand and Nixon, Ford, Reagan, and Bush on the other.[95] Yet these differences appear in only a fraction of the cases before the circuit courts. We do know that the White House, Department of Justice, members of Congress, and advocacy groups on the left and the right all *believe* these appointments matter a great deal—which means that the politics of lower court nominations and confirmations is likely to remain contentious for years to come.

Controlling Litigation

Once federal judges have taken their seats on the bench, presidents cannot fire or punish them. But this does not mean that the executive has no remaining influence in the judicial process. No litigant appears in federal court as frequently as the United States. It is the ultimate "repeat player." Presidents and their appointees in the Department of Justice have control over (1) when to file suit against private parties or subnational governments; (2) when to appeal cases the government has lost at the district court level; (3) which cases to recommend that the Supreme Court hear; and (4) what position, if any, the government should take in cases before the Supreme Court. In other words, the president has at his disposal the largest and most influential law firm in the country.

The most obvious way in which the president influences the litigational strategies of the United States is through his appointment of the solicitor general (SG). The SG is often called "the tenth justice," not only because he argues and wins so many cases before the Supreme Court, but also because the justices rely so heavily on his office for deciding when to grant *certiorari*.[96] The importance the Supreme Court attaches to the opinion of the Office of the Solicitor General is indicated by the fact that the Court frequently "invites" (i.e., commands) the SG to file an amicus brief in cases in which the government is not a party.[97] In especially important cases the president may become directly involved in the process of formulating the government's position. For example, President Eisenhower read and made editorial changes in the government's brief in *Brown v. Board of Education*.[98] President Carter decided that the United States should write a brief supporting affirmative action in the 1978 *Bakke* case. President Reagan ordered the SG's office to switch sides in *U.S. v. Bob Jones University* and to argue that the tax code does not authorize the IRS to deny tax-exempt status to schools that discriminate on the basis of race. In Reagan's second term, SG Charles Fried urged the Court to overturn *Roe v. Wade*, a decision that was obviously approved by the White House.[99]

The Office of the Solicitor General has for many years attracted highly competent attorneys who like to think of themselves as independent of politics. Academic studies of the Office dispute this claim. According to Rebecca Sakolar,

> the selection process ensures that the individuals nominated to fill the position of solicitor general will share the political ideology of the administration he serves. Although the solicitor general may appear insulated from the politics of the administration, he is no more independent than the secretary of transportation, the attorney general, or any other political appointee.[100]

President Kennedy appointed Archibald Cox, the epitome of an establishment liberal, and President Johnson selected Thurgood Marshall, the nation's leading civil rights attorney. When Nixon moved to the right in 1972, he replaced the moderate Erwin Griswold with the more conservative Robert Bork. Presidents Reagan, George H.W. Bush, and George W. Bush have all appointed well-known conservatives to the position. Franklin Roosevelt elevated two of his SGs, Stanley Reed and Robert Jackson, to the Supreme Court, where they continued to demonstrate their loyalty to New Deal principles. As SG Rex Lee (1981–1985) put it, "One of the purposes of the solicitor general is to represent his client, the president of the United States. One of the ways to implement the president's polices is through positions taken in court. When I have that opportunity, I'm going to take it."[101]

To be sure, the SG is often "in the difficult, if challenging, position of trying to serve two masters."[102] Much of the influence of the office stems from its ability to stay in tune with the Court's majority. This is particularly true in the *certiorari* process, in which the office in effect serves as the bureaucratic eyes and ears of the Court. In this respect the SG is no different from department heads who must balance their loyalty to the president with responsiveness to those members of Congress who exercise control over their budgets and authorizing legislation. Since the 1960s, when the Warren Court brought a large number of political controversies into the courtroom, presidents have placed more and more emphasis on finding SGs who will present the administration's position on those volatile and often highly partisan issues.

The Office of the Solicitor General deals primarily with cases important enough to get to the Supreme Court. Thousands upon thousands of more mundane cases are handled by the Civil Rights, Natural Resources, Antitrust, Tax, Civil, and Criminal Divisions of the Department of Justice (DOJ). The DOJ was established in 1870 to centralize control over litigation to which the government is a party. Today very few federal agencies are allowed to represent themselves in court. This means not only that DOJ attorneys compose the government's briefs and present the government's position in oral argument, but also that the DOJ has final say over when to bring enforcement actions and when to defend (or settle) cases against particular agencies. All departments and agencies have their own legal offices, but the lawyers in these offices are usually limited to advising their clients and assisting the DOJ, not litigating cases on their own. This division of counseling and litigating functions was designed to centralize executive control over litigation, to ensure that the government speaks with a single voice, and to prevent agencies from constructing autonomous areas of the law. Presidents have long supported this division of labor. According to Donald Horowitz, author of the most politically astute book on the subject,

> the White House has from time to time overruled the Justice Department in disputes over specific litigating *positions*, but it has been ardent in its support for Justice's general litigating *authority*. . . . [Presidents] apparently believe that the Justice Department, if not necessarily more responsive to the general policy orientation of the Administration, was at least more amenable to central direction.[103]

Horowitz notes that "centralized litigational authority is one of the few ready handles on the bureaucracy that a President possesses."[104]

The best example of how an administration can use the litigational authority of the Department of Justice to influence public policy is the creation of the

Civil Rights Section (later renamed the Civil Rights Division) by the Roosevelt administration in 1939. Using a combination of old statutes and innovative arguments, Civil Rights Section attorneys attacked white primaries, southern lynchings, police brutality, restrictive covenants, and school segregation. With the help of so many Roosevelt appointees on the bench, the administration was able to win victories in court that it could not possibly have won in Congress. This strategy also allowed President Roosevelt to avoid taking personal responsibility for actions that enraged many of his southern allies.[105] This serves as a useful reminder that the federal courts can be powerful allies of the president, not just the source of constraints on his power.

Conclusion

In a famous 1957 article that has gained renewed popularity among political scientists, Robert Dahl argued that "the policy views dominant on the Court are never for long out of line with the policy views dominant among the lawmaking majorities of the United States" for the simple reason that its members are nominated by the president and confirmed by the Senate.[106] While Dahl looks only at Supreme Court decisions striking down federal legislation, the Court's willingness to defer to the president's exercise of prerogative power during times of crisis seems to buttress his argument. The Court rarely upsets a well-established political consensus.

Why, then, do presidents so often find themselves at loggerheads with the Supreme Court and frustrated by the voting record of their appointees? Why do presidential appointees within the departments and agencies lose so many cases in the lower courts? The most obvious problem with Dahl's argument is that it works only in the long run: in the long run FDR transformed the Court, but during his first term the Court nearly killed his New Deal. In the long run, to paraphrase Lord Keynes, all presidents are ex-presidents. Indeed, until the Twenty-second Amendment is repealed, it is unlikely that any president will be able to equal FDR's performance in reorienting the judicial branch. It is worth noting that all nine members of the Supreme Court that decided the three 2004 cases on imprisonment of "enemy combatants" have been on the Court since 1994—before the Republicans took control of Congress, before George W. Bush became president, and before the attacks of September 11, 2001. In shaping the composition of the federal courts, the president shares power with his predecessors and his successors, with whom he is likely to have profound disagreements.

The president also shares the job of picking judges with Congress. In times of divided government—which over the past half century has meant most of the time—presidents must often nominate compromise candidates (e.g., Lewis Powell and Anthony Kennedy), stealth candidates (e.g., David Souter), and wild card candidates (e.g., Sandra Day O'Connor). Even when the president's party safely controls both houses of Congress, he must often make concessions to members of his own party—as Presidents Roosevelt, Truman, Kennedy, and Johnson learned when they were forced to swallow southern judges who had less than sterling records on civil rights. Since the 1950s the federal courts have been particularly likely to be deeply enmeshed in the "cross-cutting" issues that create bitter divisions *within* the parties. For example, since the contemporary Republican Party is a coalition of social conservatives and economic conservatives with a libertarian streak, it should come as no surprise that Republican judges frequently disagree on issues such as abortion and gay rights. One must even wonder how committed Republican presidents are to achieving a definitive victory on these issues in court, since this might end up mobilizing their opponents and alienating the center. In short, on many of the most difficult issues the Court faces, there simply is no "dominant law-making majority" capable of giving clear direction to the judicial branch.

Judges who serve for decades in an environment that discourages them from mingling with politicians and other policy makers inevitably develop new institutional and personal loyalties. They take seriously their responsibility to uphold "the rule of law," which in practice means some combination of the dictates of Congress, the precedents of past courts, and the political opinions of current judges. Since presidents live in a world whose motto is "What have you done for me lately?" they should not be surprised when the judges they select vote against them years later. Neither Congress nor the executive have any effective means for punishing judges for anything but the most egregious misconduct.

In the end, the most important factor influencing relations between presidents and the judiciary is not partisanship or institutional rivalry, not fear of punishment or the prospect of personal reward, but the extent to which the ideas that guide the incumbent administration—ideas about the proper role of the federal government and the proper instruments for turning broad goals into concrete programs—are also dominant within the judicial branch. Presidents with vision resolutely and unapologetically try to pack the courts with judges who share their vision. All great presidents have tried to do this. Only a few have succeeded. Almost all the others have found their dealings with the judiciary to be occasionally frustrating and ultimately disappointing. This might help explain why executive-judicial relations have never been very high on the agenda of presidential scholars.

Notes

1. Richard E. Ellis, *The Jeffersonian Crisis: Courts and Politics in the Young Republic* (Norton, 1971), chaps. 1–7.
2. The first and third quotations come from *Marbury v. Madison* 5 U.S. 137 (1803) at 163 and 177. The second comes from *Clinton v. Jones* 580 U.S. 681 (1997) at 688 (quoting approvingly from the opinion of the lower court).

3. Locke, *Second Treatise on Government*, chap. 14, para. 160.
4. Quoted in Fisher, *Constitutional Conflicts,* 260.
5. *Ex Parte Milligan*, 71 U.S. 2 (1866) at 120-21 (emphasis added).
6. Robert Scigliano, "The Presidency and the Judiciary," in Richard Nelson, ed., *The Presidency and the Political System,* 2nd ed. (Washington, D.C.: Congressional Quarterly Press, 1988), 453.
7. Alexis de Tocqueville, *Democracy in America,* trans. and ed., Harvey C. Mansfield and Delba Winthrop (Chicago: University of Chicago Press, 2000), p. 257.
8. *FDA v. Brown and Williamson Tobacco Corp.* 529 U.S. 120 (2000) at 133.
9. *Marbury v. Madison* at 166.
10. *Kendall v. U.S. ex rel Stokes* 37 U.S. 524 (1838).
11. James Sterling Young, *The Washington Community, 1800–1828* (New York: Columbia University Press, 1966), 27–32; James Q. Wilson, "The Rise of the Bureaucratic State," in Nathan Glazer and Irving Kristol, eds., *The American Commonwealth, 1976* (New York: Free Press, 1976), 72–84.
12. Quoted in Richard Pious, *The American Presidency* (New York: Basic Books, 1979), 58.
13. *The Prize Cases,* 2 Black 635 (1863).
14. 17 Fed. Case. No. 9487 (1861).
15. *Ex Parte Milligan* 71 U.S. 2 (1866).
16. *U.S. v. Curtiss-Wright Export Corp.* 299 U.S. 304 (1936).
17. *U.S. v. Pink* 315 U.S. 203 (1942); *U.S. v. Belmont* 301 U.S. 324 (1937); *Dames & Moore v. Regan* 453 U.S. 654 (1981). Also see Fisher, *Constitutional Conflicts,* 248–254; and Michael Genovese, *The Supreme Court, the Constitution, and Presidential Power* (Lanham, Md.: University Press of America, 1980), chap. 6.
18. *Goldwater v. Carter* 444 U.S. 996 (1979); and *Goldwater v. Carter* 617 F 2d 697 (D.C. Cir., 1979). Also see Fisher, *Constitutional Conflicts,* 242–245.
19. Fisher, *Constitutional Conflicts,* 289.
20. *In Re Debs* 158 U.S. 564 (1895).
21. *US v. Midwest Oil Co.* 236 U.S. 459 (1915).
22. *In Re Neagle* 135 U.S. 1 (1890) at 64.
23. *Myers v. U.S.* 272 U.S. 52 (1926).
24. *Yakus v. U.S.* 321 U.S. 414 (1944).
25. Pious, *American Presidency,* 53–55.
26. *Ex Parte Quirin* 317 U.S. 1 (1942).
27. *Korematsu v. U.S.* 323 U.S. 214 (1944) and *Hirabayashi v. U.S.* 320 U.S. 81 (1943).
28. Abraham, *Justices, Presidents, and Senators,* 186.
29. Alexander Bickel, *The Least Dangerous Branch* (Indianapolis: Bobbs-Merrill, 1962), chap. 4.
30. *Dames & Moore v. Regan* 453 U.S. 654 at 661.
31. *Youngstown Sheet and Tube Co. v. Sawyer* 343 U.S. 579 (1952) at 637–38. For a good recent example of the application of Jackson's analysis and the difficulty of establishing congressional intent, see *Padilla v. Rumsfeld* 352 F. 3d 695 (2nd Cir., 2003).
32. *Youngstown* at 634.
33. *Dames & Moore v. Regan* at 660.

34. Fisher, *Constitutional Conflicts*, 295.
35. Cases include *Holtzman v. Schlesinger* 414 U.S. 1304 (1993), *Holtzman v. Schlesinger* 484 F.2d 1307 (2nd Cir., 1973), *Sanchez-Espinoza v. Reagan* 568 Fed. Supp. 596 (D.D.C, 1983), *Lowry v. Reagan* 676 F. Supp. 333 (D.D.C., 1987), *Ange v. Bush* 752 F. Supp. 509 (D.D.C., 1990) and *Dellums v. Bush* 752 F. Supp. 1141 (D.D.C., 1990) (commitment of troops) and *Goldwater v. Carter* 444 U.S. 996 (1979) and *Goldwater v. Carter* 617 F 2d 697 (D.C. Cir., 1979) (termination of treaties). For a full discussion, see Fisher, *Constitutional Conflicts*, chaps. 9–10 and *Congressional Abdication on War and Spending* (College Station: Texas A&M University Press, 2000), chap. 3.
36. Peter Schuck, "The Politics of Rapid Legal Change," in Marc Landy and Martin Levin, eds., *The New Politics of Public Policy* (Baltimore: Johns Hopkins University Press, 1995), 81.
37. The quotation comes from *Nishimura Eiku v. U.S.*, cited in Daniel Tichenor, *Dividing Lines: The Politics of Immigration Control in America* (Princeton, N.J.: Princeton University Press, 2002), 110.
38. Peter Schuck, "The Transformation of Immigration Law," 84 *Columbia Law Review* 1 (1984), 1–90.
39. *Rasul v. Bush* 542 U.S. ___ (2004); *Hamdi v. Rumsfeld* 542 U.S. ___ (2004).
40. *Hamdi v. Rumsfeld*, slip opinion at 26.
41. Slip opinion at 27.
42. For example, *Whitman v. ATA* 531 U.S. 457 (2001), and *AFL-CIO v. Kahn* 618 F.2d 784 (D.C.Cir., 1979).
43. *INS v. Chadha* 462 U.S. 919 (1983).
44. Fisher, *Constitutional Conflicts*, 157. Also see Barbara Craig, *Chadha: The Story of an Epic Constitutional Struggle* (Berkeley: University of California Press, 1990); Louis Fisher, "Judicial Misjudgments about the Lawmaking Process: The Legislative Veto Case," *Public Administration Review* 45 (Nov. 1985), 705–711; and Jessica Korn, *The Power of Separation: American Constitutionalism and the Myth of the Legislative Veto* (Princeton, N.J.: Princeton University Press, 1996).
45. *Bowsher v. Synar* 478 U.S. 714 (1986). The Court had previously prohibited House and Senate leaders from appointing members of the Federal Election Commission. *Buckley v. Valeo* 424 U.S. 1 (1976).
46. *Clinton v. New York City* 524 U.S. 417 (1998). One oddity of this cases was that the Republican 104th Congress gave this power to a Democratic president. Another was that the three dissenters in the Supreme Court were the strange combination of Scalia, Breyer, and O'Connor.
47. *Morrison v. Olsen* 487 U.S. 654 (1988).
48. *U.S. v. Nixon* 418 U.S. 683 at 707 (1974).
49. *Clinton v. Jones* 520 U.S. 681 (1997).
50. *Dames & Moore v. Regan* 453 U.S. 654 (1981), at 660.
51. James Fesler and Donald Kettl, *The Politics of the Administrative Process*, 2nd edition (New York: Chatham House, 1996), 185.
52. *Udall v. Tallman* 380 U.S. 1 (1967) at 16.
53. *Chevron v. NRDC* 467 U.S. 837 (1984) at 843-44.

54. *Marbury v. Madison* at 177.

55. *INS v. Cordozo-Fonsesca* 480 U.S. 421 (1987) at 446.

56. *Calvert Cliffs Coordinating Committee v. AEC* 449 F.2d 1109 (D.C. Cir., 1971) at 1111.

57. Shapiro, *Who Guards the Guardians?*, chap. 5.

58. Marver Bernstein, *Regulating Business by Independent Commission* (Princeton, N.J.: Princeton University Press, 1955).

59. Richard Stewart, "The Reformation of American Administrative Law," 88 *Harvard Law Review* 1667 (1975).

60. Ibid., 1712.

61. R. Shep Melnick, "The Politics of Partnership," *Public Administration Review* 45 (November 1985), 653–659.

62. For examples, see Melnick, *Regulation and the Courts*, and *Between the Lines: Interpreting Welfare Rights* (Washington, D.C.: The Brookings Institution, 1994); and Jeremy Rabkin, *Judicial Compulsions: How Public Law Distorts Public Policy* (New York: Basic Books, 1989).

63. *EDF v. Ruchelshaus* 435 F.2d 584 (D.C. Cir., 1971) at 598.

64. Martha Derthick, *Agency under Stress: The Social Security Administration in American Government* (Washington, D.C.: The Brookings Institution, 1990), chap. 7.

65. Martin Shapiro, "The Presidency and the Federal Courts," in Arnold J. Metsner, ed., *Politics and the Oval Office* (San Francisco: Institute for Contemporary Studies, 1981), 142. For an extended discussion of the ideas in this paragraph, see Shapiro, *Who Guards the Guardians?*, chap. 2.

66. "Vermont Yankee: The APA, the D.C. Circuit, and the Supreme Court," 1978 *Supreme Court Review* 345, p. 371.

67. *Vermont Yankee v. NRDC* 435 U.S. 519 (1978).

68. Peter H. Schuck and E. Donald Elliott, "To the Chevron Station: An Empirical Study of Federal Administrative Law," *Duke Law Journal* 984 (1990), 984–1077.

69. *Motor Vehicle Manufacturers Association v. State Farm Mutual* 463 U.S. 29 (1983).

70. *US v. Mead* 533 U.S. 218 (2001).

71. See, on the one hand, *Heckler v. Chaney* 470 U.S. 821 (1985), *Young v. CNI* 476 U.S. 974 (1986), and *Steel Co. v. Citizens for Better Environment* (1998); and, on the other hand, *Friends of the Earth v. Laidlaw* (2000), and *Vermont Agency of Natural Reasources v. US. Ex rel Stevens* (2000).

72. Quoted in David O'Brien, "Judicial Legacies: The Clinton Presidency and the Courts," in Colin Campbell and Bert Rockman, eds., *The Clinton Legacy* (New York: Chatham House, 2000), 76.

73. Quoted in Abraham, *Justices, Presidents, and Senators*, 51.

74. Scigliano, *The Supreme Court and the Presidency*, 157; and Abraham, *Justices, Presidents, and Senators*, 51.

75. Abraham, *Justices, Presidents, and Senators*, 72–73 (McLean and Chase).

76. Ibid., p. 28.

77. John Maltese, *The Selling of Supreme Court Nominees* (Baltimore, Md.: Johns Hopkins University Press, 1994), 137–138. Also see David Yalof, *Pursuit of Justices: Presidential Politics and the Selection of Supreme Court Nominees* (Chicago: University of Chicago Press, 1999), 155–165.

78. Nancy Kassop, "The View from the President," in Mark C. Miller and Jeb Barnes, eds., *Making Policy, Making Law: An Interbranch Perspective* (Washington, D.C.: Georgetown University Press, 2004), 79.

79. Abraham, *Justices, Presidents, and Senators*, 153–155.

80. Ibid., 38–40.

81. David O'Brien, "Ironies and Disappointments: Bush and Federal Judgeships," in Colin Campbell and Bert Rockman, eds., *The George W. Bush Presidency* (Washington, D.C.: CQ Press, 2004), 139.

82. Quoted in Scigliano, *The Supreme Court and the Presidency*, 115–116. Evaluating Horace Lurton, whom he was considering nominating in 1906, TR concluded, "He is right on the Negro question; he is right on the power of the federal government; he is right on the insular business; he is right about corporations; and he is right about labor."

83. Quoted in Abraham, *Justices, Presidents, and Senators*, 209.

84. Yalof, *Pursuit of Justices*, 91.

85. Quoted in Yalof, *Pursuit of Justices*, 143–144.

86. Goldman, *Picking Federal Judges,* 285

87. Ibid., 31.

88. Ibid., 17.

89. Ibid., 292.

90. Ibid., chaps. 4, 6.

91. Ibid., chaps. 3, 5.

92. Ronald Stidham, Robert Carp, and Donald Songer, "The Voting Behavior of President Clinton's Judicial Appointments," *Judicature* 80 (1996), 16.

93. O'Brien, "Judicial Legacies: The Clinton Presidency and the Courts," 100.

94. O'Brien, "Ironies and Disappointments, 152.

95. Richard Revesz, "Environmental Regulation, Ideology, and the D.C. Circuit," 83 *Virginia Law Review* 1717 (1997), 1717–1772, and "Ideology, Collegiality, and the D.C. Circuit," 85 *Virginia Law Review* 805 (1999), 805–851; Frank Cross and Emerson Tiller, "Judicial Partisanship and Obedience to Legal Doctrines," 107 *Yale Law Journal* 2155 (1998), 2155–2176; and Cass Sunstein, David Schakade, and Lisa Michelle Ellman, "Ideological Voting on Federal Courts of Appeals: A Preliminary Investigation," Working Paper 03-9, AEI-Brookings Joint Center For Regulatory Studies (September 2003).

96. H. W. Perry, Jr., *Deciding to Decide: Agenda Setting in the United States Supreme Court* (Cambridge, Mass.: Harvard University Press, 1991), 128–133.

97. Salokar, *Solicitor General,* 143–145.

98. Richard Kluger, *Simple Justice* (New York: Vintage Books, 1975), 726–727.

99. Lincoln Caplan, *The Tenth Justice: The Solicitor General and the Rule of Law* (New York: Vintage Books, 1988), 39–48, 51–64, and 139–154.

100. Salokar, *Solicitor General*, 34. Also see Cornell Clayton, *The Politics of Justice: the Attorney General and the Making of Legal Policy* (Armonk, N.Y.: M.E. Sharpe, 1992), 54–61.

101. Quoted in Salokar, *Solicitor General*, 139.

102. Scigliano, *The Supreme Court and the Presidency*, 162.

103. Horowitz, *Jurocracy*, 104.
104. Horowitz, *Jurocracy*, 107; also see Clayton, *Politics of Justice*, 77–80.
105. The best description of this is McMahon, *Reconsidering Roosevelt on Race,* chaps. 5–6.
106. Robert Dahl, "Decision-Making in a Democracy: The Supreme Court as a National Policy-Maker," *Journal of Public Law* 6 (1957), 285.

Bibliography

Abraham, Henry. *Justices, Presidents, and Senators: A History of the U.S. Supreme Court Appointments from Washington to Clinton.* Rev. ed. Lanham, Md.: Rowman and Littlefield, 1999. A fascinating, anecdote-filled examination of how Supreme Court justices are nominated and confirmed.

Fisher, Louis. *Constitutional Conflicts between Congress and the President,* 4th ed. Lawrence: University Press of Kansas, 1997. A fair and thorough examination of legal doctrines on separation of powers by the leading authority in the field.

Goldman, Sheldon. *Picking Federal Judges: Lower Court Selection from Roosevelt through Reagan.* New Haven: Yale University Press, 1997. A detailed, well documented examination of how recent presidents have selected circuit and district court judges. Lots of great examples.

Horowitz, Donald. *The Jurocracy: Government Lawyers, Agency Programs, and Judicial Decisions.* Lexington, Mass.: Lexington Books, 1977. A politically astute assessment of a little-studied issue, relations between lawyers in the Department of Justice and those within operating agencies.

McMahon, Kevin. *Reconsidering Roosevelt on Race: How the Presidency Paved the Road to Brown.* Chicago: University of Chicago Press, 2004. A detailed, convincing account of how FDR used judicial selection and the Department of Justice to pursue his policy objectives.

Melnick, R. Shep. *Regulation and the Courts: The Case of the Clean Air Act.* Washington, D.C.: The Brookings Institution, 1983. Detailed examination of federal courts' role in limiting presidential control of the Environmental Protection Agency.

Salokar, Rebecca Mae. *The Solicitor General: The Politics of Law.* Philadelphia: Temple University Press, 1992. Balanced account of how the SG tries to act in accord with the program of the president without losing the confidence of the Court.

Scigliano, Robert. *The Supreme Court and the Presidency.* New York: Free Press, 1971. A perceptive, if somewhat dated, review of the many-faceted relationship between the presidency and the courts.

Shapiro, Martin. *Who Guards the Guardians? Judicial Control of Administration.* Athens: University of Georgia Press, 1988. Everything you ever wanted to know about administrative law, along with a convincing explanation of why this is worth knowing.

15

FEDERALISM AND
THE EXECUTIVE BRANCH

Thomas Gais and James Fossett

F EDERALISM IS OFTEN DESCRIBED AS A DECENTRALIZED
political system, a division of responsibilities between a central government and local or regional governments, in which the latter are granted
autonomy on selected matters. Such definitions of federalism are not completely
wrong. But they do not convey the fluidity of federalism in the United States, the
constant fluctuation of who uses which governments to achieve their aims.[1]
Doctrines about appropriate federal, state, and local roles rarely exert much control over American politics. When Vermont and Massachusetts extended marital
privileges to same-sex couples, many conservatives showed few qualms in using
the federal government to reverse such decisions. In the same way, when the second Bush administration limited federal research grants involving embryonic
stem cells, those who disagreed with that judgment expressed little concern
about getting state governments to support such research.[2]

Yet this opportunistic flux has not lacked structure. Constitutional processes,
the strength of state party organizations, and the administrative and political
capacities of the federal and state governments long constrained when and how
citizens and groups could turn to either the national or the state governments to
secure their objectives. These constraints, however, have eroded in recent
decades. Both federal and state governments have opened up to nearly all
domestic issues, and their policy agendas have become inextricably intertwined
and overlapped.

Convergence between state and national agendas has, along with other
changes, transformed the federal executive's role in the American federal system.
For most of the nation's history, presidents and their appointees have influenced

486

state policy choices through the legislative process, by building broad national coalitions around changes in grants, regulations, and other laws affecting states. In the last two decades, however, the executive branch has used a growing range of administrative tools to negotiate directly with states over specific policies or to alter the context of state policy making without specific congressional approval. The federal executive branch and its interactions with the states have thus become a primary locus for producing major changes in domestic policies. These developments have made American federalism more mutable, more responsive to initially small coalitions of federal political executives and groups of states supportive of a national administration's aims, quicker to react to changing conditions, and more capable of generating and diffusing policy innovations. At the same time, this executive-dominated federalism undermines checks and balances *within* the national government, avoids national debates even while major policies spread through the federal system, and creates an even more complex and varied range of policies among the states.

The Constitution and Divided Sovereignty

Rather than assigning sovereignty to either the national or the state governments, the U.S. Constitution gave it to both. Federal and state governments acted in the same territory and derived their authority from the same people. Yet both were given independent powers to govern. How to minimize friction arising from the coincident actions of sovereign governments was a problem not resolved by the Constitution, which did not clearly distinguish the responsibilities of federal and state governments. Still, most of its framers viewed the states as performing roles distinct from those of the federal government. As James Madison put it, "The federal and State governments are in fact but different agents and trustees of the people, constituted with different powers and designed for different purposes."[3]

One reason behind this expectation was the widespread view that the federal government would only exercise powers expressly granted by the Constitution. Madison argued that the jurisdiction of the national government extended "to certain enumerated powers only, and [left] to the several States a residuary and inviolable sovereignty over all other objects."[4] The powers of the federal government were "exercised principally on external objects, as war, peace, negotiation, and foreign commerce," while the powers of the states "extend[ed] to all the objects which, in the ordinary course of affairs, concern[ed] the lives, liberties, and properties of the people, and the internal order, improvement, and prosperity of the States."[5]

Maintenance of dual federalism depended also on political processes that ensured the national government would respect state prerogatives. The Senate represented the states: their legislatures selected senators, and each state was given equal representation. States established most rules for electing members of Congress. And state legislatures originally chose members of the Electoral College, which gave each state implicit representation as a sovereignty by setting the number of electors equal to the number of representatives in the House plus its two senators.

States were also protected from the federal government by its extension and institutional divisions. Madison claimed that majority factions were unlikely to form in a large and diverse republic, since the number and diversity of interests in the nation prevented a single faction from gaining control of the federal government.[6] Separation of powers within the federal government also inhibited national action, except actions commanding widespread support and, by inference, not threatening state sovereignty.

Nor were federal courts viewed as a threat to states. Supreme Court justices were selected by the president and the Senate, the two national institutions closest to the states. Federal courts were also circumscribed in dealing with state-to-state controversies by the Eleventh Amendment. In sum, though the Constitution did not clearly distinguish the functions of the national and state governments, the limited powers of the national government, its political processes, social and political barriers to national action, and past political practices were expected to ensure that divided sovereignty produced a workable regime.

Dual Federalism

These constitutional processes and structures, and the assumptions underlying them, permitted a rough dual federalism to survive until the Civil War. John Marshall's Supreme Court in *McCulloch v. Maryland* (1819) offered an opening for an expansive national government through the Court's broad interpretation of the "necessary and proper" clause of the Constitution. Yet the federal government generally refused to push its functions beyond narrow interpretations of constitutionally enumerated powers, while state and local governments dominated most domestic policies.

States, for the most part, controlled slavery. They exerted nearly exclusive control over the electoral process, apportionment, education, property rights, labor conditions, and criminal and family law. Although the national government provided some financial assistance, local and state governments controlled transportation policies and projects. And after President Andrew Jackson vetoed the recharter of the Bank of the United States in 1832, responsibility for banking, monetary policy, and commercial credit reverted to the states.[7]

Early presidents helped enforce this dualism. In a veto message concerning a bill passed by the Congress to build roads and canals, President Madison argued that "the permanent success of the Constitution depends on a definite partition of powers between the Federal and State Governments," a view that most early presidents supported.[8] Some even refused to enforce the *express* powers of the federal government. President Andrew Jackson rejected the appeals of the Cherokee Indians when Georgia forced them to leave the state, despite the fact that Georgia's actions violated federal treaties.[9] Yet presidential preferences were not the main obstacles to an expanded national government. Divisions between the Northern and Southern states over slavery, and related differences over economic policies, made vigorous actions by the federal government impossible—until events completely nationalized the slavery issue, and the divisions erupted in war in 1861.

The Civil War and the Breakdown of Dual Federalism

The Civil War had, of course, an enormous nationalizing effect. President Abraham Lincoln's wartime actions temporarily extended the powers of the federal government, especially the presidency, over the states and the people. In the course of the war, Lincoln shifted the initiative over the raising of troops from the Northern governors to the federal government.[10] He intervened in the political processes of the Northern states, as when he jailed a Democratic candidate for the Ohio governorship for suspected disloyalty. The Civil War also gave rise to the nationalization of credit mechanisms and currency as well as a temporary income tax. Passage of the Thirteenth, Fourteenth, and Fifteenth Amendments to the Constitution—and civil rights legislation enacted after the war—established, albeit briefly, a new role for the federal government in the enforcement of civil rights.

One lasting legacy of the war was Lincoln's rhetoric, which diminished the states and linked the federal government to a nearly religious conception of the nation. The word "state" was not mentioned in two of his greatest speeches, the Gettysburg Address and his second inaugural address. The combatants were not two groups of independent states but two "parties" of the same Union, who "read the same Bible and pray[ed] to the same God." Lincoln's articulation of the war's meaning and the Union's primacy helped create national citizenship; only after the Civil War was "the United States" a singular noun.

Other visions of a strong national government evolved after the war, most of which involved the role of the federal government in managing the expanding American economy. One view was represented in the U.S. Supreme Court, which, especially after the mid-1880s, interpreted the Commerce Clause in favor of increased federal power over economic transactions, often to prevent states from regulating the national economy and its multistate corporations. Congress also supported this conception by chartering and granting land to the transcontinental railroads, and by attempting to centralize business regulation through the Interstate Commerce Act (1887) and the Sherman Antitrust Act

(1890). After that, from the 1890s through the 1930s, federal judges used the Due Process Clause of the Fourteenth Amendment to strike down state laws regulating corporate activities and labor relations. Yet the Supreme Court decisions were not entirely consistent, and states continued to fashion regulations in the chinks left by the Court. In the early twentieth century, the Progressive vision called for a more positive regulatory role for the federal government. President Theodore Roosevelt argued that, "as no State has any exclusive interest in or power over [large corporations], it has in practice proved impossible to get adequate regulation through State action." To serve the whole people, then, the nation should "assume power of supervision and regulation over all corporations doing an interstate business."[11]

Congressional opposition limited Roosevelt's ability to put this view into effect, though he won some legislative victories, such as the 1906 Pure Food and Drug Act. President Woodrow Wilson was more successful by securing congressional passage of laws extending federal power over labor relations in the railroad industry, farm credit, and currency and credit (with the establishment of the Federal Reserve System). But these victories ended soon after the first years of Wilson's presidency.

Although no single vision of the national government was fully implemented, the struggle for control helped erode the institutional foundations of dual federalism. In their efforts to advance their agendas, Roosevelt and Wilson connected directly with the people, and showed that presidents could challenge the leadership of the state parties. Wilson's presidency also produced, in 1913, the Seventeenth Amendment, which completely ended the selection of senators by state legislatures; and the Sixteenth Amendment, which gave Congress the power to "collect taxes on incomes . . . without apportionment among the several States," thereby giving the federal government a large, permanent, peacetime source of stable revenues. The mobilization for World War I and Wilson's international leadership after the war further expanded the capabilities and public role of the national government.[12] Finally, the temperance movement, which culminated in the ratification of the Eighteenth Amendment in 1919, revealed the potential of moral fervor, religiosity, and social movements in overcoming the barriers to national action that Madison had expected to protect states in the "extended republic."

The Rise of Legislative Federalism: The New Deal

When Franklin Roosevelt was elected president in 1932, the institutional pillars sustaining dual federalism had thus weakened, and dualism was ready to be toppled by the economic crisis and the unifying and democratizing leadership of the new president. His first inaugural address called for a national response to the Great Depression. The president saw the day as one of "national consecration," as a "dark hour of our national life." He called for "a national scale in the redistribution" of great populations between urban and rural areas, and for "the unifying of relief activities which today are often scattered, uneconomical, and unequal."

Roosevelt's "New Deal" greatly expanded the size and scope of the federal government's control over banks and other financial institutions, labor relations, child labor, minimum wages, hours worked, agriculture, rural electrification, and other economic activities.[13] The early New Deal programs also created assistance programs to cash-strapped state and local governments, including programs distributing surplus food to the poor, free school lunches, emergency highway projects, and emergency and general relief.[14] Some of these initiatives, especially the economic regulations, were initially struck down by the U.S. Supreme Court as unconstitutional attempts to expand federal power; and many of the relief programs were only temporary efforts. However, some economic programs survived after the Court moved away from its initial hostility toward New Deal programs in 1937.

The New Deal perhaps produced its greatest effect on American federalism with the enactment of the Social Security Act in 1935. The act, especially after its expansion in 1939, created a nationally administered pension program for retirees and survivors, one available to most Americans. It thus helped democratize the federal government by establishing direct connections between the national government and the basic needs of its citizens. The Social Security Act also established several permanent grant-in-aid programs in which states were given federal money as well as substantial discretion over benefit and eligibility policies. In exchange, states paid part of the program costs and satisfied administrative requirements. Unemployment Insurance, for example, offered short-term aid to unemployed workers. Federal grants to states were also enacted to support programs for Old-Age Assistance, Aid to the Blind, and Aid to Dependent Children, which provided benefits to poor children raised by their mothers.

Grants-in-aid were not intended to change the functions of state and local governments. They were a form of cooperative federalism, that is, efforts to help states perform traditional functions despite their fiscal weakness during the Great Depression. Grants-in-aid had been a major intergovernmental tool for the federal government at least since the mid-nineteenth century.[15] However, the New Deal launched their growth as a primary mechanism by which the federal government carried out its domestic priorities. The New Deal assistance programs were typically categorical grants, which were devoted to specific purposes written into the legislation. To receive funds, states had to show a federal agency how they planned to satisfy the grant's requirements, such as their rules and procedures for determining individuals' eligibility for benefits. Once state plans were approved, the federal government reimbursed states according to a formula, such as one federal dollar for every two state dollars spent, often up to some maximum level.

Enactment of the New Deal grant programs was not easy, though federalism often made the legislation easier to pass. The Roosevelt administration maintained unity among congressional Democrats by allowing states to adjust benefits and need standards to their own political cultures and fiscal capacities. Although the original Social Security bill introduced in the Congress required states to provide "reasonable subsistence compatible with decency and health" in the aid to dependent children and old age assistance programs, those requirements were replaced before final passage with language permitting each state to assist the elderly "as far as practicable under the conditions in each State." One obstacle to the adoption of national standards was the variation in states' fiscal capacities.[16] Racial differences constituted another. Many southern members objected to federal determinations of "adequacy" because they "feared that northern standards might be forced on the South in providing for Negro and white tenant families."[17] Southern officials also believed their region's major economic draw was its low labor costs, and national standards in unemployment insurance and a minimum wage were thought to threaten this comparative advantage. By allowing states to adopt their own standards in unemployment insurance, national legislation was possible despite these regional divisions. When decentralization was rejected in favor of a single minimum wage in 1938, the Fair Labor Standards Act split the Democratic Party and effectively ended the New Deal.[18]

Once grants were enacted, they intensified interactions between the federal and state bureaucracies and the influence of federal agencies over the states. In administering grants supporting indigent elderly and dependent children, for example, states had to designate a single agency as responsible for receiving and accounting for federal funds; submit state plans to the federal agency for review; administer the program throughout the state, not just in selected localities; use merit systems to recruit, pay, and retain persons administering the grants; and submit to *post hoc* reviews by the federal agency to ensure that the state complied with its plans.[19]

Federal agencies leveraged these requirements to professionalize state agencies, centralize operations, and influence state agency missions and state policies.[20] Federal agencies convinced some states, for example, to end their reliance on local welfare boards to implement assistance programs and give greater control to professionals to ensure statewide "uniformity" in the administration of assistance programs. Once federal agencies got states to professionalize their operations, it was easier for federal officials to influence the states. For example, federal welfare administrators could more readily convince state colleagues with similar training that assistance programs ought to be operated as income support programs rather than rewards for persons who complied with social norms, such as "suitable home" requirements that had been used by local (and often volunteer) welfare boards to deny eligibility to never-married mothers.[21] Federal agencies also influenced fellow professionals in state agencies by producing and disseminating research and policy arguments, which state administrators drew on in promoting changes in their own political systems. Federal and state agencies, in short, became policy-making allies.

The Growth of Federal Grants

For four decades after the New Deal, federal grants expanded both in money spent and functional areas supported. Yet the character of grants also changed, along with the roles performed by federal executive officials. Grants generally became more prescriptive, selectively targeted, and accessible to a wider array of public and private institutions. These changes allowed federal executives to take on new functions in selecting grant recipients, approving details of plans, monitoring implementation, and generally interacting with subnational governments in a more intensive, wide-ranging manner.

Grants resumed their growth under Harry Truman's administration soon after World War II, when programs supporting hospitals, mental health, and disaster relief were added. The next major change occurred in 1956, when Dwight Eisenhower persuaded Congress to establish the interstate highway system. Spending on federal grants grew under both administrations, even after controlling for inflation and population, as they added new grants without cutting old ones. Figure 1 shows this cumulative growth by displaying per capita spending in constant (inflation controlled) dollars by the federal government on grants to state and local governments. The figure also shows the distribution of grant functions, such as education and health. Eisenhower shifted these functions dramatically in the late 1950s, from a governmental tool mostly supporting income security programs to one in which transportation spending was predominant.

Federal grants continued to grow and diversify through the 1960s and 1970s. President Lyndon Johnson's legislative skills and large Democratic Party majorities in Congress produced an explosion of grant programs, from 132 in 1960 to 379 in 1967." The greatest increase in spending, as evidenced in Figure 1, occurred in education, training, and job services. Yet the new programs were also distinctive in their ambitions. Unlike previous grants, the Great Society's Model Cities Program, Head Start, the Community Action Program, Mass Transit Aid, Educational Aid for the Disadvantaged, and the Economic Opportunity Act were designed not to support traditional state and local functions but to change their priorities in favor of goals supported by national legislative coalitions, especially the goal of expanded economic opportunity for disadvantaged people.

Because Congress and the Johnson administration suspected that states would divert federal funds from Great Society goals, the new grants stressed close federal control of state and local spending. Many were project grants, distributed competitively among applicants at the discretion of federal administrators, not

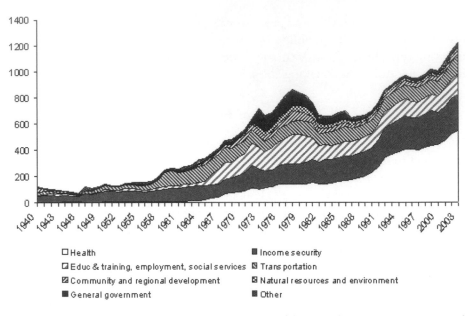

SOURCE: U.S. Office of Management and Budget, Budget of the United States Government, Fiscal Year 2005.

Figure 1   Per capita federal assistance to state and local governments, constant dollars (2000), 1940–2003

according to a fixed formula among governments, and federal administrators closely monitored their implementation. Most grants were designed to be insulated from state and local elected officials, whom federal officials distrusted, especially in their dealings with African Americans. To maintain professional control over programs without interference from local politicians, grants were often awarded to single-purpose special districts, such as mass transit and urban renewal authorities, or private nonprofit agencies.[23] When grants were made to states, they typically went to specialized agencies that were administratively isolated from other state functions. Federal agencies resisted state efforts to fold their grant programs into large departments of human services or other umbrella agencies because that gave power to agencies that did not share the federal program's particular priorities. Governors and mayors often complained that the resulting collection of fragmented state and local agencies resisted their program initiatives, using federal rules as excuses not to cooperate.[24]

The Nixon administration nudged the grant system in a different direction, away from extensive control by federal bureaucrats and in favor of local elected officials. Nixon did this in part by transforming some project grants that had been awarded competitively into grants allocated by formulas. The Community Development Block Grant (CDBG) and the Comprehensive Employment and

Training Act (CETA) consolidated several community development and job training project grant programs into two block grant programs that were distributed by formulas to cities, counties, or other governments. Block grants were not narrowly focused, like categorical grants; rather, they distributed a sum of money that state and local governments could use for a broad public purpose.

This change also spread federal money to more cities. The project grants of the Great Society had gone disproportionately to a small number of large Eastern and Midwestern cities that had invested considerable political and administrative energy into preparing grant applications and lobbying federal agencies. The new formula grants, by contrast, allocated funds according to specific criteria—unemployment, poverty, and old housing, for example—to all local governments above a certain population size, without requiring governments to apply for funds in any but the most perfunctory manner. This change increased federal financial support for local governments in the South and West, a result that assisted Nixon's effort to build his political base in these regions.

Nixon also pushed funding away from special districts and nongovernmental organizations, back toward cities, counties, and other general-purpose governmental entities. While their predecessor programs had largely gone to special districts or nonprofit agencies, CETA and CDBG funds went to city or county governments. In addition, the passage of "general revenue sharing" in 1972 increased general, noncategorical aid to state and local governments—a change that, as Figure 1 shows, pushed up spending in the 1970s on "general government" functions.

Thus, by the end of the 1970s, the federal grant system was well distributed across many purposes, reflecting cumulative efforts by presidents to impress their priorities on the federal system through fiscal incentives. As different presidents brought different goals, attitudes, and political alignments to bear on the American federal system, the national executive branch developed a variety of administrative methods in dealing with state and local governments, and dealt with an expanding range of governments, special districts, nonprofits, and other grant recipients. This accumulation of programs, administrative tools, and recipients gave presidents great flexibility in interacting with the federal system.

Intergovernmental Regulations

Executive powers over the states also grew during this postwar period of federal expansion with the expansion of federal intergovernmental regulations, which imposed new mandates on state and local governments. These regulations began to grow in the 1960s, but their growth accelerated in the 1970s. The regulations were usually cheap ways of imposing new demands on subnational governments, since the regulations were often not accompanied by significant federal funds. They also had the effect of creating new federal agencies with the authority to interpret and enforce the regulations. Rule making was thus added to the list of executive tools in federal relations with the states.

The shift toward regulation grew partly out of long-growing congressional disenchantment with positive and indirect incentives. During the 1950s and 1960s, for example, grants aimed at eliminating billboards on highways had had little impact, as did federal efforts to encourage states to address problems of environmental protection through research and demonstration grants. Yet fiscal uncertainties also encouraged federal reliance on regulations. Slower economic growth and higher inflation during the 1970s led to tighter federal budgets. These fiscal pressures increased tensions between congressional appropriations and authorizations committees as well as conflicts over budgetary issues between the White House and Congress. Annual appropriations for grants were less predictable, and one-shot enactments of new regulations became increasingly attractive as a means of producing lasting change in the federal system.

In a 1984 study, the Advisory Commission on Intergovernmental Regulation (ACIR) reported that, especially after 1969, the federal government had shifted away from reliance on positive fiscal incentives in the form of grants and toward regulatory requirements to influence state and local governments.[25] The earliest regulations were linked to federal grants. Title VI of the Civil Rights Act of 1964, for example, prohibited state and local governments from discriminating against persons on the grounds of race, color, or national origin in carrying out programs receiving federal assistance. Attaching conditions to federal grants was viewed by the courts as a constitutionally sound extension of the spending power of Congress, as long as the conditions were reasonably related to a legitimate national purpose, and the states had the option of forgoing federal dollars. However, these conditions were added after the states had created their programs, when constituencies and other political factors made it hard for states to end programs and reject federal conditions.

The ACIR labeled Title VI of the 1964 Civil Rights Act a "crosscutting requirement," one that applied to all or many federal grants, not just a single program. The method spread quickly during the 1970s. Title IX of the Education Amendments of 1972 prohibited discrimination against women in educational institutions receiving federal aid, and the National Environmental Policy Act of 1969 required states to prepare environmental impact statements before using many federal grants. The 1970s also saw the growth of crossover sanctions, regulations in which the federal government would terminate or reduce aid in a federal program unless the requirements of another program were satisfied. The Highway Beautification Act of 1965 threatened to withhold transportation funding from states if they did not stop the proliferation of billboards on federal highways; and the 1974 Federal-Aid Highway Amendments prohibited federal transportation construction projects in states that failed to establish and enforce speed limits of 55 miles per hour. The federal government also used crossover sanctions to influence states in health planning, environmental policy, and education for handicapped children.

A third form of intergovernmental regulation, partial preemptions, was not piggybacked onto existing federal grants. The federal government asserted its authority to set policy in a specific domain—perhaps by creating national goals or standards—and state governments were encouraged to implement the goals.[26] The Clean Air Act of 1970, for example, required states to submit plans adopting and enforcing national air quality standards. If a state refused, the federal government prepared the state's plan and enforced it, a loss of control most states wanted to avoid. If the state accepted responsibility for meeting the standards, the federal government paid some of the state's administrative costs. Federal officials used partial preemptions to enforce standards involving environmental protection, meat and poultry inspection, occupational safety and health, and others.

Finally, a fourth type of regulation, direct orders, mandated state or local actions under the threat of criminal or civil penalties. These orders were more constitutionally suspect than other regulations. The Fair Labor Standards Act Amendments of 1974, a direct order that extended minimum wage and overtime coverage to state and local governments, was found to be unconstitutional by the Supreme Court in *National League of Cities vs. Usery* in 1976. Yet most direct orders were found to be constitutional, such as the Public Utility Regulatory Policies Act of 1978, which required state utility officials to consider adopting various electrical energy and conservation measures.

Ironically, the Senate, once viewed as the national institution most protective of the states, initiated many of the regulations as senators responded to national news stories about widespread problems, such as mine safety and other occupational hazards, pollution scandals, and growing numbers of auto deaths.[27] Weak state parties and candidate-centered electoral politics meant that senators and governors often competed for public attention and campaign contributions from many of the same citizens and institutions, a situation that often led to a convergence in their issue agendas—which, from the states' perspective, meant an encroachment on traditional state functions.

Conservative Reaction and Its Limits

After Republican gains in the 1978 congressional elections, and especially after President Reagan's election in 1980, the expanding size and roles of the federal government became an issue in itself. As Reagan said in his 1981 inaugural speech, "government is not the solution to our problem; government is the problem"; and, "It is my intention to curb the size and influence of the Federal establishment and to demand recognition of the distinction between the powers granted to the Federal government and those reserved to the States or to the people."

In short-run fiscal terms, Reagan saw some success. The nearly uninterrupted postwar expansion of grant programs came to an end. As Figure 1 shows, the real value of federal assistance declined precipitously from 1979 to 1983. Reagan's efforts produced the 1981 Omnibus Budget Reconciliation Act (OBRA), which eliminated many Great Society grants, cut benefits and eligibility under Aid to Families with Dependent Children (AFDC), and consolidated 77 categorical programs into 9 block grants. As a result of these and other initiatives, the number of categorical grants declined from 534 in 1981 to 392 in 1984, while the number of block grants rose from 5 to 12 over the same three years.[28] During Reagan's administration, spending was cut for grants supporting education and training, employment, and social services; community and regional development; general government (including revenue sharing); and natural resources and the environment. Medicaid and other "entitlement" programs still grew, though more slowly due to cuts in eligibility or benefits. By the end of the 1980s, as Figure 1 shows, federal assistance showed a much less diverse pattern of spending than found in the late 1970s.

But the political attractions of using regulations to produce policy change in the American federal system remained strong, and the most intrusive and constitutionally suspect method of regulation, direct orders, became the most common regulatory instrument in the 1980s.[29] Most of the new regulations expanded existing programs, such as environmental requirements.[30] But some of the laws broke new policy ground, such as the Drug-Free Workplace Act of 1988, which required certification by all federal grantees and contractors that their workplaces were drug-free and that they offered anti-drug programs for employees.

In sum, Reagan and the Congresses of the 1980s did not oppose federal power as much as they opposed federal spending. But the locus of national power did shift, away from the legislative process and toward the executive branch. With respect to grants, executive power moved upward, from agency administrators to the Office of Management and Budget. Block granting enhanced the influence of central clearance processes and federal budget policies in relations between the federal executive and the states. With respect to intergovernmental regulations, the Reagan presidency was distinctive in its reliance on administrative rather than legislative means to achieve its goals.[31] Rather than asking Congress to pass new laws or amend old ones, the administration altered federal regulatory policies through administrative rule making, selective cuts in federal staffing, aggressive reviews by the Office of Management and Budget of the costs and benefits of agency actions, and appointments of ideological allies to top agency posts.[32] Sometimes these management powers were used to reduce regulatory burdens, and sometimes to tighten controls. What was clear, however, was that the choices regarding the severity and character of federal control over the states were increasingly in the hands of top political executives and the presidency.

Devolution and the New Accountability

A final period of federal expansion occurred under the George H. W. Bush administration and continued through the Clinton and George W. Bush administrations. Intergovernmental regulations were extended, including the Clean Air Act of 1990, the Religious Freedom Reformation Act of 1993 (replaced in 2000 with the Religious Land Use and Institutionalized Persons Act), and tighter blood-alcohol standards in determining drunk driving as a condition for federal highway aid. Federal spending on grants resumed rapid growth, though most of the growth came from only a few grants. Medicaid alone accounted for 63 percent of the growth in total federal grant spending between 1989 and 2003. This lopsided pattern of spending altered the distribution of federal grants. In 1989, health care spending constituted only 30 percent of total federal grants to state and local governments. By 2003, health care programs made up about half of all federal grant expenditures.

This uneven growth in federal grants produced a major divide in the financial role of the federal government in state and local functions. As Table 1 demonstrates, federal grants as a percentage of state and local expenditures fell in the 1980s and rebounded slightly in the 1990s. But these overall changes were the result of two very different trends. Federal funding of health and human service programs grew, especially between 1990 and 2000, largely as a result of Medicaid. By contrast, federal funding of all other state and local expenditures—including education, transportation, criminal justice, and environmental protection—declined from 18 percent in 1980 to 11 percent in 1990 and 2000. Thus, the federal government may use federal funding as leverage in efforts to control the states in health and human service programs, but federal fiscal bargaining power has weakened in most other policy areas.[33]

The 1990s also saw important changes in the characteristics of grants. Some have called this a period of devolution, when states were given greater discretion in how they implemented federal programs. Medicaid, for example, was used as a source of funding for an ever-expanding variety of health services and institutions. Coverage of mental health and special education services grew during these years under federal "waivers" (discussed below), as did support for health institutions, such as general-purpose grants to hospitals serving low-income people.

In addition, several block grants were created that offered state and local governments flexibility in their use of federal dollars. In 1991, President George H. W. Bush signed the Intermodal Surface Transportation Efficiency Act (ISTEA), which gave state and local governments greater control over the nation's transportation system.[34] ISTEA established a block grant, allowing state and local governments to transfer funds from one program to another—such as highways and mass transit systems—in order to implement comprehensive trans-

TABLE 1

Federal Grants-in-Aid as a Percentage of State and Local Spending, by Function, 1980, 1990, 2000.

Year	Total spending	Spending on public welfare (including health)	Spending on non–public–welfare
1980	23%	55%	18%
1990	17%	56%	11%
2000	19%	64%	11%

SOURCE: U.S. Census Bureau, Annual Survey of Government Finances.

portation strategies. These characteristics were generally retained by ISTEA's successor program, TEA-21, enacted in 1998 under the Clinton administration. Two other block grants were also enacted in the late 1990s: the Workforce Investment Act (1998), which consolidated several employment and training programs, and the Children's Health Insurance Program (1997), which allowed states to create programs covering low-income children who lacked health insurance.

State flexibility, however, was just one facet of a new model for grants. Some grants imposed a new form of accountability on states by attaching financial penalties or rewards to performance standards, that is, outcomes for people, communities, or institutions related to a program's goals.[35] One example was the 1996 block grant, Temporary Assistance for Needy Families (TANF), which replaced Aid to Families with Dependent Children (AFDC). TANF was designed to reduce long-term welfare dependency by getting low-income parents to work, discouraging out-of-wedlock births, and promoting marriage. These goals were to be achieved in part by restricting assistance to low-income families. Benefits were time-limited, adults had to work, and teen parents were to stay in school and live with their parents.

But there was also a strong experimental element in TANF. TANF delegated many policy choices to states, such as how earnings and assets were treated in calculating eligibility and benefits; whether to withhold benefits from unmarried teen mothers; and whether benefits would be in-kind supports, services, or cash. States were also given flexibility in procedures for dealing with clients and in the agencies used to deliver benefits and services. States were allowed to contract with nonprofit and for-profit organizations—including faith-based institutions, such as churches—to administer their TANF programs, in sharp contrast to AFDC, which required states to use public agencies with merit systems.

In exchange for this flexibility, states were to meet performance requirements and were encouraged to achieve other measurable outcomes. States had to increase the proportion of adults on assistance engaged in "work-related activities," such as job search and actual employment. If states failed to achieve these work requirements, their block grants were cut. A high-performance bonus rewarded top-performing states on selected outcomes, such as job retention rates among former welfare recipients—outcomes determined by federal agency officials working with state trade associations. Financial rewards were also given to states that reduced their out-of-wedlock birth rates.

Finally, another block grant, the No Child Left Behind Act (NCLB)—proposed by President George W. Bush and enacted in 2002—also stressed national accountability through performance measurement and fiscal sanctions. According to the administration's 2002 *Economic Report of the President,* NCLB expressed the basic idea that American federalism should

> create an institutional framework that will encourage the development of measurable standards to which all providers of public services— Federal and local, public and private—can be held accountable, and then to allow these providers themselves to find the best way to meet those standards.[36]

NCLB was the reauthorized version of a centerpiece of the Great Society, the Elementary and Secondary Education Act (ESEA) of 1965, which provided federal dollars to local schools serving minority and low-income students. NCLB gave states flexibility in spending federal dollars to produce educational improvements. But the flexibility came with unprecedented accountability requirements. States had to install annual reading and mathematics tests and demonstrate annual progress toward proficiency in these subjects among all students *and* among disadvantaged groups. Indeed, states were expected to achieve universal proficiency by 2014. If schools and districts did not meet these targets, they faced sanctions, including giving parents the options to leave "failing" schools, closing schools altogether, and losing federal funds.

One effect of performance requirements was a decoupling of federal funding levels from the true costs of the programs. In traditional grants, the federal government shared the costs of a grant program as long as it satisfied federal administrative and policy guidelines. Under performance-based grants, however, Congress imposed ambitious goals on states with little certainty about how much money was needed to achieve the mandated outcomes. For example, many observers believed NCLB funding was inadequate to its tasks.[37] One estimate of the costs to Texas of achieving the goals mandated by NCLB concluded that the state needed three times the actual increase in federal funding provided to Texas.[38] Some supporters of NCLB disagreed; they argued that increased accountability should suffice to improve performance.[39] But the analytical disagreement underlines the federalism problem: when performance measures are attached to grants, typically little is known about how much it costs to achieve them. By disconnecting mandated state activities and federal funding, grants like NCLB place uncertain fiscal burdens on states, create incentives for evading performance requirements, or do both.

Devolution also enhanced the powers of federal executive officials. They acquired new intergovernmental tools, such as negotiations of performance indicators, annual reviews of outcomes, and determinations of sanctions. Some programs also gave federal officials larger research budgets, which they could use to evaluate new programs and thus direct attention to particular innovations. Also, by permitting states to vary their policies and administrative approaches, devolution created a more mutable and potentially malleable system of policy making. Federal executives may, as discussed below, use various methods to influence the growing range of state choices, encouraging some policy and administrative developments and discouraging others—and do all this with little input from Congress.

Growing State Capacity and Democratization

While the federal government came to rely on states to pursue many of its domestic policies through grants and regulations, it also became more dependent on state governmental resources and their administrative, fiscal, and policy-making capacities. Strong states were, in brief, a by-product of federal activism. The increasing capabilities and political openness of the states, in turn, shifted power within the federal government, as vigorous state governments challenged congressional controls and opened opportunities for the federal executive branch to manage the increasingly complicated interactions between the national and state governments.

Federal administrative dependence on state and local governments may be seen in part by tracing the growth of their bureaucracies. In terms of employment, state and local governments are more dominant now than they were seventy years ago, before the New Deal went into effect. Table 2 reveals that the number of federal government employees grew rapidly in the 1930s and 1940s but little thereafter (see the chapter by Patricia Ingraham in this volume). The number of state and local government employees, by contrast, increased substantially every ten-year period except between 1983 and 1993. By 2003, only 15 percent of all civilian public employees in the United States worked for the federal government.

States enhanced their institutional capacities in many other ways during the twentieth century. Early in the century, improvements were driven by citizen demands for remedies to social problems that local governments were unable or unwilling to address.[40] The "good roads" movement, for example, grew out of discontent with the terrible conditions of major roads and highways and led to a great expansion of state involvement in the building of roads, highways, and parks to meet the demands of the swelling number of automobile and truck drivers. Many other reforms in state governmental institutions occurred as the federal government imposed greater demands on their operations.[41]

TABLE 2

Civilian Government Employees in Federal and in State and Local Governments, 1933–2003.

Year	Number of federal government employees (in thousands)	Number of state and local government employees (in thousands)	Percent of all public employees in federal government
1933	591	2,601	18%
1943	3,274	3,174	51%
1953	2,532	4,340	37%
1963	2,498	6,868	27%
1973	2,886	11,097	21%
1983	2,875	13,159	18%
1993	2,999	13,443	18%
2003	2,717	15,760	15%

SOURCE: U.S. Census Bureau, Annual Survey of Government Employment and Payroll.

The 1960s and 1970s saw an acceleration of the reform movement, as state governments were forced to become more responsive to a wider range of political interests. Spurred by *Baker v. Carr* (1962) and related Supreme Court decisions, states reapportioned their legislatures to comply with the "one man, one vote" standard and opened their legislatures to growing suburban and urban populations. Reapportionment produced changes in legislative leadership, which led state legislatures to adopt other reforms, including annual sessions, committee consolidation, higher pay, and more staff.[42] States also began to reorganize their executive branches in the mid-1960s.[43] They consolidated executive agencies into larger line agencies under the direct control of the governor, reduced the number of elective cabinet officers, increased the number of political executives appointed by governors, and strengthened governors' budgetary powers.[44]

Gubernatorial terms lengthened throughout the postwar period, giving governors time to formulate and build on policy initiatives. While fifteen states still had two-year gubernatorial terms in 1964, only two states did not elect governors to four-year terms by 2000. Turnover among governors declined throughout the twentieth century, especially in the second half. Reflecting in part the growing policy importance of governorships, gubernatorial elections became vigorously contested. Total gubernatorial elections expenditures more than doubled in constant dollars between 1977–1980 and 1999–2002.[45]

State governors and administrative officials also became better organized. The National Governor's Association (NGA) and other intergovernmental lobbies grew in strength and activities, as did specialized associations of state and local officials involved in specific policy areas.[46] By the 1990s, the National Governors Association had become the dominant national voice on many human service programs, a role revealed in 2003 when the NGA effectively vetoed the Bush administration's first proposal to block-grant Medicaid. State policy-making autonomy was also enhanced by the growing availability of policy expertise from national policy communities, think tanks, foundations, interest groups, and other institutions involved in formulating and diffusing policy ideas.[47]

State fiscal capacities have grown markedly in recent decades. States greatly increased their reliance on sales and income taxes since the 1950s and decreased their dependence on property taxes, which had always been politically difficult to raise. The development of a broad-based and growing tax base meant that states could sustain their own spending priorities, even in the aftermath of severe federal budget cuts, as they did in the 1980s.[48] States could even compensate for chronic federal underfunding. Since the early 1990s, for example, federal environmental grants changed little in real terms, despite the growth of state responsibilities. States responded by increasing their own spending, to the point that they now pay about 80 percent of the costs of federal environmental programs.[49]

Their greater political, administrative, and fiscal capacities have led many states to fashion their own policy responses to major problems. In the 1980s, states were on the forefront of efforts to deal with worker dislocation and retraining, when federal officials paid little attention to such issues.[50] Interest in economic development has sometimes led states to take on novel functions, such as California's decision in 2004 to fund stem cell research in order to draw academic researchers and biotech businesses unhappy with the Bush administration's restrictions on federal research grants. States showed leadership in energy policies in the 1970s, 1980s, and early 2000s—the most recent years in response to electricity reliability problems, environmental concerns, and energy price spikes.[51] Some states have even addressed the problem of global warming, while the federal government has done little, despite all the theoretical reasons that one would expect states to ignore such an issue.[52] The openness and capacities of state political institutions, combined with the growth of federal involvement in so many domestic issues, produced by the late twentieth century an extremely dynamic, less constrained system of federalism—one in which it would be difficult to identify any major domestic policy issue in the United States that has not penetrated both federal and state political agendas. Federal and state governments may be more than ever "different agents and trustees of the people." But one would be hard put to identify their "different purposes."

Congress and the States

As state and federal policy agendas converge, and as state governments increase their institutional capacities and political assertiveness, it is reasonable to ask how conflicts between the federal and state governments are resolved, if in fact they ever are. How does the federal government exercise real influence over state governments, and through which institutions, in this amorphous federal system of widespread assertions of national authority and vigorous state governments?

Despite its assertions of federal authority over so many domestic policy areas through legislation, Congress appears to play a smaller role in resolving intergovernmental issues. Indeed, the factors that made it easier for Congress to extend its authority also limited its real influence. Heavy reliance on state and local implementation, a shrinking federal domestic bureaucracy, federal funding that is poorly correlated with the costs of achieving national goals, and the failure to resolve many divisive policy issues, often by devolving major questions to state and local governments, all facilitated legislative action while weakening legislative control.

For example, members of Congress may claim credit for dealing with national problems when they impose new goals on state governments. But the same devolution that makes the enactment of such programs feasible also denies members political credit for whatever successes the programs achieve. Few votes are likely to be reaped by sustaining an "institutional framework" for *states* to succeed or fail. TANF is a good example. It was widely lauded as reducing welfare caseloads, increasing the labor participation rates of unmarried women with children, and creating a politically popular rationale (i.e., supporting work) for programs serving low-income families. However, political credit for these developments has gone largely to the states, not to Congress, with the result that many members have cared little about the program's reauthorization, which has dragged along in a fairly desultory manner since 2002.

Indeed, in recent years, Congress has failed to reauthorize many intergovernmental programs—sometimes because of difficult conflicts, sometimes because of a lack of interest among many members, and sometimes (as in the case of TANF) a combination of both. Congress has sustained some of these programs through annual appropriations or short-run reauthorizations.[53] The Child Care and Development Block Grant, the Safe Drinking Water Act, and the Clean Air Act have been sustained only through the annual appropriations process. Short-run program extensions—usually a few weeks or months, with little or no changes in the law—have been used in recent years to maintain TEA-21 (surface transportation), the Workforce Investment Act, and child nutrition programs, as well as TANF.

In addition, states' dominance of the implementation process means that states can often evade or "game" federal requirements. The federal government has few sources of in-depth information on the implementation of programs apart from what states tell them. In such circumstances, it is not surprising that states can adapt these requirements to their own ends. Job training program administrators have long been accused of "cream skimming"—of achieving high program performance scores, such as the percentage of persons served who find employment, by only serving people easy to employ.[54] Most accusations of state gaming, however, have concerned how federal dollars were used.[55] The General Accountability Office estimated that about 60 percent of federal highway grants were used, albeit indirectly, for other purposes.[56] States have been particularly creative in drawing down Medicaid funds. Some states have "taxed" hospitals serving many low-income clients, used the taxes as state matching money under Medicaid, received federal dollars as a result of the state match, and then returned the "tax" to the hospitals, while the state retained the extra federal dollars. Congress has, from time to time, clamped down on these "Medicaid maximization" strategies. But states have invented new ones.[57]

Nor are there always strong incentives among members of Congress to determine whether states satisfy requirements. Program advocates may reasonably believe that imposing penalties on noncompliant states would hurt program recipients, frustrate program goals, and further reduce states' political support for the program. Members may also have different feelings about imposing prospective costs on all states—as when they enact a new regulation—and seeing their particular states penalized for noncompliance. For example, even though Congress established strict penalties for states that made errors in determining eligibility and benefits under the Food Stamp Program, Congress has repeatedly reduced those penalties after they were levied.[58]

Finally, all of these barriers to legislative control are compounded by the declining importance of federal grant funds in most policy areas, and the discrepancies between federal funding and demanding federal mandates. In 2005, for example, Utah risked losing federal dollars offered under the No Child Left Behind Act by subordinating NCLB requirements to state policies, an action several other states were also considering as of in mid-2005. Rejection of NCLB's demands was no doubt made easier by the small role of federal funding in K-12 education systems.

Congress is not without recourse. It could give up efforts at real control and simply contain its fiscal liabilities by creating more block grants, which usually lose real value over time.[59] Or it could turn to the federal courts to enforce and adapt the laws. Congress has never funded more than a small percentage of special education services mandated under the Education for All Handicapped Children Act of 1975.[60] However, the act has had an enormous impact on state and local education budgets because Congress gave parents opportunities to challenge school decisions, and gave federal courts the authority to define which students were "disabled" and what protections they deserved. Private rights of action have been a critical enforcement mechanism against subnational governments for many other federal laws. However, the Rehnquist Court may be curtailing their use.[61]

Executive Federalism

Although the federal executive branch is, like the Congress, also limited in its ability to control the states, it nonetheless has strengths in this regard that are not found in the national legislative process. The executive branch has acquired many administrative tools that federal executives may use to influence state and local governments, including rule making or other methods of interpreting the law; discretion over project grants, demonstrations, and other grants directly controlled by federal agencies; waivers or other exemptions from the laws; contracts or grants to evaluate program innovations; and selective enforcement of federal requirements. In addition, the executive branch can apply its powers to the states in ways that Congress cannot. It can adapt quickly to state policy developments, act on selected states, and build on state reactions to federal initiatives—thereby using state changes and variations to discourage developments it opposes and to facilitate those it supports. The executive can also act in a concerted manner across several programs or even policy areas—as in the case of President Bush's Faith-Based Initiative—by using key federal appointments to bring new goals to bear on many decisions affecting the states.

The strategic exercise of executive powers to promote major changes in state policies or administrative practices is what we call "executive federalism." Its growing use has given rise to new intergovernmental dynamics. Presidents and their appointees have been able to produce significant changes in program management, coverage, and standards without new legislation. Even large policy changes depend less on major shifts in control over Congress—such as those produced by the elections of 1932–1936, 1964, and 1980—and more on control of the presidency and governorships and the conditions facing the states.

Executive federalism comes in many forms. Some involve particularistic negotiations between the federal executive and selected states over prospective policy changes, as in the case of federal waivers and demonstration projects. Most involve efforts by presidents and executive appointees to alter the context of state policy making and administration in order to influence state choices. These contextual changes may be effected through rule making and other policy interpretations, or through comprehensive managerial strategies, in which appointments, procedures, contracts, and other methods are used in combination to create new priorities in intergovernmental programs.

One common characteristic of these different forms is the fact that they do not require legions of federal staff. Waivers require a few policy and legal experts, as well as some research methodologists to review evaluation plans. Rule-making and policy memoranda demand legal and policy analysts. And management strategies, such as the Bush administration's Faith-Based Initiative, may require new staff for a few top positions. But all of these functions are consistent with the current, relatively small federal bureaucracy.

Waivers

The most common administrative device that presidents and federal executives have used to change the operation of grant programs has been the waiver. A waiver is a grant of authority by Congress to a federal agency to permit selective enforcement of a law. Acts establishing domestic grant programs often allow federal agencies to suspend normal program requirements under certain circumstances: to experiment with and evaluate demonstration programs; improve program administration; or provide services or cover groups other than those authorized in the legislation. Federal agencies have developed policies and procedures under which waivers are granted, and presidents and their appointees have manipulated these rules to pursue particular program changes.

One of the most influential series of waivers were those granted in the 1980s and 1990s permitting states to change their policies under Aid to Families with Dependent Children (AFDC).[62] Although federal authority to grant AFDC waivers had existed since 1962, they were rare until the Reagan administration established a Low Income Opportunity Advisory Board (LIOAB) in the White House to ease federal review of waiver requests. The Reagan administration did not use waivers to push particular policy preferences but focused on program evaluation and budget neutrality (waivers could not cost the federal government more than continuing the AFDC program).[63] The first Bush administration revived the practice of issuing extensive AFDC waivers in 1992, when it used them to respond to then-Governor Clinton's campaign to "end welfare as we know it."

When the Clinton administration took office, it encouraged waivers containing more radical departures from existing policies. Governors responded enthusiastically. Tommy Thompson of Wisconsin and John Engler of Michigan saw opportunities to create national reputations for policy leadership, hardly a hopeless gesture when three out of the last four presidents had been governors (now, four out of the last five).[64] Governors also saw waivers as opportunities to claim credit for getting special recognition from Washington—and as timely intergovernmental devices in dealing with state problems. Despite complaints about delays in federal approvals, waivers allowed governors to respond quickly and specifically to the circumstances they faced in the early 1990s—rising welfare caseloads in many states, and budget crises in some.

Waivers, when implemented, broke down the ideological stalemate in the national legislative process by demonstrating the political, administrative, and economic feasibility of new welfare policies, such as time limits on benefits and work requirements with severe sanctions.[65] By 1996, when President Clinton estimated that 75 percent of AFDC recipients were involved in waivers, he not unreasonably claimed that he and the states had already reformed welfare while the legislative process in Washington had bogged down. Many factors were important in explaining the enactment of federal welfare reforms in 1996.[66] But the waivers were essential, and they showed the potential for selective demonstrations and diffusion processes—encouraged and facilitated by a highly interactive form of executive federalism—to reshape a divisive national debate.

Waivers have been no less important in shaping the Medicaid program since the early 1990s. Indeed, they have constituted the primary device by which federal-state health policy changes were made. Perhaps the largest change in the operation and financing of Medicaid in the last fifteen years has been the shifting of clients, particularly low-income women and children, from the program's original fee-for-service form into managed care. Under managed care, a health maintenance organization or similar entity receives a fixed payment to serve an individual for a certain period of time. Since 1991, the percentage of Medicaid clients enrolled in managed care grew from less than 10 percent to nearly 60 percent in 2003.[67]

This enormous change was almost entirely the result of Medicaid waivers. Legislative provisions allowing managed care waivers had existed for many years, but the Health Care Financing Administration (HCFA; now the Center for Medicare and Medicaid Services, CMS) had approved only small projects in which enrollment in managed care was voluntary.[68] As governors struggled to slow the rapid growth in Medicaid spending in the early 1990s, President Clinton encouraged states to submit, and the HCFA to approve, waivers permitting large managed care programs in which enrollment by Medicaid clients was mandatory.

Beginning in the late 1980s, Medicaid waivers also allowed states to move many elderly and mentally disabled recipients out of nursing homes and state institutions and into home and community-based services. Such services were thought to be more effective and cheaper than long-term institutional care. These waivers grew dramatically during the Clinton administration, from 155 in 1991 to 263 in 2001, and the number of clients receiving home and community-based services tripled.[69]

The George W. Bush administration continued this practice of using waivers, rather than legislation, as a means of changing Medicaid policy. One of the administration's first domestic policy initiatives, announced in August 2001, was the Health Insurance Flexibility and Accountability (HIFA) waiver. These waivers allowed states to expand health insurance coverage by shifting funds from other parts of Medicaid or the Children's Health Insurance Program (CHIP), or by reducing coverage of other groups.[70] For example, the administration has granted state waiver requests to use unspent funds from the CHIP program, which was enacted to expand coverage for children, in order to expand coverage for adults.[71]

The Bush administration has also welcomed state efforts to limit coverage and benefits for Medicaid recipients through the waiver process. CMS has approved waiver requests that cap Medicaid enrollment for some groups, cut benefits, and increase the premiums and copayments charged to Medicaid patients. The agency has, for example, approved a controversial proposal from Mississippi to eliminate Medicaid coverage for some low-income elderly and disabled residents.[72] The Bush administration has also encouraged waivers to provide prescription drugs for low-income elderly while requiring states to limit spending for *all* elderly recipients.

Waivers are found in many other federal programs. For many years, legislation authorizing programs administered by the U. S. Department of Education contained no waiver provisions. In 1994, however, new legislation included waiver provisions, and the department began to grant waivers at a rapid clip, issuing more than 500 between 1995 and 1999.[73] The No Child Left Behind Act extended broad authority to the secretary of education to grant waivers to limited numbers of state and local education agencies to consolidate and redirect funds and suspend a wide range of program requirements. Waivers were also used under the Food Stamp Program to suspend time limits and work requirements for adult recipients.[74] Beginning in 1994, the U.S. Department of Labor (DOL) used workforce development waivers and demonstration grants to encourage states to establish one-stop service centers, before Congress mandated such institutions under the Workforce Investment Act of 1998—which also gave extensive waiver authority to the DOL.[75]

Some federal agencies offer instruments similar to waivers, even if they are not called such. The Environmental Protection Agency (EPA) under Clinton permitted its regional officials and state administrators to negotiate agreements and grants under the National Environmental Performance Partnership System. Performance partnership grants (PPGs) allowed states to combine funds from up to 13 different environmental protection grants to address each state's needs and to promote innovation. In 1998, forty-three states had negotiated PPGs. Performance partnership agreements covered negotiated decisions about specific goals, strategies, performance measures, and responsibilities of federal and state administrators. EPA officials have also used "differential oversight" and "accountable devolution" to give greater autonomy to states with strong enforcement histories.[76]

The popularity of waivers and other forms of selective enforcement is easy to understand. States are unequal in their administrative ability and political and financial circumstances, and waivers allow states that can operate innovative programs to move ahead without imposing burdens on states that cannot. Waivers also allow presidents to pursue controversial policy goals without seeking approval from a slow and divisive legislative process. By permitting a few, often small-scale, demonstrations to be implemented, uncertainty is reduced about the effects and feasibility of even major policy innovations, and politicians in other states and in the federal government may be led to accept the initiatives. Waivers may also allow presidents to help political friends among the nation's governors and punish enemies by withholding or delaying approval or insisting on onerous conditions attached to waivers. Finally, waivers provide governors with opportunities for political credit-claiming that are not available when they simply exercise flexibility expressly offered to all states under federal legislation.

The waiver process also neutralizes congressional scrutiny by enlisting the delegations of individual states as supporters of their states' waiver requests.[77] State delegations are expected to support waiver requests from their state and to lobby federal agencies to approve the waiver. Steven Teles observed that "members of Congress generally function as their state's advocate in Washington, protecting and advocating their state's interest much as they would in the case of a defense contract or toxic waste clean-up grant."[78]

Waivers have thus enhanced presidential control of domestic policy and have diminished congressional influence. Presidents have used the waiver process to enact significant changes in program policies and operations in many programs without legislative changes, and congressional oversight of these changes is weakened by the need for individual delegations to support requests from their own states.

Rule Making

Executive federalism is also exercised through the rule-making powers of the federal executive, as well as less formal methods of interpreting statutes to the states. Administrative rules may be overturned by Congress—though they typically are not—yet they sometimes produce major changes in intergovernmental programs.

One example was the promulgation in 1999 of rules interpreting the 1996 federal program, Temporary Assistance for Needy Families. As it was enacted by the 104th Congress and signed into law by President Clinton in 1996, TANF discouraged "dependence" on public benefits among low-income families with children. Adult recipients could receive assistance no longer than 60 months in their lifetimes. By 2002, half of each state's caseload had to be participating more than 30 hours per week in a limited number of work-related activities (which allowed few educational activities). Adults could receive assistance no longer than two years without working, and families on assistance assigned child support rights to the state. States also had to collect extensive data from people on assistance and report the information to the federal government.

If these and related requirements applied to all activities funded by TANF, states would have had little flexibility to use the block grant to supplement earnings, support education, provide job services widely, or offer child care and other work supports to families who left cash assistance rolls. But the Clinton administration promulgated a rule in 1999 interpreting the TANF legislation that made these approaches possible. A central feature was the rule's definition of "assistance" and "nonassistance." By narrowly defining assistance as benefits meeting a family's "ongoing basic needs"—such as food, clothing, shelter, and utilities—the rule allowed states to use TANF funds for many kinds of "nonassistance" without applying the time limits, narrow work requirements, or administratively costly reporting requirements for TANF "assistance." Many states could thus fashion less restrictive programs than many congressional proponents of TANF had anticipated.

For example, "assistance" did not encompass earned income tax credit programs for working families, and about one-third of the states established such programs to supplement the earnings of working families.[79] Many states expanded their child care and transportation benefits to families that left cash assistance rolls, sometimes offering years of support to former recipients. Some states also developed a variety of lump-sum "diversion" benefits that might equal three or four months of cash benefits, yet these did not count against a family's time limits. One result was an enormous shift in the types of expenditures under TANF between 1998 and 2000. In 1998, the typical or median state put 59 percent of its total TANF expenditures into basic assistance, mostly ongoing cash payments to poor families, while it put only 7 percent of its spending into child care. Just two years later, in 2000, the median state devoted only 43 percent of its TANF spending to basic assistance and 24 percent to child care. Although other factors contributed to these changes, rule making by the Clinton administration made the restrictions on assistance much less important than anticipated by the program's congressional proponents.[80]

The effects of this rule making in transforming TANF into a more flexible work support program—at least among states inclined to do so—were augmented by other actions by the Clinton administration. The administration permitted many states to continue their AFDC waiver programs after TANF was enacted. Under the waivers, a wider range of activities were counted as "work" than the TANF rules permitted, including participation in educational and training activities. The administration also allowed states to avoid having to meet the demanding work participation requirements for two-parent families by permitting them to move two-parent families to programs supported exclusively with state dollars, a shift that made the federal work participation rates inapplicable—despite language in TANF that seemed to prohibit such evasions.

Clinton's administration also mitigated the antidependency thrust found in the 1996 federal welfare reforms by using policy statements to make federal entitlements more accessible. Spurred by drops in Food Stamp and Medicaid enrollments, federal officials in the Department of Agriculture and HCFA took several administrative actions to increase access to both programs.[81] For example, HCFA officials sent a steady stream of messages to state Medicaid officials, reminding them that efforts to reduce welfare caseloads should not affect application or case closure processes for Medicaid; instructing them on legal ways of maximizing

Medicaid access; and promising lenient treatment in the federal quality-control process for state mistakes in determining eligibility. Not all states responded to federal efforts to expand participation in Medicaid and Food Stamps, but many did, and enrollments in both programs rose quickly.

Management Strategies

Another intriguing use of executive power to influence the federal system was a cluster of administrative activities that President George W. Bush labeled his "Faith-Based Initiative" (see also Chapter 1 by Scott James in this volume). President Bush was deeply interested in promoting partnerships between government and congregations or social service providers with overt religious aims and approaches. The White House supported legislation in Congress in 2001–2002 to reduce legal barriers to the direct involvement of faith-based organizations in providing social services with public (i.e., federal) funds. But the legislation languished in the Senate, which was then controlled by Democrats.

The Bush White House, however, never waited for legislation to advance the Faith-Based Initiative.[82] Nine days after his inauguration, President Bush issued two executive orders creating the White House Office of Faith-Based and Community Initiatives (WHOFBCI) and additional centers for FBCI in five federal agencies, the departments of Education, Health and Human Services, Housing and Urban Development, Justice, and Labor. Later executive orders added FBCI offices at the Agency for International Development; the Departments of Agriculture, Commerce, and Veterans Affairs; and the Small Business Administration. The combination of the White House Office and closely connected offices in ten government agencies, each with a carefully selected director and staff, was aimed at penetrating all agency operations affecting the goal of getting public financial support to faith-based groups as social service providers.

The White House and agency offices tried to get more grants to faith-based organizations (FBOs) by eliminating perceived agency barriers to their involvement and by increasing the capacity of FBOs to compete for grants at all levels of government. Administrative rules overturned two longstanding restrictions on religious institutions that received public funds: against using government money to build and renovate places of worship, and against using religious belief as a criterion in recruiting and retaining staff. The White House published reports on the "unlevel playing field" that FBOs faced in securing public dollars, and the president talked about the initiative and its aims at public occasions.

In the agencies, FBCI offices estimated the number of federal grants going to FBOs and secular organizations in order to document the "problem." They looked for federal grants—mostly project grants under the direct control of federal agencies—that could be used to expand FBO involvement. They identified barriers against religious participation and used rule making and persuasion to eliminate them. And the administration established a new program, the Compassion Capital Fund, which supported "intermediary" organizations that made "subgrants to faith-based and community organizations; train[ed] small faith-based and community groups in grant writing, staff development, and management; and help[ed] them network and collaborate."[83]

The Faith-Based Initiative did not directly change state and local laws. But the use of strategic appointments to change policies, procedures, and contracts—all to demonstrate the potential roles of FBOs, to build their skills and experiences in getting and using public funds, and to keep the issue before the public—was clearly intended to influence state and local governments, which controlled most social service contracts. The White House exploited an impressive array of administrative tools not only to demonstrate a new direction for grant making but also to mobilize and train a national constituency to compete for public funds in states and localities. Although it is too early to tell, this orchestration of administrative and presidential activities may have altered perceptions about the potential roles of FBOs at all levels of government.[84]

Conclusions

Divided sovereignty was not conceptually problematic in the early years of the republic, when constitutional, political, economic, and societal factors limited the role of the national government and its functional overlap with the states. But after many of these constraints eroded and were eventually broken by the New Deal and later waves of national legislation, the policy agendas of federal and state governments converged, as the federal government used grants and regulations to enter new domestic policy arenas.

This expansion of federal authority, however, produced an asymmetry between the federal government's authority and its fiscal and administrative powers. That is, the flip side of federal reliance on states to facilitate national action has been the dependence of the federal government on state implementation, administration, and funding. In addition to their administrative dominance, states have also increased their political capacities—their claims to political representativeness and their connections with constituencies—through, among other things, reapportionment and the increasing public salience and powers of governors.

The combination of extensive federal authority over a wide range of domestic policies, federal dependence on state implementation, and democratized and politically assertive states has contributed to a shift in national power over the federal system from the legislative process to the executive branch. Legislative processes have lost strength in controlling state bureaucracies and policy makers. Intergovernmental influence increasingly demands an adaptive, selective application of diverse tools—tools that federal administrators may marshal on priority issues but that legislative actions are less adept at manipulating. Presidents and top administrators may, if they wish, exploit a wide array of administrative mechanisms to achieve their policy aims on selected issues—through the concerted use of waivers, rule making, direct grants to selected organizations, demonstration projects, direct contracting, appointments, and other means.

This shift in the locus of national action from the legislative process to the executive branch on federalism issues also represents a culmination of changing roles performed by the federal executive with respect to the states. In the New Deal years and thereafter, the federal bureaucracy nurtured support for federal grant programs, urged states to professionalize and centralize their administration of such programs, and built bureaucratic allies within state bureaucracies to influence state policies. The Great Society years brought increasing discretion to the federal government in distributing grants—through project grants and grant provisions allowing federal agencies to give funds directly to nonprofits—and more detailed control over program planning and implementation. Then, beginning with the 1970s, intergovernmental regulations and grants with major regulatory provisions increased opportunities for federal agencies to interpret laws through administrative rules and to determine whether particular states had standards and enforcement powers sufficient to delegate regulatory powers. After waivers and other opportunities for particularized negotiations between state and federal governments began to be used widely in the 1980s and early 1990s, federal administrators and presidents had acquired a large repertoire of methods they could use to change the contexts for state decisions and to encourage the development and diffusion of major policy initiatives without congressional involvement.

This growing autonomy of federal executive powers and actions alters the dynamics of federalism. Major nationwide changes in policies no longer depend on electoral shifts in the control of the Congress, including increases or decreases in policy agreement and partisan ties between Congress and the president. Instead, control over the presidency and a few governorships can be a sufficient base to launch important policy innovations. The administrative mechanisms may often produce only small changes at each step. But federal executives may build on incremental changes—whether through rule changes, demonstration grants, waivers, evaluations, or other mechanisms—to develop new policies in sympathetic states, to focus media attention on innovative ideas, to show political opponents that the initiatives do not produce worst-case scenarios, and to demonstrate to political allies and constituencies the potential political benefits of the policies. Indeed, the ideas may originally come from the states themselves—along with critical information on how to implement them—and federal executives may selectively nurture policies they find agreeable. American federalism may thus display a more continuous process of innovation, demonstration, and diffusion.

But this mutability and flexibility may come at a price. While legislative federalism frequently produced larger coalitions than might have formed in a more centralized system, executive federalism exploits state differences in order to construct smaller policy coalitions between federal political executives and a few governors sympathetic to a national administration's goals. And while legislative federalism often created common and fairly stable frameworks within which states could exercise controlled choice and carry out long-term planning and implementation of complex policies, executive federalism may alter these frameworks with every new presidential administration—even new Cabinet and sub-Cabinet appointments—and eventually break the frameworks down altogether. By loosening the American federal system from legislative control, executive federalism may create a more uncertain, more varied, and less transparent context for state policy making. Some states may fare well under such a system, and some may not. But it is likely that differences in what they do and how effectively they do it will increase across states and over time.

Notes

*The authors wish to thank Vandana Prakash for her assistance with this chapter. They also thank David Balducchi, Bill Gormley, Scott James, Cathy Johnson, and especially Martha Derthick for excellent comments and suggestions.

1. For a dynamic, cyclical conceptualization of American federalism, see Richard P. Nathan, "Federalism—The Great 'Composition,'" 231–261. Also see Beer, *To Make a Nation,* 295–301.
2. On the lack of consistent national party positions on federalism in recent years, see R. Shep Melnick, "The New Politics of Federalism," paper presented at the Harvard Conference on the Transformation of American Politics, December 3–4, 2004.
3. *Federalist Paper* 46.
4. *Federalist Paper* 39.
5. *Federalist Paper* 45.
6. *Federalist Paper* 10.
7. McDonald, *States' Rights,* 111–114.
8. Quoted in Daniel J. Elazar, *The American Partnership: Intergovernmental Co-operation in the Nineteenth-Century United States* (Chicago: University of Chicago Press, 1962), 15.
9. McDonald, *States' Rights,* 98–103.
10. William B. Hesseltine, *Lincoln and the War Governors* (New York: A. A. Knopf, 1948).
11. President Theodore Roosevelt, "First Annual Message to Congress," December 3, 1901, excerpted in Henry Steele Commager, ed., *Documents of American History,* 3rd ed. (New York: F. S. Crofts, 1945), part 2, 201.
12. Richard L. Watson, Jr., *The Development of National Power: The United States, 1900–1919* (1976), 219.

13. For an overview of the New Deal, see David M. Kennedy, *Freedom from Fear: The American People in Depression and War, 1926–1945* (New York: Oxford University Press, 1999). On some of the federalism issues raised by the New Deal, see Patterson, *The New Deal and the States.*

14. Walker, *Rebirth of Federalism,* 99.

15. David R. Beam and Timothy J. Conlon, "Grants," in Lester M. Salamon, ed., *The Tools of Government: A Guide to the New Governance* (New York: Oxford University Press, 2002), 349.

16. Derthick, *Influence of Federal Grants,* 44–45.

17. Grace Abbott, *From Relief to Social Security* (Chicago: University of Chicago Press, 1941), 279.

18. David M. Kennedy, *Freedom from Fear: The American People in Depression and War, 1929–1945* (New York: Oxford University Press, 1999), 272, 345–346.

19. Beam and Conlan, "Grants," 353–356.

20. This discussion relies largely on Derthick, *Influence of Federal Grants.*

21. Abbott, *From Relief.*

22. Robert D. Reischauer, "Fiscal Federalism in the 1980s: Dismantling or Rationalizing the Great Society," in Marshall Kaplan and Peggy Cuciti, eds., *The Great Society and Its Legacy: Twenty Years of U.S. Social Policy* (Durham, N.C.: Duke University Press, 1986), 181.

23. On the increasing role of nonprofits in federal grant programs, see Richard P. Nathan, "The 'Nonprofitization Movement' as a Form of Devolution," in Dwight F. Burlingame, William A. Diaz, Warren F. Ilchma, et al., eds., *Capacity for Change? The Nonprofit World in the Age of Devolution* (Bloomington: Indiana University Center on Philanthropy, 1996).

24. Harold Seidman, *Politics, Position, and Power: The Dynamics of Federal Organization,* 5th ed. (New York: Oxford University Press, 1998).

25. U.S. Advisory Commission on Intergovernmental Relations, *Regulatory Federalism.*

26. For a brief discussion of preemption, see Joseph F. Zimmerman, "Trends in Congressional Preemption," *The Book of the States, 2003* (Lexington, Ky.: The Council of State Governments, 2003), 32–37.

27. Jack L. Walker, Jr., "Setting the Agenda in the U.S. Senate: A Theory of Problem Selection," *British Journal of Political Science,* 7 (October 1977), 423–445.

28. U.S. Advisory Commission on Intergovernmental Relations, *Characteristics of Federal Grant-in-Aid Programs to State and Local Governments: Grants Funded FY 1993* (Washington, D.C.: U.S. Advisory Commission on Intergovernmental Relations, 1994), 1.

29. U.S. Advisory Commission on Intergovernmental Relations, *Federal Regulation of State and Local Governments,* 47.

30. Richard J. Tobin, "Environmental Protection and the New Federalism: A Longitudinal Analysis of State Perceptions," *Publius,* 22 (Winter 1992), 93–108.

31. U.S. Advisory Commission, *Federal Regulation,* 18.

32. Richard P. Nathan, *The Administrative Presidency* (New York: John Wiley & Sons, 1983).

33. One caveat should be noted. Although direct federal assistance does not support a large part of state and local expenditures outside health and human services, the federal gov-

ernment may support these functions outside the grant system. Recipients of Medicare, an exclusively federal program, often use state and local public hospitals, and Medicare coverage reduces payments that would otherwise be required under Medicaid. Higher education is another example. A significant, though minority, share of federal support for post-secondary institutions is provided through student loans and tuition grants to students, not grants to institutions. These indirect forms of federal support help support state and local governments—and extend the reach of federal regulations. But they still leave most of the fiscal burdens to state and local governments.

34. Robert J. Dilger, "TEA-21: Transportation Policy, Pork Barrel Politics, and American Federalism," *Publius,* 28 (Winter 1998), 49–70.

35. Martha Derthick, "Inside the Devolution Revolution: The Doctrine and Practice of Grant-in-Aid Administration," unpublished manuscript, 2005.

36. U.S. Council of Economic Advisors, *Economic Report of the President; Transmitted to the Congress, February 2002* (Washington, D.C.: U.S. Government Printing Office, 2002), 191.

37. Dewayne Matthews, "No Child Left Behind: The Challenge of Implementation," in *The Book of the States, 2004* (Lexington, Ky.: The Council of State Governments, 2004), 493–496.

38. Jennifer Imazeki and Andrew Reschovsky, "Does No Child Left Behind Place a Fiscal Burden on States? Evidence from Texas," paper presented at the Annual Conference of the Association for Public Policy and Management, Atlanta, Georgia (October 2004).

39. See Eric A. Hanushek and Margaret E. Raymond, "Does School Accountability Lead to Improved Student Performance?" *Journal of Policy Analysis and Management,* 24 (Spring 2005), 297–327.

40. Teaford, *Rise of the States.*

41. See "Central Management: Personnel, Planning and Budgeting," in U.S. Advisory Commission on Intergovernmental Relations, *The Question of State Government Capability* (Washington, D.C.: U.S. Advisory Commission on Intergovernmental Relations, 1985), 160–172.

42. Teaford, *Rise of the States,* 197.

43. U.S. Advisory Commission, *Question,* 143–155.

44. Thad Beyle, "The Governors," in Virginia Gray and Russell L. Hanson, eds., *Politics in the American States: A Comparative Analysis,* 8th ed. (Washington, D.C.: Congressional Quarterly Press, 2004), 220–221.

45. Thad Beyle, "Governors: Elections, Campaign Costs, Profiles, Forced Exits and Powers," in *The Book of the States, 2004* (Lexington, Ky.: The Council of State Governments, 2004), 149.

46. Samuel H. Beer, "Federalism, Nationalism, and Democracy in America," *American Political Science Review,* 72 (March 1978), 9–21.

47. Jack L. Walker, Jr., "The Diffusion of Knowledge, Policy Communities, and Agenda Setting: The Relationship between Knowledge and Power," in John Tropman, Milan Dluhy, and Roger Lind, eds., *New Strategic Perspectives on Social Policy* (New York: Pergamon Press, 1981); Donald E. Abelson, *Do Think Tanks Matter? Assessing the Impact of Public Policy Institutes* (Montreal: McGill-Queen's University Press, 2002);

Virginia Gray and David Lowery, *The Population Ecology of Interest Representation: Lobbying Communities in the American States* (Ann Arbor: University of Michigan Press, 1996).

48. For a more detailed analysis of state compensatory actions after the budget cuts, see Nathan, Doolittle, et al., *Reagan and the States.*

49. R. Steven Brown, "Trends in State Environmental Spending," in *The Book of the States, 2004* (Lexington, Ky.: The Council of State Governments, 2004), 240–243; Michael J. Kraft, *Environmental Policy and Politics.* (New York: Harper-Collins, 2001).

50. Robert H. Wilson, *States and the Economy: Policymaking and Decentralization* (Westport, Conn.: Praeger, 1993).

51. William Prindle et al., *Energy Efficiency's Next Generation: Innovation at the State Level, Report No. E031* (Washington, D.C.: American Council for an Energy-Efficient Economy, 2003).

52. Rabe, *Statehouse and Greenhouse.*

53. U.S. Congressional Budget Office, *CBO Report: Unauthorized Appropriations and Expiring Appropriations* (Washington, D.C.: Congressional Budget Office, 2004).

54. See Gerald Marschke, "The Economics of Performance Incentives in Government with Evidence from a Federal Job Training Program," in Dall W. Forsythe, ed. *Quicker, Better, Cheaper: Managing Performance in American Government* (Albany, N.Y.: Rockefeller Institute Press, 2001), 61–97.

55. Martha Derthick, *Uncontrollable Spending for Social Services Grants* (Washington, D.C.: The Brookings Institution, 1975).

56. U.S. Government Accountability Office, *Federal-Aid Highways: Trends, Effect on State Spending, and Options for Future Program Design,* GAO-04-802 (Washington, D.C.: Government Accountability Office, 2004).

57. Beamer, *Creative Politics,* 132–135; Teresa A. Coughlin and Stephen Zuckerman, "States' Use of Medicaid Maximization Strategies to Tap Federal Revenues: Program Implications and Consequences," *Discussion Papers, Assessing the New Federalism* 02-09 (Washington, D.C.: Urban Institute, 2002).

58. U.S. House of Representatives, Committee on Ways and Means, *1996 Green Book* (Washington, D.C.: U.S. Government Printing Office, 1996), 878.

59. Most block grants decline in real (inflation-adjusted) value over time. See Kenneth Finegold, Laura Wherry, and Stephanie Schardin, "Block Grants: Historical Overview and Lessons Learned," *New Federalism: Issues and Options for States* (The Urban Institute, April 2004).

60. Tyce Palmaffy, "The Evolution of the Federal Role," in Chester E. Finn, Jr., Andrew J. Rotherham, and Charles R. Hokanson, Jr., eds., *Rethinking Special Education for a New Century* (Washington, D.C.: Thomas B. Fordham Foundation and the Progressive Policy Institute), 1.

61. R. Shep Melnick, "Both the Sword and the Purse: State Governments and Statutory Rights in the Rehnquist Court," Paper prepared for presentation at the Annual Meetings of the American Political Science Association, 2002.

62. Teles, *Whose Welfare?*

63. R. Kent Weaver, *Ending Welfare as We Know It* (Washington, D.C.: The Brookings Institution, 2000), 131.

64. Carol S. Weissert, "Learning from Midwestern Leaders," in Carol S. Weissert, ed., *Learning from Leaders: Welfare Reform Politics and Policy in Five Midwestern States* (Albany, N.Y.: Rockefeller Institute Press, 2000), 6–9.

65. Robin H. Rogers-Dillon, *The Welfare Experiments: Politics and Policy Evaluation* (Stanford, Calif.: Stanford Law and Politics, 2004).

66. See Weaver, *Ending Welfare*; and chapters by Hugh Heclo and Lawrence Mead in Rebecca Blank and Ron Haskins, eds., *The New World of Welfare* (Washington, D.C.: The Brookings Institution, 2001), 169–220.

67. For recent enrollment in Medicaid managed care, see the annual "Medicaid Managed Care Enrollment Report," published by the Centers for Medicare and Medicaid Services, at http://www.cms.hhs.gov/medicaid/managedcare/mmcss03 .asp. For earlier data, see James W. Fossett, "Managed Care in Devolution" in Frank J. Thompson and John DiIulio, eds., *Medicaid and Devolution: A View from the States* (Washington, D.C.: The Brookings Institution, 1998), 110.

68. Robert Hurley and Deborah Freund, *Managed Care in Medicaid: Lessons for Policy and Program Design* (Ann Arbor, Mich.: Health Administration Press, 1993).

69. U.S. General Accounting Office, *Long Term Care: Federal Oversight of Growing Medicaid Home and Community Based Waivers Should Be Strengthened*, GAO-03-576 (Washington, D.C.: General Accounting Office, 2003).

70. HIFA regulations may be found at Center for Medicare and Medicaid Services, "Health Insurance Flexibility and Accountability Demonstration Initiative." For a more detailed discussion of the program, see Cindy Mann, Samantha Artiga, and Jocelyn Guyer, "Assessing the Role of Recent Waivers in Providing New Coverage" (Washington, D.C.: Kaiser Commission on Medicaid and the Uninsured, December 2003).

71. For reviews of this activity, see Kaiser Commission on Medicaid and the Uninsured, "Section 1115 Medicaid and SCHIP Waivers: Policy Implications of Recent Activity" (Washington, D.C.: Kaiser Commission on Medicaid and the Uninsured, 2003); and Cindy Mann and Samantha Artiga, "The Impact of Recent Changes in Health Care Coverage for Low-Income People: A First Look at the Research Following Changes in Oregon's Medicaid Program" (Washington, D.C.: Kaiser Commission on Medicaid and the Uninsured, 2004).

72. For a critical analysis of the Mississippi proposal, see Leighton Ku, "Mississippi's Flawed Medicaid Waiver Proposal" (Washington, D.C.: Center for Budget and Policy Priorities, 2004).

73. William Gormley, "An Evolutionary Approach to Federalism in the U.S," presented at the Annual Meeting of the American Political Science Association, San Francisco, Calif., 2001.

74. U.S. General Accounting Office, *Food Stamp Waivers: How State Are Using Federal Waivers of the Work Requirement*, GAO/RCED-00-5 (Washington, D.C.: General Accounting Office, 1999).

75. See David E. Balducchi and Alson J. Pasternak, "State and Local Labor Exchange Services," in David Balducchi, Randall W. Eberts, and Christopher J. O'Leary, eds., *Labor Exchange Policy in the United States* (Kalamazoo, Mich.: W.E. Upjohn Institute for Employment Research, 2004), 64; and the report prepared by the Rockefeller

Institute for the U.S. Department of Labor, Employment and Training Administration: *The Workforce Investment Act in Eight States: State Case Studies from a Field Network Evaluation,* vols. 1 and 2 (Washington, D.C.: Employment and Training Administration, 2004).

76. See Barry G. Rabe, "Power to the States: The Promises and Pitfalls of Decentralization," in Norman J. Vig and Michael E. Kraft, eds., *Environmental Policy,* 4th ed. (Washington, D.C.: Congressional Quarterly Press, 2000), 32–54.

77. This argument is largely drawn from Teles, *Whose Welfare?,* 141–143.

78. Teles, *Whose Welfare?*

79. See Thomas Gais and R. Kent Weaver, "State Policy Choices under Welfare Reform," in Isabel V. Sawhill, R. Kent Weaver, Ron Haskins, and Andrea Kane, eds., *Welfare Reform and Beyond: The Future of the Safety Net* (Washington, D.C.: The Brookings Institution, 2002), 33–40.

80. For an example of the effects of the nonassistance rule on one state, see L. Christopher Plein, "Welfare Reform in a Hard Place: The West Virginia Experience," *Rockefeller Report* (November 2001). For another example of how the Clinton administration used rule-making to liberalize social programs—in this case, federal child care laws—see William T. Gormley and Steven J. Balla, *Bureaucracy and Democracy: Accountability and Performance* (Washington, D.C.: CQ Press, 2004), 60–63.

81. James Fossett, Thomas Gais, and Frank J. Thompson, "Federalism and Performance Management: Health Insurance, Food Stamps, and the Take-Up Challenge," in *Quicker, Better, Cheaper: Managing Performance in American Government,* edited by Dall W. Forsythe (Albany, N.Y.: Rockefeller Institute Press, 2001), 207–244.

82. This discussion relies heavily on a study by the Rockefeller Institute by Anne Farris, Richard P. Nathan, and David J. Wright, *The Expanding Administrative Presidency: George W. Bush and the Faith-Based Initiative* (Albany, N.Y.: The Roundtable on Religion and Social Policy, Rockefeller Institute of Government, 2004).

83. Ibid., 17.

84. For an overview of the legal issues, see Ira C. Lupu and Robert W. Tuttle, *The State of the Law, 2004: Partnerships between Government and Faith-Based Organizations* (Albany, N.Y.: The Roundtable on Religion and Social Welfare Policy, Rockefeller Institute/Pew Charitable Trusts, 2004).

Bibliography

Beamer, Glenn. *Creative Politics: Taxes and Public Goods in a Federal System.* Ann Arbor: University of Michigan Press, 1999.

Beer, Samuel H. "Federalism, Nationalism, and Democracy in America." *American Political Science Review* 72 (March 1978), 9–21.

Beer, Samuel H. *To Make a Nation: The Rediscovery of American Federalism.* Cambridge, Mass.: Harvard University Press, 1993.

Conlan, Timothy. *From New Federalism to Devolution: Twenty-Five Years of Intergovernmental Reform.* Washington, D.C.: The Brookings Institution, 1998.

Derthick, Martha. *The Influence of Federal Grants: Public Assistance in Massachusetts.* Cambridge, Mass.: Harvard University Press, 1970.

Derthick, Martha. *Keeping the Compound Republic: Essays on Federalism*. Washington, D.C.: The Brookings Institution, 2001.

Diamond, Martin. *As Far as Republic Principles Will Admit: Essays*. Edited by William A. Schambra. Washington, D.C.: American Enterprise Institute Press, 1992.

DiIulio, John J., and Frank J. Thompson, eds. *Medicaid and Devolution: A View from the States*. Washington, D.C.: The Brookings Institution, 1998.

Gilman, J. D. *Medicaid and the Cost of Federalism, 1984–1992*. New York: Garland, 1998.

McDonald, Forrest. *States' Rights and the Union: Imperium in Imperio, 1776–1876*. Lawrence: University Press of Kansas, 2000.

Melnick, R. Shep. "Deregulating the States: Federalism in the Rehnquist Court." In *Evolving Federalisms: The Intergovernmental Balance of Power in America and Europe*. Syracuse, N.Y.: Campbell Public Affairs Institute, Maxwell School, Syracuse University, 2003.

Nathan, Richard P. "Federalism—The Great 'Composition.'" In *The New American Political System*, 2nd version, edited by Anthony King. Washington, D.C.: American Enterprise Institute Press, 1990.

Nathan, Richard P., Fred C. Doolittle, et al. *Reagan and the States*. Princeton, N.J.: Princeton University Press, 1987.

Patterson, James T. *The New Deal and the States: Federalism in Transition*. Princeton, N.J.: Princeton University Press, 1969.

Publius: The Journal of Federalism. (A quarterly journal on federalism in the U.S. and elsewhere. See the journal's annual feature, "The State of American Federalism.")

Rabe, Barry George. *Statehouse and Greenhouse: The Emerging Politics of American Climate Change Policy*. Washington, D.C.: The Brookings Institution, 2004.

Sundquist, James L. *Making Federalism Work*. Washington, D.C.: The Brookings Institution, 1969.

Teaford, Jon C. *The Rise of the States: Evolution of American State Government*. Baltimore, Md.: The Johns Hopkins University Press, 2003.

Teles, Steven Michael. *Whose Welfare? AFDC and Elite Politics*. Lawrence: University Press of Kansas, 1996.

U.S. Advisory Commission on Intergovernmental Relations. *Regulatory Federalism: Policy, Process, Impact, and Reform*. Washington, D.C.: U.S. Advisory Commission on Intergovernmental Relations, 1984. (Also see the 1993 update, *Federal Regulation of State and Local Governments: The Mixed Record of the 1980s*. ACIR published many other fine reports on U.S. federalism through the middle 1990s.)

Walker, David B. *The Rebirth of Federalism*. 2nd ed. New York: Chatham House, 2000.

Weissert, Carol, S., ed. *Learning from Leaders: Welfare Reform Politics and Policy in Five Midwestern States*. Albany, N.Y.: Rockefeller Institute Press, 2000.

THE PAST AND FUTURE
OF THE EXECUTIVE BRANCH

16

CONTROL AND ACCOUNTABILITY: DILEMMAS OF THE EXECUTIVE BRANCH

Joel D. Aberbach and Mark A. Peterson

T HE HARD-HEADED MEN WHO DESIGNED THE AMERICAN
constitution were at once realistic and optimistic about human beings
and about their capacity to operate a state that would preserve liberty
(their primary goal) and provide an effective enough state to benefit the nation.
They assumed that people were self-interested, that they would form factions
based on their differing places in society and their differing abilities, and that
these factions would by their nature pursue goals "adverse to the rights of other
citizens, or to the permanent and aggregate interests of the community."[1]

A key question was how to control the effects of faction, since, as the author
of *Federalist* 10 (James Madison) put it, "enlightened statesmen will not always be
at the helm." The answer was a system of government that would check selfish
impulses by dividing powers, giving different interests greater say in competing
institutions and then forcing them to reach agreement before government could
act. In a classic formulation from the *Federalist Papers*: "Ambition must be made
to counteract ambition."[2]

One of the many charms of the founders is that they did not exempt themselves from their jaundiced view of human nature. In justifying the partition of
power written into the Constitution, the author of *Federalist* 51 (Alexander
Hamilton or Madison) famously said:

> The interest of the man must be connected with the constitutional
> rights of the place. It may be a reflection on human nature that such

devices should be necessary to control the abuses of government. But what is government itself, but the greatest of all reflections on human nature? If men were angels, no government would be necessary. If angels were to govern men, neither external nor internal controls on government would be necessary. In framing a government which is to be administered by men over men, the great difficulty lies in this: you must first enable the government to control the governed; and in the next place oblige it to control itself. A dependence on the people is, no doubt, the primary control on the government; but experience has taught mankind the necessity of auxiliary precautions.

This policy of supply, by opposite and rival interests, the defect of better motives, might be traced through the whole system of human affairs, private as well as public.[3]

That fabulous phrase—"the necessity of auxiliary precautions"—summarizes the philosophy behind the design of the formal institutions of government in the United States. No one, including members of the governing elite, is assumed to be motivated by anything more than self-interest. Should political leaders actually be motivated by a desire to serve the public good, so much the better; but the political system must be structured as if this is not so. All of the actors were to be bound to one another in a complex system requiring bargaining crowned by mutual assent. While no one would be totally happy with the final product of the policy process, most of those who were included in the then-prevailing definition of the active citizenry would be represented and have at least some say.

The constitutional arrangements also reflected the founders' hopes and fears about government action—the purposes and direction of public policy. The multiple checks on ambition necessarily meant that getting the government to do something would require agreement among numerous officials in many institutional settings. Although they wished to supplant the original Articles of Confederation with the Constitution so as to grant the national government the capacity to act when it needed to, the costs of inaction were still generally thought to be far less consequential than the threat of hasty choices and potentially ill-considered policies. Such were the sensibilities of the eighteenth-century experience and post-revolutionary thought. When the state had acted in most nations, or the British Crown had acted in the American colonies, it was not to protect the environment, enhance the community, or pursue the social policies and goals we identify with contemporary governments. Rather, it was to tax the general population primarily for the benefit of the monarchy and aristocracy, to wage war, or to use the military to quell civil unrest. The resulting distrust of state power lent further support to ensuring that brakes on policy making were built into the constitutional system.

There is debate about whether the founders thought that the president's motives and character would somehow be above their general characterization of the motives and character of mere mortals (see, for example, the discussion of *Federalist* 68, 70, and 71 in the chapter in this volume by Lawrence Jacobs), but there is no doubt that the institutions were structured to check the president as well as others. Presidential power was constrained in a variety of ways—for example, presidents could not formally introduce legislation in Congress, vetoes could be overridden, the design and control over the structure of the very vaguely described executive branch was to be shared with Congress (which could decide by law who would appoint the "inferior" officers of the United States), and appointments and treaties had to be consented to by the Senate. Indeed, Article 1, Section 8 of the Constitution grants Congress, not the president, a long list of enumerated powers—from taxation to declaring war, as well as the mandate to "to make all laws which shall be necessary and proper for carrying into execution the foregoing powers." The most potent explicit presidential power from the contemporary vantage point, that of commander in chief of the armed forces, did not have quite the same connotation when it was granted in a nation lacking a standing army and not widely expected to be a major military power. And even the vesting of executive power in the president's hands had a bit less grand meaning than it does today in a constitutional document that specified very little about the nation's administrative apparatus.[4]

Presidential Power

The evolution of presidential power to what we know today, along with the development of the executive branch departments and agencies, began in this challenging context. One of the most influential presidential scholars of the twentieth century, Richard E. Neustadt, famously rejected the notion that even the modern president could do much by command. (For Neustadt, in fact, a president's use of command in the constrained settings in which it is available, such as firing certain individuals, is a sign of having been proven weak or ineffective in the larger domain of politics or policy). Instead, Neustadt defined presidential power in a system of "separated institutions *sharing* power" (emphasis in the original) as "the power to persuade," that is, using bargaining to convince others "that what the White House wants of them is what they ought to do for their sake and on their authority."[5] Presidents have numerous resources to use in exerting influence. But they are hemmed in by others in the political system who have their own sources of power, derived from the Constitution and law, and whom the president needs in order to get things done, from senators and representatives in the "tandem institution" of Congress to local officials in our federal system.[6] This situation forces presidents to bargain—clearly the intention of the framers of the Constitution.

Naturally enough, presidents have not always liked this situation nor found it a viable way to operate in crisis situations (see particularly the chapter by R. Shep Melnick). Many of the authors in this volume discuss the various efforts of presidents to overcome the constraints they faced. But the basic system of institutional sharing and bargaining was rarely frontally challenged until the last third of the twentieth century. President Nixon was frustrated by his dealings with Congress and by the need to bargain with others in the system—including his own appointees to Cabinet- and sub-Cabinet-level positions who, for the most part, did not rely solely on him for political support, a common feature in the presidential system described by Neustadt. Nixon wanted control, and he slowly developed what has come to be known as the "administrative presidency" strategy to get it.[7]

The elements of this strategy were relatively simple and straightforward: Nixon aimed to put "loyalists" into Cabinet and sub-Cabinet positions, thereby putting an end to serious bargaining within his own administration. He impounded (refused to spend) unprecedented amounts of funds appropriated by Congress for endeavors he did not like in an explicit effort to stop entire programs and to downgrade others without going through the legislative process. He used administrative reorganizations for the same purposes, cutting programs off from their support and merging them with others so that they would effectively change or even cease to function effectively. Finally, he sought to use regulation writing as a tool to interpret laws so that they would conform to whatever purposes the White House had in mind, regardless of the original intent of Congress. This strategy was combined with an all-out war on the top career officials in the civil service, who were described in one particularly vivid passage from the personnel manual given to incoming political appointees as being so influenced by previous Democratic administrations (the term "rape" was actually used) that the Nixon presidency had been "left a legacy of . . . disloyalty and obstruction at high levels."[8]

The political theory behind the administrative presidency is, of course, quite different from that behind the presidency Neustadt described. A key is that the president, the one official elected by a national vote, is said to have a "mandate" to govern. In essence, the presidential election is seen as a kind of plebiscite, with the winning candidate given four years to achieve his or her objectives.[9] Other officials, lacking the mandate, are to step aside or be bowled over by the force of legitimacy imposed by the mandate, a force that allows the winner to dominate. Command is back. Neustadt's president, who governs through bargaining and persuading other officials, is no more.

Nixon's efforts were derailed by the Watergate scandal and his subsequent resignation in the face of impeachment proceedings, but his legacy endured as the first significant step in an ongoing transformation of the modern presidency. Ronald Reagan's people learned from the Nixon experience—indeed, many had studied the Nixon administration or worked in it—and they employed many of its tactics more successfully than the ill-fated creator of the administrative presidency strategy.[10] They added a systematic selection method for choosing political appointees, with an emphasis on loyalty to a set of ideas rather than only to the president as a person, and they took full advantage of changes in the civil service system to manipulate appointments to the upper level of the bureaucracy in areas of major concern.[11] Using executive orders, Reagan also brought much greater control of the regulatory process right into the Executive Office of the President.[12]

Presidents since Reagan have utilized elements of the administrative presidency (George H. W. Bush issued signing statements indicating which portions of a bill he would not enforce and Bill Clinton made creative use of regulation writing, to cite two examples), but it is in the administration of George W. Bush that the elements of the administrative presidency strategy have once again come into full flower.[13] Bush has been steadfast in asserting presidential prerogatives as seen from the perspective of one with a maximalist view of presidential power. And instead of viewing his disputed election victory in 2000 as requiring cautious, inclusive coalition building, he interpreted it as a mandate to govern assertively, pursuing a bold, ideological agenda associated with his political base.[14]

The rise of the administrative presidency as an approach to governing in the United States has been accompanied by an academic literature explaining and justifying it. Perhaps the best known article from this perspective, covered in greater detail in the chapter by Scott James, is by Terry Moe. Moe says that it is no accident of presidential personality or aberration of some other sort that has produced presidencies so unlike those expected from the Neustadt model. In brief, the public expects the president to produce. And as Steven Wayne notes in Chapter 4 in this volume: "Presidential candidates run as if they will lead in a presidential system. Rarely do they temper their promises or modify their leadership by pointing out that they cannot achieve their policy goals alone."

As a result, a serious discrepancy exists: "Expectations surrounding presidential performance far outstrip the institutional capacity of presidents to perform."[15] Such an imbalance puts the system out of equilibrium. Presidents are sorely tempted—even driven—to bridge the expectations gap by doing all they can, including going outside the bounds set by convention or the previously understood rules of the system, to sweep aside the impediments created by the system of "separated institutions sharing power."[16] In full incarnation, the imperative is to try to govern alone. Such presidents do not subscribe to the view presented in Chapter 13 of this volume by Andrew Rudalevige, among others: "The framers of the Constitution created separate branches that could not function separately." Rather, these chief executives act assertively and often independently (without the assent of others "sharing power") because—in their view—they must, and they can.

The two views of the presidency outlined above have very different implications for American democracy. In one, the president is a key actor, but not usually dominant (in legislative matters, for example, "necessary, but not sufficient," as Rudalevige notes in summarizing measures of presidential success). The president cajoles, bargains, and compromises, using the advantages of office to the best of his or her ability, but always conscious of limits. Overstepping these boundaries, in fact, can damage the reputation among other policy makers and the support among the public that the president needs to influence decision makers in the future. In the second image of the presidency, all other actors are effectively subordinate to the president and his team. If they are administrators in the executive branch, they are either totally loyal, or they depart. If they are in other institutional roles and disagree with the president, they are essentially irrelevant. Presidents, in this model, govern through legislation when they can, but they assertively exploit other means when they cannot.

In the first model, democratic control comes not only from elections, but also through the pull and haul of negotiation among actors—a sufficient number of whom must be persuaded that what the president wants them to do is also in their own interest. In the second model, the presidential election is the instrument of control. Every four years the American people get their chance to endorse or reject the candidates who run for the presidential office. Once they make their choice, the implications are profound because they have granted a mandate, no matter how tenuous the margin of victory. Reelection of the incumbent vindicates an administration's past policies. Note George W. Bush's response in a January 16, 2005, *Washington Post* interview, when asked about the possible removal or demotion of officials who had played key roles in proffering the less than perfect intelligence assessments presented during the run-up to the war in Iraq:

> *The Post*: In Iraq, there's been a steady stream of surprises. We weren't welcomed as liberators, as Vice President Cheney had talked about. We haven't found the weapons of mass destruction as predicted. The postwar process hasn't gone as well as some had hoped. Why hasn't anyone been held accountable, either through firings or demotions, for what some people see as mistakes or misjudgments?
>
> *The President*: Well, we had an accountability moment, and that's called the 2004 election. And the American people listened to different assessments made about what was taking place in Iraq, and they looked at the two candidates, and chose me, for which I'm grateful.[17]

The "accountability moment" came and went with the election. The president and his team were vindicated by their victory. End of story, though others suspected that the president was reelected despite rather strong public disapproval of his policies in Iraq.[18] Our point here is not to focus on the problems of the George W. Bush administration in particular, but to illustrate one major difficulty in what is clearly an emerging—and perhaps enduring—conception (and mode of operation) of the presidency. We will return to the important issues raised by changes in the way presidential power is conceived and executed at the end of the chapter.

The Executive Branch

The executive branch of the federal government is a complex, far-flung, and constantly evolving set of institutions and relationships. The Constitution is remarkably silent on the subject of its structure and organization, and debates at the Constitutional Convention were "almost devoid of reference to an administrative apparatus."[19] As Daniel Carpenter points out in Chapter 2, the initial executive institutions, faced with the task of structuring a government apparatus, to a large extent copied the Crown, with Americans in effect embracing many of the "organizational forms that they had attacked just decades earlier." Over time, the government grew larger and its reach increased. Substantial changes came at the time of the Civil War, and then in the latter part of the nineteenth century. The modern American bureaucratic state matured with the rise in the twentieth century of a welfare state and, eventually, World War II, and the cold war led to the colossal military power that now marks the United States as the sole remaining superpower.

James Q. Wilson, a noted authority on the American bureaucratic state, argues that "during its first 150 years, the American republic was not thought to have a 'burcaucracy,' and thus it would have been meaningless to refer to 'problems' of a 'bureaucratic state.'" What he means by this statement is that arguments about the executive branch focused on standards of appointment and on the maintenance of noncorrupt and reasonably effective organizations and policies, and not on "the extent to which political authority has been transferred undesirably to an unaccountable administrative realm." Congress, especially, and the president were seen as firmly in charge of administration, with the major political struggles over the relative power of the two. The rise of what Wilson labels a "bureaucratic state" (a state with a "bureaucracy wielding substantial discretionary powers") has been accompanied by increased concern about the powers of the broader executive branch. The focus has been on the ways in which it is controlled, with ongoing concerns about the personnel who staff it, the means by which it delivers services, and its size as well as the revenues necessary to sustain it.[20]

The discretionary powers of the bureaucracy, and its role in policy making, have made it a major target of political contention. Nixon's administrative presidency was, in part, created to counter the bureaucracy (which he and his inner circle saw as dominated by Democrats), and the burst of congressional oversight in this same period was part of Congress's answer to what it saw as presidential overreach in seeking to dominate this essential part of the government.[21] The struggle over control of administration leaves the bureaucracy "caught in the middle," as the title of Barry Weingast's chapter in this volume suggests. The Constitution itself ensures this tension. The president is granted "executive power" and charged with seeing that the laws are *"faithfully executed"* (emphasis ours). But Congress also has substantial power over administrative structure and its funding, and over policy making and the execution of laws—the very laws it creates—as well as having the authority to oversee agency actions. In the words of political scientist Norton Long: "The unanswered question of American government—'who is boss?'—constantly plagues administration."[22]

Executive Branch Characteristics: A Brief Review

Before turning to the struggle for control, we review some of the other factors that mark the executive branch. First, as Colin Campbell documents in Chapter 8, its organization is hardly a paragon of system and order. Departments and agencies, shaped or reshaped at different points in time, and influenced by different traditions, display a variety of formats and a multiplicity of organizational approaches. Political appointees are present in all of the departments and just about all of the most sensitive organizations, but the number of appointees and the positions they hold are not consistent—a function of political history, legislative whim, and interest group power, among other factors.

While the public, especially since the establishment of the welfare state in the administration of Franklin Roosevelt, has generally welcomed the benefits of public programs, it is uneasy about, and indeed often distrusts, big government and, by extension, the public servants who make it work (see the second paradox explicated in the introduction to this volume). Somewhat remarkably, despite this climate of public ambivalence, the federal public service attracts an impressive set of people. The career civil service is highly specialized. Its top officials have extraordinary educational credentials, comparing more than favorably with top executives in the private sector.[23] It has been relatively free of corruption in the era since merit became the major basis for recruitment. And its morale has remained remarkably high, even through the disruptive years that started in the late 1960s, the reinvention period of the Clinton administration, and the major overhauls proposed and implemented in civil service compensation systems during the George W. Bush administration.

A look at the figures on job satisfaction in Patricia Ingraham's chapter in this volume confirms this fact. Well over 60 percent of samples of federal civil servants (at all levels) felt satisfied with their jobs in polls taken between 1989 and 2000. An even higher percentage of them felt that they did meaningful work. In addition, data from polls of Senior Executive Service (SES) executives completed in 1970, 1987, and 1992 consistently show job satisfaction levels well above 60 percent. And a survey of career SES members (done in 2004–2005 for the Annenberg Public Policy Center as part of the Institutions of American Democracy project) shows a continuation of this satisfaction, with just over 70 percent of those sampled declaring themselves "very satisfied" with their jobs, and another 23 percent saying that they were "somewhat satisfied."[24]

However, there are also numerous problems facing the federal career service. As Ingraham points out, the federal government is not the most nimble recruiter and often faces difficulties in hiring people for highly technical jobs when there is severe competition with the private sector. While it pays competitively at lower levels, salaries for top level executives are far below those in the private sector. Personnel rules frequently create barriers to flexible management approaches. These and other problems are now being addressed in a series of controversial changes that are taking place in the federal service (see especially Chapter 9 by Ingraham and Chapter 11 by Donald Kettl in this volume).

At the political appointee level, a major problem is the sheer number of people who are involved. According to the 2004 "Plum Book" (*United States Government Policy and Supporting Positions*), there were more than 2,100 appointees, including positions appointed by the president and subject to Senate confirmation (1,137), those appointed by the president without Senate confirmation (320), and in positions in the Senior Executive service filled by noncareer appointments (701). The number of political appointees has grown significantly over the years and is part of a growing set of management layers in the government, set up to promote presidential leadership and bureaucratic responsiveness and accountability. As Paul Light points out, the federal government is now so "thick" with politically appointed presidential "helpers" that, rather than improving leadership, "more helpers clutter the message."[25] Efforts to gain political control by increasing the number of political appointees may actually be backfiring, since they complicate the process and separate those who know the most (seasoned senior career civil servants) from those who make major decisions.

Congressional Control

The dilemmas of controlling the bureaucracy are many and varied, a point made forcefully in Barry Weingast in Chapter 10. Statutes are often unclear or inconsistent due to the multiple veto points in the American system of government—the co-equal chambers of the bicameral Congress, multiple committees and subcommittees, the president's formal veto power—and the compromises that are almost always necessary to gain sufficient support to enact legislation. This ambiguity leaves it to administrators to make an initial interpretation of what is meant by a law's provisions, and magnifies the need for control in a democratic system.

However, control is not so easy to achieve. Administrators spend full time on their tasks, while members of Congress (including members of the relevant congressional committees) and the president and White House staff have a variety of policy areas they must cover simultaneously. Administrators, in other words, have huge advantages over most others in information. They also have the potential to play the president and members of Congress against one another (the multiple-principal problem). In addition, because there is relatively frequent turnover among political officials, new officials may have different ideas about what legislation means (or what they might like it to mean) from their predecessors, leading to conflict. There may also be frustration on the part of the new political appointees when these differences are perceived as evidence of the inflexibility of career civil servants.

Weingast draws on the many studies of agency supervision and oversight to lay out how the control system works, with emphasis on congressional influence over executive agencies. First, Congress may do the obvious and closely monitor (oversee) what is going on in administration. Early accounts of congressional oversight reported little such activity, but the level picked up considerably in the latter part of the twentieth century as Congress both increased its staff resources for such endeavors and also clashed vigorously with the executive over a variety of issues, including the Vietnam War and presidential prerogatives. Further, some scholars also argue that Congress does not have to play an active role in conventional terms (routinely holding hearings or conducting investigations, for example) to know what is going on in administration. It can rely on interested parties to keep it informed if there are problems—the use of "fire alarms"—thereby minimizing its need for active search. The Administrative Procedures Act (APA) helps to minimize problems in administration and to facilitate the fire alarm process by providing information and access for those with a deep interest in how programs are interpreted and administered.

The congressional control system currently in place is impressive in many ways, but it is also beset by significant problems. First, even when operating effectively, it favors established and well-organized interests that have resources available to influence members of Congress and/or to take advantage of the opportunities afforded by the APA. Second, while the tendency Weingast describes for today's political officials to solve the problem of political turnover ("political drift") by raising the costs to tomorrow's officials of meddling with the way agencies have been interpreting and administering a law may sound rather nifty (stacking the deck in favor of particular interests and disadvantaging others), it can greatly exacerbate political conflict when tomorrow's officials seek to undo what they dislike. Third, as Chapter 10 points out, the congressional oversight system may be relatively effective on a case-by-case basis, but it does nothing to solve the problem of uncoordinated policies across the executive branch, and almost certainly exaggerates the problem as individual committees push their own priorities.

A fourth major problem seems to have become prevalent in recent years. Congressional committees may be overseeing quite vigorously, but the effects of that oversight can be blunted if control over legislation intended to follow up oversight—one of the most potent tools, either threatened or used—passes from the hands of the oversight committees to the congressional leadership and the White House. That has apparently occurred over the last several years, with committee oversight hearings occurring frequently, but much legislation controlled centrally by the leadership and packaged into omnibus bills.[26] Ironically, such a process is one way to at least partially resolve the coordination problem; the cost is that committee input and especially the effects of committee expertise may be greatly diminished.

All in all, though, whatever the system's flaws, it appears that, as Weingast succinctly summarizes the thrust of the academic literature on the subject, "the bureaucracy is not out of control." However, control is imperfect, fragmented, and probably more often than not a source of frustration to most people involved in the process.

Presidential Control

That leads us back to the question of presidential power, particularly presidential control of the rest of the executive branch. One important issue in this regard focuses on the personnel of the Executive Office of the President (EOP). Originally founded because "the president needs help," Franklin Roosevelt's EOP was, as Matthew Dickinson describes it in Chapter 5, "a tightly knit grouping of institutionally oriented staff agencies that bolstered the president's managerial capacities." Staff members were said to see themselves as serving the presidency as an institution, rather than simply as tools to further the incumbent president's short-term political needs.

However, by the end of the 1970s, according to Dickinson, "Roosevelt's model for the EOP had essentially disappeared," replaced by an EOP that was "a heavily politicized and organizationally unwieldy holding company, dominated by the White House Office and related policy staffs. . . ." How and why did this happen? The answer is found in the politics of the bureaucracy and the political pressures felt by the White House. As Dickinson notes, much of the permanent government over which Roosevelt presided had been staffed during the New Deal. Bureaucrats and political appointees did not share the president's views on every subject, but they were basically people with whom Roosevelt shared much in common in political and policy terms. As a result, it was not a major problem for him to entrust professionals in the EOP with many of the staff tasks associated with the presidency and "to utilize a legislative clearance process that worked closely with departments and agencies."

Nixon and many of his successors, most especially the Republican presidents (Ford excepted by the unusual circumstances of his presidency), had a deep-seated suspicion of government careerists, including those in the EOP. They believed much of the bureaucracy was a bastion of the Democratic Party (since it had been built up under Democratic administrations), and they were reluctant to entrust career people with the task of controlling it. So they politicized the Executive Office of the President (EOP) to the extent they could, with Nixon, for example, adding a layer of politically appointed officials to oversee the Office of Management and Budget's (OMB's) budget-examining divisions, and his successors following a general politicizing strategy to bring budgetary and regulatory oversight under tighter White House control.

The negative effects of this institutional politicization can be substantial, as Dickinson points out. There is a loss of institutional memory, expertise, and organizational continuity that can cost the president dearly in certain circumstances. But the gains are also apparent. The White House can be confident that its top staff is firmly in the control of people who will look out for the current incumbent of the White House first, who will regard the president's needs and wants as their own, and who will follow the White House loyally and will share the president's views on key issues. "Neutral competence"—the presumably objective expertise and institutional memory of career professionals—may be lost, but, to use Terry Moe's optimistic formulation, "responsive competence" will be gained, helping presidents meet the short-term challenges of public expectations for leadership.[27] Even if the responsive types are not quite as administratively or analytically competent as the old neutral types may have been, they will be a major asset and therefore an improvement from the perspective of the White House. So, when faced with what Dickinson calls "the paradox of politicization," presidents often select staff for their ideological compatibility and political responsiveness, accepting the risk that a by-product of this choice may be advisors whose level of analytic skill or technical expertise is not all it could be. As to any long-term institutional or policy costs, they are either deemed relatively unimportant (especially by those who want to make big changes and may disparage such things as institutional memory and institutional caution) or well worth paying.

A second major issue in presidential control of the executive branch focuses on White House control of political appointees, a subject we have already discussed. Not only has the number of political appointees increased, but the White House has taken steps to make sure that those chosen have their primary loyalty to the president. The days when the Cabinet was a group of notables selected to forge alliances between the president and other power centers, and when sub-Cabinet appointments often served similar purposes, are now largely faded memories, especially when Republicans control the presidency. Personnel at all levels are now carefully vetted by the While House to make sure they will closely follow the president's lead.

This personnel strategy poses two central problems to effective governance. First, the ranks of appointees have become more numerous and therefore harder to monitor—a possible source of missteps, for example, if a highly ideological administration recruits overzealous officials. Second, as Dickinson suggested about staff in the EOP, executive branch appointees chosen for their political reliability are less likely to have the skills, expertise, and the political standing to give independent advice that the president and administration may need. In this system, the political leadership in the executive branch may proceed more stead-fastly than before to the glory of coherent and beneficial policy changes in line with the president's vision, but it is also easier for it to march in ordered ranks down a path to hell that, if not paved with good intentions, is at least paved with enthusiastic implementers blithely undeterred by the voice of experience or alternative advice, evidence, or visions.

Firm direction of the career civil service is a third element in presidential attempts to control the executive branch. Aside from dealing with competing congressional claims of control over agencies and the actions the legislature takes to back up those claims, plus the inherent principal-agent problems that emerge when several thousand political appointees are the immediate supervisors of the army of civil servants who do the actual work of the government, the political nature of government means that administration officials worry about the beliefs of their subordinates as well as their behavior. When presidencies change, the direction of government may also change. An incoming administration worries that what it wants may differ significantly from what the permanent workforce supports or views as consistent with existing law. Recall that President Nixon perceived the issue as a problem of "disloyalty" in the civil service, for example.

How realistic are these fears? No one can say for sure, though it is well-estab-lished that over time political appointees come to have a high regard for the competence of senior civil servants (and this despite the fact that the feeling is often not as strongly reciprocated).[28] What we do know is that many top civil servants—those in the Senior Executive Service (SES)—hold views that often put them at odds with their political masters. Earlier studies extensively documented this tendency, especially when Republican presidents were in office. (Civil servants have generally been more liberal than the political appointees chosen by the typical Republican president.) These studies also demonstrated the increas-ing effectiveness of the efforts administrations may make to put civil servants who share their views into key positions (a task made easier by provisions of the Civil Service Reform Act of 1978).[29]

As shown in Table 1, data collected for the Annenberg-sponsored Institutions of American Democracy Project indicate that the disjuncture between the views of top civil servants and those of administration appointees (especially those appointed by a Republican administration) is a continuing phe-nomenon. The table presents results from surveys conducted in 2004–2005 of

TABLE 1

Political Views of the Public and Top Executive Branch Officials.

1a. *Party ID*	General public	Career SES	Career EOP	Bush appointees	Clinton appointees
Republican	32	14	12	80	5
Independent	29	45	42	12	14
Democrat	33	32	27	5	81
No Preference	4	1	—	—	—

1b. *Liberalism-Conservatism*					
Percent conservative or very conservative	40	14	6	56	5
Percent liberal or very liberal	17	22	15	2	42
(N=)	(1500)	(407)	(33)	(113)	(152)

QUESTIONS:
In politics today, do you consider yourself a Republican, Democrat, or Independent?
In general, would you describe your political views as very conservative, conservative, moderate, liberal, or very liberal?

SOURCE: 2004–2005 surveys by Princeton Research Associations for the Annenberg Foundation Trust at Sunnylands.

the general public, career members of the Senior Executive Service in the main federal government agencies, career SES people in the Executive Office of the President, and political appointees from both the George W. Bush and Bill Clinton administrations. Not surprisingly, when it comes to party identification (Table 1a), Bush's appointees are overwhelmingly Republican and Clinton's overwhelmingly Democratic. Career civil servants were most likely to describe themselves as independents, but among those professing a party identification, they were more than 2 to 1 Democratic (and, when pressed, independents who answered a follow-up question were more likely to lean Democratic than Republican). It is in many respects reassuring that top career civil servants resemble the public more than do political appointees (though they are clearly less prone than the public to be Republican); from the standpoint of Democrats, however, top career officials must look a bit staid, and from the standpoint of Republicans they almost surely look too much like the opposition.

Table 1b goes a step further and reports data on the self-professed liberalism or conservatism of respondents to the surveys. Here one gets a confirmation of the stark differences between top career civil servants and Republican political appointees. Fifty-six percent of the Bush appointees are self-described conservatives, compared to just 14 percent of the SES career civil servants and 6 percent of the career people in the Executive Office of the President. However, we should note that the career SES respondents, while on average decidedly more liberal than the Bush appointees, are also quite a bit less liberal than the Clinton administration appointees. We should also point out that the conservative skew of the Bush officials, though demonstrably the most extreme in the table (28 to 1 conservative to liberal), comes the closest of the surveyed group to reflecting the self-identified ideological distribution of the general public (a little more than 2 to 1 conservative to liberal).

Overall, it is easy to see why executive branch politicians, particularly Republicans, may feel uneasy about the advice they receive from their career subordinates. It is a tribute to the career public service that political appointees nonetheless eventually conclude that the so-called "permanent government" has served them well. But the initial suspicion and tension have contributed to a general propensity to exclude the career service and its substantive expertise from important policy decisions and for the White House to grasp firm control over as much of the administrative apparatus of the government as possible, even if this approach means violating previous norms by limiting bargaining, appointing mainly administration loyalists to key positions, and enforcing a lock-step approach to policy making. Again, this pattern has been most manifest, at least to date, in Republican administrations since the 1960s.

A report in the *Washington Post* in the spring of 2005, for example, indicated that even in the fifth year of his administration, George W. Bush and his aides remained worried about threats to the cohesion of the administration. Indeed, Bush was busy devising mechanisms to keep the members of his Cabinet from being seduced away from his administration's message by others in the executive branch ("going native" is the operative phrase in Washington for falling into the orbit of the permanent employees and interest groups that cluster around the departments). To keep this seduction from happening, the administration decided to require Cabinet members in charge of domestic agencies to spend several hours a week at an office suite near the White House where they could meet with presidential aides and receive guidance on policy. As Paul Light said starkly to the *Post* reporter:

> This administration has been very conscious in the second term of the need to control what happens in Cabinet agencies and to make sure Cabinet officers don't get too far out there. I find it absolutely shocking that they would have regular office hours at the White House. It confirms how little the domestic Cabinet secretaries have to do with making policy.[30]

And this from an administration with unabashedly conservative, carefully chosen appointees who, as the survey data show, are hardly ready candidates for deviance from administration policy or seduction by the career civil service.

A fourth issue in presidential control of the executive branch is the use of administrative tools to increase presidential influence over policy and program administration. Chapters in this book by Andrew Rudalevige, R. Shep Melnick, Thomas Gais and James Fossett, and Scott James, among others, address the wide variety of claims and tools chosen by presidents to enhance their control. Rudalevige, writing on the president's relations with the Congress, stresses the incentives and opportunities shaping presidential actions: "[T]he fact that half of presidential proposals are scorned or ignored . . . highlights the temptation that presidents feel to go around the legislative process via unilateral action." Signing statements, adapted by presidents to tell agencies how to interpret the law or even whether to implement it at all, are one example he gives. Melnick succinctly summarizes the historical tendency of presidents, especially in the twentieth century, to claim "broad prerogative power," which he notes, "John Locke famously defined as 'the power to act according to discretion for the public good without the prescription of the Law and sometimes even against it.'" Gais and Fossett highlight the "distinctive" Reagan exercise of "administrative rather than legislative means to achieve its goals." Their chapter is replete with examples of rule making, waivers, and selective enforcement of the laws applied as ways to establish control, techniques now well ensconced in the presidential repertoire. And James laments that "the presidency today manifests a demagogic, aggrandizing, and politicizing impulse, one that feeds public perceptions of presidents as unbounded by law, standard operating procedure, and norms of official propriety."

As the authors note, what many see as the aggressive manipulation of presidential tools to control the executive branch and public policy has become the subject of great controversy. This discord is reflected in the Annenberg survey data. For example, while almost 70 percent of the George W. Bush appointees agreed that "if the president believes that something should be done about an important national issue, other policy makers should defer to him," only 43 percent of the SES career civil servants felt this way (and 39 percent of the Clinton appointees). Similar divisions emerged on some particularly controversial issues at the time of the surveys. Sixty percent of the career SES respondents disagreed with the statement that "the president should have the authority, without the consent of Congress, to take preemptive military action, even if an attack is not imminent," while only 35 percent of George W. Bush's appointees rejected this proposition. (A whopping 82 percent of the Clinton appointees opposed this idea.) And 70 percent of SES career civil servants disagreed with the suggestion that the president, without Congress's consent, could "contravene international laws or treaties to which the U.S. is a signatory." Only 44 percent of the Bush appointees said no to this (compared to 88 percent of the Clinton appointees).

Further, when one differentiates among the SES career civil servants by their political party allegiances, the differences in the views of members of the career SES and Bush administration officials reported above are almost entirely explained. Career civil servants who describe themselves as Democrats basically hold the same views on presidential unilateralism as the appointees of the previous Clinton administration: only 31 percent said that others should defer to the president on important national policy issues, while fully 83 percent responded that the president should not have the authority, without the consent of Congress, to take preemptive military action, even if an attack is imminent, and 84 percent believed the president should not be able unilaterally to contravene international treaties the U.S. has signed. On the other hand, the comparable figures for career members of the SES identified as Republicans were 66 percent, 56 percent, and 56 percent—all significant majorities supportive of acquiescence to a chief executive who not only sets the nation's agenda, but prosecutes it single-handedly. (The percentages on each of these issues for self-identified independents fall somewhere between those for the respondents who identified with either of the two parties.)

These survey responses warrant highlighting. Just as there is substantial attention and debate in the academic literature about the extent of presidential power, there is noteworthy disagreement between the average top career civil servant and the average presidential appointee in the Bush administration about the nature and extent of presidential power. Further, the disagreement is party-based, almost surely reinforcing the natural suspicions about loyalty and reliability that already exist when there is a change in administrations. This discord not only represents a source of tension in the executive branch, particularly when an activist administration bent on making major changes comes into office, but goes to the core of issues about democratic governance and accountability in the United States. Just how powerful should the modern president be? What can—and should—the president do unilaterally, and under what circumstances?

Presidents almost surely now have more control over the executive branch than ever before, an increase in dominion compared to the past that is particularly evident in those times when there is no formally declared war. They wield a more politicized EOP, place more presidential "loyalists" in key administrative positions, and exert greater control from the White House over both policy and administration. Some chief executives have asserted a set of prerogatives that would grant them power far beyond anything imagined by the founders or by scholars and practitioners as recently as a half century ago. Coupled with changes in the party system that we will discuss in the next section, the result is a muscular presidency and a political environment that a naive reader of Neustadt would have great difficulty recognizing.

The Paradoxes Revisited

Our discussion in the introduction to this volume focused on the conflict between individual interests and collective interests in the American system of government, and the ways in which this conflict has been manifested in executive branch politics. We argued that four core paradoxes define the context for shaping and evaluating the performance of the executive branch in American democracy. Taken together, they underscore the constraints that bind action and often frustrate energetic policy makers, the demands and opportunities that shape what leaders try to achieve, and the incentives that lead to their choice of strategies and instruments of influence. These paradoxes of American politics and government, set in the Constitution and its intersection with the growth of a vast, modern, industrial society, play a major role in creating the tension that motivates presidents and their appointees to pursue constitutionally or legally questionable strategies.

The four paradoxes are:

- A political ethos that at once embodies a focus on individual rights and autonomy and a call for community and concerted action.
- A more contemporary popular desire for the benefits of government programs and the security they provide, with a simultaneous fear of activist government, with its intrusive powers and its perceived lack of competence.
- Broad public and elite expectations that the president should uniquely provide energetic leadership and will know how to lead effectively, posed against the more specific and deep-seated worries about the consequences of actually granting the president the real authority to act without going through an elaborate system for gaining consent from the many other policy makers who also have constitutional or legal authority.
- A general belief that the executive branch—the bureaucracy—should be responsive to the public and its elected leaders (both legislative and executive), but a realization that a vital role for executive agencies and policy makers is to provide stable competence, not capriciousness, protecting the long-term general welfare by identifying what needs to be done rather than what may be most popular at the moment.

As noted in our introduction, the paradoxes were not much in play when the government was a relatively minor force in American life. The Madisonian tradition favors one side of each the paradoxes: individual rights and autonomy, a corresponding fear of too much government activism, a system emphasizing checks on leaders, and—to the degree that one can talk about a developed executive branch under the initial Madisonian system—a highly responsive and interactive set of institutions in which leaders would decide on a course of action after a complex process of reaching mutual agreement. But in the modern United States, the system has created great pressures in favor of the opposite side of these paradoxes: concerted action and government activism (including most recently in a conservative or neo-conservative direction on foreign policy, police powers, personal lifestyles, school standards, and the like), activist presidential leadership without checks, and presidential dominance in the service of a plebiscitary chief executive who has a mandate to serve the public interest (as it was defined by the president in the election campaign or in the course of a first term).

Presidents today tend to answer (and create) demands for action by seizing as much control over the political and policy-making system as possible. This assertiveness leads to tremendous tension because, as the third paradox on our list points out, while Americans in the modern era expect the president to provide energetic and instrumental leadership, they are also uneasy about the potentially abusive power of a chief executive unbridled by the need to accommodate numerous interests and collaborate with other institutions. In the Annenberg survey of the general public, for example, 80 percent of the public, without much difference by party identification, endorsed the statement, "Even though it may result in compromise, the president should accommodate a wide range of interests in making policy." As Scott James wrote in Chapter 1, the nation is caught "between a belief in executive leadership and a fear of executive power."

The origins of the tendency for modern presidents to reach for unilateral power are complex. Terry Moe, as noted earlier, argues that the source is a disequilibrium caused by inflated public expectations of presidential performance. Unlike presidents who were counseled by Neustadt to "teach realism" because they held sway over so little, modern presidents, in the alternative view, are effectively forced by public expectations to seize as much control as possible. Whatever the cause—the complexity and demands of modern society; the speed and reach of contemporary communications technology that always spotlights the president, compelling the holder of the office to attempt "great things" in response to public expectations; the potent and irresistible campaign imperative for candidates to promise more than they can deliver; or a combination of them all—it is clear that the public has (or quite consistently develops) high expectations of the president and presidential leadership, despite the formal institutional constraints.

Ironically, these elevated expectations are developed within a system that motivates presidents to build coalitions among relatively narrow segments of the electorate that have disparate expectations. It is another contradiction of modern American political life that many presidents, as the chapter by Lawrence Jacobs demonstrates, use opinion surveys and "narrowcasting" to develop and target messages to specific groups while simultaneously claiming that, as president, they represent the broader interests of the society through the mandate of the election result. It is a neat political trick, though one that takes them far from the bargaining, consent-oriented culture of the Madisonian political system. It risks having assertive presidential actions widely resented, and often regarded as illegitimate, by the general public.

The rise in the 1970s of political parties that are more ideologically coherent than was the case in the United States for most of the twentieth century is another factor reinforcing conflict about presidential leadership and fears about the actions of the executive branch. In earlier periods of the modern presidency (the core elements of which, most agree, came together in the administration of Franklin Delano Roosevelt), the two major parties in Congress and the country actually encompassed a three-way divide. The Republicans were usually a distinct minority, but the Democrats—holding a nominal majority in Congress—often divided into southern and non-southern wings. Most southern members were marked by a strong aversion to civil rights and generally more conservative preferences than their non-southern colleagues on many other issues, and frequently proved to be natural allies with Republicans in an informal "conservative coalition." This partisan arrangement began to break apart in the late 1940s, with its collapse accelerated by the passage of the Voting Rights Act of 1965. As more and more African-American voters in the South exercised their long-suppressed right to vote, many whites fled the Democratic Party, and its tight grip on the South disappeared. Republicans are now a growing majority in that region. This regional realignment has prompted greater ideological unity within each party and has led to a much sharper divide between the parties. In addition, groups such as Protestant Evangelicals, who were previously rather quiescent politically, now play a major role in Republican Party politics in the South and elsewhere. The earlier culture of bargaining and compromise in Congress, previously reinforced by the three-way split described above, has given way to one in which party leaders have a greater ability to enforce discipline and consequently have much less need to accommodate the opposition.

What does this change mean for the executive branch? If one party controls both the presidency and one or both chambers of Congress, there is likely to be substantial stability (especially when the Republicans, who have been the most unified party in the recent era, are in control). In this setting, administrations will be given relatively wide latitude to do what they want, and presidents are free to use the tools of the "administrative presidency," if they wish, without effective opposition or interference from Capitol Hill. The George W. Bush administration, for example, has been extraordinarily assertive about presidential prerogatives and yet has been given wide latitude by the Republican Congress.

However, with sharp ideological differences between the parties, if there is split party control of government, the political system can become extraordinarily difficult to manage. The two parties will have little incentive to cooperate, and the majority in Congress is sorely tempted to do all it can to bring down the president. This context explains much about the impeachment of President Bill Clinton by the Republican Congress in 1998 and the public's reaction to it. The impeachment was a remarkable event, not only because of the circumstances that led to it (Clinton's personal behavior and the special prosecutor's relentless investigation and graphic report), but also because it appeared to do extraordinarily little damage to Clinton's presidency or to his standing with the partisans of his own party or the public. There seemed to be an implicit understanding that politics in Washington had become so much a game of hardball that anything could be expected.

As long as cooperation between Congress and the president holds up (and especially when Congress defers to the president), stability reigns, even when the president aggressively pursues control of the executive branch and takes a variety of unilateral actions to achieve administration goals. However, the Madisonian system has the likelihood of interbranch conflict built into it. Indeed, it assumes, at minimum, a respectful distance between the two branches that requires the kind of presidential bargaining Neustadt envisions. Without such a climate, crises always loom. Imagine, for a moment, George W. Bush dealing with a Democratic House and Senate. The irony of the contemporary period for the executive branch is that presidents can now deploy numerous well-honed and effective tools to assert their power to, in effect, govern alone—based on a putative mandate coming from their elections—but they are still tremendously vulnerable if the opposition gains the majority in Congress. In fact, under divided government they are probably more vulnerable than before because the cohesion of contemporary parties and the confrontational climate of contemporary politics make compromise and a respect for the latitude of an opposition president much more difficult to achieve.

Reforming the Executive Branch

Americans, as Donald Kettl observes in his chapter in this volume, have long been reorganizers and reformers. Tinkering, both minor and major, has been common throughout American governmental history as the policy-making system has reacted and adapted to changing needs and circumstances in the society and the ebb and flow of institutional power within the constitutional framework. Not surprisingly, the evolution of presidential power in the latter part of the twentieth century has been accompanied by numerous executive branch reforms. On balance, these reforms strengthened the president's hand, especially in dealing with the rest of the executive branch.

The monumental Civil Service Reform Act of 1978 established the Senior Executive Service. Several of its provisions added significantly to the tools available to presidential administrations to control the civil service, especially the senior civil service. In particular, the act permitted an administration to appoint up to 10 percent of those in the SES. (These appointees are not permanent.) In addition, the SES system made it relatively easy to move senior civil servants from position to position within an agency, thereby allowing a savvy administration to place career civil servants favorable to its policies in key positions, something that was previously very difficult to accomplish. It also established a bonus system for those judged high performers, another tool with great potential for a determined administration with firm policy goals.

President Bill Clinton's self-proclaimed "reinvention" reforms promised a more efficient government. The reinvention campaign, as Kettl points out, had a slogan that was hard to resist: a government that "works better and costs less." While the "costs less" element took primacy after the Republican victory in the 1994 congressional elections, the "works better" part had some significant impacts in improving customer service, promoting e-government, and reducing red tape (to enable agencies to focus on results and not rules). It also served as a precursor to the determined effort of Clinton's successor, George W. Bush, to reform management practices in a way that appreciably enhances presidential power.

As Kettl mentions in his chapter, Bush shut down the Clinton reinvention office when he entered the White House. In its place Bush substituted a more focused management strategy for the somewhat "scattered," to quote Kettl, and often contradictory Clinton effort. He also abolished the Labor-Management Partnership Councils that had been formed by the Clinton administration to balance the reform initiative by including consultation with the public-sector labor unions, which are an important part of the Democratic coalition. Bush's management program consists of five elements highlighted by the administration: strategic management of human capital; an expansion of the contracting out of services (competitive sourcing); improved financial management; an expansion of e-government initiatives; and an expanded effort to measure program performance and integrate information on performance results into budget decisions. Three in particular have significant implications for presidential power, although there has been substantial resistance to them.

Strategic management of human capital includes a wide array of changes (and proposed changes) in the personnel system. For the purposes of this essay, the most important is the White House effort to accomplish "a sweeping overhaul of personnel rules that is aimed at giving managers across the federal government more flexibility to promote, punish, or fire hundreds of thousands of civil servants." Particularly central is the introduction of a new pay-for-performance system for the Senior Executive Service. According to Paul Singer of the *National Journal*:

> Together, the two new approaches give political appointees in federal agencies greater authority to reward or discipline senior managers, and

give managers the same authority over the civil servants below them. The White House calls this a "modern" personnel system, where everyone is judged on results. Critics call it a process for weeding out recalcitrant civil servants or political opponents.

The new pay-for-performance plan for the Senior Executive Service eliminates annual raises for top career managers and replaces them with a system of merit ratings. Some career executives fear that the system will allow the White House to simply push aside managers who are unenthusiastic about the president's agenda.[31]

Much of the impact of the changes in the personnel system will depend on the purposes, political will, and scruples of those implementing them. Presidents and political appointees will now have additional tools to deploy, if they wish to reward those career officials who go along with the administration's agenda without raising questions or to punish those they perceive to be inadequately enthusiastic about the incumbent president's designs. But if one endorses the proposition that a valuable role of career civil servants, especially those in high positions, is to present pertinent and objective analyses that might not always please their political bosses, then these reforms present a rather chilling prospect because many career officials will clearly be inhibited from doing so.

Competitive sourcing is also a management tool that can be employed in a more than one way. At one level, it is a tool to improve performance by making government workers compete with private-sector firms that might be able to provide the same service at lower cost. Competition may save the government substantial money and result in a superior outcome. However, it is also a tool that can be used for political purposes to inhibit civil servants and undermine their unions. In addition, effective contract management requires different and more complex administrative capabilities than direct service provision, and when private firms win substantial federal contracts, they have strong incentives to help the political party of the sitting president retain control of the White House. These features mean that increased contracting out may actually result in less effective provision of services and decreased accountability.

Finally, the expanded effort to measure program performance and integrate information on performance results into budget decisions is another management tool that can have important political effects. On the surface, it makes great sense to measure program results and then tie those results to budgeting decisions. However, as numerous critics have pointed out, under the "new management systems to grade federal agencies on the results they achieve . . . the White House [is] in charge of defining 'success.'"[32] If done in a fair a reasonably objective manner, as Donald Kettl points out in his chapter, this is a management tool with great power to improve performance. If, on the other hand, the fears of the critics are well-grounded, it can be a powerful way to, in Kettl's words, "provide analytical justification for cuts the administration wanted to make on ideological grounds." Congress has so far (as of spring 2005) been supportive of the general effort to use performance-based budgeting, but has been reluctant to change its ways of doing appropriations, thereby so far mitigating its effects.[33]

In short, management reform has been a powerful tool for promoting political, especially presidential, control of the bureaucracy (e.g., the Civil Service Reform Act of 1978), and recent management reforms and reform proposals have the potential to further increase presidential control. Whether they increase presidential aggrandizement, and thus contribute to the more complete building of a unilateral presidency, undermining the premises of checks and balances, will ultimately depend on how they are implemented and how much Congress is willing to defer to the president.

Questions for the Future

The presidency and the executive branch are at a crucial juncture in the early years of the twenty-first century. The role of the president has been evolving in fits and starts to the point at which older models are increasingly under challenge. Presidents still bargain, to be sure, but the assertive ones have acted more and more as if their elections gave them a mandate far superior to that of other office holders and a consequent right to govern as they see fit, with re-election, as President George W. Bush put it, their "accountability moment."

The "administrative presidency" style is at great variance with the political system designed by the founders. Leaders in that system were constantly to be checked by others in what the historian Richard Hofstadter termed a "harmonious system of mutual frustration."[34] The goal was to preserve liberty and to produce, through reciprocal accommodation, outcomes that would be acceptable, if not totally pleasing, to a wide range of interests.

At its best, greater control by the president represents a majoritarian strain of democratic government that permits active policy making in response to public problems. The presidential election is won by a candidate or an incumbent president who has articulated a coherent agenda; Congress does not block or inhibit presidential initiatives because it is in agreement with them; political appointees and the career civil servants of the "permanent government" support and implement the policy responses defined by the president; and the courts defer as much as possible to the rest of the government. That set of conditions is most likely when one party controls all branches of government and its congressional wing is supportive of presidential goals, a situation that has prevailed in great measure during the George W. Bush administration.

However, such a situation is hardly guaranteed. Split party government was more the norm than the exception in the last half of the twentieth century and can easily happen again. Continued party coherence is always dicey in a continental nation riven by ethnic, religious, regional, and cultural differences. Elections are not always clear and decisive. The more assertive presidential style does not necessarily sit well under these circumstances, a dilemma that has not been resolved.

Another unresolved dilemma is how to deal with a civil service that, by dint of constitutional design, statutory development, and funding, is effectively responsible to both the executive and legislative branches, and that, therefore, both the White House and Capitol Hill often suspect cannot be relied upon to do their bidding. Republican administrations, especially, have been leery of a permanent government they know is unlikely to be sympathetic to their objectives and that they suspect may not be committed to giving its all to help achieve those goals. The pendulum has swung rather dramatically since the days when Richard Nixon's administration felt the need to produce a manual instructing political appointees in ways to remove civil servants suspected of harboring unsympathetic views or of sabotaging administration plans. The rules have been changed so that such people can rather easily be moved around (though not dismissed). And the current human capital initiatives are likely to make presidential control of the civil service even easier in the future.

A key question is whether there will be a big price paid for the comfort of presidential control. Civil servants who have spent a working lifetime amassing knowledge and experience can be invaluable in alerting political leaders to pitfalls and advising them on effective ways to make policies and programs work. We also know that, over time, political appointees come to appreciate these abilities. The "paradox of politicization" that Dickinson writes about holds for both the administrative agencies of the government and the EOP. One can fill these agencies with staff who share the current administration's political and policy goals, but personnel chosen for their ideological compatibility with the president do not necessarily possess the knowledge or analytic and administrative skills needed either to help the administration achieve its own objectives or to assure a place for the enduring public interest.

One should also question whether a more unilateral, administrative presidency, even one supposedly predicated on the majoritarian impulse, is truly compatible with the constitutional design of American government. Many knowledgeable observers of our system have admired "responsible party government" of the sort practiced in parliamentary systems like the United Kingdom.[35] There, elections produce unambiguous majorities for one party. The party then "forms a government" in which the prime minister and Cabinet, all of whom continue as members of the Parliament, provide the leadership for the fully fused legislative and executive responsibilities of government (see the chapter in this volume by Richard Rose). Accountability is transparent: should the "government's" policies succeed, voters know who is responsible and reward the achievement at the polls. Should they fail, voter retribution is just as sure.

Can we experience such party government in the United States, under the direction of a more powerful presidency and consistent with our particular constitutional framework? Probably not. However decisive the election, focused the president, coherent the president's party in Congress, and partisanly unified the government, our constitutional system is intended to provide greater protections and voice to minority views than is the case in British-style parliamentary settings. A safety valve for a large and remarkably diverse society, it is supposed to engender bargaining, not acquiescence. And with the division of powers, there are no sure mechanisms for collective responsibility. As a result, assertive presidents who run into difficulties either exploit the complexity of our governing institutions to avoid blame, and thus the accountability of electoral punishment, or seek questionable extra-constitutional means to vanquish the opposition and wrest control of government in ways that undermine our system's more nuanced methods of accountability, such as congressional oversight, an independent judiciary, and an investigative press.

In the end, we are left with a set of questions that defy pat answers:

How powerful a president do we want?

How (and how much) should the executive branch be controlled? And by whom?

How should the executive branch be organized? And by whom?

How should we structure the executive branch personnel system? Should it be heavy with political appointees? How easy or hard should it be for political leaders to remove or demote civil servants, and for what causes?

A few years ago, one of us wrote an essay entitled "Sharing Isn't Easy."[36] That is the basic dilemma of executive branch government in a system designed around the idea of "separated institutions sharing power." Any notion that the president should dominate because of an electoral victory would have been anathema to the authors of *Federalist* 51 (leaving aside the fact that their president was not even going to be chosen in a popular election). They wanted "ambition to counteract ambition" in a complex and difficult struggle to contain the non-angelic impulse of the governors through competition and, ultimately, mutual accommodation. From time to time, conditions may allow presidents to ride relatively unchecked over the political and governmental terrain of the United States, but such conditions are ever subject to change in the American constitutional system. In the end, presidents need to learn to share control with others. It can be a painful lesson, for them and for the rest of us, and a central challenge of American government is that the pressures on presidents (and the temptation) to do whatever they can get away with to succeed are likely at some point to clash with the ambitions and needs of others in the political system. Democratic governance, at least in the American version, is structured on the assumption that presidents will face this reality and deal with it in ways that accommodate the interests and preferences of others. Whether and how they do this will be fundamentally important, not only in shaping the future of the executive branch, but of American democracy itself.

Notes

1. Alexander Hamilton, John Jay, and James Madison, *The Federalist Papers* (New York: The Modern Library, 1937), 54. The quotation is from *Federalist* 10 by Madison.
2. *The Federalist Papers.* The first quote is from *Federalist* 10 (p. 57) and the second from *Federalist* 51 (by either Hamilton or Madison), 337.
3. *Federalist* 51, 337.
4. See James Q. Wilson, "The Rise of the Administrative State," *Public Interest* 41 (Fall 1975), 77–103.
5. Richard E. Neustadt, *Presidential Power* (New York: Wiley, 1980; originally published in 1960). The "separated institutions" quote can be found on p. 26. "The power to persuade" is the title of chapter 3, where the last quote in this paragraph is also found (on p. 27).
6. See Mark A. Peterson, *Legislating Together: The White House and Capitol Hill from Eisenhower to Reagan* (Cambridge, Mass.: Harvard University Press, 1990).
7. Richard Nathan, *The Plot That Failed: Nixon and the Administrative Presidency* (New York: Wiley, 1975), and Richard Nathan, *The Administrative Presidency* (New York: Wiley, 1983).
8. Senate Select Committee on Presidential Campaign Activities, Executive Session Hearings on *Watergate and Related Activities, Federal "Political" Personnel Manual*, 93 Cong., 2 sess., 1974, exhibit 35 in book 19.
9. For a discussion of the plebiscitary development of the modern presidency, see Theodore J. Lowi, *The Personal President: Power Invested, Promise Unfulfilled* (Ithaca, N.Y.: Cornell University Press, 1985), and Jeffrey K. Tulis, *The Rhetorical Presidency* (Princeton: Princeton University Press, 1987).
10. Nathan, *Administrative Presidency*; Joel D. Aberbach and Bert A. Rockman, "From Nixon's *Problem* to Reagan's *Achievement*: The Federal Executive Reexamined, in Larry Berman, ed., *Looking Back on the Reagan Presidency* (Baltimore: The Johns Hopkins University Press, 1990), 175–194; and Joel D. Aberbach, "The President and the Executive Branch," in Colin Campbell and Bert A. Rockman, eds., *The Bush Presidency: First Appraisals* (Chatham, N.J.: Chatham House, 1991), 223–247.
11. Joel D. Aberbach and Bert A. Rockman, *In the Web of Politics: Three Decades of the U.S. Federal Executive* (Washington, D.C.: The Brookings Institution Press, 2000).
12. Peter M. Benda and Charles H. Levine, "Reagan and the Bureaucracy: The Bequest, the Promise, and the Legacy," in Charles O. Jones, ed. *The Reagan Legacy: Promise and Performance* (Chatham, N.J.: Chatham House, 1988), 102–142.
13. Joel D. Aberbach, "The Political Significance of the George W. Bush Administration," *Social Policy and Administration* 39, no. 2 (April 2005), 130–149.
14. See Joel D. Aberbach, "The State of the Contemporary American Presidency: Or, Is Bush II Actually Ronald Reagan's Heir?," in Colin Campbell and Bert Rockman,

eds., *The George W. Bush Presidency: Appraisals and Prospects* (Washington, D.C.: Congressional Quarterly Press, 2004), 46–72; and Mark A. Peterson, "Bush and Interest Groups: A Government of Chums," in Campbell and Rockman, eds., *The George W. Bush Presidency: Appraisals and Prospects* (Washington, D.C.: CQ Press, 2004), 240–243.

15. Terry M. Moe, "The Politicized Presidency," in John E. Chubb and Paul E. Peterson, eds., *The New Direction in American Politics*, p. 269.

16. Richard E. Neustadt, *Presidential Power*, (New York: Wiley, 1980), 26.

17. "Transcript of Bush Interview," *Washington Post*, June 16, 2005.

18. Dan Froomkin, "The No Accountability Moment," *Washington Post,* January 18, 2005.

19. Wilson, "Rise of the Administrative State," 77.

20. The quotations in this paragraph are all from Wilson, "Rise of the Administrative State." They can be found on pages 77, 80, and 103.

21. Joel D. Aberbach, *Keeping a Watchful Eye: The Politics of Congressional Oversight* (Washington, D.C.: The Brookings Institution, 1990).

22. Norton E. Long, "Power and Administration," *Public Administration Review* 9 (Autumn 1949), 257–264. Quoted in Francis E. Rourke, *Bureaucratic Power in National Politics,* 3rd ed. (Boston: Little, Brown, 1978), 16.

23. Aberbach and Rockman, *In the Web of Politics*, chap. 4.

24. The question read: "Overall, how satisfied are you with your job—very satisfied, somewhat satisfied, not too satisfied, or not satisfied at all?" Data are the percentages of all respondents in the survey, including those who said they did not know the answer to the question or who refused to answer. We follow this convention throughout this chapter.

    The surveys were conducted from August 2004 to January 2005 by Princeton Survey Research Associates International for the Annenberg Foundation Trust at Sunnylands. For ease of presentation, we did not include the 33 Bush administration SES noncareer respondents interviewed in the SES survey in the analysis. They basically resemble other Bush appointees in the attitudes discussed in this chapter.

25. Paul C. Light, *Thickening Government: Federal Hierarchy and the Diffusion of Accountability* (Washington, D.C.: The Brookings Institution, 1995), 167. See also pp. 7–13 and 181–182.

26. Joel D. Aberbach, "What's Happened to the Watchful Eye?," *Congress and the Presidency* 29, no. 1 (Spring 2002), 3–23.

27. Moe, "The Politicized Presidency," 239.

28. Data from the Annenberg surveys confirm this. For example, while 72 percent of the Bush political appointees surveyed in 2004–2005 thought that the senior civil servants they worked with were highly competent and 74 percent of the Clinton political appointees had a similar view, only 52 percent of the senior career executives questioned thought that high level political appointees in their departments or agencies were highly competent. See also Aberbach and Rockman, *In the Web of Politics*, 122–125.

    Political appointees were also asked about the perceived responsiveness of senior civil servants to the decisions and initiatives of "the president and his appointees" and to their own decisions and initiatives ("your decisions and initiatives"). Very high percentages of both Bush and Clinton appointees perceived civil servants as "very responsive" to them (74 percent in both cases). On the more general issue of their responsiveness to "the president and his appointees" (a class the respondents belonged to), 65 percent of Clinton appointees perceived the civil servants as "very responsive," but only about half of the Bush administration appointees (47 percent) said this. These data can be read in a variety of ways, with the most straightforward suggesting both a high level of actual responsiveness and a greater perception among Democrats than Republicans that top civil servants in general are responsive to the White House and presidential appointees when their party is in control of the executive branch. We will analyze these data in depth in later reports.

29. See, particularly, Aberbach and Rockman, *In the Web of Politics*, chap. 6.

30. Michael A. Fletcher, "Bush is Keeping Cabinet Secretaries Close to Home: Spending Time at the White House Required," *Washington Post,* March 31, 2005, A01.

31. Both quotes are from Paul Singer, "Bush and the Bureaucracy: A Crusade for Control," *National Journal,* March 26, 2005, p. 5.

32. Singer, "Bush and the Bureaucracy," 1.

33. Amelia Gruber, "Congressional Concerns Linger over Performance-based Budgets," *Government Executive,* March 21, 2005, www.govexec.com, accessed March 22, 2005; and Amelia Gruber, "OMB Ratings Have Little Impact on Hill Budget Decisions," *Government Executive,* June 13, 2003, www.govexec.com, accessed March 22, 2005.

34. Quoted in James MacGregor Burns, *The Deadlock of Democracy: Four-Party Politics in America* (Englewood Cliffs, N.J.: Prentice Hall, 1963), 22.

35. This goes back a long time. See, for example: American Political Science Association Committee on Political Parties, *Toward a More Responsible Two-Party System* (New York: Rinehart, 1950).

36. Joel D. Aberbach, "Sharing Isn't Easy: When Separate Institutions Clash," *Governance* 11, no 2 (1998), 137–152.

INDEX